Measuring Police Integrity Across the World

Sanja Kutnjak Ivković • M. R. Haberfeld
Editors

Measuring Police Integrity Across the World

Studies from Established Democracies and Countries in Transition

Springer

Editors
Sanja Kutnjak Ivković
Michigan State University
East Lansing
MI
USA

M. R. Haberfeld
John Jay College of Criminal Justice
New York
NY
USA

ISBN 978-1-4939-2278-9 ISBN 978-1-4939-2279-6 (eBook)
DOI 10.1007/978-1-4939-2279-6

Library of Congress Control Number: 2014960068

Springer New York Heidelberg Dordrecht London

Printed on acid-free paper

Springer is part of Springer Science+Business Media (www.springer.com)

Dedicated to Carl B. Klockars–with regrets that he is unable to share the joy of this book with us.
Sanja Kutnjak Ivković
M. R. Haberfeld

Dedicated to my loving family–thank you for your unconditional love, understanding, and patience.
Sanja Kutnjak Ivković

Dedicated to the memory of Edzia Siekiera—your life was a stream of tragedies that you handled with utmost bravery and integrity, and for this you will never be forgotten; and to my daughters, Nellie and Mia, whose love is my driving force.
M. R. Haberfeld

Preface

Police integrity, the police resistance to temptations to abuse the rights and privileges of their office, is a topic that has long held the interest of academics, practitioners, and the public. This interest has been intense not only in the USA, but also around the world. For most of the history of the police, the study of the police has been the study of their shortcomings, failures, scandals, corruption, and brutality. Although within the past twenty years, the focus of the police literature has shifted to topics of professional policy and management, community and problem-oriented policing, and the tools of technological and management sophistication, problems associated with integrity still haunt policing. Police integrity and police misconduct continue to be the topics of great concern worldwide.

Since the mid-1990s, Carl Klockars, Sanja Kutnjak Ivković, and Maria "Maki" Haberfeld have been studying police integrity, pioneering its study in a variety of ways. We have, for the first time, defined the concept of integrity in a way that distinguishes it from approaches toward defining corruption, brutality, and other forms of misconduct. We have also pioneered the measurement of integrity. In doing so, we showed that the measurement tool we devised could describe not only the contours of integrity within a particular police agency, but also how the contours of integrity could change within police agencies over time. This instrument also enables us to compare the culture of integrity in different police agencies, compare those cultures, and, for the first time in the history of policing, measure the strength of police cultures of integrity cross-nationally.

Measuring Police Integrity Across the World provides a unique perspective by conducting in-depth analyses of police integrity cross-culturally. This book moves away from the relatively narrow paradigm of police integrity viewed as resistance to for-gain misconduct, and provides a true comparative, cross-cultural exploration of police integrity, understood as resistance to *various forms* of police misconduct. It contains ten chapters describing the state of police integrity in ten countries as diverse as Croatia, Australia, South Africa, Russia, and South Korea. All these chapters follow the same format, starting with the brief introduction to the country's police, continuing with the exploration of the four dimensions of the police integrity theory and the analyses of the empirical data collected using the police integrity questionnaire, and concluding with the interpretations and implications of the findings.

In Chap. 1, Kutnjak Ivković sets the stage for the chapters studying individual countries by describing the theory of police integrity and the accompanying methodology. The chapter discusses the challenges that scholars experience while trying to study police misconduct directly and reasons why the alternative approach that focuses on its opposite—police integrity—should be used instead. The chapter presents the definition of police integrity and the theory of police integrity we employ throughout the book. Each of the four dimensions of the theory, from the emphasis on official rules, curtailing of the code of silence, and the reliance on the internal control efforts, to the influence of the society at large, is illuminated in detail. The author also incorporates a comprehensive account of the methodology used to study police integrity and describes the evolvement of the police integrity questionnaire.

In Chap. 2, Khechumyan and Kutnjak Ivković explore the contours of police integrity in Armenia, a small country in transition located in South Caucasus. The chapter describes the struggles of a country in which the transition from Soviet-dominated authoritarianism to a democracy has been ongoing since the early 1990s. It also illustrates the reforms of a centralized police agency in which implementation of community-based policing model and enhancement of police education have been top priorities. The police operate in a corrupt environment and are exposed to a close relationship between the police and the political elites. The empirical results of the study are consistent with this state of affairs; although the respondents had no problems recognizing the scenarios in the questionnaire as rule violating and evaluated most of them to be very serious, they rarely supported and expected dismissal for such behavior. The authors also present evidence of a strong code of silence.

In Chap. 3, Porter, Prenzler, and Hine explore the contours of police integrity in Australia, an established democracy. The chapter shows the evolution of the police in Australia, from the first European settlement in the eighteenth century and haphazard policing, the nineteenth century attempts of the colonial self-government to make police more professional and accountable, twentieth century policing, characterized by high levels of discretion, and the recent period of extensive reform. The chapter discusses the refinement of the laws and official rules, the development of independent police oversight mechanisms, and prior efforts to measure police culture among the police in Australia. The empirical results show that the respondents had no problems labeling cases of police misconduct as rule violations. The authors also note that despite the fact that most jurisdictions in Australia have mandatory reporting of misconduct there is a substantial minority of the respondents who would not report their fellow officers who had engaged in police misconduct.

In Chap. 4, Kutnjak Ivković explores the contours of police integrity in Croatia, an East European country in transition and the most recent member of the European Union. The chapter describes the turbulent history of one of the youngest national police agencies in Europe and argues that the events in the society at large, involving a war, strengthening of nationalism, mismanagement of economy, war profiteering, and extensive corruption, as well as transition into market economy, all affected the police and the state of police integrity. The author shows how, as time passed, the society learned to become more successful in dealing with corruption and nepotism, as well as in addressing ethnic-based violence and hostility. The empirical results show that the state of police integrity has changed over time. In particular, the chapter argues that although the code of silence is still present among the Croatian police officers, it seems to have weakened substantially since the earlier, 1995 survey. The author further finds that, although the respondents accurately evaluated examples of misconduct described in the questionnaire as rule violating, they neither supported nor expected severe discipline for such behavior.

In Chap. 5, Vallmüür explores the contours of police integrity in Estonia, a Baltic country in transition and one of the smallest and most sparsely populated members of the European Union. The author argues that the close cultural association with the Nordic countries has been a rather unique factor singling out Estonia among the other post-Soviet countries; moreover, the influence of the Protestant religion seems to have ameliorated the Soviet heritage of corruption because Estonia is perceived to be the least corrupt of all Central and East European countries. On the other hand, the chapter presents an analysis of why whistle-blowing in general, and in the police in particular, could be viewed as culturally challenging and how the recent legislative changes to the whistle-blower laws should address the shortcomings and provide more protection to the whistle-blowers. The empirical results are highly supportive of the perception of a relatively clean country. The respondents evaluated most the scenarios as serious and rule violating. At the same time, they also supported and expected dismissal for many of the behaviors described.

In Chap. 6, Cheloukhine, Kutnjak Ivković, Haq, and Haberfeld explore the contours of police integrity in Russia, a large and populous country in northern Eurasia. Based on the results of the Transparency International Corruption Perceptions Index, Russia is perceived as a highly corrupt country. In such an environment, it is not surprising that the police are perceived as one of the country's most corrupt agencies. Despite the relatively small sample of police officers participating in the survey, the results of this study, the first police integrity survey in Russia, highlight the baseline dimensions, thereby paving the road toward a future, more comprehensive study. The authors' major finding is that the majority of the respondents indeed recognized the behaviors depicted in most scenarios as violations of official rules. Given the estimates produced by Transparency International concerning corruption of governmental institutions in Russia, it is encouraging to discover that this recognition is embedded in police officer perceptions. However, the authors also report that their respondents thought that even the behaviors the majority had recognized as rule violating–use of excessive force, be it verbal or physical–neither warrant nor would receive serious disciplinary action. Finally, the existence of the code of silence is correlated with perceptions of misconduct seriousness.

In Chap. 7, Lobnikar and Meško explore the contours of police integrity in Slovenia, a transitional country in Central Europe. The chapter illustrates extensive legal changes put in place to regulate police practices, from the strengthening of the limitations on the search and seizure powers and cross-examination of witnesses, to the strengthened judicial control over police powers. The authors further describe how the legal reform has been complemented with the establishment of the Constitutional Court and the Ombudsman, both of which have shaped the conduct of Slovenian police officers. The chapter describes a captivating interplay between a complex set of domestic and transnational institutions in the control of police misconduct. The chapter compares the respondents' views about the appropriate and expected discipline and reveals that the respondents tended to view the discipline they expected their police agencies to mete out as fair. The authors also show that the police officers' evaluations of misconduct seriousness were the best predictors of the police officers' willingness to report.

In Chap. 8, Kutnjak Ivković and Sauerman explore the contours of police integrity in South Africa, a transitional country with a long history of human rights abuses. The chapter contains an in-depth exploration of the complex history of policing in South Africa and the reforms performed with the goal of changing the former apartheid regime's police force. The authors describe the twenty-year-long transition into the South African Police Service, a large national police agency. The chapter discusses questionable policies, strategies, and practices that result in an integrity-challenged organizational climate and prevent the SAPS from addressing successfully corruption and other challenges to police integrity. The results of the empirical analyses presented in the chapter show that while the respondents evaluated misconduct as rule violating and serious, they rarely expected and supported severe discipline for such rule-violating behaviors. Finally, the authors also demonstrate the presence of a rather strong code of silence.

In Chap. 9, Kang and Kutnjak Ivković explore police integrity in South Korea, an Asian democracy with a long legacy of military and autocratic regimes. In the overview of historic development of policing in South Korea, the authors argue that until about thirty years ago, the police served the interests of nondemocratic regimes and violated its citizens' human rights. The chapter explores the recent police reform—the Grand Reform. It focused primarily on police corruption and, at the same time, neglected to address the use of excessive force. The empirical results presented in the chapter demonstrate the consequences of the limited scope of the reform. The authors show that along all dimensions of police integrity, the respondents were more likely to exhibit lower levels of integrity related to the use of excessive force than to corruption and other forms of police misconduct. The chapter also shows evidence of a strong code of silence among the Korean police officers, particularly for the scenarios describing the use of excessive force.

In Chap. 10, Phetthong and Kutnjak Ivković explore police integrity in Thailand, an Asian kingdom with a turbulent history. The political instability in the country, coupled with the tradition of nepotism and corruption, create an atmosphere conducive toward police misconduct. Indeed, NGO reports suggest that corruption is widespread among the Thai police and that violations of citizens' human rights are not a rare occurrence. The empirical results seem to support these assertions. In particular, the authors show that the respondents did not evaluate most scenarios describing misconduct as serious, that they did not recognize most of them as violations of official rules, and that they neither expected nor supported severe discipline for the violations described in the scenarios. The results reveal that there is large discrepancy between the respondents' perceptions of the code of silence and its documented empirical contours.

In Chap. 11, Kutnjak Ivković, Haberfeld, and Peacock explore the contours of police integrity in the USA, a highly decentralized Western democracy. The chapter describes the 200-year-long history of policing in the United States, from the night watchmen and slave patrols to community policing and responses to terrorism. In the process, the authors review the country's heterogeneity of approaches to policing in general and police misconduct in particular. The chapter documents the existence of official rules, both federal and state laws and internal agency rules, with a particular emphasis on the role of the U.S. Supreme Court. The authors discuss how different social and political environments create different expectations of police integrity. The chapter presents empirical results of a police officer survey from a dozen municipal and sheriff police agencies. In the process, the authors show that the respondents' views about the use of excessive force scenarios match very closely with the use of force continuum. The chapter also demonstrates that police officers generally perceive their police agencies to be in line with their own views regarding appropriate discipline for misconduct.

In Chap. 12, Kutnjak Ivković and Haberfeld present a comparative view of police integrity. The authors analyze the results of the police integrity survey performed across ten countries. They find that, although absolute evaluations of seriousness and willingness to report vary across countries, relative rankings of seriousness and willingness to report seemed to be very similar. In all of these comparisons, the results from Russia and, to a certain degree, from South Korea, stand out from the remaining countries. While the respondents from most of the countries expected at least some discipline for the behaviors described in the questionnaire, the severity of the expected discipline is far from uniform. The authors conclude that police agencies across those countries create different disciplinary environments. Finally, although the authors document that the code of silence was detected in every country, the contours of the code of silence vary substantially.

About the Editors

Sanja Kutnjak Ivković is a Professor at the School of Criminal Justice, Michigan State University. She holds a doctorate in criminology (Ph.D., University of Delaware) and a doctorate in law (S.J.D., Harvard University). Her research focuses on comparative and international criminology, criminal justice, and law. Prof. Kutnjak Ivković is the author of *Reclaiming Justice: The International Tribunal for the Former Yugoslavia and Local Courts* (Oxford University Press, 2011; coauthored with John Hagan), *The Fallen Blue Knights: Controlling Police Corruption* (Oxford University Press, 2005), and *Lay Participation in Criminal Trials* (1999). She is coauthor with Carl Klockars and M. R. Haberfeld of *Enhancing Police Integrity* (Springer, 2006), and coeditor with Carl Klockars and M. R. Haberfeld of *Contours of Police Integrity* (Sage 2004), which received American Society of Criminology International Division Honorable Mention. Prof. Kutnjak Ivković's work has appeared in leading academic and law journals, such as the *Law and Society Review; Journal of Criminal Law and Criminology; Criminology and Public Policy; Law and Policy; Stanford Journal of International Law; Cornell International Law Journal; Policing and Society; Policing: An International Journal of Police Strategies and Management; Police Quarterly.*

M. R. Haberfeld is a Professor of Police Science and Chair of the Department of Law, Police Science and Criminal Justice Administration at John Jay College of Criminal Justice in New York City. She was a recipient of a National Institute of Justice grant to study Community Oriented Policing in Poland. The grant generated a number of publications on Community Policing, including an award-winning special issue of *Policing: An International Journal of Police Management and Strategies*, edited by her and titled "Community Policing around the World." Her latest books include: *Critical Issues in Police Training* (2013), *Police Organization and Training: Innovations in Research and Practice* (co-edited, 2011), *Police Leadership: Organizational and Managerial Decision Making Process* (2012) and *Policing Muslim Communities* (coauthored, 2013).

Acknowledgments

Our acknowledgments for this book go, first, to Katherine Chabalko, who provided us with the much needed understanding and support for the complex progression entailed in coauthoring and editing a comparative text; to Welmoed Spahr, who is always involved in various aspects of the process; and to other employees of the Springer who were part of the production development.

Dr. Kutnjak Ivković would like to express her gratitude to her family for their enduring support.

Dr. Haberfeld would like to extend her sincere appreciation for the work performed by her research assistant, Mr. Qasim Haq, who diligently assisted with the gathering of data collected from some of the U.S. police agencies and, internationally, for his involvement in securing all the necessary documents, and follow ups on data collection from Australia, Turkey, Cyprus, Russia, Scotland, and some other countries, where we tried to engage the police departments in our research yet, for various technical reasons, we were not successful in our attempts. Qasim's involvement in this project exemplifies the most professional academic commitment to research and his input and perseverance were beyond exemplary.

Finally, we would like to thank the leaders of the various police agencies in the countries that allowed our contributors to survey their employees and who put integrity research above other considerations. Thank you for making this research possible and for your contributions to the police profession.

Dr. Sanja Kutnjak Ivković
Dr. M. R. Haberfeld

Contents

Contributors

Serguei Cheloukhine John Jay College of Criminal Justice, New York, NY, USA

M. R. Haberfeld John Jay College of Criminal Justice, New York, NY, USA

Qasim Haq Hunter College, New York, NY, USA

Kelly Hine Griffith University, Nathan, Australia

Wook Kang Korean National Police University, Yongin-si, South Korea

Aleksandr Khechumyan Max Planck Institute for Foreign and International Criminal Law, Freiburg im Breisgau, Germany; Edmond J. Safra Center for Ethics at Harvard University, Cambridge, MA, USA

Sanja Kutnjak Ivković Michigan State University, East Lansing, MI, USA

Branko Lobnikar University of Maribor, Ljubljana, Slovenia

Gorazd Meško University of Maribor, Ljubljana, Slovenia

Robert Peacock Michigan State University, East Lansing, MI, USA

Narin Phetthong Sam Houston State University, Huntsville, TX, USA

Louise E. Porter Griffith University, Nathan, Australia

Tim Prenzler Griffith University, Nathan, Australia

Adri Sauerman Michigan State University, East Lansing, MI, USA

Birgit Vallmüür BV Consulting Ltd., Tallinn, Estonia

Chapter 1
Studying Police Integrity

Sanja Kutnjak Ivković

Abstract Police misconduct is a serious concern to scholars, police administrators, the media, and the general public. For a variety of reasons, a direct approach to the study of police misconduct poses considerable challenges. To ameliorate research hindrances, an alternative approach has been developed, focusing instead on its complement—police integrity. This chapter presents the theory of police integrity and the accompanying methodology. Each of the four dimensions of the theory, from the emphasis on official rules, curtailing of the code of silence, and the reliance on the internal control efforts, to the influence of the society at large, is described in detail. This chapter describes what an agency of high integrity should be doing along each of these dimensions. Next, a comprehensive account of the methodology has been presented and the two versions of the questionnaire described. The chapter also includes an extensive literature review of the studies that utilized the two questionnaires.

Keywords Code of silence · Police corruption · Police integrity · Rotten apple theory · Survey

Studying Police Misconduct and Police Integrity

Various forms of police misconduct and its related causes or correlates have been the focus of studies for a considerable time. Indeed, sociological studies (for a summary see, e.g., Adams 1995; Garner et al. 2002; Worden and Catlin 2002; Kutnjak Ivković 2003), independent commission reports (e.g., Knapp Commission 1972; Mollen Commission 1994; Christopher Commission 1991), and court cases (e.g., Kraska and Kappeler 1995; Harris 1997) clearly demonstrate that police officers engage in police misconduct, from police corruption, use of excessive force, racial profiling, to sexual misconduct and perjury. While the prevalence and nature of police misconduct varies from source to source and across agencies, the

---

S. Kutnjak Ivković
Michigan State University, East Lansing, MI, USA
e-mail: kutnjak@msu.edu

S. Kutnjak Ivković, M. R. Haberfeld (eds.), *Measuring Police Integrity Across the World*,
DOI 10.1007/978-1-4939-2279-6_1

common feature prevails that a certain percentage of police officers engage in some form of rule-violating behavior.

The body of research exploring each of these forms of police misconduct has grown substantially during several decades, with most of the attention devoted to the use of excessive force and police corruption. Consistent in these studies is the phenomenon that whenever direct questions about police misconduct are posed, be it about police corruption, use of excessive force, or police testifying, the researchers are bound to experience similar forms of opposition: police administrators are reluctant to open their doors to researchers raising questions about police misconduct, possibly fearing that any misconduct uncovered will be interpreted negatively for the administration/agency; police officers fearing ostracism from their colleagues if they reveal anything about the misconduct of their fellow officers or fearing disciplinary and/or criminal consequences if their own misconduct is uncovered. In addition, typical witnesses and victims of police misconduct, such as prostitutes, drug dealers, and other career criminals, may not be credible witnesses in court.

Several studies document the types of hindrances scholars or investigators encounter when police officers are confronted with direct questions about police misconduct. Numerous independent commissions (e.g., Christopher Commission 1991; Knapp 1972; Mollen 1994; Pennsylvania Crime Commission 1974) have already noted and described the presence of a strong code of silence among police officers. In fact, the Mollen Commission (1994) wrote about the code of silence as the most serious challenge to corruption control.

Similarly, there are examples of research projects in which strong codes of silence interfered with the research. Martin (1994) and Knowles (1996) planned to conduct a three-state study, asking police officers about the frequency of misconduct by other police officers in their police agencies. Because of the opposition from the police union, Pennsylvania did not participate in the study. Furthermore, even within the two participating states (Illinois and Ohio), the police union in Chicago objected, and Chicago, which accounts for about 25 % of police officers in Illinois, was excluded from the study (Martin 1994). Fabrizio (1990) conducted a study of Federal Bureau of Investigation (FBI) Academy participants—experienced police officers from police agencies across the country—about their experiences at the Academy. He asked them a series of questions, inquiring not only about their experiences but also about police misconduct. Whereas the respondents were generally eager to respond to most questions, none was willing to provide any examples of graft or corruption in their police agencies.

In 1994, Klockars and Kutnjak Ivković developed an alternative methodology to the study of police misconduct, an approach that does not face such serious challenges because it measures its opposite—police integrity. As such, it boasts several distinctive advantages (Klockars et al. 2006). First, the definition of police integrity is broad enough to allow a comparison of the contours of police integrity across different police agencies. At the same time, it is specific enough to enable scholars to engage in empirical data collection with the purpose of testing the theory. The definition is applicable not only to individual police officers but (and perhaps even more importantly) also to police agencies and groups of police officers (e.g., shifts, service areas, and units). Second, the theory of police integrity is organizational in nature. It generates specific steps that a police agency striving to be an agency of high integrity ought to follow, from creating a culture of integrity to controlling the code of silence. The theory is also amenable to empirical testing (Klockars et al. 2006). Third, the theoretical framework is accompanied by the methodological framework. The methodology can be used to measure the level of police integrity in an empirical and systematic way, both among individual police officers and within groups of police officers or police agencies. A critical feature of the methodology is that it is seldom met with the resistance that accompanies direct questions of police misconduct. Fourth, Klockars et al. (2006) have already demonstrated how to use the accompanying theoretical and methodological approach successfully to measure police integrity. As such, the integrity levels of numerous police agencies in over 20 countries have been successfully measured.

The Concept of Police Integrity

Klockars et al. define police integrity as "the normative inclination among police to resist temptations to abuse the rights and privileges of their occupation" (Klockars et al. 2006). This definition spans six dimensions.

The first dimension is the *normative* indicator, proposing that integrity is perceived to be a belief rather than a behavior (Klockars et al. 2006, p. 10), "[w]hen it is held by an individual it is often called an *attitude* or *opinion,* when it is shared by a group it is often called a *norm*." This implies that conduct may be viewed from a moral perspective as either right or wrong; it captures the belief of what police officers should do in certain circumstances. A close relation between police integrity and morality further implies that police officers who believe in "doing the right thing" should also behave in such a way and support reporting and disciplining the officers who behave contrary. However, "the norm of integrity may compete with and be tempered by norms that urge forgiveness, mercy, loyalty, reciprocity, tolerance, gratitude, compassion, and proportion, to name but a few" (Klockars et al. 2006, p. 2), resulting in a moral dilemma.

The second dimension reflects the *inclination to resist* (Klockars et al. 2006). It acknowledges that attitudes and behaviors do not always match; "people who believe in honesty sometimes lie; people who believe in fidelity sometimes are disloyal; and people of integrity sometimes do things they know are wrong" (Klockars et al. 2006, p. 2). A potential mismatch between attitudes and behavior stems from the fact that other reasons may exist (e.g., lack of opportunity, lack of imagination, fear of discovery, and fear of public punishment) that lead people to behave in a way that emphasizes high integrity. Nevertheless, attitudes and behaviors are related; attitudes of high integrity should at least partly guide police officers to behave accordingly. However, the causality of this relation between attitudes and behavior may be two-sided; attitudes could cause behavior and behavior could cause attitudes.

The third dimension is the very word *police* (Klockars et al. 2006). Its deliberate choice (instead of "police officer" or "police agency") reflects that police integrity is a characteristic of individual police officers, groups of police officers, or entire police organizations. However, the dynamics and correlates of integrity depend on the unit of analysis: "[h]ow one understands and explains the psychology of integrity of an individual police officer will most certainly differ from the understanding and explanation of the sociology, politics, or history of the evolution of a culture of integrity in a police agency" (Klockars et al. 2006, p. 3).

The fourth dimension rests on *temptation* (Klockars et al. 2006), focusing on the different environments in which police officers and police agencies operate and the specific enticements to misconduct they offer. While gain is the most obvious temptation, it is certainly not the only one. In fact, the range of possible temptations could be quite diverse and the corresponding contours of police integrity could be very different across agencies (Klockars et al. 2006, p. 4).

The fifth dimension focuses on *abuse* (Klockars et al. 2006). In severe circumstances, the abusive nature of behavior may be obvious. In other, less extreme situations, police officers may tend to offer excuses or completely deny its abusive nature. Opinions about whether certain forms of behavior should be classified as abuse could also vary from agency to agency.

The sixth dimension highlights *the rights and privileges of their occupation* (Klockars et al. 2006). Policing is a highly discretionary, coercive activity that routinely takes place in private settings, out of the sight of supervisors, and involves witnesses who are often regarded as unreliable (Klockars et al. 2006, p. 5). As such, being a police officer will create many opportunities in which the police officer may be tempted to abuse the rights and privileges of his or her occupation and succumb to temptations.

Organizational Theory of Police Integrity

In the 1970s, the views of the majority of police administrators regarding police corruption fell squarely in the doctrine of the "rotten apple" or "bad apple" theory. According to the "rotten apple" theory (Vollmer 1936; Goldstein 1977; Pennsylvania Crime Commission 1974; Knapp Commission 1972), police corruption is a result of character defects of individual police officers—"bad apples" or "rotten apples"—while the majority of the police officers ("apples in the barrel") are "healthy." Once corrupt police officers are detected, they should be swiftly removed from the agency before they "spoil" the rest of the "barrel."

The Knapp Commission (1972, p. 7), the Pennsylvania Crime Commission (1974, p. 393), and the Mollen Commission (1994) argued that the police administrators' acceptance of the "bad apple" theory presents a virtually insurmountable obstacle for meaningful reforms. By maintaining and supporting this theory, police administrators nullify efforts against police corruption because they essentially refuse to recognize and acknowledge that the problem exists in the first place. In addition, administrators' refusal to acknowledge that corruption is a widespread and serious problem in the department creates a circumstance in which official denial undermines the confidence and trust that the leadership of the police department once may have enjoyed; the administrators are perceived to be naive, incompetent, and/or corrupt (Pennsylvania Crime Commission 1974, p. 394), and the code of silence is subsequently reinforced (Knapp Commission 1972, p. 7).

An alternative theoretical view of police corruption has emerged in the late 1970s (e.g., Goldstein 1975; Punch 2009). It is organizational, occupational, and cultural in nature. Based on Goldstein's view of the organizational nature of police corruption, Klockars and Kutnjak Ivković (1999) proposed an organizational theory of police misconduct which stretches beyond the understanding of police corruption/police misconduct as a problem of individual police officers. Such an approach opens "horizons to a substantially different understanding of the problem, suggest[s] alternative control mechanisms, and allow[s] for the development of a novel methodological approach to the study" (Klockars and Kutnjak Ivković 2004, p. 1.4). This theoretical approach, upon which a substantial body of research has been built, evinces the following four dimensions.

Organizational Rules

This first dimension of the theory of police misconduct focuses on the way a police agency's organizational rules are established by the administration, how they are communicated to the police officers, and the way in which they are understood by the police officers (Klockars and Kutnjak Ivković 2004, p. 1.4). According to this theory, a police agency of high integrity is one in which the official rules prohibiting misconduct have been established, these official rules are taught and enforced, and its police officers know and support the official rules.

Typically, the conduct of police officers across the world is regulated by two types of rules. First, a country's constitution restricts the police officers' powers by establishing certain fundamental rights and guarantees of adherence to human rights in the actions of its employees. Separate laws then contain specific norms further regulating police officers' work, ranging from the limitations on the use of force to direct prohibitions of corrupt behavior. Second, regardless of whether the police agency is part of a centralized or decentralized system, additional rules, typically internal to the police agency, elaborate and determine the standards of appropriate and expected behavior of police officers. However, in decentralized police systems, such as the USA, in which each police agency makes its own official rules, the nature of official agency rules varies across police agencies to a greater extent than in centralized police systems such as Croatia, Poland, or France, in which all police agencies are part of the same police system (e.g., Croatian Police, Gendarmerie) and thus adhere to the same rules.

Virtually every country in the world evinces the basic set of laws and official agency rules. Dimensions along which countries differ, however, are reflected in the extent to which these rules prohibit misconduct, the way these official rules are made, how often they are enforced, the level of police officers' familiarity with the rules, and the extent to which police officers support them.

Quite likely, official rules would not provide equal coverage to different forms of police misconduct. By their nature, legal rules governing the use of force and the use of excessive force will be more complex to design and enforce than explicit prohibitions of corrupt behavior. Even within the same form of police misconduct, police agencies across the world will be more likely to prohibit consistently the most serious forms, such as the acceptance of bribes, kickbacks, and thefts from crime scenes (Roebuck and Barker 1974) than the lesser transgressions, the so-called *mala prohibita,* such as the acceptance of gratuities, small gifts, and discounts (Roebuck and Barker 1974).

The way in which the official rules are made influences how supportive police officers are of them. If they perceive that the rules are imposed by a detached administrator who is unaware of the realities of police work, police officers will be much less supportive of them than if they perceive the rules to be made by an administrator who understands the complexities and nuances of law enforcement. In addition, the way in which and the extent to which official rules are taught, may vary across countries, within the same country, and across time. During periods of rapid hiring, for example, the devotion to detailed knowledge and teaching of the official rules is more likely to be jeopardized, than it would be at times of steady and systematic hiring.

However, merely enacting the laws and updating the official rules is not sufficient to achieve high integrity; the enforcement of official rules is also critical as the reality shows that police agencies could differ greatly in their enforcement of these rules. In addition, whenever the police agency's official rules prohibit certain behaviors, and unofficial practice allows such actions to continue, a large discrepancy between the official rules and the unofficial policy is created (e.g., Pennsylvania Crime Commission 1974; Mollen Commission 1994) and, in the words of the Mollen Commission (1994, p. 63), "the Department's commitment to integrity is more rhetoric than reality." Police officers, particularly the new ones, will be the most likely to exhibit doubts and confusion in the situations in which "the Commander of the Internal Affairs Bureau and the officer in charge of the Police Academy cannot agree on the proper guideline" (Pennsylvania Crime Commission 1974, p. 240). By not enforcing certain rules or, even worse, by being involved in the officially prohibited behavior, police administrators are sending a very clear message to the police officers that they de facto tolerate such behavior.

Techniques of Controlling Police Misconduct

This second dimension of the theory of police misconduct focuses on various techniques used by the police agency to detect and investigate police misconduct (Klockars and Kutnjak Ivković 2004, p. 1.4). According to this theory, a police agency of high integrity is an agency which uses various mechanisms of control, be they reactive, such as investigations of misconduct and discipline of police officers who violated the official rules, or more proactive, such as education in ethics, integrity testing, and proactive investigations.

Stories of the New York City Police Department (NYPD) and the Philadelphia Police Department, depicted by independent commissions (Knapp Commission 1972; Pennsylvania Crime Commission 1974; Mollen Commission 1994), illustrate typical problems of corruption control techniques in police agencies riddled with corruption. The Mollen Commission (1994, p. 62) found that most corrupt police officers do not join the police department with the intent of becoming criminals; rather, most start as honest police officers and circumstances lead them to change their values. In accordance with the organizational theory of police misconduct, the Mollen Commission (1994, p. 63) concluded that, "[t]he Department must necessarily share the blame for this situation. It failed to take the necessary actions to keep its honest cops honest, through effective supervision, training, deterrence, personnel management and other means."

All three commissions found the cause of the collapse of the departmental machinery for investigating police corruption vested in the police departments' subscription to the "rotten apple" theory (Knapp Commission 1972; Pennsylvania Crime Commission 1974; Mollen Commission 1994), leading to the supervisors' ignorance of corruption evidence and the collapse of the principle of command accountability, thereby effectively broadcasting to the police officers that corruption is tolerated. In addition, the perceived consequences of police corruption disclosure affected the internal corruption control mechanisms; the departments did not view their mission as that of uncovering serious corruption, but, rather, as that of engaging in "damage control" (Mollen 1994, p. 71).

As the Knapp Commission (1972) and the Pennsylvania Crime Commission (1974) noted, the criminal justice system protected corrupt police officers. In the departments in which the commissions found widespread and systematic police corruption, less than one tenth of 1 % of the police officers were arrested and/or tried on charges of police corruption each year; "[i]n the view of the pervasive corruption which the Commission has uncovered, the number of arrests is very low" (Pennsylvania Crime Commission 1974, p. 446).

A recent book (Mesko et al. 2013a) on police reforms in 12 Central and East European countries in transition (Bosnia and Herzegovina, Croatia, the Czech Republic, Estonia, Hungary, Kosovo, Macedonia, Montenegro, Russia, Serbia, Slovakia, and Slovenia) demonstrates the diversity of two types of control mechanisms across a dozen countries relatively similar in a number of dimensions (Kutnjak Ivković 2013). Although the existence of internal mechanisms of control seems to be prevalent across these countries, the effectiveness of these mechanisms is quite diverse. In addition, a few countries also include a combination of internal and external mechanisms of control, both domestic (e.g., ombudsman, constitutional court, and parliament) and international (e.g., European Court of Human Rights and the European Committee for the Prevention of Torture).

The development of the control mechanisms in two countries in transition, part of the same country until 1991, illustrates this point. On the one hand, Serbia's police had a long history of protecting the regime (Kesetović 2013), violating citizens' human rights, and avoiding any accountability to either internal or external control mechanisms (Kutnjak Ivković 2013). Since 2001, however, the police have undergone a systematic reform. Yet, while the police officials evaluate the reform in positive terms, independent scholars, nongovernmental organizations (NGOs), and international police experts are critical of it (Kesetović 2013). On the other hand, Slovenia's reform of the police started very early in the country's transformation process; as the country was learning how to become a democracy, the police were also transformed. In addition to the internal control mechanisms, the Slovenian police are subject to both domestic external control (e.g., the Constitutional Court, the ombudsman, and the prosecutors) and international external control (e.g., the European Court of Human Rights and the European Committee for the Prevention of Torture; Mesko et al. 2013b).

Curtailing the Code of Silence

The third dimension of the theory of police misconduct focuses on the police code of silence, or the blue curtain, and the police agency's efforts of curtailing it (Klockars and Kutnjak Ivković 2004, p. 1.4). The code of silence, or "the unwritten rule that an officer never give incriminating information against a fellow officer," seems likely to be, "perhaps the greatest barrier to effective corruption control: the code of silence, the unwritten rule that an officer never give incriminating information against a fellow officer" (Mollen Commission 1994, p. Exhibit 6 at 6). Klockars et al. (2000, p. 2) argued that:

> The parameters of The Code—precisely what behavior it covers and to whom its benefits are extended—vary among police agencies. For example, The Code may apply to only low-level corruption in some agencies and to the most serious corruption in others. Furthermore, whom and what The Code covers can vary substantially not only *among* police agencies but also *within* police agencies. Particularly in large police agencies, the occupational culture of integrity may differ substantially among precincts, service areas, task forces, and work groups.

According to the organizational theory of police misconduct, the code of silence in a police agency of low integrity is strong, protecting various forms of police misconduct. Whereas the code of silence develops as a consequence of a semi-military police organization in each police agency, the code of silence in police agencies of high integrity is neither strong nor protects serious forms of police misconduct.

The code of silence was very strong in the NYPD in the 1990s, just as it had been in the 1970s (Knapp Commission 1972; Mollen Commission 1994). It serves as a clear illustration of the influence of the code on both honest and dishonest police officers in the department; even police officers like Michael Dowd, a drug dealer earning such staggering amounts of money from his illegal activities that he forgot to collect his from the NYPD paychecks, were never reported either by fellow police officers or by supervisors, although fellow officers silently hoped that Dowd and other officers who exhibit similar behavior would be removed from the force (Mollen Commission 1994, p. 4). Peer pressure creates solidarity which, in turn, is linked to the code of silence; honest police officers show great reluctance, if not unwillingness, to report dishonest behavior of fellow police officers (Pennsylvania Crime Commission 1974, p. 432). Indeed, the Mollen Commission (1994, p. Exhibit 6 at 7) argued that the existence of the strong code of silence and the "us versus them" mentality in some parts of the NYPD, "largely explain how groups can openly engage in corruption for long periods of time with impunity."

Klockars et al. studied police integrity in 30 U.S. police agencies (e.g., Klockars et al. 2000). They found that the majority of the police officers in the sample would protect least serious forms of corruption, while, at the same time, reporting on corruption of intermediate to high levels of seriousness (Klockars et al. 2000, p. 6). However, the findings for the overall sample masked some substantial differences across the agencies. To illustrate this, Klockars et al. (2000, p. 7) have selected two agencies from the opposite sides of the integrity spectrum:

> Agency 2, which ranked 8th in integrity of the 30 agencies surveyed, and Agency 23, which ranked in a 5-way tie for 24th place, are both large municipal police agencies. Agency 2 has a national reputation for integrity, is extremely receptive to research, and is often promoted as a model of innovation. Agency 23 has a long history of scandal, and its reputation as an agency with corruption problems persists despite numerous reform efforts. Although a local newspaper once dubbed Agency 23 "the most corrupt police department in the country," six other agencies in the sample appear to have integrity environments that are as poor or worse.

While the code of silence was similar in some aspects, the authors found systematic and dramatic differences between the codes of silence measured in the two police agencies (Klockars et al. 2000, p. 8):

> In both agencies, few officers said that they or their police colleagues would report any of the least serious types of corrupt behavior… Officers from Agency 2 reported that they and their colleagues would report the behavior described in the seven other cases. In Agency 23, however, there was *no* case that the majority of officers indicated they would report. In sum, while The Code is under control in Agency 2, it remains a powerful influence in Agency 23, providing an environment in which corrupt behavior can flourish.

Further interpretation of these dissimilarities can also be found in another publication by Klockars et al. (2004, p. 36):

> It is clear that in Agency 23 "The Code of Silence" is so strong that the officer who takes a kickback, a bribe, steals from a found wallet or a crime scene may do so without much worry that his police colleagues will expose his misconduct. By contrast, a police officer in St. Petersburg probably will not be reported for taking a free meal or a discount, accepting a holiday gift from a merchant, or for not reporting a police officer for driving under the influence, but every other offense described in the scenario runs a substantial chance of being revealed by a fellow police officer.

Klockars et al. (2004) put together a coedited book with 14 country chapters, exploring measurement of police officers' willingness to report. Although the book pertained to the measurement of police integrity in general, the measurement of the code of silence seems to reveal the most dramatic differences across the countries. Klockars et al. reported (Klockars et al. 2004, p. 17):

> In five of the countries not a single incident of the eleven described in the survey would be very likely to be reported by fellow officers. In nine out of fourteen countries fellow

officers would not be certain to report a fellow officer who took a bribe from a speeding motorist. In fact, in every one of the countries surveyed an officer could accept free drinks to overlook a bar, which remained open past the official closing time or strike a prisoner in confinement without assuming that his police colleagues who witnessed the offense would be sure to report him. It appears that in few places in the world will a police officer turn in a fellow police officer who accepts free meals, discounts, or holiday gifts.

Influence of Social and Political Environment

The fourth dimension of the police integrity theory holds that the social, economic, and political environment in which police agencies operate, influences the level of integrity in the police agency (Klockars and Kutnjak Ivković 2004). Societies shape the level of misconduct of their public servants by establishing and nurturing a culture intolerant of misconduct, promulgating governing rules for ethical behavior of its employees, and by teaching and enforcing these rules (or, conversely, failing to do so).

Since 1995, each year Transparency International has ranked countries across the world based on how corrupt their public sector is perceived by various stakeholders, ranging from citizens and business people to analysts and experts. Countries are ranked from those at the bottom of the scale, wherein the public sector is perceived as highly corrupt (e.g., Afghanistan, North Korea, Sudan, and Somalia; Transparency International 2014) to those at the top of the scale, wherein the public sector is perceived as almost clear of corruption (e.g., Finland, Sweden, Norway, Denmark, New Zealand, and Australia; Transparency International 2014). Clearly, countries at the top of the scale create very different expectations in terms of integrity of their governmental employees than countries at the bottom of the scale do. As such, police agencies are strongly affected by the views shared and control mechanisms put in place by their larger societies and, consequently, it can be expected that more police agencies of high integrity would be found in the societies that put a high premium on ethical conduct of their governmental employees, rather than in the societies that are more acceptable of misconduct of their governmental employees.

Table 1.1 helps explore this relation further. It denotes two broad categories of the integrity spectrum for both societies (rows of the table) and police agencies (columns of the table). It is expected that most police agencies of high integrity would be placed in the cell of the table associated with societies of high integrity. Conversely, it is expected that most police agencies of low integrity would be located in the cell of the table associated with societies of low integrity. Still, there might also be agencies that should be placed into one of the two remaining cells. If a police agency of low integrity is found in a country of high integrity (e.g., the NYPD), the society would create sufficient pressure to investigate the agency, propose a set of reform recommendations, and implement them (e.g., Knapp Commission 1972; Mollen Commission 1994). In other words, it is not expected that an agency of low integrity in a society of high integrity would remain

Table 1.1 Police agency integrity levels by society integrity levels

	Police agency	
Society	*High integrity*	*Low integrity*
High integrity	In societies that value ethical conduct of their governmental employees, it is reasonable to expect that the police agencies would adhere to the same standards (e.g., the police in Finland, the police in Sweden)	Society will react if the police are not able to police themselves; investigation and reform (e.g., a police reform in Singapore, NYPD in the 1990s)
Low integrity	These police agencies will be an exception; their high integrity will likely be a consequence of the police administration's determination and concentrated efforts (e.g., FBI reform under Hoover in the 1930s)	In societies that do not value ethical conduct of their governmental employees, it is reasonable to expect that police agencies will follow suit (e.g., local police agencies in Mexico, police in Pakistan)

NYPD New York City Police Department, *FBI* Federal Bureau of Investigation

at such a low level of integrity for an undetermined period of time. On the other hand, it is possible to find police agencies of high integrity in the societies of low integrity. For example, while nepotism and corruption were rampant throughout the American society in the 1920s and 1930s, the reform efforts that J. Edgar Hoover undertook as the newly appointed head of the FBI, dramatically changed not only the state of integrity within the agency but also the perceptions of the agency (Kelling and Moore 1988, p. 4).

Indeed, the results in the *Contours of Police Integrity* (Klockars et al. 2004) do reveal that police agencies from the countries typically ranked near the top of the Transparency International Corruption Perceptions Scale (e.g., Sweden, the Netherlands, and the USA) exhibit much higher levels of police integrity than police agencies from countries typically listed toward the bottom of the scale (e.g., Pakistan) or in the middle of the scale (e.g., Croatia, Poland, Slovenia, South Africa; Transparency International 2005) do. In fact, Klockars et al. (2004, p. 17) find that, "In Croatia, Hungary, Pakistan, Poland, and South Africa the code of silence is so strong that in those countries officers are actually estimating just *how unwilling* most officers are to report the misconduct described in the scenarios."

Organizational theory allows scholars to extrapolate and hypothesize that in large and diverse countries with autonomous subunits, such as the USA, social expectations could be quite different across these units. While discussing the diversity across the USA, Klockars et al. (2006, p. 10) argued that:

> Even within the same country, as United States history illustrates, there are areas with long and virtually uninterrupted traditions of persistent police corruption (e.g., Chicago, New Orleans, Key West), equally long traditions of integrity (e.g., Milwaukee, Kansas City), and still others that have undergone repeated cycles of scandal and reform (e.g., New York, Philadelphia, Oakland). From such histories we may conclude two things: not only public expectations about police integrity exert vastly different pressures on police agencies in different areas, but also police agencies of integrity may effectively resist such pressures.

The Methodology of the Measurement of Police Integrity

The theoretical approach was coupled with a novel methodology that facilitates the studying of police integrity as an organizational concept in a systematic and empirical manner. At the same time, this approach avoids the pitfalls that direct questions about police misconduct will likely stand to generate. Thus, instead of placing such questions about misconduct, scholars can rely on the measurement instrument built around the key question: *What is the level of intolerance for misconduct in the organization?*

The questionnaire solicits police officers' responses to hypothetical scenarios describing different examples of police misconduct. Prior to questionnaire completion, the respondents are informed that the police officer featured in the scenarios has 5 years of experience, that the officer has no prior disciplinary record, and that the officer has an overall satisfactory working history.

Because this project originally started as a way to measure the opposite of police corruption, the majority of the scenarios in the questionnaire (9 out of 11) describe forms of police corruption. Relying on Roebuck and Barker's typology (1974), descriptions of various forms of corruption ranging from the acceptance of gratuities and internal corruption to kickbacks and thefts from a crime scene (Table 1.2) were included in the questionnaire. In addition, the questionnaire contains one scenario describing the use of excessive force and one scenario, which may not be a violation of official rules (being employed off duty).

The goal was to create hypothetical scenarios appropriate to the functions of a line police officer walking the beat. At the same time, the scenarios should be amenable to comparative research and, thus, should be culturally natural and realistic in modern, industrial societies.

Nine out of 11 scenarios deal with examples of police corruption, a form of police misconduct characterized with the acceptance of gain (e.g., Kutnjak Ivković 2005a). Therefore, it was critical that, if at all possible, the value of the gain achieved through a corrupt transaction be incorporated into the description of the scenarios. One of the scenarios (scenario 3) includes a description of a bribe from a motorist caught speeding. The value of the bribe could have been shown in an absolute amount, described in U.S. dollars or the local currency equivalent. Such an approach would create perceptions of different seriousness in different countries, depending on the average salary of police officials. Rather, this value has been expressed in relative terms. In scenario 3, the police officer accepted a bribe "for half of the amount of the fine." Similarly, the watch stolen from the crime scene in scenario 5 is worth about 2-days' pay for the responding police officers. In addition, the auto-repair kickback in scenario 6 generates a reward equivalent to 5 % of the value of the repair.

Despite the goal of making the scenarios suitable for comparative research, several scenarios had to be modified for the sake of realism in the survey's application. For example, scenarios 7 and 8 require police officers to drive cars, but, as scholars discovered in the application of the survey in Pakistan (Chatta and Kutnjak Ivković 2004), police officers typically do not own cars. Consequently, cars were

Table 1.2 Scenario descriptions: first survey

	Scenario description
Scenario 1	A police officer runs his own private business in which he sells and installs security devices, such as alarms, special locks, etc. He does this work during his off-duty hours.
Scenario 2	A police officer routinely accepts free meals, cigarettes, and other items of small value from merchants on his beat. He does not solicit these gifts and is careful not to abuse the generosity of those who give gifts to him.
Scenario 3	A police officer stops a motorist for speeding. The officer agrees to accept a personal gift for half of the amount of the fine in exchange for not issuing a citation.
Scenario 4	A police officer is widely liked in the community, and on holidays local merchants and restaurant and bar owners show their appreciation for his attention by giving him gifts of food and liquor.
Scenario 5	A police officer discovers a burglary of a jewelry shop. The display cases are smashed and it is obvious that many items have been taken. While searching the shop, he takes a watch, worth about 2-days' pay for that officer. He reports that the watch had been stolen during the burglary.
Scenario 6	A police officer has a private arrangement with a local auto body shop to refer the owners of the cars damaged in the accidents to the shop. In exchange for each referral, he receives a payment of 5 % of the repair bill from the shop owner.
Scenario 7	A police officer, who happens to be a very good auto mechanic, is scheduled to work during the coming holidays. A supervisor offers to give him these days off, if he agrees to tune-up his supervisor's personal car. Evaluate the *supervisor's* behavior.
Scenario 8	At 2 a.m. a police officer, who is on duty, is driving his patrol car on a deserted road. He sees a vehicle that has been driven off the road and is stuck in a ditch. He approaches the vehicle and observes that the driver is not hurt but is obviously intoxicated. He also finds that the driver is a police officer. Instead of reporting this accident and offense he transports the driver to his home.
Scenario 9	A police officer finds a bar on his beat, which is still serving drinks a half hour past its legal closing time. Instead of reporting this violation, the police officer agrees to accept a couple of free drinks from the owner.
Scenario 10	Two police officers on foot patrol surprise a man who is attempting to break into an automobile. The man flees. They chase him for about two blocks before apprehending him by tackling him and wrestling him to the ground. After he is under control both officers punch him a couple of times in the stomach as punishment for fleeing and resisting.
Scenario 11	A police officer finds a wallet in a parking lot. It contains the amount of money equivalent to a full-day's pay for that officer. He reports the wallet as lost property, but keeps the money for himself.

substituted by motorbikes in Pakistan. In addition, in scenario 9, a police officer finds a bar that serves drinks after its official closing times. In Poland, the closing hours for bars are not clearly defined (Haberfeld 2004). Instead, the police officer in question encounters a situation in which the bartender serves drinks to minors.

Although the definition of police integrity includes the resistance to temptations of various sources, the scenarios in the questionnaire (with one exception) include examples of officers not being able to resist only one category of temptations—the abuse of police officer position for a gain (i.e., police corruption; Klockars et al. 1997, p. 79). To ameliorate this problem of measuring only the resistance to corruption, the second version of the questionnaire has been designed (Klockars et al. 1997, p. 79):

> Will police who steal, accept bribes or take kickbacks also succumb to the temptations to lie in court, forge records, fabricate evidence, or make unwarranted searches or unjustified arrests even though gain provides no motive for doing so? Will police who lie in court, forge records, fabricate evidence, or make unwarranted searches or unjustified arrests resist temptations to steal, accept bribes, or take kickbacks? Or will the same integrity that inclines police to resist the temptations of corruption also incline them to resist temptations to abuse their rights and privileges in most other ways and for most other reasons as well? All of these questions (and their answers) now appear quite visible on the near research horizon.

Scenarios for the second survey include police abuses motivated by a range of motives, including those driven by motivations other than gain, and have thus encapsulated different forms of police misconduct. At the same time, the motives had to be unambiguous, compelling to the officers who read them, and easily expressed within two to three brief sentences (Klockars et al. 2006, p. 137). Four scenarios describe the use of excessive force, ranging from verbal abuse to the use of deadly force (scenario 4, scenario 6, scenario 7, scenario 11; Table 1.3). Two additional scenarios describe falsification of an official report (scenario 10) and failure to execute a search warrant (scenario 2). To allow for the potential test–retest measurements of the first and second questionnaire (Klockars et al. 2006), five police corruption scenarios (scenario 1, scenario 3, scenario 5, scenario 8, and scenario 9) from the first questionnaire were kept in the second questionnaire as well. They are only slightly changed from the first survey (e.g., a police officer steals a watch in the first version and a knife in the second version; tune-up of the supervisor's personal car and the running of errands for the supervisor).

Every scenario is accompanied by a series of seven questions, each measuring the normative and proportionate reflections of police integrity (Table 1.4). Unlike the limitations of a direct study of police misconduct, these questions focus on factual issues and opinions. The questions ask for factual answers about the police officers' knowledge of the official rules, and solicit the officers' opinions about the seriousness of rule violation, the punishment such misconduct deserves or is likely to receive, and their estimates of the willingness of officers to report such behavior without asking them directly about their own or others' (mis)*behavior* (Klockars et al. 1997).

Table 1.3 Scenario descriptions: second survey

	Scenario description
Scenario 1	A police officer is widely liked in the community. Local merchants and restaurant owners regularly show their appreciation for his attention by giving him gifts of food, cigarettes, and other items of small value.
Scenario 2	A police officer is aware that there is a felony warrant for a long time friend of his. Although he sees his friend frequently over a period of more than a week and warns his friend of its existence, he does not arrest him.
Scenario 3	A police officer discovers a burglary of a hardware store. The display cases are smashed and many items have obviously been taken. While searching the store, he takes an expensive pocketknife and slips it into his pocket. He reports that the knife has been stolen during the burglary.
Scenario 4	An officer, who was severely beaten by a person resisting arrest, has just returned to duty. On patrol, the officer approaches a person standing in a dimly lit alley. Suddenly, the person throws a gym bag at the officer and begins to run away. The officer fatally shoots the person, striking him in the back. It was later determined that the person was unarmed.
Scenario 5	A police officer is scheduled to work during coming holidays. The supervisor offers to give him these days off, if he agrees to run some personal errands for the supervisor. Evaluate the *supervisor's* behavior.
Scenario 6	In responding with her male partner to a fight in a bar, a young, female officer receives a black eye from one of the male combatants. The man is arrested, handcuffed, and, as he is led into the cells, the male member of the team punches him very hard in the kidney area saying, "hurts, doesn't it."
Scenario 7	A police officer stops a motorist for speeding. As the officer approaches the vehicle, the driver yells, "What the hell are you stopping me for?" The officer replies, "Because today is 'Arrest an Asshole Day.'"
Scenario 8	At 2:00 a.m. a police officer, who is on duty, is driving his patrol car on a deserted road. He sees a vehicle that has been driven off the road and is stuck in a ditch. He approaches the vehicle and observes that the driver is not hurt but is obviously intoxicated. He also finds that the driver is a police officer. Instead of reporting this accident and offense, he transports the driver to his home.
Scenario 9	A police officer has a private arrangement with a local auto body shop to refer the owners of cars damaged in accidents to the shop. In exchange for each referral, he receives a payment of 5 % of the repair bill from the shop owner.
Scenario 10	A police officer arrests two drug dealers involved in a street fight. One has a large quantity of heroin on his person. In order to charge them both with serious offenses, the officer falsely reports that the heroin was found on both men.
Scenario 11	A police sergeant, without intervening, watches officers under his supervision repeatedly strike and kick a man arrested for child abuse. The man has previous child abuse arrests. Evaluate the *sergeant's* behavior.

Table 1.4 Wording of questions and answers

	Wording of the question and possible answers
Question 1	How serious do *you* consider this behavior to be? Not at all serious … Very serious 1 2 3 4 5
Question 2	How serious do *most police officers in your agency* consider this behavior to be? Not at all serious … Very serious 1 2 3 4 5
Question 3	Would this behavior be regarded as a violation of official policy in your agency? Definitely not … Definitely yes 1 2 3 4 5
Question 4	If an officer in your agency engaged in this behavior and was discovered doing so, what, if any, discipline do *you* think *should* follow. 1. *None* 2. *Verbal reprimand* 3. *Written reprimand* 4. *Period of suspension without pay* 5. *Demotion in rank* 6. *Dismissal*
Question 5	If an officer in your agency engaged in this behavior and was discovered doing so, what, if any, discipline do *you* think *would* follow. 1. *None* 2. *Verbal reprimand* 3. *Written reprimand* 4. *Period of suspension without pay* 5. *Demotion in rank* 6. *Dismissal*
Question 6	Do you think *you* would report a fellow police officer who engaged in this behavior? Definitely not … Definitely yes 1 2 3 4 5
Question 7	Do you think *most police officers in your agency* would report a fellow police officer who engaged in this behavior? Definitely not … Definitely yes 1 2 3 4 5

The first two questions inquire about the police officers' own and other officers' perceptions of the seriousness of each case. They are followed by a question whether the behavior described in the scenario constitutes a violation of official rules. Next, the officers are asked what discipline they think such behavior should merit and what discipline they think would be meted out by the police agency. Finally, the last two questions focus on the police officers' adherence to the code of silence by asking whether they and their fellow officers are likely to report a police officer who engaged in such behavior (Table 1.4).

Possible answers to five out of these seven questions included Likert-type scales ranging from one to five (see Table 1.4). The two questions about discipline have answers that depend upon the legal norms. Thus, they have to be adjusted to fit the legal environment. As Klockars et al. (2004) point out, these answers could range widely and even include a different number of potential answers. However, all these disciplinary scales start with "no discipline" and end with "dismissal."

Current State of Police Integrity Research

Already, the National Research Council of the National Academies (2004, p. 274) evaluated this research approach as showing "considerable promise." Indeed, since Carl Klockars and Sanja Kutnjak Ivković started the project in the mid-1990s, a significant body of research following the theory and methodology has been created. A search of various electronic sources to date uncovered four books, 14 dissertations, 20 book chapters, 42 journal articles, and eight reports published utilizing this approach.

Most of the existing research used the first questionnaire, be it exactly as it was designed (e.g., Klockars et al. 2004; Micucci and Gomme 2009; Schafer and Martinelli 2008) or in some modified form. For example, Greene et al. (2004), McDevitt et al. (2011), and White (2008) used only a few or several scenarios from the original group. On the other hand, Charles (2009) added a few scenarios, while Klockars and Kutnjak Ivković (1999), Kutnjak Ivković et al. (2004), and Rothwell and Baldwin (2006) modified the questionnaire to fit civilian employees or the general population (e.g., students). Occasionally, the focus of a project was only on some types of scenarios, such as the acceptance of gratuities (e.g., White 2008) or the use of force (Micucci and Gomme 2009). In some studies, the original set of scenarios has been indexed (e.g., Jenks et al. 2014) and regrouped (e.g., Lee et al. 2013).

The original U.S. application of the questionnaire resulted in a national sample of 3235 police officers from 30 police agencies (Klockars and Kutnjak Ivković 2004; Klockars et al. 1997, 2000, 2004). The same data set has been reanalyzed by several scholars (e.g., Marche 2009; Micucci and Gomme 2009; Raines 2010). The questionnaire has been distributed to police officers in Philadelphia (e.g., Chappell and Piquero 2004; Greene et al. 2004; Hickman 2005; Kargin 2009; Wolfe and Piquero 2011), and several other U.S. agencies (e.g., Gamarra 2011; McDevitt et al. 2011; Pogarsky and Piquero 2004; Rothwell and Baldwin 2006; Schafer and Martinelli 2008; Smith 2009) or officers from different agencies attending a police training facility (e.g., Vito et al. 2011). For the survey of U.S. studies, see Table 1.5.

Over the span of the last 20 years, the questionnaire has been applied in 23 countries (Armenia, Austria, Bosnia and Herzegovina, Canada, Croatia, Czech Republic, Eritrea, Finland, Hungary, Japan, Malaysia, the Netherlands, Norway, Pakistan, Poland, Romania, Slovenia, South Africa, South Korea, Sweden, Turkey, the UK, and the USA; see Table 1.6), spanning continents, cultures, legal systems, and economic states. The book *Contours of Police Integrity* (2004) features chapters from 14 countries (Austria, Canada, Croatia, Britain, Finland, Hungary, Japan, Netherlands, Pakistan, Poland, Slovenia, South Africa, Sweden, USA).

Most of the studies focus on the exploration of police integrity in one country (Table 1.6). However, in a handful of studies (Table 1.7) the authors compared the results from "their" country with the results from other countries, typically with

Table 1.5 Publications utilizing the first questionnaire: USA

Authors year	Country/City	Survey	Sample	Topic
Bjerregaard and Lord 2004	USA (Southeastern public university)	1st questionnaire (10 scenarios)	443 students (criminal justice and other majors)	Comparing criminal-justice majors' and other majors' views about police misconduct; gender comparisons
Chappell and Piquero 2004	USA (Philadelphia)	1st questionnaire (5 scenarios)	483 police officers	Applying social learning theory to predict citizen complaints
Charles 2009	USA (1 metropolitan police agency)	1st questionnaire (6 scenarios added)	142 police officers	Exploring police integrity and police officer race and gender
Gamarra 2011	USA (5 police agencies)	1st questionnaire	233 police officers	Studying police integrity in relation to agency-wide and individual characteristics
Greene et al. 2004	USA (Philadelphia)	1st questionnaire (6 scenarios)	499 police officers	Analyzing the district-level influence on views of police integrity
Hickman 2005	USA (Philadelphia)	1st questionnaire (6 scenarios)	499 police officers	Exploring the district-level influence and cynicism on police integrity
Jenks et al. 2014	USA (national; 30 agencies)	1st questionnaire	3235 police officers	Creating police integrity indices
Kargin 2009	USA (Philadelphia)	1st questionnaire (6 scenarios)	499 police officers	Examining influences on peer reporting intentions
Klockars and Kutnjak Ivković 2004	USA (national; 30 agencies)	1st questionnaire	3235 police officers	Elaborating on the theory of police integrity and related methodology; agency comparisons
Klockars et al. 2004	USA (national; 30 agencies)	1st questionnaire	3235 police officers	Measuring police integrity in the USA
Klockars et al. 2005	USA (national; 30 agencies)	1st questionnaire	3235 police officers	Exploring the analysis of police integrity in 30 agencies and the agency ranking
Klockars et al. 2004	USA (national; 30 agencies)	1st questionnaire	3235 police officers	Including the analysis of police integrity in 30 agencies and the agency ranking
Klockars et al. 2001	USA (national; 30 agencies; university)	1st questionnaire	3235 police officers; 375 college students	Comparing police officer and public views of police integrity

Table 1.5 (continued)

Authors year	Country/City	Survey	Sample	Topic
Klockars et al. 1997	USA (national; 30 agencies)	1st questionnaire	3235 police officers	Developing the theory and measurement; the application to the U.S. sample; agency analysis
Klockars et al. 2000	USA (national; 30 agencies)	1st questionnaire	3235 police officers	Measuring police integrity across the USA; comparing across 30 police agencies
Lee et al. 2013	USA (national; 30 agencies)	1st questionnaire	3235 police officers	Classifying scenarios into police crime and police gratuity; Hierarchical Linear Model (HLM) model measuring agency and individual characteristics (supervisory status)
Long et al. 2013	USA (national; 30 agencies)	1st questionnaire	3235 police officers	Exploring the relation between normative order, legitimacy, and fairness, and willingness to report
Marche 2009	USA (national; 30 agencies)	1st questionnaire	3235 police officers	Analyzing the data by supervisory status, length of service, and agency size
McDevitt et al. 2011	USA (7 police agencies)	1st questionnaire (3 scenarios)	Unknown	Focusing on differences by the size of community served; gender differences
Micucci and Gomme 2009	USA (national; 30 agencies)	1st questionnaire	3235 police officers	Focusing on the use of force scenario; comparison by length of service and supervisory position
Pogarsky and Piquero 2004	USA (midsized southwestern police department)	1st questionnaire (1 modified scenario)	210 police officers	Exploring the influence of deterrence considerations on the intention to commit misconduct
Raines 2006, 2010	USA (national; 30 agencies)	1st questionnaire	3235 police officers	Analyzing whether police officer tendency to report is influenced by individual, peer, or agency characteristics

Table 1.5 (continued)

Authors year	Country/City	Survey	Sample	Topic
Rothwell and Baldwin 2006	USA (Georgia)	1st questionnaire (modified for civilian employees)	198 police officers + 184 civilian employees	Focusing on predicting reporting; supervisory status most relevant; police officers less likely to stick to the code of silence
Rothwell and Baldwin 2007a	USA (Georgia)	1st questionnaire (modified for civilian employees)	198 police officers + 184 civilian employees	Focusing on willingness to report; compares police officers and civilian employees, supervisory status
Rothwell and Baldwin 2007b	USA (Georgia)	1st questionnaire	198 police officers	Examining willingness to report among police officers; supervisory status and a policy requiring reporting critical variables
Schafer and Martinelli 2008	USA ("Sunnyville Police Department")	1st questionnaire	478 police supervisors	Comparing "Sunnyville" supervisors with the U.S. sample
Servino 2013	USA (153 police agencies)	Based on 1st questionnaire, developed new scenarios	153 police chiefs/administrators	Focusing on police officer injuries in motor vehicle incidents
Smith 2009	USA (Kentucky)	1st questionnaire	50 police officers	Linking attitudes on police integrity with emotional intelligence
White 2008	USA (Florida Gulf Coast University; national; 30 agencies)	1st questionnaire (4 scenarios with gratuities)	3235 police officers; 265 students	Comparing police officer and student attitudes about police integrity with the emphasis on gratuities
Wolfe and Piquero 2011	USA (Philadelphia)	1st questionnaire (6 scenarios)	483 police officers	Examining the role of organizational justice in predicting police misconduct; association with deviant peers leads toward stronger belief in the code
Zschoche 2011	USA (8 police agencies)	1st questionnaire (3 scenarios)	1083 police officers	Application of criminological theories (anomie, moral disengagement) to police integrity

Table 1.6 Publications utilizing the first questionnaire: other countries

Authors year	Country/City	Survey	Sample	Topic
Kutnjak Ivković and Khechumyan 2014	Armenia (2 cities)	1st questionnaire	468 police officers	Comparing police integrity in rural and urban settings in Armenia
Kutnjak Ivković and Khechumyan 2013	Armenia (2 cities)	1st questionnaire	468 police officers	Exploring police integrity in Armenia
Edelbacher and Kutnjak Ivković 2004	Austria (national)	1st questionnaire	1932 police officers	Measuring police integrity in Austria
Kutnjak Ivković 2004b	Bosnia and Herzegovina (Sarajevo)	1st questionnaire	451 police officers	Comparing supervisor and line officer views of police integrity in Bosnia
Kutnjak Ivković and Shelley 2005	Bosnia and Herzegovina (Sarajevo)	1st questionnaire	451 police officers	Measuring police integrity and Herzegovina in Bosnia and Herzegovina
Alain 2004	Canada (Quebec)	1st questionnaire	455 police officers	Measuring police integrity in Canada
Kutnjak Ivković et al. 2004	Croatia (national, university, police academy, police high school)	1st questionnaire	1649 police officers; 504 college students, 511 college students; 379 police school students, 223 police academy students; 271 police academy students	Comparing evaluations of police misconduct seriousness among police officers, college students, and police academy students; measuring changes over time in their opinions
Kutnjak Ivković and Klockars 1998	Croatia (national)	1st questionnaire	1649 police officers	Exploring the relation between the code of silence and disciplinary fairness
Kutnjak Ivković and Klockars 2000	Croatia (national)	1st questionnaire	1649 police officers	Comparing the supervisor and line officer code of silence

Table 1.6 (continued)

Authors year	Country/City	Survey	Sample	Topic
Kutnjak Ivković and Klockars 2002	Croatia (university, police academy, police high school)	1st questionnaire	504 college students, 379 police school students, 223 police academy students	Comparing public views about police corruption
Kutnjak Ivković and Klockars 2004	Croatia (national)	1st questionnaire	1649 police officers	Measuring police integrity in Croatia
Kutnjak Ivković et al. 2002b	Croatia (national)	1st questionnaire	1649 police officers	Assessing the contours of police integrity; comparing supervisor and line officer views about the code of silence
Kutnjak Ivković et al. 2002	Croatia (university)	1st questionnaire	854 college students	Exploring public views about police corruption
Kutnjak Ivković and Shelley 2007	Czech Republic (1 region)	1st questionnaire	600 police officers	Measuring police integrity in the Czech Republic
Kutnjak Ivković and Shelley 2010	Czech Republic (1 region)	1st questionnaire	600 police officers	Exploring the code of silence and disciplinary fairness; comparing supervisor and line officer views about the code
Desta 2013	Eritrea (national)	1st questionnaire (9 scenarios + 1 added)	107 top police administrators	Measuring police integrity in Eritrea
Puonti et al. 2004	Finland (national)	1st questionnaire	378 police officers	Measuring police integrity in Finland
Kremer 2000	Hungary (national)	1st questionnaire	609 police officers	Comparing supervisor and line officer views about the code of silence
Kremer 2004	Hungary (national)	1st questionnaire	609 police officers	Measuring police integrity in Hungary

Table 1.6 (continued)

Authors year	Country/City	Survey	Sample	Topic
Johnson 2004	Japan (Tokyo)	1st questionnaire	182 police officers	Measuring police integrity in Japan
Yunus et al. 2013	Malaysia (local)	Based on 1st questionnaire, developed new scenarios	100 local government employees	Measuring integrity of local governmental employees in Malaysia
Punch et al. 2004	The Netherlands (3 police agencies)	1st questionnaire	795 police officers	Measuring police integrity in the Netherlands
Gottschalk 2009a, 2009b	Norway	1st questionnaire	21 police managers	Comparing scenarios with actual court cases in Norway
Gottschalk 2010	Norway	1st questionnaire	21 police managers	Measuring police integrity in Norway
Chattha and Kutnjak Ivković 2004	Pakistan (Lahore)	1st questionnaire	499 police officers	Measuring police integrity in Pakistan
Haberfeld 2004	Poland (national)	1st questionnaire	1477 police officers	Measuring police integrity in Poland
Andreescu et al. 2012b	Romania (Romanian Police Academy)	1st questionnaire (10 scenarios)	293 police officers	Comparing male and female police officers' attitudes about police integrity
Pagon and Lobnikar 2000	Slovenia (national)	1st questionnaire	767 police officers	Comparing supervisor and line officer perceptions of the code of silence
Pagon and Lobnikar 2004	Slovenia (national)	1st questionnaire	767 police officers	Measuring police integrity in Slovenia
Kutnjak Ivković and Sauer-man 2011	South Africa (national)	1st questionnaire	379 police supervisors	Studying the code of silence in South Africa
Kutnjak Ivković and Sauer-man 2012	South Africa (national)	1st questionnaire	379 police supervisors; 771 police officers	Comparing the code of silence with the 2005 and 2007 surveys

Table 1.6 (continued)

Authors year	Country/City	Survey	Sample	Topic
Kutnjak Ivković and Sauerman 2013b	South Africa (national)	1st questionnaire	379 police supervisors	Exploring the code of silence among supervisors in South Africa
Meyer et al. 2013	South Africa (Gauteng)	1st questionnaire (modified for students)	160 police officers and 186 students	Comparing police officer and student views about police integrity
Newham 2002	South Africa (Johannesburg)	1st questionnaire	104 police officers	Measuring police integrity in South Africa + qualitative interviews
Newham 2003	South Africa (Johannesburg)	1st questionnaire	104 police officers	Measuring police integrity in South Africa
Newham 2004	South Africa (Johannesburg)	1st questionnaire	104 police officers	Measuring police integrity in South Africa
Sauerman and Kutnjak Ivković 2008	South Africa (national)	1st questionnaire	379 police supervisors	Measuring police integrity in South Africa
Kutnjak Ivković and Kang 2011	South Korea (2 police academies)	1st questionnaire	329 police officers	Exploring police integrity among South Korean police officers
Yun 2003	South Korea (Chungnam Province)	1 questionnaire (4 scenarios + 4 added)	321 police officers	Studying the influence of the length of service, supervisory position, and type of community on views of police integrity
Torstensson Levander and Ekenvall 2004	Sweden (national)	1st questionnaire	1590 police officers	Measuring police integrity in Sweden
Bucak 2012	Turkey (national)	1st questionnaire (8 scenarios)	619 police cadets	Focusing on police cynicism and perceptions of corruption in Turkey; rank

Table 1.6 (continued)

Authors year	Country/City	Survey	Sample	Topic
Cetinkaya 2010	Turkey (national)	1st questionnaire (2 scenarios + 1 added)	596 police cadets	Exploring the relation between seriousness and willingness to report and socioeconomic and cultural characteristics of Turkish cadets
Dayioglu 2007	Turkey (3 cities)	1st questionnaire (modified + new scenarios)	633 police officers	Focusing on attitudes toward the use of force among the Turkish police officers
Kucukuysal 2008	Turkey (3 cities)	1st questionnaire (9 scenarios)	507 police officers	Examining the relation between police integrity and police organizational culture and individual police officer characteristics
Westmarland 2004	UK (southeast)	1st questionnaire	275 police officers	Measuring police integrity in the UK
Westmarland 2006	UK (southeast)	1st questionnaire	275 police officers	Focusing on the measures of seriousness and willingness to report in the UK
Westmarland 2006	UK (3 police agencies)	1st questionnaire	508 police officers	Measuring police integrity in the UK; comparing across gender
Wright 2010	UK (northern)	1 questionnaire (some + some new added)	723 police officers and police staff	Comparing police officer and staff views about police integrity

Table 1.7 Publications utilizing the first questionnaire: cross-country comparisons

Authors year	Country/City	Survey	Sample	Topic
Andreescu et al. 2012	Romania (Romanian Police Academy); USA (Southern Police Institute);	1st questionnaire (10 scenarios)	75 police officers; 140 police officers	Comparing the U.S. and Romanian views of police integrity
Haberfeld et al. 2000	USA (national); Croatia (national); Poland (national); Slovenia (national)	1st questionnaire	3235 police officers; 696 police officers; 1649 police officers; 1477 police officers	Comparing police officer views of appropriate and expected discipline across the USA, Croatia, Poland, and Slovenia
Huberts et al. 2003	The Netherlands (3 police agencies); USA (national); Croatia (national); Poland (national); Slovenia (national)	1st questionnaire	795 police officers	Comparing the U.S. and Dutch views on seriousness and willingness to report misconduct; some comparison across 5 countries
Johnson 2003	Japan (Tokyo); USA (national)	1st and 2nd questionnaires	182 police officers	Comparing of Japanese and the U.S. views on police integrity
Klockars and Kutnjak Ivković 1999	USA (national; university); Croatia (national, university)	1st questionnaire	3235 police officers; 375 college students; 1649 police officers; 504 college students	Comparing the U.S. and Croatian police and public evaluation of police misconduct seriousness; comparing police and public evaluations
Klockars et al. 2004	14 countries (Austria, Canada, Croatia, Finland, Hungary, Japan, Netherlands, Pakistan, Poland, Slovenia, South Africa, Sweden, UK, USA)	1st questionnaire	14 samples	Exploring the concept of police integrity; organizational theory; methodology; analysis of the police integrity in a comparative perspective
Khruakham and Lee 2013	Thailand; USA (national); Sweden (national); Finland (national); the Netherlands (3 police agencies)	1st questionnaire	295 police officers (cadets)	Measuring police integrity in Thailand and comparing with police integrity in the USA, The Netherlands, Sweden, and Finland

Table 1.7 (continued)

Authors year	Country/City	Survey	Sample	Topic
Kutnjak Ivković 2004	Croatia (national; university); USA (national; university)	1st questionnaire	1649 police officers; 504 college students; 3235 police officers; 375 college students	Studying views of police misconduct seriousness and comparing them between police officers and citizens across two countries
Kutnjak Ivković 2005b	Croatia (national); Finland (national); USA (national)	1st questionnaire	1649 police officers; 378 police officers; 3235 police officers	Exploring cross-cultural differences in perceptions of misconduct seriousness
Kutnjak Ivković et al. 2002	Croatia (national; university); Slovenia (national; university)	1st questionnaire	1649 police officers; 504 college students; 696 police officers; 215 college students	Comparing public and police views about police corruption across two countries
Kutnjak Ivković and Shelley 2008b	Bosnia and Herzegovina (Sarajevo); Czech Republic (1 region)	1st questionnaire	451 police officers; 600 police officers	Comparing the contours of police integrity in Bosnia and the Czech Republic
Pagon et al. 2000	Slovenia (national); Croatia (national); USA (national)	1st questionnaire	696 police officers; 215 college students; 1649 police officers; 3235 police officers	Analysis of police and public views of police corruption; comparing Slovenian, Croatian, and the U.S. views
Vito et al. 2011	USA (Southern Police Institute); USA (national)	1st questionnaire	307 police managers	Comparing the U.S. middle-manager views with the U.S., Croatian, and Finnish police supervisor views

the original U.S. data set (e.g., Andreescu et al. 2012; Johnson 2003; Klockars and Kutnjak Ivković 1999; Khruakham and Lee 2013; Vito et al. 2011). Most of the comparisons included two- or three-country comparisons, with an introductory chapter in the book *Contours of Police Integrity* (Klockars et al. 2004) offering a comparison across all 14 countries.

The original U.S. sample was a nonrandom national sample of U.S. police officers from 30 agencies. The samples of police officers that followed included national samples, both representative (e.g., Croatia, Slovenia) and nonrandom national samples (e.g., Finland, Poland, and South Africa), as well as samples from particular regions or cities (e.g., Bosnia and Herzegovina, Czech Republic, the Netherlands, Pakistan, and the USA; Table 1.6). Sometimes the samples were collected at police academies or training facilities (e.g., Andreescu et al. 2012; Vito et al. 2011). On several occasions, the scholars were interested in civilian employees (e.g., Rothwell and Barldwin 2006) or general populations (e.g., Klockars et al. 2000; Klockars and Kutnjak Ivković 1999; Kutnjak Ivković et al. 2002).

In addition to exploring overall contours of police integrity (see Tables 1.5–1.7), scholars sometimes focused on specific measures, such as evaluations of seriousness (e.g., Kutnjak Ivković et al. 2004; Klockars and Kutnjak Ivković 1999; Kutnjak Ivković 2004, 2005), code of silence (e.g., Kremer 2000; Kutnjak Ivković and Shelley 2010; Kutnjak Ivković and Sauerman 2012; Pagon and Lobnikar 2004; Rothwell and Baldwin 2007a), or disciplinary fairness (e.g., Kutnjak Ivković and Klockars 1998; Kutnjak Ivković and Shelley 2010). They explored district-level differences (Greene et al. 2004; Yun 2003), rank differences (e.g., Kutnjak Ivković 2004; Kutnjak Ivković and Klockars 2000; Kutnjak Ivković et al. 2002; Kutnjak Ivković and Shelley 2010; Lee et al. 2013; Pagon and Lobnikar 2000; Rothwell and Baldwin 2007a), and race and/or gender differences (e.g., Andreescu et al. 2012; Charles 2009; McDevitt et al. 2011; Westmarland 2005). On occasion, they compared hypothetical cases with actual court cases (e.g., Gottschalk 2009a, 2009b) or disciplinary records (e.g., Klockars et al. 2006).

Although the authors initially postulated the organizational theory of police integrity (see above), which has been the guiding theoretical approach in most of these studies (see Tables 1.5–1.7), they have expanded their approach since, also theorizing about the relation between the code of silence and the perceptions of disciplinary fairness (e.g., Kutnjak Ivković and Klockars 1998; Kutnjak Ivković and Shelley 2010). Others have combined the original theory with other theories or tested other theories using the police integrity approach (e.g., Bucak 2012; Chappell and Piquero 2004; Long et al. 2013; Pogarsky and Piquero 2004; Smith 2009; Zschoche 2011).

Clearly, during the last 20 years, the body of research based on the first questionnaire has grown substantially, spanning the globe. Yet, the research connected with the second questionnaire—the questionnaire, which measures the resistance to various forms of police misconduct—is still in its infancy. At present, there are only seven publications from the research team, covering three countries (Tables 1.8 and 1.9). First, the second questionnaire has been used to assess the extent of police integrity in three U.S. police agencies and measure temporal changes in their environments

Table 1.8 Publications utilizing the second questionnaire: USA

Authors Year	Country/City	Survey	Sample	Topic
Klockars et al. 2005	USA (national; 30 agencies; Charleston; Charlotte-Mecklenburg; St. Petersburg)	1st questionnaire; 2nd questionnaire	3235 police officers; 1544 police officers	Including the analysis of police integrity in 30 agencies, provides an in-depth analysis of police integrity in 3 police agencies
Klockars et al. 2006	USA (national; 30 agencies; Charleston; Charlotte-Mecklenburg; St. Petersburg)	1st questionnaire; 2nd questionnaire	3235 police officers; 1544 police officers	Including the analysis of police integrity in 30 agencies, provides an in-depth analysis of police integrity in 3 police agencies
Klockars et al. 2001	USA (national; 30 agencies; Charleston; Charlotte-Mecklenburg; St. Petersburg)	1st questionnaire; 2nd questionnaire	3235 police officers; 1544 police officers	Including the analysis of police integrity in 30 agencies, provides an in-depth analysis of police integrity in 3 police agencies
Kutnjak Ivković 2013	USA ("Rainless West" agency; Charleston; Charlotte-Mecklenburg; St. Petersburg)	2nd questionnaire	1544 police officers; 700 police officers	Exploring contours of police integrity in "Rainless West" and comparing them with the contours in Charleston, Charlotte-Mecklenburg, and St. Petersburg

Table 1.9 Publications utilizing the second questionnaire—other countries

Authors Year	Country/ City	Survey	Sample		Topic
Kutnjak Ivković 2009	Croatia (national)	2nd questionnaire	811 police officers	Paper	Exploring police integrity; police integrity and community policing
Kutnjak Ivković 2009	Croatia (national)	2nd questionnaire	1130 police officers	Paper	Comparing supervisor and line officer views about police integrity
Pagon et al. 2004	Slovenia (limited)	2nd questionnaire	95 police officers and 247 students	Paper	Comparing gender differences between police officers and students

of integrity (Klockars et al. 2006). Then, a large municipal police agency ("Rainless West") has been surveyed and the findings compared with the three U.S. agencies (Kutnjak Ivković et al. 2013). Furthermore, the second questionnaire has been used to measure the changes in a country in transition and explore the connection between police integrity and community policing (Kutnjak Ivković 2009, 2012). Finally, there was an initial application of the questionnaire to a small sample of police officers and students in Slovenia (Pagon et al. 2004). The exploration of police integrity—its contours and finesse—has only just begun.

References

Adams, K. (1995). Measuring the prevalence of police use of force. In W. A. Geller & H. Toch (Eds.), *And justice for all*. Washington, D.C.: Police Executive Research Forum.

Alain, M. (2004). An exploratory study of Quebec's police officers' attitudes toward ethical Dilemmas. In C. B. Klockars, S. Kutnjak Ivković, & M. R. Haberfeld (Eds.), *The contours of police integrity* (pp. 40–56). Thousand Oaks: Sage.

Andreescu, V., Keeling, D., Vito, G. T., & Voinic, M. C. (2012a). Romanian and American Police Officers' perceptions of professional integrity and ethical behavior. *Revista Română de Sociologie, XXIII*(3–4), 185–207.

Andreescu, V., Keeling, D. G., Voinic, M. C., & Tonea, B. N. (2012b). Future Romanian law enforcement: Gender differences in perceptions of police misconduct. *Journal of Social Research & Policy, 3*(1) http://www.academia.edu/3114941/Future_Romanian_Law_Enforcement_Gender_Differences_in_Perceptions_of_Police_Misconduct.

Bjerregaard, B., & Lord, V. B. (2004). An examination of the ethical and value orientation of criminal justice students. *Police Quarterly, 7*(2), 262–284.

Bucak, S. (2012). *An examination of police cynicism in turkey and its impacts on officers' perception of corruption*. (Order No. 3558466, University of Illinois at Chicago). *ProQuest Dissertations and Theses*, 214. http://ezproxy.msu.edu/login?url=http://search.proquest.com/docview/1343688917?accountid=12598. (1343688917).

Cetinkaya, N. (2010). *Perceptions of police corruption among Turkish police cadets*. ProQuest Dissertations and Theses, 123-n/a. http://ezproxy.msu.edu/login?url=http://search.proquest.com/docview/744399134?accountid=12598. (744399134).

Chappell, A. T., & Piquero, A. R. (2004). Applying social learning theory to police misconduct. *Deviant Behavior, 25*, 89–108.

Charles, S. (2009). *Professional integrity, modern racism, self-esteem, and universality-diversity orientation of police officers in a large urban police agency*. New York DigitalResearch@ Fordham.
Chattha, Z. N., & Kutnjak Ivković, S. (2004). Police misconduct: The Pakistani paradigm. In C. B. Klockars, S. Kutnjak Ivković, & M. R. Haberfeld (Eds.), *The contours of police integrity* (pp. 175–194). Thousand Oaks: Sage.
[Christopher Commission]. Independent Commission on the Los Angeles Police Department. (1991). *Report of the Independent Commission on the Los Angeles Police Department*. Los Angeles: Author.
Dayioglu, M. (2007). *Police officers' attitudes toward use of force in the Turkish national police. ProQuest Dissertations and Theses*, p.193. http://ezproxy.msu.edu/login?url=http://search.proquest.com/docview/304891501?accountid=12598. (304891501).
Desta, Y. (2013). Applying a US police integrity measurement tool to the Eritrean context: Perceptions of top-level Eritrean police officers regarding police misconduct. *Journal of Organizational Transformation & Social Change, 10*(3), 238–261.
Edelbacher, M., & Kutnjak Ivković, S. (2004). Ethics and the police: Studying police integrity in Austria. In C. B. Klockars, S. Kutnjak Ivković, & M. R. Haberfeld (Eds.), *The contours of police integrity* (pp. 19–39). Thousand Oaks: Sage.
Fabrizio, L. E. (1990). *The FBI national academy: A study of the change in attitudes of those who attend*. Chicago: University of Illinois. Chicagos Office of International Criminal Justice
Gamarra, A. O. (2011). Call of duty: A question of police integrity. ProQuest Dissertations and Theses, 261. http://ezproxy.msu.edu/login?url=http://search.proquest.com/docview/907104941?accountid=12598. (907104941).
Garner, J. H., Maxwell, C. D., & Heraux, C. G. (2002). Characteristics associated with the prevalence and severity of force used by the police. *Justice Quarterly, 19,* 705–746.
Goldstein, H. (1975). *Police corruption: A perspective on its nature and control*. Washington, D.C.: The Police Foundation.
Goldstein, H. (1977). *Policing a free society*. Cambridge: Ballinger.
Gottschalk, P. (2009a). Crime-based survey instrument for police integrity measurement. *Policing: An International Journal of Police Strategies & Management, 33*(1), 52–68.
Gottschalk, P. (2009b). *Knowledge management in police oversight: Law enforcement integrity and accountability*. Universal-Publishers.
Gottschalk, P. (2010). Police integrity surveys: A court-based survey approach. *International Journal of Management and Enterprise Development, 8*(3), 243–259.
Greene, J. R., Piquero, A. R., Hickman, M. J., & Lawton, B. A. (2004). *Police integrity and accountability in philadelphia: Predicting and assessing police misconduct*. National Institute of Justice. http://www.ncjrs.gov/pdffiles1/nij/grants/207823.pdf
Haberfeld, M. R. (2004). The Heritage of police misconduct: The case of the polish police. In C. B. Klockars, S. Kutnjak Ivković, & M. R. Haberfeld (Eds.), *The contours of police integrity* (pp. 95–210). Thousand Oaks: Sage.
Haberfeld, M. R., Klockars, C. B., Kutnjak Ivković, S., & Pagon, M. (2000). Police officer perceptions of the disciplinary consequences of police corruption in Croatia, Poland, Slovenia, and the United States. *Police Practice and Research: An International Journal, 1*(1), 41–72.
Harris, D. A. (1997). 'Driving While Black' and all other traffic offenses: the supreme court and the pretextual traffic stops. *Journal of Criminal Law and Criminology, 87,* 544–582.
Hickman, M. J. (2005). *Self-reported and official police problem behavior: Identifying the roles of context, individual, and data. ProQuest Dissertations and Theses*. http://ezproxy.msu.edu/login?url=http://search.proquest.com/docview/305393854?accountid=12598. (305393854).
Huberts, L., Lamboo, T., & Punch, M. (2003). Police integrity in the Netherlands and the United States: Awareness and alertness. *Police Practice and Research, 4*(3), 217–232.
Jenks, D., Johnson, L. M., & Matthews, T. (2014). Examining police integrity: Categorizing corruption vignettes. In M. Guzman, A. M. Das, & D. Das (Eds.), *The evolution of policing*. Boca Raton: CRC Press.

Johnson, D. T. (2003). Above the law? Police integrity in Japan. *Social Science Japan Journal, 6*(1), 19–37.
Johnson, D. T. (2004). Police Integrity in Japan. In C. B. Klockars, S. Kutnjak Ivković, & M. R. Haberfeld (Eds.), *The contours of police integrity*. Thousand Oaks: Sage.
Kargin, V. (2009). *An investigation of factors proposed to influence police officers' peer reporting intentions. ProQuest Dissertations and Theses*. http://ezproxy.msu.edu/login?url=http://search.proquest.com/docview/305066516?accountid=12598. (305066516).
Kelling, G. L., & Moore, M. H. (1988). *The evolving strategy of policing*. https://ncjrs.gov/pdffiles1/nij/114213.pdf
Kesetovic, Z. (2013). Serbian police: Troubled transition from police force to police service. In G. Mesko, C. Fields, B. Lobnikar, & A. Sotlar (Eds.), *Handbook on policing in central and Eastern Europe*. New York: Springer.
Khruakham, S., & Lee, J. (2013). Cross-nation comparison of the intolerance to police misconduct: Findings from a Thai police cadet survey. *International Journal of Police Science & Management, 15*(3), 237–245.
Klockars, C. B., & Kutnjak Ivković, S. (1999). The measurement of police delinquency. In W. Laufer & F. Adler (Eds.), *The criminology of criminal law. Advances in criminological theory* (Vol. 8, pp. 87–106). New Brunswick: Transaction Publishers.
Klockars, C. B., & Kutnjak Ivković, S. (2004). Measuring police integrity. In M. J. Hickman, A. R. Piquero, & J. R. Greene (Eds.), *Police integrity and ethics*. Belmont: Wadsworth.
Klockars, C. B., Kutnjak Ivković, S., Harver, W. E., & Haberfeld, M. R. (1997). *The measurement of police integrity*. Final report submitted to the U.S. Department of Justice, Office of Justice Programs, National Institute of Justice.
Klockars, C. B., Kutnjak Ivković, S., Harver, W. E., & Haberfeld, M. R. (2000). *The measurement of police integrity*. Research in brief. U.S. Department of Justice, office of justice programs, National Institute of Justice. Washington, D.C.: Government Printing Office.
Klockars, C. B., Haberfeld, M. R., Kutnjak Ivković, S., & Uydess, A. (2001). A minimum requirement for police corruption. In R. A. Silverman, T. P. Thornberry, B. Cohen, & B. Krisberg (Eds.), *Crime and justice at the millennium: Essays by and in honor of Marvin E. Wolfgang*. New York: Springer.
Klockars, C. B., Kutnjak Ivković, S., & Haberfeld, M. R. (2005). Enhancing police integrity. Research for Practice. U.S. Department of Justice, Office of Justice Programs, National Institute of Justice: Washington, D.C.: Government Printing Office. https://www.ncjrs.gov/pdffiles1/nij/209269.pdf
Klockars, C. B., Kutnjak Ivković, S., & Haberfeld, M. R. (Eds.). (2004). *The contours of police integrity*. Newbury Park: Sage.
Klockars, C. B., Kutnjak Ivković, S., & Haberfeld, M. R. (2004a). The contours of police integrity. In C. B. Klockars, S. Kutnjak Ivković, & M. R. Haberfeld (Eds.), *The contours of police integrity* (pp. 1–18). Thousand Oaks: Sage.
Klockars, C. B., Kutnjak Ivković, S., & Haberfeld, M. R. (2004b). Police integrity in the United States of America. In C. B. Klockars, S. Kutnjak Ivković, & M. R. Haberfeld (Eds.), *The contours of police integrity* (pp. 265–282). Thousand Oaks: Sage.
Klockars, C. B., Kutnjak Ivković, S., & Haberfeld, M. R. (2006). *Enhancing police integrity*. Dordrecht: Springer.
[Knapp Commission]. Commission to Investigate Allegations of Police Corruption and the City's Anti-Corruption Procedures. (1972). *Report on police corruption*. New York: G. Braziller.
Knowles, J. J. (1996). *The Ohio police behavior study*. Columbia: Office of Criminal Justice Services.
Kraska P. B., & Kappeler, V. E. (1995). To serve and pursue: Exploring police sexual violence against women. *Justice Quarterly, 12*, 85–111.
Kremer, F. (2000). Comparing supervisor and line officer opinions about the code of silence: The case of Hungary. In M. Pagon (Ed.), *Policing in Central and Eastern Europe: Ethics, integrity, and human rights* (pp. 211–219). Ljubljana: College of Police and Security Studies.
Kremer, F. (2004). Police Integrity in Hungary. In C. B. Klockars, S. Kutnjak Ivković, & M. R. Haberfeld (Eds.), *The contours of police integrity* (pp. 116–130). Thousand Oaks: Sage.

Kucukuysal, B. (2008). Determinants of Turkish Police Officers' perception of integrity: Impact of organizational culture (Doctoral dissertation, University of Central Florida Orlando, Florida).
Kutnjak Ivković, S. (2003). To serve and collect: Measuring police corruption. *Journal of Criminal Law and Criminology, 93*(2–3), 593–649.
Kutnjak Ivković, S. (2004a). Evaluating the seriousness of police misconduct: A cross-cultural comparison of police officer and citizen views. *International Criminal Justice Review, 14*, 25–48.
Kutnjak Ivković, S. (2004b). Sharing the view: Line officer and supervisor evaluations of police corruption seriousness in Bosnia and Herzegovina. In G. Mesko, M. Pagon, & G. Dobovsek (Eds.), *Dilemmas of contemporary criminal justice* (pp. 312–322). Ljubljana: Faculty of Criminal Justice, University of Maribor.
Kutnjak Ivković, S. (2005a). *Fallen blue knights: Controlling police corruption*. New York: Oxford University Press.
Kutnjak Ivković, S. (2005b). Police (Mis)behavior: A cross-cultural study of corruption seriousness. *Policing: An International Journal of Police Strategies and Management, 28*(3), 546–566.
Kutnjak Ivković, S. (2009). The Croatian police, police integrity, and transition toward democratic policing. *Policing: An International Journal of Police Strategies and Management, 32*(3), 459–488.
Kutnjak Ivković, S. (2012). Exploring the relation between police integrity and rank: A Croatian example. *International Criminal Justice Review, 22*(4), 372–396.
Kutnjak Ivković, S. (2013). Forward. In G. Mesko, C. Fields, B. Lobnikar, & A. Sotlar (Eds.), *Handbook on policing in central and Eastern Europe*. New York: Springer.
Kutnjak Ivković, S., & Kang, W. (2011). Police integrity in South Korea. *Policing: An International Journal of Police Strategies and Management, 35*(1), 76–103.
Kutnjak Ivković, S., & Khechumyan, A. (2013). The state of police integrity in Armenia: Findings from the police integrity survey. *Policing: An International Journal of Police Strategies and Management, 36*(1), 70–90.
Kutnjak Ivković, S., & Khechumyan, A. (2014). Measuring police integrity among Urban and Rural Police in Armenia: From local results to global implications. *International Journal of Comparative and Applied Criminal Justice*, Forthcoming.
Kutnjak Ivković, S., & Klockars, C. B. (1998). The code of silence and the Croatian Police. In M. Pagon (Ed.), *Policing in Central and Eastern Europe: Organizational, managerial, and human resource aspects* (pp. 329–347). Ljubljana: College of Police and Security Studies.
Kutnjak Ivković, S., & Klockars, C. B. (2000). Comparing police supervisor and line officer opinions about the code of silence: The case of Croatia. In M. Pagon (Ed.), *Policing in Central and Eastern Europe: Ethics, integrity, and human rights* (pp. 183–195). Ljubljana: College of Police and Security Studies.
Kutnjak Ivković, S., & Klockars, C. B. (2002). Public views about police corruption: The case of Croatia. In M. Pagon (Ed.), *Policing in Central and Eastern Europe: Deviance, violence, and victimization* (pp. 283–296). Ljubljana: College of Police and Security Studies.
Kutnjak Ivković, S., & Klockars, C. B. (2004). Police integrity in Croatia. In C. B. Klockars, S. Kutnjak Ivković, & M. R. Haberfeld (Eds.), *The contours of police integrity* (pp. 56–74). Thousand Oaks: Sage.
Kutnjak Ivković, S., & O'Connor Shelley, T. (2005). The Bosnian police and police integrity: A continuing story. *European Journal of Criminology, 2*(4), 428–454.
Kutnjak Ivković, S., & O'Connor Shelley, T. (2007). Police Integrity and the Czech police officers. *International Journal of Comparative and Applied Criminal Justice, 31*(1), 21–49.
Kutnjak Ivković, S., & O'Connor Shelley, T. (2008a). The police code of silence and different paths toward democratic policing. *Policing and Society, 18*(4), 445–473.
Kutnjak Ivković, S., & O'Connor Shelley, T. (2008b). The contours of police integrity across Eastern Europe: The case of Bosnia and Herzegovina and the Czech Republic. *International Criminal Justice Review, 18*(1), 59–82.

Kutnjak Ivković, S., & O'Connor Shelley, T. (2010). The code of silence and disciplinary fairness: A comparison of Czech police supervisor and line officer views. *Policing: An International Journal of Police Strategies and Management, 33*(3), 548–574.

Kutnjak Ivković, S., & Sauerman, A. (2011). Measuring the code of silence among the South African Police: Findings from a SAPS supervisor survey. In C. Gould & G. Newham (Eds.), *Toward a coherent strategy for crime reduction in South Africa Beyond 2010* (pp. 74–87). Pretoria: Institute for Security Studies.

Kutnjak Ivković, S., & Sauerman, A. (2012). The code of silence: Revisiting South African police integrity. *South African Crime Quarterly, 40,* 15–24.

Kutnjak Ivković, S., & Sauerman, A. (2013a). Threading the thin blue line: Transition toward democratic policing and the integrity of the South African Police Service. *Policing and Society*, Forthcoming.

Kutnjak Ivković, S., & Sauerman, A. (2013b). Curtailing the code of silence among the South African police. *Policing: An International Journal of Police Strategies and Management, 36*(1), 175–198.

Kutnjak Ivković, S., Klockars, C. B., Lobnikar, B., & Pagon, M. (2000). Police integrity and the code of silence: A Case of the Slovenian police force. In G. Mesko (Ed.), *Corruption in Central and Eastern Europe at the turn of millennium* (pp. 85–102). Ljubljana: College of Police and Security Studies.

Kutnjak Ivković, S., Pagon, M., Klockars, C. B., & Lobnikar, B. (2002a). A comparative view of public perceptions of police corruption. In M. Pagon (Ed.), *Policing in Central and Eastern Europe: Deviance, violence, and victimization* (pp. 297–310). Ljubljana: College of Police and Security Studies.

Kutnjak Ivković, S., Klockars, C. B., Cajner-Mraovic, I., & Ivanusec, D. (2002b). Controlling police corruption: The Croatian perspective. *Police Practice and Research: An International Journal, 3*(1), 55–72.

Kutnjak Ivković, S., Cajner-Mraovic, I., & Ivanusec, D. (2004). The measurement of seriousness of police corruption. In G. Mesko, M. Pagon, & G. Dobovsek (Eds.), *Dilemmas of contemporary criminal justice* (pp. 300–311). Ljubljana: Faculty of Criminal Justice, University of Maribor.

Kutnjak Ivković, S., Haberfeld, M., & Peacock, R. (2013). Rainless West: The integrity survey's role in agency accountability. *Police Quarterly, 16*(2), 148–176.

Lee, H., Lim, H., Moore, D. D., & Kim, J. (2013). How police organizational structure correlates with frontline officers' attitudes toward corruption: A multilevel model. *Police Practice and Research, 14*(5), 386–401.

Long, M., Cross, J. E., Shelley, T. O., & Kutnjak Ivković, S. (2013). The normative order of reporting police misconduct: Examining the roles of offense seriousness, legitimacy, and fairness. *Social Psychology Quarterly, 76*(3), 242–267.

Marche, G. E. (2009). Integrity, culture, and scale: An empirical test of the big bad police agency. *Crime, Law, and Social Change, 51,* 463–486.

Martin, C. (1994). *Illinois Municipal Officers' perceptions of police ethics*. Chicago: Illinois Criminal Justice Information Authority, Statistical Analysis Center.

McDevitt, J., Posick, C., Zschoche, R., Rosenbaum, D. P., Buslik, M., & Fridell, L. (2011). *Police integrity, responsibility, and discipline*. National institute of justice. http://www.nationalpoliceresearch.org/storage/updated-papers/Police%20Integrity%20Responsibility%20and%20Discipline.pdf.

Mesko, G., Fields, C., Lobnikar, B., & Sotlar, A. (2013a). (Eds.). *Handbook on policing in Central and Eastern Europe*. New York: Springer.

Mesko, G., Fields, C., Lobnikar, B., & Sotlar, A. (2013b). Recent developments in policing in Slovenia. In G. Mesko, C. Fields, B. Lobnikar, & A. Sotlar (Eds.), *Handbook on policing in Central and Eastern Europe*. New York: Springer.

Meyer, M. E., Steyn, J., & Gopal, N. (2013). Exploring the public parameter of police integrity. *Policing: An International Journal of Police Strategies & Management, 36*(1), 140–156.

Micucci, A. J., & Gomme, I. M. (2009). American police and subcultural support for the use of excessive force. *Journal of Criminal Justice, 33,* 487–500.

[Mollen Commission] New York City Commission to Investigate Allegations of Police Corruption and the Anti-Corruption Procedures of the Police Department. (1994). *Commission report*. New York: Author.

National Research Council. (2004). Fairness and effectiveness in policing: The evidence. Committee to review research on police policy and practices. In Wesley Skogan & Kathleen Frydl (Eds.), *Committee on law and justice, division of behavioral and social sciences and education*. Washington, D.C.: National Academies.

Newham, G. (2002, July). Promoting police integrity at station level: The case of the Hillbrow police station. *Urban Forum, 13*(3), 20–52.

Newham, G. (2003). Police attitudes and corruption. The findings of the police integrity measurement survey at three police stations in Johannesburg, Centre for the Study of Violence and Reconciliation, Braamfontein, Johannesburg, research report.

Newham, G. (2004). Out of step: Integrity and the South Africa police service. In C. B. Klockars, S. Kutnjak Ivković, & M. R. Haberfeld (Eds.), *The contours of police integrity* (pp. 232–247). Thousand Oaks: Sage.

Pagon, M., & Lobnikar, B. (2000). Comparing supervisor and line officer opinions about the code of silence: The case of Slovenia. In M. Pagon (Ed.), *Policing in Central and Eastern Europe: Ethics, integrity, and human rights* (pp. 197–209). Ljubljana: College of Police and Security Studies.

Pagon, M., & Lobnikar, B. (2004). Police integrity in Slovenia. In C. B. Klockars, S. Kutnjak Ivković, & M. R. Haberfeld (Eds.), *The contours of police integrity* (pp. 212–231). Thousand Oaks: Sage.

Pagon, M., Kutnjak Ivković, S., & Lobnikar, B. (2000). Police integrity and attitudes toward police corruption: A comparison between the police and the public. In M. Pagon (Ed.), *Policing in Central and Eastern Europe: Ethics, integrity, and human rights* (pp. 383–396). Ljubljana: College of Police and Security Studies.

Pagon, M., Lobnikar, B., & Anelj, D. (2004). Gender differences in leniency towards police misconduct. In G. Mesko, M. Pagon, & Bojan Dobovsek (Eds.), *Policing in Central and Eastern Europe–Dilemmas of contemporary criminal justice*. Ljubljana: Faculty of Criminal Justice, University of Maribor, 1–16.

Pennsylvania Crime Commission. (1974). *Report on police corruption and the quality of law enforcement in philadelphia*. Saint Davids: Author.

Pogarsky, G., & Piquero, A. R. (2004). Studying the reach of deterrence: Can deterrence theory help explain police misconduct? *Journal of Criminal Justice, 32*(4), 371–386.

Pounti, A., Vuorinen, S., & Kutnjak Ivković, S. (2004). Sustaining police integrity in Finland. In C. B. Klockars, S. Kutnjak Ivković, & M. R. Haberfeld (Eds.), *The contours of police integrity* (pp. 95–115). Thousand Oaks: Sage.

Punch, M. (2009). *Police corruption: Deviance, accountability and reform in policing*. Portland: Willan.

Punch, M., Huberts, L. W. J. C., & Lamboo, M. E. D. (2004). Integrity, perceptions, and investigations in The Netherlands. In C. B. Klockars, S. Kutnjak Ivković, & M. R. Haberfeld (Eds.), *The contours of police integrity* (pp. 161–175). Thousand Oaks: Sage.

Raines, J. B. (2006). *Ethics, integrity and police misconduct: Analyzing ethical awareness, standards and action of law enforcement officers in the united states. ProQuest Dissertations and Theses*, p. 220. http://ezproxy.msu.edu/login?url=http://search.proquest.com/docview/305292160?accountid=12598. (305292160).

Raines, J. (2010). *Ethics in policing: Misconduct and integrity*. Massachusetts: Jones & Bartlett Learning.

Roebuck, J. B., & Barker, T. (1974). A typology of police corruption. *Social Problems, 21*, 423–437.

Rothwell, G. R., & Baldwin, J. N. (2006). Ethical climates and contextual predictors of whistle-blowing. *Review of Public Personnel Administration, 26*(3), 216–244.

Rothwell, G. R., & Baldwin, J. N. (2007a). Whistle-blowing and the code of silence in police agencies policy and structural predictors. *Crime & Delinquency, 53*(4), 605–632.

Rothwell, G. R., & Baldwin, J. N. (2007b). Ethical climate theory, whistle-blowing, and the code of silence in police agencies in the state of Georgia. *Journal of Business Ethics, 70*(4), 341–361.

Sauerman, A., & Kutnjak Ivković, S. (2008). Measuring the integrity of the South African police service during transitional times. *Acta Criminologica, 2*, 21–39.

Schafer, J. A., & Martinelli, T. J. (2008). First-line supervisor's perceptions of police integrity. *Policing: An international journal of police strategies and management, 31*(2), 306–323.
Servino, C. (2013). *Driving forces: Factors affecting police officer injuries in motor vehicle incidents in the united states*. (Order No. 3590166, University of Nevada, Las Vegas). *ProQuest Dissertations and Theses*, 152. http://ezproxy.msu.edu/login?url=http://search.proquest.com/docview/1431454710?accountid=12598. (1431454710).
Smith, M. V. (2009). *Police perceptions of integrity: The relationship between emotional intelligence and moral development among police officers. ProQuest Dissertations and Theses*, 167. http://ezproxy.msu.edu/login?url=http://search.proquest.com/docview/305165879?accountid=12598. (305165879).
Torstensson Levander, M., & Ekenvall, B. (2004). Homogeneity in moral standards in Swedish police culture. In C. B. Klockars, S. Kutnjak Ivković, & M. R. Haberfeld (Eds.), *The contours of police integrity* (pp. 251–265). Thousand Oaks: Sage.
Transparency International (2005). *Corruption perceptions index 2004*. http://archive.transparency.org/policy_research/surveys_indices/cpi/2004.
Transparency International (2014). *Corruption perceptions index 2013*. http://cpi.transparency.org/cpi2013/results/.
Vito, G. F., Wolfe, S., Higgins, G. E., & Walsh, W. F. (2011). Police integrity: Rankings of scenarios on the Klockars scale by "Management Cops". *Criminal Justice Review, 36,* 152–164.
Vollmer, A. (1936). *The police and modern society*. Berkeley: University of California Press.
Westmarland, L. (2004). Policing integrity: Britain's thin blue line. In C. B. Klockars, S. Kutnjak Ivković, & M. R. Haberfeld (Eds.), *The contours of police integrity* (pp. 75–93). Thousand Oaks: Sage.
Westmarland, L. (2005). Police ethics and integrity: Breaking the blue code of silence. *Policing and Society, 15*(2), 145–165.
Westmarland, L. (2006). Police ethics and integrity: Breaking the blue code of silence. Policing and Society: *An International Journal of Research and Policy 15*(2), 145–165.
White, D. A. (2008). *Assessing the differences in opinion regarding gratuities in law enforcement. ProQuest Dissertations and Theses*, 139-n/a. http://ezproxy.msu.edu/login?url=http://search.proquest.com/docview/304836939?accountid=12598. (304836939).
Wolfe, S. E., & Piquero, A. R. (2011). Organizational justice and police misconduct. *Criminal justice and behavior, 38*(4), 332–353.
Worden, R. E., & Catlin, S. E. (2002). The use and abuse of force by police. In K. M. Lerch (Ed.), *Policing and misconduct*. Upper Saddle River: Prentice Hall.
Wright, B. (2010). Civilianising the 'blue code'? An examination of attitudes to misconduct in the police extended family. *International Journal of Police Science & Management, 12*(3), 339–356.
Yun, I. (2003). *A study of police officers' perceptions of police deviance: From an occupational socialization perspective. ProQuest Dissertations and Theses*, p. 89. http://ezproxy.msu.edu/login?url=http://search.proquest.com/docview/305329643?accountid=12598. (305329643).
Yunus, O. M., Bustaman, H., & Khalid, K. (2013). Conducive business environment: A measurement of local authority integrity. *The Journal of Interdisciplinary Networks,* 213–220.
Zschoche, R. (2011). A multilevel model of police corruption: Anomie, decoupling, and moral disengagement (Doctoral dissertation, University of South Florida).

Chapter 2
Police Integrity in Armenia

Aleksandr Khechumyan and Sanja Kutnjak Ivković

Abstract The Armenian police are a centralized police agency adjunct to the Government of Armenia. This chapter explores the contours of police integrity among the Armenian police officers. The chapter relies on the police integrity survey conducted in 2013. The sample of 969 police officers evaluated hypothetical scenarios describing various forms of police misconduct. We analyze the results across several measures of police integrity, such as the police officers' knowledge of official rules, evaluations of the seriousness of police misconduct, views about appropriate and expected discipline, and the code of silence. The results show that most of our respondents recognized behaviors described in the hypothetical scenarios as rule-violating and evaluated them to be serious. On the other hand, they thought that only lenient discipline is appropriate for such forms of misconduct. At the same time, they mostly expected their police agencies to mete out lenient discipline, indicating the presence of a relaxed disciplinary environment. Finally, our findings detect the presence of a strong code of silence, providing protection even for the behaviors evaluated to be rule violating and very serious.

Keywords Armenia · Democratization · Militia · Police integrity · Survey

---

Aleksandr Khechumyan has conducted the police integrity research as a part of his nonresidential Network Fellowship at the Edmond J. Safra Center for Ethics, Harvard University.

A. Khechumyan (✉)
Max Planck Institute for Foreign and International Criminal Law; Edmond J. Safra Center for Ethics at Harvard University, Freiburg im Breisgau, Germany
e-mail: a.khechumyan@mpicc.de

S. Kutnjak Ivković
Michigan State University, East Lansing, MI, USA
e-mail: kutnjak@msu.edu

S. Kutnjak Ivković, M. R. Haberfeld (eds.), *Measuring Police Integrity Across the World,*
DOI 10.1007/978-1-4939-2279-6_2

Introduction

The Republic of Armenia—a small country in the South Caucasus (at the junction of Eastern Europe and western Asia)—is best described as a country in transition. After the adoption of the Declaration of Independence, the former Soviet Republic has embarked on the road toward establishing a Western-style parliamentary democracy (Supreme State Council of the ASSR 1990). The Government of Armenia sought to legitimize its claim of becoming a democratic state by applying for membership in international organizations and signing major human rights treaties. Following the Declaration of Independence, the country became a member state of the United Nations (United Nations Security Council 1992). In 2001, the country became a member of the Council of Europe, subsequently ratifying the European Convention on Human Rights and Fundamental Freedoms (ECHR) (Council of Europe 2013).

In 2009, Armenia entered a new phase of transition in the way of establishing a modern democracy based on the rule of law and respect for human rights. Jointly with five other post-Soviet governments (Azerbaijan, Belarus, Georgia, the Republic of Moldova, and Ukraine), Armenian government signed a joint declaration with the European Union launching the Eastern Partnership aiming to create the necessary conditions to accelerate political association and further economic integration (Council of European Union 2009).

Democratization of the police is an integral part of transformation of the state apparatus from authoritarianism to democracy (Bayley 2006). Although the process of transition from authoritarianism to democracy in Armenia has been ongoing since the early 1990s, the police had not experienced any major reorganization until the end of the decade. Until 2001, Armenian Police was called "Militsiya" and was housed in the Ministry of Internal Affairs. After the independence from Soviet Union, the Armenian Militsiya became the successor of the Soviet Militsiya in Armenia and continued to operate under the same regulations. Most of the regulations of the Soviet Militia and the Law on Militia remained in force.

Soon after the independence, Armenia was involved in a military conflict with Azerbaijan. The conflict, which started in 1991, ended with a ceasefire in May 1994. Despite the ceasefire and continuous negotiations, no peace deal has yet been agreed between the two countries (De Wall 2003). During the active phase of the conflict, when the country was in the process of establishing military forces, police officers were not only performing their regular police work but were also regularly deployed to protect borders with Azerbaijan (Police Press Center 2012).

There was a considerable reshuffle of the police personal after the independence. Most of the police personnel, especially those who had supervisory roles, had to be members of the communist party. After the communist party lost the power in 1990, many experienced police officers—especially those in supervisory positions—were replaced by loyalists of the new government. The new appointees often were war hardened guerrilla fighters with no police experience. During this period, the Ministry of Internal Affairs was headed by Vano Siradeghyan—a writer and one of the leaders of the independence movement. Under Siradeghyan, the Militsiya had virtually unlimited powers and no accountability. It was also engaged in politics and controlled some of the most profitable sections of the economy. In 2000, after the arrest of Siradeghyan who latter fled the country and is still on the Interpol's wanted list, it became apparent that there was a special unit in the police to carry out political assassinations (Avagyan and Hiscock 2005).

In 2001, the Parliament adopted the Law on Police followed by the Law on Police Service (2002), based on which in 2003 the Ministry of the Interior was dissolved and the police were established as an independent agency adjunct to the government (Police of the Republic of Armenia 2013). In 2005, the Parliament approved the Police Disciplinary Code which clarified issues regarding police misconduct and disciplinary sanctions for such misconduct. These laws determined the legal status of the police, boundaries of policing, and accountability mechanisms. They also established the legal foundations for turning the successor of former Soviet Militsiya from an institution defending the broad range of state interests and enforcing the conformity with the state ideology (Shelley 1996) into a democratic police agency. Furthermore, in 2003, with the assistance of the Organization for Security and Co-operation in Europe (OSCE), the police conducted the strategic-needs assessment for reforms, identifying implementation of community-based policing model, improving police education, and establishing an emergency call service as priority areas for reforms (Hofstra 2010).

The police are headed by the chief of the police, who is appointed directly by the president of Armenia based on the prime minister's recommendation (Law on Police 2001, Article 9; Law on Police Service 2002, Article 13). The police have 21 units which are part of the Police Central Apparatus, including police educational complex and medical department (Police of the Republic of Armenia 2014a). Police troops—military units tasked to protect public order, state security, and defend the country—are also a part of the police (Law on Police Troops 1997). The next level down in the organizational hierarchy includes Yerevan City Department and ten provincial departments, which are further subdivided into 52 local police stations (Police of the Republic of Armenia 2014b). The majority of regular police work is performed at the level of police stations. The number of sworn police officers is still viewed as classified information in Armenia.

The first part of this chapter examines the state of police integrity in Armenia by utilizing the key components of the organizational theory of police integrity (Kutnjak Ivković and Klockars 1995; Klockars and Kutnjak Ivković 2003). The second part of this chapter provides an empirical analysis of survey data measuring the level of Armenian police integrity through evaluation of police officers' views about seriousness of police misconduct, opinions about appropriate and expected discipline such misbehavior merits, and their willingness to report it.

Theory of Police Integrity and the Armenian Police

This chapter explores police integrity among Armenian police officers based on the organizational theory of police integrity and related methodology (Klockars and Kutnjak Ivković 2003; Klockars et al. 1997). According to the organizational theory of police integrity (Klockars and Kutnjak Ivković 2003; Klockars et al. 1997), police integrity is "the normative inclination among police to resist temptations to abuse the rights and privileges of their occupation." Police integrity does not necessarily imply that police officers will have the same inclination to resist all types of temptation; rather, the contours of police integrity may vary significantly across different forms (e.g., police corruption, use of excessive force), and levels of seriousness within the same form of misconduct (e.g., within police corruption, acceptance of gratuities vs. theft from a crime scene; Klockars et al. 1997). This chapter explores the theory of police integrity in relation to the Armenian Police.

Organizational Rules

The first dimension of the organizational theory of police integrity includes organizational rule making (see, e.g., Klockars and Kutnjak Ivković 2003; Klockars et al. 1997, 2001). It requires police agencies to create, teach, and enforce rules explicitly prohibiting misbehavior, which is very important for achieving the high level of police integrity (Klockars and Kutnjak Ivković 2004, p. 1.4). According to this theory, police officers in agencies of high integrity should know and support the organizational rules.

The Armenian Police are a centralized police agency; therefore, the official rules are made at the top of the hierarchy and are applicable to all police units across the country (Law on Police 2001). According to the Law on Police Service (2002), the police service is regulated by the Constitution, the Law on Police Service, the Law on Police, other laws and legal regulations, and international treaties ratified by Armenia.

These laws provide the legal grounds for establishing a professional, politically impartial, and democratic police agency. Apart from the laws regulating the police service, there are other laws which prescribe powers and responsibilities of police as a state agency, and establish liability for individual police officers. For instance, the new Code of Criminal Procedures (1998) (hereinafter CCP) prescribed the role, responsibilities, and functions of the police in discovering, registering, and investigating crimes (Articles 27, 57). It also introduced safeguards against overreaching powers of government agencies in criminal investigations and establishes the basic rules for the protection of constitutional rights and liberties of defendants during criminal investigations. Furthermore, the new Criminal Code (2003) (hereinafter CC) introduced a special chapter on crimes committed in the official capacity.

The Law on Police (2001) defines the police as "a centralized governmental body which has the right to use force to fulfill the tasks explicitly listed in Article 2.1" (Article 1). The legal definition of the police as a governmental body concerned with the protection of life, property, and assisting individuals and organizations in protection of their rights and legitimate interests is closely associated with the democratic view of policing. Furthermore, disintegration of Ministry of Internal

Affairs and the establishment of the police as an adjunct governmental body with detailed rules regarding appointment, promotion, and service of all police personal, including the chief of the police, is an important precondition of developing professional nonpartisan police agency.

All positions at the police are grouped into following five broad categories: the top, main, senior, middle, and junior groups. The head of the police is the police chief, who should be a professional and not a political appointee. The rules require that the chief can only be a person who already has a position in the top commander group or at least 3 years of experience in the main commander group, and has the rank of police colonel or higher (Law on Police Service 2002, Article 14). The chief and his deputies are appointed and can be dismissed only by the president of Armenia (Law on Police Service 2002). The Law on Police Service (2002) establishes the criteria and the process for the appointment of all other police staff. The new Law on Police (2001), defines police powers and responsibilities (Chap. 2); it explicitly states that the use of torture, inhumane or degrading treatment, or other forms of violence by police is punishable by the law (Law on Police 2001, Article 5).

The existence of detailed and sophisticated laws demonstrates that essential legal rules prohibiting misconduct, regulating appointment, promotion, and service have been put in place. Despite creating rules prohibiting misbehavior and putting in place mechanisms to ensure that police officers are taught the rules, the key issue—the frequency with which these laws should be and actually are enforced—still remains without a clear answer. There is ground to believe that the aim of creating a nonpartisan police force has not yet been achieved: Initially the Law on Police Service (2002) required that only a police officer who holds a position in the highest commander group or has at least 3 years of experience in the main commander group may be appointed as a police chief. The Law on Police Service (2002) was amended in 2008, providing for an exception and allowing the appointee to be a former police officer or an officer with another service (e.g., military national security, prosecutors, corrections). Several days later, a governor of a Province (a former high-rank police officer) was appointed as a chief of police (Decree of the President of The Republic of Armenia 2008).

Furthermore, the familiarity with and the level of knowledge that police officers have about these new rules is an open empirical question. In 2008–2009, after the mentioned laws have been in place for more than 5 years, a survey explored officers' familiarity with official rules (Kutnjak Ivković and Khechumyan 2013a, 2014). The respondents in the study were asked to identify whether various forms of police corruption described in hypothetical scenarios violated official rules. Although the overwhelming majority of the respondents had no problems recognizing the scenarios as rule violating, the certainty with which the respondents evaluated such behaviors varied across scenarios. For instance, 80 % or more participants evaluated that a bribe from a speeding motorist and a theft from a crime scene were violations of official rules. On the other hand, about one third of participants did not evaluate a theft from a found wallet, the acceptance of gifts from merchants, and covering up drunk driving by a fellow police officer as a violation of official rules. Finally, only about three quarters of the respondents evaluated the acceptance of a kickback and the use of excessive force as rule-violating behaviors (Kutnjak Ivković and Khechumyan 2013).

In countries with decentralized police agencies, the content of the rules, in particular what behaviors are explicitly prohibited by the rules and the degree to which the rules are enforced, could vary drastically across agencies. In centralized police systems, such as the Armenian police, the same set of official rules applies to all police officers, regardless of in which agency and at what level of the organization hierarchy they work. However, what can differ is the way in which the rules are understood, taught, and applied in different parts of the country. In our prior work (Kutnjak Ivković and Khechumyan 2014), we did not find systematic and substantial differences in the police officers' knowledge of the official rules, but "we did find the largest and most systematic differences in the perceptions of disciplinary environments (i.e., police officers' estimates of discipline their agency would mete out). In particular, police officers employed in the capital consistently reported that they expected a harsher discipline than the police officers employed in a regional police department did" (Kutnjak Ivković and Khechumyan 2014).

Detection and Investigation of Police Misconduct

The second dimension of the theory of police integrity focuses on creation and maintenance of the whole range of activities that allow the detection and investigation of corrupt activities and discipline of corrupt police officers. These activities could vary from education in ethics, integrity testing, and proactive investigations, to the reactive investigations of corrupt behavior and discipline of corrupt police officers. According to the theory, there should be a strong and positive correlation between the reliance on an effective control system and the level of integrity in the agency (Klockars et al. 2004, p. 7).

The Law on Police (2001, Article 43) contains a norm concerning the right to complain against police officers to their supervisors or courts. If police officers fail to fulfill their responsibilities, do not fulfill them properly, or intentionally abuse the office, Article 43 of the Law on Police (2001) stipulates that police officers will be held liable in accordance with the legislation of Armenia. Moreover, the same article establishes the grounds for possible compensation to citizens for any damage caused by an illegal conduct of a police officer.

The disciplinary code defines that the appropriate conduct of police officers requires fulfillment of responsibilities prescribed by laws and other legal directives of the Republic of Armenia (Law on Approval of Police Disciplinary Code 2005, Article 5.1). Thus, every behavior that fits the abovementioned rules should be regarded as a disciplinary offense and, when this specific behavior fits the elements of a crime, it should be regarded as a criminal offense as well. The Police Disciplinary Code also prescribed rules of police ethics which police officers have to follow both off and on duty. Although the Law prescribes 16 rules of police ethics, it specifies that only violation of four of them can result to in a disciplinary sanction. The four rules include the prohibition of financial or other support to political parties; an obligation to support supervisors in maintaining discipline in the organization; an obligation to know and respect human rights, be reticent, polite, and respectful with people; and, finally, an obligation to refrain from establishing financial or other relationships which can affect impartiality of the police officer and hinder fulfillment of his/her service duties (Law on Approval of Police Disciplinary Code 2005, Article 10). Furthermore, the Law on Police Service specifies some additional disciplinary violations, namely the violation of constitutional rights, revealing confidential information to unauthorized persons, the acceptance of kickbacks, being under alcohol influence while on duty, as serious violations of the police discipline (2002, Article 42).

The Disciplinary Code also specifies procedures which should be followed in disciplinary investigations. The Code is clear in determining that a disciplinary investigation and the associated internal discipline do not preclude a criminal investigation and a punishment for the same conduct (Law on Approval of Police Disciplinary Code 2005, Article 8). According to the Code, the grounds for initiation of disciplinary investigations include complaints from the public, organizations, and officials, detection of disciplinary violations by supervisors, and publication of media articles alleging police misconduct (Law on Approval of Police Disciplinary Code 2005, Article 18). Based on the grounds specified in the law, only the police chief has the power to order an internal investigation to commence. There is a special unit to carry out internal investigations, but the heads of all divisional units are also eligible to carry out internal investigations within the limits of their official capacity. However, the Code also prescribes that an internal investigation involving police officers from the highest and the main commander group can be carried out *only* by the police unit specifically designed to conduct internal investigations (Law on Approval of Police Disciplinary Code 2005, Article 12).

When an internal investigation concludes that an officer had violated the norms and engaged in prohibited behavior, an official who conducted the internal investigation should write a report suggesting the type of discipline to be applied (Law on Police Disciplinary Code 2005, Article 40). According to the Article 42 of the Law on Police Service, police officers can be subject to reprimand, severe reprimand, 10–50% reduction of salary up to 3 months, declaration on unsuitability to the occupied position, demotion to a lower position or rank, or dismissal from the police. The police chief has the exclusive power to make disciplinary decisions (Law on Approval of Police Disciplinary Code 2005, Article 8) and it is his discretion to decide what discipline should be applied. According to the law, if the police officer has shown sincere remorse or significant assistance during the internal investigation, the chief can utilize his discretion and relieve the police officer of any discipline (Law on Approval of Police Disciplinary Code 2005, Article 16).

Before the decision is made in the case involving serious violations, the materials collected during the internal investigation are discussed by the Police Disciplinary Committee—a body designated by the Government of Armenia. The Police Disciplinary Code (2005) stipulates that the Committee shall include police officers, as well as representatives from other governmental bodies and nongovernmental sector. However, police officers cannot constitute more than one half of the members (Law on Approval of Police Disciplinary Code 2005, Article 43.1) The Committee has an obligation to check whether the investigation resulted in sufficient evidence to prove that the accused police officer had engaged in the rule-violating behavior and, if this were the case, then decide the appropriate discipline. The Committee does not mete out the discipline; rather, the Committee recommends a type of discipline to the police chief who has the exclusive power to met out the discipline. The Committee can also recommend the police chief to close the disciplinary investigation (if the Committee did not find sufficient evidence that the police officer engaged in rule-violating behavior) or mete out no discipline (in the cases in which the officer expressed sincere remorse or apology, or provided substantial assistance during the investigation).

The disciplinary data are not readily available.[1] The data available in an OSCE-commissioned publication demonstrate that, in the period from January 2006 to September 2009, only 856 complaints were received from the public (OSCE 2010). The annual number of cases dramatically decreased over time, coinciding with the change in police leadership. In all of these cases, disciplinary investigations resulted in the dismissal of 167 officers and less severe disciplinary sanctions were meted out for additional 625 officers. In addition, 48 cases were forwarded to criminal investigators, which resulted to conviction of 26 officers (OSCE 2010).

More recent data available on the police official website show increase in the number of the disciplinary investigations. According to the data provided on the police official website (Internal Security Department 2013), 571 disciplinary investigations were conducted in 2012, which is a 25 % increase compared to the previous year. These disciplinary investigations resulted in disciplinary sanctions in relation to 175 officers. About one quarter (43) was dismissed and the rest were subjected to less serious disciplinary sanctions (Internal Security Department of RA Police 2013). The data for the 6-month period in 2013 closely resemble the results of 2012. According to the data provided on the same website, 267 disciplinary investigations were conducted, resulting in disciplinary actions against 64 officers. About one third (19) were dismissed and less serious sanctions being meted out for the rest (Internal Security Department of RA Police 2014).

These data, which are publicly available, contain only the results of the internal investigations conducted by the Internal Security Department and do not provide a

[1] Transparency International reports that, although the laws on public access to information apply equally to the police and other public entities, the police deny to provide any disciplinary data and refer to confidentiality of requested information as a valid reason for refusing to provide them (Transparency International 2003).

complete picture: No information is available on the number of internal investigations carried out by the heads of divisional units. Although the disciplinary data are too fragmented to make any meaningful comparisons, the first impression is that the number of dismissals decreased and the proportion of less serious disciplinary sanctions increased. At least for 2012 and the first half of 2013, the most frequently applied disciplinary sanction was reprimand (Internal Security Department 2014).

According to the previous police integrity survey (Kutnjak Ivković and Khechumyan 2013), only in two scenarios (bribe from a speeding motorist; crime scene theft of watch) participants thought that both the appropriate and the expected discipline should and would be dismissal. Although the survey included descriptions of scenarios of about the same level of seriousness, the participants in the study thought that both the appropriate and expected should be less serious or no discipline at all (Kutnjak Ivković and Khechumyan 2013). Unfortunately, no information is available about the discipline meted out in actual cases similar to the ones described in the questionnaire.

The Code of Silence

The third dimension of the theory proposes that the control of the code of silence is essential for the development of high integrity (Klockars and Kutnjak Ivković 2003).The police integrity theory proposes that there is a negative correlation between the code of silence and the level of integrity in a police integrity. At the same time, supervisors in agencies of low integrity would be reluctant to investigate misconduct and eventually discipline officers (Klockars and Kutnjak Ivković 2003).

Before the 2008–2009 police integrity survey, there were no attempts to measure the code of silence in Armenian police. Our first police integrity survey (2013, 2014) demonstrated that there was a very strong code of silence among the participating Armenian police officers. For the overwhelming majority of scenarios describing police corruption, the results showed that the respondents would be reluctant to report such behavior (Kutnjak Ivković and Khechumyan 2013). Although the extent of the code of silence varied across the scenarios (being the most prominent for the less serious forms of misconduct), in only one scenario—theft of watch from a crime scene by a police officer which was evaluated by the respondents as the most serious violation and deserving the most serious discipline—the mean hardly passed the midpoint of the scale toward the reporting side (Kutnjak Ivković and Khechumyan 2013).

Moreover, the survey also revealed that the code of silence among Armenian respondents stands out in comparison with the code of silence among the U.S. and Croatian samples. When we compared the Armenian results with the results from an established democracy, such as the USA, we discovered that the code of silence in Armenia seemed to be substantially stronger than the code of silence detected in the sample of the U.S. police officers. On the other hand, when we compared the results with another East European country in transition (Croatia), the code of silence among the Armenian respondents was similar to the code of silence among the Croatian respondents for less serious scenarios. However, the code of silence covering the most serious scenarios was much stronger in Armenia than it was in Croatia (Kutnjak Ivković and Khechumyan 2013). Quite remarkably, the respondents in the Armenian sample also perceived that most of their peers would be *more* likely to report the misconduct than they were. This unusual and unique finding contrasts with findings in other police integrity surveys during more than 15 years of research in 20 countries around the world (Kutnjak Ivković and Khechumyan 2013).

It seems that police administrators in Armenia are very well aware of the strong code of silence in the Armenian police. In fact, the police code of ethics, which is included in the Police Disciplinary Code, explicitly requires of police officers to assist their supervisors in maintaining discipline in the police agency. Moreover, in the case when a police officer fails to do so, the officer can be subjected to a disciplinary sanction (Law on Approval of Police Disciplinary Code 2005, Article 10). Therefore, it could be argued that the law stipulates that not reporting a misconduct of a fellow officer is a violation of the official rules in itself.

Influence of Social and Political Environment

The fourth proposition of the theory of police integrity focuses on the society at large and argues that the integrity of a police agency is affected by the larger social and political environment in which it operates (Klockars and Kutnjak Ivković 2003). When the society at large expects ethical behavior of its officials, police agencies are also more likely to set high expectations and expect ethical behavior from its employees. In contrast, police agencies in societies where corrupt behavior of public servants is tolerated, the level of police integrity is also expected to be low.

Various surveys conducted since 2003 have demonstrated the existence of systematic corruption in Armenia. From 2003 to 2008, Armenia's Corruption Perception Index (CPI) score remained relatively stable, at about 3.0, indicating serious corruption (Transparency International 2003–2008). The majority of the respondents also evaluated the governmental actions against corruption as ineffective (Transparency International 2010/2011). In 2011, the country scored 2.6 receiving 129th place among 183 participating countries (Transparency International 2012). This reality has not changed much during 2012–2013. In 2013, Armenia scored 36 on a new 0–100 corruption perception scale and shared 94–101 place among 177 participating countries (Transparency International 2014a).

Furthermore, in 2013, 39% of the respondents in Global Corruption Barometer had a perception that the level of corruption in the country has not changed during the past 2 years (Transparency International 2014). Sixty-six percent of the participants in this survey were in the opinion that police are corrupt or extremely corrupt (Transparency International 2014b). According to the results of the 2003 Transparency International survey (2003), household bribes paid to the police ranged from

US$ 17 to 5000, with the median of about US$ 200, while businessmen paid from US$ 200 to 1000 (Transparency International 2003, p. 41). In the 2013 survey, 21 % of participants reported paying a bribe to the police (Transparency International 2014). In addition, it seems that corruption and nepotism are present also in the area of recruitment and promotion of police officers (Transparency International 2003). A respondent who participated in a Transparency International survey reported that he paid US$ 5000 to be appointed to a position in the Ministry of the Interior (Transparency International 2003, p. 40).

Activists and human rights groups have also noted widespread corruption and abuse of power among government officials pointing to law enforcement as one of the most corrupt fields (Freedom House 2010). More recently, the Ombudsman of the Republic of Armenia published an ad hoc report on widespread and systematic bribery and other types of corruption in judiciary, revealing the mechanisms and even the alleged amounts of bribes paid to judges (Ombudsman 2013). Police corrupt practices seem to be part of criminal investigations as well. According to the European Committee for Prevention of Torture and Inhuman or Degrading Treatment or Punishment (CPT), police officers tend to demand money from detained persons or their relatives in exchange for their release or for the guarantee of additional privileges in detention (CPT 2011). The topic of corruption is also present in the UN Human Rights Committee's concluding observations regarding the implementation of International Covenant on Civil and Political Rights. In this document, the Committee stated (2012, para. 22):

> The Committee is concerned at allegations of persistent corruption among all branches of State institutions, especially the police and the judiciary that undermines the rule of law. In addition, the Committee is concerned at the lack of convincing results in the fight against high-level corruption and the resulting lack of public trust in the administration of justice.

Apart from indications of widespread corruption in the society, public opinion surveys also demonstrated the lack of confidence that the public can make a difference in the fight against corruption. According to the Global Corruption Barometer, more than two thirds of the respondents disagree with the statement that ordinary people can make a difference in the fight against corruption (Transparency International 2014). This result shows that the society at large is not ready to demand ethical behavior of its officials and corruption is highly tolerated in the Armenian society.

The government's stated goal is to build a Western-style parliamentary democracy. Yet, the international observers and opposition supporters have been challenging the quality of the democracy achieved to date (U.S. Department of State 2012). Since its first report in 1998, the Freedom House has continuously evaluated the country as only "partly free" (Freedom House 1998–2013), suggesting that the full protection of political and civil rights has not been attained. The postindependence history of Armenia is full of dramatic and turbulent events, such as war, economic collapse, banning of political parties, assassination of country's leadership, and disputed parliamentary and presidential elections resulting to jailing of opposition leaders and supporters (Freedom House 1998–2013). In the aftermath of 2008 presidential elections, the riot police dispersed demonstrations in an action that resulted in jailing dozens of opposition supporters, ten dead, hundreds injured, and a 20-day state of emergency (U.S. Department of State 2011; Council of Europe 2008a). The police are perceived as a tool of the government used to suppress political opponents (e.g., Transparency International 2003, p. 40). However, violations of human rights have been occurring, not only in emergency situations such as 2008 events but also on a more regular basis. Accusations of the use of excessive force are complemented with accusations of arbitrary arrests and the use of torture to extract confessions (Freedom House 2013).

Since Armenia has joined the European Convention for the Prevention of Torture and Inhuman or Degrading Treatment or Punishment in 2002, the CPT reports a large scale of physical mistreatment of persons held in police custody (CPT 2006, 2007, 2011, 2012). These reports have detailed that police officers slap, kick, and punch to extract confessions during interrogation in police stations. Apart from international organizations, police brutality and physical ill-treatment are also confirmed by domestic sources (e.g., Ombudsman of the Republic of Armenia 2012).

Successive Armenian governments have been continually implementing reforms in order to establish a modern democracy based on the rule of law and respect for human rights. For implementation of the reform agenda including fight against corruption, governments have received substantial financial and technical assistance from the international community (e.g., EU in Armenia 2012). Despite succeeding in bringing its human rights legislation in compliance with international standards, implementation of structural reforms and some improvements in the area of human rights protection, major gaps remain between the law and practice. Armenian government has had an anticorruption strategy and action plan in place since 2003. Moreover, anticorruption rhetoric has intensified since 2009 when Armenia joined the European Union Eastern Partnership scheme and was expected to initial an agreement of association with EU (e.g., Office of the President of the Republic of Armenia 2012). Despite an increase in the number of corruption cases involving also some senior government officials, in the absence of more systematic approach, the anticorruption efforts have not had a considerable impact in the fight against deep-rooted culture of corruption (Freedom House 2014).

Data and Methods

Questionnaire

To measure the level of police integrity in Armenia, we used the questionnaires developed by Klockars et al. (2006). This questionnaire includes 11 hypothetical scenarios, 5 of which describe examples of police corruption, 4 describe examples of the use of excessive force, 1 describes a failure to execute an arrest warrant, and 1 describes a falsification of the official record and planting of evidence.

We modified the original questionnaire (Klockars et al. 2006) to adjust the scenarios to the Armenian conditions. In particular, officers working at the beat do not have the right to stop vehicles for violation of traffic rules or for routine checks: the oversight of the traffic and safety on roads is the responsibility of a specialized police agency, namely the traffic police. Our sample does not include traffic police; thus, we considered the scenario 7 (verbal abuse–"Arrest an Asshole Day") irrelevant for the present sample of Armenian police officers. In contrast, police officers patrolling the beat are often deployed to patrol various demonstrations and rallies where clashes with protestors are possible. Therefore, we replaced the scenario 7 (verbal abuse–"Arrest an Asshole Day") with a scenario describing verbal abuse of young activists.

This research uses the original methodology developed by Klockars and Kutnjak Ivković (1996, 2003). The respondents were provided with a letter asking them to assume that the officer described in the scenarios had been a police officer for 5 years, had a satisfactory working record, and had not been disciplined in the past. The questionnaires were completed anonymously, and the questions regarding demographic information were kept to the absolute minimum.

Each scenario is followed by the same set of seven questions. The follow-up questions ask about police officers' knowledge of official rules and their opinions about the seriousness of particular rule-violating behaviors, the discipline these behaviors deserve and would actually receive, and their estimates of how willing they would be to report such behavior. Each question is followed by the possible answers ranging from a five- to an eight-point Likert-scale. Most of the scales were kept in the original form, but the disciplinary scales had to be adjusted for the Armenian conditions. In particular, the original six-item scale was changed to an eight-item scale. According to the Law on Police Service (2002) for a misconduct, the following disciplinary penalties can be applied: "reprimand," "severe reprimand," "salary reduction," "incompatibility with the occupied position," "demotion to one step lower position," "demotion to one step lower rank," and "dismissal."

Finally, the questions regarding the demographic information were modified in accordance with the structure and the ranking system of the Armenian police. In addition, the questionnaire also inquired about the length of the respondents' police experience, rank, assignment, and employment in a supervisory position. These questions were kept to the minimum to increase the respondents' willingness to participate in the study and to exclude the possibility that respondents could be identified. The respondents were also asked whether they had been truthful while filling out the questionnaire. The responses from those who said that they did not answer affirmatively were excluded from the analyses.

The Sample of the Armenian Police Officers

As it was mentioned earlier in this chapter, the Armenian police include 21 specialized departments, Yerevan City Department, and ten provincial departments, which are further subdivided into 52 local police stations (Police of the Republic of Armenia 2014). Because the survey was originally designed to ensure that the scenarios describe realistic behavior for police officers—the behavior they could potentially encounter while patrolling their beats—most scenarios focus on a police officer patrolling the beat. Thus, specialized police agencies and administrative bodies that do not have direct supervisory control over officers patrolling beats were excluded from the sample. We intended to survey all officers involved in patrolling the beats at all provincial departments and the Yerevan City Department which oversee the operation of smaller administrative units such as local police stations (Law on Police 2001, Article 9). One provincial department (which includes six local police stations) was not included in the survey for technical reasons.

In the summer of 2013, we surveyed police officers employed at these local police stations. Although the number of police officers is classified information in Armenia and, thus, we could not obtain the actual number of police officers employed at these departments, we can report that, with the assistance of police administration, we approached all police officers who are involved in patrolling the beats in these departments. A total of 986 officers agreed to participate in this survey. Out of these, 969 have returned filled out questionnaires, resulting in a response rate of 97%. Table 2.1 shows the distribution of the respondents across the ten police departments. Fifty respondents said that they did not answer the questions honestly, so we eliminated their answers from the analyses.

Our respondents were quite experienced police officers; only 16.7% had less than 3 years of experience, and the majority of the respondents (64.2%) had more than 5 years of experience (Table 2.2). Similarly to the organization of the military, all police officers in Armenia have ranks. Depending on education and training, police rookies can start at the lower or middle rank and, as they progress through the ranks, could potentially reach the higher ranks. In contrast to the American police system, sergeant, lieutenant, and captain are not positions in the Armenian system, but only junior and middle ranks. The highest rank in the hierarchy is the general-

Table 2.1 Sample distribution

Provinces (marzes)	Frequency	Percent
Department 1	50	5.2
Department 2	70	7.3
Department 3	59	6.2
Department 4	30	3.1
Department 5	20	2.1
Department 6	68	7.1
Department 7	40	4.2
Department 8	99	10.3
Department 9	97	10.1
Department 10	426	44.4
Total	959	100.0

Table 2.2 Respondents' demographic characteristics

	Number of respondents	Percent of respondents
Supervisory role		
Non-supervisors	787	81.2
Supervisors	102	10.8
Length of service		
Less than 1 year	62	6.7
1–2 years	93	10.0
3–5 years	175	18.8
6–10	169	18.2
11–15	167	17.9
16–20	145	15.6
More than 20 years	116	12.5
Type of assignment		
Patrol	119	13.1
Neighborhood inspector	428	47.2
Special operations	268	29.5
Administrative	45	5.0
Other	45	5.0
Gender		
Male	809	90.8
Female	78	8.8
Rank		
Junior	138	15.1
Middle	645	70.6
Senior	118	12.9
Main	5	0.5
Highest	2	0.2
Type of police agency		
Very large to more than 500	35	3.9
Large 201–500	40	4.4
Medium 76–200	445	49.0
Small 25–75	363	40.0
Very small less than 25	24	2.6
Total	969	100.0

colonel (Law on Police Service 2002, Article 5). The majority (70.6 %) of police officers in our sample are in the middle-rank group (Table 2.2). They are mostly patrol officers (13.1 %), neighborhood inspectors (47.2 %), and special operations (juvenile inspectors, criminal inspectors; 29.5 %). Finally, only 8.8 % are female and fewer than 11 % of the respondents were employed in the supervisory positions (Table 2.2).

Analysis and Discussion

Perceptions of Misconduct Seriousness

We asked the respondents to assess how serious they consider the behavior in each scenario and how serious most officers in their agency would evaluate the behavior. They could have picked an answer on a five-point Likert scale, from 1="not serious at all" to 5="very serious."

With one exception (scenario 8: cover-up of police DUI), the results demonstrate that police officers regarded described behavior as serious (Table 2.3). Although the degree of seriousness varied among the scenarios, all scenarios apart from one scenario (scenario 8: cover-up of police driving under the influence, DUI) have mean values of four or higher on the five-point Likert scale.

Three scenarios (scenario 1: free meals, gifts from merchants; scenario 8: cover-up of police DUI, and scenario 11: Sgt. fails to halt beating) are perceived to be the least serious, with mean values either below or close to four on the five-point scale. The evaluations of scenario 8 (cover-up of police DUI accident) and scenario 1 (free meals, gifts from merchants) as the least serious behaviors among the 11 scenarios in the questionnaire is not surprising; these scenarios describe some of the mildest forms of the police corruption, namely internal corruption and the acceptance of gratuities (Barker and Roebuck 1973). These findings are consistent with prior police integrity research which demonstrates that internal corruption and the acceptance of gratuities have been classified by many police officers across the world as the least serious types of corruption (Klockars et al. 2004a). These findings are also in line with the previous police integrity survey in Armenia (Kutnjak Ivković and Khechumyan 2013).

On the other hand, it is surprising that the scenario describing a sergeant who fails to stop beating by police officers (scenario 11) is evaluated as one of the least serious ones in the questionnaire. Not stopping the use of excessive force by a supervisor was evaluated as less serious than some other forms of internal corruption (scenario 5: supervisor offers holiday for errands) and a scenario describing the verbal abuse of an activist (scenario 7: verbal abuse of young activists).

On the other end of the scale, with mean values ranging from 4.5 to 5 (Table 2.3), participants placed three scenarios which they considered to be the most serious types of misconduct. These scenarios include the theft of a knife from a crime scene (scenario 3: theft of knife from crime scene), falsification of the official report (scenario 10: false report of drugs on drug dealer), and a biased allocation of services (scenario 5: supervisor offers holiday for errands). Out of those three most serious scenarios, theft from a crime scene (scenario 3), which encompasses not only the abuse of power for personal gain, but also the abuse of trust by citizens put in a vulnerable position by a crime, was evaluated as the most serious in the group. Similarly, planting drugs on a drug dealer and falsifying the official record (scenario 10) was another scenario which well deserves to be on the serious side of the scale.

Table 2.3 Police officer perceptions of seriousness and violation of rules

Scenario number and description	Own seriousness		Others' seriousness		Mean difference (own—others)	*t*-test	Violation of rules	
	Mean	Rank	Mean	Rank			Mean	Rank
Scenario 1: free meals, gifts from merchants	4.02	2	3.78	2	0.24	6.54***	4.30	2
Scenario 2: failure to arrest friend with warrant	4.43	8	4.17	6	0.25	6.78***	4.60	8
Scenario 3: theft of knife from crime scene	4.83	11	4.68	11	0.15	5.86***	4.85	11
Scenario 4: unjustifiable use of deadly force	4.19	4.5	3.97	5	0.22	7.10***	4.39	3
Scenario 5: supervisor offers holiday for errands	4.52	9	4.33	9	0.19	5.88***	4.61	9
Scenario 6: officer strikes prisoner who hurt partner	4.19	4.5	3.92	4	0.27	7.66***	4.44	5.5
Scenario 7: verbal abuse of young activists	4.40	7	4.17	7	0.23	8.01***	4.53	7
Scenario 8: cover-up of police DUI accident	3.42	1	3.19	1	0.23	6.25***	3.88	1
Scenario 9: auto body shop 5 % kickback	4.34	6	4.19	8	0.15	5.30***	4.44	5.5
Scenario 10: false report on drug on dealer	4.67	10	4.51	10	0.15	5.84***	4.79	10
Scenario 11: Sgt. fails to halt beating	4.07	3	3.91	3	0.15	4.91***	4.40	4

Sgt Sergeant, *DUI* driving under the influence
$^{*}p<0.05$; $^{**}p<0.01$; $^{***}p<0.001$

The fact that a case of internal corruption (scenario 5: supervisor offers holiday for errands) is considered as one of the most serious scenarios is surprising, particularly in light of the fact that the questionnaire contains scenarios describing the abuse of the most severe form of force—deadly force—(scenario 4: unjustifiable use of deadly force) and another severe form of corruption—the acceptance of a kickback (scenario 9: auto body shop 5% kickback). While the other two scenarios in this group are placed in the same group also by the respondents from other countries (e.g., see Croatian chapter in this edition), it is surprising to see that scenario 5 (supervisor offers holiday for errands) is in same group. This could be probably explained by the fact that most of our participants (81.2%) are non-supervisors and that they might have identified themselves with the officers who would have replaced the corrupt officer in our scenario. In other words, our respondents are potentially reacting harshly not to the supervisor conduct, but to the direct consequences of the corrupt transaction, which they envision facing themselves or potentially might have already faced in real life.

When we explored the order of seriousness across scenarios describing instances of police corruption (scenario 1: free meals, gifts from merchants; scenario 3: theft of knife from crime scene; scenario 5: supervisor offers holiday for errands; scenario 8: cover-up of police DUI accident; and scenario 9: auto body shop 5% kickback), there was a relative order that corresponds to what we found in our previous survey (e.g., Kutnjak Ivković and Kechumian 2013a). Specifically, the acceptance of gratuities (scenario 1) and the cover-up of police DUI (scenario 8) are evaluated as the least serious and the theft from a crime scene (scenario 3) as the most serious. As discussed earlier, the case of internal corruption describing the favorable scheduling (scenario 5) was evaluated as surprisingly serious in the group, particularly compared to the kickback (scenario 9).

There are also four scenarios describing the use of excessive force (scenario 11: Sgt. fails to halt beating; scenario 4: unjustifiable use of deadly force; scenario 6: officer strikes a prisoner who hurt partner; scenario 7: verbal abuse of young activists) in the questionnaire. However, the order in which scenarios are ranked based on the mean values of seriousness is somewhat surprising (Table 2.3). Scenario 7 (verbal abuse of young activists), which is traditionally seen as the least serious violation among the violations involving the use of excessive force (National Institute of Justice 2009), was evaluated to be the most serious among the abuse of force scenarios, including the use of deadly force. A potential explanation rests in the uncomplicated nature of the scenario, which describes a plain violation of official rules, while the rest of scenarios on the use of excessive force, including the use of unjustified deadly force, have a component (e.g., police officer's prior experience) which could potentially mitigate the seriousness of the misconduct in the eyes of the respondents.

Finally, we explored the differences between the respondents' own estimates of seriousness and the estimates of seriousness they thought that the majority of the officers in their agency would provide. Although there are statistically significant differences between the respondents' own estimates and estimates of most police officers' evaluations of misconduct seriousness in all 11 scenarios (see Table 2.3), we did not find any differences to cross our rule-of-thumb threshold of 0.5, suggesting that the respondents did not perceive that the other officers in their agency would have substantially different views from their own.

Violation of the Official Rules

We asked the respondents to evaluate whether the behaviors described in each of the 11 scenarios violated official rules. After reading each scenario, the respondents could have circled an answer on a five-point Likert scale, from 1="definitely not a violation" to 5="definitely a violation." All hypothetical scenarios described in the questionnaire are violations of official rules and six of them (scenario 11: Sgt. fails to halt beating; scenario 6: officer strikes a prisoner who hurt partner; scenario 4: unjustifiable use of deadly force; scenario 2: failure to arrest friend with warrant;

Table 2.4 Views about appropriate discipline (should) and expected discipline (would)

Scenario number and description		Mode	Rank should	Rank would	None (%)	Some discipline (%)	Dismissal (%)	Chi-square test[b]	Phi
Scenario 1: free meals, gifts from merchants	*Should*	Reprimand	3–7		27.7	61.3	11.1	715.17***	0.958***
	Would	Reprimand		1–6	21.2	65.0	13.8		
Scenario 2: failure to arrest friend with warrant	*Should*	Severe rep.	8		10.3	69.9	19.9	929.80***	1.000***
	Would	Severe rep.		7–8	7.5	70.4	22.1		
Scenario 3: theft of knife from crime scene	*Should*	Dismissal	9–11		2.1	45.5	52.4	964.04***	1.000***
	Would	Dismissal		9–11	2.3	42.8	54.9		
Scenario 4: unjustifiable use of deadly force	*Should*	Dismissal	9–11		13.0	54.6	32.4	930.52***	1.000***
	Would	Dismissal		9–11	9.9	48.9	41.3		
Scenario 5: supervisor offers holiday for errands	*Should*	Reprimand	3–7		14.9	78.6	6.6	1024.78***	1.000***
	Would	Reprimand		1–6	16.7	76.6	6.7		
Scenario 6: officer strikes prisoner who hurt partner	*Should*	Reprimand	3–7		22.5	69.4	8.1	725.46***	0.956***
	Would	Reprimand		1–6	15.3	72.2	12.5		
Scenario 7: verbal abuse of young activists	*Should*	Reprimand	3–7		21.8	74.3	3.9	823.29***	1.000***
	Would	Reprimand		1–6	15.0	80.0	5.0		
Scenario 8: cover-up of police DUI accident	*Should*	None	1–2		40.9	57.1	2.1	763.25***	0.973***
	Would	Reprimand		1–6	31.0	65.2	3.8		
Scenario 9: auto body shop 5 % kickback	*Should*	Reprimand	3–7		18.4	64.2	17.3	1068.18***	1.000***
	Would	Reprimand		1–6	15.1	63.6	21.3		
Scenario 10: false report on drug on dealer	*Should*	Dismissal	9–11		7.3	63.7	29.0	1028.72***	1.000***
	Would	Dismissal		9–11	7.7	58.4	33.9		
Scenario 11: Sgt. fails to halt beating	*Should*	None	1–2		25.2	66.5	8.4	742.91***	0.966***
	Would	Severe Rep.		7–8	17.0	68.5	14.3		

Sgt Sergeant, *DUI* driving under the influence

scenario 9: false report of drug on drug dealer; scenario 3: theft of knife from crime scene) are also violations of criminal law. The remaining five scenarios are violations of official rules, but not necessarily violations of criminal law.

With one exception (scenario 8: cover-up of police DUI accident), the mean values indicate that the majority of the respondents had no problems recognizing these behaviors as examples of rule violations. The mean values for ten scenarios (Table 2.3), ranging from 4.3 to 4.9, are all clustered closely together, suggesting that there is little variation in how likely the respondents were to evaluate them as rule violating.

By far the lowest mean in the group is for scenario 1, describing the acceptance of gratuities (Table 2.3). The acceptance of gratuities is usually least likely to be recognized as a rule-violating behavior by police officers (see, e.g., Klockars et al. 2004) and is perceived to be the least serious among corrupt behaviors. At the same time, there are additional factors to take into account in Armenia. If a police officer accepts gratuities and does not do anything in exchange or does not promise anything in exchange, the acceptance of gratuities is viewed as (just) a violation of official disciplinary rules, but not of the criminal code.

Scenario 8 (cover-up of police DUI accident) does not fit well the overall pattern. Rather, it has the mean closer to the midpoint of the scale than to the end of the scale, suggesting that there was a substantial proportion of our respondents who said that this was not a violation of official rules. Such lenient attitudes toward this behavior are related to two facts. First, cases of internal corruption usually are viewed as less serious and less likely to be recognized as rule-violating behavior (e.g., Klockars et al. 2004). At the same time, this behavior does not constitute a violation of the criminal code but only of the disciplinary rules.

However, despite the overall strong likelihood that most police officers in the sample would recognize these behaviors as rule violating, the fact remains that there was still a number of respondents who had problems recognizing these behaviors as rule violating. It is possible that a substantial minority of the police officers do not know the official rules. Especially in the early 1990s, when the recruitment and promotion of police officers was driven by corruption and nepotism (Transparency International 2003, p. 40), extensive training was not provided and the trainers at the police educational establishments had no or outdated previous professional experience (Hofstra 2010). However, the Law on Police Service (2002) has been in force for more than 10 years by the time of the survey and, during this period, most, if not all police officers, have undergone some training at the police educational establishments which would have allowed them to learn at least the "basic rules." It could also be that, despite participating in police training, police officers have no motivation to learn and/or that the trainers either lack the necessary knowledge or the motivation to train those participants. For example, a paper describing OSCE's police development activities in Armenia suggests employing a moderate approach when assessing the success or failure of police reforms in Armenia. According to this source, reforms in organizations such as police often have limited success even in more developed countries where police officers are relatively better paid, trained, and motivated than in Armenia (Hofstra 2010).

Finally, the respondents' evaluations of whether the behavior constitutes a violation of official rules are strongly related to how serious they perceive the behavior; the more serious they evaluated the behavior, the more likely they were to evaluate it as rule violating. The ranking of scenarios based on their evaluations of seriousness and the ranking of scenarios based on their evaluations of rule-violating nature of the behavior are very similar (Spearman's correlation coefficient = 0.979; $p<0.001$).

Opinions About the Appropriate and Expected Discipline

The respondents were asked to assess the appropriate discipline for a police officer who engaged in the behavior described in the scenarios. They were also questioned about the discipline they expected their agencies would mete out for a police officer who engaged in the described behavior. The disciplinary options were determined based on the legal regulations governing the work of the Armenian police. Overall, there were eight disciplinary choices, ranging from "no discipline," "reprimand," "severe reprimand," "salary reduction," "incompatibility with the occupied position," "demotion to one step lower position," "demotion to one step lower rank," to "dismissal."

According to the modal values (Table 2.4), the respondents favored and expected dismissal in only three scenarios (scenario 3: theft of knife from crime scene; scenario 4: unjustifiable use of deadly force; scenario 10: false report of drug on dealer). All three scenarios were evaluated by the majority of the respondents as rule violations as well. Moreover, the respondents evaluated two out of these three scenarios (scenario 3: theft of knife from crime scene; scenario 10: false report of drug on dealer) to be the most serious types of misconduct in the questionnaire (Table 2.3). Thus, it is not surprising that the respondents were also most likely to approve and expect the most serious discipline for them.

The third scenario on this list (scenario 4: unjustifiable use of deadly force) does not quite fit the picture. Although respondents favored and expected dismissal—the most serious discipline—for such behavior, they did not see it as a very serious violation (Rank 4.5; Table 2.3) in comparison to other scenarios and had more challenges recognizing it as a violation of rules (Table 2.3). It seems that, in their evaluation of seriousness and ability to recognize as rule violation, participants identified themselves with the police officer in this scenario demonstrating sympathy to the officer who appeared in a potentially controversial situation. The description of the scenario (police officer's prior experience of being seriously hurt because he did not react on time) could potentially contribute to this evaluation and provide justification to the respondents. On the other hand, the participants realized that, for the abuse of lethal force, they cannot expect and would not get anything less than dismissal.

On the other end of the scale are two scenarios in which, according to the modal responses, our respondents did not prefer any discipline. These are scenario 8 (cover-up of police DUI accident) and scenario 11 (Sgt. fails to halt beating). The cover-up of police DUI accident (scenario 8) is evaluated to be the least serious both in terms of seriousness of the behavior and violation of rules. The scenario 11 (Sgt. fails to halt beating) is also evaluated as one of the least serious examples of misconducts described in the questionnaire with a substantial minority not recognizing it as a violation of official rules. Although the participants did not favor any discipline for the mentioned scenarios, they expected that these behaviors would meet some mild discipline, namely reprimand.

According to our respondents, the remaining six scenarios (scenario 1: free meals, gifts from merchants; scenario 2: failure to arrest a friend with a warrant; scenario 5: supervisor offers holiday for errands; scenario 6: officer strikes a prisoner who hurt partner; scenario 7: verbal abuse; scenario 9: auto body shop 5 % kickback) should and would result in "reprimand" or "severe reprimand," which are the two mildest disciplinary sanctions in the Police Disciplinary Code (2005). Although respondents evaluated that these behaviors should and would result only in a very mild discipline, they assessed some of these scenarios (scenario 7: verbal abuse; scenario 2: failure to arrest a friend with a warrant; scenario 5: supervisor offers holiday for errands) to be very serious violations. Moreover, the overwhelming majority of respondents were sure that these scenarios violate official rules.

As mentioned above, we relied not only on the modes, but also on the percentages of police officers who selected no discipline, some discipline other than dismissal, and dismissal (Table 2.4). The findings of this analysis revealed some interesting details which are not possible to see with the modal analysis. According to the modal analysis, the participants favored and expected dismissal only in three scenarios (scenario 3: theft of knife from crime scene; scenario 4: unjustifiable use of deadly force; scenario 10: false report of drug on dealer). However, the percentage analysis demonstrates that in only one of these scenarios (scenario 3: theft of knife from crime scene), the percentage of participants favoring and expecting dismissal is higher than the percentage of those who favored and expected some less severe discipline (Table 2.4). Even in this scenario, 45.5 % of participants thought that some discipline but not dismissal would be appropriate for this behavior (Table 2.4). In the other two scenarios (scenario 4: unjustifiable use of deadly force; scenario 10: false report of drug on dealer), the majority of participants (54.6 and 63.7 %, respectively) favored some milder discipline rather than dismissal. The views about appropriate and expected discipline are pretty much similar, suggesting that the police administrators are perceived to have a rather lenient approach toward some very serious forms of police misconduct.

Although the modal analysis of views about appropriate and expected discipline demonstrates that there are two scenarios in which officers did not favor any discipline, the percentage analysis revealed that there is no scenario in which the majority of participants favored no discipline; in each and every case of police misconduct included in the questionnaire, the majority of police officers expected some discipline and, for the theft from a crime scene (scenario 3), even dismissal. Even in scenario 8 (cover-up of police DUI accident), the majority of the respondents supported and expected some discipline, although there was a strong minority of the respondents who supported (40.9 %) and expected (31.0 %; Table 2.4) no discipline.

Finally, we also ranked scenarios based on the modal appropriate discipline for each scenario (Table 2.4). Because the answers are recorded on the ordinal scale with six possible categories, several scenarios share the same ranking. Nevertheless, a comparison of the ranking of appropriate discipline with the ranking for seriousness shows that they are strongly correlated (Spearman's correlation coefficient $=0.698$, $p<0.05$); the more serious the respondents evaluated the scenarios to be, the more likely they were to think that the appropriate discipline should be harsher. Similarly, a comparison of the ranking of appropriate discipline with the ranking for rule-violating behavior shows that the two are related as well (Spearman's correlation coefficient $=0.586$, $p<0.100$). The more likely the respondents were to evaluate the behavior as rule violating, the more likely they were to think that the appropriate discipline should be harsher.

We also compared the respondents' views about the appropriate discipline with discipline they expect their agency to mete out. Although we noted a few differences in the modal analysis (e.g., police officers approved of no discipline and expected reprimand for scenario 8: cover-up of police DUI accident; police officers approved of no discipline and expected severe reprimand for scenario 11: Sgt. fails to halt beating), a comparison between the appropriate and expected discipline suggested considerable similarity.[2] Furthermore, we did not find any substantial differences among the percentages of the respondents who expected no discipline, some discipline, and dismissal and those who favored no discipline, some discipline, and dismissal for such behaviors.

Willingness to Report Misconduct

The last question in each scenario of our questionnaire aims to measure the extent of the code of silence. We asked the respondents whether they personally and the most officers in their departments would report the behavior described in the questionnaire. They could pick an answer on a five-point Likert scale, from 1 = "definitely would not report" to 5 = "definitely would report."The mean value and the percentage analysis of the responses (Table 2.5) showed that the code of silence varies across scenarios. On the five-point Likert scale, in 5 out of 11 scenarios, the means were all below or close to 3.0 (midpoint), implying that most of the respondents probably would *not* report the behavior described in the questionnaire. Although this tendency varies across scenarios, being the most prominent for the protection of police DUI (scenario 8: cover-up of police DUI accident) and the least prominent for the verbal abuse of young activists (scenario 7: verbal abuse of young activists), the fact remains that the code of silence is present among our sample of the Armenian police officers. These scenarios not only involve some relatively benign forms of misconduct, such as the acceptance of gratuities (scenario 1: free meals, gifts

[2] The chi-square test of independence is statistically significant for all 11 scenarios, rejecting the null hypothesis of statistical independence. Similarly, the phi coefficients suggest that the expressed views of appropriate and expected discipline are related.

Table 2.5 Police officer perceptions of willingness to report

Scenario number and Description	Own willingness to report		Others' willingness to report		Mean difference (own—others)	*t*-test
	Mean	Rank	Mean	Rank		
Scenario 1: free meals, gifts from merchants	2.97	3	3.40	5	−0.44	−8.21***
Scenario 2: failure to arrest friend with warrant	3.36	8	3.69	8	−0.33	−6.91***
Scenario 3: theft of knife from crime scene	3.83	10	4.00	10	−0.17	−3.52***
Scenario 4: unjustifiable use of deadly force	3.93	11	4.14	11	−0.21	−5.02***
Scenario 5: supervisor offers holiday for errands;	3.27	7	3.55	7	−0.28	−5.97***
Scenario 6: officer strikes prisoner who hurt partner	2.91	2	3.25	3.5	−0.34	−7.60***
Scenario 7: verbal abuse of young activists	3.02	5	3.25	3.5	−0.23	−5.49***
Scenario 8: cover-up of police DUI Accident	2.70	1	3.04	1	−0.35	−7.87***
Scenario 9: auto body shop 5 % kickback	3.12	6	3.46	6	−0.34	−8.28***
Scenario 10: false report on drug on dealer	3.71	9	3.88	9	−0.17	−4.20***
Scenario 11: Sgt. fails to halt beating	2.98	4	3.21	2	−0.23	−5.80***

$^{*}p<0.05$; $^{**}p<0.01$; $^{***}p<0.001$

from merchants) and verbal abuse (scenario 7: verbal abuse of young activists), but also examples of severe use of excessive force (scenario 6: officer strikes prisoner who hurt partner), as well as a serious failure by supervisors to stop the use of excessive force (scenario 11: Sgt. fails to halt beating).

We find further evidence of the existence of the strong code of silence. In the remaining seven scenarios, the means are all between three and four on the five-point scale (Table 2.5). For three of them (scenario 2: failure to arrest friend with warrant; scenario 5: supervisor offers holiday for errands; scenario 9: auto body shop 5 % kickback), the means barely move away from the midpoint (Table 2.5), suggesting that the respondents were almost equally divided between those who would and would not report. Even in the case of scenarios describing the use of deadly force (scenario 4) and theft from a crime scene (scenario 3), the mean values do not get above four and close to five, the reporting side of the scale. The implications are clear: Even in the cases in which the respondents expect discipline to be meted out, there is a strong minority of our respondents who would not report even for these serious violations of official agency rules and criminal law.

We also compared the respondents' own willingness to report with their estimates of others' willingness to report (Table 2.5). The mean values suggest that, in all 11 scenarios, the respondents estimated that others to be somewhat *more* willing to report than they would. Although the differences between the means for their own willingness to report and the means for others' willingness to report are statistically significant in all 11 scenarios, the differences are not large and meaningful in any of the scenarios (i.e., they did not cross the 0.50 rule-of-thumb threshold).

Finally, a comparison of the rankings shows that their own willingness to report and their estimates of others' willingness to report are very strongly related (Spearman's correlation coefficient $=0.943$, $p<0.001$).

Conclusion

Our study demonstrated that overwhelming majority of the respondents had no problems recognizing the most of the behaviors as rule violating, but there were still police officers who did not know that these behaviors violated official rules. The perception of seriousness of the described scenarios strongly correlates to the recognition of the scenario as rule violating. When the police officers were less likely to recognize behavior described in the scenarios as rule violating, they were less likely to evaluate them as serious as well.

The evaluations of seriousness were mostly grouped on the very serious part of the scale. However, the degree of seriousness evaluation across the scenarios revealed a divergent trend. Our respondents evaluated verbal abuse (traditionally viewed as the lowest point of the use of force continuum) to be more serious than striking a handcuffed prisoner or even abusing deadly force. On the other hand, there were no surprising results in evaluation of seriousness in scenarios which were traditionally viewed as examples of police corruption. The respondents evaluated internal corruption (cover-up of police DUI accident) and acceptance of gratuities as the least serious forms of corruption, while the kickback and the theft from a crime scene were evaluate as more serious forms of corruption. These findings fit well with the previous police integrity survey in Armenia and internationally (Klockars et al. 2004a, 2004b; Kremer 2004; Kutnjak Ivković 2004b; Kutnjak Ivković and Sauerman 2012, 2013a, 2013b; Kutnjak Ivković and Khechumyan 2013, 2014)

Although the overwhelming majority of participants had no problems recognizing the behaviors as rule violating and evaluated most of them to be very serious, only in one scenario (scenario 3: theft of knife from crime scene) a narrow majority favored and expected dismissal. In the rest of the scenarios, the majority of participants supported and expected some discipline, but not dismissal. For the most scenarios, the results also demonstrated a very small difference between the appropriate and expected discipline. These findings can have two potential explanations. First, there is a possibility that police officers have misleading perceptions about the real consequences of misconduct described in the scenarios. Second, if the police officers' assessments of actual discipline are accurate, this would suggest that the police leadership is creating a relaxed disciplinary environment which does not address police misconduct adequately.

Finally, the survey shows the existence of a strong code of silence among the surveyed Armenian police officers. However, the extent of the code of silence varies across the scenarios. About one half of the participants said that they will not report a fellow police officer's DUI accident, the acceptance of gratuities, or the administration of a dose of "street justice." Even for the scenario describing the use of deadly force, there was a substantial minority of the respondents who said that they would not report.

A comparison of our findings from the 2013 survey with the results of the 2008/2009 survey on the five identical scenarios (Kutnjak Ivković and Khechumyan 2013, 2014) suggests that the code of silence might have weakened since the first survey. One tendency, which still remains, is the respondents' perception that the fellow officers would be more willing to report misconduct than they would. However, the fact remains that, even in our more recent survey, there was a substantial minority of the police officers would not report the most serious examples of police misconduct.

Our results about the contours of police integrity among the Armenian police fit well with the developments in the society at large. Armenia has been now an independent country for more than two decades after being a part of the Soviet Union for more than 70 years. The post-Soviet history of Armenia was troubled with war, transportation blockade, and economic collapse. Although a ceasefire has been in place since 1994, continued negotiations have not been successful and the threat of the war restart is still very real particularly in the light of reoccurring violations of ceasefire causing fatalities on both sides (Radio Free Europa 2014).

On the other hand, despite the stated goal of establishing a democratic state and a legal obligation of having an effective political democracy, the level of democracy achieved to date is continuously questioned by intergovernmental and nongovernmental organizations observing compliance with the treaty obligations. This is not to say that there was no effort to implement the reforms. Indeed, the legislative framework in Armenia, especially the legislation concerning the human rights, rule of law, and democratic governance, is largely in compliance with the international standards. However, major gaps still remain between the law on the books and their actual enforcement. Our results provide clear evidence to support this view. While police officers perceive cases of misconduct to be serious, they approve and expect mild discipline and are reluctant to report such behavior to the supervisors.

References

Avagyan, G., & Hiscock, D. (2005). Security sector reform in Armenia. www.saferworld.org.uk/downloads/pubdocs/Armenia_English.pdf. Accessed 23 Dec 2013.

Barker, T., & Roebuck, J. (1973). *An empirical typology of police corruption*. Springfield: Charles C. Thomas Publisher.

Bayley, D. (2006). *Changing the guard: Developing democratic policing abroad*. New York: Oxford University Press.

Code of Criminal Procedure of the Republic of Armenia. (1998). http://www.arlis.am/. Accessed 25 Feb 2014.

Council of Europe. (2008a). Resolution 1609. http://assembly.coe.int/Main.asp?link¼/Documents/AdoptedText/ta08/ERES1609.htm. Accessed 12 Jan 2014.

Council of Europe. (2013). Treaties signed and ratified or having been the subject of an accession as of 7/5/2013. http://conventions.coe.int/Treaty/Commun/ListeTraites.asp?PO=Arm&MA=999&SI=2&CM=3&CL=ENG. Accessed 7 Dec 2013.

Council of the European Union. (2009). Prague Summit Declaration. http://www.enpi-info.eu/library/content/joint-declaration-prague-eastern-partnership-summit. Accessed 12 Jan 2014.

CPT. (2006). Report to the Armenian Government on the visit to Armenia from 20 to 22 April 2004. www.cpt.coe.int/documents/arm/2006-38-inf-eng.htm. Accessed 12 Dec 2013.

CPT. (2007). Report to the Armenian Government on the visit to Armenia from 2 to 12 April 2006. www1.umn.edu/humanrts/research/armenia/Report%20to%20the%20Armenian%20Government%202007.pdf. Accessed 12 Jan 2014.

CPT. (2011). Report to the Armenian Government on the visit to Armenia from 20 to 21 May 2010. www.cpt.coe.int/documents/arm/2011-24-inf-eng.pdf. Accessed 12 Jan 2014.

CPT. (2012). Report to the Armenian Government on the visit to Armenia from 5 to 7 December 2011. http://www.cpt.coe.int/documents/arm/2012-23-inf-eng.pdf. Accessed 13 Jan 2014.

Criminal Code of the Republic of Armenia. (2003). http://www.arlis.am/. Accessed 25 Feb 2014.

De Wall, T. (2003). *Black garden: Armenia and Azerbaijan through peace and war*. New York: New York University Press.

Decree of the President of the Republic of Armenia to Appoint A. Sarkisyan as the Chief of Police. (2008, May 29). http://www.president.am/hy/decrees/. Accessed 23 Jan 2014.

EU in Armenia. (2012). http://eucentre.am/eu-in-armenia/. Accessed 23 Dec 2013.

Freedom House. (1998–2013). Country Reports: Armenia. https://freedomhouse.org/report/freedom-world/1998/armenia#.VLZKemP-J6Y. Accessed 12 Jan 2014.

Freedom House. (2010). Country Reports: Armenia. http://www.freedomhouse.org/template.cfm?page=22&year=2010&country=7772. Accessed 12 Jan 2014.

Freedom House. (2014). Country Reports: Armenia. http://www.freedomhouse.org/report/freedomworld/ 2013/armenia. Accessed 12 Jan 2014.

Hofstra, C. (2010). Police development activities of the OSCE in Armenia, pp. 155–161. In Ursel Schlichting (Edt). *The OSCE Yearbook*. http://www.core-hamburg.de/documents/yearbook/english/11/Hofstra-en.pdf. Accessed 23 Feb 2014.

Internal Security Department of RA Police. (2013). http://www.police.am/structure. Accessed 11 Jan 2014.

Internal Security Department of RA Police. (2014). http://www.police.am/news/view 2014. Accessed 11 Jan 2014.

Klockars, C., & Kutnjak Ivković, S. (1995). *A cross-cultural study of police corruption*. The 47th Annual Meeting of the American Society of Criminology, Boston, Massachusetts, November 1995.

Klockars, C. B., & Kutnjak Ivković, S. (1999). The measurement of police delinquency. In Laufer, W., & Adler, F. (Eds.). *The Criminology of Criminal Law. Advances in Criminological Theory,* Vol. 8. New Brunswick, NJ: Transaction. pp. 87–106.

Klockars, C. B., & Kutnjak Ivković, S. (2004). Measuring police integrity. In Piquero, A. R., Greene, J. R., & Hickman, M. J. (Eds.). *Police Integrity and Ethics.* Wadsworth Publishing. pp. 1.3–1.20.

Klockars, C. B., Kutnjak Ivković, S., & Haberfeld, M. R. (Eds.). (2004). *The contours of police Integrity*. Thousand Oaks, CA: Sage Publications. pp. 1–18.

Klockars, C. B., Kutnjak Ivković, S., Harver, W. E., & Haberfeld, M. R. (1997). The measurement of police integrity. Final Report Submitted to the U.S. Department of Justice, Office of Justice Programs, National Institute of Justice.

Klockars, C. B., Kutnjak Ivković, S., & Haberfeld, M. R. (2006). *Enhancing police integrity*. New York: Springer.

Kremer, F. (2004). Police integrity in Hungary. In Klockars, C. B., Kutnjak Ivković, S., & Haberfeld, M. R. (Eds.). *The contours of police integrity*. Thousand Oaks, CA: Sage Publications, 116–130.

Kutnjak Ivković, S. (2004). Evaluating the seriousness of police misconduct: A cross-cultural comparison of police officer and citizen views. *International Criminal Justice Review,* 14, 25–48.

Kutnjak Ivković, S., & Klockars, C. B. (1996). Police perceptions of disciplinary fairness and the formation of the code of silence. *The 1996 Annual Meeting of the Academy of Criminal Justice Sciences,* Las Vegas, Nevada, March 1996.

Kutnjak Ivković, S., & Sauerman, A. (2012). The code of silence: Revisiting *South African Police Integrity*. South African Crime Quarterly, 40 (June), 15–24.

Kutnjak Ivković, S., & Khechumyan, A. (2013). The state of police integrity in Armenia: Findings from the police integrity survey. *Policing: An International Journal of Police Strategies & Management, 36*(1), 70–90.

Kutnjak Ivković, S., & Khechumyan, A. (2014). Measuring Police integrity among urban and rural police in Armenia: From local results to global implications. *International Journal of Comparative and Applied Criminal Justice 38*(1), 39–61.

Kutnjak Ivković, S., & Klockars, C. B. (1995). *A cross-cultural study of police corruption*. Paper Presented at the 1995 Annual Meeting of the American Society of Criminology. Boston: November 1995.

Kutnjak Ivković, S., & Sauerman, A. (2013). Curtailing the code of silence among the South African police. *Policing: An International Journal of Police Strategies and Management,* 36(1), 175–198. doi: 10.1108/13639511311302533

Kutnjak Ivković, S., & Sauerman, A. (2015). Threading the thin blue line: Transition toward democratic policing and the integrity of the South African police service. *Policing and Society,* 25(1), 25–52. DOI 10.1080/10439463.2013.788651

National Assembly of the Republic of Armenia. (1997). Law on Police Troops. ՀՀՊՏ 1997.12.25/29. http://www.arlis.am/. Accessed 7 Feb 2014.

National Assembly of the Republic of Armenia. (2001). Law on Police Service. ՀՀՊՏ 2001.05.31/15(147) Հոդ.378. http://www.arlis.am/. Accessed 7 Feb 2014.

National Assembly of the Republic of Armenia. (2002). Law on Police Service. ՀՀՊՏ 2002.08.08/32(207) Հոդ.734. http://www.arlis.am/. Accessed 7 Feb 2014.

National Assembly of the Republic of Armenia. (2005). Law on Approval of Police Disciplinary Code. ՀՀՊՏ 2005.05.18/29(401) Հոդ. 571. http://www.arlis.am/. Accessed 7 Feb 2014.

National Institute of Justice. (2009).The use-of-force continuum. http://www.nij.gov/topics/law-enforcement/officer-safety/use-of-force/continuum.htm. Accessed 7 Jan 2014.

Office of the President of the Republic of Armenia. (2012). http://www.president.am/hy/press-release/item/2012/09/15/President-Serzh-Sargsyan-Governmernt-meeting/. Accessed 7 Feb 2014.

Ombudsman. (2013). Ad hoc report on Fair Trial Rights. http://www.ombuds.am/. Accessed 7 Feb 2014.

Ombudsman of the Republic of Armenia. (2012). Annual Report. http://www.ombuds.am/. Accessed 7 Feb 2014.

OSCE. (2010). Police accountability in the Republic of Armenia. http://194.8.63.155/yerevan/68198. Accessed 7 Feb 2014.

Police of the Republic of Armenia. (2013). http://www.police.am/about-the-police/. Accessed 7 Feb 2014.

Police of the Republic of Armenia. (2014a) http://www.police.am/en/structure/subdivisions. Accessed 7 Feb 2014.

Police of the Republic of Armenia. (2014b). http://www.police.am/en/structure. Accessed 7 Feb 2014.

Police Press Center. (2012). Independence and the Police [Անկախությունը և Ոստիկանությունը]. http://www.police.am/about-the-police/independence-and-police.html. Accessed 7 Feb 2014.

Radio Free Europe/Radio Liberty, Another Azeri Soldier Killed In Action. (2014). http://www.azatutyun.am/content/article/25256857.html. Accessed 7 Feb 2014.

Shelley, L. (1996). Policing Soviet Society: Evolution of state control. London: Routledge.

Supreme State Council of Armenian Soviet Socialist Republic. (1990). Declaration of Independence. http://www.parliament.am/legislation.php?sel=show&ID=2602&lang=eng. Accessed 16 Jan 2014.

Transparency International. (2003). National Integrity Systems Transparency International. Country Reports: Armenia (2003). http://www.transparency.org/policy_research/nis/nis_reports_by_country. Accessed 7 Feb 2014.

Transparency International. (2003–2008). Corruption Perception Index. http://www.transparency.org/research/cpi/cpi_2003/0/. Accessed 8 Feb 2014.

Transparency International. (2010/11). Global Corruption Barometer 2010 Report. http://www.transparency.org/gcb201011/results. Accessed 7 Feb 2014.

Transparency International. (2012). Corruption Perception Index. http://www.transparency.org/research/cpi/cpi_2011. Accessed 7 Feb 2014.

Transparency International.(2014a). Corruption Perception Index. http://transparency.am/en/cpi. Accessed 7 Feb 2014.

Transparency International. (2014b). Global Corruption Barometer 2013. http://www.transparency.org/gcb2013/country?country=armenia&q=1#question1. Accessed 5 Feb 2014.

United Nations Human Rights Committee. (2012). Concluding Observations adopted by the Human Rights Committee at its 105th session CCPR/C/ARM/CO2 (2012) para.22. www2.ohchr.org/english/bodies/hrc/…/CCPR.C.ARM.CO.2–3_AV.doc. Accessed 1 Feb 2014.

United Nations Security Council. (1992). Resolution 735 (1992) of 29 January 1992: Application of the Republic of Armenia. http://daccess-dds-ny.un.org/doc/RESOLUTION/GEN/NR0/010/94/IMG/NR001094.pdf?OpenElement. Accessed 7 Feb 2014.

U.S. Department of State. (2011). Armenia. www.state.gov/r/pa/ei/bgn/5275.htm. Accessed 7 Feb 2014.

U.S. Department of State. (2012). Armenia 2012 Human Rights Report. www.state.gov/documents/organization/204468.pdf. Accessed 7 Jan 2014.

Chapter 3
Police Integrity in Australia

Louise E. Porter, Tim Prenzler, and Kelly Hine

Abstract This chapter reports the results of an Australian survey of police using the international ethical climate questionnaires developed by Klockars et al. Two major police departments distributed the questionnaires to their officers on condition of anonymity. The findings from the survey—conducted in 2013—were largely positive. On the whole, respondents understood the serious nature of different types of ethics violations and expressed willingness to report violations, although willingness to report was correlated with degrees of perceived seriousness. As with the results of similar surveys, respondents tended to have a lower view of the integrity of colleagues compared to their own position. A key finding was that seriousness ratings and willingness to report tended to increase with rank. This informed the main policy implication: that the ethical perspectives adopted by more senior police need to be transmitted more widely across police ranks.

Keywords Australia · Code of silence · Discipline · Police integrity · Survey

Introduction

From the start of European settlement in the eighteenth century, law enforcement in Australia was beset by the same complex problems of unethical conduct as occurred in many locations. Expanding colonial policing was haphazard and frequently corrupt (Bryett et al. 1997). The introduction of colonial self-government in the

L. E. Porter (✉)
Griffith University, Brisbane, Australia
e-mail: l.porter@griffith.edu.au

T. Prenzler
Griffith University, Brisbane, Australia
e-mail: t.prenzler@griffith.edu.au

K. Hine
Griffith University, Brisbane, Australia
e-mail: kelly.hine@griffithuni.edu.au

S. Kutnjak Ivković, M. R. Haberfeld (eds.), *Measuring Police Integrity Across the World*,
DOI 10.1007/978-1-4939-2279-6_3

nineteenth century involved attempts to make police more professional and accountable. However, officers were generally held in low regard, discipline was erratic and discretion was difficult to manage in the highly dispersed policing environment (Bryett et al. 1997; Prenzler 2010). Victorian and post-Victorian era prohibitions or restrictions on alcohol, gambling, and prostitution set the conditions for organized protection rackets that continued well into the twentieth century.

Independence from Britain in 1901 resulted in a federal system based on the former colonial boundaries. With no local police, law enforcement responsibilities were located within the six states: New South Wales, Queensland, South Australia, Tasmania, Victoria, and Western Australia. A small commonwealth force was established in 1917, which later became the Australian Federal Police (AFP). The AFP is responsible for policing crimes against the commonwealth, such as drug trafficking, and also carries out regular police duties in the Australian Capital Territory. The eighth policing jurisdiction is the Northern Territory.

Numbers of sworn officers, as reported in police annual reports for 2012–2013, reveal the New South Wales Police to be the largest of the eight police departments, with approximately 16,000 sworn officers (around 20,000 total employees), followed by Victoria Police (13,000 sworn officers; 15,000 total staff) and Queensland (11,000 sworn; 15,000 total). Midsize departments are the AFP, Western Australia and South Australia, with between 5000 and 7000 sworn officers. Tasmania and the Northern Territory are the smallest departments with 1100 and 1500 sworn officers, respectively.

Police Integrity in Australia

Until the late 1980s, Australia's police enjoyed high levels of discretion with little oversight. After widespread allegations of police abuses, a Royal Commission into the Queensland Police Service began a period of extensive reform, not just for Queensland, but paving the way for integrity research and future inquiries (e.g., The Wood Royal Commission in New South Wales 1997; The Kennedy Commission into the Western Australia Police in 2004). In Queensland, the Criminal Justice Commission was formed in 1989 not only with responsibility for overseeing the Queensland Police, but also with an active research agenda. All Australian police departments are now subject to oversight agencies. Most agencies not only respond to allegations of police misconduct and corruption in a traditional reactive model of oversight but also proactively engage in prevention, research, and education about wrongdoing to improve the ethical health of police organizations. This has included attempts to measure ethical climate through surveying the ethical attitudes of police officers (Crime and Misconduct Commission 2010; Huon et al. 1995).

The premise of this "ethical climate" approach was the move away from the "rotten apple, theory of police misconduct and acknowledgement that integrity is the responsibility and product of agencies'' own organizational practices. In other words, organizational culture does not simply reflect the sum of individual morality. As Huon et al. (1995, p. 1) state, "the system supports corruption via (i) an opportunity structure; (ii) on-the-job socialisation; and (iii) peer group reinforcement and encouragement of certain rule violations (O'Brien 1991)." In order to build a culture of integrity, agencies must set clear expectations for behavior, with clear rules and clear consequences when rules are violated. Agencies must also combat a possible "code of silence" that can protect officers from the consequences of violations by allowing behavior to remain hidden (Fitzgerald 1989).

In the USA, the work of Klockars et al. (2000) highlighted these aspects in the form of an ethical scenario survey that has since been replicated in multiple police departments over the world (Klockars et al. 2004). The survey tapped officers' ethical attitudes not only in relation to a variety of behaviors but also in relation to their understanding of official rules, support for the code of silence (willingness to report others), attitudes towards control mechanisms (support for disciplinary responses), and expectations of others (police culture). The following sections discuss each of these aspects in relation to the Australian policing climate.

Organizational Rules

The normative frameworks of police misconduct and associated responses are primarily dependent upon two mechanisms: formal rules (societal laws, organizational policies, etc.) and informal extra-legal perspectives (societal beliefs, public opinion, police culture). The former can be enforced through formal processes, while the latter is more difficult to circumscribe. Formal rules govern behavior through describing expected standards and prescribing expected consequences for breaching those standards. Thus, rules lay down the foundations of any integrity system.

In Australia, police departments are governed by legislation at the commonwealth level and at the state (or territory) level. Each department, therefore, has a separate system of rules and processes for rule enforcement and their own codes of conduct and formal disciplinary processes. Broadly speaking, however, the evolution of police governing legislation and codes of conduct has been characterized by convergence in terms of more detailed prescriptions, consistent with the standards set out in international police codes of conduct, such as the United Nations (1979) *Code of Conduct for Law Enforcement Officials* and the International Association of Chiefs of Police (2002) *Law Enforcement Code of Conduct.*

The major inquiries outlined above, and ongoing scandals, have driven the refinement of laws and codes designed to clarify unacceptable conduct in areas such as conflicts of interest, information security, use of force, and off-duty behavior (Porter and Prenzler 2012a). This tightening of rules has included mandatory reporting of misconduct. The main substantive differences lie in enforcement practices.

As one example, in 2011–2012, a scandal forced the Queensland Police Service to adopt a more explicit policy, and an internal communications strategy, to try to reduce police acceptance of gifts and benefits (Prenzler et al. 2013). Several years earlier, the police response to a similar scandal in Victoria became lost in bureaucratic inaction.

In 1991, as part of a larger program on police integrity issues, the National Police Research Unit (NPRU) launched an ethical climate survey that tested officers' understanding of the inappropriateness of a variety of police actions (Huon et al. 1995, p. 26). A questionnaire was developed with 20 scenarios involving a hierarchy of types of misconduct—including assault, bribery, theft from a crime scene, modifying a statement, sleeping on duty, gratuities, cheating on assessment and personal identification checks. Each scenario required the respondent to rate the seriousness of the breach, their perceptions of colleagues' and the department's view, and their willingness to report incidents and to whom. Huon et al. (1995) distributed the questionnaires to police officers and recruits in the six Australian states and to senior officers attending a national training facility. A total of 683 responses were received to the survey. The overall mean for officers' personal views was 6.7 (with 10 being most serious), with the department's view put at 8.6 and the "typical officer's" view put at 5.6. Thus, on average, respondents saw a divide between the police culture and the formal organizational position, with the former taking the infractions considerably less seriously than the latter. For personal views, the highest means were 8.2 for reckless driving, 8.0 for altering a rapist's statement, and 7.9 for minor theft (cigarettes) from a crime scene. The lowest means were 5.3 for checking the ID of an attractive woman, 5.3 for a speeding officer attempting to avoid a fine, and 5.0 for an officer speaking rudely to a young person. Recruits viewed the scenarios most seriously, low- and middle-ranking officers least seriously (constables, senior constables and sergeants), and senior officers were midway. There was a similar decline across length of service, but rose back up from the 10–20 years' service mark. Female officers viewed the scenarios more seriously than males.

The other main application of ethical climate surveys in Australia has been in Queensland, where the oversight agency surveyed recruits and first-year constables each year from 1995 to 2008 in order to monitor the impact of reform. Eight scenarios based on the NPRU survey were used in 1995, with 12 scenarios in 2008. A major review covering 14 surveys to 2008 was published in 2010 (Crime and Misconduct Commission 2010). The results were similar to the NPRU study, although with slightly higher overall means. For personal views, across all surveys, on a scale of 1–10, the highest (most serious) means were 9.8 for selling confiscated drugs, 8.7 for minor theft (cigarettes) from a crime scene and 8.6 for altering a rapist's statement. The lowest means were 5.2 for accepting cartons of beer at Christmas from a publican who requested extra patrols, 5.8 for a personal job while on duty, and 6.3 for an officer speaking rudely to a young person. Indeed, the review noted an excessively tolerant attitude amongst first-year constables towards gratuities and personal jobs on police time and considerable reluctance to report misconduct—especially intermediate- and lower-level types. Across the years, recruits had fairly stable views. There was a slight trend upwards in some seriousness ratings by first-year constables. First-year constables had similar views to recruits for the four most seriously rated scenarios and lower ratings for most of the remainder—around one point on average on the 10-point scale. Females generally viewed scenarios more seriously.

Control Mechanisms

The existence of formal organizational rules, while setting expected standards, requires the establishment of enforcement mechanisms. Historically, Australian policing was characterized by recurring allegations of misconduct and a series of hamstrung, largely unsuccessful, judicial inquiries (Prenzler 2010). From the 1970s, the Victorian police ombudsman produced a series of investigative reports revealing widespread abuses, including kickbacks for emergency security notifications, unjustified shootings of mentally ill persons, violent interrogations, excessive political surveillance, sexual harassment and sex discrimination, harassment of police whistleblowers, abuse of strip searching, theft and on-selling of drugs, and leaking of information to criminals (Office of Police Integrity 2007a, 2009).

A major breakthrough in Australian police reform occurred with the Fitzgerald Commission of Inquiry in Queensland (1989), which revealed a set of police abuses centred on legal process of corruption and protection of vice. Major reforms included professional recruitment, ethics training, and civilian oversight. In New South Wales, the Wood Commission of Inquiry, which ran from 1994 to 1997, exposed diverse forms of corruption including routine assaults and excessive force, protection of organized crime, evidence tampering, opportunistic thefts, and extortionate gratuities (Wood 1997). More recently in Western Australia, the Kennedy Inquiry (2004) revealed diverse criminal conduct by police, including assaults, stealing, perjury, drug dealing, and disclosures of confidential information.

Over this period, police reform and improved accountability followed a stop–start pattern, with limited civilian oversight introduced from the 1970s. Police managers and police union leaders were generally resistant to external investigations and auditing of complaints processes (Prenzler 2010). Nonetheless, recurring scandals led to all police departments becoming subject to independent oversight. Australia has also been the site of a number of innovative integrity management strategies, including officer profiling and early intervention, covert operations and drug and alcohol testing (Porter and Prenzler 2012a). There were improvements in the reporting of complaints, and, in a number of departments, complaints were systematically analyzed to inform modified training and procedures (Porter and Prenzler 2012a).

More recently, attention has turned to the internal disciplinary systems of police departments, with increased awareness of the impact of perceived fairness and transparency on officer behavior. While traditionally punitive, for the purposes of deterrence, disciplinary systems now incorporate a number of mechanisms to improve the experience of officers, particularly for minor behavioral issues. For example, mediation and local resolution of complaints have been trialled in Queensland and Victoria in order to avoid protracted investigations with unsubstantiated findings (Porter and Prenzler 2012a). Early intervention systems have also been developed in many jurisdictions to highlight problematic behavior and deal with issues in a remedial rather than punitive manner. The acknowledgement of procedural fairness has also led to refining disciplinary processes in Queensland, New South Wales, and Victoria, providing officers with more information and opportunities to respond to allegations against them (Porter and Prenzler 2012a).

Code of Silence

Despite formal rules and control mechanisms, police culture has been raised as a powerful obstacle to rule adherence, with informal norms taking precedence over formally prescribed standards (Porter and Prenzler 2012a). The most widely cited of these is the "code of silence" that encourages officers to ignore wrongdoing they are witness to, breeding a culture of tolerance and even active workplace harassment. For example, the Queensland Crime and Misconduct Commission review (CMC 2010) of 14 ethical climate surveys identified reluctance to report misconduct as an ongoing problem, along with the view that discipline was harsh but with a low likelihood of misconduct being detected.

These types of findings support the theory that the perceived fairness of the system for responding to violations is a key factor in increased willingness to report colleagues' wrongdoing. That is, it is expected that if members view the organizational response to be too harsh, they will be less likely to report wrongdoing than if the response is understood to be legitimate and proportionate to the behavior (Klockars et al. 2004). Kutnjak Ivković and Shelley (2010) found that officers self-reported less willingness to report misconduct where the expected discipline was viewed to be harsh compared with when discipline was viewed to be fair. Similarly, "organizational justice" research shows that feelings of unfair treatment can negatively affect job performance and rule adherence (Tyler et al. 2007). In contrast, perceptions of organizational justice have been positively linked to police officers' "attitudes towards serving the public" (Myhill and Bradford 2013, p. 339) as well as a reduced likelihood of police officers supporting the code of silence and noble cause corruption (Wolfe and Piquero 2011).

Huon et al.'s (1995) questionnaires revealed a rough correlation between officer rank and willingness to report. For recruits and low- and middle-ranking officers, the preferred response was "no action" or "raise informally with a senior officer." Senior officers tended to support reporting the incident to Internal Affairs. The report remarked on the decline in standards in the early and middle years of officers' careers and concluded that training in ethics needs to be reinforced.

Public Expectations and Influences

In addition to informal influences within police organizations, the external environment has also been a powerful driver of police attitudes and behavior. In theory, negative public attitudes towards police can increase officer expectations of opposition and resistance, causing police to be less tolerant and more likely to escalate the amount of force used to do their duty (Smith and Hawkins 1973).

In Australia, there has been recurring friction between police and different groups, especially indigenous Australians and some ethnic minorities. On the whole, however, community satisfaction with police is very high (Prenzler and Sarre 2012). Surveys of the public have consistently shown general satisfaction levels around 75 %, with similar levels of support for specific questions about fair and equal treatment. For those survey respondents who had contact with police in the previous 12 months, satisfaction goes up to around 85 %. At the same time, there is clearly a very dissatisfied minority, with complaint numbers consistently high in the tens of thousands each year, including a large component concerned with excessive force.

The remainder of this chapter explores these integrity constructs in Australian policing through utilisation of a similar self-report survey to those used in the studies outlined above. Questions in response to a variety of scenarios measure both the attitudes of officers towards different infractions and their perception of the culture around these infractions (the majority of attitudes and the organizational response).

Method

Materials

The survey used in this study was based on the questionnaire developed by Klockars et al. (2000) in their U.S. National Institute of Justice study. The survey had been updated by Klockars et al. and was then reviewed by the two Australian police agencies who agreed to participate. The questionnaire contains two sections: ethical scenarios and background questions. There were 11 ethical scenarios (short descriptions of incidents) each followed by the same set of questions to measure constructs relating to perceptions of seriousness, rules, discipline, and code of silence. The 11 scenarios are provided in the introductory chapter. Minor modifications were made to suit Australian spelling and terminology. Scenario two was modified as follows (additions in italics):

> A police officer is aware that there is an arrest warrant for a long time friend of his. Although he sees his friend frequently over a period of more than a week and warns his friend of its existence, he does not arrest him *or pass on information about his friend's whereabouts to other police*.

The scenarios cover a range of behavior including rudeness, theft, receiving gifts and benefits, excessive force and failure to perform duties. Motivations for personal gain and organizational gain are represented, as well as the behavior of supervisors. Responses to the scenarios measure the following aspects of officers' views.

Seriousness Officers' perceptions of the seriousness of each scenario were measured by a single item with a 5-point scale from 1 = "not at all serious" to 5 = "very serious." Officers were also asked to rate how seriously they believe most officers would view the scenario, using the same scale. The officers' own perception of the seriousness of the scenarios sheds light on their own integrity attitudes, while their perceptions of "most officers" indicate the integrity attitudes ascribed to by the broader police culture.

Violation Officers' understanding of the scenarios in relation to agency policy was measured by a single item that asked, "Would this behavior be regarded as a violation of official policy in your agency"? Responses were measured on a 5-point scale from 1 = "definitely not" to 5 = "definitely yes." This item is an important measure of officers' understanding of agency expectations regarding behavioral standards.

Discipline Officers' views on discipline were measured by two items. For each scenario, officers were asked to indicate the level of discipline they think *should* occur in response to the behavior, and which they think *would* occur in response. For each item, officers were presented with a range of six discipline options: 1 = "none"; 2 = "verbal warning/counselling"; 3 = "written warning"; 4 = "suspension/disciplinary transfer"; 5 = "reduction in rank"; 6 = "dismissal." The first item, regarding the discipline that is believed *should* follow, is an important indicator of officers' own integrity perceptions, while the second item that measures the perception of what discipline *would* follow is an important indicator of officers' expectations of the agency response.

Further, officers' perceptions of what discipline should and would follow can be used to calculate an index of fairness (the difference between these). Fairness is an important dimension of a disciplinary system, which has been linked to employee behavior. Disciplinary fairness was calculated by subtracting the level of fairness the officers believe should follow from the level of fairness they believe would follow (would–should). If this yields a positive number, the discipline that would follow is expected to be higher than the level that should occur (harsh discipline). A negative number indicates that the level that would occur is expected to be lower than the level that should occur (lenient discipline). No difference indicates that discipline is viewed to be at the level it should be (perceived fairness).

Reporting The officers' willingness to report the behavior described in the scenarios was measured by a single item that asked, "Do you think you would report a fellow police officer who engaged in this behavior"? Responses were measured on a 5-point scale from 1 = "definitely not" to 5 = "definitely yes." One further item asked officers, "Do you think most police officers in your agency would report a fellow police officer who engaged in this behavior," using the same rating scale. These two items are important measures of the reporting culture, or the "code of silence," for the agency. While the first item indicates the officers' own comfort in reporting, the latter item refers to the officers' perception of broader agency culture (the norm).

Background Following the scenarios, questions were asked regarding the respondents' years of experience in the police, their rank, current assignment, and supervisory status.

Honesty To gauge honesty, respondents were asked if they thought most officers would give their honest opinion when completing the survey, and whether they themselves were honest in their completion. The analyses that follow did not include responses from officers who said that they were not honest in their answers.

Procedure

The survey was hosted online by Qualtrics and a weblink distributed to all police officers internally by personnel at two Australian police agencies. The agencies required confidentiality as a condition of participation (thus, they are not named specifically here) and respondents were not required to provide identifying information. The survey remained open for 3 months in 2013. At the end of this period, the survey was closed and data downloaded into statistical package for the social sciences (SPSS) for cleaning and analysis.

Response

Table 3.1 shows the characteristics of the sample of 856 officers who completed the questionnaire. Unfortunately, this represents only around 5 % of the total numbers of sworn officers employed by the agencies at the time of the survey. At the same time, the representativeness of the sample was assessed by comparing it to figures published in police agency annual reports for the 2012–2013 period. Males made up 62 % and females made up 25 % of the sample (13 % did not disclose): a figure similar to that for all Australian police agencies. Senior officers were somewhat over-represented in the sample with general duties assignments under-represented.

The modal length of service for the sample was more than 20 years. In fact, around 60 % of the sample had served more than 10 years, showing an experienced sample. Less than 5 % had served under 1 year. The distribution of experience (time in service) reflects the rank distribution of the sample, with a skew to higher ranks that would be reached after at least 5 years in service. A variety of roles were evident in the sample, including specialist assignments.

Findings

Table 3.2 provides a summary of how the 11 scenarios were scored according to the four main survey constructs: seriousness, violation knowledge, discipline, and willingness to report. The table is ordered by the officers' views of seriousness, from

Table 3.1 Characteristics of the sample ($n=856$)

Mode length of service in current post		More than 20 years	
Percentage in supervisory post		41%	
Number who said they did not give their honest opinion		11	(1.29%)
Number who said most police would not give their honest opinion		128	(14.95%)
Length of service			
	Less than 1 year	31	(3.62%)
	1–2 years	23	(2.69%)
	3–5 years	51	(5.96%)
	6–10 years	106	(12.38%)
	11–15 years	147	(17.17%)
	16–20 years	94	(10.98%)
	More than 20 years	281	(32.83%)
	Did not answer	123	(14.37%)
Length of service in current post			
	Less than 1 year	22	(2.57%)
	1–2 years	48	(5.61%)
	3–5 years	110	(12.85%)
	6–10 years	162	(18.93%)
	11–15 years	141	(16.47%)
	16–20 years	55	(6.43%)
	More than 20 years	206	(24.07%)
	Did not answer	112	(13.08%)
Rank			
	Recruit	2	(0.23%)
	Probationary constable	10	(1.17%)
	Constable	53	(6.19%)
	Senior constable	240	(28.04%)
	Sergeant/senior sergeant	230	(26.87%)
	Other non-commissioned rank	37	(4.32%)
	Inspector/chief inspector	57	(6.66%)
	Superintendent/chief superintendent	26	(3.04%)
	Other commissioned rank	2	(0.23%)
	Other	88	(10.28%)
	Did not answer	111	(12.97%)
Assignment			
	General duties	167	(19.51%)
	Community policing officer	45	(5.26%)
	Highway patrol	29	(3.39%)

Table 3.1 (continued)

	Criminal investigation	197	(23.01 %)
	Special operations	21	(2.45 %)
	Other specialist	140	(16.36 %)
	Other	151	(17.64 %)
	Did not answer	112	(13.08 %)
Gender			
	Male	532	(62.15 %)
	Female	212	(24.77 %)
	Did not answer	112	(13.08 %)

lowest to highest. It is evident that there is considerable consistency in this rank order across the remaining constructs, with some small deviations (i.e., the order of seriousness is similar to the order in which respondents would place the scenarios for severity of discipline and willingness to report, etc.). This would suggest that the constructs are highly related and part of a more general construct of integrity, as suggested in the literature (Klockars et al. 2000, 2004).

The results pertaining to each construct are reported in turn below, followed by a more detailed analysis of how the constructs relate to one another and, particularly, officers' willingness to report. Finally, differences according to sample characteristics are explored, including gender, length of service, rank, and supervisory status. Where differences are explored for significance with *t*-tests, Cohen's *d* is also provided to signify the magnitude of the difference (the effect size). An effect size of 0.2 is considered small, 0.5 medium, and above 0.8 accepted as a large effect size (Cohen 1988).

Seriousness

Table 3.3 shows that, on average, all scenarios were viewed as being at least somewhat serious (the mean being at the scale midpoint or higher). There appear to be three groups of scenarios according to the officers' own perceptions of seriousness. First are those that constitute lower levels of seriousness, which for this sample means a score of less than 4. These are scenario 7 (verbal abuse of motorist), scenario 1 (receiving gifts from small businesses), and scenario 5 (being granted leave in exchange for running errands). These constitute demeanour and personal gain infractions.

The second group represents more serious behavior, scoring between 4 and 4.6. These are scenario 6 (punching an offender in custody), scenario 8 (failure to report officer's driving under the influence, DUI), scenario 2 (failure to arrest friend with warrant), and scenario 11 (Sgt. failing to intervene in assault of suspect). These

Table 3.2 Officers' views about seriousness of misconduct, discipline it should and would receive and officers' willingness to report

Scenario number and description	Seriousness				Violation		Discipline						Willingness to report			
	Own view		Most officers				Should receive			Would receive			Own view		Most officers	
	$\bar{x}$	Rank	$\bar{x}$	Rank	$\bar{x}$	Rank	$\bar{x}$	Rank	Mode	$\bar{x}$	Rank	Mode	$\bar{x}$	Rank	$\bar{x}$	Rank
Scenario 1: free meals, gifts from merchants	3.47	2	3.27	2	4.53	3	2.59	2	Verbal warning/ counselling	2.81	2	Written warning	3.35	2	3.02	2
Scenario 2: failure to arrest friend with warrant	4.56	6	4.44	7	4.80	5	4.03	4	Suspension/ transfer	3.91	4	Written warning	4.37	7	4.04	7
Scenario 3: theft of knife from crime scene	4.94	11	4.82	10	4.98	11	5.62	11	Dismissal	5.38	10	Dismissal	4.83	10	4.52	10
Scenario 4: unjustifiable use of deadly force	4.88	10	4.86	11	4.77	4	5.34	10	Dismissal	5.44	11	Dismissal	4.89	11	4.80	11
Scenario 5: supervisor offers holiday for errands	3.94	3	3.68	3	4.34	2	3.18	3	Written warning	2.85	3	Written warning	3.76	3	3.33	3
Scenario 6: officer strikes prisoner who hurt partner	4.29	4	4.02	4	4.85	6	4.06	5	Suspension/ transfer	4.35	5	Suspension/ transfer	3.98	4	3.56	4
Scenario 7: verbal abuse of motorist	3.02	1	2.88	1	4.27	1	2.32	1	Verbal warning/ counselling	2.52	1	Verbal warning/ counselling	2.94	1	2.71	1
Scenario 8: cover-up of police DUI accident	4.39	5	4.15	5	4.87	7	4.15	6	Suspension/ transfer	4.39	6	Suspension/ transfer	4.10	5	3.73	5
Scenario 9: auto body shop 5 % kickback	4.82	8	4.68	8	4.95	9	5.18	8	Dismissal	5.08	8	Dismissal	4.69	8	4.37	8
Scenario 10: false report on drug dealer	4.85	9	4.71	9	4.95	10	5.31	9	Dismissal	5.23	9	Dismissal	4.71	9	4.40	9
Scenario 11: Sgt. fails to halt beating	4.56	7	4.33	6	4.92	8	4.65	7	Reduction in rank	4.78	7	Dismissal	4.32	6	3.97	6

DUI driving under the influence

Table 3.3 Officers' views about the seriousness of misconduct

Scenario number and description	Own view				Most officers							
	Range	*SD*	$\bar{x}$	Rank	Range	*SD*	$\bar{x}$	Rank	*t*	*df*	*p*	*d*
Scenario 7: verbal abuse of motorist	1–5	1.14	3.02	1	1–5	1.10	2.88	1	5.05	780	<0.001	0.36
Scenario 1: free meals, gifts from merchants	1–5	1.15	3.47	2	1–5	1.13	3.27	2	6.60	851	<0.001	0.45
Scenario 5: supervisor offers holiday for errands	1–5	0.96	3.94	3	1–5	1.01	3.68	3	9.74	796	<0.001	0.69
Scenario 6: officer strikes prisoner who hurt partner	1–5	0.98	4.29	4	1–5	1.02	4.02	4	9.26	787	<0.001	0.66
Scenario 8: cover-up of police DUI accident	1–5	0.86	4.39	5	1–5	0.93	4.15	5	8.89	771	<0.001	0.64
Scenario 2: failure to arrest friend with warrant	1–5	0.76	4.56	6	1–5	0.76	4.44	7	5.92	826	<0.001	0.42
Scenario 11: Sgt. fails to halt beating	1–5	0.81	4.56	7	1–5	0.92	4.33	6	8.37	756	<0.001	0.61
Scenario 9: auto body shop 5 % kickback	1–5	0.46	4.82	8	1–5	0.64	4.68	8	7.71	767	<0.001	0.56
Scenario 10: false report on drug dealer	1–5	0.49	4.85	9	1–5	0.63	4.71	9	7.19	763	<0.001	0.52
Scenario 4: unjustifiable use of deadly force	1–5	0.44	4.88	10	1–5	0.48	4.86	11	2.87	805	<0.001	0.20
Scenario 3: theft of knife from crime scene	3–5	0.25	4.94	11	1–5	0.47	4.82	10	8.05	818	<0.001	0.56

DUI driving under the influence

cases represent failures to perform duties, particularly due to internal loyalties, as well as excessive force towards offenders and suspects.

The final group was judged to be the most serious, with scores between 4.8 and 5 (the top of the scale, representing "very serious"). These are four scenarios: scenario 9 (receiving discounts for referrals), scenario 10 (falsely reporting finding evidence), scenario 4 (shooting an unarmed person), and scenario 3 (theft of knife from crime scene). These constitute a variety of examples of misconduct, including an abuse of position for personal gain as well as organizational gain (padding evidence to gain a conviction), and excessive use of lethal force.

Table 3.3 and Fig. 3.1 show that, in terms of the relative seriousness between each scenario, respondents believed their views to be similar to "most officers" (the rank order of seriousness is almost the same for officers' own view and their view of most officers). However, the degree of seriousness attached to each scenario was consistently viewed to be different: Respondents on average believed they view each scenario as being more serious than do most officers ($p<0.001$), with medium effect sizes.

Violation of Official Policy

Table 3.4 shows that, on average, respondents believed all the scenarios to be a violation of official agency policy. Across the scenarios, only small percentages of respondents (typically less than 5%) believed the behavior was not a violation (scoring 1 or 2 on the scale). A proportion of respondents was unsure (represented by the midpoint of the scale). In particular, nearly 15% were unsure that verbal abuse of motorist (scenario 7) was a violation of policy, and 10.5% were unsure that

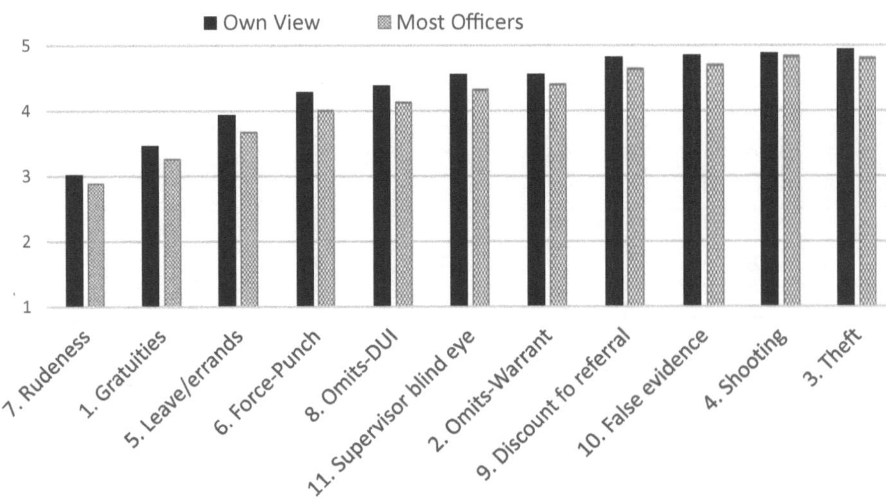

Fig. 3.1 Mean officers' ratings of seriousness and their perception of the views of most officers

Table 3.4 Would this be regarded as a violation of official policy in your agency? (rank ordered by seriousness—least serious to most serious)

Scenario number and description	Definitely not 1 (%)	2 (%)	3 (%)	4 (%)	Definitely yes 5 (%)	Mean	*SD*	Seriousness rank
Scenario 7: verbal abuse of motorist	1.2	2.8	15.3	29	51.7	4.27	0.90	1
Scenario 1: free meals, gifts from merchants	1.3	2.8	6.8	19.9	69.2	4.53	0.84	2
Scenario 5: supervisor offers holiday for errands	0.8	4.4	10.5	28.9	55.4	4.34	0.89	3
Scenario 6: officer strikes prisoner who hurt partner	0.1	0	3.0	8.3	88.5	4.85	0.45	4
Scenario 8: cover-up of police DUI accident	0.4	0.1	1.4	8.5	89.5	4.87	0.45	5
Scenario 11: Sgt. fails to halt beating	0.4	0	0.7	5.5	93.4	4.92	0.37	6
Scenario 2: failure to arrest friend with warrant	0.2	0.8	3.6	9.4	85.9	4.80	0.56	7
Scenario 9: auto body shop 5 % kickback	0.1	0.1	0.5	3.2	96.0	4.95	0.29	8
Scenario 10: false report on drug dealer	0.3	0.1	0.4	2.9	96.3	4.95	0.31	9
Scenario 4: unjustifiable use of deadly force	0.5	0.9	5.9	6.1	86.6	4.77	0.64	10
Scenario 3: theft of knife from crime scene	0.1	0	0.2	1.0	98.7	4.98	0.20	11

DUI driving under the influence

granting leave in exchange for errands was in violation of policy. These scenarios are amongst the less serious, as judged by the sample. In contrast, more than 90 % of the sample were sure that scenarios 11, 9, 10, and 3 were definitely violations. These represent some of the most serious scenarios (as rated by the sample): the supervisor turning a blind eye to violent behavior, discounts for referral of business, falsifying evidence and theft.

Discipline

Table 3.2 also shows that the discipline level that respondents' believe should be applied to each scenario largely followed the same pattern as the seriousness attributed to the scenario. The three least serious scenarios attracted mean discipline levels between 2 and 3, representing verbal and written warnings. The four scenarios rated on average as somewhat serious are prescribed sanctions amounting to suspension, transfer, or reduction in rank. Interestingly, the scenario for which respondents selected a reduction in rank as the penalty was scenario 11, which involved rating the behavior of the supervisor who did not step in when officer's assaulted a suspect. Respondents clearly saw the action as serious, but not serious enough to warrant dismissal; rather, the person is deemed to need moving down from the supervisory role as they are not exhibiting the level of responsibility appropriate to this position. This is in contrast to the supervisor in scenario 5 who grants leave in exchange for errands; that supervisor is rated as necessitating only a written warning. The remaining scenarios were the top four most serious, and all most commonly rated as warranting dismissal. These were, receiving discounts in exchange for business referrals, falsifying evidence, shooting an unarmed person and theft. These actions were, therefore, not tolerated, with those involved deemed unsuitable to continue in the service.

Table 3.5 and Fig. 3.2 show that the rank order of discipline across the scenarios was almost identical for the discipline respondents believed both should and would occur. However, there were differences between the levels of discipline respondents believed should and would occur at the case level. With the exception of scenario 10 (falsifies evidence), respondents believed, on average, that the level of discipline that *would* occur was significantly different to what they believed *should* occur. Scenarios 2, 3, 5, 9, and 10 were all considered to attract more lenient discipline than they should, while the remaining scenarios were considered to attract slightly harsher discipline than they should. However, while these differences were significant, the effect sizes were small to medium. It is interesting again to note scenarios 5 and 11, where the supervisor's behavior is the subject of judgement. In scenario 5, where the supervisor grants leave in exchange for errands, while the modal choice is the same, on average the sample thought the disciplinary response would be more lenient than it should be (perhaps suggesting that supervisors are treated more leniently overall). However, for scenario 11, where the supervisor turns a blind eye to an assault of a suspect, respondents thought the disciplinary response would be harsher than necessary; equating to a difference between a demotion (should occur) and dismissal (would occur). This suggests that, while generally not tolerated, the sample is willing to remove the individual from the position of responsibility rather than remove them from the service altogether.

Table 3.6 shows the results of this fairness calculation—as described in the method section—for each scenario. Overall, as noted above, the mean differences were small (between -1 and $+1$ out of a possible scale of -5 to $+5$). This would suggest that, on average, officers believed that fair discipline would be received. Across the scenarios, differences can be observed in the means—with five of the scenarios yielding negative means, indicating on average lenient discipline; and six scenarios yielding positive means, indicating on average harsh discipline. The scenarios found most lenient were the granting of leave in exchange for errands (scenario 5) and taking goods from a crime scene (scenario 3). The scenarios seen as most harsh were failing to report an officer's DUI (scenario 8) and punching an offender (scenario 6).

Table 3.5 Officers' views about the discipline the misconduct should and would receive

Scenario number and description	Should receive					Would receive								
	Range	*SD*	Mode	$\bar{x}$	Rank	Range	*SD*	Mode	$\bar{x}$	Rank	*t*	*df*	*p*	*d*
Scenario 7: verbal abuse of motorist	1–6	0.71	Verbal warning/ counselling	2.32	1	1–6	0.72	Verbal warning/ counselling	2.52	1	8.89	780	<0.001	0.64
Scenario 1: free meals, gifts from merchants	1–6	1.00	Verbal warning/ counselling	2.59	2	1–6	1.09	Written warning	2.81	2	5.88	851	<0.001	0.40
Scenario 5: supervisor offers holiday for errands	1–6	1.19	Written warning	3.18	3	1–6	1.18	Written warning	2.85	3	9.17	794	<0.001	0.65
Scenario 2: failure to arrest friend with warrant	1–6	1.33	Suspension/ transfer	4.03	4	1–6	1.30	Written warning	3.91	4	3.52	824	<0.001	0.25
Scenario 6: officer strikes prisoner who hurt partner	1–6	1.43	Suspension/ transfer	4.06	5	1–6	1.34	Suspension/ transfer	4.35	5	6.25	781	<0.001	0.45
Scenario 8: cover-up of police DUI accident	1–6	1.25	Suspension/ transfer	4.15	6	1–6	1.27	Suspension/ transfer	4.39	6	5.98	767	<0.001	0.43
Scenario 11: Sgt. fails to halt beating	1–5	1.28	Reduction in rank	4.65	7	1–6	1.17	Dismissal	4.78	7	3.22	756	<0.001	0.23
Scenario 9: auto body shop 5 % kickback	1–6	1.13	Dismissal	5.18	8	1–6	1.16	Dismissal	5.08	8	3.54	766	<0.001	0.26
Scenario 10: false report on drug dealer	1–6	1.03	Dismissal	5.31	9	1–6	1.09	Dismissal	5.23	9	2.61	761	0.01	0.19
Scenario 4: unjustifiable use of deadly force	1–6	1.18	Dismissal	5.34	10	1–6	1.1	Dismissal	5.44	11	2.95	788	<0.001	0.21
Scenario 3: theft of knife from crime scene	2–6	0.79	Dismissal	5.62	11	1–6	1	Dismissal	5.38	10	8.08	818	<0.001	0.57

DUI driving under the influence

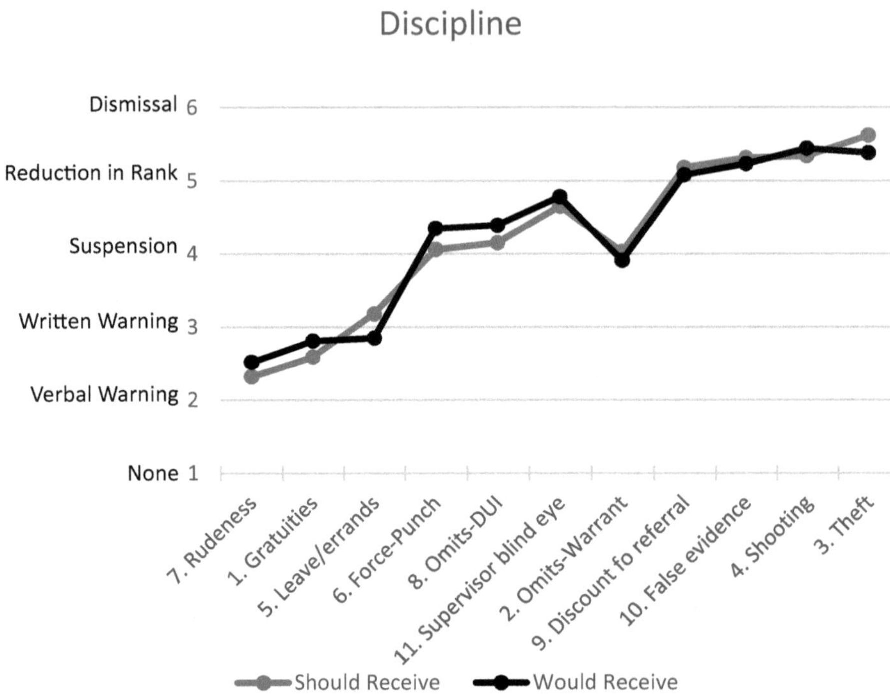

Fig. 3.2 Average score for the discipline that should and would be received for each scenario. Scenarios are ordered according to the respondents' own perception of seriousness (low seriousness to high seriousness)

Table 3.6 Difference in officers' views about the discipline the misconduct should and would receive (rank ordered from most lenient to harshest)

Scenario number and description	Min	Max	*SD*	$\bar{x}$	Rank
Scenario 5: supervisor offers holiday for errands	−4	3	1.01	−0.33	1
Scenario 3: theft of knife from crime scene	−5	3	0.82	−0.23	2
Scenario 2: failure to arrest friend with warrant	−5	5	0.99	−0.12	3
Scenario 9: auto body shop 5 % kickback	−4	4	0.84	−0.11	4
Scenario 10: false report on drug dealer	−5	3	0.78	−0.07	5
Scenario 4: unjustifiable use of deadly force	−5	5	0.82	+0.09	6
Scenario 11: Sgt. fails to halt beating	−5	5	1.14	+0.13	7
Scenario 7: verbal abuse of motorist	−2	3	0.62	+0.20	8
Scenario 1: free meals, gifts from merchants	−4	4	1.07	+0.22	9
Scenario 8: cover-up of police DUI accident	−4	4	1.13	+0.24	10
Scenario 6: officer strikes prisoner who hurt partner	−5	5	1.27	+0.28	11

DUI driving under the influence

Willingness to Report

Table 3.7 and Fig. 3.3 describe the participants' willingness to report the scenarios, and their belief about the willingness of most officers to report. On average, respondents were willing to report the majority of scenarios. Only one scenario, (scenario 7: verbal abuse of motorist) received an average score less than the midpoint of the scale—indicating unwillingness to report. Once again, this construct is related to the overall perception of seriousness of the scenarios, with the rank order of willingness to report mirroring the rank order of seriousness ratings. Those least likely to be tolerated are again, therefore, receiving discounts for referrals of business, falsifying evidence, theft and shooting an unarmed person.

For all scenarios, respondents believed they were significantly more likely to report the incident than most officers would be ($p<0.001$), with medium to large effect sizes. This shows that, on average, the sample saw their own behavior as more ethical than the majority, suggesting that, while others might subscribe to a "code of silence," they would be much less likely to do so. This discrepancy is interesting in that the perception of the code of silence may be stronger than the evidence that it actually exists. However, given the small sample, it could be the case that the respondents are indeed different from the majority of officers. Perhaps those that self-selected to complete the survey are also those more likely to report wrongdoing. The largest differences were seen for the willingness to report the theft scenario, followed by the discounts for referrals, followed by granting leave in exchange for errands and falsifying evidence. Interestingly, the smallest differences in perception of own and others' willingness to report were seen in the two scenarios they were least and most willing to report. This indicates that, at the extreme ends of the spectrum, they see their own behavior as slightly more aligned with their perception of the majority.

Correlates and Predictors of Officers' Willingness to Report

For each scenario, a percentage of officers was unwilling to report the incident (indicated by a score of 1 or 2 on the 5-point scale). Table 3.8 explores the possibility that this unwillingness may be explained by a belief that the behavior does not constitute a violation. While this may explain some of the unwillingness, it does not explain the majority. Most notably, nearly a third of respondents believed scenario 7 (verbal abuse of motorist) to be a violation of policy but were unwilling to report it, and just over a fifth of respondents believed scenario 1 (receiving gifts from small businesses) to be a violation but would not report it. Instead, reporting behavior would seem to be linked more to the perception of the seriousness of the activity, with unwillingness to report decreasing as the perceived seriousness of the incident increases.

The fairness of the discipline predicted to result from the behavior may also affect an officer's decision to report an incident. Officers who believe the result will be too lenient may feel reporting is pointless, while officers who feel the result will be too

Table 3.7 Officers' views about the willingness to report misconduct

Scenario number and description	Own view				Most officers							
	Range	*SD*	$\bar{x}$	Rank	Range	*SD*	$\bar{x}$	Rank	*t*	*df*	*p*	*d*
Scenario 7: verbal abuse of motorist	1–5	1.34	2.94	1	1–5	1.18	2.71	1	5.85	780	<0.001	0.42
Scenario 1: free meals, gifts from merchants	1–5	1.33	3.35	2	1–5	1.12	3.02	2	8.63	851	<0.001	0.59
Scenario 5: supervisor offers holiday for errands	1–5	1.21	3.76	3	1–5	1.15	3.33	3	12.09	797	<0.001	0.86
Scenario 6: officer strikes prisoner who hurt partner	1–5	1.23	3.98	4	1–5	1.16	3.56	4	10.70	786	<0.001	0.76
Scenario 8: cover-up of police DUI accident	1–5	1.13	4.10	5	1–5	1.06	3.73	5	9.77	771	<0.001	0.70
Scenario 11: Sgt. fails to halt beating	1–5	1.09	4.32	6	1–5	1.07	3.97	6	10.41	756	<0.001	0.76
Scenario 2: failure to arrest friend with warrant	1–5	0.97	4.37	7	1–5	0.97	4.04	7	10.85	824	<0.001	0.76
Scenario 9: auto body shop 5 % kickback	1–5	0.69	4.69	8	1–5	0.84	4.37	8	12.48	767	<0.001	0.90
Scenario 10: false report on drug dealer	1–5	0.71	4.71	9	1–5	0.82	4.40	9	11.60	761	<0.001	0.84
Scenario 3: theft of knife from crime scene	1–5	0.5	4.83	10	1–5	0.72	4.52	10	13.75	818	<0.001	0.96
Scenario 4: unjustifiable use of deadly force	1–5	0.47	4.89	11	1–5	0.60	4.80	11	6.84	803	<0.001	0.48

DUI driving under the influence

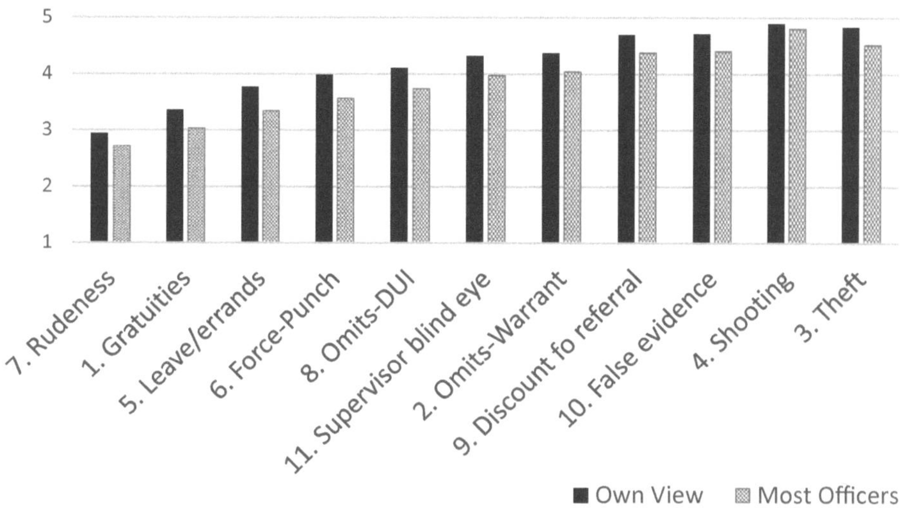

Fig. 3.3 Average responses for officers' own willingness to report and perception of most officers' willingness to report each scenario. Scenarios are ordered by the officers' perception of seriousness from least to most serious

Table 3.8 Percentage of respondents who are unwilling to report a scenario even when they believe it to be a violation of policy

Scenario number and description	Seriousness ranking	% unwilling to report	% think it is violation	% who think it is a violation but will not report
Scenario 7: verbal abuse of motorist	1	39.9	80.7	28.3
Scenario 1: free meals, gifts from merchants	2	28.1	89.1	21.4
Scenario 5: supervisor offers holiday for errands	3	17.3	84.4	9.3
Scenario 6: officer strikes prisoner who hurt partner	4	14.8	96.8	13.2
Scenario 8: cover-up of police DUI accident	5	12.3	98.1	11.1
Scenario 11: Sgt. fails to halt beating	6	9.6	98.9	9.1
Scenario 2: failure to arrest friend with warrant	7	6.8	95.3	4.6
Scenario 9: auto body shop 5 % kickback	8	2.2	99.2	1.7
Scenario 10: false report on drug dealer	9	2.9	99.2	2.5
Scenario 4: unjustifiable use of deadly force	10	0.9	92.7	0.5
Scenario 3: theft of knife from crime scene	11	0.7	99.6	0.7

DUI driving under the influence

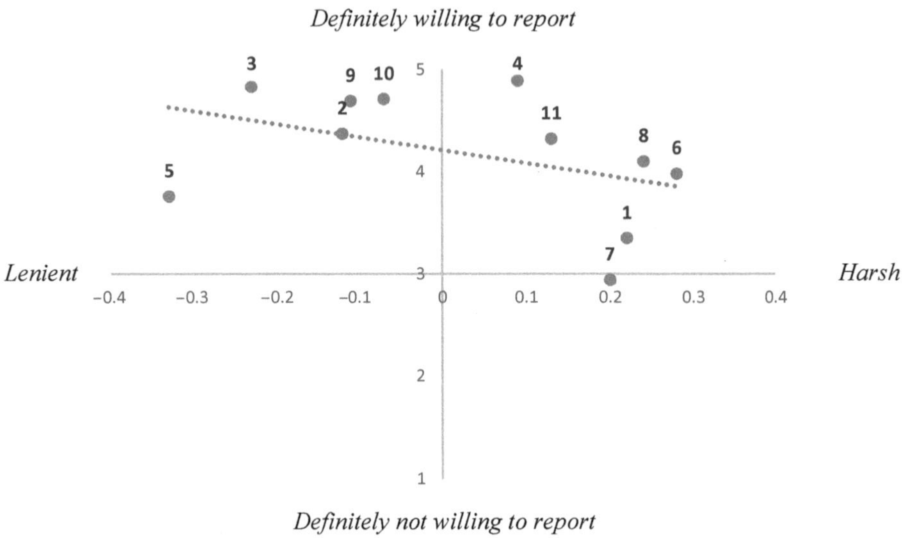

Fig. 3.4 Scenarios according to officers' perception of fairness (*horizontal axis*) and willingness to report (*vertical axis*). *Dotted line* represents the trend line

harsh may feel reporting would be unfair. Figure 3.4 shows how scores of fairness relate to willingness to report for each scenario. The trend line shows a slight negative relationship, whereby scenarios judged to have lenient-to-fair discipline will generally be more likely to be reported than those thought to incur harsh discipline.

Moving away from the individual scenarios, the survey constructs can be averaged across all scenarios to measure the relationships between them at the aggregate level (Table 3.9). Spearman's correlations reveal significant relationships between officers' willingness to report and all other measured constructs. Specifically, officers show significantly greater willingness to report when seriousness is high (in their own view and for most officers), the behavior is considered to be a violation, the discipline that should follow is higher, the discipline that would follow is higher, it is believed most officers would report and discipline is unlikely to be unfairly harsh. The strongest relationship with willingness to report is for officers' own seriousness judgments, followed by the discipline that should occur. Also high are the relationships of willingness to report with the two constructs that measure the "culture" of most officers: most officers' seriousness judgments and how likely most officers would be to report. The smallest (albeit still significant) relationships are with the discipline that would follow, the unfairness of the discipline, and the belief that it is a violation.

A step-wise linear regression confirmed these results. When all seven constructs were entered as predictors of officers' willingness to report, five were retained as significant predictors ("violation" was excluded as a non-significant predictor and "discipline (would)" was excluded due to multicolinearity), explaining 89% of the variance ($R^2=0.89$, $F(5, 731)=554.54$, $p<0.001$). Table 3.10 shows the results of the regression. All retained predictors provide a unique contribution to predicting willingness to report. Officers' perception of seriousness remains the strongest predictor, accounting for 65% of the variance.

Table 3.9 Correlations between the survey constructs averaged across all scenarios

	Report (you)	Seriousness (you)	Seriousness (most officers)	Violation	Discipline (should)	Discipline (would)	Report (most)
Seriousness (you)	0.802**						
Seriousness (most)	0.591**	0.682**					
Violation	0.396**	0.437**	0.379**				
Discipline (should)	0.635**	0.607**	0.463**	0.388**			
Discipline (would)	0.299**	0.239**	0.448**	0.352**	0.630**		
Report (most)	0.604**	0.453**	0.798**	0.257**	0.404**	0.488**	
(un)Fairness	−0.344**	−0.398**	−00.032	−00.045	−0.327**	0.433**	0.100**

n=737–757
**Spearman correlation is significant at the 0.01 level (two-tailed)

Table 3.10 Regression results for predictors of officers' willingness to report

	Unstandardised coefficients		Standardised coefficients	t	Sig.	R square change
	B	Std. error	Beta			
(Constant)	−0.836	0.122		−6.873	<0.001	
Seriousness (you)	1.021	0.043	0.695	23.505	<0.001	0.647
Report (most)	0.589	0.029	0.593	20.182	<0.001	0.078
Seriousness (most)	−0.516	0.046	−0.392	−11.219	<0.001	0.051
(un)Fairness	−0.126	0.027	−0.104	−4.632	<0.001	0.010
Discipline (should)	0.110	0.025	0.102	4.425	<0.001	0.006

Demographic/Background Differences

The constructs were averaged across all 11 scenarios before comparing for differences by years of experience, rank, gender, and supervisory status. Table 3.11 shows that, on average, years of service were significantly positively correlated with most of the integrity constructs, with the exception of fairness perceptions. However, the correlations were small to moderate. Similarly, rank was significantly positively correlated with most of the integrity dimensions, with the exception of the seriousness perception of most officers and the discipline it would attract (uncorrelated),

Table 3.11 Average construct scores across 11 scenarios; relationships with experience and rank, and differences by gender and supervisory status

	Correlations (rho)		*t*-tests							
	Years of experience	Rank	Male	Female	*p*	*d*	Non-supervisor	Supervisor	*p*	*d*
Ave report (You)	0.222**	0.311**	4.17	4.20	0.526	−0.06	4.04	4.34	0.001***	−0.46
Ave seriousness (you)	0.086*	0.137**	4.32	4.39	0.055	−0.18	4.30	4.38	0.016*	−0.18
Ave seriousness (most)	0.087*	0.061	4.21	4.03	0.001***	0.33	4.14	4.19	0.151	−0.11
Ave violation	0.121**	0.119**	4.76	4.71	0.044*	0.15	4.73	4.77	0.105	−0.12
Ave discipline (should)	0.131**	0.204**	4.26	4.13	0.012*	0.19	4.15	4.31	0.001***	−0.24
Ave discipline (would)	0.131**	0.078	4.35	4.02	0.001***	0.62	4.21	4.30	0.091	−0.13
Ave report (most)	0.162**	0.123**	3.96	3.62	0.001***	0.45	3.80	3.93	0.010*	−0.19
Ave (un)Fairness	0.007	−0.121**	0.08	−0.12	0.001***	0.33	0.06	−0.01	0.102	0.12

*Significant at the 0.05 level (two-tailed)
**Significant at the 0.01 level (two-tailed)
***Significant at the 0.0045 level (Bonferonni correction for multiple comparisons)

and a significant negative correlation between rank and unfairness, showing that, as rank increases, perceptions of unfairness decrease.

Years of service predicted willingness to report ($F(1, 723)=21.09$, $p<0.001$), although R^2 was only small (0.028). Rank also predicted willingness to report ($F(1, 610)=52.66$, $p<0.001$), but again R^2 was small (0.079). A multiple regression with both variables entered as predictors found that only rank remained a significant predictor when both were taken into account ($F(2, 607)=25.83$, $p<0.001$, $R^2=0.078$). This means that, beyond years of service (or when controlling for years of service), the rank of an officer predicts the willingness to report; such that the higher the rank, the greater the willingness.

Using a stringent alpha of 0.0045 to correct for the multiple number of comparisons (Bonferonni correction), some differences were evident by gender and supervisory status (Table 3.11). Female officers had a significantly less favourable view of 'most officers', judging most officers' seriousness perceptions and willingness to report lower than did male officers. Female officers also showed a significantly more favourable view of the discipline system, with a more lenient view on what discipline would result. However, effect sizes were small to medium. The comparison by supervision status revealed fewer differences. Supervisors were, on average, significantly more willing to report the scenarios and have a harsher view on the level of discipline that should occur in response. However, again effect sizes were small, with only the difference in willingness to report showing a medium effect size.

Discussion

Policing in Australia, like many other countries, had undergone periods of scandal and reform over the past few decades, with a changing integrity landscape. The survey reported here provides a useful comparison to previous, similar ethics surveys conducted in Australia on different samples of police officers—the NPRU survey (Huon et al. 1995) and the series of surveys conducted by Queensland's Crime and Misconduct Commission from 1995 to 2008 (CMC 2010).

In the present study, it is encouraging that mostly officers recognized the scenarios as depicting violations and viewed them as serious. For each of the scenarios, at least 80% of respondents answered that it would be a violation of agency policy. For some scenarios, this increased to around 99%. All 11 scenarios were rated as at least somewhat serious on average (all means were at or above the scale midpoint). This is similar to the findings from the NPRU survey and the CMC ethics surveys. Similar too are the types of infractions that, on average, drew the highest and lowest ratings of seriousness. The NPRU and CMC reports both highlighted that theft from a crime scene and altering a suspect's statement rated amongst the most serious of the scenarios presented. Similarly, of the current scenarios, theft from a crime scene and planting evidence were amongst the top three most serious, lower only than excessive use of lethal force. Similarly, the prior studies found gratuities and rudeness to be amongst the least serious infractions, which the current study also supports.

Most officers expressed willingness to report the scenarios. On average, respondents were willing to report 10 of the 11 scenarios, the exception being the rudeness scenario. Less than 40 % of officers were unwilling to report each scenario, although this still represents a substantial minority for some scenarios. The two scenarios least likely to be reported were the case of rudeness and also accepting gratuities. These were often seen to be violations but were not seen to be particularly serious in contrast to the other scenarios. Rudeness is often the topic of complaints against police by members of the Australian public. Indeed, some police forces have implemented strategies to particularly identify and reduce customer service complaints in contrast to other issues that demand more serious investigation. For example, triage processes of complaint handling, local resolution of complaints as well as "mystery shopper" initiatives to test front counter service at police stations (Porter and Prenzler 2012a).

The proportion of the sample unwilling to report decreased to 10 % or less for some scenarios, particularly serious behavior such as theft and shooting an unarmed suspect. This is somewhat encouraging given the CMC's finding of greater reluctance to report misconduct in Queensland over their survey period (CMC 2010). However, a proportion of officers in the current study recognised the violations, but was still unwilling to report them. This is despite the fact that most jurisdictions in Australia have mandatory reporting of misconduct, with some supporting this requirement through provision of confidential reporting channels (e.g., dedicated phone lines and support staff; Porter and Prenzler 2012a). For some scenarios, as many as 20–30 % of respondents were aware that the behavior would be considered a violation of policy, but stated they would be unwilling to report it. This was the case for the rudeness scenario and the gratuities scenario, which were also the two scenarios viewed least serious. Indeed, the primary factor that predicted officers' willingness to report the scenarios was how they perceived the seriousness of the behavior. While all integrity dimensions measured were positively associated with officers' willingness to report, the officers' own view of the seriousness of the behavior made the largest contribution to willingness to report. Further exploration of the likelihood of engaging different modes of reporting, such as informal or formal (as in the NPRU study), or even anonymous reporting, would be an interesting addition for future surveys.

Similar to previous studies, integrity was positively related to years of experience and rank. A number of relationships were observed across the dimensions of integrity with rank and years of experience as a police officer. All relationships were in the same positive direction, showing that understanding of, and support for, integrity increased with experience and rank. This is similar to the finding of the NPRU study; however, that study was also able to compare recruits to find an early decrease in ethical standards during those first few years on the job. The present study was limited only to those officers already sworn in and so was unable to explore this issue. This might be a useful focus for further exploration.

Interestingly, rank was positively related to the willingness to report, even when controlling for years in service. While rank and years of experience are highly correlated, supporting the view that officers must gain experience to be promoted, rank has a unique contribution to predicting officers' willingness to report. This suggests that attributes associated with rank affect integrity beyond the amount of experience. Exploration of the roles, attributes and training at different ranks, and their influence on ethical attitudes, would be a useful addition to this area.

In contrast, both prior Australian studies found that females viewed the scenarios as more serious than males. This was not found in the current study, with no gender difference in the overall seriousness ratings. Female officers did, however, have a dimmer view of police culture and a greater willingness to report, on average, than male officers. Further research could attempt to unpack the relationships between the integrity constructs for males and females to understand whether there are gender differences in the relative importance of, for example, police culture versus personal views in the willingness to report an infraction.

Implications and Conclusion

According to the current survey, officers' understanding of the seriousness of behavior would appear to be the most important factor in breaking the code of silence. Experience, rank, and supervisory status were positively related to respondent's own views of the seriousness of the scenarios, showing that this experience and role status may be associated with how aware officers are of the consequences of infractions. However, these individual factors do not show a large effect on officers' views. Thus, while those officers who reach positions of responsibility may reflect more on the seriousness of infractions, it is ideal to proactively engage all officers with this mindset through raising awareness of the consequences and changing the normative attitude. Incorporating ethics messages into training throughout the organization is a standard recommendation, while some agencies have also provided case-specific materials in the forms of "learning the lessons" bulletins or articles in internal publications (Porter and Prenzler 2012b) and have implemented reforms oriented towards enhancing customer service and reducing service-related complaints (Porter and Prenzler 2012a).

Indeed, the fact that the rudeness scenario rates, on average, only just above the midpoint of the scale is concerning. Annual reports of those agencies that take complaints from members of the public about police (including police agencies themselves), both in Australia and overseas, show that rudeness or incivility tend to be amongst the largest categories of complaints/allegations received (Crime and Misconduct Commission 2013; Independent Police Complaints Commission 2013; Porter and Prenzler 2012a, p. 222). Studies of police legitimacy show that such treatment can undermine public confidence in police and willingness to cooperate with police (Bayley 2002; Decker 1981; Murphy 2009). Public cooperation is essential for police effectiveness in safeguarding the public from crime (Murphy et al. 2008).

Fairness, as measured by the concordance between appropriate and likely discipline, was also important to the willingness to report and, generally, officers saw the discipline as fair (differences were small). In Australia, there have been recent attempts by some agencies at improving the procedural fairness of internal discipline systems and complaint-handling procedures (Office of Police Integrity 2007b; NSW Police Force 2012, p. 10; Queensland Government 2011).

Police culture was also important, with significant relationships between perceptions of the views and behavior of the majority and respondents' own views and likely behavior. The respondents' own views were, however, significantly different from their views of the culture (most officers), with respondents believing themselves to be more ethical than the majority. Further, respondents' own views showed higher correlation with, and greater prediction of, willingness to report than did their views of the culture.

In conclusion, on average, the respondents to the survey exhibited positive trends towards understanding the seriousness of violations and being willing to take action in reporting colleagues. In comparison to the previous Australian surveys conducted nationally by the NPRU and in Queensland by the CMC, the present survey highlighted some similar findings, despite the different samples and time periods. There seems to be consistency in views of relative seriousness of different types of infractions, as well as some consistent differences by rank and experience in the police service. It is encouraging that perceptions of fairness of discipline and willingness to report are more positive in the current sample. It is evident that respondents are somewhat cynical about police culture, viewing themselves as being more ethical than most officers in terms of both perceptions of seriousness of misconduct and willingness to take action in response. Proactive attempts to instil both personal values and cultural normative beliefs may, therefore, serve to improve police integrity systems.

References

Bayley, D. H. (2002). Law enforcement and the rule of law: Is there a tradeoff? *Criminology & Public Policy, 2,* 133–154.

Bryett, K., Harrison, A., & Shaw, J. (1997). *The role and function of police in Australia.* Sydney: Butterworths.

Cohen, J. (1988). *Statistical power analysis for the behavioral sciences* (2nd ed.). Hillsdale: Erlbaum.

Crime and Misconduct Commission. (2010). *The ethical perceptions and attitudes of Queensland POLICE SERVICE recruits and first year constables1995–2008.* Brisbane: Crime and Misconduct Commission.

Crime and Misconduct Commission. (2013). *Annual report 2012–13.* Brisbane: Crime and Misconduct Commission.

Decker, S. H. (1981). Citizen attitudes towards the police: A review of past findings and suggestions for future policy. *Journal of Police Science and Administration, 9,* 80–87.

Fitzgerald, T. (1989). *Report of a commission of inquiry pursuant to orders in council.* Brisbane: Government Printer.

Huon, G., Hesketh, B., Frank, M., McConkey, K., & McGrath, G. (1995). *Perceptions of ethical dilemmas: Ethics and policing—study 1*. Payneham: National Police Research Unit.
Independent Police Complaints Commission. (2013). Police complaints: Statistics for England and Wales 2011/12. http://www.ipcc.gov.uk/sites/default/files/Documents/research_stats/complaints_statistics_11-12.pdf. Accessed 4 Oct 2013.
International Association of Chiefs of Police. (2002). *Law enforcement code of conduct. In police chiefs desk reference* (pp. 34–39). Washington: International Association of Chiefs of Police & Bureau of Justice Assistance.
Kennedy, G. A. (2004). *Royal commission into whether there has been corrupt or criminal conduct by any Western Australian Police Officer, final report v. 2*. Perth: Government of Western Australia.
Klockars, C. B., Kutnjak Ivković, S., Harver, W., & Haberfeld, M. (2000). *The measurement of police integrity*. Washington: National Institute of Justice.
Klockars, C. B., Kutnjak Ivković, S., & Haberfeld, M. R. (Eds.). (2004). *The contours of police integrity*. Newbury Park: Sage.
Kutnjak Ivković, S., & Shelley, T. O. (2010). The code of silence and disciplinary fairness: A comparison of Czech police supervisor and line officer views. *Policing: An International Journal of Police Strategies and Management, 33*(3), 548–574.
Murphy, K. (2009). Public satisfaction with police: The importance of procedural justice and police performance in police-citizen encounters. *Australian & New Zealand Journal of Criminology, 42*(2), 159–178.
Murphy, K., Hinds, L., & Fleming, J. (2008). Encouraging public cooperation and support for police. *Policing and Society, 18*(2), 136–155.
Myhill, A., & Bradford, B. (2013). Overcoming cop culture? Organizational justice and police officers' attitudes toward the public. *Policing: An International Journal of Police Strategies & Management, 36*(2), 338–356.
NSW Police Force. (2012). *NSW police force complaint handling guidelines*. https://www.police.nsw.gov.au/about_us/policies__and__procedures/policies/nsw_police_force_complaint_handling_guidelines.pdf. Accessed 13 Jan 2015.
O'Brien, R. (1991). The individual, socialisation and police corruption. *Australian Police Journal, 45*(1), 4–8.
Office of Police Integrity. (2007a). *Past patterns—Future directions: Victoria police and the problem of corruption and serious misconduct*. Melbourne Office of Police Integrity.
Office of Police Integrity. (2007b). *A fair and effective Victoria police discipline system*. Melbourne: Office of Police Integrity.
Office of Police Integrity. (2009). *Review of the use of force by and against Victorian police*. Melbourne Office of Police Integrity.
Porter, L. E., & Prenzler, T. (2012a). *Police integrity management in Australia: Global lessons for combating police misconduct*. Boca Raton: CRC Press.
Porter, L. E., & Prenzler, T. (2012b). Police oversight in the United Kingdom: The balance of independence and collaboration. *International Journal of Law Crime and Justice, 40*(3), 152–171.
Prenzler, T. (2010). Change and continuity in Australian policing. In R. Lincoln & S. Robinson (Eds.), *Crime over time: Temporal perspectives on crime and punishment in Australia* (pp. 171–186). Newcastle upon Tyne: Cambridge Scholars Publishing.
Prenzler, T., & Sarre, R. (2012). The police. In H. Hayes & T. Prenzler (Eds.), *An introduction to crime and criminology* (pp. 258–274, 3rd edn.). Sydney: Pearson.
Prenzler, T., Beckley, A., & Bronitt, S. (2013). Police gifts and benefits scandals: Addressing deficits in policy, leadership and enforcement. *International Journal of Police Science and Management, 15*(4), 294–304.
Queensland Government. (2011).Government response to the independent review of the Queensland police complaints, discipline and misconduct system. http://www.premiers.qld.gov.au/publications/categories/reviews/assets/government-response-police-complaints-review.pdf. Accessed 4 Oct 2013.

Smith, P. E., & Hawkins, R. O. (1973). Victimization, types of citizen-police contacts and attitudes toward the police. *Law & Society Review, 8*(1), 135–152.

Tyler, T. R., Callahan, P. E., & Frost, J. (2007). Armed, and dangerous (?): Motivating rule adherence among agents of social control. *Law & Society Review, 41*(2), 457–492.

United Nations. (1979). *Code of conduct for law enforcement officials*. http://www.ohchr.org/EN/ProfessionalInterest/Pages/LawEnforcementOfficials.aspx. Accessed 4 Oct 2013.

Wolfe, S. E., & Piquero, A. R. (2011). Organizational justice and police misconduct. *Criminal Justice and Behavior, 38*(4), 332–353.

Wood, J. R. (1997). *Final report of the Royal Commission into the New South Wales police service*. Sydney: New South Wales Government Printer.

Chapter 4
Police Integrity in Croatia

Sanja Kutnjak Ivković

Abstract The Croatian police, a centralized police agency, under the auspices of the Croatian Ministry of the Interior, have had a short but turbulent history. This chapter explores the contours of police integrity among the Croatian police. The chapter relies on the police integrity survey conducted in 2008/2009. The representative stratified sample of 966 police officers evaluated hypothetical scenarios describing various forms of police misconduct. We analyze the results across several measures of police integrity, such as the police officers' knowledge of official rules, evaluations of police misconduct as serious, views about appropriate and expected discipline, and the code of silence. Our results suggest that most police officers had no problems recognizing described behavior as rule violating. The respondents' evaluations of misconduct seriousness varied substantially across the scenarios. Although the behaviors described in the questionnaire are violations not only of the administrative rules but also of criminal law, our respondents expected dismissal for only two such cases, and expected milder disciplinary options for the rest. Finally, although the code of silence has weakened since the mid-1990s, our results show that it is still present among the Croatian police.

Keywords Croatia · Democratization · Police integrity · Survey · War

Introduction

Croatia, the twenty-eighth member of the European Union, gained independence from the former Yugoslavia in 1991. Since then, the country has embarked on the road toward establishing a more democratic society, in general, and police, in particular. However, the process has been both complex and challenging (Kutnjak Ivković and Klockars 2004, p. 56):

> The journey has been far from smooth; the country has experienced a defensive war against the aggression of the Serb-dominated Yugoslav Army and various paramilitary troops, the

S. Kutnjak Ivković (✉)
Michigan State University, East Lansing, MI, USA
e-mail: kutnjak@msu.edu

S. Kutnjak Ivković, M. R. Haberfeld (eds.), *Measuring Police Integrity Across the World*,
DOI 10.1007/978-1-4939-2279-6_4

influx of refugees from Bosnia and Herzegovina, a decade-long governance of a strong, right-wing oriented political party, the strengthening of nationalism, a continued legacy of mismanagement of the economy, the transition into market economy, and a high unemployment rate. All these factors shape the environment in which the Croatian police operate and have a strong impact on the state of police integrity.

Established in the early 1990s, the Croatian police are one of the youngest police agencies in Europe. The organizational history of the Croatian police can be divided into three periods. In the first period, Croatia was still a republic within the former Yugoslavia; it did not have the legal right to establish an independent police agency in addition to the existing centralized Yugoslav police. In the early 1990s, as it became clear that the war is imminent, the Croatian Parliament passed statutory changes to establish the National Guard Corps (NGC) as a police service within the Ministry of the Interior. Police officers constituted a large portion of the man power for the NGC and, for a period of almost 2 years, the police performed both the defense role and the regular police role (Kutnjak Ivković 2000). The war-related experience exposed police officers to considerable violence, while resulting in the relaxation of official rules and strengthening of the code of silence (see, e.g., Kutnjak Ivković 2004a).

The second period in the history of Croatian policing began after the war ended in 1995. The emphasis was put on democratization of the police. During the late 1990s, the "war-is-over" attitude began to dominate the police administrators' views. The primary focus of various reforms was on demilitarization, depoliticization, professionalism, demystification, and downsizing (see Kutnjak Ivković 2004a). Eventually, there was a substantial downsizing in the police from 30,000 to 34,000 sworn in the late 1990s (Kutnjak Ivković 2000, p. 79) to 20,000 sworn in 2005 (Kutnjak Ivković 2005). The legal reform followed as well, with the enactment of the new Criminal Procedure Code in 1997 and the new Police Law in 2000.

The third period, marked by further reforms, started in the early 2000s. In 2003, the Croatian version of community policing has been introduced. The society at large put greater emphasis on accountability of police officers and police administrators, resulting in numerous firings and scandals involving top police administrators (e.g., the prime minister fired both the minister of the interior and the chief of police in 2008; the heads of the Vukovar-Srijemska Police Administration were arrested for corruption in 2013; the head of the Splitska Police Administration was removed from the position for the abuse of official position in 2013). At the same time, the country experienced considerable challenges in its attempt to deal with organized crime and widespread corruption (Nacional 2008), resulting in the decline in the level of public support for the police (Kutnjak Ivković 2008).

The Croatian police are a centralized police agency housed within the Ministry of the Interior. On top of the hierarchical structure are the minister of the interior and the chief of police (Police Law 2000), followed by 20 police administrations, and about 200 police stations at the bottom of the structure. The majority of regular police work is performed at the level of police stations, which can be either basic or specialized (e.g., airport, traffic, border). The police currently employ about 20,000 sworn officers or 4.28 police officers per 1000 inhabitants.

This chapter analyzes the societal and police-related factors in the organizational scheme of police integrity theory. The second part of this chapter provides an empirical analysis of survey data measuring the level of police integrity among the Croatian police.

Theory of Police Integrity and the Croatian Police

This chapter relies on the definition of integrity, the theory of police integrity, and the accompanied methodological approach developed by Klockars and colleagues (see, e.g., Klockars and Kutnjak Ivković 2004; Klockars et al. 1997; Klockars et al. 2004a). Police integrity is defined as "the normative inclination among police to resist temptations to abuse the rights and privileges of their occupation" (Klockars et al. 1997). It assumes that police officers are able to resist *various* forms of temptations, including corruption, use of excessive force, and other forms of abuse, the rights and privileges, to which policing as an occupation exposes them (Klockars et al. 2006). Police integrity could vary across different forms of misconduct (e.g., police corruption, use of excessive force), as well as different levels of seriousness within the same form of misconduct (e.g., within police corruption, acceptance of gratuities vs. theft from a crime scene). Consequently, the related methodological approach incorporates hypothetical scenarios describing not only a variety of forms of police misconduct but also examples of different levels of seriousness within the same form.

The organizational theory of police integrity (see, e.g., Klockars and Kutnjak Ivković 2004; Klockars et al. 1997, 2001), the theoretical organizational theme in this chapter, rests on four dimensions: quality of official rules, quality of the agency's own internal control of misconduct, curtailing the code of silence, and the influence of the larger environment. This chapter explores each of these dimensions as they apply to Croatia.

Organizational Rules

The first dimension of the theory argues that the quality of organizational rules and the way in which these rules are made, communicated, and understood by the police are critical for the high levels of police integrity (Klockars and Kutnjak Ivković 2004, p. 1.4). The theory predicts that police agencies of high integrity will not only have organizational rules explicitly prohibiting police misconduct but also teach these rules effectively and enforce them when rule-violating behavior occurs. At the same time, police officers in such agencies should know the organizational rules and also support them. The content of the rules, in particular what behaviors are explicitly prohibited by the rules, and the degree to which the rules are enforced could vary drastically across agencies. This should particularly be the case for less serious forms of misconduct, such as the acceptance of free gifts and verbal abuse.

Because the Croatian police are a centralized agency within the Ministry of the Interior, the same set of organizational rules applies to every sworn officer in the country. The evolution of the laws regulating police work in Croatia was affected by the events in the society at large. In 1990, the first Croatian Constitution was enacted, containing the basic provisions regulating citizens' civil rights. However, the war temporarily halted the changes in the criminal law, criminal procedure, and other police-related laws. The widespread reform of the criminal justice legislation occurred in the late 1990s.

The Code of Criminal Procedure was enacted in 1997 and subsequently changed several times, finally resulting in the new Code of Criminal Procedure in 2008. Other than simply reinforcing the basic civil rights established by the Constitution (1990), the two Codes of Criminal Procedure introduced extensive changes into the criminal procedure. The Codes revised the predominantly inquisitorial procedure by adding many elements of adversarial procedure. The 1997 Code gave the defendants the rights to be informed about the charges and to receive Miranda-like warnings (Kutnjak Ivković 2004a, p. 202). The 2008 Code of Criminal Procedure authorized the prosecutor to conduct the investigation, established the Office of the Criminal Investigator to assist the prosecutor, introduced plea bargaining, required of the police to audio- and videotape all suspect interrogations, and gave parties the right to select and present the evidence in the case. In addition, the 1997 Code also proscribed the level of force the police were allowed to use during the preinvestigative process (e.g., while executing a search warrant) and determined that, unless one of the conditions for the constitutional exceptions were met, the search of a residence should be performed only on the basis of a judicial warrant.

Another part of the legislation directly regulating police work is contained in the Police Laws (2000, 2011). For the first time, the Police Law of 2000 defined the police as the "public service within the Ministry of the Interior entrusted to perform the tasks enumerated by the law" (Article 2, Police Law 2000). This contemporary view of the police as a public service concerned with the protection of life and property resembles more closely the democratic view of policing. The police tasks are explicitly listed in Article 3. They include traditional police tasks such as the protection of life, rights, safety, and health of individuals; protection of property; prevention and detection of felonies and misdemeanors; and search for and apprehension of the persons who committed felonies and misdemeanors. The police right to use discretion and the police right to use force have been regulated as well (Kutnjak Ivković 2004a). As the Criminal Procedure Law has changed, the need has arisen to have the police activities during pretrial investigation regulated by a separate law, the Law on Police Activities and Rights (2009).

The new 2011 Police Law further streamlined the police toward a democratic agency. One of the most relevant changes includes the newly specified requirements for promotion and advancement, as well as the new procedure for appointment of key administrative personnel. The head of the police is the general police director, a professional (and not a political) function; the director can only be a person who has at least 15 years of experience in policing, out of which at least 10 should be at the supervisory capacity, and holds the rank of police advisor (Article 58, Police Law 2011), the highest rank. The Director is appointed for a period of 5 years and may not be fired at will (Article 59, Police Law 2011). The Police Law establishes the criteria and the process for the appointment of all other supervisory personnel. For example, the heads of the police administrations are appointed for a five-year period after a search conducted by a five-person committee. Once appointed, they are accountable to the director.

As time passed, the laws have become more detailed and sophisticated, but one of the key issues—the frequency with which these laws, should be and actually, are enforced—still remains without a clear answer. Also, familiarity with and the level of knowledge that police officers have about these new rules is an open empirical question. In 1995, a few years after the police had been established and at the time the war was ending, a survey explored officers' familiarity with official rules (Kutnjak Ivković and Klockars 2004, p. 68). The respondents in the study were asked to identify whether various forms of police corruption described in hypothetical scenarios violated official rules. Although the overwhelming majority of the respondents had no problems recognizing that a theft is a violation of official rules, at most about two thirds of police officers were able to identify the behaviors in the scenarios as rule violating. Kutnjak Ivković (2009) argues that such relatively low percentages are tied to the war-related circumstances, namely relaxed training and rapid hiring.

Results of a study conducted a few years later (Ivanović 2001) suggest that a substantial proportion of police officers, at the time, still had problems with understanding at least some of the rules. A more recent survey of police officers conducted in 2012 reveals that the majority of police officers support the idea that criminal and administrative regulation of police conduct is important for the performance of the police service and indicated that they are well versed with such regulations (Borovec 2013). At the same time, the overwhelming majority of the respondents (95 %; Borovec 2013, p. 6) assess that their knowledge of the rules regulating the use of force is "excellent" or "good," although, according to their own account, only about two thirds of respondents went through police training (Borovec 2013, p. 14).

Police Detection and Investigation of Police Misconduct

The second dimension of the theory emphasizes the police agency's own methods of detection, investigation, and discipline of rule violations. These activities could be very heterogeneous, from more reactive activities, such as investigations of corrupt behavior and discipline of corrupt police officers, to more proactive activities, such as education in ethics, integrity testing, and proactive investigations. The theory stipulates that there should be a positive correlation between the existence and use of a sophisticated system of corruption prevention and control, and the level of integrity prevailing in the agency.

The Police Law (2011, Article 5) provides citizens and organizations with the right to submit complaints against police officers. A recent study by the Ministry of the Interior revealed that about 45 % of the surveyed police officers had a complaint filed against them (Borovec 2013). Overall, the respondents evaluated the process that followed as objective. In case a citizen or an organization files a complaint, the heads of the police station or other organizational unit have the responsibility to investigate the complaint and, within 30 days since the date the complaint was filed, inform the complainant about the actions taken. If the complainant is not satisfied with the outcome and/or the procedure taken, the case will be examined by the police complaint board. The board should be composed of one police administrator and two citizens appointed by the Parliamentary Committee on Human Rights and Rights of Minorities. This provision should be the other side of the coin that established police officers' personal accountability for violation of the laws and official rules (Police Law 2011; Constitution 1990). In fact, to offer an even stronger guarantee, the Criminal Code (1997) establishes that the police officers can be charged criminally if they abuse their office with the purpose of preventing citizens from submitting complaints. Most of police officers in a 2013 study by the ministry positively evaluated the normative regulation of the process and thought that the rules provide equal protection to both the police officer and the complainant (Borovec 2013).

The Police Law (2011) explicitly distinguishes between the criminal procedure and the internal disciplinary procedure (Article 93) and states that the acquittal in criminal court does not automatically imply that the police officer will be relinquished of any responsibility in the internal disciplinary process. The Law enumerates various violations of official rules, establishes the criteria to be used in the internal procedure, and delineates the disciplinary procedure and potential outcomes.

The Police Law (Article 93, 2011) stipulates that a police officer could be held accountable for the violations of official duties if the police officer does not perform them professionally and within the stipulated deadlines; if the police officer does not adhere to the Constitution, laws, and other rules and regulations; or if the police officer, otherwise, dishonors the police occupation. The Law enumerates some less serious violations, such as being rude toward citizens and fellow coworkers, being late for work, or maintaining unprofessional appearance (Article 95). The Law also contains descriptions of serious violations of official rules, such as failing to perform police work, engaging in illegal or criminal activities, revealing confidential information to unauthorized persons, or failing to take medical tests or attend required training (Article 96, Police Law 2011).

The disciplinary process can be initiated on the basis of the written report from the head of the administrative unit or immediate supervisor (Article 104, Police Law 2011). Before initiating the official procedure, the supervisor has to provide an opportunity for the police officer to respond to the initial charge. In case a police officer is accused of committing what seems to be a less serious violation, the minister of the interior or another supervisor is in charge of conducting the internal investigation and determining the outcome of the case (Article 97, Police Law 2011). However, in case a police officer is accused of committing what seems to be a more serious violation, then the disciplinary board is in charge of conducting the investigation and making the decision (Articles 97–98, Police Law 2011).

The disciplinary process should be conducted without delay and should be public (Article 101, Police Law 2011). The police officer has an active role in the process (e.g., respond to the charges, comment on the evidence, propose evidence to be examined) and may be represented by a lawyer and/or a union member (Articles 102–108, Police Law 2011). If the police officer was accused of committing a less serious violation, the supervisor decides the outcome, while the disciplinary board makes the decision in cases in which a police officer is accused of committing a more serious violation (Article 108, Police Law 2011). Disciplinary options for less serious violations are a written reprimand and up to 10 % salary cut. For more serious violations, police officers' misbehavior can result in a pay cut of up to 20 % of the salary, prohibition of promotion for 2–4 years, reassignment to another job for 2–4 years, suspended termination for a period of 3 months to 1 year, and termination. Regardless of the severity of the charges, the police officer may appeal the decision (to the disciplinary board for the less serious violations and to the appellate disciplinary board for the more serious violations). Finally, in the cases of more serious violations, the officer could bring a lawsuit at the administrative court and appeal the appellate board decision (Article 108, Police Law 2011).

The disciplinary data are available for the period 1992–1999. In this period, administrative disciplinary procedure has been initiated against a small proportion of the police officers (between 2000 and 3500 annually; Kutnjak Ivković 2004a, p. 212). At the beginning of the period, the war was ravaging the country, and the bulk of the cases included charges of more serious disciplinary violations. As the "war-is-over attitude" started to dominate the scene in the last 1990s, the proportion of less serious charges started to increase and eventually started to constitute the majority of the disciplinary charges (Kutnjak Ivković 2004a). The most frequently applied discipline was fine.

The results of disciplinary data analyses are in complete agreement with the police officers' perceptions. The 1995 police integrity survey suggested that police officers, if they expect any discipline to be meted out at all, expected less serious forms of discipline (e.g., fine, suspension), even for the most serious forms of corruption (Kutnjak Ivković 2004a). The respondents thought that only the theft from a crime scene would probably result in a dismissal (Kutnjak Ivković 2004a), while similarly serious violations of official rules, such as stealing money from a found wallet and accepting a bribe from a motorist caught speeding, would probably result in less serious discipline.

Curtailing the Code of Silence

The third dimension of the police integrity theory focuses on the code of silence, and the efforts that the police agency is making in curtailing it. Klockars and Kutnjak Ivković (2004) argue that curtailing the code of silence is critical for agencies of integrity. According to the theory, compared to the agencies of high integrity, agencies of low integrity would have strong codes of silence in which police officers would be more likely to tolerate police misconduct without reporting it and supervisors would be more reluctant to investigate police misconduct and discipline police officers who engaged in it.

The historic events in Croatian society affected the parameters of police culture, in general, and the code of silence, in particular. Before Croatia gained independence, many police officers were of Serb ethnicity (about 70 %; Kutnjak Ivković and Klockars 2004). Once the war broke out, a large proportion of them abruptly left the police and joined the paramilitary forces fighting against the newly established Croatian state. At the same time, the Croatian Government passed the law authorizing the Ministry of the Interior to establish the National Guard Corps (NGC).

Literally overnight, the NGC started recruiting many individuals under the relaxed hiring criteria, while providing minimal police training, if any. Thus, in the early 1990s, there were very few experienced police officers who could socialize recruits into the existing police culture. Consequently, the newcomers are the ones who helped shape the police culture. The exodus of a large number of "grizzled veterans," the hiring of many people with very limited police training, and the war with the exposure to violence, conversion of police and military roles, and the relaxed disciplinary standards all resulted in the creation of a very tight-knit police culture. The war camaraderie quite likely extended beyond the war itself; after fighting shoulder to shoulder in the war, it would be difficult for a person to report a fellow combatant for any misconduct, particularly a less serious one.

The police integrity survey conducted in 1995, between the two military operations "Flesh" and "Storm," indicated the presence of the police code of silence (Kutnjak Ivković and Klockars 2004); at least 25 % of the respondents stated that they would not report for any of the behaviors described in the questionnaire, ranging from the acceptance of gratuities to the acceptance of a bribe from a speeding motorist and stealing from the crime scene. However, the code seemed to be even stronger for the forms of misconduct perceived to be the less serious; over 65 % of the respondents stated that they would not report a fellow police officer who accepted a free cup of coffee or any other gifts on his beat (Kutnjak Ivković and Klockars 2004).

Influence of Social and Political Environment

The fourth dimension of the police integrity theory (Klockars and Kutnjak Ivković 2004) focuses on the fact that police agencies are a part of the society at large and, as such, are directly influenced by the events and views held by that society at large (Klockars and Kutnjak Ivković 2004). Police agencies in societies highly tolerant of unethical behavior of public servants should have lower levels of integrity than police agencies operating in societies highly intolerant of unethical behavior of any kind. In a larger environment that supports integrity across the board, police agencies are more likely to set high expectations regarding police integrity as well.

Nepotism and corruption have been well intertwined in the core of the Croatian society. In a 2000 survey, more than 30 % of the respondents in the study reported paying a bribe to a police officer (Derenčinović 2000). A year later, in the 2001 International Crime Victimization Survey, about 15 % of the respondents reported that they were asked to pay a bribe to a governmental official *last year* (Kutnjak Ivković 2008). A more recent survey, the 2010 United Nations Office on Drugs and Crime (UNODC) survey, documents that 12 % of the Croatian respondents reported giving public officials money, gifts, or favors on at least one occasion during *last year* (UNODC 2011, p. 16).

Following the rather lukewarm efforts to deal with corruption in the early periods, the government's efforts in dealing with corruption have received a major push as the country has faced serious obstacles on the road toward the European Union membership. In the fall of 2008, the prime minister of Croatia fired the minister of the interior and the police chief in a move widely believed to have been a direct consequence of their inability to provide high-quality policing. In 2010, Ivo Sanader, the same former prime minister, has been indicted and arrested for high-level corruption. In 2012, he was convicted of corruption and sentenced to serve a 10-year prison sentence. His second trial is still ongoing. In 2013, two scandals shook the police; the heads of the Vukovar-Srijemska Police Administration were arrested for corruption and the head of the Splitska Police Administration was removed from the post for abuse of his official position.

The general public has not been impressed by the governmental efforts in dealing with corruption. The majority of the respondents in the 2010 Transparency International survey (56 %, Transparency International 2010, p. 47) evaluated the government's efforts to deal with corruption as ineffective and believed that the level of corruption in the country has increased in the past 3 years. Also, the UNODC study revealed that, while about one half of the respondents perceived that the level of corruption had remained the same in the past 2 years, about one third of the respondents thought that the level of corruption had increased (UNODC 2011, p. 44).

The country's ranking on the Transparency International's Corruption Perception Index (CPI) reflects the changes taking place in the country. Croatia's CPI score improved from 2.7 (out of 10) in 1999 to 4.4 in 2008 (Transparency International 2008), suggesting a gradual improvement in the government's dealing with corruption. However, the scores did not continue to improve; they have decreased to 4.1 in 2010 (Transparency International 2010) and 4.0 in 2011 (Transparency International 2011). The picture of corruption portrayed by the Transparency International fits well with the public perceptions hinting at the increase in corruption in the past 3 years.

As the war and war-related violence ravaged the country in the early 1990s, rules protecting human rights were not strictly enforced. The early Human Rights Watch reports (e.g., 1993, 1995, p. 3) document that the Croatian police have engaged in human rights violations, although the prevalence of such behavior seems to have been less extensive among the police officers than among military officers. The nature of the abuse—violent attacks by the police, beatings of the suspects, and failure to provide protection from either the military or the civilian violence (almost exclusively ethnically motivated)—suggests a widespread and systematic nature of the violations at the time. Although police conduct seems to have improved to some extent between 1992 and 1994 (Human Rights Watch 1995, p. 3), the two military operations in 1995 appear to have expanded the extent of the police ethnically motivated mistreatment of citizens.

Although the dominant perception during the second period in the history of Croatian police was that the human rights violations in Croatia stem from the war (Amnesty International 1998, p. 2), the reports began to include descriptions of more "traditional" human rights violations (e.g., use of force against suspects, violations of other citizens' procedural rights). Toward the end of that period, the European Commission against Racism and Intolerance (2001, Appendix 1) pointed out the positive trend, "the significant democratic changes, which have occurred after the parliamentary and presidential elections at the beginning of 2000, have contributed to the radical changes in a number of policy areas that were previously subject to criticism by various international monitoring instruments."

In the most recent time period of the Croatian police history, democratization efforts, propelled by the prospect of European Union membership, were in full swing. The nongovernmental organization (NGO) reports no longer described direct police involvement in violence and failure to protect the victims from attacks (Commission of the European Communities 2006, 2007, 2010, 2011). Although the police are still struggling with some of the issues, such as the protection of the lesbian, gay, bisexual, and transgender (LGBT) community when they exercise their right to a free assembly, over time, the police treatment of suspects improved as well. In 2003, the European Committee for the Prevention of Torture (CPT) and Inhumane or Degrading Treatment or Punishment (2007, p. 59) reported that, "the majority of persons interviewed by the CPT's delegation during the 2003 visit indicated that they had not been ill-treated by the police."

Measuring Police Integrity

Questionnaire

Our 1995 study of police integrity in Croatia, performed between two major military operations at the end of the war in Croatia, indicated that police officers seemed to be tolerant of corruption. The second version of the questionnaire, fielded in 2008/2009, constituted the empirical foundation of this chapter. It contains descriptions of 11 scenarios that cover a variety of forms of police misconduct—from police corruption and use of excessive force to planting of evidence and verbal abuse.

Each scenario is followed by the same set of questions, used in both the first and the second version of the questionnaire. The follow-up questions ask about police officers' knowledge of official rules and their opinions about the seriousness of particular rule-violating behaviors, the discipline these behaviors would deserve and would actually receive, and their estimates of how willing they would be to report such behavior. The disciplinary questions have been adjusted to fit the Croatian legal environment.[1]

Finally, the respondents were asked a few demographic questions. To increase the respondents' willingness to participate in the study, and to exclude the possibility that respondents could be identified, demographic questions have been kept to a bare minimum, inquiring about the length of the respondents' police experience, rank, assignment, and whether they were employed in a supervisory position.

The Sample

The Croatian police are a centralized police agency within the Ministry of the Interior. On top of the hierarchical structure are the minister of the interior and the chief of police (Police Law 2000), followed by 20 police administrations (which correspond to the 20 counties) and about 200 police stations at the bottom of the structure. The Police Law (2000, Article 13) prescribes the classification of police administrations into categories. Using several criteria (geographic size, population size, number of crimes known to the police, traffic patterns, and geographic location; see Ministry of the Interior 2009), the ministry classifies each police administration into one of the four categories. One of the key roles of police administrations is to oversee the operation of police stations (Police Law 2000, Article 15) in which the majority of regular police work is performed. Based on the nature of the work they perform, police stations can be divided into basic police stations and specialized police stations (e.g., airport, traffic, border). Based on the same criteria used to classify police administrations (Article 15, Police Law 2000), police stations are also classified into three categories.

In 2008/2009, the survey was administered to police officers employed in a stratified representative sample of police stations. The sample of police stations was drawn to represent both police administrations (four categories) and police stations (three categories). Because our interest is focused on regular patrol work, specialized police stations (e.g., border police, maritime police) in which police officers do not regularly patrol the beat were excluded from the sample. We created a 4×3 table by cross-tabulating four categories of police administrations with three categories of police stations. East police station was classified into one of the 12 cells (there are no class I police stations which are supervised by class IV police administrations). For the 11 categories populated by police stations, two stations were picked at random from all stations belonging to a specific category, thus yielding 22 stations in our sample. Each of the 22 stations we selected for the study participated in the study and returned questionnaires to us, resulting in a station response rate of 100 %. Most, but not all police officers working in these stations, returned

[1] The possible answers were: 1 = "None," 2 = "Public reprimand," 3 = "Fine up to 10 % of salary," 4 = "Fine up to 20 % of salary," 5 = "Reassignment to a different position," and 6 = "Dismissal."

Table 4.1 Sample distribution

	Category 1 Police stations	Category 2 Police stations	Category 3 Police stations	Total
Category I Police administrations	85	37	38	160
Category II Police administrations	37	119	97	253
Category III Police administrations	41	66	211	318
Category IV Police administrations	N/A	54	181	235
Total	163	276	527	966

completed questionnaires, yielding the officer response rate of 88%. Table 4.1 shows the overall number of officers and the distribution of officers by station and administration.

The overwhelming majority of our respondents are line officers (81%; Table 4.2) and the rest are supervisors (19%). Most officers are also very experienced; only one eighth of them have less than 5 years of experience, three quarters

Table 4.2 Respondents' demographic characteristics

	Number of respondents	Percent of respondents
Supervisory role		
Non-supervisors	742	81.0%
Supervisors	175	19.0%
Length of service		
Up to 5 years	113	12.3%
6–10 years	91	9.8%
11–15 years	298	32.0%
16–20 years	366	39.5%
Over 20 years	59	6.4%
Type of assignment		
Patrol	335	36.9%
Detective/investigative	162	17.9%
Communications	53	5.8%
Traffic	47	5.2%
Administrative	17	1.8%
Community policing	96	10.6%
Other	197	21.8%
Gender		
Male	809	88.2
Female	107	11.8

have more than 10 years of experience, and almost one half of the respondents had been police officers for more than 15 years (Table 4.2). The respondents performed a range of assignments, with patrol and detective units being the most frequent ones (Table 4.2). About 10% are women (Table 4.2).

The last questions in the questionnaire asked the respondents whether they have told the truth while filling out the questionnaire. About 5% did not provide any answer to this question. Out of the officers who responded, the overwhelming majority (92%) said that they did not lie. The analyses that follow include only the answers provided by those respondents who stated explicitly that they did not lie.

The Results

Seriousness

The respondents were asked to evaluate how serious they perceive the behaviors described in the scenarios, as well as to estimate how serious most police officers in their agencies would evaluate them. They were offered answers on a five-point Likert scale, ranging from "not at all serious" to "very serious."

The respondents' evaluations of scenario seriousness suggest that the scenarios were generally evaluated to be on the serious side (means are clustered between the midpoint of the scale and the serious end of the scale). However, these evaluations ranged in terms of seriousness, from the scenario evaluated to be the least serious, scenario 8 (describing the cover-up of police driving under the influence (DUI) with the mean at the midpoint), to the scenario evaluated as the most serious, scenario 3 (describing the theft of a knife from the crime scene with the mean very close to the serious end of the scale; Table 4.3). The average evaluations of seriousness enable the classification of these scenarios into three groups.

The four least serious scenarios (scenario 8: cover-up of police DUI; scenario 1: free meals, gifts from merchants; scenario 6: officer strikes prisoner who hurts partner; and scenario 7: verbal abuse – "Arrest an Asshole Day") all have means just above the midpoint of our scale (3.00). These scenarios describe the most benign versions of several forms of police misconduct. Scenario 1 (free meals, gifts from merchants) focuses on the acceptance of gratuities, traditionally viewed as the stepping stone toward more serious forms of police corruption. Scenario 8 (cover-up of police DUI) is also a form of police corruption, one involving internal corruption from Barker and Roebuck's classification (1973). Prior research on police integrity (Klockars et al. 2004a) shows that internal corruption has been classified as one of the least serious forms of police corruption. In this group, of least serious scenarios, there are also two scenarios involving the use of excessive force. Scenario 7 (verbal abuse – "Arrest an Asshole Day") describes the (ab)use of verbal commands, traditionally viewed as the lowest point on the use of force continuum (National Institute of Justice 2009). Although striking an arrested and handcuffed person should not be

Table 4.3 Police officers' perceptions of seriousness and violation of rules

Scenario number and description	Own seriousness		Others' seriousness		Mean difference (own–others)	*t*-test	Violation of rules			
	Mean	Rank	Mean	Rank			Yes (%)	No (%)	Not sure (%)	Rank
Scenario 1: free meals, gifts from merchants	3.48	2	2.98	2	0.50	12.74***	54.8	22.8	22.4	1
Scenario 2: failure to arrest friend with warrant	4.71	10	4.04	8	0.67	21.31***	90.7	1.7	7.6	10
Scenario 3: theft of knife from crime scene	4.74	11	4.17	10	0.57	19.95***	92.7	1.0	6.2	11
Scenario 4: unjustifiable use of deadly force	4.47	8	4.23	11	0.24	9.94***	78.4	6.2	15.5	7
Scenario 5:supervisor offers holiday for errands	4.33	6	3.67	6	0.66	17.09***	58.5	20.7	20.7	2
Scenario 6: officer strikes prisoner who hurt partner	3.59	3	3.18	3	0.41	12.74***	59.7	18.6	21.7	4
Scenario 7: verbal abuse – "Arrest an Asshole Day"	3.86	4	3.48	4	0.38	12.70***	65.6	15.4	18.9	5
Scenario 8: cover-up of police DUI accident	3.06	1	2.84	1	0.22	8.57***	59.2	19.5	21.4	3
Scenario 9: auto body shop 5 % kickback	4.46	7	3.86	7	0.60	18.16***	79.8	6.4	13.8	8
Scenario 10: false report on drug on dealer	4.54	9	4.13	9	0.41	15.61***	84.9	3.3	11.8	9
Scenario 11: Sgt. fails to halt beating	4.01	5	3.60	5	0.41	13.94***	75.0	9.5	15.6	6

DUI driving under the influence
$*p<0.05$; $**p<0.01$; $***p<0.001$

acceptable and should be evaluated, as serious (scenario 6: officer strikes prisoner who hurts partner) justification given for the activity—a dose of "street justice"—probably contributing toward making it less serious in the eyes of police officers than it should be.

Out of the four scenarios that can be classified as scenarios of intermediate seriousness (the values of means are mostly between 4.0 and 4.5), two describe misconduct by a supervisor (scenario 5: supervisor offers holiday for errands; scenario 11: Sgt. fails to halt beating). In one scenario, scenario 5 (supervisor offers holiday for errands), the supervisor is proposing a deal that could be classified as internal corruption. In the other scenario, scenario 11 (Sgt. fails to halt beating), a supervisor is not actively using excessive force himself, but is passively watching as his subordinates repeatedly strike and kick a man arrested for child abuse. In other words, his command responsibility, rather than his direct conduct, is at stake. The means for the remaining two scenarios (scenario 9: auto body shop 5 % kickback; scenario 4: unjustifiable use of deadly force) are very close to 4.5 on a five-point scale, suggesting that these scenarios have been perceived as serious. One of the scenarios, scenario 9 (auto body shop 5 % kickback) describes a traditional form of corruption in which a police officer abuses his official position to obtain an illegal kickback (Roebuck and Barker 1973). The other scenario, scenario 4 (unjustifiable use of deadly force) should be viewed as one of the most serious scenarios in the whole questionnaire, if not the most serious. What potentially mitigates the offender's responsibility in the eyes of the respondents might be the police officer's prior experience—included in the description of the scenario—in which he was seriously hurt because he did not react on time. Police officers could potentially identify with this situation.

The three most serious scenarios all have means substantially closer to 5 (the "very serious" end of the scale). These three scenarios, plain violations of criminal law, include one scenario with opportunistic theft (scenario 3: theft of knife from crime scene), a scenario illustrating a failure to execute an arrest warrant on a friend (scenario 2: failure to arrest friend with warrant), and a scenario describing falsification of the official report (scenario 10: false report of drugs on drug dealer). All three scenarios are plain violations of official rules in which a police officer does something that he was not supposed to do (e.g., steal the knife from a crime scene) or does not do something that he was supposed to do (e.g., did not arrest a friend, falsified the official report).

A comparison of the respondents' own estimates of seriousness and how serious they estimated that other police officers in the agency would evaluate the same scenarios revealed several findings. First, for each and every scenario, the respondents evaluated these scenarios as more serious than they thought the other police officers would; the means for evaluations of own seriousness were always higher than the means for others' estimates of seriousness (Table 4.3). Second, the differences between the means measuring own estimates of seriousness and the means measuring others' estimates of seriousness were all statistically significant, but were large and meaningful (above the 0.50)[2] only in five scenarios (scenario 1: free meals, gifts from merchants; scenario 2: failure to arrest friend with warrant; scenario 3: theft of knife from crime scene; scenario 5: supervisor offers holiday for errands; and scenario 9: auto body shop 5 % kickback) the differences were large and meaningful. Third, the relative order of the scenarios, measured through the ranking of the scenarios, suggests that police officers followed the same internal order of seriousness, regardless of whether they expressed their own evaluations or whether they estimated how other police officers would evaluate the scenarios. In fact, the Spearman's correlation between the rankings of own evaluations of seriousness and others' estimates of seriousness is very high (Spearman's correlation coefficient = 0.936, $p < 0.001$).

Violation of Official Rules

All of the examples of misconduct described in the questionnaire incorporate rule-violating behavior. The respondents were asked whether the behaviors described in the questionnaire could be classified as examples of rule-violating behavior. They could select an answer from three possible choices: "yes," "no," and "not sure."

Indeed, the majority of police officers recognized and labeled the (mis)behavior in each and every scenario as rule violating (Table 4.3). However, the percentages of police officers who did so varied across scenarios, from the scenarios in which a slim majority evaluated the behavior as rule violating (55 % in scenario 1: free meals, gifts from merchants) to the scenarios in which the overwhelming majority did the same (93 % in scenario 3: theft of knife from crime scene; Table 4.3). Scenarios in which two thirds or fewer officers recognized the behavior as rule violating include scenarios with minor forms of police corruption, such as the acceptance of gratuities (scenario 1: free meals, gifts from merchants), minor forms of use of excessive force (scenario 7: verbal abuse – "Arrest an Asshole Day"), scenarios involving "street justice" (scenario 6: officer strikes prisoner who hurts partner), and scenarios involving internal corruption (scenario 5: supervisor offers holiday for errands; scenario 8: cover-up of police DUI). On the other hand, scenarios in which four-fifths or more labeled the behavior as rule violating were scenarios in which the police officer in the scenario engages in severe violations of official rules and criminal laws (scenario 2: failure to arrest friend with warrant; scenario 3: theft of knife from crime scene; scenario 10: false report on drug dealer).

Why would some of the respondents have problems recognizing some of these scenarios as violations of official rules? It is possible that a substantial minority of the police officers do not know the official rules. Although extensive training was not provided in the war years to each newly hired police officer, in-service training and on-the-job experience, since those early 1990s, should have provided police

[2] Following the rule of thumb established in prior work (Klockars et al. 2006, p. 26), we consider only the differences of 0.50 or larger to be meaningful.

officers with sufficient opportunities to learn "the basic rules." The results of Veić's study conducted in 2001 indicate that a substantial portion of the officers still may have problems recognizing at least some of the rules (Ivanović 2001, p. 12). Indeed, there are at least 10% of police officers in this study, who seem to be unsure of whether the behaviors constitute violations of official rules (Table 4.3). In four scenarios (scenario 1: free meals, gifts from merchants; scenario 5: supervisor offers holiday for errands; scenario 6: officer strikes prisoner who hurts partner; scenario 8: cover-up of police DUI) the percentage even reaches 20%. In addition, in three out of these four scenarios with higher percentages of police officers not being sure whether the behavior violates official rules, about 20% of police officers flatly denied that such behavior indeed violates official rules.

Finally, the respondents' evaluations of whether the behavior constitutes a violation of official rules is strongly related to how serious they perceive the behavior; the more serious they evaluate the behavior, the more likely they are to evaluate it as rule violating. The ranking of scenarios based on their evaluations of seriousness and the ranking of scenarios based on their evaluations of rule-violating nature of the behavior are very similar (Spearman's correlation coefficient$=0.882$; $p<0.001$).

Appropriate and Expected Discipline

The respondents were also asked to express their views about the appropriate discipline for the behaviors described in the questionnaire, as well as estimate what discipline would be meted out in their agencies for such behavior. Based on the norms of the Law on Civil Servants and Public Employees (2001), the answers offered in the questionnaire included: "no discipline," "public warning," "fine in the amount of 10% of the employee's salary," "fine in the amount of 20% of the employee's salary," "reassignment," and "dismissal."

We use three ways of assessing the respondents' views. First, we rely on the modal values (Table 4.4). The respondents did not think that the same discipline would be appropriate for all scenarios. Rather, for four scenarios (scenario 1: free meals, gifts from merchants; scenario 5: supervisor offers holiday for errands; scenario 7: verbal abuse – "Arrest an Asshole Day," scenario 8: cover-up of police DUI), the modal appropriate discipline is (only) "public reprimand," the most lenient of all forms of discipline. These are the scenarios involving the least serious forms of corruption (scenario 1: free meals, gifts from merchants), the use of the excessive force on the lower end of the use of force continuum (scenario 7: verbal abuse – "Arrest an Asshole Day"), as well as internal corruption (scenario 5: supervisor offers holiday for errands; scenario 7: verbal abuse – "Arrest an Asshole Day," scenario 8: cover-up of police DUI). With the exception of scenario 5, these are the scenarios perceived to be the least serious and having the smallest number of police officers recognizing them as rule violating as well (Table 4.3). According to our respondents, two scenarios (scenario 6: officer strikes prisoner who hurts partner; scenario 11: Sgt. fails to halt beating) deserve a more severe discipline, a fine in the

Table 4.4 Views about appropriate discipline (should) and expected discipline (would)

Scenario number and description		Mode	Rank should	Rank would	None	Some discipline	Dismissal	Chi-square test[b]	Phi
Scenario 1: free meals, gifts from merchants	*Should*	Public reprimand	*1–4*		20.1 %	73.3 %	6.6 %	272.18***	0.588***
	Would	Public reprimand		*2–3*	24.3 %	65.6 %	10.1 %		
Scenario 2: failure to arrest friend with warrant	*Should*	Dismissal	*7–11*		1.0 %	61.8 %	37.2 %	245.87***	0.561***
	Would	Dismissal		*7–11*	4.2 %	62.2 %	33.6 %		
Scenario 3: theft of knife from crime scene	*Should*	Dismissal	*7–11*		0.9 %	47.0 %	52.2 %	418.51***	0.726***
	Would	Dismissal		*7–11*	3.1 %	48.6 %	48.3 %		
Scenario 4: unjustifiable use of deadly force	*Should*	Dismissal	*7–11*		9.6 %	38.1 %	52.2 %	828.64***	1.00***
	Would	Dismissal		*7–11*	7.2 %	27.8 %	65.0 %		
Scenario 5: supervisor offers holiday for errands	*Should*	Public reprimand	*1–4*		19.9 %	75.3 %	4.8 %	512.02***	0.811***
	Would	None		*1*	34.7 %	60.8 %	4.6 %		
Scenario 6: officer strikes prisoner who hurts partner	*Should*	Fine 20 %	*5–6*		25.3 %	70.0 %	4.7 %	322.90***	0.638***
	Would	Fine 10 %		*4*	18.7 %	81.3 %	0.0 %		
Scenario 7: verbal abuse – "Arrest an Asshole Day"	*Should*	Public reprimand	*1–4*		17.9 %	81.6 %	0.6 %	660.42***	0.915***
	Would	Public reprimand		*2–3*	17.0 %	81.9 %	1.2 %		
Scenario 8: cover-up of police DUI accident	*Should*	Public reprimand	*1–4*		27.7 %	69.1 %	3.1 %	607.66***	0.880***
	Would	Fine 20 %		*5–6*	19.5 %	75.2 %	5.3 %		
Scenario 9: auto body shop 5 % kickback	*Should*	Dismissal	*7–11*		7.0 %	62.5 %	30.5 %	588.26***	0.868***
	Would	Dismissal		*7–11*	9.3 %	63.9 %	26.8 %		
Scenario 10: false report on drug on dealer	*Should*	Dismissal	*7–11*		4.9 %	64.6 %	30.4 %	666.66***	0.929***
	Would	Dismissal		*7–11*	5.5 %	61.6 %	32.9 %		
Scenario 11: Sgt. fails to halt beating	*Should*	Fine 20 %	*5–6*		12.8 %	76.6 %	10.6 %	706.71***	0.959***
	Would	Fine 20 %		*5–6*	13.9 %	72.4 %	13.7 %		

DUI driving under the influence
$b < 0.10$
$*p < 0.05$; $**p < 0.01$; $***p < 0.001$

amount of up to 20% of the salary. Finally, in five scenarios (scenario 2: failure to arrest friend with warrant; scenario 3: theft of knife from crime scene; scenario 4: unjustifiable use of deadly force; scenario 9: auto body shop 5% kickback; scenario 10: false report on drug on dealer), the modal response discipline was "dismissal." Most of these scenarios were evaluated as the most serious and were most likely to have the highest percentage of police officers recognizing them as rule violating (Table 4.3).

Second, we relied not only on the modes but also on the percentages of police officers who selected no discipline, some discipline other than dismissal, and dismissal (Table 4.4). The findings of this analysis are similar to the analysis of modal responses. In addition, this analysis reveals that, out of the five scenarios classified as requiring the most severe discipline based on the modal responses, the *majority* of police officers thought that dismissal is the appropriate discipline in only two scenarios (scenario 3: theft of knife from crime scene; scenario 4: unjustifiable use of deadly force). This finding suggests that dismissal is reserved for rare situations and is only appropriate for the most serious form of corruption and the use of deadly force. For everything else, some discipline is appropriate, but it should not be dismissal.

Third, we also ranked scenarios based on the modal appropriate discipline for each scenario (Table 4.4). Because the answers are recorded on the ordinal scale with six possible categories, several scenarios share the same ranking. Nevertheless, a comparison of the ranking of appropriate discipline with the ranking for seriousness shows that they are strongly correlated (Spearman's correlation coefficient $=0.839$, $p<0.01$); the more serious the respondents evaluated the scenarios to be, the more likely they were to think that the appropriate discipline should be harsher. Similarly, a comparison of the ranking of appropriate discipline with the ranking for rule-violating behavior shows that the two are strongly related as well (Spearman's correlation coefficient $=0.897$, $p<0.001$). The more likely the respondents were to evaluate the behavior as rule violating, the more likely they were to think that the appropriate discipline should be harsher.

The second question about discipline asked the respondents to estimate what discipline their agencies would mete out. One of the options was no discipline, that is, that their agency would not discipline a police officer at all. For only one case, scenario 5 (supervisor offers holiday for errands), the modal discipline was "no discipline" at all, but a more detailed analysis across the three categories of discipline (Table 4.4) clearly suggests that, although about one third of the respondents indeed expected no discipline, about two thirds expected some discipline, but mostly minor in terms of its severity. Similarly, there are two scenarios (scenario 1: free meals, gifts from merchants; scenario 7: verbal abuse – "Arrest an Asshole Day") describing minor forms of police corruption and excessive force in which the mode was "public reprimand," and the analysis of percentages across the three discipline categories shows that the majority of the respondents expected some discipline. On the other hand, for five scenarios (scenario 2: failure to arrest friend with warrant; scenario 3: theft of knife from crime scene; scenario 4: unjustifiable use of deadly force; scenario 9: auto body shop 5% kickback; scenario 10: false report on drug on dealer) the modal discipline was dismissal. However, the analysis across the three categories of discipline reveals that in only two of these scenarios (scenario 3: theft of knife from crime scene; scenario 4: unjustifiable use of deadly force), the scenarios perceived to be most serious in the questionnaire, which over 90 % of the respondents evaluated as rule violating, the majority of the respondents expected discipline to be meted out, while in the other three scenarios (scenario 2: failure to arrest friend with warrant; scenario 9: auto body shop 5 % kickback; scenario 10: false report on drug on dealer), despite the fact that the modal discipline was dismissal, the majority of the respondents expected some discipline, but not dismissal.

We also compared the respondents' estimates of appropriate and expected discipline. First, both the analysis of modes and the analysis of percentages across three categories of discipline suggest that, in general, the views about appropriate and expected discipline are similar. The largest differences in both modal choices and differences in percentages of at least 10 % appear in two scenarios (scenario 4: unjustifiable use of deadly force; scenario 5: supervisor offers holiday for errands). In both of these scenarios, the respondents approved of somewhat less serious discipline than they expect their agencies to mete out. Second, the analysis of ranks confirms the overall findings of close relation (Spearman's correlation coefficient $=0.930$, $p<0.001$). Third, the modal discipline was the same in 8 out of 11 cases. In two of the scenarios with differences (scenario 5: supervisor offers holiday for errands; scenario 6: officer strikes prisoner who hurts partner), the appropriate modal discipline was harsher than what they expected that the agencies would mete out, thus suggesting that there is a substantial group of police officers who evaluated the actual discipline to be too lenient. On the other hand, in one of the scenarios involving internal corruption (scenario 8: cover-up of police DUI), the expected modal discipline was more severe than the modal appropriate discipline, indicating that there is a substantial group of police officers who evaluated the expected discipline as too harsh.

Willingness to Report Misconduct

The last two questions after each scenario asked the respondents to express how willing they would be to report misconduct and to estimate how willing other officers in their agencies would be to do so. The answers ranged on a five-point Likert scale from "definitely not" to "definitely yes." The answers conveying their own (un)willingness to report misconduct, help us assess the extent and nature of the code of silence.

The analysis of the results (e.g., mean values, percentage of the officers not reporting) shows that the code of silence varies across scenarios, from 51 % of the respondents saying that they would not report a cover-up of police DUI (scenario 8) to 12 % who said that they would not report a failure to arrest a friend with an outstanding warrant (scenario 2) or an unjustifiable use of deadly force (scenario 4; Fig. 4.1).

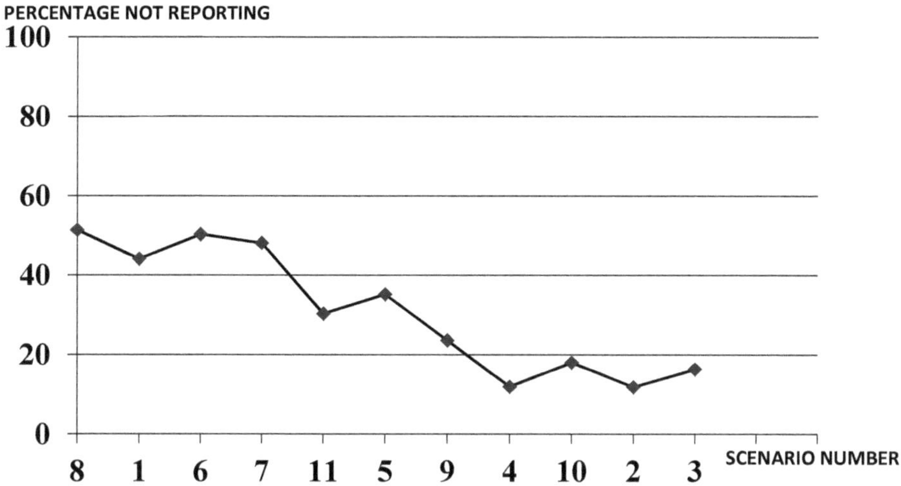

Fig. 4.1 Percentage not reporting by scenario number

The respondents' adherence to the code of silence is directly related to their perceptions of scenario seriousness (Spearman's correlation coefficient = 0.936, $p < 0.001$), likelihood of recognizing it as rule-violating behavior (Spearman's correlation coefficient = 0.809, $p < 0.01$), and the severity of appropriate discipline (Spearman's correlation coefficient = 0.839, $p < 0.01$). The analysis of the mean values suggests that scenarios could be divided into three categories (Table 4.5).

First, there are four scenarios (scenario 1: free meals, gifts from merchants; scenario 6: officer strikes prisoner who hurts partner; scenario 7: verbal abuse – "Arrest an Asshole Day"; scenario 8: cover-up of police DUI) in which the mean values are below the midpoint of the scale, suggesting that the behaviors described in these scenarios would be well protected by the code of silence. In addition, a separate analysis of the code of silence (measured as the percentage of the respondents who said that they would not report) shows that about one half of the respondents for each of these scenarios said that they would *not* report a police officer who engaged in misconduct described in the scenario. These four scenarios include the least serious forms of police corruption (i.e., the acceptance of gratuities) and the use of excessive force, as well as the two scenarios with internal corruption. These four scenarios have been perceived as the least serious, least likely to be recognized as rule-violating behavior, and deserving the least serious forms of discipline (Tables 4.3 and 4.4).

Second, there are four scenarios (scenario 5: supervisor offers holiday for errands; scenario 9: auto body shop 5 % kickback; scenario 10: false report on drug on dealer; scenario 11: Sgt. fails to halt beating) in the middle group with the means between 3 and 4 and with about one quarter of the respondents saying that they would not report (Table 4.5). These scenarios include a false report, serious forms of corruption (kickback), hitting an arrested suspect as a measure of "street justice,"

Table 4.5 Police officers' perceptions of willingness to report

Scenario number and description	Own willingness to Report		Others' willingness to Report		Mean difference (Own–others)	*t*-test
	Mean	Rank	Mean	Rank		
Scenario 1: free meals, gifts from merchants	2.84	4	2.43	4	0.41	8.37***
Scenario 2: failure to arrest friend with warrant	4.05	9	3.33	8.5	0.72	17.05***
Scenario 3: theft of knife from crime scene	4.11	11	3.53	10	0.58	15.51***
Scenario 4: unjustifiable use of deadly force	4.09	10	3.87	11	0.22	7.44***
Scenario 5: supervisor offers holiday for errands	3.04	5	2.70	5-	0.34	8.67***
Scenario 6: officer strikes prisoner who hurts partner	2.49	2	2.34	1	0.15	4.20***
Scenario 7: verbal abuse – "Arrest an Asshole Day"	2.60	3	2.42	3	0.18	5.83***
Scenario 8: cover-up of police DUI accident	2.43	1	2.39	2	0.04	1.18
Scenario 9: auto body shop 5% kickback	3.66	7	3.19	7	0.47	11.17***
Scenario 10: false report on drug on dealer	3.78	8	3.33	8.5	0.45	12.95***
Scenario 11: Sgt. fails to halt beating	3.13	6	2.88	6	0.25	7.55***

DUI driving under the influence
$*p<0.05$; $**p<0.01$; $***p<0.001$

and not reacting to the beating. They have been classified in the middle of the scale in terms of their seriousness, likelihood that the respondents will label them as rule violating, and severity of the discipline (some discipline, but not dismissal).

Third, there are three scenarios (scenario 2: failure to arrest friend with warrant; scenario 3: theft of knife from crime scene; scenario 4: unjustifiable use of deadly force) for which the means are above 4 and are on the reporting side of the scale. At the same time, the percentage of the police officers who stated that they would not report is the smallest for these scenarios (between 11 and 16%). These scenarios describe the most serious forms of corruption and use of excessive force, which are not only violations of agency rules but also violations of criminal law as well. These scenarios were evaluated as the most serious by the respondents, were most likely to be recognized as violations of the official rules, and merited dismissal from the agency.

We also compared the respondents' own willingness to report with their estimates of others' willingness to report (Table 4.5). The mean values suggest that, in all 11 scenarios, the respondents seem to be somewhat more willing to say that they would report than they estimated that others would. Although the differences between the means for their own willingness to report and the means for others' willingness to report are statistically significant in 10 out of 11 scenarios, these differences are meaningful in only two scenarios (scenario 2: failure to arrest friend with warrant; scenario 3: theft of knife from crime scene).[3] Finally, a comparison of the rankings shows that their own willingness to report and their estimates of others' willingness to report are very strongly related (Spearman's correlation coefficient = 0.980, $p < 0.001$).

Conclusion

Although Croatian police are one of the youngest police agencies in Europe, their history has been burdened with serious challenges. Not only has the transition toward a democratic agency been hampered with the war but the war experience—be it from the perspective of a victim, soldier, or both—affected the police officers as well. Hiring standards and police training have been relaxed while the enactment of the relevant legal norms has been put on hold. Eventually, relevant legal statutes (e.g., Criminal Law, Criminal Procedure Law, Police Law) have been enacted and the legal environment has been created for the successful transition. As time passed, the society at large has become more engaged and successful in dealing with corruption and nepotism, as well as in addressing ethnic-based violence and hostility.

The Ministry's recent survey revealed that the respondents' familiarity with the use of force rules was "excellent" or "good" (Borovec 2013, p. 6). Consistently, the results of our study indicate that most, but not all police officers, know the official rules. Over two thirds of police officers recognized most of the examples of misconduct as rule-violating behavior, but there was still a substantial minority of police officers who did not. Police officers were less likely to recognize as rule-violation behavior which they evaluated as less serious (e.g., acceptance of gratuities, dispensing a dose of "street justice" on a handcuffed arrestee, covering up a DUI accident, getting favors from a supervisor in exchange for running errands). In such cases, a larger percentage of our respondents tended to say that they were not sure whether the described behavior violated the official rules. Such cases indicate a potential conflict between official agency rules and the actual practice in the agency. Accordingly, an increased proportion of our respondents expected, or approved of, no discipline at all or very mild discipline for such behaviors.

The respondents' evaluations of misconduct seriousness vary substantially across the scenarios. However, the second version of the questionnaire that we used in this study allowed us, for the first time, to look at potential patterns of whether police officers differentiate across different types within the same form of misconduct. The results clearly show that the respondents had no problems distinguishing among different forms of corruption; they evaluated the acceptance of gratuities and

[3] Following the rule of thumb established in prior work (Klockars et al. 2006, p. 26), we consider only the differences of 0.50 or larger to be meaningful.

internal corruption as the least serious forms of corruption and a kickback and theft from a crime scene as the most serious forms of corruption. These findings fit well within the parameters of corruption seriousness established in our earlier work. In particular, our first questionnaire, focusing exclusively on police corruption, has been used in more than a dozen countries and overwhelmingly shows the same pattern (Alain 2004; Chatta and Kutnjak Ivković 2004; Edelbacher and Kutnjak Ivković 2004; Johnson 2004; Klockars et al. 2004a, 2004b; Kremer 2004; Kutnjak Ivković and Khechumyan 2014, 2013; Kutnjak Ivković 2004b; Kutnjak Ivković and Sauerman 2012, 2013a, 2013b; Kutnjak Ivković and Shelley 2005, 2007, 2008, 2010; Newham 2004; Pagon and Lobnikar 2004; Pounti et al. 2004; Punch 2004; Torstensson Levander and Ekenvall 2004).

The use of excessive force, on the other hand, has only been addressed in this second questionnaire. The police officers' perceptions of seriousness of different forms of (mis)use of force seem to be strongly related to the use of force continuum. The forms that violate the rules, at the lower end of the use of force continuum (e.g., abuse of a verbal command), at the same time, are evaluated to be less serious than forms of misconduct at the higher end of the use of force continuum (e.g., use of deadly force).

The behaviors described in the questionnaire are violations not only of the administrative rules but also of criminal law. Based on the results of our study, a potential outcome for a police officer who engaged in the described behaviors, and is eventually officially processed, would not necessarily involve a severe discipline. Only for the two most serious cases (i.e., the use of deadly force, theft from a crime scene) would the majority of the respondents support and expect dismissal. For all of the other forms of misconduct, the majority favored and expected some discipline, but definitely less serious than dismissal. The more lenient discipline that police officers expect the police agency to mete out—if they are reading the disciplinary threat correctly—signals that the agency is not as serious about curtailing police misconduct. On the other hand, if the police agency is actually firing police officers for a range of other forms of misconduct, the police officers are neither getting the message loudly nor clearly.

Lastly, our results constitute clear evidence that the code of silence exists among the Croatian police officers. However, the code of silence is far from a flat prohibition of reporting because it varies dramatically. On one hand, about one half of the respondents would protect in silence a fellow officer's DUI accident, administering a dose of "street justice," or verbally harassing citizens. On the other hand, about one tenth of the respondents would protect a police officer who unjustifiably used deadly force or who failed to execute an arrest warrant. Compared to the findings of the 1995 survey (Kutnjak Ivković and Klockars 2004), in which at least one quarter of the respondents said that they would not report a fellow police officer for *any* of the behaviors described in the questionnaire, the results of our 2008/2009 survey suggest that the extent of the code overall has decreased because only about one tenth of the respondents said the same. The strong code of silence that shielded the police officers who fought together during the war seems to have weakened. This is probably a combination of two factors: Improving attitudes of seasoned police officers and the arrival of the more recently trained, post-war police officers. As time passes, the war-related influences weaken, institutions of control strengthen, and the country moves along the path toward democracy.

However, our results show that, even in our more recent survey, about 10% of the police officers would not report the most serious examples of police misconduct. The good news is that the majority of the officers would not protect such behavior in silence and that the code has weakened overall. The bad news is that a nontrivial proportion of the police officers still would tolerate even the most outrageous forms of misconduct in silence. While it is not reasonable to expect that the code of silence will disappear completely as the Croatian police become a truly democratic police agency, the expectation placed before any police agency of integrity is that police culture and individual police officers will not be tolerant of serious forms of misconduct. Police officers who abuse their right to use deadly force should be certain that they would be reported by their peers and that the official disciplinary and criminal procedure would be initiated.

References

Alain, M. (2004). An exploratory study of Quebec's police officers' attitudes toward ethical dilemmas. In C. B. Klockars, S. Kutnjak Ivković, & M. R. Haberfeld (Eds.), *The contours of police integrity*. Thousand Oaks: Sage Publications.

Amnesty International. (1998). Croatia: Mirko Graorac–Shortchanging justice—War crimes trials in former Yugoslavia. http://www.amnesty.org/en/library/asset/EUR64/010/1998/en/719db05e-e75c-11dd-b8d3-c95de5982fed/eur640101998en.pdf. Accessed 24 June 2013.

Barker, T., & Roebuck, J. (1973). *An empirical typology of police corruption*. Springfield: Charles C. Thomas.

Borovec, K. (2013). An assessment of police officer satisfaction with the legal protection and support by the Ministry of the Interior. Zagreb, Croatia: Ministry of the Interior. Unpublished manuscript.

Code of Criminal Procedure. (1997). Zagreb, Croatia: Narodne novine 110/97.

Code of Criminal Procedure. (2008). Zagreb, Croatia: Narodne novine 152/08.

Commission of the European Communities, Croatia. (2006). Progress report. http://ec.europa.eu/enlargement/pdf/key_documents/2006/nov/hr_sec_1385_en.pdf. Accessed 24 June 2013.

Commission of the European Communities, Croatia. (2007). Progress report. http://ec.europa.eu/enlargement/pdf/key_documents/2007/nov/croatia_progress_reports_en.pdf. Accessed 24 June 2013.

Commission of the European Communities, Croatia. (2010). Progress report. http://ec.europa.eu/enlargement/pdf/key_documents/2010/package/hr_rapport_2010_en.pdf. Accessed 24 June 2013.

Commission of the European Communities, Croatia. (2011). Progress report. http://ec.europa.eu/enlargement/pdf/key_documents/2011/package/hr_rapport_2011_en.pdf. Accessed 24 June 2013.

Constitution. (1990). Zagreb, Croatia: Narodne novine 56/90.

Criminal Code. (1997). Zagreb, Croatia: Narodne novine 110/97.

Derenčinović, D. (2000). Kaznenopravni sadrzaji u suprotstavljanju korupciji. Zagreb, Croatia: University of Zagreb, Doctoral Dissertation.

Edelbacher, M., & Kutnjak Ivković, S. (2004). Ethics and the police: Studying police integrity in Austria. In C. B. Klockars, S. Kutnjak Ivković, & M. R. Haberfeld (Eds.), *The contours of police integrity*. Thousand Oaks: Sage Publications.

European Commission against Racism and Intolerance (2001). Second report on Croatia. http://hudoc.ecri.coe.int/XMLEcri/ENGLISH/Cycle_02/02_CbC_eng/02-cbc-croatia-eng.pdf. Accessed 24 June 2013.

European Committee for the Prevention of Torture and Inhuman or Degrading Treatment or Punishment. (2007). Report to the Croatian Government on the visit to Croatia carried out by the European Committee for the Prevention of Torture and Inhuman or Degrading Treatment or Punishment (CPT) from 1 to 9 December 2003. http://www.refworld.org/docid/45e7f0ae2.html. Accessed 24 June 2013.

Human Rights Watch. (1993). Threats to press freedom: A report prepared for the Free Media Seminar Commission on security and cooperation in Europe. http://www.hrw.org/reports/1993/11/01/threats-press-freedom. Accessed 24 June 2013.

Human Rights Watch. (1995). Civil and political rights in Croatia. http://www.hrw.org/legacy/reports/1995/Croatia.htm. Accessed 24 June 2013.

Ivanović, R. (2001). Corruption in the police? *Globus, 14,* December 2001.

Johnson, D. T. (2004). Police integrity in Japan. In C. B. Klockars, S. Kutnjak Ivković, & M. R. Haberfeld (Eds.), *The contours of police integrity*. Thousand Oaks: Sage Publications.

Klockars, C. B., & Kutnjak Ivković, S. (2004). Measuring police integrity. In A. R. Piquero, J. R. Greene, & M. J. Hickman (Eds.), *Police integrity and ethics*. Belmont: Wadsworth Publishing.

Klockars, C. B., Kutnjak Ivković, S., Harver, W. E., & Haberfeld, M. R. (1997). *The measurement of police integrity*. Final report submitted to the U.S. Department of Justice, Office of Justice Programs, National Institute of Justice.

Klockars, C. B., Kutnjak Ivković, S., Haberfeld, M. R., & Uydess, A. (2001). *Enhancing police integrity: Three case studies*. Final report submitted to the U.S. Department of Justice, Office of Justice Programs, National Institute of Justice (with contributions by William A. Geller).

Klockars, C. B., Kutnjak Ivković, S., & Haberfeld, M. R. (Eds.). (2004a). *The contours of police integrity*. Newbury Park: Sage Publications.

Klockars, C. B., Kutnjak Ivković, S., & Haberfeld, M. R. (2004b). Police Integrity in the United States of America. In C. B. Klockars, S. Kutnjak Ivković, & M. R. Haberfeld (Eds.), *The contours of police integrity*. Thousand Oaks: Sage Publications.

Klockars, C. B., Kutnjak Ivković, S., & Haberfeld, M. R. (2006). *Enhancing police integrity*. New York: Springer.

Kremer, F. (2004). Police integrity in Hungary. In C. B. Klockars, S. Kutnjak Ivković, & M. R. Haberfeld (Eds.), *The contours of police integrity*. Thousand Oaks: Sage Publications.

Kutnjak Ivković, S. (2000). Challenges of policing democracies: The Croatian experience. In D. K. Das & O. Marenin (Eds.), *Challenges of policing democracies*. Amsterdam: Gordon and Breach Publishers.

Kutnjak Ivković, S. (2004a). Distinct and different: Transformation of the Croatian police. In M. Caparini & O. Marenin (Eds.), *Transforming Police in Central and Eastern Europe*. Muenster: Lit Verlag.

Kutnjak Ivković, S. (2004b). Sharing the view: Line officer and supervisor evaluations of police corruption seriousness in Bosnia and Herzegovina. In G. Mesko, M. Pagon, & G. Dobovsek (Eds.), *Dilemmas of contemporary criminal justice. Ljubljana*. Slovenia: Faculty of Criminal Justice, University of Maribor.

Kutnjak Ivković, S. (2005). Croatia. In M. R. Haberfeld (Ed.), *Encyclopedia of Law Enforcement, Vol. 3: International*. Thousand Oaks: Sage Publications.

Kutnjak Ivković, S. (2008). A comparative study of public support for the police. *International Criminal Justice Review, 18*(4), 406–434.

Kutnjak Ivković, S. (2009). The Croatian police, police integrity, and transition toward democratic policing. *Policing: An International Journal of Police Strategies and Management, 32*(3), 459–488.

Kutnjak Ivković, S., & Khechumyan, A. (2013). The state of police integrity in Armenia: Findings from the police integrity survey. *Policing: An International Journal of Police Strategies and Management, 36*(1), 70–90.

Kutnjak Ivković, S., & Khechumyan, A. (2014). Measuring police integrity among urban and rural police in Armenia: From local results to global implications. *International Journal of Comparative and Applied Criminal Justice, 25*(1), 25–52.
Kutnjak Ivković, S., & Klockars, C. B. (2004). Police integrity in Croatia. In C. B. Klockars, S. Kutnjak Ivković, & M. R. Haberfeld (Eds.), *The contours of police integrity*. Thousand Oaks: Sage Publications.
Kutnjak Ivković, S., & Sauerman, A. (2012). The code of silence: Revisiting South African police integrity. *South African Crime Quarterly, 40*(June), 15–24.
Kutnjak Ivković, S., & Sauerman, A. (2013a). Threading the thin blue line: Transition toward democratic policing and the integrity of the South African police service. *Policing and Society*, Forthcoming.
Kutnjak Ivković, S., & Sauerman, A. (2013b). Curtailing the code of silence among the South African police. *Policing: An International Journal of Police Strategies and Management, 36*(1), 175–198.
Kutnjak Ivković, S., & Shelley, T. O.'Connor. (2005). The Bosnian police and police integrity: A Continuing story. *European Journal of Criminology, 2*(4), 428–454.
Kutnjak Ivković, S., & Shelley, T. O.'Connor. (2007). Police integrity and the Czech police officers. *International Journal of Comparative and Applied Criminal Justice, 31*(1), 21–49.
Kutnjak Ivković, S., & Shelley, T. O.'Connor. (2008). The police code of silence and different paths toward democratic policing. *Policing and Society, 18*(4), 445–473.
Kutnjak Ivković, S., & Shelley, T. O.'Connor. (2010). The code of silence and disciplinary fairness: A comparison of Czech police supervisor and line officer views. *Policing: An International Journal of Police Strategies and Management, 33*(3), 548–574.
Law on Police Activities and Rights. (2009). Zagreb, Narodne novine 76/09.
Ministry of the Interior. (2009). Police administrations. http://www.mup.hr/MainPu.aspx?id=1255. Accessed 24 June 2013.
Nacional. (2008). Survey. http://89.201.163.71/polls/result/762/. Accessed 24 June 2013.
National Institute of Justice. (2009). The use-of-force continuum. http://www.nij.gov/topics/law-enforcement/officer-safety/use-of-force/continuum.htm. Accessed 24 June 2013.
Newham, G. (2004). Out of step: Integrity and the South Africa police service. In C. B. Klockars, S. Kutnjak Ivković, & M. R. Haberfeld (Eds.), *The contours of police integrity*. Thousand Oaks: Sage Publications.
Pagon, M., & Lobnikar, B. (2004). Police integrity in Slovenia. In C. B. Klockars, S. Kutnjak Ivković, & M. R. Haberfeld (Eds.), *The contours of police integrity*. Thousand Oaks: Sage Publications.
Police Law. (2000). Zagreb, Croatia: Narodne novine 129/01.
Police Law. (2011). Zagreb, Croatia: Narodne novine 34/11.
Pounti, A., Vuorinen, S., & Kutnjak Ivković, S. (2004). Sustaining police integrity in Finland. In C. B. Klockars, S. Kutnjak Ivković , & M. R. Haberfeld (Eds.), *The contours of police integrity*. Thousand Oaks: Sage Publications.
Punch, M., Huberts, L. W. J. C., & Lamboo, M. E. D. (2004). Integrity, perceptions, and investigations in The Netherlands. In C. B. Klockars, S. Kutnjak Ivković, & M. R. Haberfeld (Eds.), *The contours of police integrity*. Thousand Oaks: Sage Publications.
Torstensson Levander, M., & Ekenvall, B. (2004). Homogeneity in moral standards in Swedish police culture. In C. B. Klockars, S. Kutnjak Ivković, & M. R. Haberfeld (Eds.), *The contours of police integrity*. Thousand Oaks: Sage Publications.
Transparency International. (2008). *Global corruption barometer*. http://archive.transparency.org/policy_research/surveys_indices/cpi/2008. Accessed 24 June 2013.
Transparency International. (2010). *Global corruption barometer*. http://www.transparency.org/content/download/57371/917572/version/2/file/Barometer_2010_web. Accessed 24 June 2013.
Transparency International. (2011). Corruption perceptions index. http://www.transparency.org/policy_research/surveys_indices/cpi. Accessed 24 June 2013.
UNODC. (2011). *Corruption in the Western Balkans: Bribery as experienced by the population*. http://www.unodc.org/documents/data-and-analysis/statistics/corruption/Western_balkans_corruption_report_2011_web.pdf. Accessed 24 June 2013.

Chapter 5
Police Integrity in Estonia

Birgit Vallmüür

Abstract This chapter addresses the context for and the nature of integrity among the Estonian police—a police agency with a long but disrupted history. The data on police corruption are based on a study carried out among the Public Order Police in Estonia in 2013. One hundred and nine respondents provided their opinions about 11 hypothetical cases of police misconduct, including seriousness of misconduct, appropriate and expected discipline for such misconduct, and the extent to which such misconduct would be protected by the code of silence. The findings suggest that, although all of the scenarios studied were seen as relatively serious, strongly believed to be violations of organizational rules, and dismissal was seen most often as the appropriate and expected outcome for such behaviors, there was a considerable reluctance toward reporting such behaviors. These results echo a wider tendency in Estonian society, namely a considerable reluctance to report corruption.

Keywords Estonia · Police integrity · Protestantism · Survey · Whistle-blower

Contemporary Estonia: A Brief Overview

The Republic of Estonia is located in northeastern Europe, bordering the Baltic Sea and the Gulf of Finland, Latvia, and Russia. Estonia regained its independence from the Soviet Union in 1991 and is a member state of the European Union (EU) since 2004, member of the Schengen area since 2007, and it joined the euro area in 2011.

With a population of 1.31 million (Statistics Estonia 2014) and the total area of 45,227 km^2, Estonia is one of the smallest and most sparsely populated countries in

---

I gratefully acknowledge the feedback given by Priit Suve for the chapter during its composition stage as well as the help provided by Sanja Kutnjak Ivković and Maria R. Haberfeld during the editorial process.

B. Vallmüür (✉)
BV Consulting Ltd., Tallinn, Estonia
e-mail: bv@bvc.ee

S. Kutnjak Ivković, M. R. Haberfeld (eds.), *Measuring Police Integrity Across the World*,
DOI 10.1007/978-1-4939-2279-6_5

the EU (Eurostat 2014a). However, the society is culturally diverse, as nationalities other than Estonian make up about 30% of the population: Russians 25.2%, Ukrainians 1.7%, Byelorussians 1.0%, Finns 0.6% (Statistics Estonia 2013a).

With the highest gross domestic product (GDP) per capita among the former Soviet republics, Estonia is listed as a "high-income economy" by the World Bank (2015), an "advanced economy" by the International Monetary Fund (2014) and has been an Organization for Economic Cooperation and Development (OECD) member since 2010 (OECD 2014). However, its GDP per capita in purchasing power standard (PPS) still reached only 71% of the EU28 average in 2012 (Eurostat 2013) demonstrating a considerable unfavorable difference with numerous European countries.

Estonian Police

History

The establishment date of Estonian police is officially considered to be November 12, 1918 (Police and Border Guard Board 2014a). On that day, the first step to take the police over from German authorities was taken under orders from the Provisional Government of Estonia, and Estonian militia was set up within a very short period and entrusted to local self-governments. In 1919, the militia in Estonia was abolished and a state-controlled police force was set up effective as of January 1, 1920 (Leps 2000, p. 92–93).

Under the Soviet rule, as of September 1, 1940, the Estonian police were disbanded (Leps 2000, p. 92–93). The Estonian police stopped to exist from the legal and administrative as well as the personnel perspectives while Soviet judicial, police, security, and other administrative institutions were established (see Raun 2001, p. 149–154). In 1990, as a result of negotiations in Moscow, the Estonian Ministry of the Interior became excluded from the Soviet-wide centrally controlled union–republic system and was subordinated to Estonian authorities solely. By the government decree of November 20, 1990, the State Police Department of the Estonian Ministry of the Interior was established (Leps 2000, p. 92–93).

The militia was replaced by police on March 1, 1991 (Police and Border Guard Board 2014a). Therefore, the reestablishing of the Estonian police started already during the Soviet era, as the independence of the country was regained later—on August 20, 1991. Nineteen police prefectures were established in November 1991. In 2004, these prefectures were reconfigured into four large prefectures: North, West, East, and South (Police and Border Guard Board 2014a).

Contemporary Organization

On January 1, 2010, the Police Board, Central Criminal Police, Public Order Police, Border Guard Board, and Citizenship and Migration Board were merged. The preconditions for the merging of the police and border guard were set already by the accession of Estonia to the Schengen visa space in 2007, as lifting border control at internal borders of the Schengen area simultaneously brought along the requirement of using compensatory measures in the border territories, making it mostly the task of Public Order Police. Merging the agencies also had the purpose of combining the resources (e.g., people, funds, and the equipment) thus bringing internal security under one management and enabling developing the field as a whole (Police and Border Guard Board 2014b).

On the basis of the former police prefectures, border guard territories and regional offices of Citizenship and Migration Board, four territorial prefectures were created and incorporated into Police and Border Guard Board forming one authority as of 2012 (Police and Border Guard Board 2014b). Thus, the director general of the Police and Border Guard Board heads the merged structure consisting of the four units of main work areas (i.e., border guard, public order, criminal police, citizenship, and migration) and the property unit, all led by the respective deputy director generals, four prefectures (North, South, East, and West) headed by the respective prefects, as well as the separate internal audit and internal control bureaus (Police and Border Guard Board 2014c).

This has led Police and Border Guard Board becoming one of the largest state agencies in Estonia (Police and Border Guard Board 2014b). According to July 1, 2013 data received from the Police and Border Guard Board (Police and Border Guard Board 2013), the total number of people employed (excluding those temporarily absent) in the Public Order Police was 2005 (1656 police officers and 349 civil service officials, including 7 employment contract employees[1]).

At the same time, the proportion of women of the total number of people employed in the Public Order Police (including those temporarily absent, e.g., due to maternity leave) was 38% (32% of police officers and 67% of civil service officials and employees) (Police and Border Guard Board 2013). As the proportion of women in Estonian police is by far the highest among European police services (Institut de Seguretat Pública de Catalunia 2013), thus making it a unique police organization, this characteristic and its possible implications for police integrity are worthy of being addressed separately, but it is out of the scope of this chapter.

The Police and Border Guard Board has no diversity policy (Institut de Seguretat Pública de Catalunia 2013). Also, no reliable data on the nationality of the police officers and employees are available, as the Police and Border Guard Board does not collect the data on the nationality (Police and Border Guard Board 2013). The

[1] The Civil Service Act (2012) is applied to the police with specifications provided for by specific laws differentiates between officials (a person who is in the public-law service) and employees (recruited for the job in an authority, which does not involve the exercise of official authority but only work in support of the exercise of official authority and working under an employment contract).

data are partly available as they were collected by the Police Board, but now they are missing for about 20–25 % of employees (Police and Border Guard Board 2013). According to a study (Drapanauskene 2013) carried out in the beginning of 2013, 15 % of the officials in the Police and Border Guard Board belonged to an ethnic minority. The same study demonstrated that the largest proportion of ethnic minorities was in the North and East prefectures (25 and 35 %, respectively) and in the central units of the Police and Border Guard Board (10 %). That can be explained by the general disproportionate geographic distribution of ethnic minorities in Estonia, as in 2011, nationalities other than Estonians formed for example 80.5 % of the population in the Ida-Viru County in the Northeast Estonia and 38.3 % in the Harju County in the northern Estonia, while only 1.5 % in the Hiiu County in the western Estonia (Statistics Estonia 2013b).

The changes of the structure of the police organization have also manifested in the salary system of the organization. The organizations that were merged in 2010 brought along different salary systems; similar positions could result in different salaries. A salary reform was carried out in the merged Police and Border Guard Board for the first time as late as in 2013. According to the Ministry of the Interior (XII Riigikogu Shorthand report 2013), the border guard was the work area with the largest proportion (90 %) of employees whose salaries were increased, indicating the police work area had relatively higher salaries under the coexisting system.

According to the same report, the fixed average salary in the Police and Border Guard Board in December 2012 was 923 €, very close to the national average of 916 € (Statistics Estonia 2013c). The average salary increased to 999 € in January 2013, when the national average was 900 € (Statistics Estonia 2013c). However, the report pointed out that the average for the police officers was about 1052 € and the average for the civil service officials was 867 €. Therefore, the average salary of police officers was higher than that of the employees in Estonia in general and thus police officers should neither complain of lack of fairness within the organization nor have justifications to engage in corrupt behavior to provide for basic necessities.

Police Integrity

This chapter provides an overview of the context and explores the nature of police integrity in Estonia. Borrowing the definition by Klockars et al. (1997), police integrity is the normative inclination among police to resist temptations to abuse the rights and privileges of their occupation. The nature of policing in any society is linked to its history, and therefore the social, economic, demographic, as well as political factors that have shaped the given state should be considered for an analysis of police work to be adequate (Haberfeld 2004).

Estonia is a post-Soviet country. Thus, the consequences of the Soviet past and the short history of democracy will be addressed. Therefore, in this chapter considerable emphasis will be put on aspects that are specific for Estonia among the other post-Soviet countries such as matters of nationality and religious legacies. However, in addition to the general context of the society, aspects specific to the police organization can be expected to influence the police integrity. An approach, labeled the theory of police integrity, that combines the organizational aspects as well as includes the influence of the larger environment, has been developed by Klockars and colleagues (e.g., Klockars and Kutnjak Ivković 2004; Klockars et al. 1997). Their framework rests on four pillars: quality of official rules, quality of the agency's internal control of misconduct, decreasing the code of silence, and the influence of the larger environment.

As the definition of police integrity implies, the nature of temptations may vary. The framework used for the survey acknowledges that police officers are faced with various forms of temptations, such as corruption, use of excessive force, and other possibilities of abusing the rights and privileges policing exposes them to (Klockars et al. 2006, 2004). Specifically, as police integrity may vary both across different forms of misconduct, as well as across different levels of seriousness within the same form of misconduct, the methodology has been designed to include scenarios describing a variety of forms of police misconduct, and also provides examples of different levels of seriousness of behaviors within the same form.

In order to provide an overview of the context of police integrity in Estonia, the first part of this chapter starts from the forth pillar of the integrity theory and analyzes societal factors, including its historic legacy, that influence corruption and reporting observed corruption in the society at large. Then, the chapter will address separately the matters of official rules, the agency's internal control of misconduct, and decreasing the code of silence. The second part of this chapter provides an overview of a survey measuring the level of police integrity among Estonian police officers.

Political Context and its Implications for Tolerating and Reporting Corruption

Estonia evolved relatively rapidly from Soviet-style command economy to the free market and integration with western Europe (Norris and Inglehart 2011). However, the country has still been categorized (see Norris and Inglehart 2011) as a newer democracy based on Freedom House ratings and the temporal criterion of less than 20 years of experience with democracy.[2] The significance of the temporal aspect of democracy is especially important when considering the context for corruption, as long the exposure to democracy has been shown to predict lower corruption (e.g., Treisman 2000). Similarly, Gerring and Thacker (2004) demonstrated that the long-term democratic rule tends to lead to lower levels of political corruption, supporting the view that the influence of democracy should be understood through its cumulative effects rather than its current actual degree. Although, part of the negative correlation between democracy and corruption has been shown to result from

[2] One should note that in 2014, the Freedom House (2014) rating continues to be "free" and the country has been democratic for 23 years.

the tendency of democracies being wealthier (Lipset and Lenz 2000), the possible influence of Estonian political past should still be considered.

Sandholtz and Taagepera (2005) suggest, communism-created structural incentives for corrupt behaviors became so widespread, that they became built into the culture of these societies as prevailing social norms and practices, thus the transition toward democracy and market economies has not yet erased the culture of corruption. Not only does it provide an explanation for the context in which public services are provided, but also it predicts the future. For example, Sandholtz and Taagepera (2005) claim that, although cultures change, the change happens relatively slowly. Thus, former communist countries can be expected to wrestle with relatively high levels of corruption for decades.

Interestingly, Inglehart and Baker (2000) demonstrated that Estonia, with the rest of the "ex-Communist/Baltic" group, has high secular–rational values on the traditional secular–rational dimension, as well as high survival values on the survival/self-expression dimension. They suggested that, contrary to other societies, Estonia with Latvia, Lithuania, Russia, Belarus, and Bulgaria appeared to be moving away from secular–rational and self-expression values, as due to the result of the collapse of the economic, social, and political systems of the Soviet Union, there was an increasing emphasis on both survival values, as well as traditional values. Namely, the former Soviet countries appear to show a bigger emphasis on values characterizing a perceived need for moving quickly toward Western prosperity (Jackson 2002). These orientations, however, are linked to corruption as a stronger survival orientation increases corruption, while a stronger secular–rational orientation has an opposite effect (Sandholtz and Taagepera 2005).

In case of Estonia, there is one more factor that plays a role in shaping the views toward corruption—the Nordic influence. Many Estonians have felt a strong affinity for Scandinavia for decades and the interaction between Estonians and Finns, supported by proficiency in Finnish language among numerous Estonians, provided familiarity with western way of life and making it easier to shed the Soviet cultural legacy and increase the connections after regaining independence (Panagiotou 2001). Continuing close ties with the Nordic countries (ranking low on corruption) shapes Estonian political and social life; however, according to Uslaner (2008), even that should not be expected to change the Estonian mindsets in the near future.

The example of the Nordic influence, which has been a factor specifically influencing Estonia among other post-Soviet countries, suggests there can be other, country-specific factors. Similarly, Rees and Miazhevich (2009) point out that although the conceptualization and research of ethics in post-Soviet countries often assume universality of ethical norms, placing these countries under the general umbrella of former Soviet states ignores the influence of sociocultural factors in these societies by overlooking the significant differences of nationality and religious legacies. Therefore, also the cultural background of Estonia should be considered when addressing ethical norms and integrity.

Cultural Context and its Implications for Tolerating Corruption

According to Gallup 2009 ranking, Estonia was the least religious country in the world. In 2011, the most prevalent religion was reported to be Orthodoxy (16 % are affiliated with it) with Lutheranism (10 % are affiliated with it) being the second for the first time (Statistics Estonia 2011). Therefore, looking beyond the latest data and considering the religious past is of notable importance to characterize the cultural background of Estonia.

Especially so, when considering its influence on corruption, as the two most dominant religions have different views on values and individual responsibility. Namely, the Orthodox Churches tend to be more accepting of human weakness as the clergy have the authority to free the individual of some sense of responsibility resulting in the acceptance of human frailty and of the assumption that no one can be saint (Lipset and Lenz 2000). On the other hand, the Protestant ethos, suggesting individuals are personally responsible for avoiding sin, causes norm-adhering behavior and is more likely to foster adherence to absolute values, especially so with respect to morals, and thus encourages attaining and institutionalizing virtue and destroying, or at least reducing, the influence of evil people, wicked institutions, and practices (Lipset and Lenz 2000).

Estonia is considered Protestant when classified by its historically predominant major religion (Norris and Inglehart 2011) and thus some authors (e.g., Davie 2003) claim Estonia belongs to Western (Lutheran) Europe, while others (e.g., Norris and Inglehart 2011) see Estonia as a Protestant ex-Communist society. At the same time, Martin (2005) argues Estonia with its post-Protestant secularity is one of the "secularist indoctrination" countries as religion in Estonia was historically out of alignment with ethnic tradition and national solidarity, and thus failed to reproduce itself under communist pressure. On the other hand, Madeley (2003) categorized Estonia due to the historic multi-confessional cultural background (Protestant and Orthodox) among territories of mixed confession.

Acknowledging the interplay of religious and ethnic differences and similarities, secularization tendencies, simultaneous identification with western and eastern Europe, the effect of national solidarity and communist pressure, makes the exercise of determining the dominant sources of moral standards and integrity complex and contradictory.

The Level of Corruption and Informing of Corrupt Behavior in Estonia

As suggested above (e.g., Inglehart and Baker 2000; Sandholtz and Taagepera 2005; Uslaner 2008), the Soviet legacy continues to influence the cultural context of corruption. However, possibly due to the combination of the various factors discussed above, Estonia has had the least corruption among the central and eastern European countries from 2009 to 2013 according to the Transparency International Corruption Perception Index. It reached for the first time the score of 6.0 in 2004 and a score of 68 in 2013[3] (Transparency International 2014). The biggest shortcomings influencing the ranking for the recent years (i.e., in 2011 and 2012) stemmed from political corruption. The increase in the score in 2013 was possibly influenced by the new Anti-Corruption Act (2012) coming into force in April 2013 and the new Anti-Corruption Strategy 2013–2020 being approved by the government in October 2013 (Transparency International Estonia 2013a).

Assessing how common whistle-blowing in Estonia is very difficult, as related research is minimal and there are no statistics on the subject other than the respective telephone hotline and corruption surveys. The 2009 country report (Transparency International Estonia 2009) could still claim that there was neither any known case of whistle-blower harassment in the public sector nor were there examples of public officials having been prosecuted for not reporting corrupt activities. According to a more recent similar report, there are still no statistics or data on instances where an official has informed the authorities about corruption, nor are there any cases where sanctions have been applied for not reporting but there has been wide media coverage on a case concerning removal of Narva[4] city's Property and Economy Department's director placeholder, which is one of the few public cases where an official's whistle-blowing has resulted in potential retaliation (Asso Prii 2012).

Previous studies have shown that the readiness to report corruption in Estonia has been one of the lowest in the EU and reporting corruption has been considered unnecessary (Transparency International Estonia 2013b). For example, surveys conducted by the Ministry of Justice (2007; 2010) showed that only 1 % of the general population reported corruption that they had personally experienced to law enforcement authorities in both 2006 and 2010 while the number among civil servants was somewhat higher (5 % in 2006 and 13 % in 2010). Even prosecutors and judges have admitted they are not keen on reporting wrongdoing to law enforcement (Ministry of Justice 2011).

However, according to the latest poll (i.e., Saar Poll 2013c), the attitudes toward whistle-blowing have improved and the general attitude toward whistle-blowers is positive (Transparency International Estonia 2013c). Namely, when asked whether people would be approving toward a whistle-blower, 80.5 % of the society would be approving and only 10.9 % condemning. Interestingly, the Estonian society in general is rather equally split based on whether people believe that it is possible to report corruption or the possibility of it without negative consequences to the whistle-blower (43.0 %) or not (45.5 %).

The 1999 Anti-Corruption Act guaranteed the whistle-blower anonymity only if formally requested, unless the whistle-blowing was motivated by personal gain or other "low motives," or if the criminal process required questioning the whistle-blower as a witness in a criminal case. Therefore, there was no direct regulation on

[3] On the scale from 1 to 100 following an updated methodology that has been used since the Transparency International Corruption Perception Index 2012 (Transparency International 2012).

[4] A city located at the eastern extreme point of Estonia in the Ida-Viru County in Northeast Estonia.

whistle-blowers' protection (other than guarantees of anonymity is so requested) but, in the case when the disciplinary sanction (including the dismissal from the office) had been imposed on the public official, the person had a right to contest that decision in court and a right to be restored in the office or be awarded damages if the person decided to forgo the option of being restored in office (Transparency International Estonia 2009).

The new Anti-Corruption Act (2012) has replaced the obligation to inform of any knowledge of corruption with prohibition to conceal acts. Although the old law was more stringent on the book, it has not been enforced and remained dead letter on paper; there were no cases of someone being punished for failing to report a corrupt activity. The new law is expected to be a rule that can be followed and implemented (Transparency International Estonia 2009). Thus, the future effect of this change can be considered ambiguous and the willingness to inform of corruption may become even more important than previously.

The new act also increased regulation on ensuring the anonymity of the whistle-blower by guaranteeing confidentiality of the information, unless the whistle-blower signs a release document. Furthermore, the act also strengthens the whistle-blower's role by ensuring that, if the whistle-blower is included in the investigation of the case, it is done in a manner that will not violate his/her confidentiality. The whistle-blower's protection is also increased by the court's enforcement of the principles of equal treatment (although whistle-blowing is not mentioned in the Equal Treatment Act, it is not excluded either) and by applying the reversed burden of proof regarding motives of the alleged discrimination. These changes could lead to higher willingness to report cases of corruption in the future.

Organizational Rules on Misconduct in Estonia's Police

The Police and Border Guard Act (2009) regulates what is considered disciplinary misconduct in the police and what types of disciplinary sanctions can be used. The act states that a police officer who has committed a disciplinary offense should have a disciplinary sanction imposed in proportion to the nature and gravity of the offense committed. The act lists disciplinary offenses as: wrongful nonperformance or unsatisfactory performance of functions; wrongful causing of danger of or actual damage to the property of an administrative agency; an indecent act, meaning a wrongful act which is in conflict with generally recognized moral standards or ethical standards set for officials, or which discredits an official or administrative agency, regardless of whether the act is committed in or out of the service.

The disciplinary sanctions that can be imposed for disciplinary violations on police officers in Estonia according to the Police and Border Guard Act (2009) are: a reprimand; a fine of up to ten times the daily wage of the officer; reduction of salary up to 30% for up to 3 months; demotion in service rank by one service rank for 1 year; and release from the service.

Internal rules of procedure of the Police and Border Guard Board (Politsei- ja Piirivalveameti töökord 2010) outline the concepts of "serious violations of duties," "loss of trust," and "dishonorable acts." The list of "serious violations of duties" is not fixed and only the examples are provided in the document (e.g., liable nonperformance of duties; performing duties in violation of the norms; if the act harms another person either materially or physically; not being present at duty for more than 3 h if serious consequences arose; being on duty under the influence of alcohol; forgery of documents; passing on information with restricted access or making it public). A police officer can be dismissed for engaging in any of these.

According to the same document, "loss of trust" may be caused by liable nonperformance of duties that caused a destruction, damage, or a loss of goods belonging to or under the responsibility of the Police and Border Guard Board. A "dishonorable act" is an act, performed either on or off duty, which contradicts common moral standards or ethical requirements expected from officials, or discredits the official or the police.

Corruption in Estonia's Police

The number of corruption crimes in Estonia has remained relatively stable from 2009 to 2012. In 2012, out of the 193 corruption crimes registered, 32 were cases of abuse of authority,[5] 105 were cases of bribery (accepting and granting of gratuities and bribes), and 28 were cases of embezzlement. The area with the highest number of registered corruption cases (46 in 2012), excluding the abuse of authority, is legal protection (i.e., Security Police Board, Policc, Tax and Customs Board) (Sööt 2013).

However, the offering of money or services is not always followed by accepting these and, thus, the statistics of registered cases may provide a distorted view about the integrity of the officials. In 2012, the officials of the public service were the suspects in 66 % of the cases; legal protection was the area with the smallest respective proportion (52 % or 24 out of 46) (Sööt 2013). As corruption crimes are often committed by the same individuals, the sole statistics do not provide an accurate understanding on how many officials were involved. According to the same report (Sööt 2013), in the legal protection area, there were 25 separate incidents, but 54 % of the cases involved the same officials. Particularly interesting is one incident in the Security Police Board that resulted in registering 12 corruption crimes forming a fourth of all cases registered in the legal protection area (Sööt 2013). In 2012, out of the 46 corruption cases (excluding abuse of authority) registered in the legal protection area, 41 % (19 cases) involved the police (Sööt 2013). Out of these, police

[5] Abuse of authority is not considered as corruption in its classic sense in Estonia and thus viewed separately in statistics (Sööt 2011).

officers were the suspects in 12 cases[6] (Ministry of Justice 2013). In addition, police officers were also the suspects in 18 cases of abuse of authority (Ministry of Justice 2013), making the abuse of authority the most widespread type of registered misconduct among the police.

As abuse of authority, which is not seen as classic type of corruption in Estonia, as mentioned above, is strongly represented in general statistics as well as in police statistics, it should be viewed separately. The cases of abuse of authority tend to involve the police or security guards. For example, of the 40 cases registered in 2010, police officer was the suspect in the majority (20) of the cases, while in addition to these other suspects were an assistant police officer (1), a municipal police officer (2), a security guard (5), a prison guard (3), a tax and customs official (2), and for the remaining cases the suspect could not be determined based on the statistics. Thus, in 2010, the abuse of authority formed the majority of the 29 police corruption cases registered (Sööt 2011).

However, a large number of cases of abuse of authority have throughout the years been terminated upon the occurrence of circumstances precluding criminal proceedings based on the Code of Criminal Procedure (Sööt 2010). For example, in 2010, out of the 63 cases that were taken to the court and closed, 41 were terminated upon occurrence of circumstances precluding criminal proceedings, and 3 subjects were convicted of abuse of authority (Sööt 2011).

These absolute numbers may be part of a reason why Estonians trust their rescuers and police—combining the "full confidence" and "mostly trust" categories of a poll carried out in 2012, the rescuers came in first with the 95 % of the respondents showing a lot of confidence and the police being second with the 83 % of the respondents showing confidence as well (ERR 2013). According to another set of studies (Saar Poll 2013a, b) on public confidence in the national defense agencies, the most trusted was the rescue service, followed by the defense forces and the police; police were the third most trusted institution with 77–83 % of the respondents expressing a lot of confidence in the police (Saar Poll 2013a, b). The police and the rescue service have had the most stable level of support in recent years (Saar Poll 2013a). The trust in the police is not only general but also transcends to specific issues, such as the fair treatment of rich and poor victims by the police. This is the area in which Estonia, like the Netherlands, Denmark, and Finland, scores relatively well compared to other European countries (European Social Survey 2010).

Addressing the prevalence of misconduct in the police also requires considering the context and ease of reporting observed violations. A Transparency International country report published in 2009 on whistle-blower's protection concluded that, compared to other public sector organizations in Estonia, the Police Board's system for whistle-blowing was the most advanced one with very detailed internal disclosure systems.

[6] Out of these twelve cases, was charged with accepting gratuities, four for accepting a bribe, one for accepting a bribe by a group, one for arranging the receipt of gratuities, one for granting of gratuities, and four for counterfeiting or falsifying documents (Ministry of Justice 2013).

Measuring the Level of Tolerance of Corruption in the Police

Discussing the complex set of factors that have influenced the context for police work and corruption in Estonia indicates that police culture could be intolerant to moderately tolerant of corruption. The Estonian context also indicates that police officers may not be willing to report misconduct because of the small size of the country and its police. Also, the relatively negative view on whistle-blowing due to the Soviet past and the fear of negative consequences in general can be detrimental in curtailing police officers' willingness to report misconduct. However, these claims do not rely on the results of actually measuring the views on misconduct among the Estonian police or comparing these to the views of police officers in other countries. Therefore, using the survey instrument developed by Klockars and colleagues (e.g., Klockars and Kutnjak Ivković 2004; Klockars et al. 1997) to carry out a larger cross-cultural study of police integrity, the level of tolerance of police misconduct and related opinions among the Estonian police are measured.

The questionnaire, consisting of 11 hypothetical scenarios, is designed to measure and gain an understanding of officers' perceptions of the seriousness of different types of misconduct, their support for disciplinary consequences for it, as well as their willingness to report misconduct and beliefs about the attitudes of their colleagues. The 11 hypothetical scenarios were used in their original wording in the Estonian study, as no adjustments were needed to use these in the Estonian context. Also, no changes were made in the wording of disciplinary options (i.e., none, verbal reprimand, written reprimand, period of suspension without pay, demotion in rank, dismissal) to enable international comparison. The options included in the survey enabled differentiating between reprimands to include a less formal sanction between "none" and a "written reprimand" and replaced the Estonian two monetary sanctions (a fine of up to ten times the daily wage of the officer and the reduction of salary up to 30 % for up to 3 months) with a "period of suspension without pay."

The Sample

All police officers and employees in the field of Public Order Police are assigned an e-mail account, which is included into a general e-mail list of Public Order Police, providing a full coverage of the population. In April 2013, all officials from the Public Order Police were sent an e-mail invitation to participate in the survey. The invitations included a link to the web survey (using the SurveyMonkey tool). An e-mail reminder was sent by the head of the Public Order Police (i.e., deputy director general in the field of the Public Order Police) to the same list in the beginning of May 2013. However, the IP addresses were not collected to guarantee the full anonymity to respondents, especially because of the sensitivity of the subject being studied.

The size of the population receiving the survey can be estimated using the total number of people employed according to the July 1, 2013, data. There were 2005 total employees, including 1656 (82.6%) police officers and 349 (17.4%) civil service officials (including 7 (0.3%) employment contract employees). The e-mail list covers the whole Public Order Police including police officers, civil service officials, and the few employment contract employees.[7] The civil service officials and employment contract employees were not excluded from the population, as their duties are closely linked with police work, although not exercising police authority. The examples of the positions civil service officials in the Public Order Police hold are not only data input specialists and issuers of permits but also front desk officials and detention house personnel (Police and Border Guard Board 2014d). These positions exercise official authority, and may provide access to police data and thereby a possibility for misusing it, personal access to citizens with the possibility of verbally abusing them, as well as a possibility of engaging in excessive use of force.

In the end, 147 respondents started the survey, but numerous respondents did not complete the questionnaire. However, the respondents who did not complete the scenario typically did so relatively early (e.g., 12 quit after answering the first scenario, 4 additional ones after the second scenario) well before they reached the background questions. This would suggest that they decided to quit ahead of time and not to avoid answering background questions. Finally, 112 respondents completed the questionnaire. Out of these 112 officers who completed the survey, 3 were excluded from the analysis because they responded that they were not honest while they filled out the questionnaire. However, as one of the respondents who reported having filled in the questionnaire honestly, specified that "honest answer is a relative concept. Everything cannot be evaluated so specifically. You do not know how you would behave in reality," it cannot be concluded that the three excluded ones were purposefully dishonest, as they may have been unsure also. Regardless, in the end, the analyses will include 109 complete responses. Traditionally, the nonresponses tend to be a considerable concern in web surveys (Couper 2000). Indeed, this survey has a low response rate as well, between 5.4% (excluding partial completions) and 7.3% (including partial questionnaires) of the population.

The respondents came from all four prefectures: North (28.4%), South (29.4%), East (16.5%), and West (25.7%). The most widely represented assignment was constable (32.1%), followed by patrol (27.5%), administrative (18.3%), other, e.g., detention house personnel and control station officials (11.9%), detective/investigative (5.5%), juvenile (4.6%). The most widely represented rank was commissar (23.9%). Slightly less than one half of the respondents (45%) belonged to lower ranks than the commissar, and about one third (31%) to the higher ranks. The overwhelming majority of the respondents (63.3%) reported having no subordinates, while about one quarter (28.4%) had six or more.

While 31.2% of the respondents reported more than 20 years of service and only 11.9% reported 5 years of service or less, 22.9% reported being employed at

[7] For the sake of simplicity, the respondents are referred to as "police officers" when discussing the results of the survey.

the current police agency for more than 20 years and 22 % reported having been there 5 years or less. When considering years of service and time employed in the current agency, one should keep in mind that Estonian police was reestablished 22 years ago, which would suggest that about one quarter to one third of our officers have been police officers from the very beginning of the new Estonian police. Also, attending the academy is traditionally included in the years of service.

About three quarters of the respondents (72.5 %) were men and one quarter (27.5 %) were women. Although the percentage of female respondents in the sample is relatively high compared to the proportion of women in other police agencies across the world (Institut de Seguretat Pública de Catalunia 2013), it is on the lower side for Estonia where women account for about 38 % of the Public Order Police (Police and Border Guard Board 2013). Women were part of the new Estonian police since its reestablishment in 1991. The proportion of women increased steadily from 12.4 % in 1992, to 26.0 % in 2000, and 33.3 % in 2006. However, the presence of women in police was largely unnoticed until the beginning of 2000, when they became the majority among the applicants to the police school (Resetnikova 2006). By 2008, the proportion of women reached 35.4 %, but decreased by 2012 to 33.9 %, still leading among European police services, followed by the other two Baltic countries, Sweden and the Netherlands all below 29 % (Institut de Seguretat Pública de Catalunia 2013).

The majority of the respondents (91.7 %) identifying themselves as Estonians, 4.6 % as Russian, and 3.7 % as other. It is possible that the sample is biased toward Estonians and that various ethnic minorities are underrepresented in the sample. However, there are no reliable data on nationality in the Public Order Police. On the other hand, there is information about ethnic composition of the whole Police and Border Guard Board, although it is based on partial data. In particular, in 2013, about 15 % of the officials, whose nationality was known, belonged to an ethnic minority.

It is possible to argue that there is no ground to reason that those who refused to participate in the survey are somehow systematically different from respondents. However, due to the low response rate, it is possible that a unit nonresponse error occurred, but the magnitude of the potential bias cannot be assessed. Therefore, as the response rate is often used to measure how well the survey results can be generalized, the current study does not encourage generalizing.

The low response rate leads to consider the sample to be a voluntary sample. However, this creates the possibility of a voluntary response bias. Namely, although every member of the population had the possibility of being included in the survey and, thus, the probability that every respondent included in the sample could be determined, it was fully left up to each individual to decide whether to participate in the survey. As a probability-based sampling methodology is required to conduct statistical inference (Fricker 2008), no quantitative statements about the unobserved population are made based on this study and only the sample will be characterized.

The Results

Seriousness

The 11 scenarios were perceived to range in terms of seriousness—from the least serious scenario 1, describing gifts of food and other items of small value, to the most serious scenario 3, describing a theft of an expensive pocketknife from a crime scene. However, the variation was not extensive.

The rankings for the least serious and the most serious case were the same when assigning the rankings from respondents' own point of view and when estimating that of others. Comparing the means of respondents' own estimates of seriousness to how serious they expected other police officers in their agency to evaluate the same scenarios, revealed that for each scenario, the respondents evaluated themselves to consider these serious as more serious than they thought their colleagues would. In case of each and every scenario, the means for evaluations of own seriousness were higher than these for others. However, considering the rule of thumb established by Klockars et al. (2006), only the differences of 0.50 or larger are considered as meaningful. In the current study, none were considered.

The scenario of gifts of food and other items of small value (scenario 1) was perceived as the least serious both from own perspective (M=3.77) and according to what was expected of other police officers (M=3.28). The second least serious case was perceived to be an insulting of a motorist (scenario 7: M=3.98), closely followed by the case of a cover-up of a car accident (scenario 8: M=4.02).

The analysis of others' estimates of seriousness revealed that four cases had nearly identical mean values: a cover-up of a car accident (scenario 8: M=3.83); insulting a motorist (scenario 7: M=3.86); punching a handcuffed man (scenario 6: M=3.87); offering days off for errands (scenario 5: M=3.88). Interestingly, it is the lack of variety from the perspective of seriousness that can be considered noteworthy in this case. Namely, striking a handcuffed man and covering up a car accident of a police officer caused while driving under the influence are expected to be seen similar in seriousness by most police officers in their agency with insulting a motorist and offering days off for errands.

Therefore, one could say that it is the case of gifts of food and other items of small value that clearly stands out as the least serious. It is noteworthy regarding the scenario that two respondents found it necessary to comment on it at the end of the questionnaire. One of them pointed out that this case was the most difficult to evaluate as the police organization has contracts with partnering organizations that offer discounts on services to police officers and some restaurants offer all police officers free coffee. The respondent suggested that seriousness would be completely different, if only some select police officers would receive small gifts for a behavior that specifically favors a specific restaurant they have a connection with. Another respondent pointed out that diners, petrol stations, and similar, try to attract police officers, so police would be more visible in the area and the location would feel safer, with half-priced coffee or discount on lunch. However, as one still has to pay for these, it is not perceived as a considerable violation by the respondent.

The most serious violation was perceived to be the case of taking an expensive pocketknife from a crime scene (scenario 3) both according to the own perception of the respondents (M=4.89) and that expected from the majority of the colleagues (M=4.59). The case of false report on drug on dealer (scenario 10) was perceived as the second most serious violation both according to the own perception of the respondents (M=4.63) and according to what was expected from the majority of the colleagues (M=4.51). Thus, a common characteristic of the case judged as the most serious (a theft of an expensive pocketknife from a crime scene), and the second most serious case (false reporting of possession of heroin), is providing false evidence to frame a suspect for a crime they did not commit. Also, in both of these scenarios, the respondents expected other police officers to share their views on the seriousness of these cases and similarly for the majority of other cases.

Interestingly, the case of fatally shooting the person in the back (scenario 4: M=4.56) was ranked as serious as the case of referral to auto body shop (scenario 9: M=4.56). Thus, these two scenarios share the third and fourth rank of seriousness from the point of view of the respondents. However, two comments by respondents may explain why police officers appear to be somewhat forgiving when evaluating the seriousness of the scenario of shooting. One of them asked for the reason why the description of the case of a police officer who had been attacked previously did not mention anything about psychological counseling. The other pointed out the questionnaire lacked an option of making suggestions and added that, in every organization there should definitely be a psychologist, as it would decrease pressure, and enable talking about worries and problems. Thus, one could suspect that, considering the system of psychological counseling being insufficient, responses to this scenario may reflect perceptions among the police officers, that in such post-traumatic situations the blame is seen as solely not only on the person but also on the organization.

Yet, when considering the seriousness the respondents expected their colleagues to assign to these cases, then while the third most serious violation was the unjustifiable use of deadly force (scenario 4: M=4.43), and the case of failing to arrest a friend (scenario 2: M=4.18) was fourth, and the case of receiving a kickback for auto body shop referral (scenario 9: M=4.16) was fifth. Thus, in sum, it may be argued that framing a suspect by either false reporting of finding drug on a person or by adding to their crime an additional pocketknife, and also thereby stealing, as well as unjustifiable use of deadly force by shooting an unarmed man in the back are seen as the most serious violations.

The standard deviation (SD) of the sample is included to indicate how large the stretch of opinions was—the wider the stretch, the less the respondents shared the views of others. The answers to scenario 1 were the most diverse (SD=1.39) and the respondents agreed to most on the seriousness of the scenario 11 (SD=0.58). Table 5.1 indicates there is a relationship between how serious a case is considered and the diversity of opinions on it: The opinions differed the most on the least serious cases and were the most similar in the most serious cases.

Table 5.1 Officers' views about the seriousness of misconduct, violation of rules, and officers' willingness to report it: the Estonian sample

Scenario number and description	Own seriousness			Others' seriousness			Mean difference (own–others)	Violation of rules			Own willingness to report			Others' willingness to report			Mean difference (own–others)
	M	SD	Rank	*M*	SD	Rank		*M*	SD	Rank	*M*	SD	Rank	*M*	SD	Rank	
Scenario 1: free meals, gifts from merchants	3.77	1.39	1	3.28	1.29	1	0.49	4.39	1.06	1–2	3.14	1.38	2	2.66	1.10	1	0.48
Scenario 2: failure to arrest friend with warrant	4.40	1.05	7	4.18	1.04	8	0.22	4.72	0.69	8	3.86	1.22	8	3.50	1.05	8	0.36
Scenario 3: theft of knife from crime scene	4.89	0.58	11	4.59	0.77	11	0.30	4.93	0.44	11	4.41	1.03	11	4.01	0.98	10	0.40
Scenario 4: unjustifiable use of deadly force	4.56	1.01	8–9	4.43	0.99	9	0.13	4.60	0.87	5	4.39	1.09	10	4.31	1.04	11	0.08
Scenario 5: supervisor offers holiday for errands	4.31	1.15	5	3.88	1.30	5	0.43	4.39	1.04	1–2	3.68	1.29	6	3.28	1.27	6	0.39
Scenario 6: officer strikes prisoner who hurt partner	4.27	1.15	4	3.87	1.27	4	0.39	4.54	0.96	3	3.35	1.43	3	3.04	1.26	3	0.31
Scenario 7: verbal abuse of motorist	3.98	1.24	2	3.86	1.16	3	0.12	4.55	0.84	4	3.00	1.44	1	2.75	1.26	2	0.25
Scenario 8: cover-up of police DUI accident	4.02	1.26	3	3.83	1.14	2	0.19	4.64	0.87	6	3.36	1.44	4	3.10	1.17	4	0.26
Scenario 9: auto body shop 5 % kickback	4.56	0.88	8–9	4.16	1.06	7	0.40	4.67	0.84	7	3.66	1.35	5	3.22	1.24	5	0.44
Scenario 10: false report on drug on dealer	4.63	0.85	10	4.51	0.88	10	0.12	4.82	0.64	10	4.20	1.15	9	3.77	1.11	9	0.43
Scenario 11: Sgt. fails to halt beating	4.39	1.11	6	4.02	1.28	6	0.37	4.74	0.77	9	3.75	1.27	7	3.40	1.21	7	0.35

SD standard deviation, *DUI* driving under the influence

However, it should be noted that, for each case of the 11 scenarios, the answers on how serious these case was perceived by the respondents or how serious they expected their colleagues to consider these ranged from 1 to 5. That suggests that for each and every case there was at least one respondent in the sample who considered that scenario to be "not at all serious" and at least one respondent who expected that most police officers in their agency would consider that case as "not at all serious." At the same time, for each and every scenario there were also respondents who considered these cases as "very serious" or who expected most police officers in their agency to hold that opinion.

Violation of Official Rules

Behaviors described in all 11 scenarios would violate official rules in Estonia. The respondents tended to hold the same view. It is noteworthy, that the mean of the case being seen as a violation was very high in all cases ranging from 4.39 (scenario 1: free meals, gifts from merchants, and scenario 5: supervisor offers holiday for errands) to 4.93 (scenario 3: theft of knife from crime scene). In case of the former, 66 and 65 % of the respondents, respectively, were convinced that it would definitely be regarded as a violation of official policy in their agency, while in case of the later, the case that is also seen as the most serious scenario, 96 % of the respondents were of that opinion.

As seen with the opinions of seriousness, the SD of the sample demonstrates that the opinions differed the most (SD = 1.04 and SD = 1.06) on cases where the respondents on average were the furthest away from considering it to be definitely a violation (scenario 5: supervisor offers holiday for errands $M = 4.39$ and scenario 1: free meals, gifts from merchants $M = 4.39$, respectively) and were the most similar (SD = 0.44) in the case (scenario 3: theft of knife from crime scene) that was considered most definitely to be a violation ($M = 4.93$).

However, again, for each case of the 11 scenarios, the answers on if these cases were regarded as a violation of official policy in their agency ranged from 1 to 5. This demonstrates that, for each and every case, there was at least one respondent in the sample who considered that this behavior would "definitely not" be were regarded as a violation of official policy in their agency.

Appropriate and Expected Discipline

Ordinal scales were used for questions about discipline respondents considered appropriate for the hypothetical scenarios and what they expected to follow in their organization. Thus, their modal responses were analyzed, followed by the analysis of percentages in more detail to characterize the whole range of options selected by respondents as well as to look more closely at the least and most serious discipline options.

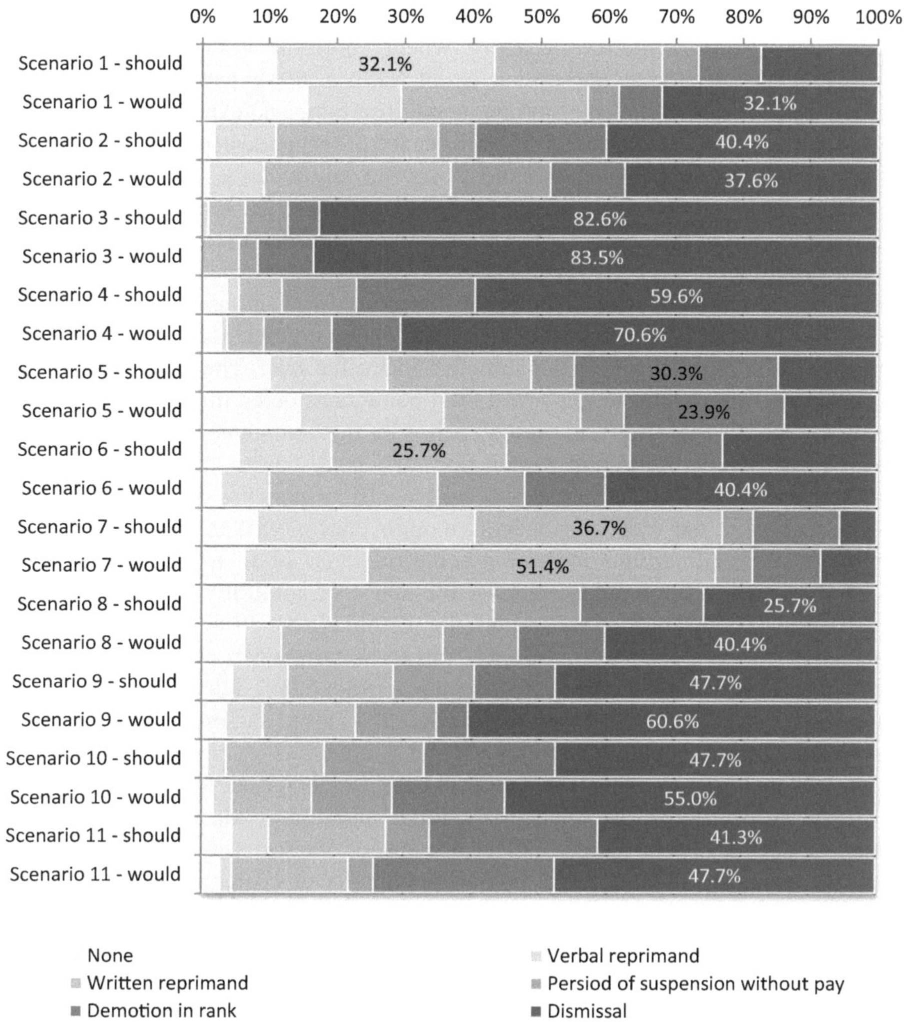

Fig. 5.1 Officers' views about the discipline the scenarios should and would receive: the Estonian sample

The general finding, as Fig. 5.1 illustrates, is that "dismissal" was the most frequent option both to be expected and perceived as appropriate—in 9 cases out of 11, the largest number of respondents expected a "dismissal" to follow and in 7 cases they also considered that to be an appropriate discipline. This may indicate that, according to the respondents, there is a somewhat greater general organizational intolerance toward misconduct, while as individuals, police officers tend to be more tolerant of misconduct.

Only in two cases, a discipline other than "dismissal" was expected to follow by the largest number of respondent. For scenario 5, where the supervisor offered days off for errands, the appropriate and expected discipline was considered to be "demotion in rank," while for scenario 7, where a motorist was insulted, a "written reprimand" was seen as an appropriate result that was also expected to follow.

In 9 cases out of 11, the appropriate modal discipline and expected modal discipline did not diverge, suggesting the preferences of respondents match the severity of disciplines that in their view are most likely to follow in the organization. Only in two scenarios (scenario 1: gifts of food and other items of small value; and scenario 6: punching a handcuffed man) the appropriate modal discipline and expected modal discipline diverged. In both cases, the respondents expected a dismissal to follow, while the most widely preferred discipline for such behavior would have been "verbal reprimand" for accepting gifts of food and other items of small value and a "written reprimand" for punching a handcuffed man. The less formal discipline for the former may be explained by it being considered the least serious violation (M=3.77; SD=1.39), as well as partly by the comments respondents made about the difficulty of differentiating it from official discounts.

The case of the scenario in which police officer punches a handcuffed man (scenario 6) and the most respondents though that a "written reprimand" is an appropriate discipline, thus indicating some tolerance of such behavior, is noteworthy. Namely, as pointed out above, the abuse of authority is the most widespread type of police misconduct reported in Estonia (Sööt 2011). However, a large number of cases of abuse, of authority tend to be terminated upon occurrence of circumstances precluding criminal proceedings (Sööt 2010). For example, in 2010, 41 cases out of 63 that were taken to the court and closed and only 3 subjects were convicted of abuse of authority (Sööt 2011).

However, it is noteworthy that, for every case, except for one, the answers for the preferred and expected disciplinary sanctions ranged from "dismissal" to "none." Thus, for each and every case out of 11, except for one scenario, there was at least one respondent in the sample who considered that for this behavior no discipline at all should or would follow. More specifically, across these ten scenarios from 0.9 to 11 % of respondents did not think a sanction should follow and 0.9 to 15.6 % did not think a sanction would follow, suggesting that although "dismissal" is the modal discipline, opinions range considerably across scenarios and among respondents.

As mentioned, for every case, except for one, the answers for the preferred and expected disciplinary sanctions ranged from "none" to "dismissal." The exceptional case was scenario 3 (theft of knife from crime scene). In this case, there were no respondents in the sample to suggest that no discipline should follow and the mildest preferred discipline was "verbal reprimand." Also, there were no respondents in the sample to expect no discipline or "verbal reprimand" to follow such behavior and the mildest expected discipline was "written reprimand."

This exceptional case echoes a tendency demonstrated in previous studies. Namely, the officers' views on appropriate and expected discipline tend to be related to their evaluations of the seriousness of the misconduct—generally, the more serious the behavior is considered, the more serious is the discipline that is considered to be appropriate (Kutnjak Ivković and Klockars 2004). Indeed, considering that all of the scenarios were seen as rather serious (e.g., none of the 11 cases would fall into the least serious group of having means of seriousness below or just above the midpoint of the scale 3; see Kutnjak Ivković and Klockars 2004), the harsh modal discipline—dismissal as the most frequent option both to be expected and perceived as appropriate—can be expected.

The most prominent view that "verbal reprimand" would be appropriate for accepting gifts of food and other items of small value (scenario 1) is an expected result, taking into consideration that it was seen as the least serious scenario as well. Interestingly, two written comments by respondents may be used to explain it, as one pointed out that the police organization has contracts with partnering organizations that offer discounts on services to police officers and some restaurants offer all police officers free coffee suggesting it makes the seriousness of the violation very difficult to evaluate. And the other claimed that diners, petrol stations, etc., try to attract police officers with half-priced coffee or discount on lunch, but as one still has to pay for these, it is not perceived as a considerable violation.

However, when looking at the general distribution of answers (see Fig. 5.1) and not only modes, another pattern emerges. In case of nine scenarios, respondents tend to find the expected discipline to be stricter than what is seen as appropriate. Namely, when combining the more formal sanctions (i.e., leaving out the option of no sanctions at all and "verbal reprimand") then the proportion of police officers who thought formal sanctions would follow was larger (ranging from 1.0% for scenario 3 to 13.7% for the scenario 1 and 15.7% for the scenario 7) than the proportion of police officers who thought these formal sanctions should follow. It seems that the general tendency is that police officers prefer somewhat milder discipline as appropriate than they expect their agencies to mete out. Potentially, they may personally tend to be more forgiving of misconduct than they expect the organization to be.

The general pattern does not apply to two scenarios. In case of one of these (scenario 10, false report on drug on dealer) the difference is minute (1.1%). However, when asked what disciplines should follow if a supervisor offered days off for running personal errands (scenario 5), a considerably larger percentage (8.2%) of police officers thought formal sanctions would be appropriate (72.5%) than they expected (64.3%) these to follow. The most widely chosen discipline for this violation was "demotion in rank," but while 30.3% of the respondents suggested it to be appropriate, only 23.9% believed it really be meted out. This suggests police officers believe that supervisors would be given more lenient discipline for using their position within the organization than they believe should follow.

Officers' Willingness to Report Misconduct

The respondents were asked about both their own willingness to report various types of misconduct described by the 11 cases as well as their perceptions of others' willingness to report such acts.

The data provide insight into the extent of the code of silence among the sample when examining the prevalence of police officers choosing not to report observed misconduct. Values 1 (i.e., "definitely not"[8]) and 2 are added together to characterize the code of silence among the sample while values 4 and 5 are combined to characterize the proportion of police officers who would report. The results characterizing the choice of not reporting, confirm that code of silence is certainly present among the surveyed police officers. The proportion of police officers who would not report a violation ranges from 7.3 to 38.5 % across scenarios and, depending on the scenario, between 6.4 and 45.9 % of respondents believed that the majority of the police officers in their organization would not report such acts. On the positive note, 36.7–85.3 % of police officers stated that they would report depending on the scenario and 21.1–80.7 % of the respondents expect the majority of police officers in their organization to report these violations.

While as much as 38.5 % of respondents would not report (with 21.1 % definitely not reporting) a police officer insulting a motorist (scenario 7) and 42.2 % do not expect their colleagues to report such behavior, the same proportion (38.5 %) would not report if their colleague accepted gifts of food and other items of small value (scenario 1) and 45.9 % believe the majority of police officers in their organization would not report it either.

Not as many but surprisingly close to one third (30.3 %) of police officers would not report witnessing a police officer punching a handcuffed man (scenario 6) and more than one third (33.9 %) believe the majority of the police officers in their organization would not report it. Similarly, a large proportion (28.4 %) of police officers would not report a colleague covering up a car accident of a police officer (scenario 8) and 30.3 % believe the majority of their colleagues would adhere to the code of silence is such a situation (see Fig. 5.2).

It is noteworthy, that both of these two cases involve a police officer violating rules by informally protecting or seeking revenge for harming another police officer. Namely, in the first of these two, it was a male partner of a young, female officer who received a black eye when responding to a bar fight, who punched the handcuffed combatant later saying, "Hurts, doesn't it." In the other case, where, instead of reporting an accident and offense, the person is driven home by a police officer on duty, the intoxicated driver was a police officer. That may indicate that violations performed to adhere to the code of silence or to revenge injustice toward other police officers are among these that may be seen as worthy of being protected by code of silence in turn.

The results of previous similar studies in other countries (e.g., Kutnjak Ivković and Klockars 2004) have shown the willingness to report misconduct appears to be directly related to the perceptions of the seriousness of the given act—the more serious the misconduct is perceived to be, the more likely the respondents were to claim they would report it. Similar results can be found in the Estonian study. In the two scenarios, the police officers considered the least serious (scenario 1: accepting gifts of food and other items of small value $M=3.77$, and scenario 7: insulting a motorist $M=3.98$), they were also the scenarios with the lowest means for willingness to report ($M=3.14$ and $M=3.00$, respectively), suggesting that the

[8] On the five-point scale, where five denoted "definitely report."

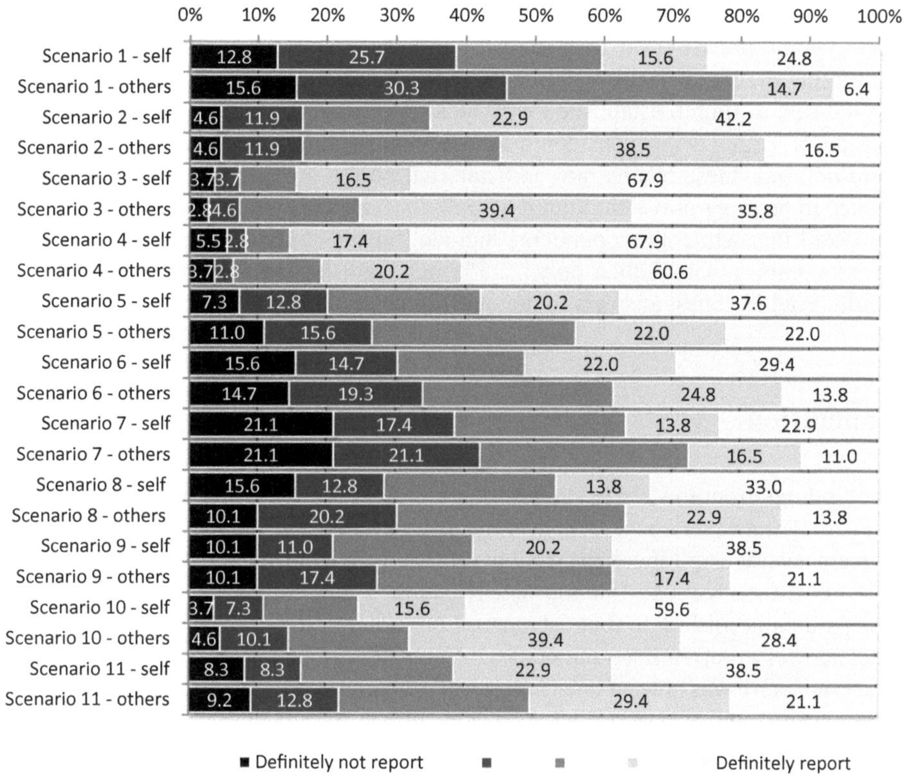

Fig. 5.2 The prevalence of code of silence among the officers of the Estonian sample and their expectations for others

cases considered the least serious would less likely be officially reported by the respondents. The scenario that was considered the most serious ($M=4.89$) by the respondents (scenario 3: theft of knife from crime scene) was also the one with the highest mean ($M=4.41$) for willingness to report among the respondents. The case (scenario 4: unjustifiable use of deadly force) with the second highest mean ($M=4.39$) for willingness to report by the respondents themselves was the one that the respondents expected other police officers to report the most likely ($M=4.31$), followed by scenario 3 (taking an expensive pocketknife $M=4.01$) that they themselves were most willing to report.

Again, the two cases where the willingness to report was the highest both among the respondents themselves, as well as anticipated from colleagues, had the smallest SDs indicating respondents holding most similar opinions. However, for every single case, the answers on the willingness to report by the respondents and on the expectation of willingness to report by most colleagues, vary from as little as one to as high as five with numerous respondents falling into each of these choices.

With no exceptions, when comparing the attitudes both toward seriousness and willingness to report, respondents expected to have higher moral standards than their colleagues—in case of each scenario the means for seriousness and willingness to report are lower (on average 0.29 for the former and 0.34 for the latter) when comparing their own views with the expectations about their colleagues. Considering the rule of thumb established by Klockars et al. (2006) of only the differences of 0.50 or larger being considered as meaningful, the differences in this sample were not. Yet, these results may indicate that police officers perceive the code of silence to be more prevalent than it actually is. The same tendency is supported by the detail that while all respondents included in the study reported answering the questionnaire honestly, then only 72.5% believed the majority of police officers would provide honest answers to the questionnaire.

Conclusion

The findings from this study suggest that although the scenarios were perceived to range in terms of seriousness on average, the variation was not extensive. While the officers' average opinions regarding the seriousness of misconduct have previously been used (see Kutnjak Ivković and Klockars 2004) to classify cases into three groups then according to that categorization, none of the cases would fall into the least serious group in Estonian context. Yet, it should be noted that for each of the scenarios there was at least one respondent who considered that situation to be "not at all serious" and at least one who expected that most police officers in their agency would consider that case as "not at all serious." At the same time, for each and every scenario there were also respondents who considered these cases as "very serious" or who expected most police officers in their agency to hold that opinion. Therefore, there is a considerable variety among the police officers regarding opinions on the seriousness of the scenarios as well as regarding their beliefs on what is the opinion of the majority of their colleagues. Also, for each scenario, the respondents believed that they consider these more serious than their colleagues would. However, these differences were not big enough to be considered meaningful (Klockars et al. 2006).

Similarly to considering all of the scenarios relatively serious, the respondents tended to consider these as violations of official rules with the mean of the case being seen as a violation ranging from 4.39 to 4.93. Yet, again, for each of situations described, there was at least one respondent in the sample who considered that this behavior would "definitely not" be regarded as a violation of official policy in their agency.

As all of the cases were seen as relatively serious and strongly believed to be violations of official rules, it is not unexpected that dismissal was the most frequent option expected and seen as appropriate—in 9 out of 11 scenarios, the largest number of respondents expected a dismissal to follow and in 7 cases they also considered that to be an appropriate discipline. This may suggest that, according to the respondents, there is a general organizational intolerance toward misconduct, while they individually are at times more forgiving. Namely, in two scenarios the appropriate modal discipline and expected modal discipline diverged. In both of these cases, the respondents expected a dismissal to follow. While the most widely preferred discipline for accepting gifts of food and other items of small value would have been verbal reprimand, which can be expected considering the gray area that is caused by official discounts available from some partnering organizations. Then surprisingly, a written reprimand was considered appropriate for punching a handcuffed man, suggesting the most respondents supported such a behavior not to be punished with one of the more serious options.

Yet, again, for every case, except for one, the answers for the preferred and expected disciplinary sanctions ranged from dismissal to none—for ten scenarios there was at least one respondent in the sample who considered that for this behavior no discipline at all should or would follow. The proportion of respondents who were of such opinions ranged across these ten scenarios with 0.9–11 % not thinking a sanction should follow and 0.9–15.6 % not thinking a sanction would follow. Thus, although dismissal is the modal discipline, opinions range considerably across scenarios and between respondents and at times considerable proportion of respondents believe a violation should or would not be disciplined.

However, when asked what disciplines should follow if a supervisor offered days off for running personal errands, 8.2 % more police officers thought formal sanctions would be appropriate compared to what they expected to follow. This suggests respondents believe that supervisors would be given less formal disciplines for using their position within the organization toward subordinates than they believe should follow, indicating possible intolerance toward injustice within the organization among the police officers.

A tendency of the respondents to form a close group and adhere to the code of silence also became evident from the results characterizing the choice of not reporting, with the proportion of police officers who would not report a violation ranging from 7.3 to 38.5 % across scenarios and 6.4 to 45.9 % believing that the majority of the police officers in their organization would not report such acts. On the other hand, 36.7–85.3 % of police officers claimed they would report and 21.1–80.7 % expected the majority of police officers in their organization to report these violations. Notably, some of the violations that were seen as worthy of code of silence in turn, were the ones that were performed to adhere to the code of silence in the first place or to revenge injustice toward other police officers.

Similarly to previous studies in other countries (e.g., Kutnjak Ivković and Klockars 2004) that have shown the willingness to report misconduct appears to be directly related to the perceptions of the seriousness of the given act, the cases considered the least serious would less likely be officially reported by the respondents, and the scenario that was considered the most serious was also the one with the highest mean for willingness to report among the respondents. However, for every single case the answers on the willingness to report by the respondents and on the expectation of willingness to report by most colleagues, varied between the extremes with numerous respondents falling into each of these choices. Therefore, it is possible to conclude that the code of silence is certainly present among the surveyed police officers regardless of the fact that violations were seen as relatively serious, strongly believed to be violations of organizational rules, and dismissal was seen most often as the appropriate and expected outcome of such behaviors.

References

Anti-corruption Act. (2012). RT I, 29.06.2012, 1; 01.04.2013.

Asso Prii. (2012). Providing an alternative to silence: Towards greater protection and support for whistleblowers in the EU. Country report: Estonia (Estonia: September 2012).

Avaliku teenistuse seadus [Civil Service Act]. (2012). RT I, 06.07.2012, 1; 01.04.2013.

Couper, M. P. (2000). Web surveys. A review of issues and approaches. *Public Opinion Quarterly, 64,* 464–494.

Davie, G. (2003). Patterns of religion in Western Europe: An exceptional case. In R. K. Fenn (Ed.), *The Blackwell companion to sociology of religion*. Malden: Blackwell.

Drapanauskene, O. (2013). Rahvusvähemuste esindatus Eesti sisejulgeolekustruktuurides, Sisekaitseakadeemia, Tallinn [Representation of ethnic minorities in Estonia internal security structures] Master's thesis.

ERR. (2013). Survey: Estonians trust rescuers and police, distrust the prime minister and political parties. ERR. January 3 2013. http://news.err.ee/politics/9cbf1203-8927-4682-80c2-cfee-4ac62af4. Accessed 29 July 2013.

European Social Survey. ESS5– (2010). Edition 3.0.

Eurostat. (2013). GDP per capita in PPS. http://epp.eurostat.ec.europa.eu/tgm/table.do?tab=table&init=1&plugin=1&language=en&pcode=tec00114. Accessed 9 March 2014.

Eurostat. (2014a). Population density. Inhabitants per km². http://epp.eurostat.ec.europa.eu/tgm/table.do?tab=table&init=1&plugin=1&language=en&pcode=tps00003. Accessed 9 March 2014.

Freedom House. (2014). http://www.freedomhouse.org/country/estonia. Accessed 9 March 2014.

Fricker, R. (2008). Sampling methods for web and e-mail surveys. In N. Fielding, R. M. Lee, & G. Blank (Eds.), *The SAGE handbook of online research methods*. London: SAGE Publications Ltd.

Gallup. (2009). What Alabamians and Iranians Have in Common. http://www.gallup.com/poll/114211/Alabamians-Iranians-Common.aspx. Accessed 29 March 2014.

Gerring J., & Thacker S. C. (2004). Political institutions and corruption: The role of unitarism and parliamentarism. *British Journal of Political Science, 34*(2), 295–330.

Haberfeld, M. R. (2004). The heritage of police misconduct. The case of the polish police. In C. B. Klockars, S. Kutnjak Ivković, & M. R. Haberfeld (Eds.), *The contours of police integrity*. Thousand Oaks: Sage.

Inglehart, R., & Baker, W. E. (2000). Modernization, cultural change, and persistence of traditional values. *American Sociological Review, 65*(1), 19–51.

Institut de Seguretat Pública de Catalunia. (2013). Women in Police Services in the EU. Facts and Figures. 2012. Edit. Lola Vallès. http://www20.gencat.cat/docs/interior/Home/MS%20-%20Institut%20de%20Seguretat%20Publica%20de%20Catalunya/02%20ambits%20dactuacio/3_Recerca/Projectes%20europeus/Women%20in%20Police%20Services/WOMEN%20IN%20POLICE%20SERVICES%20EU_2012.pdf. Accessed 9 March 2014.

International Monetary Fund. (2014). Republic of Estonia and the IMF. http://www.imf.org/external/country/EST/index.htm. Accessed 9 March 2014.

Jackson, T. (2002). The management of people across cultures: Valuing people differently. *Human Resource Management, 41*(4), 455–475.

Klockars, C. B., & Kutnjak Ivković S. (2004). Measuring police integrity. In A. R. Piquero, J. R. Greene, & M. J. Hickman (Eds.), *Police integrity and ethics*. Belmont, CA: Wadsworth/Thomson Learning.

Klockars, C. B., Kutnjak Ivković, S., Harver, W. E., & Haberfeld, M. R. (1997). *The measurement of police integrity*. Final report Submitted to the U.S. Department of Justice, Office of Justice Programs, National Institute of Justice.

Klockars, C. B., Kutnjak Ivković, S., & Haberfeld, M. R. (2004). The contours of police integrity. In C. B. Klockars, S. Kutnjak Ivković, & M. R. Haberfeld (Eds.), *The contours of police integrity*. Thousand Oaks: Sage.

Klockars, C. B., Kutnjak Ivković, S., & Haberfeld, M. R. (2006). *Enhancing police integrity*. New York: Springer.

Korruptsioonivastane seadus [Anti-corruption Act]. R. T. I. (1999). 16, 276; 28.02.1999; latest provision RT I 2004, 71, 504; 29.10.2004.

Kutnjak Ivković, S., & Klockars, C. B. (2004). Police integrity in Croatia. In C. B. Klockars, S. Kutnjak Ivković, & M. R. Haberfeld (Eds.), *The contours of police integrity*. Thousand Oaks: Sage.

Leps, A. (2000). Estonian police. In O. Marenin & D. K. Das (Eds.), *Challenges of policing democracies: A world perspective*. Amsterdam: Gordon and Breach.

Lipset, S. M., & Lenz, G. S. (2000). Corruption, culture, and markets. In S. P. Huntington & L. E. Harrison (Eds.), *Culture matters: How values shape human progress*. New York: Basic Books.

Madeley, J. T. S. (2003). A framework for the comparative analysis of church-state relations in Europe. *West European Politics, 26*(1), 27–31.

Martin, D. (2005). *On secularization: Towards a revised general theory* (pp. 77–78). Aldershot: Ashgate.

Ministry of Justice. (2007). Korruptsioon Eestis: Kolme sihtrühma uuring 2006. [Corruption in Estonia: Study of three target groups 2006] Kriminaalpoliitikauuringud 6. Tallinn.

Ministry of Justice. (2010). Korruptsioon Eestis: Kolme sihtrühma uuring 2010. [Corruption in Estonia: Study of three target groups 2010] Kriminaalpoliitika uuringud 13. Tallinn.

Ministry of Justice. (2011). Eesti kohtunike ja prokuröride mõjutamine. [Influencing of judges and prosecutors in Estonia]. http://www.korruptsioon.ee/orb.aw/class=file/action=preview/id=53634/Eesti+kohtunike+ja+prokur%F6ride+m%F5jutamine.pdf. Accessed 23 March 2014.

Ministry of Justice. (2013). Response to the inquiry. *August, 7,* 2013.

Norris, P., & Inglehart, R. (2011). *Sacred and secular: Religion and politics worldwide*. Cambridge: Cambridge University Press.

Organisation for Economic Co-operation and Development (OECD). (2014). List of OECD Member countries—Ratification of the convention on the OECD. http://www.oecd.org/general/listofoecdmembercountries-ratificationoftheconventionontheoecd.htm. Accessed 9 March 2014.

Panagiotou, R. A. (2001). Estonia's success: Prescription or legacy? *Communist and Post-Communist Studies, 34*(2), 261–277.

Police and Border Guard Act. (2009). 06.05.2009 RT I 2009, 26, 159, latest amendment 12.06.2013 RT I, 02.07.2013, 1.

Police and Border Guard Board. (2013). Response to the inquiry August 30 2013.

Police and Border Guard Board. (2014a). Politsei ajalugu. [History of the police]. https://www.politsei.ee/et/organisatsioon/politsei-ja-piirivalveamet/ajalugu/politsei-ajalugu/. Accessed 9 March 2014.

Police and Border Guard Board. (2014b). Police and Border Guard Board—in cooperation we create security. https://www.politsei.ee/en/organisatsioon/organization/. Accessed 9 March 2014.

Police and Border Guard Board. (2014c). Politsei- ja Piirivalveameti struktuur. [The structure of the Police and Border Guard Board]. https://www.politsei.ee/et/organisatsioon/politsei-ja-piirivalveamet/struktuur/. Accessed 8 March 2014.

Police and Border Guard Board. (2014d). Response to the inquiry March 17 2014.

Politsei- ja Piirivalveameti töökord. (2010). [Rules of Procedure of the Police and Border Guard Board] Approved by the Director General of the Police and Border Guard Board order of March 26th 2010 No. 145.

Raun, T. U. (2001). *Estonia and the Estonians*. Stanford: Hoover Institution Press, Stanford University.

Rees, C. J., & Miazhevich, G. (2009). Socio-cultural change and business ethics in post-Soviet countries: The cases of Belarus and Estonia. *Journal of Business Ethics, 86*(1), 51–63.

Resetnikova, A. (2006). Women in policing in a transforming organization: The case of the Estonian Police, The Journal of Power Institutions in Post-Soviet Societies [Online], Issue 4/5 | 2006, Online since 27 November 2006. http://pipss.revues.org/502. Accessed 30 June 2013.

Saar Poll. (2013a). Public Opinion and National Defence. Ordered by: Ministry of Defence of Estonia. March 2013. Tallinn.

Saar Poll.(2013b). Public Opinion and National Defence. Ordered by: Ministry of Defence of Estonia. October 2013. Tallinn.

Saar Poll. (2013c). Arvamusküsitlus korruptsioonist teavitamisega (ehk vilepuhumisega) seotud hoiakute kohta. [Survey on attitudes towards reporting corruption (i.e. whistle blowing)]. Ordered by: Transparency International Estonia.

Sandholtz, W., & Taagepera, R. (2005). Corruption, culture, and communism. *International Review of Sociology, 15*(1), 109–131.

Sööt, M.-L. (2010). Korruptsioonikuriteod. Kuritegevus Eestis 2009. [Corruption crimes. Crimes in Estonia in 2009]. Kriminaalpoliitika uuringud 12. Justiitsministeerium Tallinn 55–62.

Sööt, M.-L. (2011). Korruptsioonikuriteod. Kuritegevus Eestis 2010. [Corruption crimes. Crimes in Estonia in 2010]. Kriminaalpoliitika uuringud 15 Justiitsministeerium Tallinn 85–93.

Sööt, M.-L. (2013). Korruptsioonikuriteod. Kuritegevus Eestis 2012. [Corruption crimes. Crimes in Estonia in 2012]. Kriminaalpoliitika uuringud 17. Justiitsministeerium, Tallinn. 83–89.

Statistics Estonia. (2011). Population and Housing Census 2011.

Statistics Estonia. (2013a). Population by ethnic nationality, 1 January, years. http://www.stat.ee/34278. Accessed 14 March 2014.

Statistics Estonia. (2013b). Rahva ja Eluruumide Loendus 2011. Ülevaade Eesti Maakondade Rahvastikust. [Population and Housing Census 2011. Overview of the population in the counties of Estonia].

Statistics Estonia. (2013c) Keskmine palk tõusis mullu kõigil tegevusaladel. June 17. Press release. http://www.stat.ee/65289.

Statistics Estonia. (2014). Main indicators January 1. 2014 data. http://www.stat.ee/main-indicators. Accessed 8 March 2014.

Transparency International. (2012) Corruption Perception Index 2012: An updated methodology. http://www.transparency.org/files/content/pressrelease/2012_CPIUpdatedMethodology_EMBARGO_EN.pdf. Accessed 16 Jan 2015.

Transparency International. (2013). Whistleblowing in Europe: Legal protections for whistleblowers in the EU. http://www.transparency.org/whatwedo/pub/whistleblowing_in_europe_legal_protections_for_whistleblowers_in_the_eu. Accessed 22 March 2014.

Transparency International. (2014). Corruption perception index. http://www.transparency.org/research/cpi/. Accessed 16 March 2014.

Transparency International Estonia. (2009). Whistleblower protection assessment report on Estonia. Country report. http://www.transparency.ee/cm/files/whistleblower_protection_assessment_report_on_estonia_1.pdf. Accessed 9 March 2014.

Transparency International Estonia. (2013a). Korruptsioonitajumise indeks 2013. Press release 3.12.2013.

Transparency International Estonia. (2013b). Ühing tutvustab korruptsioonist teavitajate kaitse raportit. Press release 1.11.2013.

Transparency International Estonia. (2013c). Ühing: Korruptsioonist teavitajad vajavad paremat kaitset, kuid hoiakud juba paranevad. Press release 5.11.2013.

Treisman, D. (2000). The causes of corruption: A cross-national study. *Journal of Public Economics, 76*(3), 399–457.

Uslaner, E. M. (2008). *Corruption, inequality, and the rule of law: The bulging pocket makes the easy life*. Cambridge: Cambridge University Press.

World Bank (2015). Country and Lending Groups. http://data.worldbank.org/about/country-and-lending-groups#High_income. Accessed 16 Jan 2015.

XII Riigikogu [Parliament] Shorthand report. (2013). V Session Monday, 11. March 2013 15:00 18:33 Inquiry about the salaries of the police. Minister of the Interior Ken-Marti Vaher. http://www.riigikogu.ee/?op=steno&stcommand=stenogramm&date=1363006648&pkpkaupa=1&paevakord=12333.

Chapter 6
Police Integrity in Russia

Serguei Cheloukhine, Sanja Kutnjak Ivković, Qasim Haq, and Maria R. Haberfeld

Abstract This chapter explores the contours of police integrity in Russia. The Transparency International Corruption Perceptions Index suggests that Russia is perceived as a highly corrupt country. With about 1 million employees, the Russian police are one of the largest police agencies in the world. This chapter relies on the police integrity survey conducted in 2012–2013. Questionnaires were distributed to the police officers in two regions of the Russian Federation: Southern District–Rostov Region and North Caucasus–Karachaevo Cherkessia. With two exceptions, the respondents did not perceive the behaviors described in the scenarios as very serious. While most of the respondents did not have any problems recognizing these behaviors as rule violating, they supported and expected police agencies to mete out no discipline for the majority of these behaviors. Finally, the results suggest that the code of silence covers all of the behaviors described in the questionnaire.

Keywords Militia · Police integrity · Russia · Soviet Union · Survey

Introduction

The Russian Federation, commonly known as Russia, extends over a substantial part of northern Eurasia (Asia and Europe). Russia is the largest country in the world by land area, and its population is the ninth largest in the world. About three

S. Cheloukhine (✉)
John Jay College of Criminal Justice, New York, NY, USA
e-mail: scheloukhine@jjay.cuny.edu

S. Kutnjak Ivković
Michigan State University, East Lansing, MI, USA
e-mail: kutnjak@msu.edu

Q. Haq
Hunter College, New York, NY, USA
e-mail: qhaq@jjay.cuny.edu

M. R. Haberfeld
John Jay College of Criminal Justice, New York, NY, USA
e-mail: mhaberfeld@jjay.cuny.edu

S. Kutnjak Ivković, M. R. Haberfeld (eds.), *Measuring Police Integrity Across the World*,
DOI 10.1007/978-1-4939-2279-6_6

quarters of the 142.5 million people in Russia are Russian; in addition, there are more than 190 ethnic groups represented in Russia (The World Factbook 2014). Levels of religiosity are relatively low, an enduring legacy of the Soviet era; about 15–20 % of the Russian population belong to the Russian Orthodox Church, about 10–15 % are Muslim, and 2 % belong to other Christian denominations (The World Factbook 2014).

During the Soviet era, Russia (Russian Soviet Federative Socialist Republic) was a constituent republic of the Union of Soviet Socialist Republics (USSR). Following the dissolution of the Soviet Union in December 1991, Russia became the Russian Federation, with the land area, population, and industrial production of the Soviet Union located in Russia. The Constitution of the Russian Federation (1993) determines that the Russian Federation comprises of 85 federal subjects:

- 47 *oblasts* (provinces)
- 21 republics (states), enjoying a high degree of autonomy on most issues and corresponding to some of Russia's numerous ethnic minorities
- 8 *krais* (territories)
- 6 *okrugs* (autonomous districts)
- 2 federal cities (Moscow and St. Petersburg)
- The Jewish Autonomous Oblast.

The history of Russia traces back to the ninth century. By the thirteenth century, Moscow surfaced as an influential cultural center. Following more than two centuries of Mongol domination (thirteenth–fifteenth centuries), the principality of Muscovy reemerged and gradually conquered the surrounding princedoms (The World Factbook 2014). In the subsequent centuries, the boundaries of the Russian Empire extended across Siberia to the Pacific and, from the eighteenth century, to the Baltic Sea. During the nineteenth century, additional conquests extended the borders of the Empire throughout Europe and Asia (The World Factbook 2014).

In 1917, in the midst of World War I, the Russian Empire was overthrown and the USSR formed (The World Factbook 2014). Turbulent events unfolding at the time established Vladimir Lenin as the leader and communism as the prevailing ideology of the newly established Soviet Union. Following Lenin's death in 1924, Joseph Stalin emerged as the undisputed leader of the Soviet Union until his death in 1953. Over a period of nearly three decades, marked by considerable brutality and disregard for human rights, millions of people have been imprisoned in correctional labor camps and deported to remote areas (Getty et al. 1993). Departing from Lenin's New Economic Plan, Stalin favored a highly centralized economy. The ensuing *industrialization* and collectivization served to facilitate a swift transformation of the USSR from a primarily agrarian society to an industrial power (Wheatcroft et al. 1986). The three decades following Stalin's death in 1953 were marked mainly by economic stagnation. In the 1980s, Mikhail Gorbachev introduced domestic policies known as *glasnost* (openness) and *perestroika* (restructuring; The World Factbook 2014), leading toward some degree of modernization of Soviet ideology. His shifts in foreign policy contributed to the end of the Cold War. However, the economy faltered and a crisis ensued, leading to increasing political instability and crisis. Following the August 1991 coup and subsequent events, the USSR dissolved in December of 1991. In the post-Soviet era, Russia (the Russian Federation) experienced a multifaceted crisis, including a financial collapse in 1998, followed by a period of economic growth (The World Factbook 2014). Recent events in Russian history are reviewed throughout the remainder of this chapter as they pertain to the key subject matter of police integrity.

This chapter examines the contours of police integrity in Russia. The chapter first explores the larger social and political context of the Russian police integrity and then focuses on the empirical part of the study. In 2012–2013, questionnaires aiming to measure police integrity were distributed to police officers in two regions of the Russian Federation: Southern District–Rostov Region and North Caucasus–Karachaevo Cherkessia. The chapter explores how police officers view hypothetical scenarios describing examples of police misconduct. They were asked to assess how serious misconduct is, what they think that the appropriate and expected discipline is, and whether they would be willing to report for such behavior.

The Police in Russia

The first police force in Saint Petersburg was established as the Main Police on June 7, 1718 by decree from Peter the Great. Anton de Vieira was appointed as the first General Polizmeister. On January 19, 1722, the Governing Senate established the Moscow Police. The Detective Department was founded in 1866 operating under the police department of the Ministerstvo Vnutrennikh Del (MVD; the Ministry of the Interior) and, by 1907, similar departments had been created in other major cities of the Russian Empire, including Moscow, Kiev, Riga, Odessa, Tiflis, Baku, and Rostov-on-Don. Other districts were policed by rural police or gendarmerie units (Cheloukhine and Haberfeld 2011).

The 3500 strong police force of Saint Petersburg provided the main opposition to the rioting, which marked the initial outbreak of the February Revolution in 1917. After the army units garrisoning the city defected, the police became the main target of the revolutionaries and a number were killed. The Police of the Russian Empire was dissolved on March 10, 1917, and on April 17, 1917, the Provisional Government established the People's Militia (*Militsiya*) as a new law enforcement body. The name *Militsiya* originates from the early Soviet history, when the Bolsheviks intend to associate their new policing authority with the self-organization of the people and distinguish it from the "bourgeois class protecting" police. *Militsiya* was created in 1917 under the official name "the Workers' and Peasants' *Militsiya.*"

The Police Service in today's Russia is the most powerful and multifunctional Russian law enforcement agency. The legal basis for its operations is the Law on *Militsiya*, passed on April 18, 1991 (with subsequent amendments), in accordance with which the Militia protects the life, health, rights, and freedoms, as well as the property and interests of individuals, legal entities, society, and the government (Cheloukhine and Haberfeld 2011).

In 2009, then President Medvedev announced a new law on the Russia's police service and the beginning of the police reform. The focus of the police reform was on increased efficiency of the police, decreasing the level of corruption in the country, and improving the public image. The 2008 European Social Survey showed that, compared to their counterparts in other European countries, the Russian public showed one of the lowest levels of trust in the police. This low level of confidence was directly related to the people's willingness to contact the police and their responses to the crimes. Kosals (2010, p. 2) elaborated:

> According to public opinion polls, less than 40 % of crime victims contact the police to register a crime, to request that they open a criminal case, or to seek compensation for damages that they have suffered. Most people report that they were unhappy with the police reaction to their inquiry, and only slightly more than a quarter expressed satisfaction (nearly one third claimed that the police did nothing at all in response to their request for help). Victims who contacted the police seeking assistance evaluate police activity more negatively than those who have no personal contact with them.
>
> Victims who did not report crimes to the police cited a variety of reasons for their reluctance to seek help. Two percent said that they had suffered from police criminality. While 2 % seems like a small number, taking into account that 2.3 million people filed official complaints…nearly 70,000 Russians suffered from the unreported crimes committed by policemen.
>
> Distrust in the police is so high in Russia that more than a tenth of the victims polled do not report crimes to the police and try to take care of the problem on their own. If these numbers are accurate, more than 200,000 people annually go around the police system to seek their own form of justice.

During the reform, the militia were expected to downsize by 20 %, salaries would be increased by 30 %, and police officers with connections to organized crime should be fired (Russia Today 2011). However, the number of police officers before the reform remains a secret and the targeted number of police officers post-reform is not known. Russia participated in the Fifth UN Survey of Crime Trends and Operations of the Criminal Justice Systems and, according to the information provided there, the number of police officers increased from 1.5 million in 1990 to 1.8 million in 1994 (UN Office on Drugs and Crime 1994). After 2000, there are no systematic data on the number of sworn police officers in the country (Kosals 2010, p. 2). Occasional accounts provide some estimates (e.g., about 1.4 million police officers in 2009). However, as Kosals (2010, p. 2) emphasizes, "[a]ll police statistics and data gathered through sociological surveys done in-house or by external research centers are classified and only a few facts and figures are provided to the public after police approval."

The most obvious change resulting from that reform has been the service's name—it changed from the Soviet-era term *Militsiya* to the more universal *Politsiya* (police). The police are now the federal law enforcement agency in Russia, operating under the Ministry of Internal Affairs. It was established in 2011 replacing the *Militsiya*, the former police service. The reform also resulted in a more centralized control over the police; the responsibility for the oversight of the police agencies in the regions was removed from regional and municipal authorities and put under the direct control of the MVD in Moscow (Kulikov 2011).

Among the very recent restructuring moves, some key departments from the MVD were transferred to other ministries and vice versa. For example, the responsibility for the correctional institutions was transferred to the Ministry of Justice, firefighting was subordinated to a newly created the Ministry for Emergency Situations. Currently, the main components of the Ministry include the following units: The MVD central administration, the MVD federal/regional administration, the Police Service, Internal Military Troops (*Vnutrennie Voyska*), Federal Migration Service (*Federal'naya Migratsionnaya Sluzhba*), and the MVD forensic, logistical, research, and educational institutions of central subordination (Cheloukhine and Haberfeld 2011).

Theory of Police Integrity and the Russian Police

Organizational Rules

The first dimension of the theory of integrity emphasizes the existence of the official rules. Klockars and Kutnjak (2004, p. 1.4) argue that it is relevant not only that the official rules are made but also how they are communicated and understood by the police officers (Klockars and Kutnjak 2004, p. 1.4). Police agencies of high integrity are expected to have the official rules that prohibit misconduct, as well as to enforce them when the violations occur (Klockars 2006).

Little has been known about the *Militsiya*'s organizational rules because their work has been covered by the veil of secrecy. Officially, the police operate according to the Law on Police, which has been approved by the Federal Assembly and was subsequently signed into law on February 7, 2011 by the then President of Russian Federation Dmitry Medvedev. The Police Law was based on the one adopted in 1991 (Semukhina 2013). Medvedev's 2011 Law on the Police, reflected a serious effort to make the MVD more legitimate and effective. However, Galeotti (2012) asserts that this attempt was indeed very weak, including the lack of a powerful constituency for change within the MVD and a clear concept of the reform.

Between 1989 and 1991, work on legislation addressing the growing crime phenomenon (particularly in the post-Soviet economy and privatization of Soviet property) was underway in the Supreme Soviets of the USSR and the Russian Federation. After the collapse of the USSR, these state institutions, including the MVD of the USSR, disappeared, as did their drafts. To empower the unpopular *Militsiya,* the new Russian state has tried to resume this unfinished legislative process. While the privatization of the former Soviet State property was ongoing, in 1995, the state Duma of the Russian Federation considered simultaneously three drafts of the Law on the Fight of (Organized[1]) Crime, two of which were published in the media. The

[1] The concept of organized crime was foreign to Militsiya; officers could not operate or press charges because the Criminal Code did not prohibit such behavior. Thus, growing organized crime activity in the newly established capitalist economy and the old Soviet Criminal Code put *Militsiya* in a bystander position.

Council of the Federation rejected all of those bills. The reason was related to the unacceptability of certain provisions, which were classified (Cheloukhine 2008).

It was not until January of 1997 that the Criminal Code of the Russian Federation, Chap. 22, defined "offenses in the area of economic activity." The definition was included in the chapter sections of the Criminal Code of the Russian Federation and comprised a structure of crimes, the majority of which were relevant to the developing market economy. An essential characteristic of the new criminal code is the specific targeting of organized crime. Article 35 provides the legal definition and establishes that a group of persons, a group of persons having a prior agreement, an organized group, or a criminal association can be held responsible for participating in the organized crime. For example, a person who creates or supervises a criminal association (criminal organization) is subject to criminal responsibility for his or her organization and supervision, and for all the crimes committed by the association if the crimes were within the person's intent. The commission of crimes by a criminal association entails more severe punishment (Cheloukhine and Haberfeld 2011). The new offenses appear to be typical responses to white-collar crime, but, in the Russian context, they are closely associated with organized crime and corruption. They include related crimes combined into the following categories: illegal entrepreneurship; illegal banking activity; fraudulent entrepreneurship; legalization (laundering) of money assets or other property acquired by illegal means; illegal receipt of credit; compulsion to conclude or refuse to conclude a transaction; and production or sale of counterfeited credit cards or other payment documents.

A very novel feature of the special part of the criminal code is the introduction of legal rules prescribing punishment for economic crimes (Chap. 22), crimes by corporate executives in violation of their official duties (Chap. 23), environmental crimes (Chap. 26), and computer crimes (Chap. 28). With a few exceptions (such as smuggling and consumer fraud, traditionally called "economic" crimes in Soviet criminal law), the majority of the specified crimes are new phenomena in Russia, and the difficult process of building a market economy has dictated the necessity to create some responsibility for committing these transgressions. All these were new and major challenges to the police. Despite significant changes in the Russian Criminal Code, between the years 1996 and 2004, the success in combating crime was very limited. Both white-collar and organized crimes referred to under the same umbrella of "corruption," continued to rise and Militsiya still operated within the context of the old criminal code.

Police Detection and Investigation of Police Misconduct

The second dimension of the theory emphasizes the police agency's own methods of detection, investigation, and discipline of rule violations (Klockars and Kutnjak 2004; Klockars 2006). Methods of controlling misconduct could be either reactive (e.g., reactive investigations, discipline of officers who violated the rules) or proactive (e.g., education in ethics, training, and integrity testing). Police agencies of high integrity are expected not only to have an elaborate system put in place but also to use it efficiently.

The above theoretical assumption is predicated on the notion that the organization is truly interested in the investigation of the police misconduct and imposition of the proper discipline. As McCarthy (2014, p. 6) elaborated on the accountability system by the Russian police:

> Police are not accountable to any local, regional, or national government officials or to the public. All accountability is vertical and within the MVD. Officers answer to both their local/regional superiors as well as to all of the people above them in the sub-unit that they belong to, all the way up to the federal level.... In practice, this system of multiple accountability leads to excessive bureaucratic reporting requirements with each boss asking for multiple, often duplicative information.

The Russian police, as a large semi-military organization, have the capacity to deal with misconducts of its employees. Empirical studies suggest that they would have their work cut out for them. The data on the number of employees investigated and disciplined/punished for misconduct are not publicly available. The publicly available Annual Report of the Ministry of the Interior for 1994 revealed that, out of all the "personnel of the law enforcement structures," 29 % were involved in corrupt and illegal activities. President Medvedev reported that, during the first 6 months of 2009, out of the more 4500 cases of corruption were brought to prosecution and individuals eventually convicted, more than 700 were police officers (Cheloukhine and Haberfeld 2011).

Furthermore, the most frequent complaint by the citizens (32 %) expressed in the VTIOM's (All-Russia Public Opinion Research Center *(Всероссийский центр изучения общественного мнения)*) 2010 public opinion survey "about the work of personnel of the organs of the Ministry of the Interior" was that "[t]hey have no respect for the law and they break the law, they are engaged in illegal activites" (Russian Analytical Digest 2010). In the same survey, more than 80 % of the respondents perceived that the "illegal activity of militia personnel [is] a regular occurrence, or…merely isolated cases of illegal activity" (Russian Analytical Digest 2010, p. 11). At the same time, about 35 % thought that the illegal activities are a regular occurrence and about 45 % thought that they are occurring only occasionally (Russian Analytical Digest 2010, p. 11). Moreover, the majority of the respondents who provided answers to the question about the need to reform the Ministry of the Interior agreed that such a reform is necessary (Russian Analytical Digest 2010, p. 11). When asked about the specific elements that should be included in such a reform, the three most frequent choices were "human resources policy (stricter selection criteria, higher level of professionalism)," "increased transparency and control by society," and "fight against corruption" (Russian Analytical Digest 2010, p. 11). At the same time, the overwhelming majority of the respondents (73 %) thought that a radical reform of the militia will not occur and that "everything will boil down to decorative renaming and a reshuffle of the leadership of the militia" (Russian Analytical Digest 2010, p. 12).

However, according to Pustintsev (2000), despite the reforms introduced by Medvedev, two fundamental dilemmas remain in place. Pustintsev (2000) stipulates that the public in Russia views its police as the enforcer of the will of those in power who are not necessarily interested in the role change of police organization, and are fine with the way the police operates so far, with primary interest of protecting the racketeers or corrupt officials.

Curtailing the Code of Silence

The third dimension of the theory of police integrity discusses the code of silence and the police agency's efforts in curtailing it (Klockars and Kutnjak 2004). Although the code of silence exists in each and every police agency, undertaking serious efforts in curtailing it is a sign of an agency of high integrity (Klockars and Kutnjak 2004). Consequently, police agencies of low integrity would have a strong code of silence that would protect almost all behavior. By contrast, in police agencies of high integrity, police officers would be willing to report misconduct and supervisors would be willing to investigate it and discipline police officers who have engaged in misconduct.

Kosals (2010) argues that the marketization—the development of large-scale informal economic activities by police officers—is a feature and a problem of policing in Russia. According to the studies such as the Open Society Institute (Kosals 2010), police officers not only engage in economic activities outside their regular work hours, but also during their regular hours. In particular, Kolennikova et al. (Kolennikova et al. 2008) reported that about one half of the respondents engaged in after hours work and that about one fifth engaged in additional income-producing activity during their regular hours. Similar results were reported in the study by Gudkov and Dubin (2006); about 60% of the respondents interviewed in the study are earning off-duty income and about 20% earned additional income during regular work hours. Kosals (2010, p. 3) states that this process of marketization has clear consequences, including the institutionalization of bribery:

> For example, if a traffic officer wants to patrol in a lucrative area (for example, where he potentially can collect personal payments in lieu of fines), he has to pay his direct boss for this privilege; if an inquiry officer wants to meet his arrest quota, but there are no true crimes in the region that he patrols, he has to pay an investigator to avoid punishment, and so on. Another important area of marketization is one's personal career. In some cases, officers must pay to win promotion to a higher post (especially, if this post opens the path to informal earnings). Sometimes these fees can be as high as hundreds of thousands of dollars. Of course, then the newly-promoted officer must develop large-scale business activities to recoup his investments.

In the case of such institutionalized and entrenched misconduct, very few officers would be motivated to blow the whistle. McCarthy (2014, p. 6) explains why police officers may not be motivated to do so:

> The strong hierarchical subordination also makes it difficult for well-meaning lower-ranking officers to refuse to participate in corruption schemes if they do exist. For example, it may fall to a lower-ranking officer to collect bribes from local businessmen for police protection, but usually a large part of that money gets set up the police hierarchy… When

> the bosses are corrupt but allow their subordinates to benefit from the corruption, whistle-blowing becomes even less likely since everyone benefits just enough to keep the corrupt practices going.

If police officers dare to do so, they would probably face severe consequences. For example, Sergei Magnitsky was a lawyer who learned about organized and widespread corruption among public officials (Poduzov 2010). Rather than leading into a scandal, investigation by an independent committee, and a subsequent reform of the police, the events have taken a different turn. Magnitsky was arrested, spent almost a year in pretrial detention, and eventually died in prison (Poduzov 2010).

The most famous whistle-blower in the recent Russian police history is Major Aleksey Dymovsky. He and several other police officers "jeopardized their careers to appeal directly to the Russian president to end the lawlessness inside the police system" (Poduzov 2010, p. 8). In his video appeal to Putin, Dymovsky claims that corruption is endemic and that other forms of misconduct, such as framing innocent citizens to meet the official arrest quotas, are widespread (2009). In the video, Dymovsky speaks directly to Putin: "You talk about reducing corruption… You say that it should not be just a crime, that it should be immoral. But it is not like that. I told my boss that the police are corrupt. And he told me that it cannot be done away with." Dymovsky (2009) also stated that, "I'm sick and tired of being told to solve crimes that don't exist. I'm sick and tired of being told to put [innocent] people in jail. I'm sick and tired of made-to-order criminal cases." Dymovsky was eventually fired, arrested, and prosecuted (Levy 2010).

The videos received widespread public support and thousands of people posted comments online supporting police officers (Harding 2009). As a reaction, on July 22, 2010, the Russian Criminal Code was amended. The revised Article 286.1 now contains a norm that makes it criminal for the subordinate police officers to criticize the decisions of the superiors. Poduzov (2010, p. 9) related the whistleblower videos and the legislative changes, "[u]ndoubtedly, this norm appeared in response to Dymovsky's Youtube video and the widespread public reaction to it. However, the effect is to paralyze any public discussion about the police by policemen because they will always be under the threat of criminal prosecution." This norm has also effectively eliminated any realistic hope that scholars seeking to study the code of silence empirically would be successful in their endeavors.

Influence of Social and Political Environment

The fourth dimension of the theory puts the emphasis on the fact that each and every police agency is directly influenced by the society at large (Klockars and Kutnjak 2004). A police agency in a society which tolerates misconduct of its public employees should have a lower level of integrity than a police agency in a society which is critical and addresses misconduct by its public employees.

Corruption and bribery during Soviet times appeared to represent a universal system and, in this sense, the roots of contemporary corruption had been established already. By the 1970s, illegal resale of scarce goods by retail employees had become widespread. It also included bribes to officials responsible for the allocation of consumer goods and other recourses, quotas for scholarships in the education system, and the falsification of official reports. Within the Soviet legal system, the battle against corruption was practically nonexistent, although there was a system of punishments, in addition to public and party censure, for the abuse of official positions. The fundamentals of Soviet corruption were structured by a totalitarian system and, in particular, by the system of resource allocations during conditions of constant shortages of goods and services. Therefore, the major spheres of corruption were logistics, capital investments, and the drawing of plans and reports on their performance, accompanied by huge falsifications of official data. This system, from one viewpoint, was the social illness corrupting the morals of society. From another point of view, the plan-distribution system in the economy could not function without this "lubricant," without decisions being made in the allocation of funds and "limits" (Cheloukhine and Haberfeld 2011).

The Russian democratic transition, a combination of ill-designed legal, economic, and moral actions, fed organized crime and corruption, which was now aspiring to absorb the state. Russia has become a state with continuous anarchy, where people, radioactive materials, weapons, and narcotics are easily bought and sold. As if these threats were not troublesome enough, the truly frightening aspect of the new Russia is the cold-blooded organized crime groups and corrupt government executives working together to generate not so much a new market economy as a truly new criminal state. Kosals (2010, p. 4) argued:

> …the police who were essentially competing with the criminals reached a kind of symbiosis with the mob. Ultimately, they began "racketeering the racketeers" and captured the criminal business. Step by step they accumulated economic wealth, initially spending their money on consumer goods… Then, during the second part of the 1990s, they started to invest, first in retail trade…and other sectors. This was potentially damaging to the authorities' efforts to maintain control over the police.

The new Russian elite who came to power after the collapse of the USSR played a key role in the criminalization of Russian society at the post-Soviet stage of its development (Cheloukhine and Haberfeld 2011). If the party and administrative control restricted the activities of the old Soviet *nomenklatura*, the new, market-oriented elite who did not abide by any restrictions, because they could easily get around laws, would not have emerged. Russia's new ruling class consisted of corrupt officials who freely mixed government service with business activities. The emerging market economy, which began to gain strength in the late 1980s and was legalized in the early 1990s, was inevitably permeated with criminality. The market economy effectively deformed and neutralized the new state, undermining its capacity to act against crime and corruption (Cheloukhine and Haberfeld 2011).

The post-Soviet Russian state proved to be incapable of effective resistance to the onslaught of criminal elements in different spheres of society. It undermined its own policing agencies such as MVD, courts, and *Federalnaya Sluzhba Bezopastnosti* (FSB, formerly known as KGB), which initially were assigned to fight crime. No reforms in either structure or in the courts were implemented until 1995 (the reform of the court), which also led to the tremendous increase of crime and corruption. The failed state generated a monetary starvation and a subsequent pervasive corruption that was a direct consequence of the governmental malfunction, therefore creating new conditions for economic crimes (Cheloukine and Haberfeld 2011). The publicly available 1994 Annual Report of the Ministry of the Interior suggests that 47% of the public servants in the ministries, committees, and other institutions, 29% of the police, and 13% of the employees of the financial and banking system were involved in corrupt and illegal activities.

Despite some successes against crime (the 2008 headline figures saw a 10.2% drop in total crimes, although in part this was because of under-reporting rather than a genuine decline), most Russians continue to see the police as at best incompetent, at worst corrupt extortionists and heavy-handed Kremlin goons. According to a number of Russian researchers, between 30 and 35% of the public prefers to avoid any police contact, even in life threatening situations (Makarova 2011; Semukhina 2014a). Semukhina (2014b, p. 1) summarized the results of the existing empirical studies on the public support of the police:

> Longitudinal studies examining levels of trust and satisfaction with police in Russia indicate that at least 50% of Russians do not trust the police in any given year; in some years the levels of public trust and satisfaction plummeted to 30%. International studies, including the International Crime Victimization Survey (ICVS), New Europe Barometer (NEB), European Social Survey (ESS), Gallup World Poll, and World Value Survey (WVS) consistently rank Russia as one of the lowest countries in both public trust in and satisfaction with police.

On November 12, 2009, then President Dmitry Medvedev, during his address to the Federal Assembly of the Russian Federation, assessed the current state of corruption as one of the main obstacles to his government. He expressed a conviction that it is quite clear that the fight against corruption must be waged on all fronts: from legislation, through law enforcement, and the judicial system to the social intolerance of these evil phenomena, including domestic ones.

As then President Medvedev stated, during the first 6 months of 2009, more than 4500 cases of corruption were brought to prosecution, 532 officials of government authorities and local self-government bodies were convicted, as were more than 700 law-enforcement officers (Cheloukhine and Haberfeld 2011). One of the speakers during the same Assembly session, the Minister of the Interior, provided additional figures: during the first 10 months of 2009, his ministry alone investigated 40,000 cases, up by 11% from the previous year. Russians pay US$ 300 billion in bribes each year, according to the government's own figures. According to the most recent interview with two-star General Alexander Bastyrkin, head of the Inquiry Committee of the Main Public Prosecutor Office, and the two-star General Alexei Anchikhin, head of the Investigative Committee of the Ministry of the Interior, it appears that corruption, referred to as a cancerous phenomenon in Russia is spreading with an excessive speed. The generals provided quite well-documented facts during the interviews (Cheloukhine and Haberfeld 2011).

Kosals (2010, p. 4) argues that the reforms in the 2000s (e.g., removing the penitentiary system out of the Ministry of the Interior; removing the firefighters out of the Ministry of the Interior; the 2003–2006 criminal campaign and prosecution of "werewolves in uniform"; the 2009 political drive against corruption and the police reform) have not been very effective:

> All these actions were not reforms aimed to provide better security services to the public and to cut criminality. The main content of these measures were, and remain, organizational restructuring, criticizing corrupt officers in the media, and punishing select individuals according to various political needs. During the 2000s the police did not provide better security services to the public or change the bad habits developed by officers. The police force remains a militarized, opaque system focused on making money while ignoring the needs of the public.

As recently as February 2010, the newly unveiled great corruption scandal created a shock in the public opinion in Russia. This time it concerned the (*Otryad Militsii Osobogo Naznachenia–Отряд милиции особого назначения*) OMON (special purpose police squad), the elite Russian police (*Militsiya*) formation. According to "The New Times" (*Novoye Vremya*), a prestigious Moscow's weekly newspaper, within the OMON formation, a gigantic and systemic corruption phenomenon was firmly in place, which involved practically all OMON members, from the very top commands to the lowest bottom level. The scandal was exposed when a group of variously ranking officers from the formation sent a report to the president of the Russian Federation and to the main prosecutor office providing, in detail, facts about what was going on within the unit (The New Times 2010). Given the current situation in Russia, where corruption is so common and so far-reaching, including even a great part of law-enforcement high-ranking officers, Medvedev's appeal to the Russian Federal Assembly (…zero tolerance of corruption should become part of our national culture, and an intrinsic part of who we are)," appears to be a truly ambitious goal.

Measuring Police Integrity

Questionnaire

The questionnaire used in this chapter includes hypothetical scenarios originally developed by Klockars and colleagues (Klockars 2006). The scenarios describe various examples of police misconduct, ranging to both types and severity. Five scenarios describe police corruption, four scenarios describe the use of excessive force, one scenario describes a failure to execute an arrest warrant, and one scenario describes the planting of evidence and the falsification of the official report. Scenarios describing the same type of misconduct vary in terms of their seriousness. For example, scenarios focusing on police corruption range from the least serious forms of police corruption, such as the acceptance of gratuities, to the most serious forms of corruption, such as a theft from a crime scene and the acceptance of a bribe.

The scenarios were translated into Russian and prepared for pre-testing. In the process, we discovered that scenario 6 (officer strikes prisoner who hurt partner) does not fit well with the Russian conditions. In particular, the scenario states that:

> In responding with her male partner to a fight in a bar, a young, female officer receives a black eye from one of the male combatants. The man is arrested, handcuffed, and, as he is led into the cells, the male member of the team punches him very hard in the kidney area saying, "hurts, doesn't it."

Yet, police officers in Russia have control of the arrestees for a very short period of time and have to transfer them to the detention centers, which are not run by the police agencies. Although police officers would have an opportunity to hit the arrestee while making an arrest, they would not have an opportunity to lead the arrestee into the cell and punch the person there. Therefore, we omitted scenario 6 from the Russian version of the questionnaire.

Each scenario is followed by the set of seven questions. These questions inquire about the police officers' knowledge of the official rules, their views about the seriousness of the described behavior, views about the appropriate and expected discipline, and their willingness to report this misconduct. Questions about the appropriate and expected discipline had to be adjusted to fit the Russian conditions. Thus, the Russian version of the questionnaire includes a six-point Likert scale: 1= "none," 2= "public reprimand," 3= "fine up to 10% of salary," 4= "fine up to 20% of salary," 5= "reassignment to a different position," and 6= "dismissal." The questionnaire concluded with a few demographic questions. In particular, the questionnaire asked about the respondents' gender, length of service, assignment, and rank, as well as whether they were employed in a supervisory position.

The Sample

In 2012–2013, questionnaires were distributed to the police officers in two regions of the Russian Federation: Southern District–Rostov Region and North Caucasus–Karachaevo Cherkessia. The *South Federal District*, an administrative region of Russian southern part, has a population of about 13,910,000 (Russian Federal State Statistics Service 2011). The administrative center of South Federal District is Rostov-on-Don city. *Karachay-Cherkessia Republic* (also spelled *Karachaevo-Cherkessia*) is part of North Caucasian Federal District, that has a population of about 472,000 (Russian Federal State Statistics Service 2011). The capital of the region is Cherkessk. The number of the police employed in each district is classified.

Both districts underwent a reform from the *Militsiya* into the police. The reforms process was initiated in 2011, with a plan to conclude it by 2013. By the end of the period, both MVD District Headquarters reported to Moscow on successful transformation. It was required that all personnel take specific tests and attestation according to responsibilities and the new law on police. By the end of the time frame set by the central MVD administration, all Militsiya departments and personnel

Table 6.1 Respondents' demographic characteristics

	Number of respondents	Percent of respondents
Length of service		
Up to 5 years	12	11.3%
6–10 years	61	57.5%
11–15 years	32	30.2%
16–20 years	1	0.9%
Supervisory role		
Non-supervisors	49	46.2%
Supervisors	57	53.8%
Type of assignment		
Patrol	1	0.9%
Detective/investigative	33	31.1%
Communications	6	5.7%
Special operations	16	15.1%
Administrative	46	43.4%
Community policing	4	3.8%
Gender		
Male	85	80.2%
Female	21	19.8%

went through the required reform and change. During informal interviews, several potential survey respondents expressed mixed feelings about the reforms. They mentioned that they had been trained at the Police Academy by the supervisors who served in Soviet *Militsiya* and who rejected and disapproved of the new reforms.

The Russian sample includes 106 police officers. Police officers were surveyed at the Rostov Police University (3rd year of study; all were at the rank of Junior Lieutenant), local police precinct stations, and district headquarters. About 90% of the sample includes police officers from the Rostov Police University. Police officers attending the Rostov Police University were enrolled in a 5-year program leading to the Juris Doctor Degree and a rank of the Police Lieutenant. They were surveyed during their regular classes. All participants in the survey went through a mandatory internship in the precincts.

Most of the respondents in the study were experienced police officers (Table 6.1); only 11% had been police officers for 5 years or fewer. The majority of the respondents (57.5%; Table 6.1) had between 6 and 10 years of experience. At the same time, about one half were supervisors (Table 6.1). There is a clear relation between the length of service and the supervisory position; the more years they have served as police officers, the more likely they were to be supervisors (Table 6.2).

In terms of their assignment, the respondents were mostly employed as detectives/investigators (31.1%) or administrators (43.4%; Table 6.2). Only a few respondents worked as either patrol officers or community policing officers (Table 6.2). Finally, the overwhelming majority of the respondents were men (80.2%, Table 6.2).

Table 6.2 Years in service by supervisory position

Years in service	Supervisory position	
	No	Yes
3–5 years	7 (58.3%)	5 (41.7%)
6–10 years	33 (54.1%)	28 (45.9%)
11–15 years	9 (28.1%)	23 (71.9%)
16–20 years	0 (0.0%)	1 (100%)

The Results

Seriousness

The first question the respondents in the study were asked inquired about the seriousness of the behavior described in the scenario. They were also asked to estimate how serious most police officers in their agencies would evaluate them. The respondents were offered answers on a five-point Likert scale, ranging from "not at all serious" to "very serious."

The respondents' evaluations of scenario seriousness suggest that there is very little variation in the perceived seriousness of the ten scenarios. In particular, in eight out of ten scenarios (Table 6.3), the mean values of the responses are all clustered on the nonserious side of the scale, between 1.25 and 2. This implies that the respondents did not perceive any of the eight scenarios as serious, regardless of the fact that a number of them included not only violations of official rules but also explicit violations of criminal laws (e.g., scenario 3: theft of knife from crime scene; scenario 9: auto body shop 5% kickback).

On the other hand, there are two scenarios with the means on the serious side of the scale. The scenario describing unjustifiable use of deadly force (scenario 4)—the most severe type of force available—was evaluated as very serious (with the mean value of 4.46; Table 6.3). However, the scenario evaluated as the most serious of all ten scenarios involved (only) verbal abuse (scenario 7: verbal abuse—"Arrest an Asshole Day"). It is a rather surprising finding that an instance of verbal abuse, which corresponds to the lowest point on the use of force continuum, is evaluated as more serious than the use of deadly force, which corresponds to the highest point on the use of force continuum.

A comparison of perceptions of seriousness across the scenarios belonging to the same form of misconduct reveals illuminating conclusions. All five scenarios describing examples of police corruption (scenario 1: free meals, gifts from merchants; scenario 3: theft of knife from crime scene; scenario 5: supervisor offers holiday for errands; scenario 8: cover-up of police DUI accident; scenario 9: auto body shop 5% kickback) were evaluated as not very serious at all. In fact, regardless of whether the scenarios described a kickback, theft, or the acceptance of gratuities, the respondents evaluated them to be about the same in terms of their seriousness. Although it may be surprising that the respondents really did not differentiate across different examples of police corruption, it comes as no surprise that the respondents did not perceive cases of

Table 6.3 Police officer perceptions of seriousness and violation of rules

Scenario number and description	Own seriousness		Others' seriousness		Mean difference (own—others)	*t*-test	Violation of rules	
	Mean	Rank	Mean	Rank			Mean	Rank
Scenario 1: free meals, gifts from merchants	1.82	7	1.52	2	0.30	6.738***	4.42	6.5
Scenario 2: failure to arrest friend with warrant	1.53	2	1.64	6	−0.11	−1.692	4.10	2
Scenario 3: theft of knife from crime scene	2.02	8	1.82	7	−0.20	3.354**	4.17	4
Scenario 4: unjustifiable use of deadly force	4.46	9	4.69	10	−0.23	−4.819***	3.15	1
Scenario 5: supervisor offers holiday for errands	1.55	3	1.55	4	0.00	0.00	4.47	8
Scenario 6: officer strikes prisoner who hurt partner	N/A	N/A	N/A	N/A	N/A	N/A	N/A	N/A
Scenario 7: verbal abuse—"Arrest an Asshole Day"	4.98	10	3.98	9	1.00	43.070***	4.16	3
Scenario 8: cover-up of police DUI accident	1.27	1	1.56	5	−0.28	−6.438***	4.42	6.5
Scenario 9: auto body shop 5% kickback	1.77	5.5	1.53	3	0.24	5.842***	4.96	10
Scenario 10: false report on drug on dealer	1.76	4	2.01	8	−0.25	−5.842***	4.18	5
Scenario 11: Sgt. fails to halt beating	1.77	5.5	1.25	1	0.52	10.261***	4.93	9

$^{*}p<0.05$; $^{**}p<0.01$; $^{***}p<0.001$

police corruption as very serious. In a country that has consistently ranked in the bottom third of the Transparency International Corruption Perceptions Index (2014), and in which close to 90% of the respondents on the Global Corruption Barometer (2013) perceived that the police are corrupt/extremely corrupt, corruption—particularly public sector corruption—seems to be a way of life. In an environment in which corruption is tolerated by the society at large and it permeates through all aspects of society, it is by no means surprising that our respondents evaluated scenarios describing police corruption as not serious as all. In the broader context, these scenarios are so low on the grand seriousness scale of corruption that, in the eyes of our respondents, the differences among them may be so small that our scale did not capture them.

The questionnaire featured three scenarios describing the use of excessive force (scenario 4: unjustifiable use of deadly force; scenario 7: verbal abuse—"Arrest an Asshole Day," scenario 11: Sgt. fails to halt beating). The scenario describing the supervisor's omission (failure to intervene and stop the beating) was evaluated to be by far less serious than both the explicit use of deadly force and the explicit verbal abuse. On the other hand, the respondents provided little differentiation between verbal abuse and use of deadly force. This is rather surprising because these two match the opposite ends of the use of force continuum. At the same time, both of these behaviors, unlike cases of police corruption, were evaluated as serious.

A comparison of the respondents' own estimates of seriousness with their estimates of how serious others would evaluate the same behaviors revealed several key findings. To begin, the differences were statistically significant in seven out of ten scenarios (Table 6.3). At the same time, these differences were mostly below the threshold of 0.50, established in prior research as a gauge for substantive importance.[2] In fact, these differences were above 0.50 for only two scenarios (scenario 7: verbal abuse—"Arrest an Asshole Day"; scenario 11: Sgt. fails to halt beating; Table 6.3). Respondents' evaluations of seriousness of these scenarios were higher than their respective assessments of others' evaluations of seriousness. While both scenarios describe variations on the abuse of force theme, they were evaluated as being of quite different levels of seriousness (i.e., verbal abuse in scenario 7 was evaluated as the most serious behavior in the questionnaire and the Sergeant's failure to stop the beating in scenario 11 was evaluated to be in the middle of the range).

The exploration of the two sets of rankings—a relative measure suggestive of how serious the scenario was perceived compared to other scenarios in the questionnaire—yielded that these rankings are similar, but, at the same time, that they are far from identical. For example, the scenario describing the failure to arrest a friend with an arrest warrant (scenario 2) was evaluated as one of the least serious scenarios according to their own estimates of seriousness, while they perceived that it would be evaluated by others to be somewhere in the middle of the scale. Similarly, the scenario describing the Sergeant's failure to stop the beating (scenario 11) was evaluated as being in the middle of the scale by their own accounts, while they

[2] Following the rule of thumb established in prior work (Klockars 2006, p. 26), we consider only the differences of 0.50 or larger to be meaningful.

assumed that the others would evaluate it as the least serious scenario in the questionnaire.

Violation of Official Rules

The next question inquired of the respondents to state whether the behaviors described in the questionnaire could be classified as examples of rule-violating behavior. The respondents could have selected an answer on a five-point Likert scale, ranging from "definitely not" to "definitely yes."

All of the behaviors selected for inclusion in the questionnaire constitute violations of official rules and many are violations of criminal law as well. Indeed, the respondents seemed to have no problems recognizing and acknowledging this fact; with one exception, the behavior in all scenarios was evaluated as rule violating (i.e., the mean values were all above 4; Table 6.3). In fact, two scenarios (scenario 9: auto body shop 5% kickback; scenario 11: Sgt. fails to halt beating) had means very close to 5 and approached the end of the scale. Nonetheless, despite being recognized as definite violations of official rules by virtually all police officers in the sample, our respondents did not regard these scenarios as serious at all (Table 6.3).

The only scenario that does not fit the broad pattern of being recognized as a violation of official rules is the scenario describing the use of deadly force (scenario 4). While it provides an example of use of deadly force—the most severe use of force on the use of force continuum—and has been evaluated by the respondents both in relative and absolute terms as one of the most serious violations in the questionnaire (Table 6.3), the respondents were quite ambivalent about whether it constitutes a violation of the official rules. A more detailed analysis of their answers revealed that this mean, lower than any of the other means in Table 6.3 was not driven by a few outliers. Rather, it represents the majority view (71% of the officers selected "3" which is the middle choice on the five-point scale). It is quite possible that the history of serious violations of human rights, committed with the approval and even request of the politicians, created an atmosphere in which the use of excessive force is tolerated and had not been considered a "big issue" (Maxim 2010).

A comparison of the respondents' answers about the rule violations with their estimates of seriousness for the same scenarios point toward a rather weak similarity between the rankings (Table 6.3). It almost appears as if, the more likely the respondents were to evaluate the behavior as rule violating, the less likely they were to evaluate it as serious. For example, while they definitely evaluated the kickback (scenario 9: auto body shop 5% kickback) as a rule-violating behavior, they did not view it as very serious. On the other hand, they had most problems evaluating the use of deadly force as rule violating, yet, they perceived this scenario as very serious.

The correlation (Spearman's correlation coefficient = −0.323; n.s.) which was not statistically significant, further confirms the conjecture of a weak and negative relation between their perceptions of misconduct seriousness with their evaluations of the behavior as rule violating. However, the relation was stronger for their estimates of others' evaluations of seriousness and knowledge of the official rules (Spearman's correlation coefficient=−0.839; $p<0.01$).

Appropriate and Expected Discipline

The next two questions asked the respondents to share their views about the appropriate discipline for the behaviors described in the questionnaire, as well as estimate what discipline would be meted out in their agencies for such behavior. As discussed earlier, the answers were adjusted to fit the Russian conditions and included: "no discipline," "public reprimand," "fine up to 10% of the employee's salary," "fine up to 20% of the employee's salary," "reassignment to a different position," and "dismissal." The respondents' views were evaluated in three different ways. The results were first presented for the respondents' views of the discipline the respondents thought was appropriate and then for the discipline the respondents expected to be meted out by the police agencies.

First, the assessment of the appropriate discipline relies on modal values (Table 6.4). To begin, there is very little variability across the scenarios, with the respondents most likely selecting either no discipline at all ("none") or most lenient discipline possible. In particular, in six out of ten scenarios the respondents thought that no discipline should be appropriate (scenario 1: free meals, gifts from merchants; scenario 4: unjustifiable use of deadly force; scenario 5: supervisor offers holiday for errands; scenario 8: cover-up of police DUI accident; scenario 10: false report on drug on dealer; scenario 11: Sgt. fails to halt beating), in three out of ten scenarios (scenario 2: failure to arrest friend with warrant; scenario 3: theft of knife from crime scene; scenario 9: auto body shop 5% kickback) they thought that the least severe discipline should be used ("public reprimand"), and in only one out of ten scenarios (scenario 7: verbal abuse—"Arrest an Asshole Day") they thought that "reassignment" was appropriate.

The six scenarios in which the respondents thought that no discipline should be appropriate encompass a heterogeneous set of behaviors, from the acceptance of free meals (scenario 1) and the cover up of police DUI and accident (scenario 8) to the use of deadly force (scenario 4) and falsifying an official report (scenario 10; Table 6.4). While a number of them are on the less serious side and are evaluated as such by the respondents (e.g., scenario 1: free meals, gifts from merchants; scenario 8: cover-up of police DUI accident), some of them are very serious forms of misconduct (scenario 4: unjustifiable use of deadly force; scenario 10: false report on drug dealer) and may have been evaluated as such by the respondents as well (scenario 4: unjustifiable use of deadly force, but not scenario 10: false report on drug dealer). At the same time, five out of six scenarios were recognized by the majority of the respondents as violations of the official rules. Strikingly, despite their knowledge of the official rules, the respondents thought that the police officer who engaged in such obvious rule violating should not be disciplined.

Table 6.4 Views about appropriate discipline (should) and expected discipline (would)

Scenario number and description		Mode	Rank should	Rank would	None	Some discipline	Dismissal	Chi-square test	Phi
Scenario 1: free meals, gifts from merchants	Should	None	1–6		99.1 %	0.9 %	0.0 %	0.19	0.140
	Would	Public reprimand		6–9	1.9 %	98.1 %	0.0 %		
Scenario 2: failure to arrest friend with warrant	Should	Public reprimand	7–9		47.2 %	52.8 %	0.0 %	106.00***	1.000
	Would	Reassignment		10	47.2 %	52.8 %	0.0 %		
Scenario 3: theft of knife from crime scene	Should	Public reprimand	7–9		0.0 %	100 %	0.0 %	N/A[a]	N/A[a]
	Would	Public reprimand		6–9	0.9 %	97.2 %	0.0 %		
Scenario 4: unjustifiable use of deadly force	Should	None	1–6		100 %	0.0 %	0.0 %	N/A[a]	N/A[a]
	Would	None		6–9	96.2 %	1.9 %	0.0 %		
Scenario 5: supervisor offers holiday for errands	Should	None	1–6		100 %	0.0 %	0.0 %	N/A[a]	N/A[a]
	Would	None		1–5	100 %	0.0 %	0.0 %		
Scenario 6: officer strikes prisoner who hurt partner	Should	N/A	N/A	N/A	N/A	N/A	N/A	N/A	N/A
	Would	N/A	N/A	N/A	N/A	N/A	N/A		
Scenario 7: verbal abuse—"Arrest an Asshole Day"	Should	Reassignment	10		0.0 %	100 %	0.0 %	N/A[a]	N/A[a]
	Would	Public reprimand		6–9	0.0 %	100 %	0.0 %		
Scenario 8: cover-up of police DUI accident	Should	None	1–6		99.1 %	0.9 %	0.0 %	N/A[a]	N/A[a]
	Would	None		1–5	100 %	0.0 %	0.0 %		
Scenario 9: auto body shop 5 % kickback	Should	Public reprimand	7–9		100 %	0.0 %	0.0 %	N/A[a]	N/A[a]
	Would	None		1–5	75.5 %	0.0 %	24.5 %		
Scenario 10: false report on drug on dealer	Should	None	1–6		100 %	0.0 %	0.0 %	N/A[a]	N/A[a]
	Would	None		1–5	100 %	0.0 %	0.0 %		
Scenario 11: Sgt. fails to halt beating	Should	None	1–6		99.1 %	0.9 %	0.0 %	52.50***	−0.704
	Would	Public reprimand		6–9	1.9 %	98.1 %	0.0 %		

$*p<0.05$; $**$; $p<0.01$; $***$; $p<0.001$

[a] The chi-square test could not be computed because there was no variability in either should and/or would measure (i.e., all the respondents selected the same answer)

For the scenarios for which respondents thought that some discipline should be appropriate, the most frequently selected disciplinary option was "public reprimand," the least serious form of discipline possible (scenario 2: failure to arrest friend with warrant; scenario 3: theft of knife from crime scene; scenario 9: auto body shop 5% kickback). In one scenario (scenario 7: verbal abuse—"Arrest an Asshole Day"), they picked "reassignment," one of the harshest forms of discipline. The behaviors described in these scenarios (with the exception of scenario 7) are some of the most serious forms of police misconduct (e.g., stealing from the crime scene, accepting kickbacks); they surely violate official rules in any country. However, although the respondents were able to recognize them as rule-violating behaviors, they typically did not perceive them as very serious (with the exception of scenario 3).

Second, the respondents' views about the appropriate discipline were further analyzed via the percentages of police officers who selected either "no discipline," "some discipline," or "dismissal" (Table 6.4). There was not a single scenario in which not even a slim minority of the respondents thought that dismissal was appropriate. In fact, in seven out of ten scenarios (scenario 1: free meals, gifts from merchants; scenario 4: unjustifiable use of deadly force; scenario 5: supervisor offers holiday for errands; scenario 8: cover-up of police DUI accident; scenario 9: auto body shop 5% kickback; scenario 10: false report on drug on dealer; scenario 11: Sgt. fails to halt beating) the overwhelming majority—99 or even 100%—thought that the police officer who engaged in such behavior should not be disciplined at all (Table 6.4). In one additional scenario (scenario 2: failure to arrest friend with warrant), about one half of the respondents (47.2%; Table 6.4) thought that no discipline should be the appropriate response. In other words, there was only one scenario (scenario 3: theft of knife from crime scene) in which the majority of the respondents (100%; Table 6.4) thought that some discipline should be appropriate. In that case, describing a serious form of police corruption that definitely violates official rules, all of the respondents uniformly selected "public reprimand"—the least serious form of discipline—as the appropriate discipline.

Third, the relation between the respondents' perceptions of the appropriate discipline and their perceptions of misconduct seriousness was explored as well. However, the comparison proved to be difficult because the respondents' views of the appropriate discipline were so tightly clustered in only three categories and many scenarios shared the same ranking (six scenarios had the same modal value of "none" and shared the rankings 1–6; three scenarios had the same modal value of "public reprimand" and shared the rankings of 7–9). Consequently, although the size of the Spearman's correlation coefficient (0.344, n.s., for own perceptions of seriousness and 0.284, n.s., for others' evaluations of seriousness) suggests at least some positive correlation between the respondents' views of the misconduct seriousness and the appropriate discipline, neither correlation was statistically significant. The results were very similar for the relation between the respondents' views of the appropriate discipline and evaluations of behavior as rule violating, with the opposite direction of the relation (−0.242, n.s.).

The second question about discipline tapped into the potential discipline that the police agency would mete out for such misconduct. The results are again presented by using modal values, percentages, and correlations.

First, the analysis of data using modal values of expected discipline (Table 6.4) showed that the respondents thought that police officers who engaged in any of the behaviors described in the questionnaire—including very serious forms of police misconduct that violate not only official rules but the rules of criminal law as well—would not be dismissed for such behavior. In fact, in five out of ten scenarios, including use of deadly force and acceptance of a kickback (scenario 4: unjustifiable use of deadly force; scenario 5: supervisor offers holiday for errands; scenario 8: cover-up of police DUI accident; scenario 9: auto body shop 5 % kickback; scenario 10: false report on drug on dealer), the respondents did not expect their police agencies to mete out any discipline. In the one half of the scenarios in which they expected some discipline to be meted out, modal values indicated that the respondents expected the most lenient form of discipline. In particular, in four out of five scenarios (scenario 1: free meals, gifts from merchants; scenario 3: theft of knife from crime scene; scenario 7: verbal abuse—"Arrest an Asshole Day," scenario 11: Sgt. fails to halt beating), they expected "public reprimand." The only scenario in which they expected the more severe discipline of "reassignment" was scenario 2 (fail to arrest friend with warrant).

Second, the percentage analysis confirmed the basic findings from the modal analyses and further refined the findings. Indeed, in none of the scenarios did the majority of the respondents expect dismissal to follow. In only one scenario (scenario 9: auto body shop 5 % kickback) was there a substantial minority of the respondents (21 %; Table 6.4) who thought that their police agency would fire police officers who accepted a kickback and the majority of the respondents expected that the police officer who engaged in this behavior should be reassigned (Table 6.4).

However, our respondents' dominant view about the possible discipline was far from dismissal. In five out of ten scenarios (scenario 4: unjustifiable use of deadly force; scenario 5: supervisor offers holiday for errands; scenario 8: cover-up of police DUI accident; scenario 9: auto body shop 5 % kickback; scenario 10: false report on drug on dealer), or one half of the scenarios, the overwhelming majority of the respondents—at least 75 % and in some instances, even 100%—expected no discipline to be meted out (Table 6.4). Additionally, about one half of the respondents did not expect any discipline for scenario 2 (fail to arrest friend with warrant). The results imply that the respondents felt comfortable engaging in these types of misconduct, including some very serious forms of misconduct such as the use of deadly force and the acceptance of a kickback, without fear of discipline from their agencies.

Finally, there were four scenarios (scenario 1: free meals, gifts from merchants; scenario 3: theft of knife from crime scene; scenario 7: verbal abuse "Arrest an Asshole Day," scenario 11: Sgt. fails to halt beating) in which the overwhelming majority of the respondents—97 % or more—expected some discipline. In all these cases, they expected the most lenient form of discipline, namely "public reprimand," despite the fact that some of them included very serious forms of police misconduct, such as stealing from a crime scene.

Third, the exploration of the relation between the expected discipline and respondents' views of misconduct seriousness was also confounded with the fact that there was very limited variability in modal answers, resulting in a large number of scenarios sharing the same rank (five scenarios had the same modal value of "none" and shared the rankings 1–5; four scenarios had the same modal value of "public reprimand" and shared the rankings of 6–9). Although the sizes of the Spearman's correlation coefficients (0.373, n.s., for own perceptions of seriousness and 0.141, n.s., for others' evaluations of seriousness) are suggestive of a positive correlation between the respondents' own views of the misconduct seriousness and the appropriate discipline, these correlation coefficients are not statistically significant.

On the other hand, the correlation between the respondents' evaluations of rule-violating behavior and the expected discipline is statistically significant and negative. Specifically, the more likely they were to recognize the behavior as rule violating, the less likely the respondents were to state that harsher discipline would follow (Spearman's correlation coefficient −0.589, $p<0.05$). This relation could be sensitive to the potential methodological and substantive issues affecting the measurement of the rule-violating behavior (e.g., with one exception, the mean values were clustered very closely between 4 and 5; the respondents had most problems recognizing the use of deadly force as rule-violating behavior).

Finally, a comparison of the results for the appropriate and expected discipline indicates that the respondents' views about appropriate discipline and the discipline they expect their agencies to mete out are similar. In particular, modal analysis indicates that the modes were identical in five out of ten scenarios. In three scenarios (scenario 1: free meals, gifts from merchants; scenario 2: failure to arrest friend with warrant; scenario 11: Sgt. fails to halt beating), the modal expected discipline was harsher than the modal appropriate discipline, suggesting that the respondents would evaluate such discipline as too harsh. For two of the scenarios, the respondents thought that there should be no discipline, while they expected their police agencies to apply some discipline, albeit the least severe discipline possible. On the other hand, there were two scenarios (scenario 7: verbal abuse—"Arrest an Asshole Day"; scenario 9: auto body shop 5% kickback) in which the respondents thought that the harsher discipline is appropriate than the discipline they expected their agencies to mete out.

In eight out of ten scenarios, the distribution of answers across "none," "some discipline," and "dismissal" categories was almost identical, to the point that it was not even possible to calculate the chi-square test (Table 6.4). For example, 100% of the respondents selected "none" as their answer on the question about the appropriate discipline for scenario 10 (false report on drug on dealer) and 100% of the respondents selected "none" as their answer to the question about the expected discipline. In two scenarios (scenario 1: free meals, gifts from merchants; scenario 11: Sgt. fails to halt beating), the distribution of answers for the appropriate and expected discipline differed substantially. In both scenarios, the overwhelming majority of the respondents (99%) thought that a police officer who engaged in this behavior should not be disciplined at all, while about the same percent of the respondents (98%) expected that the police agency would mete out some discipline—public reprimand—for such behavior (Table 6.4). In these two scenarios, the respondents thus perceived any discipline, including the most lenient discipline such as public reprimand, as too harsh.

Finally, the correlation coefficient measuring relation between the respondents' views of the appropriate and expected discipline indicates a moderate correlation (0.357, n.s.) that, at the same time, is not statistically significant.

Willingness to Report Misconduct

The last two questions after each scenario asked the respondents to express how willing they would be to report the described misconduct and to estimate how willing other officers in their agencies would be to do so. The answers ranged on a five-point Likert scale from "definitely not" to "definitely yes."

An analysis of the means of their own reporting suggests that the code of silence would protect almost all of the behaviors described in the questionnaire (Table 6.5). Specifically, in nine out of ten scenarios, the mean values are clustered on the non-reporting side (all are between 1 and 2), suggesting that the majority of the respondents would be reluctant to report a police officer who engaged in any of these behaviors. In fact, some of the scenarios (e.g., scenario 8: cover-up of police DUI accident; scenario 10: false report on drug on dealer) had means of 1 or very close to 1, indicating a very strong homogeneity of the views. Even in the only scenario with a mean value of above 2 (scenario 4: unjustifiable use of deadly force), the mean value is not even reaching the midpoint of the scale. In other words, even for this scenario describing the abuse of the most severe type of force, the mean value stays on the non-reporting side of scale, suggesting that even such behavior would be covered by the code of silence.

The analysis by the type of misconduct is simple. The code of silence seems to be strong and protects all forms of police corruption described in the questionnaire, regardless of whether they include the acceptance of free meals (scenario 1) or the acceptance of a kickback (scenario 9) and the theft from a crime scene (scenario 3). There is some minimal variation within the use of force types of misconduct. In particular, all abuses of the right to use force described in the questionnaire would be protected (scenario 4: unjustifiable use of deadly force; scenario 7: verbal abuse—"Arrest an Asshole Day"; scenario 11: Sgt. fails to halt a beating), with the abuse of the deadly force (scenario 4: unjustifiable use of deadly force) being the least likely to be protected (Table 6.5).

The respondents' unwillingness to report was closely related to how serious they evaluated the behaviors (Spearman's correlation coefficient $=0.590$, $p<0.05$); the more serious they perceived the behavior to be, the more likely they were to say that they would report it. Their reporting preferences were also negatively correlated with the likelihood that the behavior is a violation of the official rules (Spearman's correlation coefficient $=-0.677$, $p<0.05$); in a counterintuitive manner, the more likely they were to evaluate the behavior as rule violating, the more likely they were to say that they would not report it. Furthermore, the reporting preferences were

Table 6.5 Police officer perceptions of willingness to report

Scenario number and description	Own willingness to report		Others' willingness to report		Mean difference (own—others)	*t*-test
	Mean	Rank	Mean	Rank		
Scenario 1: free meals, gifts from merchants	1.37	4	1.28	2.5	0.09	0.895
Scenario 2: failure to arrest friend with warrant	1.80	8	1.75	6.5	0.05	0.587
Scenario 3: theft of knife from crime scene	1.78	7	1.86	8	−0.08	−1.421
Scenario 4: unjustifiable use of deadly force	2.87	10	2.84	10	0.03	1.000
Scenario 5: supervisor offers holiday for errands	1.56	6	1.75	6.5	−0.19	−2.311*
Scenario 6: officer strikes prisoner who hurt partner	N/A	N/A	N/A	N/A	N/A	N/A
Scenario 7: verbal abuse—"Arrest an Asshole Day"	2.00	9	2.00	9	0.00	N/A[a]
Scenario 8: cover-up of police DUI accident	1.00	1	1.55	5	−0.55	−6.289***
Scenario 9: auto body shop 5 % kickback	1.28	3	1.28	2.5	0.00	N/A[a]
Scenario 10: false report on drug on dealer	1.01	2	1.29	4	−0.28	−6.438***
Scenario 11: Sgt. fails to halt beating	1.51	5	1.05	1	−0.46	7.029***

[a] *t*-test cannot be computed because the difference was zero and the standard error of the difference was also zero

related to the perceived severity of the expected discipline (Spearman's correlation coefficient = 0.704, $p < 0.05$); the more severe the discipline they expected, the more likely they were to say that they would report such behavior. At the same time, the estimate of the strength of the relation with the perceptions of severity of appropriate discipline, though non-trivial in magnitude, was not statistically significant (Spearman's correlation coefficient = 0.409, n.s.).

The analysis of the means for the estimates of others' willingness to report yields very similar results to the analysis of the means for their own willingness to report. Specifically, the results indicate that the code of silence is strong and that it would protect almost all of the behaviors described in the questionnaire (Table 6.5); in nine out of ten scenarios, the mean values are all between 1 and 2, suggesting that the majority of the respondents perceived that their colleagues would be reluctant to report a police officer who engaged in any of these behaviors. The only scenario with a mean above 2 is the only scenario describing the use of deadly force (scenario 4: unjustifiable use of deadly force). In this scenario, the mean is above 2, but does not cross the midpoint into the reporting side of the scale. Simply put, the mean value suggests that even abusing deadly force would be protected by the code of silence.

Similarly, the analysis by the type of misconduct reveals little variability. All five scenarios with police corruption examples (scenario 1: free meals, gifts from merchants; scenario 3: theft of knife from crime scene; scenario 5: supervisor offers holiday for errands; scenario 8: cover-up of police DUI accident; scenario 9: auto body shop 5% kickback) have means below 2, suggesting that the officers perceived that other police officers would protect them in silence. Although all three examples of the abuse of force (scenario 4: unjustifiable use of deadly force; scenario 7: verbal abuse—"Arrest an Asshole Day;" scenario 11: Sgt. fails to halt beating) would be protected by the code, the mean value for the use of deadly force scenario (scenario 4) is the highest and, thus, least likely to be protected by the code.

The respondents' estimates of the code of silence among other officers were strongly related to how serious they perceived that other officers would evaluate the scenarios (Spearman's correlation coefficient = 0.854, $p < 0.01$). The relation with their own estimates of seriousness was neither strong nor was it statistically significant (Spearman's correlation coefficient = 0.388, n.s.). Their estimates of others' willingness to report yielded statistically significant correlations with neither appropriate discipline (Spearman's correlation coefficient = 0.349, n.s.) nor expected discipline (Spearman's correlation coefficient = 0.283, n.s.).

A comparison of the respondents' own willingness to report and their estimates of others' willingness to report reveals that these estimates are very close (Table 6.5);[3] in all but one scenario, the differences are small, below the cutoff of 0.50. The cor-

[3] The *t*-test could not be computed in two scenarios (scenario 7 and scenario 9) because the difference between the means was zero. The differences were not statistically significant in four scenarios (Table 6.5), and were statistically significant in four scenarios (scenario 5, scenario 8, scenario 10, and scenario 11). However, out of the latter four scenarios, the application of the rule of thumb suggests that the differences were large and meaningful in only one case—scenario 8.

relation analysis also supports the view that these two measures are closely related (Spearman's correlation coefficient = 0.744, $p < 0.01$).

The only scenario in which the difference is above 0.50 is scenario 8 (cover-up of police DUI accident). In this scenario, the respondents assumed that others would be somewhat more likely to report than they would. The respondents evaluated this scenario as the least serious by the respondents, but they also thought that the others would evaluate it as somewhat more serious. At the same time, the respondents both expected no discipline and supported such a disciplinary outcome.

Conclusion

As Cheloukhine and Haberfeld (2011) assert, the phenomenon of corruption in Russia has penetrated political, economic, judicial, and social systems so thoroughly that is has ceased to be a deviation from the norm and has become the norm itself. A government plagued by corruption will tend to rely on a corrupt law enforcement agency that will not only facilitate the existence of such government but, in addition, will develop its own modality of misconduct. The effects of the larger environment and the culture tolerant of police misconduct are traceable in our empirical findings. On the one hand, the overwhelming majority of the officers were able to recognize that all the forms of misconduct included in the questionnaire constitute violations of the official rules. On the other hand, with the exception of the use of deadly force, they did not perceive that any of the described forms of misconduct were serious and, accordingly, approved and expected no severe discipline. In the environment in which corruption is entrenched into everyday life and everything is for sale (see, e.g., Kosals 2010), the acceptance of kickbacks (scenario 9) and thefts from the crime scene (scenario 3) are the new "normal." In the situation in which planting of evidence on innocent people and falsification of official records to bust the arrest records are occurring on a regular basis (see, e.g., Dymovsky 2009), falsification of a police record (scenario 10) and a failure to exercise an arrest warrant on a friend (scenario 2) are also becoming the new "normal."

For the past two decades, the perceptions of Russian citizens of its police force have been consistently negative (e.g., Semukhina 2014b). Various international surveys, from the International Crime Victimization Survey and the World Value Survey, to the New Europe Barometer and the European Social Survey, demonstrate that, compared to the level of confidence in the police in other countries, the level of confidence in the Russian police is quite low (Semukhina 2014b). Despite the police reforms carried over the years (e.g., Kosals 2010), distrust toward the police remains very high, to the point that citizens actually avoid all contacts with the police, both as an organization and with the police officers are its representatives (Semukhina and Reynold 2014).

Some highly publicized police scandals may have had an additional influence on the way the Russian citizens view its police. Such negative perception of the organization and its employees can become a self-fulfilling prophecy, in which police officers whose behaviors are already condemned by the population they serve become more tolerant of its own misconduct. The subcultural themes of “being on the side of the angels” (Crank and Caldero 2001) can contribute to the way police officers interpret violations of organizational rules, especially under constant criticism and distrust from the public they are charged to protect.

On a positive note, despite the corrupt governmental institutions in Russia, it is encouraging to discover that there is indeed a quite clear recognition, at least in police officer perceptions, that the behaviors described in our questionnaire represent various kinds of professional misconduct. On a more somber note, however, it is also quite clear that the respondents, despite the awareness of rule-violating behaviors, did not think that serious disciplinary action should be applied.

References

Barabanov, I., & Aronov, N. (2010). Raby OMONa, The New Times, January 2, 2010.

Burger, E., & Cheloukhine, S. (2013). *Counterterrorism in areas of political unrest: The case of Russia's Northern Caucasus*. New York: Springer.

Cheloukhine, S. (2008). Problem of policing economic crime in Russia. *Law Enforcement Executive Forum Journal, 8*(4), 185–193.

Cheloukhine, S. (2009). Corruption as a Condition Promoting Infiltration of Organized Crime into the System of Public Service. In G. Barkovsky & V. Vereschsagin (Eds.), *Russian anti-corruption policy*. Russia: Rostov Law School Press.

Cheloukhine, S., & Haberfeld, M. R. (2011). *Russian organized corruption networks and its international trajectories*. New York: Springer.

Cheloukhine, S., & King, J. (2007). Corruption networks as a sphere of investment activities in modern Russia. *Communist and Post-Communist Studies, 40*(1), 107–122.

Crank, J., & Caldero, M. (2001). *Police Ethics: The Corruption of Noble Cause*. Cincinnati: LexisNexis.

Dymovsky, A. (2009). Russian police officer's message to Vladimir Putin. https://www.youtube.com/watch?v=38Ma_kSJWS4. Accessed 22 Jan 2014.

European Social Survey. (2008). ESS Round 4. www.europeansocialsurvey.org.

Galeotti, M. (Ed.) (2010). *The politics of security in modern Russia*. Ashgate.

Galeotti, M. (2011). Medvedev's Law on Police: A quiet revolution? https://www.opendemocracy.net/od-russia/mark-galeotti/medvedev%E2%80%99s-law-on-police-quiet-revolution. Accessed 9 Sep 2014.

Galleotti, M. (2012). Purges, power and purpose: Medvedev's 2011 police reforms. *The Journal of Power Institutions in Post-Soviet Societies, 13,* 1–32.

Getty, A., Rittersporn, G. T., & Zemskov, V. N. (1993). Victims of the Soviet penal system in the pre-war years: a first approach on the basis of archival evidence. *The American Historical Review,* 98(4), 1017–1049.

Gudkov, L., & Dubin, B. (2006). Privatizatsiya Politsii//Index proizvola pravoohranitelnyh organov:otsenki sotciologov I kommentarii pravozashitnikov. M. Obshestvennyi verdict. 2005. p. 11–13 (*Гудков Л., Дубин Б.* Приватизация полиции // Индекс произвола правоохранительных органов: оценки социологов и комментарии правозащитников. М.: Общественный вердикт, 2005. С. 11–33).

Harding, L. (2009). Russian police officer sacked after exposing corruption on home videoblog. *The Guardian*. http://www.theguardian.com/world/2009/nov/09/russia-police-videoblog. Accessed 9 Nov 2009.
Klockars, C. B. (2006). The contemporary crises of marxist criminology. *Criminology*. DOI: 10.1111/j.1745-9125.1979.tb01389.x (7 Mar 2006).
Kolennikova, O., Kosals, L., Ryvkina, R., Simagin, Y., & Wilson, D. G. (2008). The 'economic activities' of the Russian police. *International Journal of Police Science and Management, 10*, 37–40.
Kosals, L. (2010). Police in Russia: reform or business restructuring? *Russian Analytical Digest, 84*(19), 2–7.
Levy, C. J. (2010). Videos rouse Russian anger toward police. *New York Times*. http://www.nytimes.com/2010/07/28/world/europe/28russia.html?pagewanted=all&_r=0. Accessed 28 July 2010.
Maxim, T. (2010). Moscow cop jailed over supermarket rampage. CNN, February 19, 2010. http://www.cnn.com/2010/WORLD/europe/02/19/russia.cop.jailed/
McCarthy, L. (2014). The day-to-day work of the Russian police. *Russian Analytical Digest, 151*(30), 5–8.
New World Encyclopedia. (2013). Russian Federation. http://www.newworldencyclopedia.org/entry/Russian_Federation. Accessed 24 Jan 2014.
Poduzov, S. (2010). Is police reform taking place in Russia: a view from the regions. *Russian Analytical Digest, 84*(19), 8–9.
Pustintsev, B. (2000). Police reform in Russia: Obstacles and opportunities. *Policing and Society: An International Journal, 10*(1), 79–90.
Russia Today. (2011). Russia's rebranded police initiated with major layoffs. http://rt.com/politics/police-reform-major-layoff/. Accessed 24 Jan 2014.
Russian Analytical Digest. (2010). Reputation and reform: opinions on the Russian militia. *Russian Analytical Digest, 84*(19), 10–13.
Russian Federal State Statistics Service. (2011). http://www.gks.ru/wps/wcm/connect/rosstat_main/rosstat/en/main/
Semukhina, O. (2014a). Public contacts with Russian police in life-threatening situations. *Policing: An International Journal of Police Strategies & Management, 3*(2), 12.
Semukhina, O. (2014b). From militia to police: the path of Russian law enforcement reforms. *Russian Analytical Digest, 151*(30), 1–4.
Semukhina, O. B., & Reynolds, K. M. (2013). *Understanding the Modern Russian Police*. Boca Raton: CRC Press, Taylor&Francis Group.
Slade, G. (2010). Russia: crisis, crime, and police reform. https://www.opendemocracy.net/gavin-slade/russia-crisis-crime-and-police-reform. Accessed 28 Jan 2014.
The Constitution of the Russian Federation. (1993). http://www.constitution.ru/en/10003000-02.htm. Accessed 22 Jan 2014.
Transparency International. (2013). Global Corruption Barometer. http://www.transparency.org/gcb2013/country/?country=russia. Accessed 29 Jan 2014.
Transparency International. (2014). Corruption Perceptions Index. http://www.transparency.org/search. Accessed 29 Jan 2014.
UN Office on Drugs and Crime. (1994). *The Fifth United Nations Survey of Crime Trends and Operations of Criminal Justice Systems (1990–1994)*. http://www.uncjin.org/Statistics/WCTS/WCTS5/wcts5.html. Accessed 30 Jan 2014.
Wheatcroft, S. G., Davies, R. W., & Cooper, J. M. (1986). Soviet Industrialization Reconsidered: some preliminary conclusions about economic development between 1926 and 1941. *Economic history review, new series, 39*(2), 264–294.
(CIA) World Factbook. (2014). Russia. https://www.cia.gov/library/publications/the-world-factbook/index.html. Accessed 2 Mar 2014.

Chapter 7
Police Integrity in Slovenia

Branko Lobnikar, Gorazd Meško

Abstract Slovenia is a Central European democracy, independent since 1991. With a population of approximately two million and above 17,000 € gross domestic product (GDP) per capita, it is considered to be quite a successful transitional country from a former socialist republic to a functional democracy. The Slovenian police service employs 8808 personnel, one police officer for every 267 inhabitants. The survey, conducted in spring 2011 on a representative sample of 550 Slovenian police officers, provides an in-depth exploration of police integrity among Slovenian police officers after two decades of Slovene independence and 13 years after the first survey on police integrity with the same methodology was performed. The survey analyzes police integrity from the organizational/occupational culture theory of corrupt behavior perspective. The questionnaire, developed by Klockars and colleagues, consists of 14 hypothetical case scenarios. One of the main findings is that the officers' own perception of the seriousness of corruption was the most significant determinate of their willingness to report corruption. Expected discipline had no influence on willingness to report corruption. We believe that these results demonstrate a high level of police integrity among police officers in Slovenia. Nevertheless, our results also contain some evidence of the code of silence among the Slovenian police officers.

Keywords Civilian oversight · Democratization · Police integrity · Slovenia · Survey

Introduction

Slovenia is a Central European country covering 20,237 km². On 1 July 2010, Slovenia had 2,049,261 inhabitants, and, according to the 2002 census, the majority of whom were Slovenians (83.1 %), Serbs (2 %), Croats (1.6 %), and Muslims—

B. Lobnikar (✉) · G. Meško
University of Maribor, Ljubljana, Slovenia
e-mail: Branko.Lobnikar@fvv.uni-mb.si

G. Meško
University of Maribor, Ljubljana, Slovenia
e-mail: Gorazd.Mesko@fvv.uni-mb.si

S. Kutnjak Ivković, M. R. Haberfeld (eds.), *Measuring Police Integrity Across the World*,
DOI 10.1007/978-1-4939-2279-6_7

Bosnians (1.6%) the most populous minorities. The 2002 Census revealed that 58% of inhabitants are Roman Catholic. The official language is Slovenian. The capital city is Ljubljana with about 300,000 inhabitants (Government of the Republic of Slovenia 2012).

Slovenia declared independence from Yugoslavia on June 25, 1991. This was followed by the 10-day Slovenian war for independence, the departure of the Yugoslav People's Army from Slovenia (October 1991), adoption of the constitution (December 1991), and broad international recognition of the country (December 1991–May 1992). Slovenia became a member of the United Nations and in the following years also joined other major international political, security, and economic organizations, such as, the Council of Europe (1993), the European Union (2004), North Atlantic Treaty Organization (NATO; 2004), and the Organization for Economic Cooperation and Development (OECD; 2010). In 2007, Slovenia joined the eurozone.

The origins of the Slovenian police go back to the period of the Austro-Hungarian monarchy, when in 1849 the Gendarmerie Corps was founded. After World War I, and the disintegration of Austro-Hungarian Empire, Slovenia, along with its existing gendarmerie, became a part of the newly established Kingdom of Serbs, Croats, and Slovenes. Between the years 1945 and 1991, the Slovenian police were a part of the Yugoslav police force called "Milica" (militia). At that time, the Slovenian police force was subordinated directly to the Slovenian Secretariat of Interior and was decentralized to some extent—police station commanders were appointed by local authorities with approval of the Secretary of the Interior. After 1991, when Slovenia gained its independence, a period of institutional changes began and in 1992 the militia was renamed the police (Kolenc 2003; Meško and Klemenčič 2007). Unlike other Eastern European countries, the police in Slovenia were not associated with political oppression before 1991. This fact and the role of the police in the struggle for independence from Yugoslavia contributed to an interesting phenomenon—the public "approval rating" of the Slovenian police, as indicated through public surveys, was unusually high at the beginning of the transition period, decreasing until 2001 when the trend stabilized.[1]

The Slovenian police service employs 8852 personnel—one police officer per 267 inhabitants (Police 2012). The police are a (semiautonomous) body within the Ministry of the Interior, led by the director general of the police. The police are organized into state, regional, and local levels. Since 2011, there have been eight police directorates (regional level) responsible for organizing police activities and performing criminal investigations as well as coordinating police activity at a local level. The majority of police work is done at 111 police stations. There are different types of police stations: (general) police stations, traffic police stations, border police stations, maritime police stations, airport police stations, mounted police sta-

[1] The conclusions are based on the results of public opinion surveys conducted regularly by the Centre for Research of Public Opinion at the Faculty of Social Sciences, University of Ljubljana, which included questions related to the police such as "How much do you trust the police?" and "How satisfied are you with the performance of the police?" (Toš 1999, 2004).

tions, service dog handler stations, and police stations for compensatory measures (Police 2012)[2]. Police tasks at the state level are performed by the general police directorate, which is the highest body within the police organization and is represented by the director general of the police, who is appointed by the government and responsible to the Minister of the Interior. The Police Act of 1998 introduced the office of director general of the police, while formerly the Minister of Interior had been the head of the police force. This position is reserved for a professional and not a political appointee (Meško and Klemenčič 2007).

Theory on Police Corruption and Integrity

It is assumed that corruption is omnipresent in the so-called transitional societies where strain and social conditions create a greater susceptibility to corruption (Meško 2000). From that point of view, management of police corruption has always been a serious problem, particularly since police work is a highly discretionary activity that contains elements of repression and which is carried out mostly in the absence of direct supervision of senior police officials. In addition to police officers' reluctance to report their peers (the *Code of Silence*), the management of corruption is hindered by the fact that a police officer's corrupt behavior frequently involves a transaction that benefits both sides. This means that for all intents and purposes, there is no victim (in the classic sense of the word) who would have an interest in reporting this kind of offense.

If police corruption is one side of the coin, police integrity is the other. Government and accountability of the police, police integrity, and related aspects are important aspects of contemporary policing which are believed to have a central role in policing as a profession (Pagon and Lobnikar 2004). Delattre (1996) defines integrity as "the settled dispositions, the resolve and determination, the established habit of doing right where there is no one to make you do it but yourself." Further, Vicchio (1997) defines integrity at the individual level as a coherent and relatively stable set of core moral values and virtues to which one is freely and genuinely committed and which are reflected in one's actions and speech. We find the same definition given by Becker (1998): "Integrity is the principle of being principled, practicing what one preaches regardless of emotional or social pressure, and not allowing any irrational consideration to overwhelm one's rational convictions."

Girodo (2003) described integrity as simultaneously a personal attribute and a social construct. Integrity is not only a personal but also an organizational notion, as appropriate expectations and standards of operation also arise in and around organizations with regard to the tasks and operations of the organization or the people working for it. An organization's integrity can be understood as the degree to which its employees are encouraged to behave responsibly. Klockars et al. (2000; 2004)

[2] More information about the Slovenian police is available at http://www.policija.si/eng/index.php/publication.

define police integrity as the normative inclination among police to resist temptations to abuse the rights and privileges of their occupation. When discussing the normativity of integrity, authors claim: first, integrity is a belief rather than a behavior (an opinion at an individual level and a norm at group level); second, the idea of police integrity is morally charged, and police conduct is, at least to a certain degree, right or wrong; and finally, it is characteristic of integrity to be virtually inseparable from moral attitudes, since it combines a belief with an inclination to behave in accordance with that belief (Klockars et al. 2004, pp. 2–3). Integrity in policing, then, means that a police officer genuinely accepts values and moral standards of policing, possesses the virtues of the profession, and consistently and voluntarily acts in accordance with those values, standards, and virtues, even in the face of external pressures.

Contemporary theories increasingly highlight the significance of the four dimensions of sources of police corruption which, in contrast to the classic individualist approach, focus on organizational and social elements. These approaches highlight the organization's obligation to create an environment that promotes integrity and a professional culture that does not tolerate corruption. The following sections deal in brief with these dimensions (Haberfeld et al. 1999, p. 14).

Organizational Rules

Organizational rules set out in detail what is deemed corrupt behavior by the organization (the police force). Here, however, one of the main problems is defining what exactly corruption is. This applies especially to marginal corruption-related offenses such as the performance of off-duty work, acceptance of favors and small gifts, free meals, and discounts. As a matter of fact, there is no single document in Slovenia where these organizational rules would be described precisely. As the police officers are civil servants, the disciplinary misconducts are defined in Civil Servants Act in general. In particular, the integrity is mentioned in the paragraph 17 of the Police Tasks and Powers Act (2013), where it is stated that police officers in performing police tasks shall observe the code of professional conduct and strengthen police integrity. In the Organisation and Work of Police Act (2013), there is paragraph 31 on integrity and internal security within the police. According to this paragraph, the police shall ensure internal security by applying internal security procedures so as to prevent, detect, evaluate, and analyze potential risks threatening the internal security of the police, and implement measures to reduce the risks of degrading the integrity of police employees and police units. The types and methods of implementing the procedures and measures are prescribed by the minister upon a proposal of the director general of the police. Besides the laws (e.g., Penal Code), there are some bylaws on the issue (e.g., the Police Rules from 2013). The Code of Police Ethics (2008) is also important, where professional conduct of police officer is discussed in a concrete and understandable way.

Some rules of professional conduct of police officers are also defined in police officer's employment contract, and there are some organizational rules and bylaws on special issues (like on compatibility of work of a police officer with other professions) regulating police officers' behavior. Although it does not have the status of a law or bylaw, there is a document entitled The Anticorruption Program in Police[3] from 2005, where different forms of police corruption and police misconduct are explained, and accompanied with tasks for police corruption management. This document on anticorruption measures, accompanied with code of ethics, represents the foundation for strategic approach to reinforce police integrity in Slovenian police. We discuss this in the next subsection.

As the changes in the Slovenian political system were driven by demands for democratization and the respect for human rights, these changes brought about significant changes in the criminal justice system in general and in policing in particular. Meško et al. (2013) summarized these reforms. The 1991 Constitution put a high emphasis on the protection of human rights and fundamental liberties (and included a number of rights directly relevant to police practices: *Miranda*-type rights, strong limitations on pretrial detention and search and seizure powers, habeas corpus, protection of privacy and fundamental rights in criminal procedure such as the right to counsel, right to cross-examine a hostile witness, etc; Meško and Klemenčič 2007). The 1991 Constitution gave birth to two institutions, the Constitutional Court and the ombudsman, both of which greatly influenced police practices in Slovenia. During the 1990s, the Constitutional Court ruled unconstitutional a number of laws and regulations governing various police powers and practices, especially in the areas of deprivation of liberty, covert surveillance, access to lawyers, use of physical force, stop and frisk, and identity checks (Zupančič et al. 2000). These rulings further limited police powers and made them subject to more strict conditions and the principle of proportionality. On the other hand, the ombudsmen, having unrestricted access to places of custody and persons in custody as well as to all official documents regardless of the level of confidentiality, has contributed substantially to the improvements of the legal and material conditions related to police custody (Klemenčič et al. 2002).

New legislation in 1995 on criminal procedure, in particular pretrial investigation, introduced adversarial elements in the pretrial and trial stage of procedure and strengthened judicial control over police powers through wide judicial powers (and mandate) of exclusion of illegally obtained evidence and strict warrant requirements. A telling, and in comparison to other countries rather unique, example of this change is represented by the statistic regarding warrant requirements for search of premises: In the 1980s more than 80 % of all searches of premises were conducted without a warrant under the "exigent circumstances" rule, while between 2001 and 2004 only 1 % of all searches were without a warrant (Meško and Klemenčič 2007).

In 1993, when Slovenia became a member of the Council of Europe and ratified the European Convention of Human Rights, the country became subject to the jurisdiction of the European Court and later to oversight by the European Committee for the Prevention of Torture, which has (among others) the power to conduct on-site inspection of places of police custody. The Police Act of 1998 significantly

[3] Accessible only in Slovene version at www.policija.si: http://www.policija.si/images/stories/KatalogInformacijJavnegaZnacaja/PDF/akti/program_protikorupciji.pdf.

changed basic police powers, limiting the powers to stop and frisk, abolishing preventive identification checks and preventive detentions, as well as notably raising the threshold for the use of coercive measures. In 2013, new police legislation on police powers and police organization was adopted, adding some new police powers (e.g., on maintaining peace and order at sports events and prohibiting known aggressive offenders from attending sports events) and restricting police use of deadly force to the circumstances involving attacks on human life. In 2001, the public prosecutors were given stronger control over the criminal police in the process of investigating crimes, and, while remaining within the institutional framework of the police organization, they have become fully operationally subordinated to the prosecution service. Apart from contributing to the efficiency of criminal investigations, this move, given the nonpolitical and independent nature of the prosecution service, has arguably also symbolically strengthened the independence, professional status, and nonpolitical nature of the criminal police. In 2013, new acts on police organization and police powers were adopted: Police Tasks And Powers Act (2013) and Organisation And Work Of The Police Act (2013), the culmination of two decades of deliberation on the best organizational and legislative forms for police function.

Approaches to Corruption Control

The next organizational dimension addressing police corruption comprises a spectrum of measures and activities that a specific police organization uses to prevent and control corruption. Among other things, these measures include training in the area of ethics, proactive and reactive investigations of corrupt behavior, tests of integrity, and general prevention based on the use of disciplinary procedures and sanctions for violators. Within the investigation, understanding, and management of corruption, we must first abandon the belief that the term corruption exclusively denotes moral degradation of individuals. This approach is known as the "rotten apple theory."

Lobnikar et al. (2006) presented the evaluation of a case study of police officer integrity training in Slovenia. The results of the survey indicate that most of the police officers were acquainted with the concept of integrity. Moreover, those police officers who believed that high levels of integrity were crucial for performing police work also believed that high levels of integrity were the main factor in dealing with deviant behaviors within the police organization. Those whose behavior was shaped by their superiors' behavior were more satisfied at work. Of the participants, 59.1 % agreed with the statement that the unethical behavior of police officers is encouraged by supervisors showing low levels of integrity. In addition, 65.2 % agreed with the statement that indifference to integrity is shown by a bad example of police managers or supervisors. In assessing the level of police integrity, most of the participants indicated that levels of integrity in their environment are high. The participants responded that integrity of 75 % of their supervisors at police stations is very high, and that of 59.1 % of their first-line supervisors is high.

In Slovenia, civilian oversight in the resolution of complaints of ill-treatment by the police was introduced by the Police Act of 1998 and reinforced by legislation in 2013. Following the ruling of the European Court of Human Rights in the cases of *Rehbock v. Slovenia* (in 2000) and *Matko v. Slovenia* (in 2006), a department for the prosecution of officials with special authorizations within the specialized department in the Office of the State Prosecutor General was established in 2007. This took investigations of police officers suspected of committing criminal offenses out of the hands of the police organization. In 2011, this department conducted 80, and in 2010, 137 cases of criminal offenses investigation, where the suspect was a police officer. In 2011, there were 19 police officers dismissed because of they were suspected of committing a crime[4].

The Constitutional Court ruled unconstitutional a number of laws and regulations governing various police powers and practices, especially in the areas of deprivation of liberty, covert surveillance, access to lawyers, use of physical force, stop and frisk, and identity checks (Zupančič et al. 2000). These rulings further limited police powers and made them subject to stricter conditions and the principle of proportionality. Besides that, the ombudsmen, having unrestricted access to places of custody and persons in custody as well as to all official documents regardless of the level of confidentiality, has contributed substantially to the improvements of the legal and material conditions related to police custody (Klemenčič et al. 2002).

All that resulted in a well-developed process of dealing with complaints against the work of police officers[5], defined in Organisation and Work of the Police Act. A person, who disagrees with an action of a police officer or thinks a police officer failed to act while performing police tasks, which could constitute a violation of human rights or fundamental freedoms, is entitled to file a complaint. The Ministry of the Interior is responsible for the overall monitoring and supervision of the resolution of complaints, and the police are responsible for considering complaints in conciliation procedures and for certain other tasks in the complaint procedure. A complaint has to be filed within 45 days of the day when a police officer by an action or by failing to act while performing police tasks allegedly violated the human rights or fundamental freedoms of the complainant (Organisation And Work Of The Police Act 2013).

The police officer against whom a complaint was made must be served with a copy of the complaint. Throughout the procedure, the police officer must participate in the examination of the complaint and may prepare a written statement on the complaint within 5 working days of the serving of the complaint. If this is necessary to clarify the circumstances of the complaint, he can be invited to clarify additional facts in relation to the complaint. The invitation may be given to the police officer in writing, directly verbally, by telephone, or by electronic mail. The interview with

[4] Police annual report for 2011: http://www.policija.si/images/stories/Statistika/LetnaPorocila/PDF/LetnoPorocilo2011.pdf.

[5] In 2011, 627 complaints against police officers were addressed: http://www.policija.si/images/stories/Statistika/LetnaPorocila/PDF/LetnoPorocilo2011.pdf.

the police officer must take place at least 5 working days after the invitation; however, this period may exceptionally be shortened with his consent.

Submissions in a complaint procedure could be considered in a conciliation procedure or before a panel. In a conciliation procedure, a complaint is considered in the police unit within which the complainant's human rights or fundamental freedoms were allegedly violated, and a complaint is considered before a panel if the conciliation procedure was not concluded successfully. A conciliation procedure is a meeting between the head of police unit to which the police officer against whom the complaint was made is assigned and the complainant. The police supervisor must allow the complainant to present facts in relation to the complaint and propose evidence for establishing the actual situation. At the conciliation procedure meeting, the complainant is informed of his or her rights, and about the course of the complaint procedure. Police powers and the conduct of the police officer in the incident are explained and, if the complaint is justified, the complainant is informed of the measures that have been or will be taken (apology, written or oral caution to the police officer, proposal for the initiation of disciplinary procedure, minor offense proceedings or criminal proceedings, etc.).

The police officer against whom the complaint was made must be informed about the scheduled conciliation procedure meeting. However, the attendance at the conciliation procedure meeting is voluntary. If the police officer attends the conciliation procedure meeting, the police officer must be allowed to present facts and evidence related to the complaint. In some cases, a complaint is considered directly before a panel (e.g., if anybody suffered serious bodily injury, grievous bodily injury, or lost their lives in the police procedure; if the complaint concerns a police procedure in which instruments of restraint were used against more than three persons and slight bodily harm was caused).

The Ministry of the Interior designates a reporter to establish the facts of the complaint. In order to perform tasks smoothly and efficiently, a reporter has many rights, including the right to have access to the police premises, examine documents, and interview the police officers and any witnesses. Police employees must deliver to the reporter all the necessary data and documents they possess or to which they have legal access and facilitate their examination, copying and printing, that is, facilitate the examination of the complaint and provide any other assistance necessary.

A panel is appointed by the Minister of the Interior and consists of the authorized representative of the minister as the head of the panel and two representatives of the public as panel members. Any adult citizen of the Republic of Slovenia who has not been convicted by a final judgment for an intentionally committed criminal offense for which the perpetrator is prosecuted ex officio, *or* is not in criminal proceedings for an intentionally committed criminal offense for which the perpetrator is prosecuted ex officio *and* has not been convicted by a final judgment for two or more minor offenses with elements of violence or three or more serious offenses against road traffic safety for which penalty points are imposed may be appointed a representative of the public.

Invitations to the meeting are issued to the complainant, the police officer against whose work the complaint was made, authorized representatives, the reporter, witnesses, experts, and interpreters. At the meeting, the reporter presents the report on findings. The complainant and the police officer express their views on the content of the complaint and facts related to the complaint and, through the head of the panel, pose questions to the invitees or propose that additional evidence be presented. On the basis of established the facts and circumstances, the panel decides on the merits of the complaint. A decision is adopted if at least two panel members vote for it. When voting is concluded, the head of the panel immediately informs everybody present of the decision of the panel; the decision of the panel is final (Organisation and Work of The Police Act 2013).

The police in Slovenia developed a step-by-step approach to reinforce police integrity. At the beginning of this century, some surveys on police integrity were conducted (Lobnikar et al. 2000, 2004, 2006; Banutai et al. 2011), mainly supported by the police administration. Based on the knowledge gained, the National Working Group on Police Integrity was established within the police (2008–2010). This group was converted into the Integrity and Ethics Committee in the police in 2011, first as a consulting body of the director general of the police and in 2014 as a special department within the police academy. The main task of the department is systematic examination of strategic proposals, innovations, questions, and dilemmas in the field of ethics and integrity (based on the Code of Police Ethics), resolving conflict situations in all organizational levels, developing projects connected to police integrity (e.g., ethical phone, measuring organizational climate in police), taking an active role in the European Police College (CEPOL) projects (updating new curriculum on police ethics and integrity, seminars, workshops, etc.), intensifying cooperation with universities and active participation on conferences, roundtables.

Existence of the Informal Code of Silence

The Code of Silence involves the informal prohibition, inherent in the professional culture among police officers, against reporting any irregularities or violations committed by peers. Two particular characteristics of the *Code of Silence* call for special attention: first, opinions in police organizations are divided as to the issue of what kind of behavior the *Code of Silence* covers. In some organizations, it merely covers milder forms of corruption, while in others it can refer to the most severe forms of corruption. Second, the *Code of Silence* varies among individual organizations in terms of to whom it applies, in other words, what groups within the police organization it covers. In some environments, this relationship is confined to police officers' partners, where it is characterized by a high level of mutual trust, while in other places the *Code of Silence* may be extended to cover officer relationships much more comprehensively. It has been proven, however, that the *Code of Silence* is the result of the focus on punishment inherent in paramilitary forms of organization and management of the police (Pagon and Lobnikar 2001).

Lobnikar et al. (2004) conducted a survey on the frequency and the causes of violence and aggressive behavior at the workplace. It has been found that victimization of Slovenian police officers can, above all, be accounted for by social undermining by peers and superiors. Therefore, authors conclude that it is social undermining that most probably leads to victimization at the workplace (Lobnikar et al. 2004). Research has shown that these categories—the victimized (nonvictimized) or the proponents (nonproponents) of violence and aggressive behavior—partly mutually overlap, and this even further obstructs the process of violence and aggression management at workplace (Lobnikar et al. 2004).

In the first comprehensive study on police integrity in Slovenia (Pagon et al. 1998; Kutnjak Ivković et al. 2000; Pagon and Lobnikar 2004; Pagon et al. 2003, 2000), the willingness to report police misconduct (*Code of Silence*) was analyzed. The police officers were the most willing to report the most serious police misconducts—such as, theft of watch from crime scene, theft from the found wallet, and bribe from speeding motorist. The two cases where the police officers were the least willing to report were running an off-duty security system business and accepting holiday gifts from local merchants. The regression analyses revealed the officers' own perception of the seriousness of corrupt behavior was the most significant determinant of their willingness to report corruption, accounting for as much as 43.6 % of the variance. Although some cases of Code were discovered, authors concluded that police officers in Slovenia possess high integrity (Pagon and Lobnikar 2004).

The Impact of Public Expectations

The last dimension refers to the social and political environments in which the police are performing their activity. Public expectations relating to police corruption put different pressures on the police in different environments; it can be said that, as far as the management of corrupt behavior is concerned, police organizations in different environments resist public pressure in different ways.

According to Škrbec and Dobovšek (2012), both the Slovenia public opinion[6] and the statistics of courts, prosecution offices, police, and anticorruption commission show that corruption is increasing, developing into new forms and is spread throughout all areas of the society, particularly in the public sector. The results of Corruption Perceptions Index (CPI) carried out by Transparency International[7], were relatively good. CPI survey data show that the level of corruption in Slovenia

[6] Commission for the Prevention of Corruption since 2002 runs annual public surveys on corruption (Stališča o korupciji). Retrieved August 15, 2012 from http://www.kpk-rs.si/index.php?id=48.

[7] http://www.transparency.org/policy_research/surveys_indices/cpi.

in the period from 2003 to 2008 steadily declined.[8] A drop of almost ten points in 1 year is not an indicator of the worsening of the Slovenian situation but shows a more realistic situation (Dobovšek and Škrbec 2012).

The role of Commission for the Prevention of Corruption of the Republic of Slovenia established in 2004 is also worth discussing. From its establishment, the Commission adopted 237 opinions of principle[9] showing if specific conducts or actions met the definition of corruption. Out of these 237 cases, the Commission found in 167[10] cases that the analyzed conducts of individual persons, in public or private sectors, met the definition of corruption. All cases are publicly available on the Commission Internet homepage[11] in the Slovenian language.

Policing in Slovenia after 1991 has been characterized by several attempts at police reform in order to move closer to a democratic style of policing. Despite organizational, professional, and cultural obstacles, some notable changes have been achieved. While it would be an overstatement to say that the reform of the Slovenian police was successful, one can claim reasonable optimism and characterize the Slovenian police as a relatively modern and professional law enforcement service far closer to its Western counterparts than to the "militia" of communist times. The present orientation is based on the slogan "to protect and serve" and community policing is the foundation of its declared strategy (Police 2013). This transformation has been the result of a complex set of processes that have not always delivered the promised results—while community policing, professionalism, protection of human rights, and restrains on the arbitrary use of force top the official agenda, understanding of the underlying principles of problem-oriented policing and its practical implementation remains weak, and human rights monitoring mechanisms continue to voice their concerns over the inadequate system of accountability of police officers for ill-treatment of citizens (Meško and Klemenčič 2007).

Institutional reforms were closely linked to the centralization of the police in Slovenia. This was partially a by-product of a separate reform in the local self-government but was also driven by the notion that the in-depth reform of the police requires a clear hierarchy and central "command." Under the socialist system, the organization of the Slovenian police was quite decentralized (Meško and Lobnikar 2005)—prior to 1991, all police stations in the country were considered community-level units. The commanders of local and regional stations were appointed by

[8] In 2003, it reached a score of 5.9 (occupying the 29th place) and 6.7 in 2008 (occupying the 26th place). In 2009, it reached 6.6; in 2010, 6.4; and in 2011, 5.9.

[9] The Commission prepares a document called opinion of principle, where simply identifying and reviewing corruptive practices and does not evaluate criminal or other liabilities of the individual, but is assessing the actions of individuals to see if they meet the criteria, conditions, and definition of corruption, as defined in article 4 of IPCA. Opinions of principle are based on actual cases and reports (Škrbec and Dobovšek 2012).

[10] We should remind the readers that one opinion of principle may contain several conducts of corruptive practices. The opinion of principle 219 deals with four different conducts of corruptive practices and several perpetrators, so that their number is not equal to the number of opinions of principle, where corruption has been detected.

[11] http://www.kpk-rs.si/sl/nadzor-in-preiskave/odlocitve-in-mnenja-komisije.

local authorities after such appointments were approved by the Secretary of the Interior. The current police organization in Slovenia is centralized, with one national, state-funded police force, leaving local authorities with almost no influence; all police stations are state-level units which operate at the local level. The local government has no oversight in their operation or in the appointment of their commanders. While such centralization arguably facilitated the management of reforms, it soon conflicted with the new policing strategy that the police wanted to adopt: community policing (Police 2013). The involvement of local municipalities in the planning and evaluation of police work at the local level was therefore re-reintroduced to some extent with the legislation of 2013. This, accompanied with new complaining procedure, explained prior in the text, forms a new approach, attempting also to have influence on police officers misbehavior.

Methods, Data Collection, and Description of the Sample

Questionnaire

Klockars and Kutnjak (2004) developed a survey instrument that measures the extent of police integrity. Their questionnaire includes descriptions of 11 hypothetical scenarios, the majority of which address various forms of police corruption, from the acceptance of gratuities and gifts to opportunistic thefts and shakedowns. The questionnaire has been used to survey police offices in a number of countries across the world, from the USA, England, and Canada to Japan and Pakistan (see Klockars et al. 2004). Of the East-European countries in transition, it has been used in Croatia, Slovenia, Bosnia and Herzegovina, Poland, Hungary, and the Czech Republic (see Klockars et al. 2004; Kutnjak and Shelley 2005, 2007).

Klockars et al. argued that their original survey needed to be augmented if inquiry into police misconduct were to be extended beyond corruption motivated by personal gain (2000, pp. 9–10). The second version of their questionnaire includes scenarios that cover a variety of forms of police misconduct, from police corruption and use of excessive force to the planting of evidence and verbal abuse. In consultation with the Croatian police, Kutnjak (2009) added three scenarios to the questionnaire. The first added scenario describes the failure to note on a report that a crime could be classified as a hate crime, while the second one focuses on one of the more frequent forms of police corruption in East-European countries: the acceptance of a bribe from a motorist caught speeding. Finally, the third added scenario involves a failure to intervene when the police officer sees juveniles writing graffiti on a wall. These additional three scenarios were also used in the Slovenian version of questionnaire. The descriptions of scenarios correspond to various forms of police corruption and misconduct.

Each scenario is followed by the same set of questions used in both the first and the second version of the questionnaire. The follow-up questions ask about police officers' knowledge of official rules, their opinions about the seriousness of particular rule-violating behaviors, the discipline these behaviors would deserve and would actually receive, and their estimates of how willing they would be to report such behavior (Kutnjak 2009).

The methodology used in both questionnaires is the same. To facilitate comparisons across questionnaires, the authors retained five scenarios from the original questionnaire in the second questionnaire (the acceptance of gratuities, theft from a crime scene, internal corruption, cover-up of a police driving under the influence (DUI) accident, and a 5% kickback). The wording of the questionnaire is either identical or slightly changed (e.g., theft of a knife instead of a watch from a crime scene).

The last part of the questionnaire contains a few demographic questions. To increase the respondents' willingness to participate in the study and to exclude the possibility that respondents could be identified, the number of demographic questions has been kept at the minimum. These questions inquired about the length of the respondents' police experience, rank, assignment, and whether they were employed in a supervisory position.

Sample

Data were obtained from 583 police officers from all three levels of the police organization (national, regional, and local). Data were collected from all police stations (102) at the local level and from all regional police administrations (11 at the time of data collection). All the data were collected in spring 2011. The questionnaires were administered to all police officers in the shift on a particular day along with letters disclosing the intent of the survey and envelopes for return mail. We asked police officers to fill out the questionnaire, seal the envelope, and return it to the research institution. Confidentiality and anonymity were guaranteed and participation was voluntary. All community policing officers (CPOs) received personally addressed mail[12] and the same procedure as at the local police stations was used.

The majority of police officers' sample consists of male police officers, working in a medium-sized police department with 11–20 years of service within the police. The vast majority held various ranks within the category of police officers (from junior police officer to senior police officer). The sample is presented in detail in Table 7.1. In the sample, the number of CPOs is overrepresented. However, due to the fact that CPOs also perform other police tasks (e.g., crime investigation), the sample reflected the population of police officers in Slovenia (Table 7.2).

Table 7.2 data on demographic characteristics of police population in Slovenia are presented. The structure of the sample (all three organizational levels), its size, and the demographic features of questioned police officers indicate that we can generalize the findings to the entire population of police officers in Slovenia.

[12] The list of CPOs was obtained from police internet homepage: http://www.policija.si/index.php/dravljani-in-policija/vodje-policijskih-okoliev.

Table 7.1 Respondents' demographic characteristics

	Number of respondents	Percent of respondents (%)
Gender		
Male	516	88.5
Female	57	9.8
N/A	10	1.7
Agency size		
Small (up to 25)	145	24.9
Medium (26–75)	251	43.1
Large (over 75)	178	30.5
N/A	9	1.5
Length of service		
Up to 10 years	129	22.2
11–20 years	243	41.6
Over 20 years	204	35.0
N/A	7	1.2
Rank		
Police officer (from junior police officer to senior police officer)	459	78.8
Police inspector (from junior inspector to senior police inspector)	103	17.7
N/A	21	3.5
Type of assignment		
Public order	91	15.6
Crime investigation	63	10.8
Dispatch	35	6.0
Traffic	43	7.4

Table 7.1 (continued)

	Number of respondents	Percent of respondents (%)
Community policing	111	19.0
Administration	20	3.4
Other	139	23.8
N/A	81	13.9
Supervisors		
Yes		73.3
No		26.5

Table 7.2 The police force in numbers

No. of employees in the police force (on 1 October 2011)	8852
No. of police officers	7666
No. of criminal officers	885
No. of members of the special forces	91
Average age	40.7 years old
Average age of employees with police powers	38.9 let
No. of women with police powers (2012)	1142 (17.8%)
No. of employees with a Ph.D. or M.A.	167 (1.9%)
No. of employees with university or high education	2042 (23.2%)
No. of employees with higher education	564 (6.2%)
No. of employees with secondary education	5675(64.1%)
No. of employees with lower education (primary, occupational)	404 (4.6%)

Results

Assessment of Violation of Official Rules

All forms of police misconduct described in the questionnaire not only constitute violations of the official rules but also represent violations of criminal laws. Engaging in any of the forms of misbehavior described in the questionnaire should result in a disciplinary response by the police agency and, in most of the scenarios, in a response from the criminal justice system as well. The respondents could select an answer from three possible choices: "yes," "no," and "don't know." The results are presented in Table 7.3.

Respondents' opinions about whether these behaviors constitute violations of official rules vary greatly across the 14 scenarios. For each scenario, the majority of the respondents recognized that the described behavior is a violation of the official rules, although the percentage of police officers who stated that the behavior violates the official rules ranges across scenarios. In three scenarios (72% in scenario 8: cover-up of police DUI accident, 81.5% in scenario 1: free meals, gifts from merchants, and 80.4% in scenario 12: failing to report hate crime), we find some variations in answers, while there were more scenarios in which the answers were almost unanimous (e. g., scenario 3: theft of knife from crime scene with 98.9%; scenario 13: taking bribe from speeding motorist with 98.7%; and scenario 10: false report on drug dealer with 97.6% of *yes* answers regarding respondents' assessment whether behavior qualifies as a violation of official rules). There is only one case in which the level of uncertainty is high: scenario 12: failing to report hate crime (13.4% of police officers do not know if this will violate organizational rules). According to the Slovenian criminal law and court practice, the hate crime is a relatively new area, with little or no court rulings on the issue. So it is not surprising that police officers are to some extent unsure whether the case presented in scenario 12 would violate organizational rules. The results are also presented in Fig. 7.1.

Table 7.3 Respondents' assessment whether behavior qualifies as violation of official rules

	Rank	Percentage	
		Yes	No
Scenario 1: free meals, gifts from merchants	12	81.5	12.3
Scenario 2: failure to arrest friend with warrant	5	96.5	2.2
Scenario 3: theft of knife from crime scene	1	98.9	0.7
Scenario 4: unjustifiable use of deadly force	10	87.9	3.9
Scenario 5: supervisor offers holiday for errands	11	81.9	8.2
Scenario 6: officer strikes prisoner who hurt partner	7	95.1	3.1
Scenario 7: verbal abuse—"Arrest an Asshole Day"	9	89.8	6.9
Scenario 8: cover-up of police DUI accident	14	72	18.9
Scenario 9: auto body shop 5 % kickback	6	95.4	1.5
Scenario 10: false report on drug dealer	3	97.6	0.9
Scenario 11: Sgt. fails to halt beating	4	96.7	2.4
Scenario 12: failing to report hate crime	13	80.4	6.2
Scenario 13: bribe from speeding motorist	2	98.7	0.6
Scenario 14: not reacting to graffiti	8	95	1.8

DUI driving under the influence

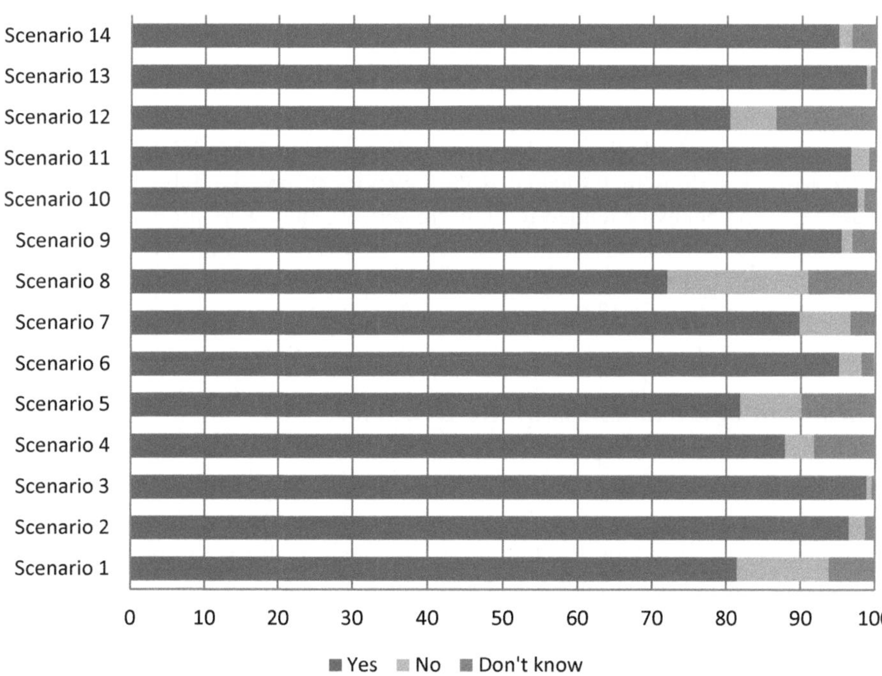

Fig. 7.1 Respondents' assessment whether behavior qualifies as a violation of official rules

Table 7.4 Police officer perceptions of seriousness

Scenario number and description	Own seriousness		Others' seriousness		*t*-test
	Mean	Rank	Mean	Rank	
Scenario 1: free meals, gifts from merchants	3.64	13	3.0	12	14.208***
Scenario 2: failure to arrest friend with warrant	4.76	3	4.3	4	15.598***
Scenario 3: theft of knife from crime scene	4.87	1	4.64	1	10.069***
Scenario 4: unjustifiable use of deadly force	4.55	6	4.35	3	8.197***
Scenario 5: supervisor offers holiday for errands	4.45	7	4.19	6	8.432***
Scenario 6: officer strikes prisoner who hurt partner	4.13	9	3.57	10	14.959***
Scenario 7: verbal abuse—"Arrest an Asshole Day"	3.66	12	3.19	11	13.768***
Scenario 8: cover-up of police DUI accident	2.87	14	2.51	13	9.744**
Scenario 9: auto body shop 5 % kickback	4.63	5	4.18	7	12.322**
Scenario 10: false report on drug dealer	4.67	4	4.3	4	12.236**
Scenario 11: Sgt. fails to halt beating	4.34	8	3.86	8	13.570**
Scenario 12: failing to report hate crime	4.01	11	3.57	10	12.659**
Scenario 13: bribe from speeding motorist	4.85	2	4.64	1	7.51**
Scenario 14: not reacting to graffiti	4.13	9	3.8	9	11.243**

** $p = 0.01$;
***$p = 0.000$

The respondents' labeling of a particular behavior as rule violating is closely related to how serious they evaluated the behavior to be (see Table 7.4): if they thought that the behavior tended to be more serious, they were more likely to say that it violated official rules (for each scenario, the correlation was statistically significant, and Cramer's *V* coefficient varied from lowest 0.257 in scenario 7 to highest 0.464 in scenario 13).

Evaluation of Seriousness of the Behavior

The respondents were asked to evaluate how serious they perceive the behaviors described in the scenarios to be. Two questions probed the respondents about the seriousness of the behavior; the first question sought their own evaluations of seriousness, while the second one asked about their estimates of how the majority of police officers in their agency would evaluate the behavior. Answers were recorded on a five-point Likert scale, ranging from "not at all serious" to "very serious."

The respondents' evaluations of scenario seriousness suggest that the scenarios were generally evaluated to be on the serious side (means are clustered between the midpoint of the scale and the "very serious" end of the scale). However, these evaluations ranged in terms of seriousness from the scenario evaluated to be the least serious, scenario 8 (describing the cover-up of a police DUI), to the scenario evaluated as the most serious, scenario 3 (describing the theft of a knife from the crime scene with the mean very close to the very serious end of the scale; see Table 7.4). We can see that the case scenarios fall into three categories of perceived seriousness: three scenarios (scenario 1: free meals, gifts from merchants; scenario 8: cover-up of police DUI accident; and scenario 7: verbal abuse—"Arrest an Asshole Day") were not considered very serious by Slovenian police officers—cover-up of police DUI accident was the only case in which the mean was lower than 3. For the other two cases in this category, the mean was somewhere between 3 and 4. Scenario 1 (free meals, gifts from merchants) focuses on the acceptance of gratuities—traditionally viewed as the stepping stone toward more serious forms of police corruption. Scenario 8 (cover-up of police DUI) is classified as internal corruption in Barker and Roebuck's classification system (1973; cit. in Kutnjak Ivković, this book). Prior research on police integrity in Slovenia (Pagon and Lobnikar, 2004) shows that internal corruption was also viewed as one of the least serious forms of police corruption in 1998, with a mean score 2.41, and was the second least serious scenario. "Free meals and gifts from merchants" was evaluated as the least serious scenario by Slovenian police officers in 1988 with a mean score of 2.00.

Respondents considered five other cases (supervisor offers holiday for errands officer strikes prisoner who hurt partner, Sgt. fails to halt beating, failing to report hate crime, and not reacting to graffiti) to be at an intermediate level of seriousness.

The three most serious scenarios have means substantially closer to 5 (the "very serious" end of the scale). These three scenarios, plain violations of criminal law, include one scenario with opportunistic theft (scenario 3: theft of knife from crime scene), a scenario involving a failure to execute an arrest warrant on a friend (scenario 2: failure to arrest friend with warrant), and scenario 13: taking bribe from speeding motorist. All three scenarios are plain violations of official rules in which a police officer does something that he/she was not supposed to do (e.g., steal the knife from a crime scene) or does not do something that he/she was supposed to do (e.g., arrest a friend). The case of shooting a runaway suspect and taking 5% of the repair bill from a local auto body shop owner are also included in this group.

A comparison of the respondents' own estimates of seriousness to their estimate of how serious the other police officers in the agency would evaluate the same scenarios revealed several findings. For each and every scenario, the respondents evaluated scenarios as more serious than they thought the other police officers would; the means for evaluations of "own seriousness" were always statistically significantly higher than the means for "others' seriousness" (see Table 7.3). Following the precedent established by Klockars et al. (2006, p. 26), we consider only differences of 0.50 or larger to be meaningful. These large and meaningful differences appeared only in three scenarios (scenario 1: free meals, gifts from merchants; scenario 6: officer strikes prisoner who hurt partner; and scenario 9: auto-body shop 5% kickback). In most cases, there is a statically significant positive correlation with work experience (except in scenarios 2, 4, and 8)—those with more work experience evaluated the majority of cases as more serious. Police chiefs/supervisors evaluate eight cases as a more serious violation when compared to the evaluations of line officers (no statistically significant differences in scenarios 3, 4, 14, and 12).

Opinions About the Appropriate and Expected Discipline

The respondents were also asked what they thought the appropriate discipline for the behaviors described in the questionnaire should be as well as what they thought the actual discipline meted out by their agencies would be. The possible responses were "no discipline," "public warning," "fine in the amount of 10 % of the employee's salary," "fine in the amount of 20 % of the employee's salary," "reassignment," and "dismissal." The percentages of the respondents who picked each disciplinary option and the modal values for each scenario are shown in Table 7.5.

The opinions on the appropriate discipline vary across scenarios, as in the case of evaluation of seriousness. Based on modal values, we can form three categories: in the first group, dismissal was most frequently regarded as an appropriate discipline (this is the fact in six scenarios: scenario 2: failure to arrest friend with warrant; scenario 3: theft of knife from crime scene; scenario 4: unjustifiable use of deadly force; scenario 9: auto body shop 5 % kickback; scenario 10: false report on drug dealer; and scenario 13: bribe from speeding motorist), the second group (reassignment ad appropriate discipline) includes two scenarios (scenario 11: Sgt. fails to halt beating, and scenario 5: supervisor offers holiday for errands), and in the third group public reprimand or no discipline were selected as appropriate (scenario 1: free meals, gifts from merchants; scenario 6: officer strikes prisoner who hurt partner; scenario 7: verbal abuse—"Arrest an Asshole Day"; scenario 12: failing to report hate crime; scenario 14: not reacting to graffiti; and scenario 8: cover-up of police DUI accident—the only scenario where police officers indicated that the perpetrator deserved no discipline). The respondents indicated that the severity of discipline will be the lowest for those offenses they perceive as less serious ("verbal abuse—'Arrest an Asshole Day'," "free meals, gifts from merchants, and cover-up of police DUI accident), and will be highest for the most serious cases (e. g., theft of knife from crime scene and bribe from speeding motorist). We can say that respondents' views on police misconduct are very consistent: The scenarios for which the modal response is dismissal were the scenarios which the respondents were most likely to evaluate as "very serious."

The perceived fairness of discipline was then analyzed. To measure how officers perceived the fairness of discipline, the scores on the "discipline *would* receive" scale were subtracted from the scores on the "discipline *should* receive" scale. A difference of zero was interpreted to mean that the respondent thought the discipline was fair. If the difference was greater than zero (positive), the respondent thought that the discipline was too lenient. Conversely, if the difference was less than zero (negative), the respondent thought that the discipline was too harsh. The results are presented in Fig. 7.2.

Table 7.5 Views about appropriate discipline (should) and expected discipline (would)

Case scenario	Should receive			Would receive			
	Mean	Rank	Mode	Mean	Rank	Mode	*t*-test sig.
Scenario 1: free meals, gifts from merchants	2.68	3	Reprimand	2.65	3	Reprimand	No sig.
Scenario 2: failure to arrest friend with warrant	4.93	11	Dismissal	4.36	8	Dismissal	$t=7.82$ $p=0.000$
Scenario 3: theft of knife from crime scene	5.72	14	Dismissal	5.50	13	Dismissal	$t=5.32$ $p=0.000$
Scenario 4: unjustifiable use of deadly force	5.29	12	Dismissal	5.53	14	Dismissal	$t=-5.63$ $p=0.000$
Scenario 5: supervisor offers holiday for errands	3.52	7	Reassignment	2.58	2	None	$t=13.24$ $p=0.000$
Scenario 6: officer strikes prisoner who hurt partner	3.32	6	Reprimand	3.59	7	Reprimand	$t=-4.15$ $p=0.000$
Scenario 7: verbal abuse—"Arrest an Asshole Day"	2.22	1	Reprimand	2.16	1	Reprimand	No sig.
Scenario 8: cover-up of police DUI accident	2.26	2	None	2.81	6	Reprimand	$t=-7.67$ $p=0.000$
Scenario 9: auto body shop 5 % kickback	4.90	9	Dismissal	4.56	10	Dismissal	$t=5,56$ $p=0.000$
Scenario 10: false report on drug dealer	4.92	10	Dismissal	4.72	11	Dismissal	$t=3.89$ $p=0.000$
Scenario 11: Sgt. fails to halt beating	4.38	8	Reassignment	4.42	9	Reassignment	No sig.
Scenario 12: failing to report hate crime	2.85	4	Reprimand	2.73	4	Reprimand	No sig.
Scenario 13: bribe from speeding motorist	5.60	13	Dismissal	5.47	12	Dismissal	$t=3.01$ $p=0.003$
Scenario 14: not reacting to graffiti	3.06	5	Reprimand	2.77	5	Reprimand	$t=4.01$ $p=0.000$

DUI driving under the influence

As we can see, in most scenarios, police officers perceive discipline to be fair, especially in the cases that were perceived to be the most serious (e.g., unjustifiable use of deadly force, taking bribe or theft from crime scene). There are only three cases where the percentage of those perceiving the discipline too harsh is higher than 20 %. Of the surveyed police officers, 31.5 % believe that discipline for covering up a fellow police officer's DUI is too harsh. This case scenario is the only one for which police officers think they should not be punished at all for their behavior and was also evaluated as the least serious scenario. In the same group, we can add the scenario describing the use of excessive use of force, and accepting free meals

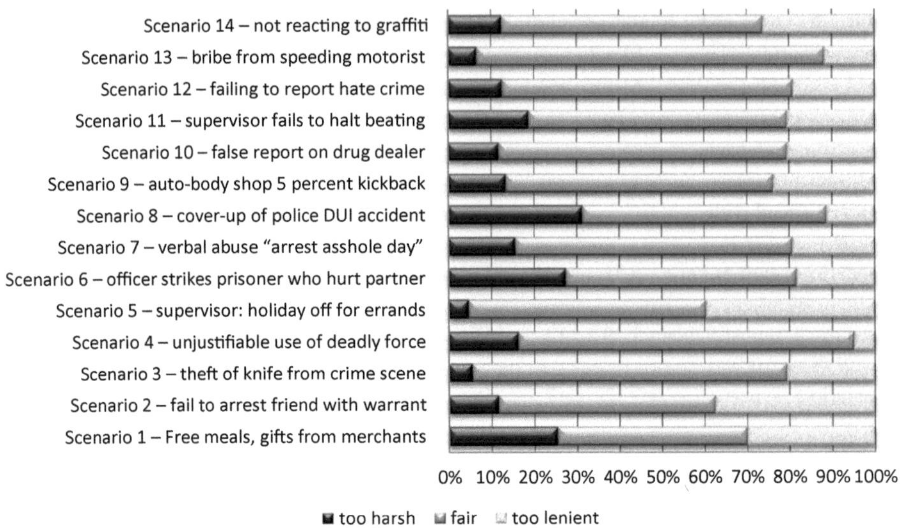

Fig. 7.2 Perceived fairness of discipline

and gifts from local merchants. On the opposite site, there are some scenarios, where discipline was perceived as too lenient. Of police officers surveyed, 39.5 % believe that discipline for a police supervisor abusing his/her power by asking a police officer to do some private work for the supervisor is too lenient (scenario 5: supervisor offers holiday for errands). They indicated that they believed the supervisor would receive no discipline. This is the only case in which respondents indicated that the perpetrator will receive no discipline, with less experienced police officers more frequently indicating that their supervisor will get no discipline.

Willingness to Report Misconduct

The last two questions after each scenario asked the respondents to indicate how willing they would be to report misconduct and to estimate how willing other officers in their agencies would be to do so. The answers ranged on a five-point Likert scale from "definitely not" to "definitely yes." The answers conveying the officers' own (un)willingness to report misconduct help us assess the extent and nature of the Code of Silence.

The scenarios also fall into three categories according to officers' willingness to report misconduct. In the cases of verbal abuse (scenario 7), accepting gifts from merchants (scenario 1), and covering up a police officer DUI (scenario 8), the respondents were less willing to report (mean score less than 3), while we observe a high willingness to report in cases of theft (scenario 3), taking bribes (scenario 13), protecting a friend from prosecution (scenario 2), falsification of evidence (scenario

10), taking money for arranging business (scenario 9), and shooting a runaway suspect (scenario 4).

Willingness to report is for all scenarios statistically significant and positively correlated with the perceived level of seriousness of the misconduct (all correlations were statistically significant at the level 0.000; Pearson "*r*" correlation coefficient varies from lowest 0.251 in scenario 13: "bribe from speeding motorist" to highest 0.709 in scenario 8: cover-up of police DUI accident)—the less serious the misconduct is perceived by police officers, the less willing they are to report the misconduct and vice versa—the more serious the behavior is evaluated, the higher is the willingness to report it. Furthermore, respondents with more work experience are in all scenarios more willing to report police misconduct compared to those with less work experience (all correlations were statistically significant at the level of 0.000; the lowest correlation in scenario 4: "unjustifiable use of deadly force": $r=0.141$ and scenario 8: "cover-up of police DUI accident": $r=0.130$; the highest correlation occurs in scenario 13: "bribe from speeding motorist": $r=0.312$). Also, as was the case in the evaluation of seriousness of scenarios, in each scenario police supervisors (all those police officers in any managerial position or with managerial duties) are more willing to report police misconduct compared to those with no managerial responsibilities (all mean differences were statistically significant at the level of 0.000).

We also compared the respondents' own willingness to report with their estimates of others' willingness to report (Tables 7.6 and 7.7). The mean values suggest that, in all 14 scenarios, the respondents seem to be somewhat more willing to report than they estimated that others would be. Although the differences between the means for their own willingness to report and the means for others' willingness to report are statistically significant in all scenarios, these differences are meaningful in only four scenarios (scenario 2: "failure to arrest friend with warrant;" scenario 3: "theft of knife from crime scene;" scenario 9: "auto body shop 5% kickback;" and scenario 11: "Sgt. fails to halt beating").[13]

As we see in Table 7.6, there are three scenarios in which the mean values are below the midpoint of the scale (scenario 1: "free meals, gifts from merchants;" scenario 8: "cover-up of police DUI accident;" and scenario 7: "verbal abuse—" 'Arrest an Asshole Day') suggesting that the behaviors described in these scenarios would be well protected by the Code of Silence. In addition, a separate analysis of the Code of Silence (measured as the percentage of the respondents who said that they would not report) shows that for each of these scenarios about one third to almost one half of the respondents said that they would *not* report a police officer who engaged in the misconduct described in the scenario (see Fig. 7.3). These three scenarios include the least serious forms of police corruption (i.e., the acceptance of gratuities), the use of verbal assault as the first step of an excessive use of force, as well as the scenario involving internal corruption. These three scenarios have been perceived as the least serious, least likely to be recognized as rule-violating behavior, and deserving the least serious forms of discipline.

[13] Following the precedent established in prior work (Klockars et al. 2006, p. 26), it can be considered only the differences of 0.50 or larger to be meaningful.

Table 7.6 Police officer perceptions of willingness to report

Scenario number and description	Own willingness to report			Others' willingness to report		*t*-test sig.
	Mean	S.D.	Rank	Mean	S.D.	
Scenario 1: free meals, gifts from merchants	2.76	0.064	12	2.27	0.047	$t=9.77$ $p=0.000$
Scenario 2: failure to arrest friend with warrant	4.14	0.051	4	3.51	0.046	$t=14.55$ $p=0.000$
Scenario 3: theft of knife from crime scene	4.6	0.037	1	4.08	0.041	$t=14.69$ $p=0.000$
Scenario 4: unjustifiable use of deadly force	4.42	0.043	2	4.15	0.045	$t=8.67$ $p=0.000$
Scenario 5: supervisor offers holiday for errands	3.47	0.06	9	3.04	0.052	$t=9.73$ $p=0.000$
Scenario 6: officer strikes prisoner who hurt partner	3.16	0.63	11	2.6	0.052	$t=12.28$ $p=0.000$
Scenario 7: verbal abuse—"Arrest an Asshole Day"	2.7	0.061	13	2.25	0.05	$t=10.72$ $p=0.000$
Scenario 8: cover-up of police DUI accident	2.27	.057	14	2.05	0.071	$t=3.32$ $p=0.001$
Scenario 9: auto body shop 5% kickback	4.06	0.051	6	3.43	0.049	$t=14.68$ $p=0.000$
Scenario 10: false report on drug dealer	4.14	0.049	4	3.6	0.048	$t=14.44$ $p=0.000$
Scenario 11: Sgt. fails to halt beating	3.61	0.06	7	3.11	0.055	$t=11.83$ $p=0.000$
Scenario 12: failing to report hate crime	3.3	0.057	10	2.83	0.049	$t=11.60$ $p=0.000$
Scenario 13: bribe from speeding motorist	4.42	0.045	2	3.99	0.047	$t=12.11$ $p=.000$
Scenario 14: not reacting to graffiti	3.49	0.056	8	2.98	0.049	$t=12.86$ $p=0.000$

S.D. standard deviation

Table 7.7 Hierarchical regression for dependent variable OWRALL

Model	*R*	R^2	Adjusted R^2	Std. Error of the estimate	df	Mean square	*F*	Sig.
1	0.828[a]	0.69	0.68	7.14	4	12851.79	252.29	0.000[b]

[a] Dependent variable: OWRALL
[b] Predictors: (Constant), MWRALL, EDALL, OSALL, MSALL

To evaluate the level of police integrity within the Slovenian police force, we used an aggregate measure (a sum of all 14 scenarios) of the "own perception of the seriousness of corrupt behavior" (OSALL), "beliefs about other officers' perception

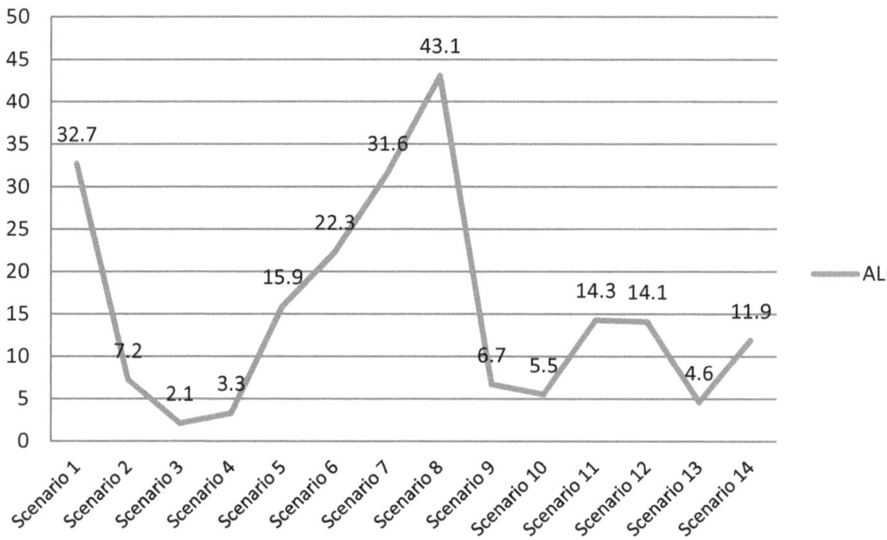

Fig. 7.3 Percentage of police officers definitely not willing to report

of corrupt behavior" (MSALL), "expected discipline" (EDALL), "own willingness to report" (OWALL) and "beliefs about other officers' willingness to report" (MWRALL). The results of regression analyzes (with "own willingness to report" as dependent variable) are presented in Tables 7.7 and 7.8.

As shown, we can explain up to 68 % of variance of the officers' willingness to report police corruption and misconduct with the four entered variables. In the following table, the contribution of each of the variables is further analyzed, and we can see that the officers' own perception of seriousness has the strongest influence on willingness to report (β=0.714), followed by beliefs about other police officers' willingness to report (MWRALL; β=0.690). We can also see that expected discipline (EDALL) is not significant, and that officers' beliefs about others' perception of corrupt behavior (MSALL) is even negatively correlated.

Table 7.8 Hierarchical regression for dependent variable OWRALL Coefficients[a]

Model		Unstandardized coefficients		Standardized coefficients	*t*	Sig.
		B	Std. error	Beta		0.000
1	(Constant)	−12.508	2.859		−4.374	0.000
	OSALL	1.152	0.062	0.714	18.712	0.000
	MSALL	−0.768	0.070	−0.491	−10.985	0.620
	EDALL	0.015	0.031	0.014	0.497	0.000
	MWRALL	0.809	0.039	0.690	20.611	0.000

[a] Dependent variable: OWRALL

Discussion

The results of the survey revealed that the majority of the respondents recognized described behavior as a violation of the official rules. In three scenarios (cover-up of police DUI accident, taking free meals and gifts from merchants, and failing to report hate crime), we find some variations in answers, while there were more scenarios in which the answers of the respondents whether behavior qualifies as a violation of official rules were almost unanimous (e.g., theft of knife from crime scene and false report on drug dealer). The respondents' labeling of a particular behavior as rule violating is closely related to how serious they evaluated the behavior to be—if they thought that the behavior tended to be more serious, they were more likely to say that it violated official rules. The respondents' evaluations of scenario seriousness suggest that the scenarios were generally evaluated to be on the serious side; means were clustered between the midpoint of the scale and the "very serious" end of the scale. As we have seen, in most scenarios, police officers perceived discipline to be fair—especially in the cases that were evaluated to be the most serious. As was seen, willingness to report was for all scenarios statistically significant and positively correlated with the perceived level of seriousness of the misconduct.

The survey was intended to assess police integrity according to the approach described in the introduction. We believe that an officer's perception of the seriousness of corruption is a moral judgment and, as such, an indirect indicator of the set of moral principles guiding such judgments. An officer's willingness to report corruption reflects an intention that is a precursor of action (Pagon and Lobnikar 2004). To the extent that a person's willingness to report corruption is a consequence of their perception of its seriousness, the person demonstrates integrity, that is, congruence between their moral beliefs and their propensity for action. If the willingness to report corruption is influenced more by exogenous variables (such as other people's beliefs and actions, fairness of the discipline, rank, assignment, etc.) than by the person's own perception of the seriousness of corruption, the person does not demonstrate integrity. The officers' own perception of the seriousness of corruption was the most significant determinate of their willingness to report corruption, followed by their estimation of other police officers' willingness to report (see Table 7.8). Expected discipline had no influence on willingness to report corruption. We believe that the results demonstrate a high level of police integrity among police officers in Slovenia.

A practical implication of this study's findings is that efforts to manage police corruption and other forms of police misconduct are most likely to be successful if they are directed at changing perceptions and moral beliefs about the seriousness of corruption. Although the results of the survey revealed a high level of police integrity, there are some issues where additional work has to be done. First is the case of covering up a police officer DUI (scenario 8), where 23.6 % of respondents selected answer 1 ("not at all serious"). This is a form of police corruption involving internal corruption from Barker and Roebuck's classification (1973 cit. in Kutnjak Ivković, this book). Early research on police integrity in Slovenia conducted in 1998 (Pagon and Lobnikar 2004) also showed that internal corruption was viewed by officers as one of the least serious forms of police corruption. We can conclude that there has been little change in the past 15 years in this regard, and some managerial intervention is needed.

Results also constitute some evidence of the existence of the Code of Silence among Slovenian police officers. However, the Code of Silence is far from a universal prohibition on reporting. Rather, it varies dramatically. There are three issues (represented by scenario 1: "free meals, gifts from merchants;" scenario 8: "cover-up of police DUI accident;" and scenario 7: "verbal abuse"—"Arrest an Asshole Day") where an analysis of the Code of Silence shows that about 32–43 % of the respondents for each of these scenarios said that they would *not* report a police officer who engaged in the misconduct described in the scenario (see Fig. 7.3). These three scenarios include the least serious form of police corruption (i.e., the acceptance of gratuities) and the use of verbal assault as a first step of excessive use of force as well as the scenario involving internal corruption. On the other hand, our results show a very low number of police officers who would not report the most serious instances of police misconduct.

We believe that police leaders have to foster the desired character development and moral habits of police officers by educating and training them in police ethics. Leadership based on rules and punishment does not produce desirable outcomes. To conclude, in trying to change police officers' perceptions in the areas of internal corruption and the Code of Silence, police managers will discover that setting an example is of the utmost importance.

References

Banutai, E., Šifrer, J., & Meško, G. (2011). Deviance and police organisational culture in Slovenia. In G. Meško, A. Sotlar, & J. Winterdyk (Eds.), *Policing in central and Eastern Europe—Social control of unconventional deviance: Conference proceedings* (pp. 379–400). Ljubljana: Faculty of Criminal Justice and Security.

Becker, T. E. (1998). Integrity in organizations: Beyond honesty and conscientiousness. *Academy of Management Review, 23*(1), 154–161.

Code of Police Ethics (2008). http://www.policija.si/eng/images/stories/Publications/Kodeks.pdf. Accessed 11 Jan 2015.

Delattre, E. J. (1996). *Character and cops: Ethics in policing* (3rd ed.). Washington, D.C.: The AEI Press.

Dobovšek, B., & Škrbec, J. (2012). Corruption prevention model in the Republic of Slovenia. *Cah. politiestudies, 3*(24), 165–180.

Girodo, M. (2003). Evaluating risk behavior and strategic systems: new tools for preventing corruption and strengthening integrity. In M. Pagon et al. (Ed.), *Ethics, integrity and human rights from the perspective of police activity*. Ljubljana: College of Police and Security Studies.

Government of the Republic of Slovenia. (2012). *About Slovenia*. http://www.vlada.si/en/about_slovenia/.

Hren, B. (2011). Slovenija po dohodkovni (ne)enakosti še v socializmu [Slovenia regarding the income (in)equality still in socialism]. *Dnevnik*, March 12 2011. http://dnevnik.si/objektiv/vec_vsebin/1042430243.

Klemenčič, G., Kečanović, B., & Žaberl, M. (2002). *Vaše pravice v policijskih postopkih* [*Citizens Rights in Police Proceedings*]. Ljubljana: Pasadena Publishing.

Klockars, C. B. & Kutnjak Ivković, S. (2004). Measuring police integrity. In A. R. Piquero, J. R. Greene, & M. J. Hickman (Eds.), *Police integrity and ethics*. Belmont: Wadsworth.

Klockars, C. B., Kutnjak Ivković, S. K., Harver, W. E., & Haberfeld, M. R. (2000). *The Measurement of Police integrity*. Washington, D.C.: National Institute of Justice, Research in Brief.

Klockars, C. B., Kutnjak Ivković, S. K., & Haberfeld, M. R. (2004). *The contours of police integrity*. Washington, D.C.: SAGE.

Klockars, C. B., Kutnjak Ivković, S., & Haberfeld, M. R. (2006). *Enhancing police integrity*. New York: Springer.

Kolenc, T. (2003). *The Slovene police*. Ljubljana: Ministry of the Interior of the Republic of Slovenia, Police, General Police Directorate.

Kutnjak Ivković, S. (2009). The Croatian police, police integrity, and transition toward democratic policing. *Policing: An International Journal of Police Strategies and Management, 32*(3), 459–488.

Kutnjak Ivković, S., & O'Connor Shelley, T. (2005). The Bosnian police and police integrity: A continuing story. *European Journal of Criminology, 2*(4), 428–454.

Kutnjak Ivković, S., & O'Connor Shelley, T. (2007). Police integrity and the Czech police officers. *International Journal of Comparative and Applied Criminal Justice, 31*(1), 21–49.

Kutnjak Ivković, S., Klockars, C. B., Lobnikar, B., & Pagon, M. (2000). Police integrity and the code of silence: The case of the Slovenian police force. In G. Meško et al. (Eds.), *Corruption in central and Eastern Europe at the turn of millennium* (pp. 85–102). Ljubljana: Open Society Institute Slovenia.

Lobnikar, B., Pagon, M., Duffy, M. K., & Ganster, D. C. (2000). Dejavniki deviantnega vedenja slovenskih policistov [Factors of police deviance]. *Organizacija: revija za management, informatiko in kadre, 33*(2), 77–93.

Lobnikar, B., Pagon, M., & Ovsenik, M. (2004). The frequency and the causes of violence and aggressive behavior at the workplace: The case of Slovenian police. *Organizacija: revija za management, informatiko in kadre, 37*(6), 371–378.

Lobnikar, B., Koporec, A., & Šumi, R. (2006). Evaluation of police officer integrity training. *Varstvoslovje: revija za teorijo in prakso varstvoslovja, 8*(3/4), 303–308.

Meško, G. (2000). Introduction. In G. Meško et al. (Eds.), *Corruption in central and Eastern Europe at the turn of millennium* (pp. 7–9). Ljubljana: Open Society Institute Slovenia.

Meško, G., & Klemenčič, G. (2007). Rebuilding legitimacy and police professionalism in an emerging democracy: The Slovenian experience. In T. R. Tyler (Ed.), *Legitimacy and criminal justice* (pp. 84–115). New York: Russell Sage Foundation.

Meško, G., & Lobnikar, B. (2005). The contribution of local safety councils to local responsibility in crime prevention and provision of safety. *Policing: An International Journal of Police Strategies and Management, 28*(2), 353–373.

Meško, G., Lobnikar, B., Jere, M., & Sotlar, A. (2013). Recent developments of policing in Slovenia. In G. Meško, C. B. Fields, B. Lobnikar, & A. Sotlar (Eds.), *Handbook on policing in central and Eastern Europe* (pp. 263–286). New York: Springer.

Organisation And Work Of The Police Act. (2013) Official Gazette of the RS, No. 15/2013. Ljubljana.

Pagon, M., & Lobnikar, B. (2000). Comparing supervisor and line officer opinions about the code of silence: The case of Slovenia. In M. Pagon (Ed.), *Policing in Central and Eastern Europe. Ethics, integrity, and human rights* (pp. 197–209). Ljubljana: College of Police and Security Studies.

Pagon, M., & Lobnikar, B. (2004). Police integrity in Slovenia. In C. B. Klockars, S. Kutnjak Ivković, & M. R. Haberfeld (Eds.), *The contours of police integrity*. Thousand Oaks: Sage.

Pagon, M., Kutnjak Ivković, S., & Klockars, C. (1998). The measurement of police integrity in Slovenia. Crime control policies: political rhetoric or empirical reality? Academy of Criminal Justice Sciences Annual Meeting Albuquerque, New Mexico, March 10–14 (p. 221).

Pagon, M., Kutnjak Ivković, S., & Lobnikar, B. (2000). Police integrity and attitudes toward police corruption: a comparison between the police and the public. In M. Pagon (Ed.), *Policing in Central and Eastern Europe. ethics, integrity, and human rights* (pp. 383–396). Ljubljana: College of Police and Security Studies.

Pagon, M., Kutnjak Ivković, S., & Branko, L. (2003). Policijska integriteta in stališča do policijske korupcije: primerjava med policisti in študenti. In M. V. Pagon, G. Meško, & B. Lobnikar (Eds.), *Etika, integriteta in človekove pravice z vidika policijske dejavnosti* pp. 149–162. Ljubljana: Ministrstvo za notranje zadeve, Visoka policijsko-varnostna šola.

Police. (2012). *About the police*. http://www.policija.si/eng/index.php/aboutthepolice.

Police (2013). *Policijsko delo v skupnosti. [Community Policing]*, Doc. no. 2214-41/2012/4 (pp. 207–07). Ljubljana: MNZ, GPU.

Police Tasks And Powers Act. (2013). Official Gazette of the RS, No. 15/2013. Ljubljana.

Škrbec, J., & Dobovšek, B. (2012). The impact of corruption on the rule of law in the Republic of Slovenia—Facts versus public fiction. In G. Meško, A. Sotlar, & B. Tominc (Eds.), *Contemporary criminal justice practice and research: Conference proceedings* (pp. 36–37). Ljubljana: Faculty of Criminal Justice and Security.

Toš, N. (ur.) (1999). *Vrednote v prehodu II: slovenskojavno mnenje 1990–1998* [Values in transition II: Slovene public opinion 1990–1998]. Ljubljana: Fakulteta za družbene vede, Inštitut za družbene vede, Center za raziskovanje javnega mnenja.

Toš, N. (ur.) (2004). *Vrednote v prehodu III: slovensko javnomnenje 1999–2004* [Values in transition III: Slovene public opinion 1999–2004]. Ljubljana: Fakulteta za družbene vede, Inštitut za družbene vede, Center za raziskovanje javnega mnenja.

Vicchio, S. J. (1997). Ethics and police integrity. Keynote address. National Institute of Justice., National Symposium on Police Integrity. Washington, D.C. (July, 14–16). http://www.fbi.gov/leb/july972.htm. Accessed 1 Sept 1998.

Zupančič, B. M., et al. (2000). *Ustavno kazensko procesno pravo [Constitutional Criminal Procedure]*. Ljubljana: Pasadena.

Chapter 8
Police Integrity in South Africa

Adri Sauerman and Sanja Kutnjak Ivković

Abstract The South African Police Service (SAPS) is a large, nationally centralized police agency resorting under the minister of police in the government department of the SAPS. Formerly known as the SA police force, the agency has experienced vast reform since its years as the apartheid regime's policy enforcer. This chapter explores the contours of police integrity among the agency, based on a police integrity survey conducted from 2010 to 2013. The sample of 871 police officers from all nine South African provinces evaluated hypothetical scenarios describing various forms of police misconduct. Our results suggest that the majority of police officers had no problems recognizing the described behavior as rule violating and evaluated all 11 hypothetical cases as serious. At the same time, they supported and expected some discipline less severe than dismissal to be meted out for such behavior. Only for the serious misconduct of stealing from the crime scene they supported and expected dismissal. Finally, our results also indicate the existence of the code of silence among the respondents although the code did not cover all behaviors equally. Our respondents seem least likely to protect a theft from a crime scene and unjustifiable use of deadly force.

Keywords Apartheid · Police integrity · South Africa · South African Police Service · Survey

Introduction

The subject of Dutch rule (1652–1795 and 1803–1806) and British colonization (1795–1803 and 1806–1910), South Africa's colonial history is marked with inordinately many bitter and bloody conflicts prior to it becoming a Union in 1910 and, in severing its ties with the Commonwealth, a truly independent republic in 1961

S. Kutnjak Ivković (✉)
Michigan State University, East Lansing, MI, USA
e-mail: kutnjak@msu.edu

A. Sauerman
Michigan State University, East Lansing, MI, USA
e-mail: sauerman@msu.edu

S. Kutnjak Ivković, M. R. Haberfeld (eds.), *Measuring Police Integrity Across the World*,
DOI 10.1007/978-1-4939-2279-6_8

(Thompson 2001). Considering its embattled past and the fact that South Africa would only hold its first democratic elections in 1994, the country could likely be hailed as the poster state for the doctrine of past behavior predicting future actions. In fact, in their comprehensive analyses of South Africa's past, the historians Gilliomee and Mbenga (2007) acknowledge this principle in identifying one particular conflict from the period 1899–1902:

> The South African War (a.k.a. the Anglo-Boer War) remains the most terrible and destructive modern armed conflict in South Africa's history. It was an event that in many ways shaped the history of 20th Century South Africa. The end of the war marked the end of the long process of British conquest of South African societies, both Black and White.

Shortly after this predisposing and devastating war, and in step with most colonial police forces, the South African Police (SAP) entered into law enforcement during 1913 with a primary task of policing race relations within the country (Malan 1999). Forebodingly, the Natives Land Act or "the Black Land Act" was passed during the same year (Thompson 2001) which, in imitation of preceding British policy, legislated territorial segregation based on race. The SAP would continue to be developed within this context of discriminatory law enforcement whilst serving and protecting the interests of selected sectors of the South African society (Rauch and Marais 1992). Under the auspices of the National Party, which came into power in 1948, the SAP's transformation to a paramilitary force would eventually reach its apex during the 1980s as a pivotal part of the *total strategy* response to a government perceived *total onslaught* on its apartheid policies (Rauch and Marais 1992). In considering the prevailing world politics of the Cold War at the time, Bruce (2002) reflects:

> Rather than fighting crime the South African government and thus SAP members saw themselves as being involved in fighting against a "communist threat," and used this to provide a blanket justification for the various extreme and cruel measures they applied.

During this period, ten police agencies in the ethnic "independent homelands" operated parallel to the SAP within South Africa. Established between 1976 and 1981 under the apartheid policy, these "homelands" were considered as independent states by the South African government, but had no international recognition as such (Thompson 2001, Chronology). Acting thus as self-governing territories but still under the rule of the South African government, their police forces similarly operated to curb the *total onslaught,* albeit with lesser degrees of ideological and political enthusiasm. In terms of their effectiveness as law enforcement agencies, Bruce (2002) notes that their recruitment and training standards were lower than those of the SAP, and that "incompetence, callousness, and corruption" were common traits of these "homeland" police forces.

Within this context of paramilitary policing and an unprecedented rise in political violence, the African National Congress (ANC) coalition came to power in 1994, and, as apartheid policies were officially replaced by a democratic constitution, this new government faced the immediate challenge of transforming the SAP and the attitudes of its employees into a police agency that would serve all the people of South Africa. A key element to a peaceful political transition, this process of transformation was already a negotiation topic between the National Party and the ANC in the years leading up to the 1994 elections (Bruce 2002), with researchers offering advice at the time:

> The process of transition, though it provokes fear and insecurity, can itself contribute to the creation of a new ethos. The management of the transition for the police force is therefore itself a crucial process, on which the success or failure of future policing may rest. (Rauch and Marais 1992)

By 1995, with the promulgation of the South African Police Service Act (SAPS Act), the "homeland" police forces were formally amalgamated with the SAP in forming the South African Police Service (SAPS). A police agency of considerable size with around 120,000 members (Newham and Faull 2011, p. 25), the SAPS showed strong experience in regime maintenance, but was otherwise poorly versed in crime detection and investigation (Malan 1999). After democratic elections, however, its process of reform had assistance from the international community,[1] and it increasingly encompassed an improvement to the SAPS' battered public image, the agency's size and command structures, and its demilitarization. These goals were achieved by, among other actions, substituting the archaic military rank structure for a configuration of civilian titles, unified conduct regulations, endeavors toward higher adherence to the rule of law, and a determination toward professionalism (Bruce 2002). Even though the majority of SAP members (prior to the integration of the "homeland" police forces) were not white, another SAPS reform centered on limiting the numbers of whites within its new structures, as they were considered overrepresented in comparison to their numbers in the country's population (Bruce 2002). Without the benefit of mirroring any precedents of legitimate police agencies created in post-conflict transitional societies (Shaw 2002), some researchers still assessed the reforms as positive:

> …South Africa is generally considered a heartening success. Following the 1994 elections, the first truly free and representative elections in South African history, the Mandela government initiated not just reform but what is described as a "transformation" of the police. The transformation involved increasing the representation of blacks at senior ranks, developing a national-crime prevention strategy, introducing community policing, emphasizing responsive service delivery, reforming public order policing, promoting affirmative action for women and minorities, and strengthening internal discipline and accountability. (Bayley 2005, p. 113)

Conversely, criticisms also abound, ranging from concerns over "general weaknesses in policing in South Africa" due to "limited resources, an overly centralized and bureaucratic hierarchy, a general lack of appropriate skills and training, and a dearth of managerial and investigative expertise" (Pelser et al. 2000) to claims that the SAPS is "…'out of step' as far as integrity is concerned" (Newham 2004, p. 232).

Currently, after two decades of seemingly equivocal reform under a transformation process that, according to the agency's administration is still ongoing, the current SAPS is a nationally centralized police organization resorting under the minister of police in the department of the SAPS and headed operationally by a national commissioner with the military rank of general (SAPS 2013). Across the country's nine provinces, 1134 police stations are found in which the majority of the 155,531 SAPS Act employees (functional police personnel) and 42,415 Public Service Act employees (civilian personnel) are employed with a correlating population ratio of 1:341 (SAPS 2013).

[1] The major donors during the initial police reform period included Belgium, Denmark, the UK, Sweden, Canada, France, Germany, the Netherlands, and the USA (Malan 1999).

Its origin, initial development, and function thus established, the following chapter examines the SAPS in accordance with the societal and police-related aspects of the police integrity theory. The second part of the chapter offers an empirical analysis of survey data in the measuring of the level of police integrity within the SAPS.

Theory of Police Integrity and the SAPS

Organizational Rules

One of the initial reform focuses—a uniform set of internal rules in terms of police conduct (Bruce 2002)—appears after 20 years to be well established in the SAPS. Since 1997, every member is expected to sign a standardized code of conduct that has them warrant, among several behavioral and ethical matters, that they shall "act with integrity…"; "work towards preventing any form of corruption and to bring the perpetrators thereof to justice"; exercise their conferred powers "in a responsible and controlled manner"; and more rhetorically, "contribute to the reconstruction and development of, and reconciliation" of the country (SAPS Code of Conduct 1997).

Internally, the SAPS regulates the behavior of their members through the SAPS disciplinary regulations (SDR) of 2006[2], prohibiting a range of possible misconducts by SAPS Act and civilian personnel alike (Regulation 20, SDR 2006), and stating "the support constructive labour relations in the Service" as one of its purposes (Regulation 3(a), SDR 2006). Whether this objective is met seems unclear; Newham and colleagues (2003) reported that commanders have struggled to apply the SDR since its promulgation and that they believed that discipline within the agency had generally deteriorated as a result. Masuku is evenly skeptical and identifies impeding absences of official attention and resources to the disciplinary system (2005, p. 16).

Another purpose of the SDR states that the regulations should ensure "a mutual understanding of misconduct and discipline among supervisors and employees" (Regulation 3(c), SDR 2006). Although this objective underscores the organizational theory of police integrity's proposed correlation between a police agency of high integrity and its members' ability to identify misconduct in accordance with the agency's rules and regulations (see, e.g., Klockars and Kutnjak Ivković 2004; Klockars et al. 1997, 2001), it remains uncertain whether it is realized at the operational level. With limited information available on the extent to which SAPS members recognize incidents of SDR-violating behavior, our 2005 research attempted to shed some light on this aspect (Kutnjak Ivković and Sauerman 2008). In measuring the levels of integrity among 379 mostly supervisory SAPS members, our results indicated a substantial majority who acknowledged police misconduct

[2] The latest set of disciplinary regulations within the agency, it has significantly evolved from the first transformational disciplinary system instituted during 1991 which was substantively based on the South African Criminal Procedure Act (Newham 2000).

within a provided set of regulation-violating scenarios. Disconcertingly, we also found a considerable minority of supervisors who did not recognize the most severe violations of regulations, even though such violations would usually be subject to criminal investigation (p. 31).

Policing the SAPS: Detection and Investigation of Police Misconduct

The years of initial police reform witnessed the establishment of several independent entities that endeavored to formally monitor policing within the country. Lacking any direct authority over police disciplinary processes, and struggling with organizational impediments such as understaffing, these civilian-led bodies would always struggle in achieving their ambitious objectives. Add to these difficulties the expected obstacle of police resistance to any external investigations, and their positive effects on the SAPS' service delivery, and corruption complaints appear to be sporadic at best (Newham 2004, pp. 235–236).

Arguably the most effective independent institution of the time, the Independent Complaints Directorate (ICD), was established in terms of the SAPS Act, and had to ensure that police officers act in accordance with the country's 1996 constitution. As such, the ICD could investigate any complaint of misconduct or offense against members of the police, refer such investigations to the police, and make recommendations as to how offenses by officers should be dealt with, both departmentally and criminally (SAPS Act 1995, Section 53(2)(a–c)). An inherent flaw in its operation would prove to be the absence of legal obligations that could compel the SAPS to comply with its commendations (Burger and Adonis 2008, p. 30).

In 2011, the ICD was replaced by the Independent Police Investigative Directorate (IPID; SA IPID Act 2011). This strengthened investigative body holds more executive powers than its predecessor did (Section 24) and may even oblige SAPS cooperation in certain investigative instances (Section 29). With such ameliorated authority, it is hoped that the IPID will reach its mission of "effective, independent and impartial investigating…, …committed to justice and acting in the public interest while maintaining the highest standards of integrity and excellence" (IPID, Vision and Mission 2014).

Focusing inwardly, the SAPS unveiled its National Crime Prevention Strategy during 1996, which identified corruption within the criminal justice sector "as the greatest threat to the governance of safety and security" (Faull 2007, p. 2). With an emphasis on this risk, the SAPS established a dedicated Anti-Corruption Unit (ACU) with a mandate "to engage with corruption within the SAPS both proactively and reactively in all of the country's nine provinces" (Faull 2007, p. 2). Although, by its own account, it experienced serious capacity limitations, insufficient witness information, and had to accommodate flawed legislation that established problematic legal proof of corruption (Newham et al. 2003), the unit was undoubtedly effective in its directive. By the end of 2001, after 20,779 investigations of police corruption, the ACU had arrested 3045 SAPS members, and had assisted in the convictions of 576 (SAPS 2002 as cited in Masuku 2004). Unfortunately, these successes in ridding itself of internal corruption would prove to be mere passing phenomena for the SAPS. In early 2002, the national police commissioner at the time closed the ACU under the politically induced pretense that its functions were being duplicated by the SAPS' various "organized crime units" (OCUs). At the same time, ominously indicative of future integrity problems, the provincial head of an OCU was convicted on corruption charges on the basis of yet another, thorough ACU investigation (News24 2008).

The SDR of 2006 propose a disciplinary system of "progressive" discipline (Regulation 4(b)), in which the type of discipline must correlate with the severity of the misconduct. As such, a clear distinction is made between "less serious misconduct" (Regulation 7) and "serious misconduct" (Regulation 12). For the former, progressive discipline entails an application of various discipline steadily growing in severity, such as corrective counseling (Regulation 8), verbal warnings (Regulation 9), written warnings (Regulation 10), and final written warnings (Regulation 11). Depending on whether the police officer admits to the misconduct, these disciplines might be applied with or without a formal disciplinary hearing (Regulations 9–11). In cases of serious misconduct, the array of discipline is more limited. If found guilty[3] at a disciplinary hearing in such instances, the police officer may be suspended without remuneration for up to 3 months, be dismissed, receive a suspended sanction of dismissal or suspension, receive a fine of up to R(and)500,[4] or receive a combination of these sanctions (Regulation 15(1)(e–i)). All findings and discipline are subject to appeal by the police officer (Regulation 17). The SDR also provides a list of serious offenses for which the discipline of suspension without remuneration may be considered. This list is inclusive of acts of corruption, bribery, extortion, defeating the course of justice, and, peculiarly, theft "of a serious nature."

Whilst it may appear that integrity-related offenses are frowned upon by the SAPS management, the reality of the void left by the closure of the ACU suggests a more lenient response. During the unit's swansong year, the SAPS' annual report reflected the investigation of 2370 cases of corruption, resulting in 641 departmental disciplinary hearings (SAPS 2002 as cited in Newham 2005). The very next year, the only information supplied by the SAPS indicates the suspension of 347 members, vaguely attributed to their involvement in corruption-related activities (SAPS 2004). The 2007/2008 report shows an even lower suspension "for corruption" of 192 police members (News24 2008), with the 2009/2010 suspension numbers nearly unchanged at 193 (SAPS 2010). The SAPS' 2012/2013 annual report specifies 319 members charged under the SDR for corruption with a mere 22 suspensions for the period (SAPS 2013). Seen as a litany, these low and dwindling numbers indicate that all is not well with the SAPS' internal detection and investigation of integrity-related

[3] Although terminology more at place in criminal cases, the SDR nevertheless stipulates such jargon for SAPS disciplinary hearings (Regulation 20), an anomaly inherited from its predecessors which were in turn strongly influenced by the South African Criminal Procedure Act (Newham 2000).

[4] At the time of writing, 1 U.S. $ exchanged between the range of 11/12 (latest exchange put it at 11.50) South African Rand.

offenses. In comparing these figures with research of the public's experiences of police corruption, Newham and Faull (2011 p. 33) acknowledge this worrisome situation and add that "the vast majority of members involved in corruption and other offences escape both detection and formal punishment."

Ultimately, these declining detection and discipline statistics, coupled with researcher conclusions, challenge the SDR and its application. In our 2005 measurement of 379 SAPS members' opinions about appropriate and anticipated discipline at the hand of 11 scenarios of police misconduct ranging in seriousness, "written reprimands" were found to be the most frequently selected disciplinary option, even for SDR offenses that are also violations of criminal law (Kutnjak Ivković and Sauerman 2008). Furthermore, the respondents overwhelmingly felt that accepting bribes and receiving kickbacks should only result in suspensions without pay of the involved SAPS members. More troubling still, our research indicates that a substantial minority of SAPS supervisors believed in either verbal reprimands or no discipline at all for even the most serious forms of police corruption (Kutnjak Ivković and Sauerman 2008, p. 32).

Deciphering the SAPS' Code of Silence

The initial composition of the newly formed SAPS resembled a police organization of dissimilarity rather than a well-integrated police agency of uniformity. To maintain the loyalty of the armed forces during the period of initial transformation, quick-fix political agreements dictated that vastly opposing groups, both in ideology and historical backgrounds, were placated with employment within the new police service. As such, a "sunset clause" assured continued employment to SAP members for a period of 5 years after the 1994 democratic elections (Newham 2004, p. 235). Members of the ANC party's military wing and, thus, former enemies of the SAP, were also included. Former "homeland" police officials similarly joined the fray from regions "dominated by ethnic political elite and controlled by illegitimate and often overtly corrupt homeland administrations" (Malan 1999). Parallel to this process, voluntary retrenchment packages were offered to senior SAP officers, some of whom were suspected of past atrocities. Precise information regarding those who left the agency in this manner, however, remains obscure (Bruce 2002). In analyzing this diverse workforce of the SAPS, Newham and Faull (2011) reflect:

> Certainly the new national police service was far from homogenous. Its members spoke different languages, wore different uniforms, carried different types of firearms, used different ranking systems, and had received different levels of training. Approximately one third of the 120,000 members were functionally illiterate, 30,000 did not have driver's licences, and 20,000 had criminal records. (p. 25)

After a brief staffing cessation during its amalgamation and retrenchment phase, the SAPS started an en masse recruitment process in 1996, during which stringent screening and selection procedures were ostensibly neglected in favor of sheer induction numbers (Bruce 2008, p. 8). Not surprisingly, the questionable integrity of the fledgling SAPS' workforce exacerbated by 2000, when as many as 14,600 members faced criminal charges "ranging from murder, rape, armed robbery, assault, theft, and bribery to reckless driving" (Newham and Faull 2011, p. 25). Clearly, the "working assumption" held by the SAPS administration that the organization's traditionally strict hierarchy, code of conduct, and level of internal discipline would naturally establish standards and procedures that enhance democratic transition was "notably insufficient" (Vigneswaran and Hornberger 2009, p. 6). Nonetheless, the notion may indicate one reason for a code of silence among SAPS members, albeit through an unintentional result of police agencies' traditionally punitive, authoritarian approaches (Newham and Faull 2011, p. 43). In such rigidly managed agencies, the code strengthens with every draconian, exemplary sanction against police officers caught and similarly in the assumed, subsequent public outcry (Kutnjak Ivković and Sauerman 2013, p. 179). Notwithstanding these indicative factors, when considering the apparent criminality within the SAPS' ranks over a mere 5-year period ending in 2000, a presence of the code within the agency can be reasonably expected (Mollen Commission 1994). As such, several research studies have since attempted to expose the extent of the code of silence within the SAPS.

In his measurement of 104 SAPS members' adherence to the code at the hand of 11 scenarios of police misconduct ranging in seriousness, Newham (2004) reports that the majority would observe the code of silence in six of the postulations. Perceptions of their colleagues' responses reflected an even stronger code of silence within this inner-city police station in Johannesburg, with respondents indicating that they were either "unsure or that their colleagues would not report violations" in ten of the scenarios (Newham 2004, p. 246). In our 2005 research, we utilize a slightly altered version of the same survey instrument on 379 mostly supervisory members and find that a sizable minority of the respondents was less than enthusiastic to report even the most severe forms of police corruption and/or expected their colleagues to also turn a blind eye (Kutnjak Ivković and Sauerman 2011, p. 84).

Influence of Social and Political Environments: South Africa's Struggle with Corruption

At first glance, corruption and a general lack of accountability for integrity-challenged actions appear endemic to the South African political and police landscapes. Closer analyses reveal an even more dire reality. Although little is known about the extent of SAP corruption prior to 1994, Newham and Faull point to "sufficient evidence that the abuse of power for personal gain was relatively widespread and occurred at the highest levels" (2011, p. 19). Their reference to top echelons also suggests that the politicians heading the apartheid government were involved in such unethical activities, for they did issue the SAP's directives.

With the Truth and Reconciliation Hearings (TRC)[5] that followed the end of apartheid, South Africa had a unique opportunity to rid itself from enduring, disreputable political and police behavior. Ultimately, though, the TRC process would affect "only a very small minority of police who were mainly more senior members of the SAP associated with the Security Branch," while unfortunately failing "to hold any of the politicians answerable" (Bruce 2002). The power-abusive apartheid authorities, who without hesitation sent thousands of South African Defence Force (SADF) and SAP conscripts in harm's way, whilst ordering the assassinations of political opponents with impunity, in the end did little more than deny and cover while blaming the foot soldiers (TRC Report 1998). More significantly, they were "allowed" (whether by proxy or intent) to get away with it, which would prove to be a foreboding introduction to political and administrative accountability in the new, democratic South Africa. Not surprisingly, when the historians Giliomee and Mbenga (2007) reflect on the prevalence of this issue during the country's initial transformation period:

> Corruption of high-ranking officials partly stemmed from the arms deals…, but pervaded other sectors as well, such as massive social welfare fraud and patronage arrangements. Parliamentarians, managers, and executives allocated themselves disproportionately large salaries and perks in the face of widening income gaps. Ordinary South Africans were dismayed. When Desmond Tutu criticized this practice, an ANC spokesperson replied: "The Archbishop should stick to religion." (p. 432)

The unprecedented political violence of the early 1990s did not cease after the 1994 democratic elections. On the contrary, crime escalated to such levels that it not only affected the public and police morale but also emerged as a key political issue in the country. Unfortunately, the new political leadership seemed indecisive in dealing with this phenomenon and, until 1999, followed an approach of rhetoric rather than addressing the problem through resolute and effective action (Bruce 2002). As a result, foreign observers of the country's reform still consider this crime wave as the dominant "blotch" on the South African image, followed closely by widespread corruption (Giliomee and Mbenga 2007, p. 432).

While the government has gradually learned that it needs to "demonstrate seriousness about tackling the [crime] problem in order to retain credibility and popular support" (Bruce 2002), the curbing of corruption has been met with somewhat less official recognition. As a result, a National Victims of Crime Survey (NVCS), conducted by the Institute for Security Studies in 2003, had respondents ranking corruption as the second most prevalent crime in the country (Van Vuuren 2004, p. 12). Considering the trends in national surveys since then, it is clear that the South African public is acutely aware of their government's integrity challenges. In an analysis of the annual South African Social Attitudes Surveys for the 5-year period between 2006 and 2011, Newham (2014) reports a near doubling in the percentage of respondents who believe that the government must address corruption as a matter of national priority. This urgency of the situation is also reflected in Transparency

[5] The Truth and Reconciliation Commission hearings, conducted in Cape Town from 1996 to 1998. For the full report, see the Truth & Reconciliation Commission, 1998.

International's 2013 Global Corruption Barometer that shows that South Africa has dropped 34 places in its global integrity standing since 2001, with half of the recorded freefall occurring since 2009 (Newham 2014). With a ranking of 72 out of 175 countries, it does not appear as if South Africa is heading upwards on the integrity scale, especially with results indicating politicians as second among the "extremely corrupt" groups within the country (Transparency International 2013). Even the current national president and head of the ANC, Jacob Zuma, has been criminally accused of corruption. Peculiarly, the charges related to his involvement in the "arms deal" were dropped mere weeks before his election to office, with the prosecution insisting that the case was "tainted by political meddling" (News24 2011).

Cascading from the top levels of government, the SAPS—the starting point of the criminal justice system—could hardly be left unaffected by such extensive corruption. In fact, already in 1998, Syed and Bruce analyze corruption-related media releases over a 15-month period and reach the conclusion that "the occurrence of reports on so many different types of corrupt activities in the South African press in little over a year may indicate that police corruption in South Africa is fairly extensive as well as being varied in nature" (p. 11). The premature closure of the ACU in 2002 drew further criticisms from researchers. Newham (2004, pp. 232–233) states that, "when it comes to tackling police corruption and building integrity, the SAPS has yet to develop a coherent strategy." Similarly, reflecting on the ACU's demise and what followed for internal governance, Bruce offers that "not only has the SAPS actively undermined its corruption control mechanisms but it has done so whilst management systems, which constitute the basic mechanism of control, have been undermined" (2008, p. 9).

With the SAPS rapidly developing a reputation of a police agency beset by corruption, the United Nations Office on Drugs and Crime's Country Assessment Report of 2003 identified the agency as the country's most corrupt public service in the public's perception (Masuku 2004, p. 8). Domestic surveys on public opinions of the SAPS' integrity appeared evenly damning with respondents from both the 2003 and 2007 NVCS, recognizing the police as the leading initiator of corruption among public service departments (Bruce 2008, pp. 6–7). The public's already negative view of SAPS integrity was further reinforced during 2008, when the national police commissioner and Interpol president at the time was charged with corruption and defeating the ends of justice related to his association with organized crime syndicates (Joubert et al. 2008). In considering that this police commissioner was a political appointee with no previous police experience, his role as the impetus in the sinister closure of the ACU should have prompted the ANC government into serious reconsideration of its selection criteria for such key positions. Instead, more of the same occurred when the national prosecuting authority's (NPA) investigating unit in charge of this corruption case was publically accused by the government of "Hollywood style tactics," which led to the suspension of the NPA head on the grounds of incompetence and, finally, the disbanding of the division (Joubert et al. 2008).

Within such an integrity-challenged organizational climate, it comes as little surprise that, in their review of studies of SAPS personnel perceptions for the period 2001–2009, Newham and Faull observe that members' views on corruption within the agency mirrors the pessimism of the larger public, indicating its extensive nature as a "serious challenge facing the SAPS" (2011, p. 22). Meanwhile, Bheki Cele, another police commissioner without any law enforcement experience, was appointed from the political ranks of the ANC. His tenure would prove to be more fleeting than that of his predecessor, albeit similarly controversial. Early in 2011, the Office of the Public Protector issued a damning report, in which the police commissioner was accused of "conduct [that] was improper, unlawful and amounted to maladministration" because of the violation of governance laws and regulations in the leasing of police offices (News24 2012).

By now the norm, the SAPS reacted with coercion tactics by arresting the journalist who exposed the lease scandal and then releasing him without any charge. Shortly afterwards, the SAPS showed up at the office of the Public Protector and demanded documents relating to the allegations—an action "widely perceived as police intimidation" (Newham and Faull 2011, p. 24). In June 2012, after a lengthy investigation into the report's allegations, the police commissioner's services were officially terminated (News24 2012). To date, and now employed as the country's deputy minister of Agriculture Forestry and Fisheries, he has not faced any criminal charges in connection with this scandal.

Ignoring the battered image of the country's police, the ANC insisted on appointing a political ally and yet another civilian commissioner, Mangwashi Victoria "Riah" Phiyega, who, when questioned at her media introduction about her lack of police experience, offered that "you do not need to be a drunkard to own a bottle store" (SowetonLive 2012). Nonsensical analogies notwithstanding, she did acknowledge that corruption was not only a problem in the police but also a general tendency in the country. Incredulously, she also pledged that, under her mandate, the SAPS "will build on the momentum created by the previous leadership" (SowetonLive 2012).

The SAPS soon found itself in even murkier waters as the vilified party in the Marikana Massacre of August 2012 (Dixon 2013; Newham 2013).[6] In a dismal display of police integrity that followed, the new leader's testimony at the ensuing commission of inquiry[7] was sharply criticized for being evasive and, at times, outright dishonest (Newham 2013).

Despite the SAPS' 2013 introduction of a new ACU "aimed at fighting fraud and corruption" within the agency (Politicsweb 2013), reports of SAPS corruption seemed to intensify still with one media report summarizing the sordid state of police integrity:

> …the chief of police is accused of criminal behaviour; a provincial police boss is allegedly on the payroll of a drug-dealer; the acting head of crime intelligence allegedly bamboozled his qualifications and the suspended head of crime intelligence, who stands accused of murder and corruption, is set to return to his job. SAPS is in deep trouble. The only people who benefit from it are criminals. (News24 2013)

[6] Dubbed the "Marikana Massacre" by the media, the incident refers to the SAPS shooting of 112 striking mineworkers on 16 August 2012 near the town of Marikana in the North West province, which left 34 dead on the day. With several of the survivors seriously wounded, the death toll would eventually rise to 44 (Dixon 2013). In the ongoing investigation by the Farlam Commission, the SAPS claimed self-defense (Newham 2013).

[7] The Farlam Commission was appointed by the country's president on 23 August 2012 with Ian Farlam was a retired judge of the Supreme Court of Appeal, as chairperson (Dixon 2013).

In late 2013, the SAPS announced the establishment of its own university in the Western Cape province that would emphasize the administration's commitment in transforming the agency "into a professional entity, with employees of integrity" (SAPS, Department of Police 2013). There, students will pursue undergraduate degrees in policing, whilst following a curriculum that includes military drill exercises (SAPS, Department of Police, 2013). Considering the brutality of the Marikana shootings, the agency's present training in crime suppression conducted in China (SAPS 2013, Part E: Financial Information), and the administration's ostensible persistence in remilitarizing the SAPS, it appears that the agency is slowly returning to the ways of the former SAP, a phenomenon that, by all accounts, poses a serious concern for such a young democracy.

Measuring the SAPS' Integrity

Questionnaire

Our 2005 study of the agency's integrity among 379 mostly supervisory SAPS members across seven provinces indicated an integrity-challenged police service. Here, we utilize a questionnaire depicting 11 scenarios of police misconduct, ranging from corruption and use of excessive force, to the planting of evidence and falsifying the official record. Each scenario is followed by a standard set of questions, a format used in both versions of the questionnaire. These questions solicit answers to the respondents' knowledge of official rules and their opinions about the seriousness of particular rule-violating behaviors, the discipline these behaviors subjectively deserve and might actually receive, and their evaluations in terms of their own willingness to report such behavior. The disciplinary questions have been adjusted to mirror the sanctions contained both in the SDR and at operational level. The possible answers were: 1 = "none," 2 = "verbal reprimand," 3 = "written reprimand," 4 = "reassignment to a different position," 5 = "demotion in rank," and 6 = "dismissal."

Lastly, demographic questions are posed to the respondents. To increase participation, answers that may lead to the individual identification of respondents have been kept to a minimum. Subsequently, these questions address essential information only, such as policing experience, rank, assignment, race, gender, and whether they are employed in a supervisory position. We excluded from the analyses all answers provided by respondents who did not explicitly state that they were truthful in completing the questionnaire.

The Sample

During 2010–2013, we distributed questionnaires to commissioned and noncommissioned officers across all nine provinces. In our first sweep of the survey, covering the period 2010/2011, we collected 771 questionnaires. In our second survey

Table 8.1 Respondents' demographic characteristics

	Number of sworn officers	Percent of sworn officers (%)
Type of police agency		
SAPS	757	86.9
Metro police	62	7.1
Traffic police	52	6.0
Police agency size		
Very large (more than 500 sworn)	196	22.5
Large (201–500 sworn)	120	13.8
Medium (76–200)	241	27.7
Small (25–75)	161	18.5
Very small (fewer than 25)	152	17.5
Province		
Western Cape	196	22.5
Eastern Cape	87	10.0
Northern Cape	49	5.6
Free State	80	9.2
Kwazulu-Natal	120	13.8
Gauteng	144	16.5
Mpumalanga	53	6.1
North West	75	8.6
Limpopo	67	7.7
Gender		
Men	611	70.8
Women	254	29.2
Race		
White	151	17.3
Black	482	55.3
Colored	238	27.3
Type of assignment		
Patrol	243	27.9
Detective/investigative	289	33.2
Communications	50	5.7
Traffic	36	4.1
COP	112	12.9
Administrative	65	7.5
Other	76	8.7
Supervisory position		
No	544	62.5
Yes	324	37.5

Table 8.1 (continued)

	Number of sworn officers	Percent of sworn officers (%)
Length of service		
Up to 5 years	157	18.0
6–10 years	230	26.4
11–15 years	72	8.3
16–20 years	117	13.4
More than 20 years	295	33.9
Rank		
Constable + student constable	374	42.9
Sergeant	64	7.3
Warrant officer	173	19.9
Lieutenant	24	2.8
Captain	149	17.1
Major	4	0.5
Lieutenant colonel	51	5.9
Colonel	19	2.2
Other	13	1.5

run during 2012, we collected 100 more questionnaires. Consequently, the total number of questionnaires was 871, with a response rate of 87.5 %.

Our sample contains police officers from three different police agencies from all nine South African provinces (Table 8.1). The majority of the respondents are employed in the SAPS (86.9 %; Table 8.1), with some respondents from the metro police (7.1 %) and the traffic police (6.0 %; Table 8.1). The respondents were generally stationed in larger police agencies (22.5 % from very large agencies, 13.8 % from large agencies, and 27.7 from medium-sized police agencies; Table 8.1). Although the respondents were inclusive of all nine South African provinces, the most populated provinces were also the most represented with the Western Cape (22.5 %), Eastern Cape (10.0 %), Kwazulu-Natal (13.8 %), and Gauteng (16.5 %; Table 8.1) reflecting the lion's share of respondents.

The majority of the respondents were men (70.8 %; Table 8.1) and black (55.3 %; Table 8.1). Overall, our respondents were quite experienced, with only one in five (18 %; Table 8.1) having fewer than 5 years of experience and almost one half (47 %; Table 8.1) having more than 15 years of experience. The respondents were mostly employed as detectives or investigators (33.2 %), patrol officers (27.9 %), and community-policing officers (12.9 %; Table 8.1). About two thirds were employed in nonsupervisory positions and mostly of the lower ranks of the hierarchy; they were most frequently at the rank of a constable (42.9 %) or warrant officer (19.9 %).

The Results

Seriousness

The respondents were asked to evaluate the seriousness of 11 hypothetical examples of police misconduct. These hypothetical scenarios include instances of police corruption, use of excessive force, planting of evidence and writing a false report, and failing to execute a search warrant. The instructions invited the respondents to read the description of the behavior and evaluate how serious they view the conduct, as well as how serious they think other police offices in their police agency would view the depicted conduct. In answering these two questions, the respondents could select answers from a five-point scale, ranging from 1 = "not at all serious" to 5 = "very serious."

The respondents evaluated all 11 scenarios as serious forms of misconduct (Table 8.2); the mean values for all 11 scenarios were well above the midpoint of the scale and toward the seriousness end of the scale. Not all behaviors however were evaluated to be equally serious. Three scenarios were perceived to be the least serious, with means below 4 (scenario 1: free meals, gifts from merchants; scenario 7: verbal abuse—"Arrest an Asshole Day"; scenario 8: cover-up of police DUI accident). These results are not surprising as the three scenarios describe the least serious forms of corruption and abuse at the lowest level of the use of force scale. On the other hand, the respondents evaluated four scenarios as the most serious, with means above 4.5 (scenario 2: failure to arrest friend with warrant; scenario 3: theft of knife from crime scene; scenario 4: unjustifiable use of deadly force; scenario 10: false report on drug dealer). These four scenarios incorporate violations not only of the official rules but also of the norms of criminal law. As such, they depict serious forms of corruption (i.e., opportunistic theft in scenario 3; Roebuck and Barker 1974), abuse at the highest level of the use of force scale (i.e., deadly force in scenario 4), falsification of an official record, and a failure to execute an arrest warrant.

Police officers' perceptions of seriousness differentiated within forms as well. In accordance with prior research in South Africa (Kutnjak Ivković and Sauerman 2013) and across the world (Klockars et al. 2004), among the five scenarios describing police corruption (scenario 1: free meals, gifts from merchants; scenario 3: theft of knife from crime scene; scenario 5: supervisor offers holiday for errands; scenario 8: cover-up of police DUI accident; and scenario 9: auto body shop 5 % kickback), the acceptance of gratuities was evaluated as the least serious form of corruption and theft from a crime scene as one of the most serious forms. Conversely, the covering up of a fellow police officer's DUI accident and accepting a kickback from a towing company were evaluated somewhere between these two extremes, both in the present study and in 2005 (Kutnjak Ivković and Sauerman 2013).

Four scenarios included in the questionnaire capture the use of force continuum (scenario 4: unjustifiable use of deadly force; scenario 6: officer strikes prisoner who hurt partner; scenario 7: verbal abuse—"Arrest an Asshole Day"; and scenario 11: Sgt. fails to halt beating). Verbal abuse, misconduct that mirrors the lowest steps

Table 8.2 Police officer perceptions of seriousness and violation of rules

Scenario number and description	Own seriousness		Others' seriousness		Mean difference (Own–others)	*t*-test	Violation of rules	
	Mean	Rank	Mean	Rank			Mean	Rank
Scenario 1: free meals, gifts from merchants	*3.88*	*1*	*3.37*	*1*	*.51*	*11.92****	*4.22*	*3*
Scenario 2: failure to arrest friend with warrant	*4.61*	*10*	*4.00*	*7.5*	*.61*	*16.32****	*4.57*	*10*
Scenario 3: theft of knife from crime scene	*4.77*	*11*	*4.27*	*10*	*.50*	*14.43****	*4.74*	*11*
Scenario 4: unjustifiable use of deadly force	*4.56*	*9*	*4.35*	*11*	*.21*	*6.51****	*4.48*	*8*
Scenario 5: supervisor offers holiday for errands	*4.33*	*6*	*3.86*	*5*	*.47*	*11.25****	*4.33*	*5*
Scenario 6: officer strikes prisoner who hurt partner	*4.29*	*4*	*3.81*	*4*	*.48*	*13.28****	*4.35*	*6*
Scenario 7: verbal abuse—"Arrest an Asshole Day"	*3.90*	*2*	*3.56*	*2*	*.34*	*10.62****	*3.96*	*1*
Scenario 8: cover-up of police DUI accident	*3.98*	*3*	*3.66*	*3*	*.32*	*10.16****	*4.03*	*2*
Scenario 9: auto body shop 5% kickback	*4.30*	*5*	*3.92*	*6*	*.38*	*10.73****	*4.30*	*4*
Scenario 10: false report on drug dealer	*4.50*	*8*	*4.15*	*9*	*.35*	*11.21****	*4.47*	*7*
Scenario 11: Sgt. fails to halt beating	*4.47*	*7*	*4.00*	*7.5*	*.47*	*13.11****	*4.49*	*9*

*$p<.05$; **$p<.01$; ***$p<.001$
DUI driving under the influence

in the use of force continuum, was evaluated to be the least serious in this group. The abuse of deadly force, mirroring the top steps in the use of force continuum, was evaluated as the most serious in the group. These findings were quite similar to the findings from the U.S. application of the survey; among the use of force-related misconduct, verbal abuse was perceived to be the least serious, abuse of deadly force the most, and the rest of the use of force misconduct was perceived to lie between the two extremes (Klockars et al. 2006, p. 147).

We also compared the respondents' own evaluations of seriousness with how serious they thought other police officers in their agencies would assess these scenarios (Table 8.2). In all 11 scenarios, the results show that the respondents perceived that they would evaluate these behaviors as more serious than their fellow officers (Table 8.2). Although these perceptional differences were statistically significant in all 11 scenarios (Table 8.2), they were not of substantive importance in any of the scenarios if the established rule of thumb (Klockars et al. 2006) is followed that only the differences between the means in excess of 0.50 should be considered as substantively important. The differences cross this cutoff in three scenarios (scenario 1: free meals, gifts from merchants; scenario 2: failure to arrest friend with warrant; scenario 3: theft of knife from crime scene); while in three additional scenarios (scenario 5: supervisor offers holiday for errands; scenario 6: officer strikes prisoner who hurt partner; scenario 11: Sgt. fails to halt beating), the differences are very close to it.

Violation of Official Rules

Our questionnaire also focuses on whether the respondents recognized the described behaviors, all of which violates the official rules, as rule violating. In response to this question, posed for each scenario, the respondents could have selected answers ranging from 1 = "definitely not a violation" to 5 = "definitely a violation."

The majority of the respondents had no problems recognizing and labeling the behaviors described in the scenarios as rule violating (Table 8.2); the mean values for every scenario were at least 4 or even closer to 5 on our five-point scale, ranging from about 4 (for scenario 7: verbal abuse—"Arrest an Asshole Day") to almost 5 (for scenario 3: theft of knife from crime scene).

Accepting gratuities (scenario 1: free meals, gifts from merchants), verbally abusing citizens (scenario 7: verbal abuse—"Arrest an Asshole Day"), and the covering up of a DUI accident (scenario 8: cover-up of police DUI accident) were the least likely to be recognized as rule-violating behaviors, while stealing from a crime scene (scenario 3: theft of knife from crime scene), abusing deadly force (scenario 4: unjustifiable use of deadly force), failing to execute an arrest warrant (scenario 2: failure to arrest friend with warrant), and failing to stop a beating (scenario 11: Sgt. fails to halt beating) were the most likely to be recognized as violations of official rules. These estimates correspond very closely with how the respondents evaluated the scenarios in terms of their seriousness. Indeed, there is a strong positive correlation between the respondents' own evaluations of seriousness and whether they evaluated the behavior to be rule violating (Spearman's correlation coefficient $=0.918$; $p<0.001$).

Appropriate and Expected Discipline

The questionnaire contains two questions about the potential discipline for such behaviors. The first question inquired about the respondents' views of the appropriate discipline for the depicted conduct. The second question asked them to assess what discipline their agency would mete out for such behaviors. The answers we offered to the respondents are based on the sanctions contained both in the SDR and at the agency's operational level. The options included: 1= "none," 2= "verbal reprimand," 3= "written reprimand," 4= "reassignment to a different position," 5= "demotion in rank," and 6="dismissal."

Because the scale used for disciplinary questions is ordinal, we use modal values and percentages to analyze the results. The results show that for the majority of the behaviors, the modal value is the least serious official discipline—"written reprimand" (Table 8.3); in 8 out of 11 scenarios, respondents thought that "written reprimand" should be the adequate discipline, regardless of whether the police officer only verbally abused the citizens or actually hit the citizens. Only for the acceptance of gratuities did the officers think that "verbal reprimand," the least severe disciplinary option that does not leave a permanent blemish on the record, should be appropriate. In only two scenarios (scenario 3: theft of knife from crime scene; scenario 4: unjustifiable use of deadly force), the modal response indicated that the respondents though that "dismissal" was the most appropriate discipline. These two scenarios describe the most serious forms of corruption (theft from a crime scene) and abuse of force (deadly force).

We also examined the percentages of the respondents who selected each of the disciplinary options by reclassifying their responses into "no discipline," "some discipline other than dismissal," and "dismissal" (Table 8.3). Our analysis of the percentages yields very similar results to the analysis based on the modes. The majority of the respondents, from as low as 50% to as high 85%, argued that some discipline, "less serious than dismissal," should be appropriate in each and every scenario (Table 8.3). None of the scenarios indicated either a majority or a substantial minority (20% or more) of respondents who thought that "no discipline" should be appropriate for these behaviors.

In only one scenario, depicting an opportunistic theft, evaluated to be the most serious in the group and most likely to be recognized as a rule-violating behavior (scenario 3: theft of knife from crime scene), about one half of the respondents argued that "dismissal" should be the appropriate form of discipline. There were also five additional scenarios (scenario 2: failure to arrest friend with warrant; scenario 4: unjustifiable use of deadly force; scenario 9: auto body shop 5% kickback; scenario 10: false report on drug on dealer; and scenario 11: Sgt. fails to halt beating) in which there was a substantial minority, from about 20 to 42%, who argued that "dismissal" was appropriate. These scenarios share some features: they are typically evaluated to be more serious and more likely to be regarded as a violation

Table 8.3 Views about appropriate discipline (should) and expected discipline (would)

Scenario number and description		Mode	Rank should	Rank would	None (%)	Some discipline (%)	Dismissal (%)	Chi-square test
Scenario 1: free meals, gifts from merchants	*Should*	Verbal rep.	1		9.6	74.3	16.1	1022.06***
	Would	Written rep.		1–9	12.4	74.2	13.4	
Scenario 2: failure to arrest friend with warrant	*Should*	Written rep.	2–9		2.8	76.4	20.8	874.95***
	Would	Written rep.		1–9	3.9	74.6	21.5	
Scenario 3: theft of knife from crime scene	*Should*	Dismissal	10–11		0.8	49.5	49.7	933.45***
	Would	Dismissal		10–11	1.1	49.5	49.4	
Scenario 4: unjustifiable use of deadly force	*Should*	Dismissal	10–11		3.1	55.1	41.8	1417.11***
	Would	Dismissal		10–11	2.6	54.6	42.8	
Scenario 5: supervisor offers holiday for errands	*Should*	Written rep.	2–9	1–9	4.4	84.7	10.9	1021.16***
	Would	Written rep.			7.3	79.7	13.0	
Scenario 6: officer strikes prisoner who hurt partner	*Should*	Written rep.	2–9		4.8	80.1	15.1	1143.81***
	Would	Written rep.		1–9	6.7	78.6	14.7	
Scenario 7: verbal abuse—"Arrest an Asshole Day"	*Should*	Written rep.	2–9		14.5	79.3	6.2	1328.64***
	Would	Written rep.		1–9	14.2	79.3	6.5	
Scenario 8: cover-up of police DUI accident	*Should*	Written rep.	2–9		13.0	74.4	12.6	1278.89***
	Would	Written rep.		1–9	13.0	72.5	14.5	
Scenario 9: auto body shop 5% kickback	*Should*	Written rep.	2–9		11.5	64.3	24.2	1000.94***
	Would	Written rep.		1–9	14.1	61.2	24.7	
Scenario 10: false report on drug dealer	*Should*	Written rep.	2–9		4.5	62.2	33.3	1238.67***
	Would	Written rep.		1–9	5.6	62.3	32.1	
Scenario 11: Sgt. fails to halt beating	*Should*	Written rep.	2–9		4.0	69.9	26.1	1295.53***
	Would	Written rep.		1–9	4.0	70.2	25.8	

***$p < 0.001$

of the official rules. Scenario 4 (unjustifiable use of deadly force) was particularly revealing because it describes the abuse that mirrors the most serious part of the use of force continuum and only a very strong minority (42 %) believed that "dismissal" should be an appropriate discipline.

The second disciplinary question in the questionnaire inquired about the discipline that agency would mete out for such behavior. Clearly, because of the SDR's focus on the confidentiality of disciplinary hearings, police officers do not have direct access to the actual cases and outcomes and, thus, are not always familiar with the specific discipline that the agency meted out in instances of misconduct.

Based on the modal responses, the results indicate that the respondents expected that "written reprimand" would be the agency's choice of discipline in 9 out of 11 scenarios (Table 8.3). In only two scenarios (scenario 3: theft of knife from crime scene; scenario 4: unjustifiable use of deadly force), which were both very serious violations of not only agency rules but also criminal law, the modal responses indicated that, according to the respondents, "dismissal" would be the discipline that the agencies would mete out. The analysis of the percentages leads toward the same conclusion: The majority of the respondents, from as low as 50 % (scenario 3: theft of knife from crime scene) to as high as 80 % (scenario 5: supervisor offers holiday for errands), expected the agencies to mete out some discipline, but not as harsh as "dismissal." About one half of the respondents expected "dismissal" only for the theft of knife from the crime scene (scenario 3), while there was a larger group of respondents, but still only a minority ranging from about 20 to 43 %, who expected "dismissal" in five additional scenarios (scenario 2: failure to arrest friend with warrant; scenario 4: unjustifiable use of deadly force; scenario 9: auto body shop 5 % kickback; scenario 10: false report on drug on dealer; and scenario 11: Sgt. fails to halt beating).

We also compared the respondents' views of the appropriate discipline with their views of the expected discipline. We first compared the modal values (Table 8.3) and concluded that the modes were identical in all but one scenario. Our respondents thought that a police officer who accepts gratuities (scenario 1: free meals, gifts from merchants) should receive only a "verbal warning." At the same time, they expected that the agency would discipline somewhat more harshly, meting out a "written reprimand" instead. Our exploration of the percentages (Table 8.3) pointed toward an even more uniform picture. A comparison of percentages for appropriate and expected discipline suggested that the distributions were related (Table 8.3). Furthermore, they were very small (all were below 5 %) and, thus, not of substantive importance.

Willingness to Report Misconduct

The last aspect of police integrity measured in the questionnaire is the code of silence. The first question inquired about the respondents' own willingness to report a police officer who engaged in the misconduct described in the questionnaire and the second question asked the respondents to assess how likely other

Table 8.4 Police officer perceptions of willingness to report

Scenario number and description	Own willingness to report		Others' willingness to report		Mean difference (Own–others)	*t*-test
	Mean	Rank	Mean	Rank		
Scenario 1: free meals, gifts from merchants	3.61	3	2.91	1	.70	14.99***
Scenario 2: failure to arrest friend with warrant	4.20	9	3.48	9	.72	16.61***
Scenario 3: theft of knife from crime scene	4.36	11	3.59	10	.77	17.52***
Scenario 4: unjustifiable use of deadly force	4.32	10	3.82	11	.50	13.62***
Scenario 5: supervisor offers holiday for errands	3.84	6	3.43	7	.41	12.27***
Scenario 6: officer strikes prisoner who hurt partner	3.80	5	3.27	5	.53	13.42***
Scenario 7: verbal abuse—"Arrest an Asshole Day"	3.33	1	2.99	2	.34	10.23***
Scenario 8: cover-up of police DUI accident	3.47	2	3.05	3	.42	11.73***
Scenario 9: auto body shop 5% kickback	3.68	4	3.20	4	.48	12.27***
Scenario 10: false report on drug dealer	4.07	8	3.44	8	.63	16.17***
Scenario 11: Sgt. fails to halt beating	3.92	7	3.36	6	.56	13.20***

*$p<0.05$; **$p<0.01$; ***$p<0.001$

officers in their agencies were to report such misconduct. The respondents could select answers from 1 = "definitely would not report" to 5 = "definitely would report."

The results, shown in Table 8.4, paint the contours of the code of silence. As the mean values do not approach 5 (the reporting side of the scale) for any of the scenarios (Table 8.4), in each instance there was a certain percentage of police officers who would not report for such misconduct, thus indicating the existence of the code of silence.

Furthermore, the code of silence does not cover all behaviors equally (Table 8.4); the mean values ranged from as low as 3.33 for the scenario describing the verbal abuse (scenario 7: verbal abuse—"Arrest an Asshole Day") to as high as 4.36 for the scenario describing the theft of knife from a crime scene (scenario 3: theft of knife from crime scene). Two scenarios, with mean values below 3.5, stand out as those covered by the code of silence most extensively (scenario 7: verbal abuse—"Arrest an Asshole Day"; scenario 8: cover-up of police DUI accident). One of them (scenario 7: verbal abuse—"Arrest an Asshole Day") describes the verbal abuse of a citizen and, as such, was evaluated by our respondents to be among the least serious and, at the same time, was least likely to be recognized as a violation of the official rules. Similarly, the cover-up of a police DUI accident (scenario 8: cover-up of police DUI accident), certainly a form of internal corruption, was viewed as one of the least serious forms of misconduct in the questionnaire, one that was least likely to be labeled as rule violating.

On the other end of the scale are four scenarios (scenario 2: failure to arrest friend with warrant; scenario 3: theft of knife from crime scene; scenario 4: unjustifiable use of deadly force; and scenario 10: false report on drug dealer) with the mean values of 4 or more (Table 8.4). Based on the values of these means, the respondents seemed much less likely to tolerate such behavior in silence. At the same time, they were more likely to evaluate these behaviors as the most serious ones, most likely to recognize them as rule violating, and, for at least two of them, more likely to expect and support dismissal.

The respondents' adherence to the code of silence (their (un)willingness to report) seems to be strongly related to the other measures of police integrity. The more serious the respondents evaluated the behavior, the more likely they were to say that the code of silence would not protect it (Spearman's correlation coefficient = 0.955, $p < 0.001$). Also, the more likely they were to recognize the behavior as a violation of official rules, the more likely they were not to adhere to the code of silence (Spearman's correlation coefficient = 0.945, $p < 0.001$).

A comparison of the respondents' own willingness to report and their estimates of the extent to which other police officers in their agency would be willing to report (Table 8.4) yielded statistically significant differences in all 11 scenarios. The mean values for their own willingness to report are higher than the mean values for the estimated willingness of others to report for all the 11 scenarios, suggesting that the respondents perceived that they would be less likely to participate in the code of silence than other police officers in their agencies would. An application of the rule of thumb that only differences of 0.50 or larger would be substantively important

(Klockars et al. 2006) suggests that, in the majority of the scenarios (7 out of 11), these differences were not only statistically significant but also substantively important. With two exceptions (scenario 1: free meals, gifts from merchants; scenario 6: officer strikes prisoner who hurt partner), these five scenarios were evaluated to be the most serious in the questionnaire.

Conclusion

Since the early 1990s, South African governments and transitional administrations have engaged in an encompassing transformation of the national police agency. The success of the 1994 commenced, ANC-led law enforcement makeover has however been considerably debated in the media (News24 2008, 2013; IOLNews 2013) and among researchers (Bruce 2002; Bayley 2005; Newham 2004; 2013; Faull 2010; Newham and Faull 2011; Kutnjak Ivković and Sauerman 2008, 2011, 2012, 2013) with mostly negative assessments on especially issues of police conduct and integrity. The ANC coalition[8] government itself is under even more scrutiny and criticism in terms of its questionable prevention of and dubious reactions to corruption from within its own ranks (see Bruce 2002; Van Vuuren 2004; Giliomee and Mbenga 2007; News24 2011; Transparency International 2013; Newham 2014).

After 20 years of SAPS reform, at least one of the initial transformation objectives—a uniform set of internal rules to regulate police conduct—seems to be acknowledged in the agency through the functioning of the SDR of 2006. As such, our research results suggest that the majority of the police officer respondents had no difficulties in recognizing the hypothetical police behavior as rule violating and had evaluated all 11 hypothetical cases as serious transgressions. However, it is interesting that in all the scenarios, the respondents supposed that their colleagues would consider the behaviors as less severe. Several reasons might exist for such perceptions and the subsequent lack of trust in the judgment of fellow officers. The politically induced, initial makeup of the agency which forced former enemies to work together could prove explanatory, as would the agency's ill-conceived promotion policy. Based on ambiguous national equity strategies and widely criticized in both political and police circles as "a source of fraudulent and corrupt employment" (Parliament of the Republic of South Africa (Parliament RSA 2012)), the policy's function was eventually suspended by a High Court ruling in 2013, only through the intervention of a trade union on the grounds of its lack in transparency, fairness, and recognition of work experience (IOLNews 2013). With one half of our respondents having more than 15 years of police experience, and with the vast majority being employed in nonsupervisory positions faced with a long-standing system of advancement not based on merit, their unbridled confidence in the operational judg-

[8] The ANC governs with the support of its tripartite alliance with the Congress of South African Trade Unions (Cosatu) and the South African Communist Party (SACP; SouthAfrica.info 2014).

ments of fellow officers and senior ranks would have been somewhat of a novel response.

Evenly troubling is our finding of the respondents' support and expectations of very mild discipline in terms of serious rule-violating actions. Generally, they believed that less severe disciplinary sanctions than "dismissal" should be meted out for the majority of scenarios regardless whether the scenarios were also indicative of criminal conduct. Only for the serious misconduct of stealing an item from a crime scene did they support and expect a sanction of dismissal. Such perceptions bring into question the presence of "a mutual understanding of misconduct and discipline among supervisors and employees" as proposed by the SDR (Regulation 3(c)). On the other hand, the complexity of disciplinary proceedings in the SAPS might very likely explain these responses. With only the National Defence Force, the National Intelligence Agency, and the South African Secret Service excluded from the country's labor dispensation (Labour Relations Act 66 of 1995 (LRA), the SDR contains sector-specific derivatives of this legislation. As such, organized labor has become entrenched in the disciplinary processes of the SAPS and with the SDR stating that the agency may be represented by "any employee who is impartial…to the alleged misconduct" (Regulation 4(d)), members often lack the necessary skills and experience to effectively conduct hearings when confronted with trained labor union representatives who might also be legal practitioners (Regulation 14(5)(a)). Add to this imbalance the strict adherence to challenging concepts in law, two recognized labor unions, and a Safety and Security Sectoral Bargaining Council agreement that all but financially forces SAPS members to belong to an organized labor union, it comes as no surprise that bewilderment often accompanies the initialization of disciplinary procedures (Sauerman 2001, p. 182). In such circumstances, it is certainly doubtful whether severe disciplinary sanctions are frequently and consistently applied in the agency.

Similar to our 2005 study, our results further expose the code of silence among the respondents even though it appears not to be protective of all behaviors equally. As such, our present respondents seem to be least likely to protect a theft from a crime scene and an unjustifiable use of deadly force. This status quo in the code over a period of 7 years further indicates that the SAPS' 2010 strategy to improve the agency's discipline (South African Government Information 2010) had little immediate effect. According to the minister of police at the time, the plan bizarrely entailed the reintroduction of military ranks and the acquiring of "force" (rather than "service") characteristics (South African Government Information 2010). Not only was this new approach conflicting with the agency's initial reform focuses, but with the code of silence an expected consequence of militarized policing environments (Kutnjak Ivković and Sauerman 2008, p. 28), it is very likely that instead of "improving discipline," the strategy actually strengthened the code within the agency. Correspondingly, Faull (2010) warns that the SAPS should be careful that the "military ranks and 'war on crime' do not create police officials who alienate the citizens they serve" (p. 40).

Finally, our research indicates that the SAPS is not in the process of shaking its reputation as a police agency beset by corruption. Seen in the context of the country's integrity dilemmas, this inability to rid the SAPS of corruption is not necessarily the result of its operational members' efforts or lack thereof. On the contrary, they seem acutely aware of this "serious challenge facing the SAPS" (Newham and Faull 2011, p. 22). Casual comments made by our respondents after their survey completions corroborated their awareness of the situation: "You should hand out these [questionnaires] at the [SAPS] Head Office, there you'll find the real crooks" and "serious corruption is [coming] from the top, we try to make a difference, but it's always a losing battle."

The integrity dilemmas of the SAPS are merely symptoms of larger organizational and government problems. The continuous political appointments of former civilians in the role of national police commissioner have consistently resulted in corruption scandals, certainly exacerbating the already tarnished public image of the SAPS. The SAPS. officials encountered in our research projects are mostly ready to be led from this; they are waiting on their captain. Alas, with politicians perceived as one of the "extremely corrupt" groups within the country (Transparency International 2013), it might be a very long wait indeed.

References

Bayley, D. (2005). *Changing the guard: Developing democratic police abroad.* New York: Oxford University Press.

Bruce, D. (2002). New wine from an old cask? The South African Police Service and the process of transformation. Paper presented at John Jay College of Criminal Justice, New York, 9 May 2002. Cape Town, South Africa, Centre for the Study of Violence and Reconciliation.

Bruce, D. (2008). Benign neglect? The policies and practice of controlling police corruption in South Africa. Paper presented at the Special Session: Crime, poverty and police corruption of the Annual Bank Conference on Development Economics, Cape Town, South Africa, 9–11 June.

Burger, J., & Adonis, C. (2008). A watchdog without teeth? The Independent Complaints Directorate. *South African Crime Quarterly, 24.*

Constitution of the Republic of South Africa. Act 108 of 1996.

Department: Independent Police Investigative Directorate, South Africa. Vision and Mission. http://www.ipid.gov.za/about%20us/vision_mission.asp.

Dixon, B. (2013). Waiting for farlam: Marikana, social inequality and the relative autonomy of the police. *South African Crime Quarterly, 46,* 5–11.

Faull, A. (2007). Corruption and the South African Police Service: A review and its implications. Paper 150, September. Pretoria: Institute for Security Studies.

Faull, A. (2010). 'When I see them I feel like beating them': Corruption and the South African Police Service. *South African Crime Quarterly, 34,* 33–40.

Giliomee, H., & Mbenga, B. (2007). *New history Of South Africa.* Cape Town: Tafelberg.

IOLNews. (2013). Cops frustrated over 'unfair' promotion policy. http://www.iol.co.za/news/crime-courts/cops-frustrated-over-unfair-promotion-policy-1.1484331.

Joubert, P., Basson, A., Brümmer, S., & Sole, S. (2008). Scorpions lose Selebi sting. In Mail & Guardian, April 11–17. South Africa.

Klockars, C. B., & Kutnjak Ivković, S. (2004). Measuring police integrity. In M. J. Hickman, A. R. Piquero, & J. R. Greene (Eds.). *Police integrity and ethics* (pp. 1.3–1.20). Belmont: Wadsworth.

Klockars, C. B., Kutnjak Ivković, S., & Haberfeld, M. R. (1997a). *The contours of police integrity.* Thousand Oaks: Sage.

Klockars, C. B., Kutnjak Ivković, S., Harver, W. E., & Haberfeld, M. R. (1997b). The measurement of police integrity. Final report submitted to the U.S. Department of Justice, Office of Justice Programs, National Institute of Justice.

Klockars, C. B., Kutnjak Ivković, S., Haberfeld, M. R., & Uydess, A. (2001). Enhancing police integrity: Three case studies. Final report submitted to the U.S. Department of Justice, Office of Justice Programs, National Institute of Justice. (with contributions by Geller, W. A.).

Kutnjak Ivković, S., & Sauerman, A. (2008). Measuring the integrity of the South African Police Service during transitional times. *Acta Criminologica, CRIMSA Conference, 2,* 21–39.

Kutnjak Ivković, S., & Sauerman, A. (2011). Measuring the code of silence among the South African police: Findings from a SAPS supervisor survey. In C. Gould (Ed.), *National and international perspectives on crime and policing: Toward a coherent strategy for crime reduction in South Africa beyond 2010* (pp. 74–87). Pretoria: Institute for Security Studies.

Kutnjak Ivković, S., & Sauerman, A. (2012). The code of silence: Revisiting South African police integrity. *South African Crime Quarterly, 40,* 15–24.

Kutnjak Ivković, S., & Sauerman, A. (2013). Curtailing the code of silence among the South African police. Policing—An International Journal of Police Strategies & Management, 36 (1).

Malan, M. (1999). Police reform in South Africa: Peacebuilding without peacekeepers. *African Security Review, 8*(3), 32–44.

Marais, E., & Rauch, J. (1992). Policing South Africa: Reform and prospects. Paper presented at IDASA conference, Policing in South Africa in the 1990s, Van der Bijl Park, Johannesburg, October 1992. Cape Town, South Africa: Centre for the Study of Violence and Reconciliation.

Masuku, T. (2004). Numbers that count: National monitoring of police conduct. *South African Crime Quarterly, 8,* 5–10.

Masuku, T. (2005). Strengthening democratic policing in South Africa: Enhancing and coordinating the internal and external accountability of the South African Police Service. Research report, July. Braamfontein: Centre for the Study of Violence and Reconciliation.

Mollen Commission. (1994). The city of New York commission to investigate allegations of police corruption and the anti-corruption procedures of the police department: Commission report, Mollen Commission, New York, NY.

Newham, G. (2000). Transformation and the internal disciplinary system of the South African Police Service. Research report written for the Centre for the Study of Violence and Reconciliation, November.

Newham, G. (2004). Out of step: Integrity and the South African Police Service. In C. B. Klockars, S. Kutnjak Ivković, & M. R. Haberfeld (Eds.), *The contours of police integrity* (pp. 232–250). Thousand Oaks: Sage.

Newham, G. (2005). Internal police systems for officer control: A strategic focus area for improving civilian oversight and police accountability in South Africa. Research report written for the Criminal Justice Conference, February 7–8.

Newham, G. (2013). Why have the police learned nothing from Marikana? ISS Today. http://www.issafrica.org/iss-today/why-have-the-police-learned-nothing-from-marikana.

Newham, G. (2014). ISS: Why is corruption getting worse in South Africa? DefenceWeb, Governance. http://www.defenceweb.co.za/index.php?option=com_content&view=article&id=33113:iss-why-is-corruption-getting-worse-in-south-africa&catid=54:Governance&Itemid=118.

Newham, G., & Faull, A. (2011). Protector or predator? Tackling police corruption in South Africa. Monograph No. 182. Pretoria: Institute for Security Studies.

Newham, G., Masuku, T., Gomomo, L., & Maroga, M. (2003). The police integrity management report. Research report. Braamfontein: Centre for the Study of Violence and Reconciliation.

News24. (2008). SAPS 'full of criminals'. www.news24.com/SouthAfrica/News/SAPS-full-of-criminals-20080509.

News24. (2011). High-level corruption cases mount. http://www.news24.com/SouthAfrica/News/High-level-corruption-cases-mount-20110509.

News24. (2012). Bheki Cele fired. http://www.news24.com/SouthAfrica/News/Bheki-Cele-fired-20120612.

News24. (2013). Is SAPS the Mafia? http://www.news24.com/Columnists/GuestColumn/Is-SAPS-the-Mafia-20131029

Open Society Justice Initiative. (2003). South Africa: Enhancing police accountability. www.justiceinitiative.org/activities/ncjr/police/sa_police.

Parliament of the Republic of South Africa. (2012). Blame Rules for Corrupt Cops. http://www.parliament.gov.za/live/content.php?Item_ID=2246.

Pelser, E., Louw, A., & Ntuli, S. (2000). Poor safety: Crime and policing in South Africa's rural areas. Monograph No. 47, May. Pretoria: Institute for Security Studies.

Politicsweb. (2013). SAPS anti-corruption unit to be launched—Riah Phiyega. http://www.politicsweb.co.za/politicsweb/view/politicsweb/en/page71651?oid=391555&sn=Detail&pid=71651.

Sauerman, A. (2001). Labour negotiations: Rewarding the carriers and the trackers. In F. Reynecke & M. Fourie (Eds.), *Police management beyond 2000* (pp. 167–194). Lansdowne: Juta & Co.

Shaw, M. (2002). *Crime and policing in post-apartheid South Africa: Transforming under fire*. London: Hurst.

South African Government Information. (2010). Statement: Police Ministry announces new police ranks. 11 March. http://www.info.gov.za/speech/DynamicAction?pageid=461&sid=9243&tid=9260.

South African Independent Police Investigative Directorate Act. (Act 1 of 2011).

SouthAfrica.info. (2014). South Africa's political parties. http://www.southafrica.info/about/democracy/polparties.htm#anc#ixzz2qkB2MC4A.

South African Labour Relations Act. (1995). (Act no. 66 of 1995).

South African Police Service. (1997). Code of Conduct. Promulgated on 31 October.

South African Police Service (SAPS). (2002). Annual Report: 2001/2002. Pretoria, South Africa.

South African Police Service (SAPS). (2004). Annual Report: 2003/2004. Pretoria, South Africa.

South African Police Service (SAPS). (2009). Annual Report: 2008/2009. Pretoria, South Africa.

South African Police Service (SAPS). (2013). Annual Report: 2012/2013. Pretoria, South Africa.

South African Police Service (SAPS), Department of Police. (2013). The Department of Police announces partnership with UNISA to establish SAPS University in Paarl. Media Statement from the office of the National Commissioner, 22 October. http://www.saps.gov.za/_dynamicModules/internetSite/newsBuild.asp?myURL=3766.

South African Police Service Act. (1995). (Act No 68 of 1995).

South African Police Service Disciplinary Regulations. (2006). In Government Gazette no. 28985, dated 3 July 2006. Pretoria, South Africa.

SowetonLive. (2012). Corrupt cops on our radar—Phiyega. http://www.sowetanlive.co.za/news/2012/06/15/corrupt-cops-on-our-radar--phiyega.

The Star. (2010). A national embarrassment—Selebi gets 15 years as actions ruled 'incomprehensible'. South Africa: 4 August.

Thompson, L. (2001). A history of South Africa (3rd ed.). New Haven: Yale University Press.

Transparency International. (2013). Global Corruption Barometer 2013. http://www.transparency.org/whatwedo/pub/global_corruption_barometer_2013.

Truth & Reconciliation Commission. (1998). The TRC Report. http://www.justice.gov.za/Trc/report/index.htm.

Van Vuuren, H. (2004). Small bribes, big challenge: Extent and nature of petty corruption in South Africa. *South African Crime Quarterly, 9,* 11–16.

Vigneswaran, D., & Hornberger, J. (2009). Beyond good cop/bad cop: understanding informality and police corruption in South Africa. FMSP Research Report for the African Centre for Migration and Society, October.

Chapter 9
Police Integrity in South Korea

Wook Kang and Sanja Kutnjak Ivković

Abstract South Korea is an Asian democracy with the history of military and autocratic regimes. The police served the regimes and engaged in various forms of police misconduct, from the use of excessive force and violation of human rights to corruption. Recent reforms of the South Korean police primarily targeted police corruption and mostly neglected the use of excessive force. This chapter presents the results of the 2009 police integrity survey of 379 South Korean police officers. The respondents had no problems recognizing most of the behaviors described in the questionnaire as rule violating. The instances in which they had problems were mostly focused on the scenarios describing the use of excessive force. The respondents evaluated most of the scenarios as serious. They also expected, and approved of, some discipline milder than dismissal for such behavior. We uncovered a strong code of silence among our respondents that protects not only violations of official rules but also violations of criminal law. Our results indicate that the respondents' own views about the described behavior and their estimates of how others would evaluate the same behavior are very similar. We argue that these results should be interpreted in light of the Confucianism and the collective culture of homogeneity widespread in South Korea.

Keywords Grand Reform · Korean National Police Agency · Police integrity · South Korea · Survey

Introduction

South Korea is an Asian democracy with a highly developed economy (e.g., Global Competitiveness Report 2009–2010). Unlike the current democratic regime, South Korean political history is replete with long periods characterized by the governance

W. Kang (✉)
Korean National Police University, Yongin-si, South Korea
e-mail: kangw@police.ac.kr

S. Kutnjak Ivković
Michigan State University, East Lansing, MI, USA
e-mail: kutnjak@msu.edu

S. Kutnjak Ivković, M. R. Haberfeld (eds.), *Measuring Police Integrity Across the World*,
DOI 10.1007/978-1-4939-2279-6_9

of the military and authoritarian regimes. In the early 1900s, Korea was first declared a Japanese protectorate and, within a few years, officially annexed by Japan in 1910 (Kwon 1999). For more than three decades, until its surrender to the Allied Forces at the end of World War II, Japan occupied and controlled Korea. With Japanese demise at the end of World War II, Korea was split at the 38th parallel into the Soviet and the U.S. zones of occupation. In 1948, the elections in the U.S. zone of occupation led toward the establishment of the Republic of South Korea (Song 2011). As South Korea has faced constant military threat from North Korea, military governments remained in power until 1987 when a civilian government was finally established (Kim 2007). This long history of military governments has shaped the way police operated and were perceived by the citizens.

Throughout history, the police in Korea were controlled by and served the military and autocratic regimes. During the colonial period, the Korean police served the Japanese government. The modern Korean police, established in the 1940s, were controlled by the U.S. Army Government in Korea and, after South Korea was established as a separate state in 1948, also by the South Korean military government. In the 1960s, the police were accused of participating in manipulations of various elections (Moon 2004; Nalla and Kang 2011). The police continued to serve the regime and routinely violated human rights of their own constituency (Lee 1990). Continuing police corruption and blatant violations of human rights kept the public support for the police low (Pyo 2002). Eventually, one such critical incident involved a student who was tortured and killed during a police investigation about an antigovernment organization (Cohen and Baker 1991). The brutality and gross violations of human rights in this case resulted in a public outcry that eventually led the government to initiate the police reform.

When Kim Youngsam was elected as a civilian president in 1993, the South Korean police maintained political neutrality and began to change the negative image associated with the brutality of the colonial police and authoritarian police (Nalla and Kang 2012). Following his appointment as the head of the South Korean police, Mooyoung Lee embarked upon a substantial reform of the police, including changes to the system, practice, and culture of the police (Pyo 2002). This Grand Reform of police was conducted with the purpose of democratizing and civilianizing the South Korean police (Nalla and Kang 2012). The Reform also aimed to curtail police corruption by providing higher salaries and better working environment, as well as opening communication channels between supervisors and officers (KNPA 2005). Through concentrated efforts, from creating a friendly animated character "Podori" to establishing the Police Service Charter, the police also worked on improving its public image and confidence in the police.

However, although fewer citizens believed in 2000 than in 1997 that the police were corrupt (35.8% vs. 52.2%; Kim 2002), the police were still perceived as the most corrupt part of the government. Even in 2013, the situation did not improve dramatically. The results of the 2013 Anti-Corruption & Civil Rights Commission (ACRC) Integrity Assessment Program, which surveys about 220,000 government employees and citizens about corrupt practices at public organizations, reveal that the police are still perceived as corrupt, sharing the lowest rank with the prosecutors' office (ACRC 2013).

The South Korean police have a centralized police system under the auspices of the Ministry of Security and Public Administration. The Korean National Police Agency (KNPA) is the headquarters of South Korean police. The KNPA controls state police agencies, and each state police agency supervises police departments in their areas. As of December 2013, there were 16 state police agencies, 249 police departments, and 1947 police boxes. This hierarchical organization employs 102,386 sworn officers, yielding a rate of 1 police officer per 498 inhabitants.

This chapter analyzes the key elements of the organizational theory of police integrity (Klockars et al. 1997, 2001, 2004, 2005) as they apply to the conditions in South Korea. South Korea is a particularly poignant case because it is a relatively new democracy with a long history of military and authoritarian governments. Furthermore, the chapter also provides an analysis of a survey of South Korean police officers' data, based upon the police integrity questionnaire developed by Klockars et al.

Police Integrity and South Korea

The organizational theory of police integrity (e.g., Klockars et al. 1997, 2001, 2004, 2005) rests upon the premise that police integrity is a feature of individuals, groups, and organizations. It defines police integrity as "the normative inclination among police to resist temptations to abuse rights and privileges of their occupation" (Klockars et al. 1997, 2001, 2004, p. 2). Klockars et al. developed four key dimensions of their organizational theory, ranging from the way official rules are made and understood by the police to the influence of the society at large on the police.

Organizational Rules

Organizational theory of police integrity proposes that it is critical that police agencies have official rules that prohibit misconduct. At the same time, the theory acknowledges that it is relevant not only whether the police agency has such rules but also how they are established, educated, understood, and obeyed by the police (Klockars and Kutnjak Ivković 2003; Klockars et al. 1997, 2001, 2004). A police agency characterized by high integrity should be able to communicate the official rules to the police officers effectively. Moreover, police officers employed in such agencies are expected to know, understand, and support the official rules.

The reality is that, in a highly decentralized country like the USA, the range of behaviors prohibited by police misconduct could vary dramatically from one police agency to the next. In a centralized country like South Korea, the official rules are made at the top of the organization and apply to all sworn officers, be they employed in a state or a local police agency. However, as the research on police integrity from Armenia demonstrates, despite the existence of the same rules applying to all police officers in a centralized system, the way the rules are interpreted and enforced could vary substantially across the country (Kutnjak Ivković and Khechumyan 2013), creating different levels of integrity among police agencies.

The conduct of police officers in South Korea is regulated by both laws and administrative rules. The South Korean Criminal Code (2013) consists of 42 chapters and 372 articles. The seventh chapter of the Code incorporates prohibitions of governmental officials' abuse of power; its 14 articles criminalize a range of behaviors by public officials, including police officers. They cover various types of misconduct, including the abandonment of official duties (Article 122), abuse of authority (Article 123), illegal arrest (Article 124), and bribery (Article 129–134). In addition, the Code further states that government officials who abuse their official authority and commit a crime other than the ones listed in the seventh chapter will be punished 50% more severely than other offenders who have committed the same crime (Article 135).

Police officers' use of force is regulated by the Act on the Performance of Duties by Police Officers (1981, revised 2011). The Act tries to establish the demarcation line between excessive and legitimate use of force. According to the Act, a police officer is authorized to use the official weapon only to protect a citizen's life or to make an arrest of a citizen who is resisting the police. Under these conditions, the police officer should use his or her "reasonable discretion." In addition, the police officer should be cautious not to create any danger or injury to bystanders (Article 10).

The basic set of rules dealing with internal discipline is contained in the Police Disciplinary Code (1969, revised in 2013). The Code determines the decision maker, the procedure to be used, and the possible outcomes. Initial investigations upon citizen complaints are performed by the police agency's internal affairs unit. If the investigator concludes that the complaint is sustained, the decision about the appropriate discipline should be made by a different body, a disciplinary committee. The Code prescribes that the disciplinary committee should be established in police agencies to address violations of internal rules. Finally, the Code provides the guidelines for the application of discipline in individual cases and enumerates four different kinds of discipline, ranging from written reprimand to dismissal. It also limits the discretion of the disciplinary committee in some cases. For example, when a police officer engages in what is evaluated as an intentional and severe violation of the official rules, the officer will receive more serious discipline, namely suspension or dismissal. The Rule on Extent of Police Discipline (2009, revised in 2013) provides further details on the application of discipline in individual cases.

Following a traditional model of police education, official rules are taught as part of the basic police training at the Police Academy. The content of the rules is incorporated in different classes. In 2005, the KNPA decided that an ethics seminar should be a required part of not only the basic police education but also of all the police training courses offered at the Police Academy (KNPA 2005). The police ethics seminar includes multiple discussions of official rules as they relate to police misconduct and police integrity. The seminar also incorporates discussions of recent cases, but the personal information, such as name, affiliation, and ranks, is not revealed because of the confidentiality rules.

In 2013, the Korean National Police University (KNPU) established the Character Training Institute because police officers who graduated from the KNPU committed a series of rule violations. The institute develops the ethics program for the students at the KNPU and educates them periodically. In addition, the institute examines the students' personality characteristics.

Police Detection and Investigation of Police Misconduct

The second dimension of the organizational theory of police integrity includes the police agency's methods used to detect and investigate police misconduct and disciplining of police officers who have engaged in misconduct (Klockars and Kutnjak Ivković 2003; Klockars et al. 1997, 2001, 2004). The nature of control mechanisms used by a police agency is very heterogeneous; proactive mechanisms include training in ethics and police integrity testing, whereas reactive mechanisms include investigations and disciplining of police officers who have engaged in police misconduct (Klockars et al. 2004). The expectation is that the police agency of high integrity will have a highly operational and sophisticated system that incorporates both proactive and reactive control mechanisms.

The history of the police in South Korea is dominated with the servitude to, and support for, the military and authoritarian regimes. Such regimes prefer to keep the control over the troops within the agency and neither favor nor approve any citizen involvement in the oversight of the police. If and when they deal with misconduct, such investigations are covered by the veil of secrecy and, as such, lack transparency. Historically, the situation in South Korea fits this stereotype well; internal affairs units, composed of police officers and responsible to the police administration, were in charge of such investigations. Not surprisingly, the citizens displayed low levels of trust and confidence in their work (Baek 2000).

As part of the Grand Reform in the 1990s, the police have experienced a complete overhaul of the internal disciplinary system. In accordance with the goal of increasing public confidence in the police, the Grand Reform made a substantial change in the way citizen complaints are handled. In 2000, the South Korean police established a separate and independent internal affair unit, called the Office of Hearing and Inspection (OHI) or "Chungmun Gamsagwan" in South Korea. The OHI is housed in every police department and entrusted to investigate citizen complaints and address police misconduct (Moon 2004). Although the OHI is housed within the police agency, it is completely independent from the chief of police or the top police administration in the police agency. Rather, all OHI offices are directly responsible to and supervised by the director general for audit and inspection at KNPA; the director general for audit and inspection is supervised by commissioner general directly (Fig. 9.1).

The OHI in each police agency is entrusted to receive citizen complaints about any form of police misconduct (Choi and Ma 2008). In addition, they are required to investigate potential cases of police corruption. Once the investigation is complete,

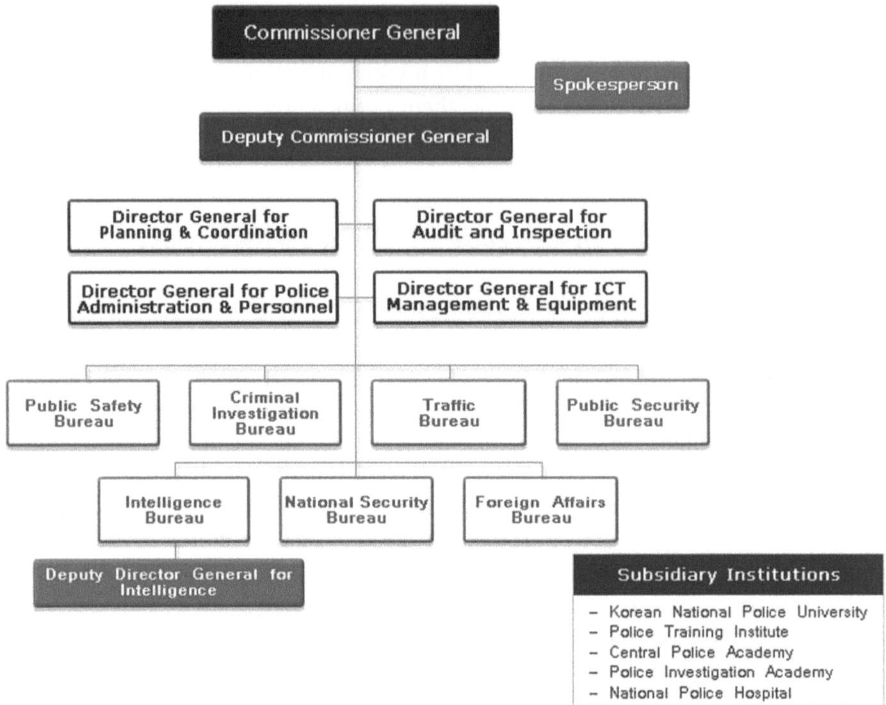

Fig. 9.1 Organization of Korea National Police Agency (KNPA). (Source: http://www.police.go.kr/eng/main/contents.do?menuNo=500017)

the OHI makes the decision about the complaint. If the complaint is sustained, the disciplinary committee reviews the case and determines the appropriate discipline.

However, the OHIs are still composed only of police officers, with no citizen participation in the investigation and review of complaints. Consequently, it comes as no surprise that the results of research studies show that citizens still distrust the investigations performed by the local OHIs (e.g., Yang and Lee 2006). At the same time, the police officers are not satisfied with the decisions either; they perceive that the OHIs are biased and unnecessarily harsh toward police officers in their zeal to please the citizens and avoid criticism (e.g., Kim 2008). In response, the KNPA instituted a rule that provides both the complainants and the involved police officers with the right to appeal to the upper-level OHI, established at the level of the state police agency (KNPA 2008).

The Reform also included changes related to complex and/or sensitive cases of police misconduct. Specifically, if the cases involve two or more state agencies, the jurisdiction for such cases lies in the hands of the director general for audit and inspections. If the complaint alleges misconduct by two local police departments, the state police agency handles the case because it has an authority to supervise local police departments. Similarly, if the complaints allege the involvement in misconduct by the chiefs of state or local police agencies, jurisdiction for such sensitive cases rests with the outsider, namely the director general for audits and inspections.

Once the OHI determines that the complaint is sustained, the disciplinary committee takes over. Depending on the rank of the police officer, disciplinary committee can be either ordinary (rank of captain or below) or central (ranks above captain). Disciplinary committees, formed ad hoc, are composed of five to seven police officers. All members, appointed by the commissioner general (for the central committees) or by the police chief (for the ordinary committees), should have a rank higher than the police officer whose case is decided. The highest-ranked member becomes the chair of the disciplinary committee.

Before making a decision, the disciplinary committee discusses the case at a hearing. Both the investigator from the OHI and the police officers against whom the complaint has been sustained are invited to attend the meeting and present their side to the committee. After the hearing, the committee makes the decision about the appropriate discipline by the majority vote. The lack of disciplinary committees' independence seriously threatens the objectivity of the findings and results in the public's low level of trust in the decisions they make (KNPA 2008).

In 2008, the police received 16,859 citizen complaints, of which 83 % have been dismissed based on the results of the internal affairs' investigation and 17 % have been sustained (KNPA 2010). The sustained complaints entered the next stage in the process, including the disciplinary hearing and the disciplinary decision made by the discipline committee. Out of the cases with sustained complaints, the overwhelming majority of the police officers involved in these cases (96 % of sustained cases) received only verbal reprimand, a discipline not even listed as a potential discipline in the Police Disciplinary Code (1969, revised in 2013). In other words, police officers received discipline more serious than verbal reprimand in only 4 % of the cases with sustained complaints (KNPA 2010).

The OHIs perform other functions, namely audits and unscheduled inspections. Unscheduled inspections are sometimes triggered by the information that the OHI receives. If the OHI receives a tip that their police officers employed in a particular agency might be corrupt, the OHI may decide not only to inspect these individual officers but also to inspect the whole police agency. This practice is probably grounded in the idea that corruption is related to a structural issue within the police agency and should be addressed as such.

The disciplinary data, obtained from the KNPA, include the data based on citizen complaints, audits, and unscheduled inspections. The data from 2003 to 2009 show that, depending on the year, about 600–1,000 officers have been disciplined every year (KNPA 2010). These data suggest that only a miniscule proportion of all police officers (1,000 out of 100,000 or less than 1 %) have been disciplined every year. Written warning—the least serious disciplinary option included—is the most frequently exercised disciplinary option, with percentages ranging from as low as 34 % in 2008 and 2009 to as high as 47 % in 2005. The most serious disciplinary option—dismissal—has been exercised in as few as 18 % of the cases in 2006 to as many as 28 % of the cases in 2009.

However, more officers have been disciplined based on the OHI audits and inspections than based on citizen complaints. For example, in 2008, there were 16,859 citizen complaints, of which 83 % or 13,993 have been dismissed based on the results of the internal affairs' investigation and 17% or 2,866 were sustained. Out of the sustained complaints, 96% or 2,751 police officers received a verbal reprimand, while only 4% or 115 police officers received a more serious discipline. However, the KNPA data on disciplined officers for the same year show the total number of 801 police officers who had received discipline more serious than verbal reprimand. The difference of 686 officers (801 police officers from the KNPA data vs. 115 police officers from the citizen complaints) is the result of OHI audits and inspections. Among the 801 disciplined officers from the KNPA reports, written warning was the most frequent option (34%), followed by dismissal (24%), decrease in salary (21%), and suspension (21%).

If a police officer is dissatisfied with the disciplinary decision meted out by the disciplinary committee, the officer has the right of appeal to the Request and Review Committee (RRC). The RRC, established by the Ministry of Public Administration and Security, is composed of seven members, appointed by the president. The officer's last stage of appeal involves a regular court, whose decision is final.

The KNPA overall efforts to further improve public confidence in the police include the establishment of the Human Rights Committee of Police (HRCP) and the Civilian Review Committee. The HRCPS, established at the police headquarters, are entitled to investigate police misconduct thoroughly (KNPA 2006). The 14 members of the HRCP are appointed directly by the commissioner general of KNPA. According to the Rule on the Protection of Human Rights in Police (2005, revised 2013), members of HRCP, intended to be experts in human rights, include lawyers, professors, and NGO representatives.

The role of the HRCP is twofold. First, the HRCP has the authority to investigate cases in which citizens allege police misconduct related to human right violations. However, the HRCP does not have the authority to investigate each and every case that comes before the OHIs. Rather, they are entrusted to investigate only the cases that become public issues and recommend the appropriate discipline for each case to the chief of police (Kutnjak Ivković and Kang 2012). In 2007, the HRCP members voted to review only 11 cases (KNPA 2008). In 2012, the number of cases had increased to 54 (KNPA 2013). The decisions of the HRCP are mainly made by the majority agreement. The HRCP asks the commissioner general to examine the case and report the results. Recently, a high-ranked officer was reported to the HRCP by his subordinate because of the sexual harassment. The HRCP unanimously agreed that the case should be examined.

Second, the HRCP has the capacity to review cases and recommend changes to the official policies related to human rights. Although the number of the policy recommendations is not available publicly, the major policy recommendations are typically publicly announced. For example, the HRCP suggested that the detention facilities in police should be improved to protect the human rights of the detainees. The KNPA accepted the suggestion and began to improve the detention facilities (KNPA 2013).

Therefore, in the parlance of the terminology developed by Walker and Wright (1995) for American citizen review boards, the HRCP performs both the case-by-case complaint function *and* the policy review function. Just like the American citizen reviews, the HRCP has only advisory powers; in case-by-case reviews, it only recommends specific discipline to the police chief; similarly, in the domain of policy changes, the HRCP only recommends the policy change to the police commissioner general.

The KNPA has also established the Citizen Review Committee (CRC). Like the name suggests, the CRC is also composed of citizens. However, it is smaller than the HRCP; the CRC includes only nine members who are experts or scholars. Like the HRCP members, the CRC members are also appointed by the commissioner general of KNPA. Like the HRCP, the CRC members serve a 2-year mandate and can be reappointed. The leading idea behind the establishment of the CRC was that the internal affairs offices within police agencies would not be able to provide objective investigations of their immediate supervisors and chiefs of these police agencies and, accordingly, an independent agency should be entrusted with this task. Thus, the CRC's mandate is limited only to the review of a selected number of cases and has no policy review powers at all. As for the cases the CRC can review, it is entrusted to review the cases involving allegations of misconduct by highly ranked police officers (i.e., chiefs of police agencies) and, once the review is completed, recommend the appropriate discipline to the commissioner general of KNPA. In 2005, the CRC recommended that the commissioner general dismiss two police chiefs who had received a US$ 600 bribe; the commissioner general accepted the recommendations and dismissed the two police chiefs (KNPA 2007).

Whereas the idea behind the HRCP and the CRC was to allow for independent citizen review of the complaints in selected subset of cases and, consequently, enhance citizen trust in the police, the way these two institutions are defined limits the likelihood of its realization. First, both the HRCP and the CRC are established only at the highest organizational level (the KNPA level) and do not exist at the level of individual police agencies. Second, although both the HRCP and CRC have the power to review cases, they do not have their own investigative units. Consequently, they have to depend on the internal affairs units and the results of their investigations. Third, even when they do succeed and either recommend discipline or propose policy changes, the HRCP and CRC are toothless lions because their findings are advisory, not mandatory. The commissioner general—a highly-ranked police officer—has a final say in the matter.

Curtailing the Code of Silence

The third dimension of the organizational theory of police integrity emphasizes the agency's willingness and ability to curtail the code of silence (Klockars and Kutnjak Ivković 2003; Klockars et al. 2004; Klockars et al. 1997, 2001). Although the code of silence—the informal prohibition of reporting misconduct by fellow police officers—exists in every police agency, the contours of the code of silence may vary substantially from one agency to the next. The expectation is that the police agency of high integrity would be more aggressive and successful in curtailing the code of silence among its police officers than the agency of low integrity. Consequently, the code of silence is expected to be weaker in police agencies of high integrity.

Empirical studies exploring the contours of the code of silence in South Korea are rare. In 2002, Lee reported the results of his dissertation targeting investigative policies and practices. The results of his study, involving a survey of 600 South Korean police officers, showed that the minority of the surveyed police officers (about 40 %) admitted that the code of silence exists among the South Korean police officers, but 60 % flatly denied the existence of the code. Furthermore, a strong minority of the respondents (40 %; Lee, 2002) indicated that their supervisors did not report police officers' misconduct and thereby participated in the code of silence themselves.

Influence of Social and Political Environment

The last dimension of the theory of police integrity focuses on the influence of the social, political, and economic environment (Klockars and Kutnjak Ivković 2003). Police agencies are part of the larger society and what occurs in the society at large influences the conduct of police officers as well.

Kang (2002, p. 1) argues that corruption scandals are a frequent theme in South Korean history and that "the exchange of money for political influence has not been just an open secret, but it has been common knowledge." Kang (2002, p. 1) further emphasizes that corruption has been a part of South Korean history since its establishment in 1948, that it has been rampant, and that the list of those convicted for corruption includes two former presidents; "members of many presidential staffs, and a slew of military officers, politicians, bureaucrats, bankers, businessman, and tax collectors." In 1995, the trial of two former presidents and numerous businessmen uncovered the existence of bribes in the excess of US$ 1 billion (Kang 2002).

Corruption in South Korea consists of the elite cartel corruption, involving businessmen, high-ranking government officials, and politicians, sometimes even the president (Johnston 2008). Such state of affairs has started to develop relatively early in South Korea's history. In the 1960s, Park Chunghee, a former general, became the president via a coup and remained in the position for the next two decades until another military general, Chun Doohwan, took over the Office of President in 1981 by means of another coup. While Park established the cartel, Doohwan strengthened in and only the elite received keys to admission to the cartel (Johnston 2008). Kang argues that extensive and contradictory regulatory and tax policies at the time (2002, p. 9) allowed a lot of discretion over companies and provided both Park and Chun with opportunities to reward selected development winners. Membership in the cartel was based on productivity, export growth, and loyalty (Johnston 2008). Over time, despite widespread corruption, South Korea's GDP continued to grow (see Table 9.1).

Table 9.1 South Korea's rankings. (Sources: Transparency International (2014); Freedom House (2014); International Monetary Fund (2013)

Year	CPI score	Freedom house ranking political rights	Freedom house ranking civil liberties	GDP
1995	4.3	2 Free	2 Free	531,001
1996	5.0	2 Free	2 Free	573,001
1997	4.3	2 Free	2 Free	532,239
1998	4.2	2 Free	2 Free	357,510
1999	3.8	2 Free	2 Free	461,808
2000	4.0	2 Free	2 Free	533,385
2001	4.2	2 Free	2 Free	504,584
2002	4.5	2 Free	2 Free	575,930
2003	4.3	2 Free	2 Free	643,760
2004	4.5	1 Free	2 Free	721,976
2005	5.0	1 Free	2 Free	844,866
2006	5.1	1 Free	2 Free	951,773
2007	5.1	1 Free	2 Free	1,049,239
2008	5.6	1 Free	2 Free	931,405
2009	5.5	1 Free	2 Free	834,060
2010	5.4	1 Free	2 Free	1,014,890
2011	5.4	1 Free	2 Free	1,114,472

In the 1980s, the end of the military regime and the transition into a democratic regime dispersed the power of the leading politicians (Kang 2002, p. 10):

> This led to increased for political payoffs as politicians began to genuinely compete for electoral support and to decreased ability of the state to resist or contain the demands of the business sector. The small number of massive Korean firms, unrestrained by any market forces because of their size, made increasingly risky decisions. Thus "too much" democracy combined with a still collusive business–government relationship resulted in increasingly ineffectual policy making, and the Asian financial crisis of 1997 brought this to the light.

The elite cartel corruption has included the police as well. At least several highly ranked police officers have been arrested for bribery annually (Kim 2002). Most recently, in 2013, the chief of police department in Chungbook province was indicted for receiving a bribe totaling around US$ 80,000 (Choi 2013).

The attempts at reforming the level of corruption in the country started with some of the first democratic presidents, namely Kim Youngsam (1993–1998), Kim Dae-Joong (1998–2003), and Roh Moohyun (2003–2008). Kim Youngsam started to develop first anticorruption policies (Quah 2006), and signed the Ethics Law of 1993, which requires of highly ranked public officials and their family members to declare publicly their assets (Kim 1998). The Law also required of police officers to declare their assets, *regardless* of their rank. The rationale was that, because of the nature of their profession, police officers may have plentiful opportunities for corruption and every police officer should be required to declare their assets to minimize chances that they would engage in unlawful increase of their wealth. The reforms continued and, in 2001, the Anti-Corruption Act was passed, opening the doors for the establishment of the Korean Independent Commission against Corruption (KICAC). Few years later, the KICAC, the ombudsman for Korea, and the Administrative Appeals Commission were merged into the newly established Anti-Corruption and Civil Rights Commission.

These anticorruption efforts have been noted by both the international community and the public at large. While South Korea's score on the Freedom House Freedom of the World Ranking (measuring the extent to which the country protects civil liberties and political rights) remained relatively stable (indicating a true democracy), its score on the Transparency International's Corruption Perceptions Index (measuring the degree to which the country is perceived to be free from public-sector corruption) seems to have improved over the last two decades (Table 9.1). Furthermore, the percentage of citizens who believe that the police are corrupt has decreased. For example, about 52 % of the respondents surveyed in 1999 believed that the police were corrupt, compared with 36 % surveyed in 2000 (Kim 2002).

Measuring Police Integrity

Questionnaire

Klockars and Kutnjak Ivković (2003; Klockars et al. 2004) developed a questionnaire that contains descriptions of 11 hypothetical scenarios, mostly describing police corruption, to measure police integrity. The questionnaire was subsequently administered in 17 countries across the world (see Klockars et al. 2004; Kutnjak Ivković and Shelly 2007, 2008a, 2008b). However, Klockars et al. indicated that their original survey, if it was to be used for measurement of police integrity, needed to be augmented because it did not include abuses of discretion in arrests, order maintenance, discourtesy to citizens, or other police misconduct not usually motivated by temptations of gain (Klockars et al. 2001).

In the course of carrying out our study in South Korea, we made several steps to insure its validity. First, we translated the questionnaire, both the scenario descriptions and the related questions and answers, into Korean. This was done by one of the coauthors, who is a native speaker. Furthermore, we discussed the applicability of the situations described in the questionnaire to the conditions in South Korea. One of the coauthors is a ranked South Korean police officer who initially analyzed the scenarios and later discussed their appropriateness with several police officers. We also explored the applicability of the questions and answers offered after each scenario and made adjustments to the disciplinary questions (see below). In addition, we pretested the questionnaire in South Korea to ensure that all cultural, legalistic, and linguistic issues have been addressed.

The respondents were asked to assume that the officer in question has been a police officer for 5 years, has not been previously disciplined, and has a good track record on the job. Each scenario was followed by the same series of questions. The follow-up questions are about police officers' knowledge of official rules, their opinions about the seriousness of particular rule-violating behaviors, the discipline these behaviors should deserve and would actually receive, and their estimates of how willing they would be to report such behavior.

Questions about potential discipline had to be adjusted to fit the legal conditions. Police Disciplinary Code (2009) determines that there are four possible disciplinary options: written warning, decreased salary (the officer receives 50% of the salary for 1–3 months), suspension (the officer receives 30% of the salary for 1–3 months), and dismissal. Consequently, our disciplinary options in the questionnaire were: "no discipline," "written warning," "decreased salary by 50%," "suspension for 1–3 months," and "dismissal."

We minimized the number of demographic questions to prevent potential identification of our respondents. We asked about the respondents' gender, police experience, rank, assignment, and whether they were employed in a supervisory position. Finally, we wanted to gauge the respondents' willingness to answer truthfully. We first asked whether the respondents estimated that the majority of the respondents would answer truthfully while filling out the questionnaire. Then, we asked the respondents directly whether they themselves had answered truthfully. Unless they noted that they answered truthfully, we excluded their answers from the analyses.

The Sample

We surveyed police officers attending classes at two South Korean police educational facilities: the KNPU and the Police Comprehensive Academy (PCA). As a general rule, the KNPU mainly trains managers, while the PCA trains line officers. There are also exceptions from this rule and managers are sometimes educated at the PCA and line officers at the KNPU. Various specialized training courses are simultaneously provided at both the KNPU and the PCA. Typically, upon promotion or transfer to a new position, officers would need to undergo additional police training. Participation in the training is mandatory, supervisors are required to allow their subordinates to take part in the required training, and the training should be completed within a year or two of the promotion or reassignment. In addition, police officers may also participate in the training voluntarily.

In summer of 2009, questionnaires were distributed to the police officers taking classes at the KNPU and the PCA as part of either mandatory or voluntary police training. At the end of the class period, we distributed 500 questionnaires to police officers. Three hundred and seventy officers agreed to participate in the study, resulting in the response rate of 74%.

The majority of our sample are male police officers (92%; Table 9.2). This is by no means surprising because men constituted about 94% of the South Korean

Table 9.2 Sample demographic characteristics. (Source: Kutnjak Ivković and Kang 2012)

Survey items	*N*	%
Gender		
1=Male	308	92
2=Female	28	8
Age		
1=23–35	110	33
2=36–45	165	50
3=46–56	58	17
Years of Experience		
1=less than 10	142	43
2=11–20	158	47
3=more than 21	34	10
Education		
1=High school	61	18
2=Associate degree	100	30
3=BA	166	49
4=MA or more	8	3
Type of assignment		
1=Patrol	157	46
2=Detective/investigative	60	18
3=Traffic	27	7
4=Police administration	46	14
5=Public security or intelligence	47	14
6=National security or foreign affairs	2	1
Supervisory role		
1=No	301	90
2=Yes	34	10

police in 2009 (KNPA 2009) and 92.5% in 2013 (KNPA 2013). The respondents are mostly middle-aged (50% of the respondents were between 36 and 45 years of age; Table 9.2), holding a bachelor's degree (49%; Table 9.2), typically with 11–20 years of experience (47%; Table 9.2), and working in patrol (46%; Table 9.2). The overwhelming majority of our respondents are line officers (90%; Table 9.2), and only 10% are supervisors. Finally, 41 respondents (or 11%) explicitly told us that they had lied while filling out the questionnaire or did not answer the question about their own truthfulness. Consequently, we excluded their answers from further analyses.

The Results

Seriousness

Police officers who participated in our study were asked to assess how seriously they consider the behavior in each scenario and how seriously they estimate that other police officers in their agency would assess these same behaviors. Possible answers ranged on a 5-point Likert scale from 1 = "not at all serious" to 5 = "very serious."

Although the respondents evaluated these scenarios to vary in terms of their seriousness (Table 9.3), most scenarios (6 out of 11) were evaluated to be rather serious (mean values are between 4 and 5). Several scenarios were evaluated to be the least serious, namely scenario 4 (unjustifiable use of deadly force), scenario 6 (officer strikes prisoner who hurt partner), and scenario 7 (verbal abuse—"Arrest an Asshole Day"). On the other hand, three scenarios evaluated to be the most serious included, scenario 5 (supervisor offers holiday for errands), scenario 9 (auto body shop 5 % kickback), and scenario 3 (theft of knife from crime scene).

We also compared the perceived severity of different forms of misconduct. Out of four scenarios addressing different abuses of the use of force continuum, three

Table 9.3 Police officers' perceptions of seriousness

	Own seriousness		Others' seriousness		Mean Difference	
	Mean	Rank	Mean	Rank	(Own–others)	*t*-test
Scenario 1: free meals, gifts from merchants	3.78	5	3.54	5	0.24	1.32
Scenario 2: failure to arrest friend with warrant	4.25	7	4.04	7	0.21	4.42**
Scenario 3: theft of knife from crime scene	4.77	11	4.64	11	0.13	5.04**
Scenario 4: unjustifiable use of deadly force	3.34	1	3.30	1	0.04	0.63
Scenario 5: supervisor offers holiday for errands	4.44	9	4.24	8	0.20	4.82**
Scenario 6: officer strikes prisoner who hurt partner	3.42	2	3.31	2	0.12	2.78**
Scenario 7: verbal abuse—"Arrest an Asshole Day"	3.59	3	3.51	4	0.08	3.41**
Scenario 8: cover-up of police DUI accident	3.64	4	3.46	3	0.18	3.34**
Scenario 9: auto body shop 5 % kickback	4.68	10	4.56	10	0.08	4.91**
Scenario 10: false report on drug dealer	4.40	8	4.33	9	0.07	3.35**
Scenario 11: Sgt. fails to halt beating	4.05	6	3.94	6	0.11	5.25**

DUI driving under the influence
$^{*}p<0.05$ $^{**}p<0.01$

scenarios were evaluated to be among the least serious (scenario 4: unjustifiable use of deadly force; scenario 6: officer strikes prisoner who hurt partner; and scenario 7: verbal abuse—"Arrest an Asshole Day"). In fact, the unauthorized use of deadly force—the most severe type of force on the use of force continuum—is evaluated as the *least* serious type of police misconduct among all 11 scenarios, including acceptance of gratuities (scenario 1: free meals, gifts from merchants) and verbal abuse (scenario 7: verbal abuse—"Arrest an Asshole Day").

On the other hand, five scenarios describing police corruption (scenario 1: free meals, gifts from merchants; scenario 3: theft of knife from crime scene; scenario 5: supervisor offers holiday for errands; scenario 8: cover-up of police driving under the influence (DUI); scenario 9: auto body shop 5 % kickback) were evaluated to be among the more serious scenarios. In fact, three of them (scenario 3: theft of knife from crime scene; scenario 5: supervisor offers holiday for errands; scenario 9: auto body shop 5 % kickback) were perceived to be the *most* serious among all 11 scenarios. Based on its rank among the 11 scenarios, even the scenario describing the acceptance of gratuities (scenario 1: free meals, gifts from merchants) was placed somewhere in the middle of the group.

A comparison of the respondents' own evaluation of seriousness and how serious they estimated that other police officers in the agency would evaluate the same scenarios revealed a number of findings. First, the respondents' own evaluations of seriousness were higher than the estimated evaluations of seriousness by others. This was true for all 11 scenarios (Table 9.3). Second, the differences between the means for own seriousness and others' seriousness were statistically significant in 9 out of 11 scenarios (Table 9.3); they were not statistically significant for scenario 1 (free meals, gifts from merchant) and scenario 4 (unjustifiable use of deadly force). However, following the rule of thumb established by Klockars et al. (204, p. 26), these differences were large and meaningful (above the 0.50 threshold) in none of the scenarios. The largest differences were about 0.24, that is, about half of the size required for the threshold. Third, the relative order of seriousness, evaluated as a relative ranking of scenarios within the group of 11 scenarios, revealed that police officers probably followed the same internal order of seriousness when providing their own assessments and when estimating how seriously other police officers in their agency would evaluate them. In other words, regardless of considering the ranking for their own estimates of seriousness or their estimates of how others would evaluate these behaviors, the conclusion is that the same four scenarios were evaluated as the least serious and the same four scenarios as the most serious. Finally, there was a very strong correlation between their own estimates of seriousness and estimates of seriousness by others (Spearman's rho = 0.982; $p < 0.001$).

Violation of Official Rules

Police officers were asked to assess whether the behaviors described in the scearios violated agency's official rules. A 5-point Likert scale was employed, ranging from 1 = "definitely not" to 5 = "definitely yes."

The respondents' evaluations of specific behavior as rule violating varied substantially from the scenarios in which only about one third of the respondents labeled the behavior as rule violating (e.g., scenario 4: unjustifiable use of deadly force) to the scenarios in which nine tenth of the respondents did the same (e.g., scenario 3: theft of knife from crime scene). Respondents' estimates of whether the behavior is rule violating were very strongly related to how seriously they perceived the behavior to be (Spearman's rho $=0.991$; $p<0.001$).

There were four scenarios (scenario 4: unjustifiable use of deadly force; scenario 6: officer strikes prisoner who hurt partner; scenario 7: verbal abuse—"Arrest an Asshole Day;" and scenario 8: cover-up of police DUI) in which only the minority or just about one half of the respondents were successful in recognizing the described behavior as rule violating. It is particularly striking that the majority (over 60 %) of the respondents did not label unjustifiable use of deadly force (scenario 4) as a violation of official rules, while the majority had no problem recognizing the acceptance of gratuities (scenario 1: free meals, gifts from merchants) as such.

The second group of scenarios (scenario 1: free meals, gifts from merchants; scenario 11: Sgt. fails to halt beating) features a strong majority—typically about two thirds of the respondents—who managed to recognize the described behaviors as violations of official rules (Table 9.4). Finally, there were four scenarios (scenario 2: failuer to arrest friend with warrant; scenario 5: supervisor offers holiday for errands; scenario 10: false report on drug dealer; and scenario 3: theft of knife from crime scene) in which three quarters or more of the respondents correctly classified these behaviors as violations of official rules. The nature of the behaviors described in these four scenarios includes very serious forms of corruption, failure to perform, and falsification of official record.

Table 9.4 Respondents' assessment of rule violation

	Percentage		
	Yes (%)	No (%)	Rank
Scenario 1: free meals, gifts from merchants	64.7	35.3	5
Scenario 2: failure to arrest friend with warrant	78.7	21.3	7
Scenario 3: theft of knife from crime scene	94.7	5.3	11
Scenario 4: unjustifiable use of deadly force	39.5	60.5	1
Scenario 5: supervisor offers holiday for errands	80.3	19.7	8
Scenario 6: officer strikes prisoner who hurt partner	48.1	51.9	2
Scenario 7: verbal abuse—"Arrest an Asshole Day"	50.1	49.9	3
Scenario 8: cover-up of police DUI accident	53.7	46.3	4
Scenario 9: auto body shop 5 % kickback	87.0	13.0	10
Scenario 10: false report on drug dealer	82.2	17.8	9
Scenario 11: Sgt. fails to halt beating	67.3	32.7	6

DUI driving under the influence

Appropriate and Expected Discipline

Respondents were also asked what they thought that the appropriate discipline for the behaviors in the scenarios should be and what they thought that the actual discipline in their agencies would be. Answers offered to the respondents were based on the possible disciplinary options listed in the Police Disciplinary Code (1969, revised in 2013). In particular, they were: "no discipline," "written warning," "salary decrease by 50 %," "suspension," and "dismissal."

The results, shown in Table 9.5, suggest that the opinions about the appropriate discipline vary across the scenarios and that they are related to respondents' evaluation of violation of official rules and perception of seriousness. For seven scenarios (scenario 1: free meals, gifts from merchants; scenario 2: failure to arrest friend with warrant; scenario 5: supervisor offers holiday for errands; scenario 6: officer strikes prisoner who hurt partner; scenario 8: cover-up of police DUI accident; scenario 10: false report on drug dealer; scenario 11: Sgt. fails to halt beating), the modal appropriate discipline is (only) "written warning." According to the Police Disciplinary Code (2013), this is the most lenient form of discipline. In addition, respondents reported that police officers who engaged in the behaviors described in scenario 4 (unjustifiable use of deadly force) and scenario 7 (verbal abuse—"Arrest an Asshole Day") should deserve *no* discipline at all.

On the opposite end of the spectrum are the scenarios for which the respondents thought that harsh discipline, such as suspension and dismissal, was appropriate or expected (scenario 2: failure to arrest friend with warrant; scenario 3: theft of knife from crime scene; scenario 5: supervisor offers holiday for errands; scenario 9: auto body shop 5 % kickback; scenario 10: false report on drug dealer; scenario 11: Sgt. fails to halt beating). These scenarios include different forms of misconduct, from corruption to failure to make an arrest and failure to stop the beating.

We also analyzed the distribution across the answers (Table 9.5). The results show that the respondents did not have a clear preference for a particular form of discipline for each of these behaviors; rather, with one exception (scenario 7: verbal abuse—"Arrest an Asshole Day"), the majority of the respondents thought that some discipline but less severe than dismissal (i.e., "written warning," "salary decrease by 50 %," or "suspension"), should be appropriate (Table 9.5). The percentages ranged from as low as 60 % for scenario 1 (free meals, gifts from merchants) to as high as 86 % for scenario 10 (false report on drug dealer). "No discipline" was the majority choice in only one case (scenario 7: verbal abuse—"Arrest an Asshole Day"), which depicts the (mis)use of force on the lowest level of use of force continuum. However, there was a strong minority push (between one third and one half of the respondents) toward "no discipline" in four other scenarios (scenario 1: free meals, gifts from merchants; scenario 4: unjustifiable use of deadly force; scenario 6: officer strikes prisoner who hurt partner; and scenario 8: cover-up of police DUI accident). Two of these scenarios involve less serious forms of police corruption (scenario 1: free meals, gifts from merchants; scenario 8: cover-up of police DUI accident). The remaining two involve cases of use of excessive force (scenario 4: unjustifiable use of deadly

Table 9.5 Views about appropriate discipline (should) and expected discipline (would)

		None	Written warning	Salary decrease 50 %	Suspension	Dismissal	Chi-Square
Scenario 1: free meals, gifts from merchants	Should	35.0 %	41.2 %	11.9 %	6.5 %	5.3 %	193.4**
	Would	30.5 %	36.2 %	15.3 %	10.8 %	7.2 %	
Scenario 2: failure to arrest friend with warrant	Should	11.6 %	33.4 %	17.4 %	21.7 %	15.9 %	497.65**
	Would	12.4 %	27.7 %	18.5 %	22.6 %	18.8 %	
Scenario 3: theft of knife from crime scene	Should	1.2 %	20.8 %	24.2 %	25.1 %	28.7 %	566.5**
	Would	2.2 %	20.0 %	21.6 %	24.6 %	31.6 %	
Scenario 4: unjustifiable use of deadly force	Should	39.0 %	26.3 %	20.1 %	11.5 %	3.1 %	473.1**
	Would	23.0 %	26.5 %	24.3 %	19.9 %	6.3 %	
Scenario 5: supervisor offers holiday for errands	Should	19.8 %	42.9 %	19.4 %	10.5 %	7.4 %	651.1**
	Would	29.6 %	40.3 %	16.0 %	8.5 %	5.7 %	
Scenario 6: officer strikes prisoner who hurt partner	Should	40.6 %	41.6 %	8.4 %	6.6 %	2.8 %	531.5**
	Would	34.0 %	40.3 %	13.3 %	8.3 %	4.1 %	
Scenario 7: verbal abuse—“Arrest an Asshole Day”	Should	50.0 %	38.0 %	7.3 %	3.8 %	0.9 %	733.1**
	Would	41.9 %	44.7 %	7.3 %	3.8 %	2.2 %	
Scenario 8: cover-up of police DUI accident	Should	29.3 %	36.7 %	17.9 %	10.2 %	5.9 %	596.1**
	Would	22.9 %	34.5 %	19.1 %	12.2 %	11.3 %	
Scenario 9: auto body shop 5 % kickback	Should	4.3 %	21.7 %	25.7 %	22.9 %	25.4 %	749.3**
	Would	5.1 %	21.6 %	23.2 %	22.5 %	27.6 %	
Scenario 10: false report on drug dealer	Should	8.0 %	36.9 %	21.5 %	27.7 %	13.8 %	752.6**
	Would	8.5 %	29.3 %	17.4 %	27.8 %	17.0 %	
Scenario 11: Sgt. fails to halt beating	Should	19.4 %	37.8 %	22.5 %	13.2 %	7.1 %	693.1**
	Would	19.7 %	34.1 %	24.4 %	14.4 %	7.5 %	

DUI driving under the influence

* $p < 0.05$; ** $p < 0.01$; *** $p < 0.001$

force; scenario 6: officer strikes prisoner who hurt partner). The surprising finding is that the (mis)use of deadly force is an example of a case in which four out of ten respondents argued that no discipline should be meted out at all.

Finally, in none of these 11 scenarios did the majority of the respondents select "dismissal" as the appropriate discipline (Table 9.5), regardless of the fact that all of these behaviors violate official rules and that the majority of them are violations of criminal law as well. In only two scenarios (scenario 3: theft of knife from crime scene; scenario 9: auto body shop 5 % kickback) there was a strong minority (about one quarter of the respondents) who argued that police officers who engaged in such behavior should be dismissed. Both of these scenarios describe examples of severe police corruption and constitute violations of not only official rules but also criminal law.

The differences between the respondents' views of what they considered to be the appropriate discipline and what discipline they thought their agencies would mete out were statistically significant in all scenarios. In most of these cases, the chi-square test indicated that the two distributions are similar. In only one scenario (scenario 5: supervisor offers holiday for errands) did the respondents think that the police agency would be less likely to discipline the supervisor than they thought would be appropriate (19.8 % selected "no discipline" as the appropriate discipline and 29.6 % selected "no discipline" as the expected discipline; Table 9.5). Although there were a few scenarios (scenario 6: officer strikes prisoner who hurt partner; scenario 7: verbal abuse—"Arrest an Asshole Day"; scenario 8: cover-up of police DUI accident) with differences of about 5 %, the only scenario with a substantial difference of more than 10 % was scenario 1 (free meals, gifts from merchants). In this scenario, depicting the least serious form of police corruption, the respondents though that the police agency would be more likely to discipline the police officer who accepted gratuities than they thought would be appropriate (39.0 % selected "no discipline" as the appropriate discipline and 23.0 % selected "no discipline" as the expected discipline; Table 9.5). Finally, in no scenarios there were substantially large differences (10 % or more) between the selection of "dismissal" as the appropriate and expected discipline (Table 9.5).

Willingness to Report Misconduct

Lastly, we asked the respondents to report how willing they would be to report their fellow police officers' misconduct and to estimate how willing other officers in their agencies would be to do so. The answers ranged on a 5-point Likert scale from 1 = "definitely not" to 5 = "definitely yes." We provide both the mean values in Table 9.6 and the percentage of officers who would not report in Fig. 9.2 (answers 1 and 2 coded together).

The results, shown in Table 9.6 and Fig. 9.2, indicate that the code of silence is present in the South Korean culture of policing; at least one quarter of police officers would not report for any misconduct described in our questionnaire. However, the code of silence does not cover all forms and types of misconduct equally.

Table 9.6 Police officer perceptions of willingness to report

	Own willingness to report		Others' willingness to report		Mean difference (own–others)	*t*-test
	Mean	Rank	Mean	Rank		
Scenario 1: free meals, gifts from merchants	2.36	3	2.28	3	0.08	1.95*
Scenario 2: failure to arrest friend with warrant	2.98	7	2.92	7	0.06	1.67
Scenario 3: theft of knife from crime scene	3.57	11	3.42	11	0.15	1.64
Scenario 4: unjustifiable use of deadly force	3.20	10	3.24	10	0.04	1.70
Scenario 5: supervisor offers holiday for errands	2.84	6	2.69	6	0.15	4.12**
Scenario 6: officer strikes prisoner who hurt partner	2.20	2	2.18	2	0.02	0.79
Scenario 7: verbal abuse—"Arrest an Asshole Day"	2.05	1	2.05	1	0.00	0.01
Scenario 8: cover-up of police DUI accident	2.41	4	2.42	4	0.02	0.60
Scenario 9: auto body shop 5% kickback	3.19	9	3.18	9	0.01	0.80
Scenario 10: false report on drug dealer	3.18	8	3.12	8	0.06	2.47**
Scenario 11: Sgt. fails to halt beating	2.72	5	2.68	5	0.04	1.55

DUI driving under the influence
$*p<0.05$, $**p<0.01$

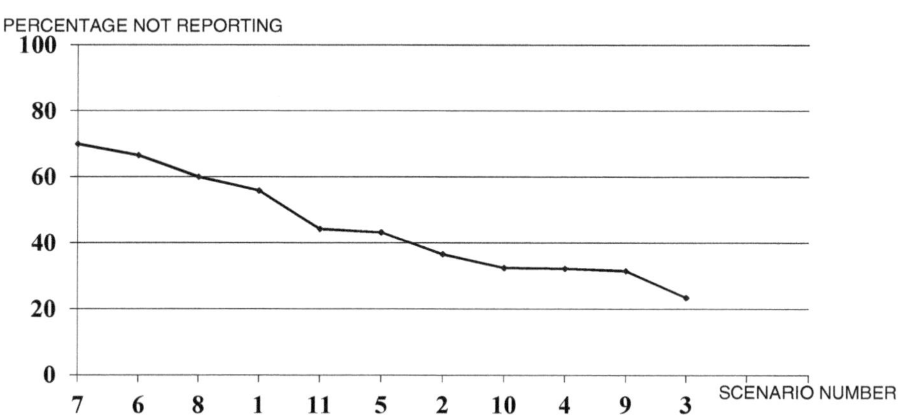

Fig. 9.2 Percentage not reporting by scenario number

There were three scenarios (scenario 1: free meals, gifts from merchants; scenario 6: officer strikes prisoner who hurt partner; scenario 7: verbal abuse—"Arrest an Asshole Day") in which the majority of the officers clearly indicated that they would not report such behavior (the means are all around 2 and close to the nonreporting side of the scale; Table 9.6; between 55 and 70 % of police officers said that they would not report; Fig. 9.2). Two of these scenarios (scenario 1: free meals, gifts from merchants; scenario 7: verbal abuse—"Arrest an Asshole Day") describe the least serious versions of a particular form of misconduct—the acceptance of gratuities for corruption and the abuse of verbal command for the use of excessive force. The third scenario (scenario 6: officer strikes prisoner who hurt partner) describes a case of "street justice" which we assume police officers would not only tolerate in silence but also support. This is the scenario in which the highest percent of police officers—seven out of ten (Fig. 9.2)—explicitly stated that they would protect such behavior.

There were additional four scenarios (scenario 2: failure to arrest friend with warrant; scenario 5: supervisor offers holiday for errands; scenario 8: cover-up of police DUI accident; and scenario 11: Sgt. fails to stop beating) with the means below the midpoint of the scale (below 3.0; Table 9.6), suggesting that there is a substantial group of police officers who would tolerate such behaviors in silence as well. Indeed, the data displayed in Fig. 9.2 show that for three scenarios (scenario 2: failure to arrest friend with warrant; scenario 5: supervisor offers holiday for errands; and scenario 11: Sgt. fails to stop beating) there was a strong minority group who would not report, ranging from about one third to almost one half of all police officers. However, the cover-up of police DUI accident (scenario 8) would receive an even stronger protection; the majority of police officers—six out of ten—would tolerate such behavior in silence (Fig. 9.2).

Finally, there were four scenarios with the means above the median of our scale, suggesting that police officers would be more likely not to tolerate such behaviors in silence. However, in three scenarios (scenario 4: unjustifiable use of deadly force; scenario 9: auto body shop 5 % kickback; and scenario 10: false report on drug dealer) the means barely cross the midpoint (Table 9.6), suggesting that there is a large group of police officers who would still protect such behavior in silence. In fact, the data in Fig. 9.2 show that at least one third of police officers would tolerate such behavior, including the use of deadly force, serious corruption, and false reporting, without reporting it.

The scenario describing a serious form of police corruption (scenario 3: theft of knife from crime scene) is perceived to be least likely to be protected by the code of silence. In particular, the mean for this scenario is the highest (Table 9.6) and the percentage of police officers who said that they would not report is the lowest (Fig. 9.2). However, even for this scenario, there was a group of about one quarter of police officers who would not report.

We also compared the respondents' own willingness to report with their estimates of others' willingness to report. Overall, the differences between their own estimates and how they estimated that others would be willing to report were very similar. The differences in mean values were statistically significant in only three scenarios (scenario 1: free meals, gifts from merchants; scenario 5: supervisor offers holiday for errands; scenario 10: false report on drug dealer) and, even in these scenarios, they were small and not meaningful (they did not cross the 0.50 threshold established).

Conclusion

Today, South Korea is a developed and democratic country. Until about three decades ago, South Korea had a long history of governance of military and authoritarian regimes, which allowed and even required of the police to serve the regimes and, when required, violate citizens' human rights. The country has also experienced widespread corruption, particularly cartel elite corruption, which resulted in a widespread web of connections between businessmen and politicians, sometimes at the highest ranks of government (Kang 2002). In the 1990s, the government decided to start curtailing corruption, reform the police, and improve the public image. The efforts targeting corruption have been noticed by both the international community (e.g., Transparency International 2013) and by the public at large (Kim 2002).

The Grand Reform of the police put a lot of emphasis on dealing with police corruption, while the use of excessive force remained dormant, despite the long history of extensive violations of human rights and the fact that one of the cases involving the use of deadly force created a public outcry which triggered the reform of the police (Kutnjak Ivković and Kang 2012). The results of our police integrity survey strongly support the view that the society at large sends different messages about corruption and the use of excessive force. In a nutshell, police officers in our study had much fewer problems recognizing police corruption than use of excessive force as a violation of official rules, evaluating it as a serious misbehavior, expecting and supporting some discipline for such behavior, and, potentially, even being willing to report it.

The percentage of our respondents able to recognize whether certain behaviors violate the official rules was substantially higher for scenarios describing police corruption than for the ones describing the use of excessive force. In particular, the overwhelming majority of our respondents—more than two thirds—had no problem recognizing that four out of five police corruption scenarios indeed are violations of official rules. Even in the scenario depicting the acceptance of gratuities, traditionally the least serious form of police corruption, about two thirds of the respondents recognized such behavior as rule violating. On the other hand, in three out of four scenarios describing the use of excessive force, a slim majority, or maybe even a minority of the respondents, recognized such scenarios as rule violating. In fact, the scenario describing the use of deadly force, the most serious form of force, has been recognized as a rule-violating behavior by *only* four out of ten respondents.

Our results about the respondents' evaluation of scenario seriousness support this view as well; three out of four scenarios with the use of excessive force were evaluated to be among the least serious and the use of deadly force was evaluated as the *least* serious type of police misconduct among all 11 scenarios. It was evaluated to be less serious than the acceptance of gratuities or verbal abuse. On the other hand, all five scenarios describing police corruption were evaluated to be at least of the medium seriousness. More precisely, three out of five corruption scenarios were perceived to be the *most* serious scenarios in the questionnaire.

While the respondents in general did not approve of harsh discipline for any of these behaviors, we also uncovered differences in the respondents' views of what the appropriate discipline should be, depending on whether the behavior in question is a form of corruption or use of excessive force. In particular, in three out of four scenarios with the use of excessive force, at least four out of ten officers thought that no discipline should be used at all, even in the scenario describing the use of deadly force. The percentage of police officers who favored no discipline in corruption scenarios tended to be much lower, typically below 30 %. When we looked at the opposite side of the disciplinary scale, namely dismissal, fewer than one in ten respondents thought that dismissal was appropriate for any of the scenarios describing the use of excessive force, while one out of four respondents advocated for dismissal for two out of the five corrupt scenarios.

The measurement of the code of silence points in the same direction, although the differences are not as large as they are with other questions. However, more than two thirds of the respondents would tolerate when a police officer strikes a prisoner who hurt their partner or verbal abuse by the police officer. A somewhat smaller percentage, closer to one half of the respondents, would not report officers who engaged in what was perceived to be the least serious form of corruption in the questionnaire, specifically the acceptance of gratuities and the cover-up a police DUI accident.

Another finding about the code of silence emerges from our analyses. The code of silence seems to be rather strong among the surveyed police officers. With one exception, at least one in three police officers would not report a fellow police officer who is engaged in any described misconduct, ranging from verbal abuse of citizens and acceptance of gratuities to receiving kickback, striking a prisoner, falsifying an official report, and abusing deadly force. For the behaviors with the greatest degree of protection, such as striking a prisoner or verbally abusing citizens, the substantial majority—two out of three police officers—would not report. The current police culture seems to be highly tolerant of various forms of misconduct, typically, regardless of how serious they are perceived to be.

At first glance, our results pointing toward the presence of a strong code of silence are quite different from the findings reported by Lee (2003). According to Lee (2003), the majority of the respondents declared that the code of silence among the South Korean police officers does not exist. However, a careful interpretation of Lee's (2003) results reveals that 40 % of his respondents also agreed that their *supervisors* do not report line officers' misconduct. This indicates that at least 40 % of the supervisors did participate in the code of silence. Furthermore, when the line officer code and the supervisor code differ, the supervisor code seems to be narrower (e.g., Huon et al. 1995; Kutnjak Ivković and Klockars 2000; Kutnjak Ivković and Shelley 2008; Pagon and Lobnikar 2000; Weisburd et al. 2001). This further suggests that a larger proportion of line officers than supervisors participates in the code, and that the code among the line officers in South Korea is stronger than the results Lee's study (2003) suggest at first glance.

The presence of a strong code of silence may be linked with several factors. First, the reforms did not address the issue of the use of excessive force at all. In the society used to police officers using excessive force, such behavior would be tolerated among the police officers as well. Second, current regulations, such as the Act on the Performance of Duties by Police Officers (1981, revised 2006), leave a lot of discretion in the hands of the police. In particular, police officers are allowed to use firearms when "there is a sufficient reason." Third, although the Anti-Corruption Act provides protection to the whistleblowers, which should include police officers who report misconduct by fellow officers as well, whistleblowers are not really protected by their organizations and colleagues (Choi 2013). Fourth, Confucianism is one of the building blocks of the social values in South Korean society. It emphasizes a harmonious relationship with others; reporting a fellow colleague for misconduct breaks this harmony. Whistleblowers would have to go against the key values of their own culture.

Finally, our results show that there is an extraordinary degree of similarity between what our respondents report they would do and what they thought that others in their agencies would do. We have observed this pattern for their views about misconduct seriousness, as well as for their estimates of the code of silence. In all these comparisons, the differences between their own views and their estimates of others' views were rather small, suggesting that the officers try to fit their views with what they perceive to be the views of the majority in their agencies. Unlike western individualist societies, in which self-serving bias leads people to believe that they are morally better than their counterparts, Asian countries, such as South Korea, China, and Vietnam, rely on Confucianism. The reliance on the collectivist culture, which integrates principles of harmonious relationships and conformity (Bui and Morash 2008; Cheung and Kwok 1998; Morash et al. 2008), creates situations in which pressure is created to fit in rather than stand out. Our results clearly support this notion; the responses indicate that the respondents were trying to fit in rather than stand out in their views. In the grand scheme of things, these findings confirm the importance of incorporating the potential influence of the society at large into shaping the views and attitudes among police officers.

References

ACRC. (2012). *ACRC's integrity assessment program wins the UN public service awards*. Seoul: ACRC.

ACRC. (2013). *2013 Results of integrity assessment for public institutions*. Seoul: ACRC.

Act on the Performance of Duties by Police Officers (1981). 12,600 KC, §§ 1–12.

Baek, H. (2000). *The analysis of police reform*. Seoul: Police Science Institute.

Bui, H., & Morash, M. (2008). Immigration, masculinity, and intimate partner violence from the standpoint of domestic violence service providers and Vietnamese-origin women. *Feminist Criminology*, 3(3), 191–215.

Cheung, C., & Kwok, S. (1998). Social studies and ideological beliefs in mainland China and Hong Kong. *Social Psychology of Education*, 2, 217–236.

Choi, D. (2013, December 23). Indictment of police chief for bribery. *Chungbook Daily News*.

Choi, O., & Ma, K. (2008). A study on the operation and improvement in Korea police-ombudsman. *Journal of Korean Public Safety and Criminal Justice, 31,* 255–286.

Cohen, J., & Baker, E. (1991). U.S. foreign policy and human rights in South Korea. In W. Shaw (Ed.), *Human Rights in Korea: Historical and Policy Perspective* (pp. 171–220). Boston: Harvard University Press.

Freedom House. (2014). Freedom in the World, 2014. https://freedomhouse.org/report/freedom-world/freedom-world-2014#.VMNC5ct0yUk. Accessed 24 Jan, 2015.

Huon, G. F., Hesketh, B. L., Frank, M. G., McConkey, K. M., & McGrath, G.M. (1995). *Perceptions of ethical dilemmas: Ethics and policing study I.* Payneham: National Police Rese arch Unit.

International Monetary Fund. (2013). World economic outlook database. http://www.imf.org/external/pubs/ft/weo/2013/01/weodata/weorept.aspx?sy=1995&ey=2011&scsm=1&ssd=1&sort=country&ds=.&br=1&c=542&s=NGDP_R%2CNGDP_RPCH%2CNGDP%2CNGDPD&grp=0&a=&pr.x=34&pr.y=11.

Johnston, M. (2008). Japan, Korea, the Philippines, China: Four syndromes of corruption. *Crime, Law and Social Change, 49,* 205–223.

Kang, D. (2002). *Crony capitalism: Corruption and development in South Korea and the Philippines*. Cambridge: Cambridge University Press.

Kim, B. (1998). Corruption and anti-corruption policies in Korea. *Korea Journal, 38*(1), 46–69.

Kim, C. (2002). The practical corruption situations of policemen and their countermeasures.
Korean Association of Public Safety and Criminal Justice Journal, 14, 57–79.

Kim, Y. (2007). Democratization of the constitutional debate regime in South Korea. *Journal of Korean Political Science, 10*(2), 97–116.

Kim, T. (2008). *Police ombudsman for Korea*. Kyungi: Police Science Institute.

Kwon, S. (1999). The critical analysis of annexation. *Journal of Modern History in Korea, 10,* 398–420.

Klockars, C. B., & Kutnjak Ivković, S. (2003). Measuring police integrity. In A. R. Piquero, J. R. Greene, & M. J. Hickman (Eds.). *Police integrity and ethics* (pp. 1.3–1.20). Belmont Wadsworth Publishing.

Klockars, C. B., Kutnjak Ivković, S., Harver, W. E., & Haberfeld, M. R. (1997). The measurement of police integrity. Final report to the National Institute of Justice (NIJ Grant# 95-IJ-CX-0058, The Cross Cultural Study of Police Corruption). Washington, DC: National Institute of Justice, U.S. Department of Justice.

Klockars, C. B., Kutnjak Ivković, S., Haberfeld, M. R., & Uydess, A., with contributions by Geller, William A. (2001). Enhancing police integrity: Three case studies. Final Report Submitted to the U.S. Department of Justice, Office of Justice Programs, National Institute of Justice.

Klockars, C. B., Kutnjak Ivković, S., & Haberfeld, M. R. (2004). *The contours of police integrity.* Newbury Park: Sage.

Klockars, C. B., Kutnjak Ivković, S., & Haberfeld, M. R. (2005). *Enhancing police integrity. Research for practice*. U.S. Department of Justice, Office of Justice Programs, National Institute of Justice: Washington, D.C.: Government Printing Office.

Korea National Police Agency. (2005). *Annual police policy manual for reform*. Seoul: KNPA.

Korea National Police Agency. (2006). *Korea Police Annual Report.* Seoul: KNPA.

Korea National Police Agency. (2007). *Korea Police Annual Report.* Seoul: KNPA.

Korea National Police Agency. (2008). *Korea Police Annual Report.* Seoul: KNPA.

Korea National Police Agency. (2009). *Korea Police Annual Report.* Seoul: KNPA.

Korea National Police Agency. (2010). *Korea Police Annual Report.* Seoul: KNPA.

Korea National Police Agency. (2013). *Korea Police Annual Report.* Seoul: KNPA.

Kutnjak Ivković, S., & Kang, W. (2012). *Police integrity in South Korea. Policing: An International Journal of Police Strategies & Management, 35*(1), 76–103.

Kutnjak Ivković, S., & Khechumyan, A. (2013). Measuring police integrity among urban and rural police in Armenia: From local results to global implications. *International Journal of Comparative and Applied Criminal Justice*, Forthcoming. doi:10.1080/01924036.2013.777869.

Kutnjak Ivković, S., & Klockars, C. B. (2000). Comparing police supervisor and line officer opinions about the code of silence: The case of Croatia. In M. Pagon (Ed.), *Policing in Central and Eastern Europe: Ethics, integrity, and human rights* (pp. 183–195). Ljubljana: College of Police and Security Studies.

Kutnjak Ivković, S., & Shelley, T. O. (2007). Police integrity and the Czech police officers. *International Journal of Comparative and Applied Criminal Justice, 31*(1), 21–49.
Kutnjak Ivković, S., & Shelley, T. O. (2008a). The contours of police integrity across Eastern Europe: The case of Bosnia and Herzegovina and the Czech Republic. *International Criminal Justice Review, 18*(1), 59–82.
Kutnjak Ivković, S., & Shelley, T. O. (2008b). The police code of silence and different paths toward democratic policing. *Policing and Society, 18*(4), 445–473.
Lee, G. (2003). *A study on influencing factors and control strategies of police corruption. Unpublished dissertation*. Seoul: Gwangoon University.
Lee, S. Y. (1990). Morning calm, rising sun: National character and policing in South Korea and in Japan. *Police Studies, 13*(3), 91–110.
Lee, Y. (2002). *A cross-national comparative study of police: Criminal investigative policies and practices in the U.S. and South Korea*. Unpublished doctoral dissertation, East Lansing: Michigan State University.
Moon, B. (2004). The politicization of police in South Korea: A critical review. *Policing: An International Journal of Police Strategies & Management, 27*(1), 128–136.
Morash, M., Kwak, D., Hoffman, V., Lee, C., Cho, S., & Moon, B. (2008). Stressors, coping resources and strategies, and police stress in South Korea. *Journal of Criminal Justice, 36,* 231–239.
Nalla, M. K., & Kang, W. (2011). An assessment of South Korean police officers' perceptions of organizational characteristics in the post-reform era. *Policing: An International Journal of Police Strategies & Management, 34*(2), 326–346.
Nalla, M. K., & Kang, W. (2012). Organizational climate, perceived citizen support, and job satisfaction of police officers: Findings from the post-grand reform era in South Korea. *Asian Journal of Criminology, 7*(2), 153–171.
Pagon, M., & Lobnikar, B. (2000). Comparing supervisor and line officer opinions about the code of silence: The case of Slovenia. In M. Pagon (Ed.), *Policing in Central and Eastern Europe: Ethics, integrity, and human rights*. Ljubljana: College of Police and Security Studies, 197–209.
Police Disciplinary Code. (1969). 3,723 KC, §§ 1–23.
Police Disciplinary Code. (2009). 21,166 KC, §§ 1–21.
Police Disciplinary Code. (2013). 25,751 KC, §§ 1–21.
Protection of Human Rights in Police. (2005). 465 PO, §§ 1–93.
Pyo, C. (2002). *An empirical research on the public perception of the police and various police reform initiatives in Korea: 1999–2001*, paper presented at the Asian Association of Police Studies, Hong Kong.
Quah, J. T. (2006). Curbing Asian corruption: An impossible dream? *Current History, April,* 176–179.
Song, D. (2011). *Confrontation of Rhee Syng-man and Kim Gu Regarding Separate Government in the Post-Liberation Period: From the Perspectives of Power Struggle*. Unpublished doctoral dissertation. Seoul: Soongsil University.
The Rule on Extent of Police Discipline. (2009). 412 PC, §§ 1–9.
The South Korean Criminal Code. (2013). 12,898 KC, §§ 122–144.
Transparency International. (2013). Corruption Perception Index. http://www.transparency.org/cpi2013/results. Accessed 24 Jan 2015.
Transparency International. (2014). Corruption Perception Index. http://www.transparency.org/cpi2014. Accessed 24 Jan 2015.
Walker, S., & Wright, B. (1995). Citizen Review of the Police, 1994: A National Survey. Police Executive Research Forum.
Weisburd, D., Greenspan, R., Hamilton, E. E., Bryant, K. A., & Williams, H. (2001). *The abuse of police authority: A national study of police officers' attitudes*. Washington, DC: Police Foundation.
Yang, M., & Lee, D. (2006). A study on the strategic internal affairs system against corruption in Korean police. *Korean Association of Public Safety and Criminal Justice Journal, 22,* 291–320.

Chapter 10
Police Integrity in Thailand

Narin Phetthong and Sanja Kutnjak Ivković

Abstract The Royal Thai Police, a police agency decentralized by law, yet centralized in reality, is under the umbrella of the office of the prime minister. This chapter explores the forms of police integrity among the Thai police officers. The representative stratified sample of 280 police officers, collected in 2013, evaluated hypothetical scenarios describing various forms of police misconduct. Results suggest that police officers evaluated the behaviors described in the scenarios to vary in their seriousness. Only one scenario—an opportunistic theft—was evaluated as very serious and, at the same time, was recognized by the overwhelming majority as rule violating. The respondents thought that most of the described behaviors deserve a milder form of discipline. At the same time, they also expected relatively mild discipline for most of the scenarios. They thought that dismissal was the appropriate and expected discipline only for the opportunistic theft. We also detected the code of silence and concluded that it is not a flat prohibition of reporting. The more serious the respondents perceived the scenarios, the less likely they were to cover it by the code. Finally, the police officers expected that other officers in their agencies would be much more likely to protect all these behaviors in silence than they themselves would.

Keywords Martial law · Police integrity · Royal Thai Police · Survey · Thailand

Introduction

Thailand is a member of the Association of Southeast Asian Nations (ASEAN), located in Southeast Asia. According to the latest national census in 2010, it has a population of approximately 66 million (National Statistical Office 2010). The

N. Phetthong (✉)
Sam Houston State University, Huntsville, TX, USA
e-mail: nxp012@shsu.edu

S. Kutnjak Ivković
Michigan State University, East Lansing, MI, USA
e-mail: kutnjak@msu.edu

S. Kutnjak Ivković, M. R. Haberfeld (eds.), *Measuring Police Integrity Across the World*,
DOI 10.1007/978-1-4939-2279-6_10

number of women in the population slightly exceeds the number of men (1:0.96; National Statistical Office 2010). The overwhelming majority of Thais practice Buddhism (about 94%). The second most dominant religion is Islam, practiced by about 5% of the population, followed by Christianity with approximately 1% (National Statistical Office 2010). Almost all citizens (96%) are Thai native, and the remaining 4% are either Burmese, Laotian, Cambodian, or Chinese (National Statistical Office 2010).

The country is ranked third on the index of economic freedom in the region, following Singapore and Malaysia (The Heritage Foundation 2014). The gross domestic product (GDP) growth of 2013 was around 8%, with an even higher GDP growth expected in 2014 (Bhaopichitr et al. 2014). In 2014, Thailand's per capita income is 174,319 Thai Baht (approximately US$ 5800; Office of the National Economic and Social Development Board 2014).

Though the country's political system had changed from an absolute monarchy to a constitutional monarchy since the 1932 revolution, the country still does not completely function as a democratic system. There were 18 military coups since 1932. The 19th coup took place on May 22, 2014. It was a successful overthrow of the elected government by a group of four military generals and a police general (called the National Council for Peace and Order (NCPO); The Heritage Foundation 2014). After the coup in May, Army General Prayuth Chan-o-cha, the coup leader, was appointed prime minister by appointed members of the parliament (MPs are appointed by the NCPO's method which in its entirety is not derived by elections). The coup and the new cabinet claimed that they stopped the political turmoil and the daily casualties inflicted over the past 6 months by the two divided political groups (one side supporting the ex-prime minister, the "Red-Shirts," composed of people from rural areas, and the other side supporting the coup, the "Yellow-Shirts," composed of people from the middle-class society in urban areas, especially based in Bangkok, the capital of Thailand). So far, the NCPO and the junta government are still coping with the country's political problems by enforcing martial law in which all political activities are banned. Martial law is enforced and, as a recent report by the Human Rights Watch revealed, a "[f]ailure to comply with censorship orders could result in prosecution before a military court" (Human Rights Watch 2014).

Because of the political instability in the country, and the police subordinate role to the politicians, the police have long been controlled and governed by the majority party that heads the government. The history of the Royal Thai Police (RTP) can be dated back to the reign of King Rama IV (1851–1868). The establishment of the RTP started when the king appointed Captain Joseph Byrd Ames, an Englishman, to form the police force for the protection of Thai people's lives and properties (ASEANAPOL n.d.). However, there have been several human rights scandals related to the RTP. There is widespread belief that the police support every government and that they violate citizens' human rights. For example, in early 2003, Prime Minister Thaksin Shinawatra announced that the war on drugs would be waged (Human Rights Watch 2004). Over the course of the next few months, as part of the war on drugs by the Thaksin government, more than 2000 people were brutally and wrongfully killed by the Thai police, and more than 70,000 people were arrested

(Human Rights Watch 2004). However, there are no official records about these abuses (Phillip 2007).

The Thai police are headed by a commissioner, who is required to have served in the police for at least 30 years before becoming the chief of police. The police chief is appointed by National Police Committee, which includes the prime minister, deputy prime minister, secretary of defense,[1] permanent secretary, budget director of the Budget Bureau, and two specialized committee members. He[2] who will become a chief of police must be actively serving in the police. Most importantly, he must be an individual with a good connection with the current prime minister. In August 2014, RTP's chief of police has been appointed after the meeting of the Police Commission chaired by Army General Prayuth Chan-o-cha, the now coup leader and prime minister.

According to the National Police Act of 2004, the organizational structure of the Thai police is decentralized. However, in reality, the police force of approximately 230,000 officers is still controlled by the chief of police located in Bangkok, the capital of Thailand. Therefore, decentralization did not occur, and the RTP is actually a centralized police organization. The National Police are divided into ten geographical regions. Each region has a police commissioner,[3] who holds the rank of police lieutenant general, overseeing the Regional Police Agency. Further, there are several divisions within each regional police agency and several police stations within each division. In sum, there are six categories within the organizational structure, including special operations, crime prevention and suppression, crime prevention and suppression support, education, service, and general staff (INTERPOL n.d.).

There are approximately 6000–7000 stations across the country. Most of the traditional police work takes place at the level of police stations under the crime prevention and suppression category. The police stations are the heart of all police operations that maintain peace and order, as well as law enforcement. Most police stations consist of five sections: administration, inquiry, investigation, traffic control, and patrol. The larger police stations are headed by a police colonel, while the smaller police stations may be headed by a police lieutenant colonel or a police major, depending on the size of the population in that area.

This chapter focuses on police integrity among the RTP officers. It begins with the examination of the dimensions of the police integrity theory, and their application to the conditions in the RTP. The chapter continues with the empirical study of the contours of police integrity in the RTP. Based on the police integrity survey, the chapter explores the police officers' perceptions of misconduct seriousness, their assessments of rule-violating behavior, their views about the appropriate and expected discipline, as well as their views about the code of silence.

[1] The NCPO includes the secretary of defense as a new committee which allow the army general to have control over the appointment of the chief of police.

[2] There is no "she" because a person eligible to be appointed the chief of police must hold the rank of police general. To date, the highest rank obtained by female police officers has been police lieutenant general.

[3] This does not include other bureaus that do not have a patrol function, such as the Police Education Bureau, Police Cadet Academy, Bureaus under Command, and General Staff.

Dimensions of the Police Integrity Theory and the Royal Thai Police

This chapter relies on the police integrity theory originated by Klockars et al. (1997). Police integrity "[is] the normative inclination among police to resist temptations to abuse the rights and privileges of their occupation" (Klockars et al. 2006, p. 1). Policing, as an occupation, creates many temptations and, as the authors wrote, "police officers [of high integrity] are able to resist *various* forms of temptations, including corruption, use of excessive force, and other forms of abuse, the rights and privileges to which policing as an occupation exposes them" (Klockars et al. 2006). Klockars and Kutnjak Ivković (2004) suggest that the theory of police integrity has four dimensions, including "quality of official rules, quality of the agency's own internal control of misconduct, restraining the code of silence, and the influence of the larger environment."

Organizational Rules

The theory of police integrity emphasizes that police agencies should have written rules prescribing appropriate behavior and proscribing inappropriate behavior. At the same time, Klockars et al. (2004a, 2006) emphasize that the extent to which official rules regulate police officers' behavior varies across police agencies. According to Klockars and Kutnjak Ivković (2004), police agencies of high integrity will have extensive rules. In addition, they will teach these rules and enforce them when police officers violate them (Klockars and Kutnjak Ivković 2004).

While the RTP used to be under the department of interior, the National Police Act (NPA) of 2004, Section 6, puts the RTP under the administration of the prime minister. In other words, the RTP are under the auspices of neither the department of interior nor the department of justice. Thus, their first priority is to provide security to the king, queen, and the royal family. The next level of responsibility for the RTP includes the duty to enforce the criminal code and other legal codes, maintain peace and order, and provide safety in the country.

The Thai Criminal Procedural Code of 1934 (2004 revision) provides the basic set of legal rules used to balance the police powers of arrest, search, and seizure with the rights of the Thai people, as determined by the Thai Constitution. The constitution has enacted the rights of the citizens to be detained by the police no longer than 48 hours; however, under the recent political turmoil of the country (December 2013–May 2014) and after the 2014 coup d'état, the Thai police or the Thai military can detain suspects for interrogation purposes for up to a maximum of 7 days under the martial law (in effect across the country).

The 2014 temporary constitution does not mention the right of the Thai citizens against unreasonable search or arrest. However, the police still rely on Section 33 of the 2007 Constitution, which states that "[the] arrest and custody of a person are prohibited, except directed by court order or another virtue of the law" and combines these constitutional norms with rules contained in the Criminal Procedural Code section about search, seizure, and detention. Moreover, Sect. 2, Article 8 of Notice of Proposed Amendment (NPA) 2004 further reinforces the protection of citizens' rights and establishes that, "a police officer must strictly respect the right and freedom of people as endorsed by the Constitution and other laws with due process and rule of law."

In addition to the 2007 Constitution and the 2004 Criminal Procedural Code, there are two other official sets of rules that regulate police operations. The RTP has enacted the so-called regulations on noncriminal cases of 2004 and the regulations on criminal cases of 2004. The 2004 regulations on noncriminal cases have 57 categories and regulate many aspects of police behavior. For example, proper behavior and discipline are regulated in category 1, recruitment of police officers and the process of becoming a police officer are regulated in categories 2–4, ranks are defined in category 7, decorations on the uniforms are described in category 10, and the police training is elaborated upon in category 11. In a nutshell, these regulations on noncriminal cases cover almost every aspect of a police officer's life, from day one in the RTP until retirement. Despite the complexity and extent of these rules, there are no specific rules addressing police corruption or integrity issues. Furthermore, none of the 2004 regulations addressed the use of force issues or violations. However, the NPA 2004 Act vaguely mentions excessive force violations under Section 79(3), which regulates that the police must refrain from such actions toward citizens, including abusing, oppressing, or injuring people during the performance of their official duties.

Nonetheless, the Thai Criminal Code of 1956 in Section 149 prohibits public officials (which includes police officers), members of the parliament, and local government officials from demanding, accepting, or agreeing to accept any bribes. The prohibition covers both monetary gain and any benefit for either the official or another person. The official could be punished if he does something he was not supposed to do or does not do something he was supposed to do, regardless of whether his behavior constitutes a violation of the official rules. Section 149 of the Thai Criminal Code of 1956 prescribes the appropriate punishment for criminal behavior as well; punishment can include imprisonment for up to 12 years, fine of up to 40,000 Thai baht (approximately US$ 1000), and/or the death penalty. For police misconduct that does not fall into any category by Thai law, there is Section 157 of the 1956 Thai Criminal Code that is regularly enforced to crack down on police wrongdoings. Section 157 states that "[w]hoever, being an official, wrongfully exercises or does not exercise any of his functions to the injury of any person, or dishonestly exercises or omits to exercise any of his functions, shall be punished with imprisonment of 1–10 years or fined of two thousand to twenty thousand Baht, or both" (United Nations Office on Drugs and Crime 2011).

In addition, the National Anti-Corruption Commission (NACC), an independent organization under the 1997 Thai Constitution and the most important agency that fights corruption in Thailand, has enacted a regulation on the acceptance of gift and/or benefits by governmental officials. Under the Act on prevention and suppression of corruption of 2000 (attached to the 1997 Thai Constitution), Section 103 specifies that government officials (including police officers) shall not accept gifts or benefits equal to or in excess of 3000 Thai Baht (approximately US$ 100) from individuals who are not their relatives. Otherwise, officials may be prosecuted for the acceptance of bribes.

Police Detection and Investigation of Police Misconduct

The second dimension of the integrity theory focuses on the police agency's own methods toward rule-violation management, including "detection, investigation, and discipline of rule violations" (Klockars and Kutnjak Ivković 2004). The police agency of high integrity is expected to have set up and use a complex set of methods of such control.

Corruption cases are categorized as typical criminal cases; thus, the process is similar to other common cases. This process involves four major agencies: the RTP, the prosecutors or the Office of the Attorney General, the courts of Thailand, and the Department of Corrections under the Thailand Department of Justice. The process is rather similar to the U.S. criminal process, except that prosecutors in Thailand are not involved in the investigation stage as the district attorneys (DAs) are in the USA. Thus, most of the criminal investigation in the Thai criminal justice system is performed by police officers. However, the protection of individual rights is similar to the protection in the USA (e.g., the police must obtain search or arrest warrants from Thai courts). The RTP have the Counter Corruption Division set up under the Central Investigation Bureau (CIB). The CIB and, particularly, the Counter Corruption Division have jurisdiction all over the country, similar to the Federal Bureau of Investigation (FBI) in the USA. The division's work in corruption cases extends not only to police officers but also to all government officials.

The statistics on corruption cases, the NACC investigated in a period of 5 years (between the fiscal years of 2007 and 2011), suggest that the number of cases has increased by about 200 cases from 2819 to 3092 cases. About 65 % of these cases involve governmental officials (except members of parliament) charged with corruption by taking advantage of their position of power in the criminal justice system (Office of Justice Affairs 2011). However, most corruption cases that were investigated and in which charges were brought forward, target other government officials; only about one fifth of all NACC corruption cases were filed against police officers (Office of the National Anti-Corruption Commission n.d.). For example, one of the most recent cases involved an investigation into the rice scheme corruption. The corruption investigation targeted the government of Ms. Yingluck Shinawatra, Thailand's former prime minister ousted by the military coup on May 22, 2014.

The Office of Inspector General (OIG), another police bureau, deals with matters related to police corruption. The OIG is a part of the RTP and serves as an office where citizens may file a complaint about any form of police misconduct. Everybody has the right to submit or file complaints to the OIG. By law, the complaint must include facts and other evidence that will allow the police to further investigate the issues raised in the complaint. The OIG provides three channels for people to file complaints, including telephone, fax, and a website. The police complaint process involves two agencies of the RTP (the OIG and Counter Corruption Division) and the NACC. After the OIG has received the complaint, it will collect the information and report to the director of the OIG. If the case shows any evidence of potential corruption, the chief of police will order the Counter Corruption Division to investigate it further. The case will also fall under the provision of the NACC. If the case seems to be just a violation of the official rules, the RTP has discretion depending on the severity of the violation. Potential outcomes range from the least serious disciplinary options, such as a warning, detention, or cutting wages, to the most severe disciplinary options, such as a dismissal. There was a recent case against highly ranked police officers (a police major general and a police lieutenant colonel)[4] for corruption. These police officers were charged with corruption.

Although the police in Thailand are infamous for their low integrity, there were few charges brought against the police officers; even if the officers were charged, justice would be slow. Statistics from the NACC show that in only one fifth of the cases, the accused were police officers (Officer of the National Anti-Corruption Commission n.d.). As the Global Advice Networks on Integrity Solutions (2014) writes:

> Police officers are being paid relatively low wages, creating an incentive for 'earning' additional money by demanding bribes and extorting money from offenders. The same report states that an owner of a transportation business accused police of demanding bribes from his drivers; when the driver refused, the officers allegedly pushed the truck into a canal and the driver and his wife disappeared.... The police in Thailand is characterized by a climate of impunity and rare prosecution, as described by the Human Rights Report 2013. The Human Rights Report 2012 states that 211 Royal Thai Police (RTP) officers were criminally charged during the second half of 2012.

During the 2010 fiscal year, there were about 7000 cases on police misconduct within the RTP. The Human Rights Report of 2012 indicated that there were two police generals involved in the torture of suspects in the separatist/insurgency cases in the southern part of Thailand (U.S. Department of State 2012). On April 1, 2014, the NACC indicted police commanders in charge of the police motorcycle procurement. The NACC charged the officers under Section 12 of Governmental Procurement Act 1999 and Section 157 of the Thai Penal Code of 1956. This case is being processed, and it will take 4–5 years under the Thai justice system before it will be completed (Officer of the National Anti-Corruption Commission n.d.).

Curtailing the Code of Silence

The third aspect of the police integrity theory is concerned with the code of silence within the police organization, and how the agency restrains it (Klockars et al.

[4] NACC's black color case no. 50440327 and 51442126 retrieved from http://www.nacc.go.th/culpability.php.

2004a, 2006). The theory suggests that high-integrity police agencies are less likely to have the strong code of silence. In contrast, lower police integrity can be seen in police agencies with the stronger code of silence. Klockars and Kutnjak Ivković (2004) claimed that "curtailing the code of silence is critical for agencies of integrity."

There are signs that the Thai police subculture exists and that it contains the code of silence. To become a police officer in Thailand does not necessarily require a completely clean criminal record. Article 2(4) of the Police Code of Conduct of 2003 clearly stipulates that the successful applicants for the police officer position should not have been prosecuted, tried, and punished with imprisonment, *except* if they were tried and convicted of the offenses of negligence or misdemeanors which resulted in a fine of under 1000 Thai Baht (approximately US$ 33) and/or imprisonment for less than a month.

Suwanmala described a broadcasting from 2003, which he claimed was the first one in Thailand in which the public could see actual bribery on TV. It involved the infamous highway patrol case of police corruption. The so-called highway patrol police, a police division within the Bureau of Central Investigation of the RTP, have jurisdiction over all the highways in the country. The TV footage captured by the independent TV channel (ITV) showed that every truck driver who has passed through the highway checkpoints must throw the 20 Thai Baht bill (approximately US$ 0.25) into the bucket in front of the checkpoints or hand the bill directly to a policeman. Then, the bribery money collected this way was later gathered and disseminated to every police officer within the chain of command (Suwanmala n.d.). He claimed that there was a highway patrol officer, named Police Senior Sergeant Major Chit Thongchit, who broke the code of silence and disclosed the highway bribery to the public almost 10 years ago. After the incident, he was forced to resign from the RTP and later was assassinated by fellow police officers on January 15, 2009 (Suwanmala n.d.). A Bangkok Post reporter interviewed a police deputy commander from the CIB in charge and investigated Thongchit's assassination, who stated that:

> …from our field investigations, we realized that no policeman liked him because he tried to expose their extortion activities…on the other hand, every villager loved him because he always lent them a hand every time they had problems with police (Ngamkham 2009).

Indeed, breaking the code of silence seems to be a highly risky activity. Assassinations are used to deter anyone who would consider breaking the code of silence. As Suwanmala (n.d.) revealed, there were at least six other whistle-blowers who were killed in connection with several criminal cases involving police corruption.

We were not able to find any existing empirical studies measuring the contours of the code of silence among the Thai police officers directly. Instead, we found only one study measuring the level of police integrity among the Thai police. In the foreword to the study of police integrity, Khruakham and Joongyeup (2013, p. 238) wrote that, "[a] number of studies worldwide have examined police or public attitudes toward misconduct…no such research has been implemented for Thailand despite the relatively high prevalence of the problem."

Khruakham and Lee (2013) surveyed 295 police cadets at the Royal Police Cadet Academy in Thailand. Using the first questionnaire developed by Klockars and Kutnjak Ivković (2004), the respondents were asked to evaluate 11 hypothetical scenarios mostly focusing on police corruption. The authors found that, "the police cadets in Thailand were relatively tolerant of misconduct when compared with police officers in the other countries [U.S.A., the Netherlands, and Croatia]" (Khruakham and Joongyeup 2013, p. 243). Unfortunately, Khruakham and Lee (2013) did not use all the measures of police integrity and, for example, the willingness to report misconduct variables were not used in the analyses. However, previous research using the same questionnaire (e.g., Klockars et al. 2004b) reported that the seven measures of police integrity were strongly correlated. Thus, the findings about the lack of seriousness that the respondents expressed when evaluating these hypothetical scenarios probably resemble the findings on the willingness to report.

Influence of Social and Political Environment

The fourth dimension of the police integrity theory explores the influence of the larger social and political environment on the police agencies and police officers. The theory suggests that different societies create different expectations of the appropriate police conduct (Klockars and Kutnjak Ivković 2004).

According to the results of research on corruption and Thai democracy, by Phongpaichat et al. (n.d.), there are four types of corruption in Thailand: (1) syndicate corruption, (2) *kin tām nām*[5] or voluntary bribes, (3) bribes paid to get a national concession, and (4) corruption from government procurement. Police corruption is categorized into the first type—the syndicate corruption. This comes in the form of corruption in which subordinate officials collect bribes or unofficial taxes from businesses, either illegal or legal, for their supervisors. The bribes are then divided among the police officers in the agency (Phongpaichat et al. 1991).

Phongpaichit and Piriyarangsan (1996) pointed out that, from ancient times, the Thai culture has been influenced by the beliefs and values supportive of corruption. They further argued that, based on the traditional Thai beliefs, corruption is spreading among the police or government officers all over the country (Phongpaichit and Piriyarangsan 1996). Similarly, the Human Rights Report 2012 stated that, "corruption remained widespread among members of the police" (U.S. Department of State 2012).

This tendency is particularly enhanced with the lack of labeling of such actions as corruption and, generally, something that is viewed as wrong. Phongpaichit and Piriyarangsan (1996) described the ancient Thai administrative system called Sakdina (similar to the feudal system), in which government officers may legally accept gifts or money from citizens (as cited in Ariyabuddhiphongs and Hongladarom 2014, p. 185). Phongpaichit and Piriyarangsan (1996, pp. 112–113) gave the following description about the historical roots of police corruption:

[5] *kin tām nām* is a Thai slang which means take the usual/rake-off/payoff even though the payoff came from the bribery money.

> The establishment of the police force was one element of the administrative reforms fashioned by King Chulalongkorn in the late nineteenth century. One of the main purposes of these reforms was to regularize and centralize the system of revenue collection, so as to reduce the leakage into the pockets of tax collectors under the *gin muang* system [This system allows local officials obtain their income from a percentage of the taxes they had collected]. In the reforms, the king took away the function of taxation from local governors.... He [the King] replaced these local officials with men appointed and controlled from Bangkok. These new bureaucrats were paid a regular salary and were no longer supposed to obtain their income from a percentage of the taxes they collected.

Currently, corruption continues to be a problem in the Thai society. Indeed, the 2013 Corruption Perceptions Index (CPI) shows a low score of 35/100 for Thailand and ranks the country as the 102nd among the 177 countries ranked. Ariyabuddhiphongs and Hongladarom's (2014) revealed that "bribe-taking [in Thailand] was slightly acceptable and they somewhat agreed that bribe-payment was a reciprocal obligation" (p. 184). In accordance with the trend in the society at large, the 2013 Human Right Report reports that corruption is widespread within police agencies as well (U.S. Department of State 2012). The 2013 Transparency International Global Corruption Barometer revealed that 71 % of the respondents evaluated the Thai police as either "corrupt" or "extremely corrupt." Phongpaichit and Piriyarangsan (1996) wrote that, "police officers pay their superiors in order to advance up to more important positions. Subordinates are then held to extort money from the people on behalf of the officers" (Phongpaichit and Piriyarangsan 1996, p. 111). Furthermore, Khruakham and Lee's study (2013) found that "public-assessed police corruption is more serious in Thailand than in Western countries, such as the USA, Sweden, Finland, the Netherlands and Norway, among others" (p. 237).

The extent to which the Thai police officers use excessive force is not known. Phongpaichit and Piriyarangsan (1996) stated that, "General Pho Sriyanon, the most notorious director of the police at this time [1951 through 1957], created a squad of special aides known as *aswin waen phet* (knights of the diamond ring), who basically acted as his private hit men" (p. 116). Recently, in 2011, a group of plainclothes police officers shot and killed an alleged drug trafficker, Pairote; the police planted drugs in his pants and argued that Pairote was armed with a gun and shot at the police first. The subsequent inquiry revealed that he was unarmed and was not involved in any drug trafficking (Human Rights Watch 2012).

At present, there are serious attempts in campaigning against corruption in the civil service in Thailand. However, Thailand is under the control of the junta government and the NCPO has enacted order no. 69/2014 about the surveillance on the protection and solution of corruption. Under this initiative, the NCPO has used the Office of Public Sector Anti-Corruption Commission (PACC), first established in 2012, in accordance with the enactment of the Administration Measurement in Prevention and Suppression Corruption Act of 2008. This new agency is under the provision of the department of justice and will be the agency that deals with corruption cases similar to the NACC. However, the PACC will investigate corruption cases that involve public servants who hold positions lower than senior executives. Cases involving senior executives are still under the investigative division within the NACC.

There are two major aspects and six measurements that the PACC must prepare in the initiative process, which are to improve the overall transparency of Thailand, and increase Thailand's CPI ranking. The six measurements include (1) investigation of corruption cases and formulation of preliminary reports within 30 days, (2) punishment of public servants under strict disciplinary violation, (3) prosecution of corruption cases through PACC or NACC, (4) establishment of a network of corruption watchdogs, (5) establishment of corruption-free organizations, and (6) instilling the anticorruption awareness among the Thai citizens (Office of Public Sector AntiCorruption Commission 2014).

Measuring Police Integrity

Questionnaire

The questionnaire, developed by Klockars et al. (2006), contains descriptions of 11 hypothetical scenarios. The nature of the behaviors described in the questionnaire ranges in their severity from the very mild examples of misconduct, such as the acceptance of free food and a verbal abuse of a citizen, to the very serious examples of misconduct, such as the use of deadly force and a theft of an item from a crime scene. The questionnaire also includes various forms of police misconduct. Specifically, there are five scenarios containing examples of police corruption, four scenarios containing examples of the use of excessive force, and two scenarios containing examples of other forms of police misconduct (e.g., falsification of the official report, failure to execute an arrest warrant). Scenarios were translated into Thai by a native speaker.

After the respondents read the description of each example, they were asked to provide answers to the same seven questions. The first two questions asked the respondents to assess how serious they evaluate the described misconduct and how serious other police officers in the agency would assess it. The respondents were also asked to ascertain whether the described violation violates the official agency rules. Then, the respondents needed to state what they thought that the appropriate and expected discipline should and would be for such behavior. Finally, the respondents were asked whether they would be willing to report the behavior, and whether other police officers in their agency would likely do the same. The answers for most questions relied on the Likert-type scale from 1 to 5. Questions about the appropriate and expected discipline are country dependent. However, we assessed that the original U.S. version of the answers worked well for the Thai conditions (1="none," 2="verbal reprimand," 3="written reprimand," 4="period of suspension without pay," 5="demotion in rank," 6="dismissal") and kept these answers in the questionnaire. The questionnaire also contained several demographic questions. In particular, the respondents were asked about the length of their service, the supervisory position, rank, assignment, and gender.

The Sample

In 2013, questionnaires were distributed to the police officers employed in a stratified representative sample of Thai police stations. The sample of police stations was drawn to represent both police administrations and police agencies in northern Thailand. The questionnaires were distributed in seven police stations in the northern region (see Table 10.1). In addition, they were distributed to the police officers attending training sessions at the Police Education Bureau (Table 10.1). This course was conducted in Bangkok by the RTP Bureau of Education. The course that was held at the time was the Superintendents' Course, a required training for every future police superintendent, a chief of a police station. The length of the course is 4 months; the course intends to strengthen their knowledge about the rules and laws, and teach them about new investigation techniques, or even well-known police theories such as community policing. This course prepares them for their new role as the head of police stations across the country.

The Thai sample, featuring the response rate of 94 %, consists of 280 police officers (Table 10.1). The overwhelming majority of the officers were experienced officers (Table 10.2). Specifically, 90 % of the officers had more than 5 years of experience, and about 70 % had more than 15 years of experience (Table 10.2). About one half of the respondents were supervisors. Their supervisory position was related to their rank (Table 10.3); all lance corporals, corporals, sergeant, sergeant majors, senior sergeant majors, and sublieutenants in the sample were not supervisors, while all lieutenants, captains, majors, lieutenant colonels, and colonels were supervisors (Table 10.2).

Most of the respondents were employed in patrol (40 %), detective/investigative units (27 %), or administrative positions (20 %; Table 10.2). About 10 % worked as community-policing officers. In addition, the overwhelming majority of the respondents (91 %) were men (Table 10.2).

Finally, the last question asked the respondents whether they were truthful in filing out the questionnaire. If the respondents did not answer affirmatively, their answers were excluded from further analysis. About 3 % of the respondents wrote that they did not answer the questions honestly and additional 1 % did not provide any answer to the question; their answers were excluded from further analyses.

Table 10.1 Police stations

Questionnaires distribution	Region
Muang police station 28	Northern
Mae Ping police station 30	
Phu Phing police station 30	
Chiang Mai traffic police 30	
Crime investigation division region 5 30	
Mae Jun police station 30	
Chiang Klong police station 30	
Police Education Bureau 90	All regions
Total 298	

Table 10.2 Respondents' demographic characteristics

	Number of respondents	Percent of respondents (%)
Length of service		
Up to 5 years	30	10.7
6–10 years	22	7.9
11–15 years	34	12.1
16–20 years	75	26.8
Above 20 years	119	42.5
Supervisory role		
Non-supervisors	148	52.9
Supervisors	132	47.1
Type of assignment		
Patrol	113	40.4
Detective/investigative	76	27.1
Special operations	4	1.4
Traffic	2	0.7
Administrative	57	20.4
Community policing	26	9.3
Gender		
Male	250	91.2
Female	24	8.8

Table 10.3 Respondents' rank by the supervisory position

Rank	Supervisory position		Total
	No	Yes	
Police lance corporal	7 (100%)	0 (0%)	7
Police corporal	8 (100%)	0 (0%)	8
Police sergeant	1 (100%)	0 (0%)	1
Police sergeant major	8 (100%)	0 (0%)	8
Police senior sergeant major	28 (100%)	0 (0%)	28
Police sub-lieutenant	96 (100%)	0 (0%)	96
Police lieutenant	0 (0%)	49 (100%)	49
Police captain	0 (0%)	16 (100%)	16
Police major	0 (0%)	10 (100%)	10
Police lieutenant colonel	0 (0%)	10 (100%)	10
Police colonel	0 (0%)	46 (100%)	46
Total	148	132	280

The Results

Seriousness

The respondents were asked to evaluate how serious they perceived the behaviors described in the scenarios, as well as to estimate how serious most police officers in their agencies would evaluate them. They were offered answers on a five-point Likert scale, ranging from 1 = "not at all serious" to 5 = "very serious."

The results suggest that the respondents thought that these scenarios vary substantially in terms of their seriousness, with a number of scenarios having the means close to the nonserious side of the scale, such as scenario 1 (free meals, gifts from merchants; Table 10.4), to the scenarios with the means close to the serious side of the scale, such as scenario 3 (theft of knife from crime scene). Based on the values of their means, scenarios could be divided into three groups.

The least serious group, below the midpoint of the scale, includes acceptance of free meals and gifts from merchants (scenario 1), verbal abuse of citizens (scenario 7), the cover-up of police driving under the influence (DUI) and accident (scenario 8), and the auto body shop kickback (scenario 9). It is somewhat surprising that kickback, traditionally a serious form of corruption, is classified into the least serious forms of misconduct in the questionnaire. On the other hand, prior research on police integrity (Klockars et al. 2004b) shows that acceptance of gratuities, internal corruption, and verbal abuse have been perceived among the least serious scenarios in the questionnaire by the American respondents.

The middle group (means above the midpoint of 3 and into the serious side of the scale up to 4) includes six scenarios (scenario 2: failure to arrest friend with warrant; scenario 4: unjustifiable use of deadly force; scenario 5: supervisor offers holiday for errands; scenario 6: officer strikes prisoner who hurts partner; scenario 10: false report on drug on dealer; scenario 11: Sgt. fails to halt beating; Table 10.4), as diverse as failure to execute an arrest warrant (scenario 2), use of deadly force (scenario 4), and offer of internal corruption (scenario 5).

The most serious group (above four and well into the serious side of the scale) includes only scenario 3, describing the theft of a knife from the crime scene (Table 10.4). In this scenario, the police officer not only violates the official rules but also the norms of criminal law, so it is not surprising that such a scenario has been evaluated among the most serious in the questionnaire. On the other hand, it is surprising *not* to find the use of deadly force (scenario 4) in the same group.

The respondents were quite able to distinguish among the scenarios within the same forms of police misconduct. Acceptance of free meals and gifts from merchants (scenario 1), cover-up of police DUI accident (scenario 8), and acceptance of a kickback arrangement (scenario 9) were evaluated as the least serious forms of corruption in the questionnaire (Table 10.4), while theft of a knife from the crime scene (scenario 3) was evaluated as the most serious (Table 10.4). A case of internal corruption, in which the police sergeant offers a police officer to have holiday off if he runs errands for the supervisor (scenario 5), was evaluated as the corruption case of intermediate seriousness.

Table 10.4 Police officer perceptions of seriousness and violation of rules

Scenario number and description	Own seriousness		Others' seriousness		Mean difference (Own—Others)	*t*-test	Violation of official rules		
	Mean	Rank	Mean	Rank			Mean	Rank	Percent violation (%)
Scenario 1: free meals, gifts from merchants	1.42	1	1.41	1	0.01	0.355	1.52	1	3.2
Scenario 2: failure to arrest friend with warrant	3.58	8	3.59	8	−0.01	−0.187	3.87	10	67.3
Scenario 3: theft of knife from crime scene	4.47	11	4.39	11	0.08	3.04**	4.51	11	91.2
Scenario 4: unjustifiable use of deadly force	3.38	7	3.41	7	−0.03	−1.07	3.42	7	50.6
Scenario 5: supervisor offers holiday for errands	3.23	6	3.17	5	0.06	1.51	3.23	5	44.8
Scenario 6: officer strikes prisoner who hurts partner	3.20	5	3.18	6	0.02	0.492	3.37	6	50.8
Scenario 7: verbal abuse –"Arrest an Asshole Day"	2.37	3	2.39	3	−0.03	−1.09	2.41	3	17.4
Scenario 8: cover-up of police DUI accident	2.09	2	2.11	2	−0.02	−0.565	2.27	2	14.5
Scenario 9: auto body shop 5 % kickback	2.57	4	2.47	4	0.10	3.99***	2.58	4	24.9
Scenario 10: false report on drug on dealer	3.77	10	3.75	10	0.03	1.05	3.85	9	66.9
Scenario 11: Sgt. fails to halt beating	3.64	9	3.64	9	0.00	0.00	3.74	8	61.2

DUI driving under the influence
*$p<0.05$; **$p<0.01$; ***$p<0.001$

In accordance with the use of force continuum, the scenario describing verbal abuse of a citizen (scenario 7) was evaluated as the least serious form of the use of excessive force in the questionnaire (Table 10.4). Hitting a prisoner (scenario 6) or failing to stop the beating (scenario 11) were evaluated as more serious. However, the surprising finding is that use of deadly force, the most serious force on the use of force continuum, is not uniformly evaluated as the most serious of the use of excessive force scenarios (Table 10.4). In fact, abusing deadly force (scenario 4) was evaluated as less serious than failing to stop the beating (scenario 11).

There were also two scenarios in the questionnaire describing other forms of police misconduct, namely falsifying the official record (scenario 10) and failing to exercise an arrest warrant (scenario 2). Both of these scenarios were evaluated to be on the serious side (mean values between 3 and 4).

A comparison of the respondents' own estimates of seriousness and how serious they estimated that other police officers in the agency would evaluate the same scenarios revealed several findings. First, the mean values of the respondents' own estimates of seriousness and others' estimates of seriousness were very similar in all 11 scenarios; the largest difference was only 0.10 in scenario 9 (auto body shop 5% kickback). Second, the differences between the means measuring own estimates of seriousness and the means measuring others' estimates of seriousness were statistically significant in only 2 out of 11 scenarios (Table 10.4), but they were not large and meaningful (above the 0.50)[6] in any of the scenarios. Third, the relative order of the scenarios, measured through the ranking of the scenarios, suggests that police officers followed the same internal order of seriousness, regardless of whether they expressed their own evaluations or whether they estimated how other police officers would evaluate the scenarios. The Spearman's correlation of the ranking of the respondents' own estimates of seriousness and the ranking of others' estimates of seriousness was very high (Spearman's correlation coefficient $=0.964$, $p<0.001$), suggesting an extremely strong connection between the two measures.

Violation of Official Rules

The respondents were asked to assess whether the behavior described in the scenario violates the official rules in their police agencies. The possible answers ranged on a scale from 1="definitely not" to 5="definitely yes." The respondents' assessments of whether the described behaviors violate the official rules varied greatly across the scenarios (Table 10.4). The mean values for four scenarios (scenario 1": free meals, gifts from merchants; scenario 7: verbal abuse –"Arrest an Asshole Day," Scenario 8: cover-up of police DUI accident; scenario 9: auto body shop 5% kickback; Table 10.4) were below the midpoint of the scale (i.e., 3), suggesting that the respondents hesitated to label these behaviors as rule violating. To eliminate the

[6] Following the rule of thumb established in prior work (Klockars et al. 2006, p. 26), we consider only the differences of 0.50 or larger to be meaningful.

possibility that a few outliers are affecting the mean value, we also analyzed the percentages of police officers who said that these behaviors violate official rules[7] (Table 10.4). The results show that the overwhelming majority of the officers did not think that such behaviors violated official rules. In fact, less than one quarter of the respondents confirmed that these behaviors indeed are violations of official rules. At the same time, all four scenarios describe the behaviors evaluated as the least serious in the questionnaire.

Another group of scenarios had mean values between 3 and 4 (scenario 2: failure to arrest friend with warrant; scenario 4: unjustifiable use of deadly force; scenario 5: supervisor offers holiday for errands; scenario 6: officer strikes prisoner who hurts partner; scenario 10: false report on drug on dealer; scenario 11: Sgt. fails to halt beating), indicating that the respondents were more likely to evaluate them as rule violating. However, there is variation within this group; while only the minority of the respondents (45 %; Table 10.4) recognized internal corruption (scenario 5: supervisor offers holiday for errands) as rule violating, as many as two thirds (67 %; Table 10.4) recognized as rule violating the failure to exercise an arrest warrant (scenario 2: failure to arrest friend with warrant) and falsification of the official report (scenario 10: false report on drug on dealer). Some of the forms of misconduct included in this middle group include very serious examples of misconduct (e.g., failure to exercise an arrest warrant, falsifying the official report, abusing deadly force) and it is rather surprising that between one third and one half of the respondents did *not* recognize these behaviors as rule violating.

Finally, there was only one scenario (scenario 3: theft of knife from crime scene) in which the mean was above 4 and more than 90 % of the respondents recognized this behavior as rule violating. This scenario describes one of the most serious forms of police corruption, one in which a police officer steals from a crime scene. The overwhelming majority of the respondents had no problems recognizing it as a violation of official rules.

The respondents' evaluations of whether the behavior violates official rules are very strongly associated with how serious they evaluated these behaviors. The two sets of rankings (own seriousness ranking and ranking of rule violating) are very similar, resulting in a high correlation (Spearman's correlation coefficient $=0.964$, $p<0.001$). The more serious the respondents' evaluated the behavior, the most likely they were to say that the behavior violates official rules.

Appropriate and Expected Discipline

The next two questions in the questionnaire focused on the views about the appropriate and expected discipline. The respondents were asked to express their views about the appropriate discipline for the behaviors described in the questionnaire, as well as to estimate what discipline their agency would mete out for such behavior.

[7] Answers by the respondents who selected either 4 or 5 on the scale were grouped together.

Possible answers included: "no discipline," "verbal reprimand," "written reprimand," "period of suspension without pay," "demotion in rank," and "dismissal."

The respondents' views about the appropriate and expected discipline were analyzed using three analytical approaches. First, based on modal values, the respondents thought only mild discipline should be appropriate (typically "verbal reprimand") and that dismissal is not appropriate for *any* of behaviors described in the scenarios (Table 10.5). In fact, the respondents supported verbal reprimand as the appropriate discipline for the overwhelming majority of the scenarios (in 9 out of 11 scenarios; Table 10.5). Only in the scenario describing theft from a crime scene (scenario 3: theft of knife from crime scene) did they express that only a somewhat harsher discipline, such as written reprimand, would be appropriate. On the other hand, the respondents thought that no discipline should be given to the police officer who accepted free meals and gifts from merchants (scenario 1).

Second, the analysis of the percentages of respondents who selected either no discipline, some discipline other than dismissal, and dismissal led toward similar conclusions (i.e., the majority preferred no discipline in only one scenario, the majority expected dismissal in only one scenario; in 9 out of 11 scenarios, the majority expected some discipline, but more lenient than dismissal). It also revealed that views are more complex than the modal analysis would suggest. In particular, just like the modal analysis revealed, the percentage analysis implies that majority of the respondents thought that no discipline was appropriate in only one scenario (scenario 1: free meals, gifts from merchants). In addition, there was also a substantial minority of the respondents—between 30 and 40 %—who thought that the police officer should not be disciplined for engaging in the behaviors described in three additional scenarios (scenario 7: verbal abuse – "Arrest an Asshole Day"; scenario 8: cover-up of police DUI accident; scenario 9: auto body shop 5 % kickback; Table 10.5). Similarly, while there is only one scenario (scenario 3: theft of knife from crime scene) in which the majority of the respondents thought that dismissal was appropriate, there were three more scenarios (scenario 2: failure to arrest friend with warrant; scenario 10: false report on drug on dealer; scenario 11: Sgt. fails to halt beating) in which between 20 and 30 % of the respondents advocated for dismissal.

Third, the scenarios were ranked based on the modal appropriate discipline for each scenario (Table 10.5). A comparison of the ranking of appropriate discipline with the ranking for own seriousness shows that they are correlated (Spearman's correlation coefficient $=0.674$, $p<0.05$). The more serious the respondents evaluated the scenarios, the more likely they were to advocate for the reliance on a harsher discipline. Similarly, a comparison of the ranking of appropriate discipline with the ranking for rule-violating behavior shows that the two are correlated (Spearman's correlation coefficient $=0.674$, $p<0.05$). The more likely the respondents were to evaluate the behavior as rule violating, the more likely they were to advocate for harsher discipline.

The respondents were also asked to assess what kind of discipline their agency would mete out for the behaviors described in the questionnaire. The analysis of the respondents' modal responses indicated that, in most of the scenarios, respondents expected only "verbal reprimand" as the discipline that their police agency would

Table 10.5 Views about appropriate discipline (should) and expected discipline (would)

Scenario number and description		Mode	Rank should	Rank would	None (%)	Some discipline (%)	Dismissal (%)	Chi-square test
Scenario 1: free meals, gifts from merchants	*Should*	None	1		81.9	17.0	1.1	411.5***
	Would	None		1	80.8	17.7	1.5	
Scenario 2: failure to arrest friend with warrant	*Should*	Verbal reprimand	2–10		5.2	72.0	22.9	449.1***
	Would	Verbal reprimand		2–10	5.2	70.5	24.4	
Scenario 3: theft of knife from crime scene	*Should*	Written reprimand	11		1.5	42.4	56.1	341.2***
	Would	Written reprimand		11	1.8	42.1	56.1	
Scenario 4: unjustifiable use of deadly force	*Should*	Verbal reprimand	2–10		7.7	79.3	12.9	434.00***
	Would	Verbal reprimand		2–10	7.0	78.2	14.8	
Scenario 5: supervisor offers holiday for errands	*Should*	Verbal reprimand	2–10		19.2	73.1	7.7	427.8***
	Would	Verbal reprimand		2–10	21.4	70.8	7.7	
Scenario 6: officer strikes prisoner who hurts partner	*Should*	Verbal reprimand	2–10		12.9	81.2	5.9	431.8***
	Would	Verbal reprimand		2–10	13.3	80.8	5.9	
Scenario 7: verbal abuse – “Arrest an Asshole Day”	*Should*	Verbal reprimand	2–10		37.3	62.0	0.7	481.8***
	Would	Verbal reprimand		2–10	38.4	60.9	0.7	
Scenario 8: cover-up of police DUI accident	*Should*	Verbal reprimand	2–10		43.5	54.2	2.2	467.3***
	Would	Verbal reprimand		2–10	44.6	53.5	1.8	
Scenario 9: auto body shop 5 % kickback	*Should*	Verbal reprimand	2–10		36.9	60.1	3.0	444.5***
	Would	Verbal reprimand		2–10	38.0	59.0	3.0	
Scenario 10: false report on drug on dealer	*Should*	Verbal reprimand	2–10		8.9	60.9	30.3	472.8***
	Would	Verbal reprimand		2–10	9.2	58.7	32.1	
Scenario 11: Sgt. fails to halt beating	*Should*	Verbal reprimand	2–10		7.7	73.1	19.2	464.8***
	Would	Verbal reprimand		2–10	8.5	73.8	17.7	

DUI driving under the influence
*$p<0.05$; **$p<0.01$; ***$p<0.001$

mete out (Table 10.5). The only scenario in which they expected more serious discipline than "verbal reprimand" was the scenario describing theft from a crime scene (scenario 3). On the other hand, they expected no discipline in the case of a police officer who accepted free meals and gifts from merchants (scenario 1). The analysis of percentages of respondents who expected no discipline at all, some discipline more lenient than dismissal, and dismissal yielded similar conclusions. In addition, the percentage analysis also brought to the attention the existence of strong minority views (e.g., a strong minority of the respondents expected no discipline in scenario 7: verbal abuse – "Arrest an Asshole Day"; scenario 8: cover-up of police DUI accident; scenario 9: auto body shop 5 % kickback; a strong minority of the respondents expected dismissal in scenario 2: failure to arrest friend with warrant; scenario 10: false report on drug dealer). Finally, the respondents' views of the expected discipline were correlated with their estimates of misconduct seriousness (Spearman's correlation coefficient = 0.674, $p < 0.05$) and estimates of rule violation (Spearman's correlation coefficient = 0. 674, $p < 0.05$).

The respondents' views of the expected discipline were very similar to their views of the appropriate discipline. First, there was a very strong correlation between the ranking of the respondents' views of the appropriate discipline and the ranking of the respondents' estimates of the expected discipline (Spearman's correlation coefficient = 1.00). Second, the modal values of appropriate discipline and expected discipline were virtually identical for all 11 scenarios. Third, the analysis of percentages across the three categories of discipline suggests that the views about appropriate and expected discipline were quite similar[8] (Table 10.5).

Willingness to Report Misconduct

The last two questions focused on the code of silence. In particular, the respondents were asked how willing they would be to report misconduct and to estimate how willing other officers in their agencies would be to do the same. The answers ranged on a five-point Likert scale from "definitely not" to "definitely yes."

The analysis of the mean values for the respondents' own willingness to report shows very clearly that the code of silence is far from a flat prohibition of reporting (Table 10.6). The respondents' willingness to report is positively related to their evaluations of scenario seriousness (Spearman's correlation coefficient = 0.934, $p < 0.001$), perceptions that the behavior violates the rules (Spearman's correlation coefficient = 0.929, $p < 0.001$), and severity of the appropriate discipline (Spearman's correlation coefficient = 0.676, $p < 0.05$). The mean values ranged from as low as 1.26 for the scenario describing acceptance of gratuities (scenario 1) to as

[8] The chi-square test of independence was statistically significant in all 11 scenarios, suggesting that the null hypothesis that these two variables are statistically independent should be rejected. Both the chi-square test and the Phi coefficient suggest that the views of appropriate and expected discipline were related.

Table 10.6 Police officer perceptions of willingness to report

Scenario number and description	Own willingness to report		Others' willingness to report		Mean difference (Own—Others)	*t*-test
	Mean	Rank	Mean	Rank		
Scenario 1: free meals, gifts from merchants	1.26	1	1.07	1	0.19	4.82[c]
Scenario 2: failure to arrest friend with warrant	3.44	7.5	1.62	7.5	1.82	23.94[c]
Scenario 3: theft of knife from crime scene	4.27	11	1.85	11	2.42	36.9[c]
Scenario 4: unjustifiable use of deadly force	3.84	10	1.72	9	2.12	31.7[c]
Scenario 5: supervisor offers holiday for errands	2.84	5	1.46	6	1.38	16.9[c]
Scenario 6: officer strikes prisoner who hurts partner	2.88	6	1.41	5	1.47	18.8[c]
Scenario 7: verbal abuse – "Arrest an Asshole Day"	2.01	3	1.22	3	0.79	11.7[c]
Scenario 8: cover-up of police DUI accident	1.92	2	1.21	2	0.71	11.7[c]
Scenario 9: auto body shop 5 % kickback	2.35	4	1.35	4	1.00	13.1[c]
Scenario 10: false report on drug on dealer	3.75	9	1.75	10	2.00	26.3[c]
Scenario 11: Sgt. fails to halt beating	3.44	7.5	1.62	7.5	1.82	23.8[c]

DUI driving under the influence
* $p < 0.05$; ** $p < 0.01$; *** $p < 0.001$

high as 4.27 for the scenario describing theft from a crime scene (scenario 3). Based on the mean values, scenarios could be classified into three categories (Table 10.6).

First, six scenarios (scenario 1: free meals, gifts from merchants; scenario 5: supervisor offers holiday for errands; scenario 6: officer strikes prisoner who hurts partner; scenario 7: verbal abuse – "Arrest an Asshole Day"; scenario 8:" cover-up of police DUI accident; scenario 9: auto body shop 5 % kickback; Table 10.6) have means below 3 (the midpoint of the scale), suggesting that the respondents would be unwilling to report such behaviors and that the code of silence would cover them. However, even within this group, the respondents were more likely to stick to the code of silence for the behaviors they evaluated as the least serious (i.e., scenario 1: free meals, gifts from merchants; scenario 7: verbal abuse—"Arrest an Asshole Day"; scenario 8: cover-up of police DUI accident) than for the other behaviors in this category (i.e., scenario 5: supervisor offers holiday for errands; scenario 6: officer strikes prisoner who hurts partner; scenario 9: auto body shop 5 % kick-back). These behaviors describe the least serious forms of police corruption, such as acceptance of gratuities (scenario 1: free meals, gifts from merchants) and internal corruption (scenario 8: cover-up of police DUI accident), as well as the least serious forms of misconduct related to the use of force continuum (scenario 7: verbal abuse – "Arrest an Asshole Day"). On the other hand, the code seems to be somewhat weaker (but still very strong) for the more serious forms of police corruption, such as the kickback (scenario 9: auto body shop 5 % kickback) and the use of excessive force (scenario 6: officer strikes prisoner who hurts partner).

Second, there are four scenarios (scenario 2: failure to arrest friend with warrant; scenario 4: unjustifiable use of deadly force; scenario 10: false report on drug on dealer; scenario 11: Sgt. fails to halt beating) with the means between 3 (the middle point) and 4 (Table 10.6). In these scenarios, the mean values are crossing into the reporting side of the scale, suggesting that the respondents would be less likely to tolerate such behaviors without reporting them. Most of these scenarios involve very serious forms of the use of excessive force (scenario 4: unjustifiable use of deadly force; scenario 11: Sgt. fails to halt beating) or other forms of misconduct (scenario 2: failure to arrest friend with warrant; scenario 10: false report on drug on dealer). However, even for such serious forms of police misconduct, there is a substantial proportion of the respondents who would protect such behavior without reporting it.

Third, there is only one scenario (scenario 3: theft of knife from crime scene) in which the mean value is above 4, thus suggesting that the respondents would be much less likely to tolerate such behavior in silence. This scenario (scenario 3: theft of knife from crime scene) describes one of the most serious forms of corruption. It has been evaluated as the most serious scenario in the questionnaire, the scenario most likely to be evaluated as rule violating (over 90 % of the respondents recognized it as rule violating), and the only scenario in which the majority of the respondents expected dismissal. Therefore, it is not surprising that it is also the scenario in which the respondents were least likely to say that they would protect such behavior without reporting it.

The respondents' views of their own willingness to report were also compared with their estimates of the other officers' willingness to report (Table 10.6). Although the views are highly correlated (Spearman's correlation coefficient = 0.982, $p < 0.001$), the mean values show a remarkable finding: The respondents expected that other police officers would be much more likely to protect such behavior in silence than the respondents themselves would. In fact, the respondents expected that their fellow officers would not be willing to report the behavior described in *any* of the 11 scenarios (the mean values for the others' willingness to report are all below the midpoint of the scale; Table 10.6). The differences between the respondents' own willingness to report and the others' willingness to report are not only statistically significant, but also substantively important[9] in ten scenarios. In fact, these differences tended to be unusually large in some scenarios. For example, in three scenarios (scenario 3: theft of knife from crime scene; scenario 4: unjustifiable use of deadly force; scenario 10: false report on drug on dealer), evaluated as some of the most serious scenarios, they were larger than two points on the scale from 1 to 5 (see Table 10.6).

Conclusion

The story of the Thai Royal Police (TRP) illustrates the importance of the role that the society, at large, plays in shaping the ethical behavior of police officers. Scholars (e.g., Phongpaichit and Piriyarangsan 1996) described the long history of corruption in the Thai society, from the ancient Thai system *Sakdina,* in which government officers were legally allowed to accept gifts or money from citizens, to the modern times, in which bribe taking is still an acceptable practice (e.g., Ariyabuddhiphongs and Hongladarom 2014). These scholarly descriptions suggest that police corruption is highly organized (e.g., syndicate corruption; Phongpaichat et al. 1991), affecting many ranks within a police agency. On the other hand, the "tradition" of military coups as an acceptable way of obtaining power, without any negative consequences, and the encouragement of the police to engage in the war on drugs, without a concern for human rights violations, create the impression that the use of (excessive) force is tolerated as well.

The results of our empirical study should be analyzed with a larger context in mind. Of the various forms of misconduct included in the questionnaire—ranging from acceptance of gratuities and verbal abuse to use of deadly force, kickbacks, and thefts—the respondents evaluated only theft from a crime scene as a truly serious example of misconduct and were certain that it violates official rules. There were a few other examples of misbehaviors (e.g., failure to exercise an arrest warrant, falsifying an official report) in which most of the officers perceived that the behavior is serious and that it violates official rules, but, as a norm, most of the

[9] Following the rule of thumb established in prior work (Klockars et al. 2006, p. 26), we consider only the differences of 0.50 or larger to be meaningful.

behaviors in the questionnaire were neither evaluated as very serious nor viewed as severe violations of the official rules—nor perceived as deserving harsh discipline. Such findings should not be surprising in a society in which corruption seems to be a part of the cultural tradition and force is used regularly to overthrow governments.

The results also show that the code of silence is present among the respondents and that it does not cover all behaviors equally. The degree to which the respondents' own willingness to report and the estimates of others' willingness to report differ is no less than remarkable. One potential explanation is that the respondents do not have a good perception about the extent of the code and that they are misled into believing that the code is much stronger than it really is. If that is the case, the police administration faces a substantial challenge in teaching the officers what the code really looks like. An alternative explanation is that police officers asked to participate in the study have much higher levels of police integrity than the average police officers. This might have been the case for some of the respondents, particularly those surveyed, while taking a course for the future chiefs of police stations. However, this should not have been the case for the majority of the police officers surveyed in their respective police stations. The code of silence is one area in which the police administrators, who are presumably interested in controlling misconduct, could make substantial strides toward addressing it.

References

Ariyabuddhiphongs, V., & Hongladarom, C. (2014, Jan 1). Bribe taking acceptability and bribe payment among Thai organizational employees: The mediating effect of reciprocity obligation. *International Perspectives in Psychology: Research, Practice, Consultation, 3*(3), 184–196.

ASEANAPOL. (n.d.). *The royal thai police*. ASEANAPOL: http://www.aseanapol.org/information/royal-thai-police. Accessed 29 Aug 2014.

Bhaopichitr, K., Thitisakmongkol, C., Anantavrasilpa, R., & Mohib, S. (2014). *Thailand Economic Monitor—February 2014*. Washington: The World Bank. http://www.worldbank.org/content/dam/Worldbank/document/EAP/Thailand/thailand_economic_monitor_february_11_2014_english.pdf. Accessed 29 Aug 2014.

Global Advice Networks on Integrity Solutions. (2014). *Thailand country profile: Thai police*. Retrieved from http://www.business-anti-corruption.org/country-profiles/east-asia-the-pacific/thailand/corruption-levels/police.aspx.

Human Rights Watch. (2012). *Thailand: Police blamed for killing drug suspect*. Bangkok: Human rights watch. http://www.hrw.org/news/2012/03/16/thailand-police-blamed-killing-drug-suspect. Accessed 29 Aug 2014.

Human Rights Watch. (2004). Human rights abuses and the war on drugs. http://www.hrw.org/reports/2004/thailand0704/4.htm.

Human Rights Watch. (2014, Aug 22). *Thailand: Junta leader named prime minister*. Bangkok: Human Rights Watch. http://www.hrw.org/news/2014/08/22/thailand-junta-leader-named-prime-minister. Accessed 29 Aug 2014.

INTERPOL. (n.d.). Thailand. INTERPOL: http://www.interpol.int/Member-countries/Asia-South-Pacific/Thailand. Accessed 29 Aug 2014.

Khruakham, S., & Joongyeup, L. (2013). Cross-nation comparison of the intolerance to police misconduct: Findings from a Thai police cadet survey. *International Journal of Police Science & Management, 15*(3), 237–245.

Klockars, C. B., & Kutnjak Ivković, S. (2004). Measuring police integrity. In A. R. Piquero, J. R. Greene, & M. J. Hickman (Eds.), *Police integrity and ethics*. Belmont: Wadsworth.

Klockars, C. B., Kutnjak Ivković, S., Harver, W. E., & Haberfeld, M. R. (1997). *The measurement of police integrity*. Final Report Submitted to the U.S. Department of Justice, Office of Justice Programs, National Institute of Justice.

Klockars, C. B., Kutnjak Ivković, S., & Haberfeld, M. R. (Eds.). (2004a). *The contours of police integrity*. Newbury Park: Sage.

Klockars, C. B., Kutnjak Ivković, S., & Haberfeld, M. R. (2004b). Police integrity in the United States of America. In C. B. Klockars, S. Kutnjak Ivković, & M. R. Haberfeld (Eds.), *The contours of police integrity*. Thousand Oaks: Sage.

Klockars, C. B., Kutnjak Ivković, S., & Haberfeld, M. R. (2006). *Enhancing police integrity*. New York: Springer.

National Statistical Office. (2010). The 2010 Population and housing census (Whole Kingdom). Bangkok, Thailand: National Statistical Office of Thailand. http://popcensus.nso.go.th/file/popcensus-10-01-56-E.pdf. Accessed 29 Aug 2014.

Ngamkham, W. (2009, Feb 2). Caught in the crossfire of love and hate. B. http://www.global-report.com/pattaya/a354159-caught-in-the-crossfire-of-love-and-hate.

Office of Justice Affairs. (2011). Criminal Justice System Statistics 2007–2011. Bangkok, Thailand: Office of Justice Affairs. http://www.oja.go.th/. Accessed 29 Aug 2014.

Office of the National Economic and Social Development Board. (2014). *Thailand economic indicators*. Bangkok: Office of the National Economic and Social Development Board. http://www.nesdb.go.th/Default.aspx?tabid=456.

Officer of the National Anti-Corruption Commission. (n.d.). Cases that NACC files against corruption. Officer NACC: http://www.nacc.go.th/culpability.php.

Phillip, S. (2007, Nov 30). Southeast Asia: Most killed in Thailand's 2003 drug war not involved with drugs, Panel Finds. Stop The Drug War Organization: http://stopthedrugwar.org/chronicle/2007/nov/30/southeast_asia_most_killed_thail. Accessed 29 Aug 2014.

Phongpaichit, P. (n.d.). Plan to solve corruption in the bureaucracy. http://pioneer.netserv.chula.ac.th/~ppasuk/paenkan.doc.

Phongpaichit, P., & Piriyarangsan, S. (1996). *Corruption and democracy in Thailand*. Bangkok: Silkworm Books.

Suwanmala, C. (n.d.). Fighting corruption from the bottom: The case of Thailand. Asian Human Rights Commission: http://www.humanrights.asia/resources/journals-magazines/article2/0901/07fighting-corruption-from-the-bottom-the-case-of-thailand. Accessed 29 Aug 2014.

The Heritage Foundation. (2014). *The index of economic freedom of Thailand*. Washington, DC: The Heritage Foundation. http://www.heritage.org/index/country/thailand. Accessed 29 Aug 2014.

U.S. Department of State. (2012). Country Reports on Human Rights Practices. http://www.state.gov/j/drl/rls/hrrpt/2012humanrightsreport/index.htm?year=2012&dlid=204241#wrapper. Accessed 29 Aug 2014.

United Nations Office on Drugs and Crime. (2011, July 12). Thailand Penal Code. UNODC: https://www.unodc.org/tldb/pdf/Thailand/THA_Pena_CodeEN.pdf. Accessed 29 Aug 2014.

Chapter 11
Police Integrity in the United States

Sanja Kutnjak Ivković, M. R. Haberfeld, and Robert Peacock

Abstract This chapter explores the contours of police integrity in the United States. The 11 local police departments, surveyed across the United States in the period from 2013 to 2014, constitute a convenience sample of a diverse range of police departments, with both large and small municipal agencies and sheriff's departments. The questionnaire is built around 11 scenarios covering a variety of forms of police misconduct, including police corruption, use of excessive force, planting of evidence, and failure to execute an arrest warrant. After reviewing each scenario, the respondents were asked to report own and others' evaluation of its seriousness, appropriate and expected discipline, as well as own and others' willingness to report the misconduct. The respondents evaluated scenarios described in the questionnaire to range in seriousness from the least serious (acceptance of gratuities and verbal abuse of citizens) to the most serious (opportunistic theft, unjustifiable use of deadly force, and official report falsification). Although most of the respondents expected and supported some discipline for all the scenarios described in the questionnaire, they expected police officers to be dismissed from service only for the three most serious scenarios. We also measured the contours of the code of silence and found that the code of silence is far from the flat prohibition of reporting. The code was much stronger for the behaviors evaluated as the least serious and the weakest for the behaviors evaluated as the most serious.

Keywords Code of silence · Civilian oversight · Organizational rules · Police integrity · Survey

S. Kutnjak Ivković (✉)
Michigan State University, East Lansing, MI, USA
e-mail: kutnjak@msu.edu

R. Peacock
Michigan State University, East Lansing, MI, USA
e-mail: r.peacock@icitapeurasia.org

M. R. Haberfeld
John Jay College of Criminal Justice, New York, NY, USA
e-mail: mhaberfeld@jjay.cuny.edu

S. Kutnjak Ivković, M. R. Haberfeld (eds.), *Measuring Police Integrity Across the World,*
DOI 10.1007/978-1-4939-2279-6_11

Introduction

With around 18,000 law-enforcement agencies (LEMAS 2007), the American police system is probably the most decentralized one in the world. In addition to having a large number of police agencies, the United States is characterized by a range of policing agencies at different levels, from local agencies and state agencies to federal agencies (LEMAS 2007). Agencies vary in terms of their size as well, from the smallest ones, employing a handful of police officers, to the largest ones, with tens of thousands of police officers. In addition, public policing includes a diversity of police agencies, from municipal police agencies and sheriff's departments, to the transportation police, park police, and university police. Some agencies specialize (e.g., Federal Bureau of Investigation handles only violations of federal laws), while others have more general jurisdiction (e.g., municipal police agencies). To complicate matters further, jurisdiction of various police agencies can overlap.

Police officers employed by these police agencies are subject to federal and state laws, as well as the official agency rules created by their agency. Because each of these agencies has its own set of rules and regulations, the approach to ethics and integrity differs not only across, but also within the jurisdictions. This chapter explores the contours of police integrity among the police in the United States. It begins with a short history of policing in the United States, with particular emphasis on the nature of police misconduct and the conditions that allow misconduct to continue. Then, it analyzes the conditions in the United States through the prism of the police integrity theory. Finally, the chapter provides a measurement of the level of police integrity among the U.S. police officers, based upon empirical analyses of the responses police officers provided in a survey we conducted for that purpose.

Short History of Policing in the United States

American policing stems from the arrival of the earliest colonists, bringing with them Saxon roots and the seventeenth century English police traditions. The colonist first engaged in a system of mutual protection. Soon, town constables, sheriffs, and night watchmen were established. Early settlement patterns favored the northeast and the south of today's United States of America. In the North, more towns and cities developed and, promulgating the system of watchmen patrolling force. The agrarian settlers in the South favored law enforcement styles that had developed in the countryside of England, including the county sheriff. With its earliest appearance around 1634 in Virginia, the institution of the American sheriff became the most powerful and significant law enforcement entity in the southern United States. The western areas of America, settled later, adopted the sheriff as the primary police agent (Moore and Kelling 1985).

Industrialization in the north fostered rapid growth of towns and cities. The sheriff system did not appear to suffice there and, consequently, the night watchmen system was imported from England. Aside from their primary task—crime prevention—watchmen were often in charge of other duties such as lighting street lamps, watching for fires, chasing runaway animals, or assisting in family disputes (Moore and Kelling 1985). Early watchmen's principal policing strategy was to alert the community by raising "hue and cry" if they saw a crime being committed. Boston organized the first watchmen system in 1631, which in 1712 became the first full-time night watch force (Bopp and Schultz 1972). It was originally organized as a military structure, with one commanding officer and six watchmen (Lane 1967).

The concept of a modern police department permeated America relatively late. The challenges associated with an enormous increase in the inflow of immigrants were mounting. Moreover, several riots that had occurred in 1834 (Costello 1972) prompted the media and citizens to start campaigning for a police system similar to the Metropolitan Police Force in England. Consequently, in 1845, New York became the first city in America that introduced a modern police department. Cincinnati and New Orleans followed the New York standard in 1852. Boston and Philadelphia followed in 1854, Chicago the year after, and Baltimore in 1857 (Ketcham 1967).

The new police forces had to overcome several problems, including increased crime rates and the public suspicion and distrust towards the police, prompted by the economic depression in the mid-1850s. The creation of various private law enforcement agencies added additional dimensions to the way the public viewed law enforcement. In Chicago, Allan Pinkerton started the Pinkerton Protective Patrol (Morn 1977), performing all the same functions as the regular police department did. Pinkerton expanded his offices after the civil war, opening up in New York City (1865) and Philadelphia (1866). Pinkerton's officers focused on detection work, not on patrolling and prevention. The agency was successful and, by 1895, nine offices were established in different cities in America.

Another form of policing early in the U.S. history was slave patrols. They were established in the early eighteenth century in the southern States in response to the perception that the slaves constituted a threat to the southern States in at least three ways. First, slaves were running away from their owners and thus undermined the Southern economy. Second, slaves could conspire, organize themselves, and revolt against their owners. Finally, slaves engaged in crimes, such as theft, robbery, crop destruction, arson, and poison. The main functions of slave patrols were patrolling and policing. From the standpoint of law enforcement, they had a couple of limitations, ranging from duty avoidance (elite members of different districts often avoided duty by paying a fine or finding a substitute), inappropriate behavior (e.g., being drunk on duty, using excessive force), to infrequent and often very poor training. Slave patrols disappeared in the aftermath of the 1865 Emancipation Proclamation, but they left a lasting legacy of tensions between minority groups and police agencies, continuing into the twenty-first century.

A typical classification of the history of modern policing in the United States features three periods: the political period (1840s–1900s), the reform era (1930s–1970s), and the community era (1970s-present; Kelling and Moore 1988). A wealth of information exists in the literature about the three eras; in this chapter, we focus on illustrating the nature of police misconduct and the specific historic conditions that allow misconduct to flourish.

The Political Era

From about the middle of the eighteenth century to the 1920s, local policing was dominated by politics; there was a close connection between the local politicians and the police administrators (Kelling and Moore 1988) and politics influenced every aspect of law enforcement, from employment, through promotion, appointment of the police commissioner or chief of police to some police arrest practices and services. Police jobs became an important part of the political patronage system that developed in the cities. The police were particularly useful during elections because they maintained order at polling booths and were able to determine who voted and who did not (Roberg et al. 2000). The amount of policing received, if any, was dependent upon one's political connections (Walker 1977).

Walker (1999) argues that nineteenth century policing in America was characterized by corruption of epidemic proportions. The police routinely received payoffs for not enforcing laws on drinking, gambling, and prostitution. Officers themselves often had to pay bribes for promotion (Walker 1999). More broadly, corruption was one of the main functions of local government. The deeply engrained corruption that permeated every aspect of police work was but one problem in the grand scheme of things. Although political reformers made police corruption a major issue during the nineteenth century, their success in such a toxic environment was quite limited (Walker 1999).

At the same time, legislators enacted racially biased laws and the police were in charge of enforcing them (Williams and Murphy 1990). In 1863, the Emancipation Proclamation promised freedom to the slaves in the Confederacy states and, in 1865, the Thirteen Amendment to the U.S. Constitution abolished slavery except as a punishment for a crime. A year later, in 1866, the Fourteenth Amendment established a guarantee to equal protection under the laws. Following the Civil War, however, "Black Codes," a series of State laws severely restricting the rights of African Americans, were passed in Southern States. A body of laws and legal practice that promulgated the "separate but equal" legal doctrine enabled racial segregation to continue well into the 1900s, until its official abolishment with the U.S. Supreme Court decision in *Brown v. Board of Education* (1954).

The Reform Era

The second period, "the professional era" or the "reform era" of policing, commenced in early twentieth century, but is formally recognized as the period from the 1920s to—depending on the source—the early 1960s or the late 1970s. The slogan "get politics out of the police and get the police out of politics" formed a foundation for hiring professional administrators and, thereby, seeking to limit political influences.

This period is associated with notable names such as Richard Sylvester (founder of the International Association of Chiefs of Police), August Vollmer (police chief of Berkley, the founder of American Society of Criminology, and an avid advocate of higher education and extensive training for police officers), and Orlando W. Wilson (author of one of the most influential texts in police science, "Police Administration"). Despite the reformers' power and influence, however, success in "getting the politics out of the police and getting the police out of politics" was lackluster. From the organizational standpoint, professionalization of the police force prompted the troublesome move of distancing the police force from the beat functions and close interaction with the public, in the direction of seclusion and isolation inside the police car.

A major challenge, inherited from the political period, was attainment of better policing practices aimed toward actual racial equality. The aforementioned legal doctrine and practice of "separate but equal" coexistence—a de facto segregation—prompted unabated practice of racially-biased policing. Laws were biased against African Americans in general, as were the professional criteria for participation and career advancement in the law-enforcement profession (Williams and Murphy 1990). The tension between minority communities and the police had been growing steadily, escalating in a series of riots in the 1960s. Civil rights movement and riots were coupled with war protests, increase in street crime, and unrest on college campuses (Hunter et al. 2000).

The Community Era

The third period in the history of U.S. policing has started in the late 1960s/early 1970s. It has been strongly affected by Supreme Court's judicial activism in the 1960s. In the period from 1961 to 1966, the Supreme Court made several decisions that directly influenced how the police perform their tasks and drew the line between proper and improper police conduct. In *Mapp v. Ohio* (1961), the Supreme Court banned the use of illegally seized evidence in criminal cases in state courtrooms by applying the Fourth Amendment guarantee against unreasonable searches and seizures. In *Gideon v. Wainwright* (1963), the Supreme Court found that legal counsel must be appointed for all indigent defendants in all criminal cases. In *Escobedo v. Illinois* (1964), the Supreme Court ruled that suspects are entitled to consult an attorney once the police investigation shifts from investigatory to accusatory. Finally, in *Miranda v. Arizona* (1966), the Supreme Court established that, before questioning suspects, police officers have to inform them of their Fifth Amendment rights.

In the 1960s/1970s, inner cities were disintegrating at a rapid pace, the level of crime and social order increased, and racial tensions gained momentum. The Kerner Commission (1968) was formed to investigate the causes of the series of riots in America's inner cities. In its report, the Kerner Commission argued that the riots were caused by a long history of racism in America and that the "the riots had been precipitated by police actions, often cases of insensitivity, sometimes incidents of outright brutality" (Williams and Murphy 1990, p. 11). Several of the Commission's recommendations directly address the topic of police misconduct. The Commission required of the police agencies to change the way policing was carried out in minority communities and reduce the likelihood that police would engage in misconduct. Furthermore, the Commission asked of the police to "[p]rovide adequate police protection to inner city residents to eliminate the high level of fear of crime" (Williams and Murphy 1990, p. 11). Finally, the Commission pushed police agencies to create official rules that would regulate police conduct and establish official mechanisms citizens could use to file complaints.

The late 1960/early 1970s were characterized with a formation of a number of commissions, foundations, and programs. Commissions, formed in response to urban riots and Vietnam protests (e.g., Kerner Commission 1968; National Advisory Commission on the Causes and Prevention of Violence 1969; National Advisory Commission on Criminal Justice Standards and Goals 1973; President's Commission on Campus Unrest 1970), opened the door for researchers to analyze police departments' practices and led to the formation of the Police Foundation and the Police Executive Research Forum (PERF)(Oliver 1998). Some of the fundamental research had been carried out at the time, addressing effectiveness of popular random patrol (e.g., Kelling et al. 1974), patrol work (President's Crime Commission 1967), rapid police response (Spelman and Brown 1981), detective work (Chaiken et al. 1976), and police officer attitudes and behavior (e.g., Skolnick 1966).

As police scholars were researching, analyzing, and writing about the future of American policing, considering various modalities of Community Oriented Policing, the events of 9/11 shifted the emphasis of law enforcement research and practices away from various modalities of Community Oriented Policing, and toward mounting concerns of the newly emerged global threat. The Homeland Security office was created to prevent terrorist attacks; protect Americans, key resources, and critical infrastructure; respond to and recover from incidents; and, finally, continue to strengthen the foundation of homeland security to ensure long-term success (Kappeler and Gaines 2011). As many local law enforcement agencies responded, through actual organizational restructuring or, at minimum, through explicit language in their new mission statements, misconduct and integrity violations continued unabated. Indeed, the National Police Misconduct Reporting Project (NPMSRP), compiled from the accredited media resources throughout the United States, indicated that in 2010 there were approximately 4861 reports of police misconduct involving 6613 sworn police officers, and almost 7000 victims (Fig. 11.1, CATO Institute 2010).

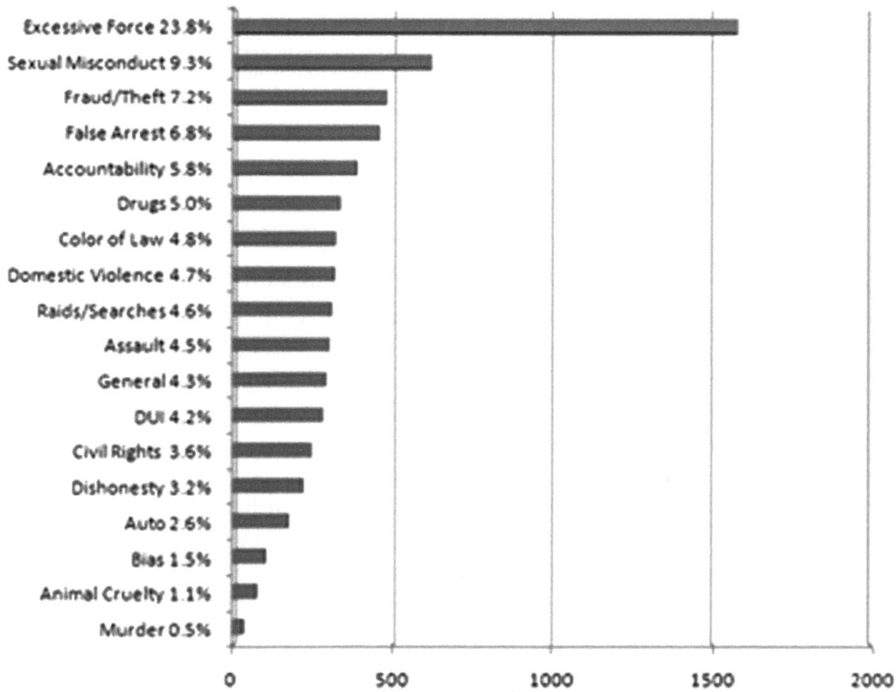

Fig. 11.1 National police misconduct reporting project, 2010

Theory of Police Integrity and Policing in the United States

This chapter relies on the definition of integrity, the theory of police integrity, and the accompanied methodological approach developed by Klockars and colleagues (see, e.g., Klockars and Kutnjak Ivković 2004; Klockars et al. 1997; Klockars et al. 2004a). Police integrity is defined as "the normative inclination among police to resist temptations to abuse the rights and privileges of their occupation" (Klockars et al. 1997). It assumes that police officers are able to resist *various* forms of temptations, including corruption, use of excessive force, and other forms of abuse the rights and privileges to which policing as an occupation exposes them (Klockars et al. 2006). Police integrity could vary across different forms of misconduct (e.g., police corruption, use of excessive force), as well as different levels of seriousness within the same form of misconduct (e.g., within police corruption, acceptance of gratuities v. theft from a crime scene). Consequently, the related methodological approach incorporates hypothetical scenarios describing not only a variety of forms of police misconduct, but also examples of different levels of seriousness within the same form.

The organizational theory of police integrity (see, e.g., Klockars and Kutnjak Ivković 2004; Klockars et al. 1997, 2000), the theoretical organizational theme in this chapter, rests on four dimensions: quality of official rules, quality of the agency's own internal control of misconduct, curtailing the code of silence, and the influence of the larger environment. This chapter explores each of these dimensions as they apply to a number of police organizations surveyed by the authors in the period from 2013 to 2014 in the United States.

Organizational Rules

The first dimension of the theory argues that the quality of organizational rules and the way these rules are made, communicated, and understood by the police are both critical for the high levels of police integrity (Klockars and Kutnjak Ivković 2004, p. 1.4). The theory predicts that police agencies of high integrity will not only have organizational rules explicitly prohibiting police misconduct, but also teach these rules effectively and enforce them when rule-violating behavior occurs. At the same time, police officers in such agencies should know the organizational rules and also support them. The content of the rules, particularly what behaviors are explicitly prohibited by the rules and the degree to which the rules are enforced, could vary drastically across agencies. This should especially be the case for less serious forms of misconduct such as the acceptance of free gifts and verbal abuse.

Relevant legal rules governing police conduct are made at the federal, state, and local levels. Appropriate conduct of police officers in the United States is regulated by federal and state criminal and civil statutes (e.g., Title 18 of the U.S. Code, Chap. 11, Sect. 201, 1999; Title 18 of the U.S. Code, Sect. 872, 1999; Title 18 of the U.S. Code, Sect. 242, 1999). Federal codes directly prohibit a number of different types of police misconduct, from bribery (Title 18 of the U.S. Code, Chap. 11, Sect. 201, 1999) and extortion (Title 18 of the U.S. Code, Sect. 872, 1999), to the deprivation of civil rights (Title 18 of the U.S. Code, Sect. 242, 1999).

The Supreme Court has been instrumental in testing the constitutionality of various legal rules, determining their application on specific cases, and delineating acceptable from unacceptable police conduct. One of the most difficult issues has been defining the legal standard to be used to evaluate cases involving the use of (excessive) force. In *Graham v. Connor* (490 U.S. 386 (1989)), the Supreme Court argued that the decision about whether the police officer used excessive force in the specific case should be based on the standard for the specific right that has been violated. In addition, the Supreme Court has been active in regulating the use of deadly force, the most severe type of force. In *Tennessee v. Garner* (471 U.S. 1 (1985)), the Supreme Court declared the old fleeing-felon rule (which authorized police officers to use "all the means necessary to effect an arrest") as unconstitutional and established a stricter standard. In particular, police officers are authorized to use deadly force *only* in the cases in which the police officer has a probable cause to believe that the citizen presents "a significant threat of death or serious physical injury to the officer or others." Since 1985, the use of deadly force that does not fulfill all of the requirements established by the Supreme Court should be viewed as the use of excessive force.

The Supreme Court also made a number of decisions addressing police violations of the Fourth Amendment right to be free from unreasonable searches and seizures. In *Mapp v. Ohio* (367 U.S. 643 (1961)), the Supreme Court imposed direct negative consequences on the police searches and seizures in violation of the Fourth Amendment, banned the use of illegally seized evidence in state criminal cases, and established the so-called "exclusionary rule." Empirical studies conducted shortly after the decision showed mixed results about the effect of this rule on police conduct (e.g., Canon 1974; Oaks 1970; Skolnick 1966), but the more recent studies (e.g., Cannon 1991; Orfield 1987) suggested stronger deterrent effects on police officer conduct.

Furthermore, the Supreme Court made key decisions involving the police misconduct involving violations of the Fifth Amendment rights. In one of the most famous decisions, *Miranda v. Arizona* (372 U.S. 436 (1966)), the Supreme Court declared that a suspect's confession obtained during custodial police interrogation constitutes a violation of the Fifth Amendment right against self-incrimination, unless the police provided specific warnings to the persons that they have the right to remain silent, that anything they say could be used against them, and that they have the right to counsel. At the time the decision was made, police officers rarely gave Miranda warnings (Black and Reiss 1967). However, more recent studies (Leo 1998; Leo and Thomas 1998) show that the Miranda warnings have become a norm.

The decentralized nature of American policing implies that each police agency also makes its own internal official rules that regulate the work of police officers employed by the agency. Municipal and state agencies use their official rules to regulate police officer conduct and prohibit inappropriate conduct such as the acceptance of bribes, gifts, gratuities, rewards (see, e.g., National Research Council 2004; Walker and Katz 2013). In the 2000s, more than 95 % of local police agencies have written policies covering the code of conduct and appearance, use of lethal force, and use of non-lethal force (Reaves 2010). However, with around 18,000 police agencies regulating the work of their employees, the content of the rules and their extent vary greatly across police agencies. On the one hand, there are police agencies that barely have written rules, while, on the other hand, there are others that have standard operating procedure manuals several hundred pages long (e.g., Barker and Wells 1982).

The effectiveness of the internal agency regulation in controlling police misconduct varied across different forms. Administrative rules have been used successfully to control several different aspects of police work: use of deadly force, high-speed pursuits, and domestic violence. Before the Supreme Court decided *Tennessee v. Garner* (471 U.S. 1 (1985)), individual police agencies started regulating the use of deadly force more stringently. Results of several empirical studies (e.g., Fyfe 1979; Geller and Scott 1992) reported that the frequency of the use of deadly force decreased after the introduction of the more restrictive internal official policy. In addition, the launch of more restrictive high-speed pursuit internal rules in a police agency resulted in the decline of high-speed pursuits (e.g., Alpert 1997). On the other hand, the introduction of stricter use of force rules was not as successfully supported by empirical research (e.g., National Research Council 2004, p. 285).

The reality is that the establishment of internal agency rules by itself does not guarantee that police misconduct will decrease. If the rules are not clear or are conflicting, police officers will have problems learning what behavior is appropriate (Kutnjak Ivković 2005). In one study, police officers from the police agencies characterized by widespread corruption tended to emphasize that the rules are not clear more often than police officers from less corrupt police agencies did (Fishman 1978). Intentionally or unintentionally, police administrators may allow the creation of unofficial rules in conflict with the official ones (e.g., Kutnjak Ivković 2005). Independent commissions investigating police misconduct in New York and Philadelphia (e.g., Knapp Commission 1972; Mollen Commission 1994; Pennsylvania Crime Commission 1974) uncovered numerous instances in which the top administrators tacitly allowed the development of the unofficial rules that were in conflict with the official rules prohibiting misconduct.

Lastly, the codes of ethics contain professional standards of appropriate conduct. The International Association of the Chiefs of Police developed the code of ethics. When police officers take an oath, they explicitly state that they will not engage in acts of corruption or bribery (Barker 2002, p. 4).

Police Detection and Investigation of Police Misconduct

The second dimension of the theory emphasizes the police agency's own methods of detection, investigation, and discipline of rule violations (Klockars and Kutnjak Ivković 2004; Klockars et al. 1997, 2001). These activities could be very heterogeneous, from the more reactive activities, such as investigations of corrupt behavior and discipline of corrupt police officers, to the more proactive activities, such as education in ethics, integrity testing, and proactive investigations. The theory stipulates that there should be a positive correlation between the existence and use of a sophisticated system of corruption prevention and control, and the level of integrity prevailing in the agency.

As a consequence of the 1967 *Garrity* ruling (*Garrity v. New Jersey*, 385 U.S. 483 (1967), an investigation of potential cases of police misconduct is separated into two: an administrative investigation (run by the internal affairs office) and a criminal investigation (run by the detectives in the detective unit). The Supreme Court decided that, while the full set of constitutional rights applies in the criminal investigation, these constitutional rights to not apply in administrative investigations. In other words, the accused police officer has to answer the questions truthfully and may not claim the Fifth Amendment rights in an administrative investigation.

A typical administrative or internal process includes multiple steps: the receipt of complaints, investigation, and decision-making. Depending on the police agency size, available resources, the number of complaints received annually, and the overall public service demands, the agency administrative control could be performed by a range of organizational structures, (e.g., Carter 1994, p. 361). In the 2000s, the majority of state police agencies (84 %) and local police agencies (79 %) have permanent internal affairs offices (Reaves and Hickman 2004, p. 66).

While the work performed by the internal affairs offices could be either proactive (e.g., integrity testing; Baueris 1997; Giulianni and Bratton 1995) or reactive (e.g., investigations), the reality is that it is mostly reactive in nature (e.g., Kutnjak Ivković 2005). Reactive investigations can start with the report filed by a supervisor or a complaint submitted by a citizen or a fellow police officer. Typically, however, a reactive investigation starts with a citizen filing a complaint. How often citizens complain seems to vary substantially. In 1991, Pate and Hamilton described the complaint rates across the six largest U.S. cities (p. 144) and found that they vary from 5.5 per 100 sworn officers in Philadelphia to 36.9 per 100 sworn officers in Houston. Pate and Fridell (1993) included not only municipal, but also other types of police agencies in their study. They found that municipal agencies have the highest use of force complaint rates; the complaint rates per 1000 police officers were 16 for state agencies, 21 for sheriff's departments, 34 for county agencies, and 48 for municipal agencies.

After the complaint is submitted, the official investigation will be opened. The investigators will interview witnesses, the victims, and the accused police officer, collect physical evidence, and examine the official records (Carter 1994). After the investigation has been completed, the case file will be sent to the decision-making body. Typically, the decision will be made either through an administrative review conducted the police officer's chain of command or through a disciplinary hearing by the administrative board (Carter 1994).

The decision-maker may reach several possible decisions (i.e., not sustained, exonerated), but only the decision that the complaint has been sustained (i.e., there is sufficient evidence to prove that the police officer engaged in the rule-violating behavior) may yield any discipline for the police officer. The severity of the discipline depends on several factors, including the seriousness of misconduct, officer prior discipline history, as well as mitigating and aggravating circumstances. The frequency with which police agencies sustain complaints is low; studies showed that the rate is somewhere between 0 and 25 % (e.g., Hickman 2006, p. 4; Klockars et al. 2006; Pate and Fridell 1993, p. 42; Perez 1994). However, because of the agency differences in complaint rates, methods of complaint filing, and effectiveness of investigations, scholars have warned about the difficulty of cross-agency comparisons (e.g., Klockars et al. 2006; Pate and Hamilton 1991).

Numerous examples reported in the literature (e.g., Christopher Commission 1991; Knapp Commission 1972; Mollen Commission 1994; Pennsylvania Crime Commission 1974) suggest that police agencies may be reluctant to accept complaints, investigate police (mis)conduct, and discipline police officers. The independent commission reports (e.g., Christopher Commission 1991; Knapp Commission 1972; Mollen Commission 1994; Pennsylvania Crime Commission 1974) documented instances in which police agencies did not investigate police misconduct, ignored relevant information, and actively hid the complaints. The reality seems to be that the internal systems of control may be more likely to malfunction in the police agencies what would need them the most, such as agencies characterized by widespread police misconduct (Kutnjak Ivković 2014). Complaint rates and rates of sustained complaints would be gross underestimates of the extent and nature of police misconduct in such agencies (e.g., Christopher Commission 1991; Knapp Commission 1972; Mollen Commission 1994; Pennsylvania Crime Commission 1974).

The *criminal* investigation typically would be performed either by the detectives from the same police agency or by the police officers from another agency. The investigation would start after the detectives had learned about a potential violation of the federal or state criminal laws. There is no nationwide statistics on the overall number of criminal investigations into police violations of criminal laws or the number of police officers found guilty and convicted across U.S. courtrooms. The heterogeneity of the criminal laws across the country complicates matters further.

Studies suggest that the prosecution and conviction rates for the cases with the use of excessive force are low (e.g., Adams 1999; Cheh 1995, p. 241; Human Rights Watch 1998). Similarly, the prosecution and the conviction rates for corruption cases in both federal and state courtrooms tend to be low (e.g., Kutnjak Ivković 2005). However, independent commission findings clearly show that low conviction rates should not be interpreted automatically to indicate that the actual rates of police officer criminal behavior are low. At the time when the independent commission reports showed that corruption was widespread throughout the New York Police Department and the Philadelphia Police Department (e.g., Knapp Commission 1972; Pennsylvania Crime Commission 1974), there were very few prosecutions and convictions of police officers. In the two police agencies employing thousands of police officers and in which independent commissions found corruption to be widespread, there were fewer than 50 police officers who were prosecuted and convicted for corruption annually (Knapp Commission 1972; Pennsylvania Crime Commission 1974).

One of the most recent additions to the arsenal of detection and investigation of police misconduct in the U.S. police agencies includes the early warning systems, one of the best practices included in "Principles for Promoting Police Integrity" (U.S. Department of Justice 2001). The underlying idea is to identify potential problem officers—those who generate an unusually large number of complaints—and try to intervene before they become problem officers and engage in police misconduct. Although U.S. Commission on Civil Rights (1981) recommended their introduction in 1981, it took over a decade for the early warning systems to gain nationwide acceptance. A nationwide survey of municipal police agencies conducted in the late 1990s (Walker et al. 2000) uncovered that about one third of the police agencies have already established early warning systems in their agencies or are in the process of developing it. A number of decrees between the U.S. Department of Justice and individual police agencies (Walker and Katz 2008, p. 489) further increased the number of agencies with the early warning systems. Scarce research on the topic suggest that the use of early warning systems results in the reduction in the number of citizen complaints and the use of force reports (e.g., Walker et al. 2000; Vera Institute of Justice 2002).

Curtailing the Code of Silence

The third dimension of the police integrity theory focuses on the code of silence and the efforts that the police agency is making in curtailing it. Klockars and Kutnjak Ivković (2004) argue that curtailing the code of silence is critical for agencies of integrity. According to the theory, compared to the agencies of high integrity, agencies of low integrity would have strong codes of silence in which police officers would be more likely to tolerate police misconduct without reporting it and supervisors would be more reluctant to investigate police misconduct and discipline police officers who engaged in it.

The code of silence in the U.S. police agencies has been studied since the 1950s. Studying police officers in a Midwest police agencies in the 1950s, Westley (1970, p. viii) found a very strong code of silence; he reported that three quarters of police officers would not report a fellow police officer who took money from a citizen arrested for drunkenness. Many independent commissions also uncovered the existence of the strong code of silence in the police agencies which were investigated (e.g., Christopher Commission 1991; Knapp Commission 1972; Mollen Commission 1994; Pennsylvania Crime Commission 1974). Bernard Cawley, a corrupt police officer in New York, testified before the Mollen Commission (1994) investigating the nature and extent of police corruption in the NYPD. When asked whether he was afraid that any of the fellow police officers might report him for his corrupt behavior, Calwey flatly denied and explained why (Mollen Commission 1994, p. 53),

> Because it was the Blue Wall of Silence. Cops don't tell on cops. And if they did tell on them, just say if a cop decided to tell on me, his career's ruined. He's going to be labeled as a rat. So if he's got 15 more years to go on the job, he's going to be miserable because it follows you wherever you go.

In the 2000 National Institute of Justice nationwide survey of police officers (Weisburd et al. 2000), the majority believed that it was not unusual for the police officers to tolerate police misconduct without reporting it (Weisburd et al. 2000) and over 60 % agreed that police officers do not always report serious violations of criminal law committed by their fellow officers. At the same time, more than three quarters of police officers stated that they do not accept the code of silence. Furthermore, about one quarter thought that whistle-blowing is not worth it and more than two-thirds agreed that police officers who do report incidents of misconduct will likely encounter a "cold shoulder" by fellow officers (Weisburd et al. 2000, p. 3).

It seems that "an atmosphere in which the dishonest officer fears the honest one, and not the other way round," as Frank Serpico, the most famous whistle-blower in the history of the U.S. policing, had hoped (Knapp Commission 1972, p. 51), is still not within the reach of police agencies plagued by excessive police misconduct. In fact, the Mollen Commission (1994, p. 53) reported that the code seems to be the strongest in the precincts in which the corruption was the most pervasive:

> The pervasiveness of the code of silence is itself alarming. But what we found particularly troubling is that it often appears to be strongest where corruption is most frequent. This is because the loyalty ethic is particularly powerful in crime-ridden precincts where officers most depend upon each other for their safety every day-and where fear and alienation from the community are most rampant. Thus, the code of silence influences honest police officers in the very precincts where their assistance is needed most.

Klockars and colleagues used the first questionnaire, focusing primarily on examples of police corruption, to survey 3250 police officers from 30 U.S. agencies (Klockars et al. 2000, p. 6). The survey revealed that the code of silence was indeed present among our respondents. However, the code did not cover all types of police corruption equally; "the majority would not report a police colleague who had engaged in behavior described in the four scenarios considered the least serious. At the same time, a majority indicated that they would report a fellow police officer who had engaged in behavior they deemed to be at an intermediate or high level of seriousness" (Klockars et al. 2000, p. 6).

The subsequent cross-agency analysis revealed substantial differences in the contours of the code of silence (Klockars et al. 2000, p. 6). To illustrate the size and nature of differences in the code of silence among the agencies in the sample, Klockars and colleagues emphasized the differences in the codes using the data from two agencies:

> The most systematic and dramatic differences between Agencies 2 and 23, however, is evident in their attitudes toward The Code of Silence. In both agencies, few officers said that they or their police colleagues would report any of the least serious types of corrupt behavior (Cases 1, 2, 4, and 8). Officers from Agency 2 reported that they and their colleagues would report the behavior described in the seven other cases. In Agency 23, however, there was *no* case that the majority of officers indicated they would report. In sum, while The Code is under control in Agency 2, it remains a powerful influence in Agency 23, providing an environment in which corrupt behavior can flourish.

Klockars et al. (2006) also used the second survey to explore the contours of the code of silence in three police agencies of high integrity. A comparison across the three agencies showed that, despite the fact that all three agencies were classified as agencies of high integrity, police officers in one agency were substantially more likely to adhere to the code of silence than police officers in the other two agencies (Klockars et al. 2006, p. 149). Finally, Kutnjak Ivković et al. (2013) found that the code of silence in "Rainless West" police agency was strongly negatively related to the perceptions of seriousness. Furthermore, the code in this new agency was similar to the codes of silence in the three agencies of integrity (Kutnjak Ivković et al. 2013).

Influence of Social and Political Environment

The fourth dimension of the police integrity theory (Klockars and Kutnjak Ivković 2004) connects police agencies with the society at large. It argues that police agencies are directly affected by the social, economic, and political environments. Police agencies in societies highly tolerant of unethical behavior of public servants should have lower levels of integrity than police agencies operating in societies highly intolerant of unethical behavior of any kind. In a larger environment that supports integrity across the board, police agencies are more likely to set high expectations regarding police integrity as well.

In societies as large and diverse as American, we could expect variation across communities and police agencies which are serving them. Indeed, some police agencies, such as Milwaukee and Kansas City, have long traditions of minimal corruption. Other police agencies in the United States, such as New Orleans, Key West, and Chicago, have almost uninterrupted traditions of police corruption (Klockars and Kutnjak Ivković 2004, p. 1.5).

Several scholars documented the turbulent history of policing in Chicago. Lindberg (2008, p. xviii) covered the period from the 1855 to 1960 and found that, "[f]or 100 years, the evils of the system were endemic: graft, spoils, and political treachery at the highest levels." After analyzing 5 decades of newspaper reports about police misconduct in Chicago (from 1960 until 2013), Hagedorn and colleagues (2013, p. 1) concluded that, "Chicago has a checkered history of police scandals and an embarrassingly long list of police officers who have crossed the line to engage in brutality, corruption and criminal activity." The authors summarized their major findings (Hagerdorn et al. 2013, p. 1):

> First, corruption has long persisted within the CPD and continues to be a serious problem... Second, police officers often resist reporting crimes and misconduct committed by fellow officers. The 'blue code of silence,' while difficult to prove, is an integral part of the department's culture and it exacerbates the corruption problems.
> Third, over time a large portion of police corruption has shifted from policemen aiding and abetting mobsters and organized crime to officers involved in drug dealers and street gangs. Fourth, internal and external sources of authority, including police superintendents and Mayors, have up to now failed to provide adequate anti-corruption oversight and leadership.

Finally, some cities, such as New York and Philadelphia, have experienced cycles of scandal and reform (Klockars and Kutnjak Ivković 2004, p. 1.5). For over a century, New York—the largest and the oldest police agency in the country—has had "the history of police corruption investigations in New York has run in 20-years cycles of scandal, reform, backslide, and fresh scandal" (Mollen Commission 1994, Exhibit 2, p. 2). The 20-year cycles include the Lexow Committee Report (1895), the Curran Committee Report (1913), the Seabury Investigation Report (1932), the Helfand Investigation Report (1955), the Knapp Commission Report (1972), and the Mollen Commission Report (1994). Chin (1997, p. xvii) argued that these reports illuminate the changes and similarities in police behavior over time:

> Reading the reports is sobering. Anyone with even a passing familiarity with big city criminal justice knows that the system rarely works with absolute perfection. However, these reports describe problems far beyond occasional peccadillos. They reveal persistent, serious criminal misconduct by police officers of all ranks, as well as an apparent indifference by the department about whether its officers obey the law. While details change, the problems remain over time.

One of the consistent themes across the reports was the existence of the code of silence. The adherence to the code was visible from the time commissions were established; their appointments were typically followed by lawsuits challenging their existence (Chin 1997, p. xxvii). The underlying rationale is that the outsiders do not have the right to interfere in police business. This would continue with honest police officers being unwilling to talk about or report misconduct committed by their fellow officers (Chin 1997).

Methodology

Questionnaire

During 2013–2014, we used the second version of the questionnaire to measure the contours of police integrity among officers from 11 diverse police agencies located in the Midwest and East Coast of the United States. The survey's questionnaire is built around 11 scenarios covering a variety of forms of police misconduct, including police corruption, use of excessive force, planting of evidence, and failure to execute an arrest warrant.

Upon reading description of each hypothetical case, the respondents answered seven questions designed to measure the officers' personal views, as well as their assessments of their colleagues' views, regarding the case. In particular, the respondents were asked to provide assessments of scenario seriousness, the anticipated and appropriate disciplinary action, and willingness to report misconduct. At the end of the questionnaire, the respondents were asked to answer a few demographic questions. To obfuscate identification of individual police officers taking part in the survey, and thus entice participation in it, these demographic questions have been kept at a minimum. Finally, the very last two questions asked the respondents to assess whether other police officers in their agency would have provided truthful answers and whether they had done so themselves. We used the response to the latter question as a screen, eliminating from further analyses the respondents who had stated openly that their answers were not truthful.

The Sample

With 17,985 independent police organizations operating in the U.S.A. (BJS 2011), it is elusive to measure police integrity across the entire population of these organizations. Moreover, in light of their heterogeneity, an almost equally challenging undertaking would be to collect data from a representative sample of these organizations. Instead, researchers have relied on a realistic approach—convenience samples composed of a range of police agencies. The 11 police agencies surveyed in this study constitute such a convenience sample (Table 11.1). The sample consists of a diverse range of police departments, with both large and small municipal agencies and sheriff's departments. A Bureau of Justice Statistics (2011) survey of local police agencies suggests that the 11 agencies taking part in the study generally reflect the range of law enforcement officers working in large, medium, and small cities in the U.S.A.

In each agency, the police chief or his designee emailed all sworn police officers an invitation to participate in the study; the email message also included our cover letter describing the study, informing the respondents that their participation is voluntary and that they can withdraw from the study at any point, and enlisting potential risks and benefits from participation in the study. The email message also contained the link to the Survey Monkey location and a password (each agency received a separate link and password). When potential respondents followed the provided link to Survey Monkey, they first saw our welcoming letter, containing all the elements of the consent form. About 2–3 weeks after the initial email, the police chief or his designee emailed all police officers again, reminding them to compete the survey if they choose to do so.

Table 11.1 Sample distribution

Agency's jurisdiction size	Number of agencies	Total sworn officers	Respondents	Percent responding (%)
Very large (>500+ sworn officers)	1	726	123	16.9
Large (201–500 sworn officers)	1	230	164	71.3
Medium (76–200 sworn officers)	4	664	315	47.4
Small (25–75 sworn officers)	2	128	46	35.9
Very small (<25 sworn officers)	3	28	16	57.1
All agencies	11	1776	664	37.4

Our overall response rate for the 11 police agencies was 37.4 % (see Table 11.1),[1] consistent with what the literature suggests for one-time web surveys (e.g., Shih and Fan 2008). However, the response rates were not uniform across the agencies. The response rate was substantially lower in one police agency serving a large city than in ten police agencies serving smaller communities (Table 11.1).

Most of those participating in the study were line officers (72.6 %), primarily assigned to patrol functions (55.2 %). At the same time, about one in sixth was a detective (16.5 %). The respondents from the 11 agencies were quite experienced; the overwhelming majority of our respondents have been police officers for 10 years or longer (Table 11.2); almost one half have been police officers for 15 years or longer (Table 11.2).

The last question in the questionnaire asks respondents whether they and their fellow police officers responded honestly while filling out the questionnaire. The overwhelming majority (83 %) thought that their fellow officers would provide truthful answers. This percentage corresponds very closely to the percentage of police officers in our earlier survey of police officers in three U.S. agencies (84 %; Klockars et al. 2006, p. 20).

Ten officers (1.5 % of the sample) reported that they personally had not answered honestly, so we excluded their responses from the further analyses. The percentage of officers who indicated that they had lied while filling out the questionnaire was comparable to, perhaps somewhat lower than, the percentage embedded in previous samples of U.S. metropolitan agencies such as Klockars and colleagues (2006) and Kutnjak Ivković and colleagues (2013); found that 2.2–2.6 % of officers in four large metropolitan police forces had indicated not honestly answering the survey questions.

[1] Web-based surveys traditionally have lower response rates than the surveys which are mailed, emailed, faxed, or phoned (e.g., Manfreda et al. 2008). In their comparison of survey modes, Shih and Fan (2008) found that the average web-based survey had a response rate of 34 %.

Table 11.2 Respondents demographic characteristics

	Number of respondents	Percent of respondents (%)
Supervisory role		
Non-supervisors	445	72.6
Supervisors	168	27.4
Length of service (current agency)		
Up to 5 years	91	14.6
6–10 years	113	12.3
11–15 years	298	32.0
16–20 years	366	39.5
Over 20 years	59	6.4
Type of assignment		
Patrol	314	55.2
Detective/investigation	94	16.5
Community policing officer	21	3.7
Special (vice, juvenile, etc.)	74	13.0
Administrative	66	11.6

Results

Perceptions of Misconduct Seriousness

After reviewing each scenario, the respondents were asked to report their evaluation of its seriousness. They could select one answer from a five-point Likert scale, ranging from "not at all serious" (1) to "very serious" (5). The results, shown in Table 11.3, indicate that the respondents viewed each of these violations of their agency's rules as serious. Specifically, the mean assessment of seriousness for each of the 11 scenarios was greater than the midpoint (3) of the scale; in 8 scenarios, the mean was well above 4.0 (Table 11.3).

The degree to which the officers considered the scenarios serious, though high on average, varied greatly across the scenarios. Respondents evaluated three behaviors (scenario 1: free meals, gifts from merchants; scenario 7: verbal abuse of motorist; and scenario 8: cover-up of police DUI accident) as the least serious forms of police misconduct covered by the questionnaire. The acceptance of gratuities, described in scenario 1 (free meals, gifts from merchants) is traditionally viewed as the least serious form of corruption and, to some extent, the beginning of the "slippery slope" of corruption. In Roebuck and Barker's typology of police corruption (1974, p. 429), the abuse of authority—in this instance, the acceptance of gratuities—is viewed to have the strongest support from the group, rational-

Table 11.3 Police officer perceptions of seriousness and violations of rules

Scenario number and description	Own seriousness		Others' seriousness		Mean differen ce (own-others)	Paired *t*-test	Violation of rules[a]			
	Mean	Rank	Mean	Rank			Yes (%)	No (%)	Not sure (%)	Rank (%)
Scenario 1: free meals, gifts from merchants	3.16	1	2.77	1	0.61	13.17***	75.9	12.6	11.4	1
Scenario 2: faiurel to arrest friend with warrant	4.35	5	4.16	7	0.19	9.13***	86.8	4.3	8.8	5
Scenario 3: theft of knife from crime scene	4.97	11	4.88	11	0.09	6.80***	99.4	0.2	0.5	11
Scenario 4: unjustifiable use of deadly force	4.84	9	4.81	10	0.03	3.02**	88.2	2.6	9.2	6
Scenario 5: supervisor offers holiday for errands	4.24	4	3.97	6	0.27	10.44***	81.4	6.1	12.4	3
Scenario 6: officer strikes prisoner	4.40	6	4.17	8	0.23	9.54***	97.0	0.8	2.2	9
Scenario 7: verbal abuse of motorist	3.41	2	3.44	2	0.03	8.10***	86.7	4.8	8.5	4
Scenario 8: cover-up of police DUI accident	3.70	3	3.71	3	0.01	7.87***	78.4	6.1	15.6	2
Scenario 9: auto body shop 5 % kickback	4.64	8	3.86	5	0.81	9.60***	94.3	2.3	3.4	7
Scenario 10: false report of drug possession	4.91	10	4.28	9	0.63	6.83***	98.2	0.5	1.3	10
Scenario 11: Sgt. fails to halt beating of child abuser	4.56	7	3.85	4	0.71	7.80***	94.5	0.6	4.9	8

*$p<0.05$; **$p<0.10$; ***$p<0.001$

[a] Answers "4" and "5" were grouped together as "yes," answers "1" and "2" as "no," and answer "3" as "not sure"

ized as an informal reward, and the official reaction varies from acceptance to mild disapproval. It is by no means surprising to see that the police officers in our sample evaluated this behavior as the least serious among all the cases of police corruption and other forms of police misconduct described in the questionnaire. The second least serious scenario addresses verbal abuse of a citizen (scenario 7: verbal abuse of motorist). Like the acceptance of gratuities, verbal abuse is the abuse of force at the lowest level of use of force continuum (if the continuum does not include the use of force situations which require a physical contact).

On the other hand, our respondents assessed three scenarios (scenario 3: theft of knife from crime scene; scenario 10: false report of drug possession; and scenario 4: unjustifiable use of deadly force) as the most serious forms of police misconduct. They each represent not only violations of agency rules, but criminal law as well. The 2013–2014 results are closely aligned with past studies of U.S. policing agencies. In a comparative analysis of four large metropolitan police departments, Kutnjak Ivković and colleagues (2013) find that those officers judged the same three scenarios as the least serious (though in a different order) and the same three scenarios as the most serious forms of misconduct (p. 158).

Theft from a crime scene (scenario 3) has also been included in the first version of the questionnaire (theft of a watch instead of theft of a knife). Current results closely resemble those from our earlier, police corruption study, wherein we found that, among all 11 examples of police corruption described in the first questionnaire, theft from a crime scene has been evaluated as *the* most serious of all (Klockars et al. 2000). Similarly, in our current study, theft from the crime scene is viewed as *the* most serious not only among all the police corruption scenarios, but also among all 11 scenarios included in the questionnaire (Table 11.3).

The second scenario that belongs to the most serious group is scenario 4, describing unjustifiable use of deadly force. Keeping in mind that deadly force is at the top of the use of force continuum, it is by no means surprising to see that the respondents evaluated the use of deadly force as the most serious scenario describing the use of force scenarios and, at the same time, one of the three most serious scenarios overall, regardless of the type of police misconduct (Table 11.3).

Five scenarios addressed acts of personal gain categorized generally as police corruption (scenario 1: free meals, gifts from merchants; scenario 3: theft of knife from crime scene; scenario 5: supervisor offers holiday for errands; scenario 8: cover-up of police DUI accident; and scenario 9: auto body shop 5 % kickback). The acceptance of gratuities (scenario 1: free meals, gifts from merchants) was evaluated as the least serious form and the theft from a crime scene (scenario 3: theft of knife from crime scene) as the most serious form of corruption. Two other traditional forms of corruption, kickback (scenario 9: auto body shop 5 % kickback) and internal corruption (scenario 5: supervisor offers holiday for errands) were also evaluated as serious, although not as serious as a committing the additional transgression of theft (scenario 3).

The questionnaire also includes four scenarios that involve officer misuse of force (scenario 4: unjustifiable use of deadly force; scenario 6: officer strikes prisoner; scenario 7: verbal abuse of motorist; scenario 11: Sgt. fails to halt beating of child abuser). The four scenarios used in the survey could be modeled along the use of force continuum traditionally used to model force in police training (NIJ 2009). The verbal coercion (scenario 7: verbal abuse of motorist) can be viewed as belonging to the start of the force continuum while the use of deadly force (scenario 4: unjustifiable use of deadly force) would occupy the end of the force continuum. The other two examples (scenario 6: officer strikes prisoner; scenario 11: Sgt. fails to halt beating of child abuser) are examples of the empty hand control, located in the middle of the continuum.

Our respondents' evaluations of seriousness closely match the use of force continuum: they evaluated the verbal abuse of citizens as the least serious (scenario 7: verbal abuse of motorist), misuse of the empty hand control as substantially more serious (scenario 6: officer strikes prisoner; scenario 11: Sgt. fails to halt beating of child abuser), and the misuse of deadly force as the most serious (scenario 4: unjustifiable use of deadly force). In line with the previous evaluations of U.S. agencies (Klockars et al. 2006; Kutnjak Ivković et al. 2013), the officers from the 11 agencies viewed the unjustifiable use of deadly force (scenario 4) as the most serious of the coercive misbehaviors but considered stealing a knife (scenario 3) and the false report of drug possession (scenario 10) as more serious overall.

The last two of the 11 scenarios (scenario 2: failure to arrest friend with warrant; scenario 10: false report of drug possession) address a failure to make an arrest and a falsification of the official report. Falsifying the official report (scenario 10: false report of drug possession) was evaluated as the second most serious scenario overall. On the other hand, the scenario addressing the failure to make an arrest (scenario 2: failure to arrest friend with warrant) was evaluated as much less serious.

Finally, the seriousness evaluations offer an opportunity to compare the difference between officers' own perceptions of seriousness and their prediction of how serious their fellow officers would view the same behavior. The results, shown in Table 11.3, indicate that in all 11 scenarios the differences between the two means were statistically significant. However, because of the large sample size (664 respondents) and the increased power of the test, differences of only 0.01 or 0.03 between the two means (scenario 7: verbal abuse of motorist; scenario 8: cover-up of police DUI accident; respectively, Table 11.3) were statistically significant.

As a rule of thumb, researchers using the police integrity survey focus on differences of substantive importance—those differences of more than 0.50 between the mean responses to a paired set of questions.[2] Four scenarios from this survey (scenario 1: free meals, gifts from merchants; scenario 9: auto body shop five percent kickback; scenario 10: false report of drug possession; and scenario 11: Sgt. fails to halt beating of child abuser) had differences between the means of greater than 0.50 and, thus, should be considered as having substantial differences. A com-

[2] Klockars and colleagues (2004, p. 26) "employed a rule of thumb which was to regard mean differences of less than 0.5 as not meaningful even though a simple *t*-test establishes the difference as significant." With more than 650 completed questionnaires, nearly every mean response in this study differed from the mean responses to other questions by a statistically significant margin ($p<0.001$).

mon feature across the four scenarios is that police officers evaluated behavior described in the questionnaire to be more serious than they thought that their fellow police officers would have done.

Assessment of Rule Violations

As part of the evaluation of each scenario, the officers from the 11 agencies were asked whether the hypothetical cases violates the official rules. Specifically, the respondents were asked, "Would this behavior be regarded as a violation of official policy in your agency?" The officers were given a choice of five possible answers displayed across a uniformly-spaced spectrum line. On the extreme left, they could select 1 = "definitely not" on the extreme right 5 = "definitely yes" while the options for 2–4 were placed between the two extremes with 3 in the exact center of the answer continuum.

The portion of affirmative answers, shown in Table 11.3, demonstrates that most of the police officers from the 11 agencies correctly evaluated the described behaviors as violations of official rules. More than three fourths of the respondents (89.2 % on average across the 11 scenarios) selected either "4" or "5" on the questionnaire and, thus, affirmed that the behavior described in the scenarios violated the agency's rules. However, despite the overall high percentage of police officers who correctly recognized the described behavior as rule-violating, the percentages of respondents who viewed each scenario as a violation varied across the scenarios. The respondents were most likely to label as a violation of the rules a theft from a crime scene (scenario 3: theft of knife from crime scene), falsifying a drug report (scenario 10: false report of drug possession), and hitting a prisoner (scenario 6: officer strikes prisoner). The officers were least likely to rule as a violation the acceptance of gratuities (scenario 1: free meals, gifts from merchants), a failure to arrest a friend (scenario 2: failure to arrest friend with warrant), and a case of internal corruption (scenario 8: cover-up of police DUI accident).

Evaluations of whether the behavior violates the official rules were also strongly related to the respondents' evaluations of misconduct seriousness (Spearman's rho $=0.882$, $p<0.001$); the more serious the respondents evaluated the behavior, the more likely they were to say that it was the violation of the official rules. Also, the more likely they were to say that the behavior violates the official rules, the more likely they were to evaluate the behavior as serious.

The two scenarios in which fewer than 80 % of the respondents were confident that the scenario was a violation were from the three scenarios evaluated as less serious by the same officers (scenario 1: free meals, gifts from merchants; scenario 8: cover-up of police DUI accident). The third of the less seriously ranked behaviors (scenario 7: verbal abuse of motorist) was viewed by 86.7 % as a violation, which was nearly equal to the mean assessment for the 11 behaviors. The two scenarios with the greatest uncertainty (scenario 1: free meals, gifts from merchants; scenario 8: cover-up of police DUI accident) were also the two scenarios evaluated to be among the three least serious scenarios (Table 11.3). The acceptance of free meals and gifts, which could be classified as “corruption of authority” in Roebuck and Barker’s typology (1974, p. 429), is most likely to be accepted among the all forms of corruption. Furthermore, it is also a form that may result in the clash of official and unofficial rules in the agency; “[m]any police departments, though publicly disavowing this behavior, accept it as a system of informal rewards, particularly if the officers receiving the gratuities are otherwise acceptable to the department, and if the corruptors are respectable citizens” (Roebuck and Barker 1974, p. 429).

Although the overwhelming majority of respondents had no problems labeling the cover-up of police DUI (scenario 8) as rule-violating, this scenario had the second highest percentage of police officers who were not sure whether such behavior is a violation of the official rules. Although the scenario does not directly specify that the police officer has engaged in DUI, it implies that the police officer has driven the police car in to a ditch while intoxicated. Potentially, this indirect implication may be confusing for some respondents.

Perceptions of Appropriate and Expected Discipline

In addition to emphasizing the communication of official rules, the organizational theory of police integrity (Klockars et al. 2006) predicts that the disciplinary actions taken by an agency play a key role in shaping that department’s overall integrity levels. Accordingly, the respondents were asked to select the discipline appropriate for the behaviors described in the scenarios as well as to select the discipline they thought their agency would mete out in such cases.[3] The respondents were given six possible answers: “none” (no discipline), “verbal reprimand,” “written reprimand,” “suspension,” “demotion in rank,” and “dismissal.”

We first explored the respondents’ views of the appropriate discipline for the misbehaviors described in the questionnaire. We used four different approaches: modes, ranks, means, and percentages.[4] Regardless of the method we use to analyze the data, the results point in the same direction: the overwhelming majority of respondents approved of at least some discipline for all examples of police misconduct listed in the questionnaire and, in only a few highly selected cases, they thought that dismissal was the appropriate discipline (Table 11.4). The acceptance of gratuities (scenario 1: free meals, gifts from merchants) was evaluated to deserve the least serious discipline (i.e., the mean of 2.2 close to “verbal reprimand,” “verbal reprimand” as the mode, and about one out of five respondents selecting “no discipline”). On the other hand, theft from a crime scene (scenario 3: theft of knife from crime scene), the use of deadly force (scenario 4: unjustifiable use of

[3] The two questions were worded: “If an officer in your agency engaged in this behavior and was discovered doing so, what if any, discipline do you think SHOULD follow?” and “If an officer in your agency engaged in this behavior and was discovered doing so, what if any, discipline do you think WOULD follow?”

[4] The answers were reclassified the following way: “none” remained “none,” “dismissal” remained “dismissal,” and all the other disciplinary options (“verbal reprimand,” “written reprimand,” “suspension,” “demotion in rank”) were reclassified as “some discipline other than dismissal.”

Table 11.4 Views about appropriate discipline (should) and expected discipline (would)

Scenario number and description		Mode	Rank should	Rank would	Mean	None (%)	Discipline (%)	Dismiss (%)	Cramer's V (%)
Scenario 1: free meals, gifts from merchants	*Should*	Verbal	1		2.20	18.6	80.0	1.4	0.654***
	Would	Verbal		1	2.32	19.9	78.4	1.8	
Scenario 2: fail to arrest friend with warrant	*Should*	Written	2–4		3.41	4.9	85.4	9.7	0.682***
	Would	Written		2–4	3.35	6.0	84.0	10.0	
Scenario 3: theft of knife from crime scene	*Should*	Dismissal	9–11		5.44	0.5	25.7	73.8	0.616***
	Would	Dismissal		9–11	5.31	0.8	31.5	67.7	
Scenario 4: unjustifiable use of deadly force	*Should*	Dismissal	9–11		5.36	5.3	17.2	77.5	0.674***
	Would	Dismissal		9–11	5.43	4.3	17.0	78.7	
Scenario 5: supervisor offers holiday for errands	*Should*	Written	2–4		3.47	6.6	90.4	3.0	0.686***
	Would	Written		2–4	3.15	13.4	83.6	3.0	
Scenario 6: officer strikes prisoner	*Should*	Suspension	5–7		*3.84*	3.0	82.4	14.6	0.659***
	Would	Suspension		5–7	*3.15*	2.4	79.8	18.0	
Scenario 7: verbal abuse of motorist	*Should*	Written	2–4		2.59	8.3	90.9	0.8	0.641***
	Would	Written		2–4	2.85	4.5	94.1	1.4	
Scenario 8: cover-up of police DUI accident	*Should*	Suspension	5–7		3.12	16.4	75.2	8.4	0.611***
	Would	Suspension		5–7	3.49	9.1	79.2	11.7	
Scenario 9: auto body shop 5 % kickback	*Should*	Suspension	5–7		4.35	3.1	61.8	35.1	0.684***
	Would	Suspension		5–7	4.36	2.3	63.2	34.5	
Scenario 10: false report of drug possession	*Should*	Dismissal	9–11		5.21	0.7	35.4	63.9	0.647***
	Would	Dismissal		9–11	5.13	1.1	37.7	61.2	
Scenario 11: Sgt. fails to halt beating of child abuser	*Should*	Demotion	8		4.50	4.0	71.7	24.3	0.604***
	Would	Demotion		8	4.55	3.0	71.7	25.3	

*$p<0.05$; **$p<0.10$; ***$p<0.001$

deadly force), and falsifying the official report (scenario 10: false report of drug possession) deserved “dismissal” (i.e., the mean above 5, “dismissal” as the mode, and the majority of respondents selecting “dismissal” as the appropriate discipline; Table 11.4).

By comparing the respondents’ views on the appropriate discipline and their expectation of the agency’s actual response, the police integrity survey offers a gauge of whether the officers perceive the agency’s discipline as fair. The officers’ modal judgments on what they viewed as appropriate and what they expected the agency to choose to implement for a discipline did not differ for any of the scenarios (see Table 11.4). The Cramer’s V coefficients, calculated using the 6×6 matrix of potential pairs of categorical disciplinary responses, indicate a very strong association between the two judgments. Similarly, the correlation between the two rankings of modal values suggests a very strong correlation (Spearman’s rho $= 1.00$, $p < 0.001$). In the 1996 survey of the 30 U.S. police agencies, the two judgments also were closely associated (Klockars et al. 2004). The 2013–2014 survey further supports the conclusion that police officers generally do not view their agencies as out of line with their own views on appropriate discipline for misconduct.

The police integrity survey allows for a test of whether the officers’ evaluation of the seriousness of the misconduct influenced their advocacy and expectation of more severe discipline. In this study of 11 agencies, the officers’ assessments of both appropriate and expected discipline were closely related to their evaluations of scenario seriousness. Support for a strong positive relation was demonstrated by the Spearman’s rank correlation coefficient between modal appropriate discipline and the mean seriousness of the misconduct ($\rho = 0.898$, $p < 0.001$) and between modal expected discipline and the mean seriousness of the misconduct ($\rho = 0.898$, $p < 0.001$).

To further compare the respondents’ views on appropriate versus expected agency discipline, we compared the respondents’ mean responses (see Table 11.4). Generally, mean responses were in line with past police integrity surveys of U.S. agencies (see Klockars et al. 2006; Kutnjak Ivković et al. 2013) which found that most officers perceived the appropriate discipline to be slightly lighter than the discipline they expected their police agency would mete out. Nonetheless, the results of this survey have four exceptions (scenario 2: fail to arrest friend with warrant; scenario 3: theft of knife from crime scene; scenario 6: officer strikes prisoner; scenario 10: false report of drug possession) in which the officers expected agency discipline on average would be milder than they perceived as appropriate. Moreover, one of those cases (scenario 6: officer strikes prisoner) has a difference between mean responses that meets the Klockars and colleagues’ rule of thumb on meaningful differences between mean survey responses of 0.5 (2004, p. 26), with the respondents expecting that the discipline the agency would mete out would be less severe than it should have been (Table 11.4).

Willingness to Report Misconduct

The police integrity questionnaire offers a means to assess the extent and nature of the police code of silence. The blue wall of silence refers to the existence of an unwritten rule that police officers do not report on the misconduct of their colleagues (Kutnjak Ivković 2005). The respondents in the 11 agencies were asked whether they would report a fellow officer who engaged in the behavior described in the scenario.[5] They were asked to choose from a five-point Likert scale, ranging from "definitely not" to "definitely yes."

The results (Table 11.5) show, as expected, that the code of silence exists in the 11 surveyed agencies. However, our results illustrate the point that the code of silence does not protect all behaviors equally. We can conclude that, because the means are close to 3 and below the midpoint of our scale, the code is most likely to

Table 11.5 Police officer perceptions of willingness to report

Scenario numbers and description	Own willingness to report		Others' willingness to report		Mean difference (own-others)	*t*-test
	Mean	Rank	Mean	Rank		
Scenario 1: free meals, gifts from merchants	2.39	1	2.16	1	0.2	7.32***
Scenario 2: failure to arrest friend with warrant	3.61	4	3.32	4	0.29	9.11***
Scenario 3: theft of knife from crime scene	4.65	10	4.33	10	0.32	12.97***
Scenario 4: unjustifiable use of deadly force	4.79	11	4.70	11	0.09	5.90***
Scenario 5: supervisor offers holiday for errands	3.67	5	3.45	5	0.22	6.94***
Scenario 6: officer strikes prisoner	3.79	6	3.47	6	0.32	10.10***
Scenario 7: verbal abuse of motorist	2.83	2	2.56	2	0.27	7.86***
Scenario 8: cover-up of police DUI accident	3.07	3	2.87	3	0.20	6.24***
Scenario 9: auto body shop 5% kickback	4.15	8	3.83	7	0.32	10.70***
Scenario 10: false report of drug possession	4.59	9	4.26	9	0.33	11.66***
Scenario 11: Sgt. fails to halt beating of child abuser	4.12	7	3.85	8	0.27	9.40***

*$p<0.05$; **$p<0.10$; ***$p<0.001$

[5] The question was worded: "Do you think you would report a fellow police officer who engaged in this behavior?"

protect the acceptance of gratuities (scenario 1: free meals, gifts on beat), a verbal abuse of the citizen (scenario 7: verbal abuse of motorist), and a cover-up of police DUI (scenario 8: cover-up of police DUI accident). On the other hand, the means are all close to 5: our reporting side of the scale—for three scenarios. This indicates that the code of silence is least likely to protect the theft from a crime scene (scenario 3: theft of knife from crime scene), the use of deadly force (scenario 4: unjustifiable use of deadly force), and falsifying an official report (scenario 10: false report of drug possession; Table 11.5). The code is also less likely to protect a kickback (scenario 9: auto body shop five percent kickback) and the failure to stop beating an alleged child abuser (scenario 11: Sgt. fails to halt beating of child abuser).

The extent of the code of silence is strongly negatively related to the perceptions of seriousness (Spearman's correlation coefficient $=-0.964$, $p<0.001$). The more serious the officers evaluated the behavior, the less likely they were to say that they would protect it. For example, the mean evaluations for the three most serious scenarios (scenario 3: theft of knife from crime scene; scenario 4: unjustifiable use of deadly force; scenario 10: false report drug possession) from Table 11.3 are also the three scenarios ranked in Table 11.5 as the least likely to be tolerated by police officers. This finding is consistent with past studies on U.S. police integrity (Klockars, et al. 2006; Kutnjak Ivković, et al. 2013), suggesting that willingness to report misconduct is negatively related to the officers' perceptions that the behavior was serious.

Conclusion

Modern policing in the U.S.A. commenced more than a century ago. A gradual evolution, often divided into three distinct periods, has been complex and multifaceted. Political era, characterized with rampant corruption and abuse of citizens' human rights, was followed by the professional era. Although the policing profession has experienced some progress, there have been no significant advances of the ethical aspects of policing. The subsequent era of community policing transformation, marked by reforms and changes of paradigm, as well as recent emphasis on dealing with terrorism, still has not addressed integrity issues completely. Throughout history, there have been countless examples of police misconduct, many of which have been documented by independent commissions and illustrated in newspaper accounts. At the same time, despite the long history riddled with integrity challenges, empirical exploration of police integrity has not been extensive.

Our current study provides the first broad study of the contours of police integrity in the United States. The results indicate that police integrity is a complex phenomenon and that police officers do not treat all misconduct equally. On the one hand, the acceptance of free meals and gratuities, verbal abuse of citizens, and cover-up of police DUI accident have been evaluated as the least serious forms of misconduct featured in the questionnaire, requiring the most lenient discipline, and the most likely to be covered by the code of silence. On the other hand, theft from a crime scene, the unjustifiable use of deadly force, and the falsification of the official report have been evaluated as the most serious forms of misconduct in the questionnaire, requiring dismissal of the police officer, and lacking strong support by the code of silence.

That our respondents evaluated verbal abuse as the least serious form and the use of deadly force as one of the most serious forms of police misconduct is far from surprising. If the use of force continuum is regarded to include non-physical contact, verbal commands constitute the lowest end of the continuum, just above the police mere presence. On the other hand, the use of deadly force constitutes the other end of the continuum (NIJ 2009). Abusing verbal commands should not be viewed to be as serious and should not be disciplined as severely as abuses of the higher ends of the use of force continuum. Consistent with this ranking is the notion, manifested in our respondents' evaluations, that abusing the level of the use of force in the middle of the continuum, such as striking a person, should be viewed as less serious than abusing the deadly force, but, at the same time, more serious than abusing verbal commands. It appears that, explicitly or implicitly, the respondents in our sample adhered to the use of force continuum and made a connection between the seriousness of the act with its location on the use of force continuum. These findings are consistent with our results exploring police integrity in four police agencies (Kutnjak Ivković et al. 2013).

Our questionnaire also contains several scenarios describing police corruption, spanning a range of seriousness. Our respondents evaluated the acceptance of free meals and gratuities as the least serious form of corruption, followed by internal corruption and a kickback, culminating in the most serious form of corruption in the questionnaire—opportunistic theft. The policing literature typically views the acceptance of gratuities as the stepping stone toward more serious corruption, in itself tolerated by the police culture, seen as easily justifiable, and rarely severely disciplined by police agencies (Roebuck and Barker 1974). Empirical studies support this view. In an application of the police corruption questionnaire, Klockars et al. (2004) found that police officers from 30 U.S. agencies evaluated the acceptance of gratuities as one of the least serious forms of corruption. Similarly, in a comparative analysis of four large metropolitan police departments, Kutnjak Ivković and colleagues (2013, p. 158) reported that police officers from four large metropolitan police agencies also judged the acceptance of free meals as the least serious forms of corruption. On the other end of the spectrum, Roebuck and Barker (1974) characterized opportunistic theft as one of the most serious types of corrupt activities, typically triggering a negative reaction from the police agency. Consistent with our results regarding seriousness of opportunistic theft are findings from both Klockars et al. (2004) and Kutnjak Ivković et al. (2013).

Most of the respondents in our sample had no problems recognizing these behaviors as rule-violating. However, only about three quarters of the respondents were able to articulate that acceptance of free meals and gifts was a violation of official rules in the agency; one eighth of the respondents thought these behaviors not to be violations of official agency rules, and the remaining respondents were unsure.

This dispersion of opinion may be related to multiple factors. First, official rules may not be clear on whether the acceptance of gratuities is prohibited. A police agency may even have a general rule prohibiting the acceptance of gifts, but may not specify whether the prohibition applies to any gifts or only larger gifts. If the prohibition applies only to larger gifts, the cutoff may not be clear. Second, there may be a discrepancy between the official rules prohibiting acceptance of gratuities and the unofficial rules allowing it. Roebuck and Barker (1974, p. 429) elaborated on the police agencies' view of acceptance of gratuities as an integral part of the internal rewards systems. Third, the official rules may clearly prohibit acceptance of gratuities, but may be rarely enforced. Overall, the message sent by the police administration could be that official rules are not relevant and that they should not be followed. Consequently, it is quite plausible that some police officers may have been confused and conflicted as they evaluated acceptance of gratuities from our questionnaire.

Although the majority of the respondents recognized use of deadly force as rule-violating, about 10% of the respondents were unsure. This finding is particularly troubling because use of deadly force is not only a firing offense, but can also result in criminal punishment and civil judgment determining police liability. Still more troubling is that about 20% of our respondents did not think that a police officer who abused deadly force should be fired. Such views suggest the presence of integrity-challenged police officers whose knowledge of official rules and the consequences of their violations should be reinforced and who should be carefully monitored.

Our results also demonstrate that the code of silence exists in the surveyed police agencies. This finding is in agreement with the results of the 2000 National Institute of Justice nationwide survey police officers (Weisburd et al. 2000), indicating that police officers believed that it was not unusual for the police to adhere to the code of silence. Furthermore, our findings emphasize that the code does not protect all forms of misconduct equally. The code provides the strongest protection to the types of police misconduct evaluated as the least serious and the weakest protection to the types of police misconduct evaluated at the most serious. These results provide further evidence in support of Klockars and colleagues' (2000, p. 6) empirical finding of the negative relation between perceptions of misconduct seriousness and the code of silence.

Finally, we found that the respondents' views about misconduct seriousness were closely associated with their views about rule violations. They were also closely related to the severity of discipline and negatively related to their willingness to report. These findings are consistent with past studies on U.S. police integrity (Klockars et al. 2006; Kutnjak Ivković et al. 2013). Therefore, the analyses of our data showed that different measures of police integrity we use in the questionnaire—assessments of misconduct seriousness, views about expected and appropriate discipline, and willingness to report misconduct—measure the same underlying phenomenon. Despite the complexity of the task, we were able to capture the contours of the police integrity across a dozen of police agencies.

References

Adams, K. (1999). What we know about police use of force. *Use of force by police: Overview of national and local data*. Washington, DC: Office of Justice Programs.

Alpert, G. P. (1997). *Pursuit policies and training*. Washington, DC: Government Printing Office.

Barker, T. (2002). Ethnical police behavior. In K. Lersch (Ed.), *Police misconduct*. Upper Saddle River: Prentice Hall.

Barker, T., & Wells, R. O. (1982). Police administrator's attitudes toward definition and control of police deviance. *FBI Law Enforcement Bulletin, 51,* 8–16.

Baueris, V. (1997). New York Police Department: Preventing crime and corruption. http://www.icac.nsw.gov.au/frame_pub.htm. 10 Jan 2014.

Black, D., & Reiss, A. J. (1967). Patterns of behavior in citizen and police transactions. In Studies of crime and law enforcement in major metropolitan areas, field surveys III, Vol. 2. President's commission on law enforcement and the administration of justice. Washington, DC: U.S. Government Printing Office.

Bopp, W. J., & Schultz, D. O. (1972). *A short history of American law enforcement*. Springfield: Thomas.

Bureau of Justice Statistics (2011). Census of state and local law enforcement agencies, 2008. Washington, DC: U.S. Department of Justice. http://www.bjs.gov/content/pub/pdf/csllea08.pdf. Accessed 10 Jan 2015.

Canon, B. C. (1974). Is the exclusionary rule in failing health? Some new data and a plea against a precipitous conclusion. *Kentucky Law Journal, 62,* 681–730.

Canon, B. C. (1991). Courts and policy: Compliance, implementation, and impact. In J. B. Gates & C. A. Johnson (Eds.), *American courts: A critical assessment*. Washington, DC: Congressional Quarterly Press.

Carter, D. L. (1994). Police disciplinary procedures: A review of selected police departments. In T. Barker & D. L. Carter (Eds.), *Police deviance* (3rd ed.). Cincinnati: Anderson.

CATO Institute (2010). National police misconduct reporting project. http://www.policemisconduct.net/2010-q2-npmsrp-national-police-misconduct-statistical-report/. Accessed 10 Jan 2015.

Chaiken, J. M., Greenwood, P. W., & Petersilia, J. (1976). The criminal investigation process: A summary report. http://www.rand.org/content/dam/rand/pubs/papers/2006/P5628-1.pdf. Accessed 10 Jan 2015.

Cheh, M. M. (1995). Are law suits an answer to police brutality? In W. A. Geller & H. Toch (Eds.), *And justice for all*. Washington, DC: Police Executive Research Forum.

Chin, G. (1997). *New York City police corruption investigation commissions, 1894–1994*. Buffalo: William S. Hein & Co.

[Christopher Commission]. Independent Commission on the Los Angeles Police Department. 1991. Report of the independent commission on the Los Angeles Police Department. Los Angeles: Author.

Costello, A. E. (1972). *Our police protectors: A history of New York police*. Montclair: Patterson Smith.

Curran, C. (1913). Report of the special committee of the board of aldermen of the city of New York appointed August 5, 1912 to Investigate the police department. New York: Author.

Fishman, J. E. (1978). *Measuring police corruption*. New York: John Jay College of Criminal Justice.

Fyfe, J. J. (1979). Administrative interventions on police shooting discretion: An empirical examination. *Journal of Criminal Justice, 7,* 303–323.

Geller, W. A., & Scott, M. S. (1992). Deadly force: What we know: A practitioner's desk reference on police-involved shootings. Washington, DC: Police Executive Research Forum.

Giuliani, R. W., & Bratton, W. J. (1995). *Police Strategy No. 7: Rooting out corruption. Building organizational integrity in the New York Police Department*. New York: New York Police Department.

Hagedorn, J., Kmiecik, B., Simpson, D., Gradel, T. J., Zmuda, M. M., & Sterrett, D. (2013). Crime, corruption and cover-ups in the Chicago Police Department. Anti-Corruption Report Number 7. University of Illinois Chicago, Department of Political Science. http://www.uic.edu/depts/pols/ChicagoPolitics/policecorruption.pdf. Accessed 10 Jan 2015.

Helfand, J. (1955). Report of special investigation by the district attorney of kings county, and the December 1949 grand jury. New York: Author.

Hickman, M. J. (2006). Citizen complaints about police use of force. Washington, DC: Bureau of Justice Statistics. http://bjs.ojp.usdoj.gov/content/pub/pdf/ccpuf.pdf. Accessed 10 Jan 2015.

Human Rights Watch (1998). *Shielded from justice: Police brutality and accountability in the United States*. New York: Human Rights Watch.

Hunter, R. D., Mayhall, P. D., & Barker, T. (2000). *Police-community relations and the administration of justice*. Englewood Cliffs: Prentice Hall.

Kappeler, L., & Gaines, V. E. (2011). *Policing in America* (7th ed.). Cincinnati: Anderson.

Kelling, G. L., & Moore, M. H. (1988). The evolving strategy of policing. https://ncjrs.gov/pdffiles1/nij/114213.pdf. Accessed 10 Jan 2015

Kelling, G. L., Pate, T., Dieckman, D., & Brown, C. E. (1974). The Kansas City preventive patrol experiment. http://www.policefoundation.org/sites/g/files/g798246/f/Kelling%20et%20al.%20%281974%29%20%20THE%20KANSAS%20CITY%20PREVENTIVE%20PATROL%20EXPERIMENT.pdf. Accessed 10 Jan 2015.

Kerner Commission [National Advisory Commission on Civil Disorders]. (1968). Report of the National Advisory Commission on civil disorders. Washington, DC: Govt. Printing Office.

Ketcham, G. A. (1967). Municipal police reform, a comparative study of law enforcement in Cincinnati, Chicago, New Orleans, New York and St. Louis, 1844–1877. Ph.D. dissertation, University of Missouri.

Klockars, C. B., & Kutnjak Ivković, S. (2004). Measuring police integrity. In M. J. Hickman, A. R. Piquero, & J. R. Greene (Eds.), *Police integrity and ethics*. Belmont: Wadsworth.

Klockars, C. B., Kutnjak Ivković, S., Harver, W. E., & Haberfeld, M. R. (1997). The measurement of police integrity. Final Report Submitted to the U.S. Department of Justice, Office of Justice Programs, National Institute of Justice.

Klockars, C. B., Kutnjak Ivković, S., Harver, W. E., & Haberfeld, M. R. (2000). The measurement of police integrity. Research in brief. U.S. Department of Justice, Office of Justice Programs, National Institute of Justice. Washington, DC: Government Printing Office.

Klockars, C. B., Kutnjak Ivković, S., & Haberfeld, M. R. (Eds.). (2004a). Police integrity in the United States of America. In C. B. Klockars, S. Kutnjak Ivković, & M. R. Haberfeld (Eds.), *The contours of police integrity*. Thousand Oaks: Sage.

Klockars, C. B., Kutnjak Ivković, S., & Haberfeld, M. R. (Eds.). (2004b). The contours of police integrity. In C. B. Klockars, S. Kutnjak Ivković, & M. R. Haberfeld (Eds.)., *The contours of police integrity* (pp. 1–18). Thousand Oaks: Sage.

Klockars, C. B., Kutnjak Ivković, S., & Haberfeld, M. R. (2006). *Enhancing police integrity*. New York: Springer.

[Knapp Commission]. Commission to Investigate Allegations of Police Corruption and the City's Anti-Corruption Procedures. (1972). *Report on police corruption*. New York: G. Braziller.

Kutnjak Ivković, S. (2005). *Fallen blue knights*. New York: Oxford University Press.

Kutnjak Ivković, S. (2014). Police misconduct. In M. Reisig & R. Kane (Eds.), *Handbook on police and policing*. New York: Oxford University Press.

Kutnjak Ivković, S., Haberfeld, M., & Peacock, R. (2013). Rainless west: The integrity survey's role in agency accountability. *Police Quarterly, 16*(2), 148–176.

Lane, R. (1967). *Policing the city: Boston 1822–1885*. Cambridge: Harvard Univesity Press.

LEMAS. (2007). Local police departments. http://www.bjs.gov/content/pub/pdf/lpd07.pdf. Accessed 10 Jan 2015.

Leo, R. A. (1998). The impact of Miranda revisited. In R. A. Leo & G. C. Thomas (Eds.), *The Miranda debate: Law, justice, and policing*. Boston: Northeastern University Press.

Leo, R. A., & Thomas, G. C. (1998). *The Miranda debate: Law, justice, and policing*. Boston: Northeastern University Press.

Lexow, C. (1895). Report of the special committee appointed to investigate the police department of the city of New York. Albany: Author.
Lindberg, R. C. (2008). *To protect and to serve: Chicago politics and police corruption from the lager beer riot to the summerdale scandal, 1855–1960*. New York: Praeger.
Manfreda, L. K., Bosnjak, M., Berzelak, J., Haas, I., & Vehovar, V. (2008). Web surveys versus other survey modes: A meta-analysis comparing response rates. *International Journal of Market Research, 50*(1), 79–104.
[Mollen Commission] New York City Commission to Investigate Allegations of Police Corruption and the Anti-Corruption Procedures of the Police Department. (1994). Commission report. New York: Author.
Moore, M. H., & Kelling, G. L. (1985). To serve and protect: Learning from police history. In A. S. Blumberg & E. Niederhoffer. *The ambivalent force*. New York: Holt, Rinehart and Winston.
Morn, F. T. (1977). *Allan Pinkerton, private police influence on police development*. Montclair: Patterson Smith.
National Advisory Commission on Criminal Justice Standards and Goals. (1973). Reports of the National Advisory Commission on Criminal Justice Standards and Goals. Washington, DC: Govt. Printing Office.
National Advisory Commission on the Causes and Prevention of Violence. (1969). *To establish justice, to insure domestic tranquility*. Washington, DC: Govt. Printing Office.
National Institute of Justice (NIJ). (2009). The Use-of-Force Continuum. http://www.nij.gov/topics/law-enforcement/officer-safety/use-of-force/Pages/continuum.aspx. Accessed 20 Jan 2015.
National Research Council. (2004). Fairness and effectiveness in policing: The evidence. Committee to Review Research on Police Policy and Practices. Wesley Skogan and Kathleen Frydl, editors. Committee on Law and Justice, Division of Behavioral and Social Sciences and Education. Washington, DC: The National Academies Press.
Oaks, D. H. (1970). Studying the exclusionary rule in search and seizure. *University of Chicago School Law Review, 37,* 655–757.
Oliver, W. M. (1998). *Community-oriented policing: A systemic approach to policing*. Upper Saddle River: Prentice-Hall.
Orfield, M. W. Jr (1987). The exclusionary rule and deterrence: An empirical study of chicago narcotics officers. *University of Chicago Law School Review, 54,* 1016–1069.
Pate, A., & Fridell, L. (1993). *Police use of force: Official reports, citizen complaints, and legal consequences*. Washington, DC: Police Foundation.
Pate, A., & Hamilton, E. E. (1991). *The big six: Policing America's largest cities*. Washington, DC: Police Foundation.
Pennsylvania Crime Commission. (1974). Report on police corruption and the quality of law enforcement in Philadelphia. Saint Davids: Author.
Perez, D. W. (1994). *Common sense about police review*. Philadelphia: Temple University Press.
President's Commission on Campus Unrest. (1970). Report of the president's commission on campus unrest. Washington, DC: Govt. Printing Office.
President's Crime Commission [President's Commission on Law Enforcement and Administration of Justice] (1967). The challenge of crime in a free society. Washington, DC: Government Printing Office. www.ncjrs.gov/pdffiles1/nij/42.pdf. Accessed 10 Jan 2015.
Reaves, B. A. (2010). Local Police Departments. Washington, D.C.: Bureau of Justice Statistics. http://bjs.ojp.usdoj.gov/content/pub/pdf/lpd07.pdf. Accessed 10 Jan 2015.
Reaves, B. A., & Hickman, M. J. (2004). Law enforcement managementand administrative statistics, 2000: Data for individual state and local agencies with 100 or more officers. Washington, DC: Bureau of Justice Statistics. http://bjs.ojp.usdoj.gov/content/pub/pdf/lemas00.pdf. Accessed 10 Jan 2015.
Roberg, R. R., Crank, J. P., & Kuykendall, J. (2000). *Police & society*. Los Angeles: Roxbury.
Roebuck, J. B., & Barker, T. (1974). A typology of police corruption. *Social Problems, 21*(3), 423–437.
Seabury, S. (1932). Final report of samuel seabury, referee, in the matter of the investigation of the magistrates' courts in the first judicial department and the magistrates thereof, and of attorneys-at-law practicing in said courts. New York: Author.

Shih, T., & Fan, X. (2008). Comparing response rates from web and mail surveys: A meta-analysis. *Field Methods, 20,* 249–271.
Skolnick, J. (1966). *Justice without trial: Law enforcement in a democratic society*. New York: Wiley.
Spelman, W., & Brown, D. K. (1981). *Calling the police: Citizen reporting of serious crime*. Washington, DC: Police Executive Research Forum.
U.S. Commission on Civil Rights. (1981). *Who is guarding the guardians?* Washington, DC: Government Printing Office.
U.S. Department of Justice. (2001). Principles for promoting police integrity. https://www.ncjrs.gov/pdffiles1/ojp/186189.pdf. Accessed 10 Jan 2015.
Vera Institute of Justice. (2002). Pittsburgh's experience with police monitoring. http://www.vera.org/project/project1_1asp?section_id=2&proejct_id=13. Accessed 10 Jan 2015.
Walker, S. (1977). *A critical history of police reform*. Lexington: Lexington Books.
Walker, S. (1999). *The police in America: An introduction* (3rd ed.). New York: McGraw-Hill.
Walker, S., & Katz, C. M. (2008). *The police in America: An introduction* (6th ed.). Boston: McGraw-Hill.
Walker, S., & Katz, C. (2013). *The police in America: An introduction* (8th ed.). New York: McGraw-Hill.
Walker, S., Alpert, G., & Kenney, D. (2000). *Responding to the problem officer: A national evaluation of early warning systems*. Washington, DC: National Institute of Justice.
Weisburd, D., Greenspan, R., Hamilton, E. E., Williams, H., & Bryant, K. A. (2000). Police attitudes toward abuse of authority: Findings from a national survey. Washington, DC: United States Department of Justice, National Institute of Justice, Research in Brief. http://www.ncjrs.gov/pdffiles1/nij/181312.pdf. Accessed 10 Jan 2015.
Westley, W. (1970). *The police*. Boston: MIT Press.
Williams, H., & Murphy, P. V. (1990). The evolving strategy of police: A minority view. https://www.ncjrs.gov/pdffiles1/nij/121019.pdf. Accessed 10 Jan 2015.

Chapter 12
A Comparative Perspective on Police Integrity

Sanja Kutnjak Ivković and M. R. Haberfeld

Abstract This chapter presents a comparative view of police integrity. The authors analyze the results of the police integrity survey performed across ten countries. We find that, although absolute evaluations of seriousness and willingness to report vary across countries, relative rankings of seriousness and willingness to report (i.e., how scenarios are evaluated compared to other scenarios in the questionnaire) tend to be similar across most of the ten countries. Behaviors evaluated as more serious were also more likely to be viewed as violations of official rules. Although the majority of the respondents from nine countries support and expect some discipline for all forms of misconduct featured in the questionnaire, police agencies create vastly different disciplinary environments. Police officers differentiate across scenarios and neither expect nor support the same type of discipline for every type of misconduct. While the code of silence is present in each and every country, what seems to be protected by the code varies greatly across the ten countries. We conclude that the contours of police integrity are quite heterogeneous; what is acceptable and tolerated in one country or one police agency may not be acceptable at all in another, and may be disciplined severely. As the results from Russia and South Korea demonstrate, historical, political, social, and economic conditions in a country are closely tied with the level of integrity in the country.

Keywords Discipline · Police integrity · Sample · Survey · Theory of police integrity

S. Kutnjak Ivković (✉)
Michigan State University, East Lansing, MI, USA
e-mail: kutnjak@msu.edu

M. R. Haberfeld
John Jay College of Criminal Justice, New York, NY, USA
e-mail: mhaberfeld@jjay.cuny.edu

S. Kutnjak Ivković, M. R. Haberfeld (eds.), *Measuring Police Integrity Across the World*,
DOI 10.1007/978-1-4939-2279-6_12

Introduction

Police integrity is a virtue of individual police officers, police units, and police agencies as such. In the early 1990s, Klockars and Kutnjak Ivković (2004) developed a way to measure police integrity empirically and opened the doors for both the explorations within and across countries. Once cross-country or comparative analyses have become a reality, many methodological issues should be considered and taken into account.

Studying police integrity across countries is riddled with challenges. To begin, police agencies are part of their societies at large and, as such, are regulated by the cultural and legal norms of those societies. What is viewed as "appropriate" or "legitimate" conduct could vary greatly from country to country. Not only do the official rules defining what constitutes a violation or a crime vary but so does the procedure used to determine whether the officer engaged in misconduct and its potential outcome. Indeed, various countries employ a range of disciplinary options (e.g., suspension for a certain period of time, administrative leave, monetary punishment, reassignment). Furthermore, linguistic issues may become relevant in cross-country comparisons. An additional complication is that the behaviors described in the questionnaire may not be realistic in a particular country, yet very real in other countries. The value of the bribe or the item stolen could have different implications, depending on the affluence of the society. The nature and the composition of the samples may also lead to potential difference.

Having all these caveats in mind, this chapter explores the contours of police integrity across ten countries. It starts with a short overview of comparative exploration of police integrity. Then, it provides a description of the methodology used to collect the data and discusses potential methodological differences. Finally, the chapter analyzes police integrity across the countries, focusing on the respondents' evaluations of misconduct seriousness, assessments of rule-violating behavior, views about appropriate and expected discipline, and the respondents' willingness to report misconduct.

Studying Police Integrity in Individual Countries

Since the first police corruption questionnaire has been designed in the early 1990s (Klockars and Kutnjak Ivković 2004), it has been used in 23 countries (Armenia, Austria, Bosnia and Herzegovina, Canada, Croatia, Czech Republic, Eritrea, Finland, Hungary, Japan, Malaysia, Netherlands, Norway, Pakistan, Poland, Romania, Slovenia, South Africa, South Korea, Sweden, Turkey, the UK, and the USA) from four continents. However, most of the studies using the questionnaire explored for-gain facets of police integrity in just one country.

Based on the police corruption questionnaire, most single-country studies focused on describing and analyzing the contours of for-gain facets of police integrity in their country. Table 12.1 contains the list of 23 countries with selected publications following this mold. They vary based on their level of democratization from established democracies, such as the USA, the UK, Finland, Sweden, and South Korea to countries in transition such as Croatia, Slovenia, Poland, and South Africa (Table 12.1). The countries span across four continents: North America (e.g., Canada, the USA), Europe (e.g., Sweden, the Netherlands, the UK, Bosnia and Herzegovina), Africa (e.g., Eritrea, South Africa), and Asia (e.g., Armenia, Japan, South Korea). Their legal systems are based on civil law (e.g., Finland, Sweden, Croatia, Poland), common law (e.g., the UK, the USA), or a combination of laws (e.g., Eritrea, South Africa, Malaysia). Countries' police agencies range from centralized (e.g., Croatia, Slovenia, Sweden) to decentralized (e.g., UK, USA).

A number of studies supplemented exploration of police integrity in their country with an in-depth study of a particular issue. Studies provided more detailed accounts of evaluations of seriousness (e.g., Kutnjak Ivković et al. 2004; Klockars

Table 12.1 Single-country publications utilizing the first questionnaire

Country	Representative references
Armenia	Kutnjak Ivković and Khechumyan (2013)
Austria	Edelbacher and Kutnjak Ivković (2004)
Bosnia and Herzegovina	Kutnjak Ivković (2004)
Canada	Alain (2004)
Croatia	Kutnjak Ivković and Klockars (2004)
Czech Republic	Kutnjak Ivković and Shelley (2007)
Eritrea	Desta (2013)
Finland	Puonti et al. (2004)
Hungary	Kremer (2004)
Japan	Johnson (2004)
Malaysia	Yunus et al. (2013)
The Netherlands	Punch et al. (2004)
Norway	Gottschalk (2010)
Pakistan	Chattha and Kutnjak Ivković (2004)
Poland	Haberfeld (2004)
Romania	Andreescu et al. (2012)
Slovenia	Pagon and Lobnikar (2004)
South Africa	Newham (2004); Sauerman and Kutnjak Ivković (2008)
South Korea	Kutnjak Ivković and Kang (2011)
Sweden	Torstensson Levandar and Ekenvall (2004)
Turkey	Kucukuysal (2008)
The UK	Westmarland (2004)
The USA	Klockars et al. 2000; Klockars, Kutnjak Ivković et al. 2004; McDevitt et al. 2011

and Kutnjak Ivković 1999; Kutnjak Ivković 2004, 2005), the code of silence (e.g., Kremer 2000; Kutnjak Ivković and Shelley 2010; Kutnjak Ivković and Sauerman 2012; Pagon and Lobnikar 2000; Rothwell and Baldwin 2007), and perceptions of disciplinary fairness (e.g., Kutnjak Ivković and Klockars 1998; Kutnjak Ivković and Shelley 2010). They also explored district-level differences (Greene et al. 2004; Yun 2003), rank-differences (e.g., Kutnjak Ivković 2004; Kutnjak Ivković and Klockars 2000; Kutnjak Ivković et al. 2002; Kutnjak Ivković and Shelley 2010; Lee et al. 2013; Pagon and Lobnikar 2000; Rothwell and Baldwin 2007), and race and/or gender differences (e.g., Andreescu et al. 2012; Charles 2009; McDevitt et al. 2011; Westmarland 2005).

Studying Police Integrity Across Countries

The body of police integrity research that grew over the course of the past two decades has also included about a dozen comparative studies (Table 12.2). Of those, about one half featured a comparison across only two countries (Table 12.2). It seems that, as the number of countries in the analyses increases, the number of publications decreases. In particular, there were six studies comparing two countries, and three studies comparing three countries, and there was only one study comparing four countries, two studies comparing five countries, and only one study comparing 14 countries (Table 12.2).

Some of the studies included the analysis that covered all measurements of police integrity (i.e., views about misconduct, seriousness, assessment whether the behavior is rule violating, opinions about the appropriate and expected discipline, and willingness to report misconduct) in the selected countries (e.g., Klockars et al. 2004; Kutnjak Ivković and Shelley 2007; Khruakham and Lee 2013). Other studies targeted a specific measure, such as seriousness (e.g., Klockars and Kutnjak Ivković 1999; Kutnjak Ivković 2004, 2005; Huberts et al. 2003), appropriate and expected discipline (e.g., Haberfeld et al. 2000), or willingness to report (e.g., Huberts et al. 2003).

Most of the studies included police officers as respondents, but the nature of the samples differed, from students attending the police academy to grizzled veterans. Researchers used opportunities to collect the data in police stations (e.g., Kutnjak Ivković et al. 2002; Kutnjak Ivković and Shelley 2007) or surveyed them while the respondents—be they novice line officers or newly promoted middle managers—were taking a course at a police academy (e.g., Khruakham and Lee 2013; Vito et al. 2011). Sometimes, scholars compared police officers' views about police misconduct with the public's views about police misconduct (e.g., Pagon et al. 2000; Kutnjak Ivković 2004; Kutnjak Ivković et al. 2002).

Most of the comparisons (11 out of 13 publications) included the U.S. data, funded by the National Institute of Justice and are readily accessible. Some authors focused their paper on the measurement of police integrity in one country (e.g., Johnson 2004; Khruakham and Lee 2013; Vito et al. 2011) and devoted a smaller section

Table 12.2 Publications utilizing the first questionnaire-cross-country comparisons

Countries	Reference	Topic
Two-country comparisons		
Bosnia and Herzegovina and the Czech Republic	Kutnjak Ivković and Shelley (2008)	Comparing the contours of police integrity in Bosnia and Herzegovina and the Czech Republic
Croatia and Slovenia	Kutnjak Ivković et al. (2002)	Comparing public and police views about police corruption across Croatia and Slovenia
The USA and Croatia	Klockars and Kutnjak Ivković (1999)	Comparing the U.S. and Croatian police and public evaluation of police misconduct seriousness; comparing police and public evaluations
The USA and Croatia	Kutnjak Ivković (2004)	Studying views of police misconduct seriousness and comparing them between police offices and citizens across Croatia and the USA
The USA and Japan	Johnson (2003)	Comparing of Japanese and U.S. police officers' views on police integrity
The USA and Romania	Andreescu et al. (2012)	Comparing the U.S. and Romanian police officers' views of police integrity
Three-country comparisons		
The USA, Croatia, and Finland	Kutnjak Ivković (2005)	Exploring cross-cultural differences in police officer perceptions of misconduct seriousness across Croatia, Finland, and the USA
The USA, Croatia, and Finland	Vito et al.(2011)	Comparing U.S. middle-manager views with the U.S., Croatian, and Finnish police supervisor views
The USA, Croatia, and Slovenia	Pagon et al. (2000)	Analyzing police and public views of police corruption; comparing Slovenian, Croatian, and the U.S. views
Four-country comparisons		
The USA, Croatia, Poland, and Slovenia	Haberfeld et al. (2000)	Comparing police officers' views of appropriate and expected discipline across the USA, Croatia, Poland, and Slovenia
Five-country comparisons		
USA, Croatia, The Netherlands, Poland, andSlovenia	Huberts et al. (2003)	Comparing the U.S. and Dutch police officer views on seriousness and willingness to report misconduct; some comparison across 5 countries
USA, Finland, Sweden, the Netherlands, Thailand	Khruakham and Lee (2013)	Measuring police integrity in Thailand and comparing with police integrity in the USA, The Netherlands, Sweden, and Finland

Table 12.2 (continued)

Countries	Reference	Topic
Fourteen-country comparisons		
Austria, Canada, Croatia, Finland, Hungary, Japan, Netherlands, Pakistan, Poland, Slovenia, South Africa, Sweden, UK, USA	Klockars et al. (2004)	Exploring the concept of police integrity; organizational theory; methodology; analysis of the police integrity in a comparative perspective

of the paper to the comparative analyses. On the other hand, some papers contained the comparative analyses only (e.g., Andreescu et al. 2012; Haberfeld et al. 2000; Klockars et al. 2004; Kutnjak Ivković and Shelley 2007; Kutnjak Ivković et al. 2002; Pagon et al. 2000).

The most comprehensive study was the 14-country project by Klockars et al. (2004). It was a comparative book chapter next to 14 individual country chapters (Klockars et al. 2004). In each chapter, the authors discussed methodological challenges in designing the questionnaire that could be used in different countries (i.e., in modern, industrialized societies), the solutions they have incorporated in the questionnaire to address a number of challenges, and the problems they encountered in applications of the questionnaire in different countries.

The authors concluded that, although there is a substantial heterogeneity in the absolute measures of police integrity (e.g., mean values), the relative measures (i.e., ranking of scenarios within a country) tend to be rather similar across countries (Klockars et al. 2004, p. 13). This overall similarity of rankings across countries was noted not only for the measures of seriousness but also for the assessments of appropriate and expected discipline and willingness to report. However, they argued (Klockars et al. 2004, p. 13) that the willingness to report data show most volatility because,

> …in some countries the code of silence is strong enough to confound the data on officers' willingness to report. In Croatia, Hungary, Pakistan, Poland, and South Africa the code of silence is so strong that in those countries officers are actually estimating just how *unwilling* most officers are to report the misconduct described in the scenarios.

The authors also wrote about potential relations between different measures of police integrity (Klockars et al. 2004) and noted that the assessments of seriousness are always higher than the assessments of discipline or willingness to report. The reason, according to Klockars et al. (2004, p. 13) lies in the fact that, unlike assessments of appropriate discipline and willingness to report, estimates of seriousness do not carry with them any behavioral consequences. Consequently, officers may have a tendency to overestimate seriousness. Furthermore, the authors documented that various measures of police integrity are related; the harsher the discipline expected to be meted out by the police agency, the more pronounced the perception of its seriousness.

Finally, the authors found the largest differences across countries in their estimates of the respondents' willingness to report misconduct. Klockars et al. 2004, p. 17) elaborated:

> In 5 of the countries, not a single incident out of the 11 incidents described in the survey would be very likely to be reported. In 9 out of 14 countries, officers would not be certain to report a fellow officer who took a bribe from a speeding motorist. In fact, in every one of the countries surveyed, an officer could accept free drinks to overlook a bar that remained open past the official closing time or strike a prisoner in confinement without assuming that his or her police colleagues who witnessed the offense would be sure to report it. It appears that there are few places in the world where a police officer will turn in a fellow police officer who accepts free meals and discounts, or holiday gifts.

At the same time, the second questionnaire—measuring police integrity as the opposite of temptations of various sources—has not been utilized in comparative studies. There are a handful publications on the topic (Klockars et al. 2006; Kutnjak Ivković 2009, 2012; Kutnjak Ivković et al.2013; Pagon et al. 2004), but all of them are single-country studies. This chapter provides the first comprehensive analysis of findings from ten countries.

Measuring Police Integrity

Questionnaire

Scholars studying police integrity across ten countries all used the same police integrity questionnaire developed by Klockars and colleagues (Klockars et al. 2006). Based on the definition of police integrity as normative inclination to resist temptations of one's office (Klockars et al. 2006), the questionnaire contains 11 hypothetical scenarios describing different forms of police misconduct, from police corruption and use of excessive force to planting of evidence and falsifying official reports. Five scenarios describe police corruption (scenario 1, scenario 3, scenario 5, scenario 8, and scenario 9), four scenarios describe use of excessive force (scenario 4, scenario 6, scenario 7, scenario 11), and two additional scenarios describe official report falsification (scenario 10) and failure to execute a search warrant (scenario 2 Table 12.3).

Questionnaires were translated into local languages and back translated by native speakers to ensure quality of translation. Typically, descriptions of the scenarios and wording of the questions were checked with the local police administrators and line officers to make sure that all cultural, legal, and linguistic issues have been resolved (e.g., Kang and Kutnjak Ivković 2015). If English was the dominant language in the country (e.g., South Africa, Australia), the wording was adjusted for spelling and local terminology (Porter et al. 2015).

Although the scenarios were originally designed to fit the conditions in modern, industrialized societies, researchers in several countries had to modify some of the

Table 12.3 Scenario descriptions: second survey

	Scenario description
Scenario 1	A police officer is widely liked in the community. Local merchants and restaurant owners regularly show their appreciation for his attention by giving him gifts of food, cigarettes, and other items of small value
Scenario 2	A police officer is aware that there is a felony warrant for a long-time friend of his. Although he sees his friend frequently over a period of more than a week and warns his friend of its existence, he does not arrest him
Scenario 3	A police officer discovers a burglary of a hardware store. The display cases are smashed and many items have obviously been taken. While searching the store, he takes an expensive pocketknife and slips it into his pocket. He reports that the knife has been stolen during the burglary
Scenario 4	An officer who was severely beaten by a person resisting arrest, has just returned to duty. On patrol, the officer approaches a person standing in a dimly lit alley. Suddenly, the person throws a gym bag at the officer and begins to run away. The officer fatally shoots the person, striking him in the back. It was later determined that the person was unarmed
Scenario 5	A police officer is scheduled to work during coming holidays. The supervisor offers to give him these days off, if he agrees to run some personal errands for the supervisor to evaluate the *supervisor's* behavior
Scenario 6	In responding with her male partner to a fight in a bar, a young, female officer receives a black eye from one of the male combatants. The man is arrested, handcuffed, and, as he is led into the cells, the male member of the team punches him very hard in the kidney area saying, "hurts, doesn't it."
Scenario 7	A police officer stops a motorist for speeding. As the officer approaches the vehicle, the driver yells, "What the hell are you stopping me for?" The officer replies, "Because today is 'arrest an asshole day.'"
Scenario 8	At 2:00 a.m. a police officer, who is on duty, is driving his patrol car on a deserted road. He sees a vehicle that has been driven off the road and is stuck in a ditch. He approaches the vehicle and observes that the driver is not hurt but is obviously intoxicated. He also finds that the driver is a police officer. Instead of reporting this accident and offense, he transports the driver to his home
Scenario 9	A police officer has a private arrangement with a local auto body shop to refer the owners of cars damaged in accidents to the shop. In exchange for each referral, he receives a payment of 5% of the repair bill from the shop owner
Scenario 10	A police officer arrests two drug dealers involved in a street fight. One has a large quantity of heroin on his person. In order to charge them both with serious offenses, the officer falsely reports that the heroin was found on both men
Scenario 11	A police sergeant, without intervening, watches officers under his supervision repeatedly strike and kick a man arrested for child abuse. The man has previous child abuse arrests. Evaluate the *Sergeant's* behavior

scenarios to make them more realistic for the police in their countries. For example, regular police in Armenia are not in charge of traffic, so scenario 7 (verbal abuse –"Arrest an Asshole Day") was reworded to verbal abuse of young activists (Khechumyan and Kutnjak Ivković 2015). In the Australian application of the survey, Porter and colleagues expanded scenario 2 (failure to arrest friend with felony warrant) by adding "or pass on information about his friend's whereabouts to other police" at the end of the sentence (Porter et al. 2015). Scenario 6 (officer strikes prisoner) was not included in the Russian version of the questionnaire. Police officers in Russia have to transfer arrestees to the detention centers immediately and have control of the arrestees and prisoners only for a short period of time. To avoid potential complaints that this scenario is not applicable in Russia because police officers do not have access to the prisoners, scenario 6 was excluded from the Russian questionnaire.

Upon reading each scenario, the respondents were asked the same seven questions: two about evaluations of seriousness, one about violation of agency rules, two about discipline, and two about willingness to report. Questions about seriousness and willingness to report and their answers were left in each country as they were; these questions are inquiring about the respondents' views and opinions and do not require knowledge of any facts.

Wording of the question which asks the respondents to recognize whether the described behavior violates official rules was left unchanged in all surveys. However, several countries (Armenia, Australia, Estonia, Russia, Thailand, and South Africa) used the 5-item Likert scale with 1= "definitely not" and 5= "definitely yes" (which Klockars et al. 2004, used in the first police corruption questionnaire). On the other hand, several other countries (Croatia, Slovenia, South Korea, and the USA) used the revised 3-item Likert scale with 1= "yes," "2= no," and "3= not sure." In the comparative analyses that follow, the 5-item Likert scale was dichotomized (values 1–3 as "no" and values 4–5 as "yes").

Questions about appropriate and expected discipline are dependent upon the legal environment in each country. The original scale, developed for the U.S. conditions, included 6 items: "1=none," "2=verbal reprimand," "3=written reprimand," "4= period of suspension without pay," "5= demotion in rank," and "dismissal." Although most of the other countries include 6-item scales (see Table 12.4), Armenia has an 8-item scale and South Korea has a 5-item scale. The common features across the countries are that the scales: (1) have no discipline on one end; (2) have dismissal on the opposite end; and (3) between the two ends, the scales have discipline that becomes progressively harsher. For the purposes of comparative analyses, we group disciplinary options as "no discipline," "some discipline other than dismissal," and "dismissal" (see Table 12.4).

Finally, the questionnaire also contained several questions about the respondents' demographic measures. A number of questions included standardized scales used in all countries: length of service, supervisory status, and gender. Potential answers to the question about the type of assignment have been adjusted to fit the assignment type in a typical country/police agency surveyed. The last two questions in the questionnaire, inquiring about the truthfulness of respondents' answers and estimates of truthfulness of the answers provided by others in the agency, were standardized.

Table 12.4 Disciplinary answers by country

Country	"No discipline"	"Some discipline other than dismissal"	"Dismissal"
Armenia	1="none"	2="reprimand," 3="severe reprimand," 4="salary reduction," 5="incompatibility with the occupied position," 6="demotion to one step lower position," 7="demotion to one step lower rank"	8= "dismissal"
Australia	1="none"	2= "verbal warning/counseling," 3="written warning," 4= "suspension/disciplinary transfer," 5="reduction in rank"	6="dismissal"
Croatia	1="none"	2= "public reprimand," 3="fine up to 10% of salary," 4="fine up to 20% of salary," 5="reassignment to a different position"	6="dismissal"
Estonia	1="none"	2= "verbal reprimand," 3="written reprimand," 4="period of suspension without pay," 5="demotion in rank"	6="dismissal"
Russia	1="none"	2="public reprimand," 3="fine up to 10% of salary," 4="fine up to 20% of salary," 5="reassignment to a different position"	6="dismissal"
Slovenia	1="none"	2="public warning," 3="fine in the amount of 10% of the employee's salary," 4="fine in the amount of 20% of the employee's salary," 5="reassignment"	6="dismissal"
South Africa	1="none"	2= "verbal reprimand," 3="written reprimand," 4="reassignment to a different position," 5="demotion in rank"	6="dismissal"
South Korea	1="none"	2="written warning," 3="decreased salary by 50%," 4="suspension for 1–3 months"	5="dismissal"
Thailand	1="none"	2= "verbal reprimand," 3="written reprimand," 4="period of suspension without pay," 5="demotion in rank,"	6="dismissal"
The USA	1="none"	2="verbal reprimand," 3="written reprimand," 4="period of suspension without pay," 5="demotion in rank,"	6="dismissal"

The Samples/Populations

The nature of policing structure in these ten countries is quite different, from the centralized police structures prevailing in Armenia, Croatia, and Slovenia to the highly decentralized police structure in the USA. In the centralized systems, such as Croatia, it was possible to draw a representative sample of police agencies. In several other centralized systems (e.g., Armenia, Estonia, Slovenia), the authors decided to survey whole populations of police officers in either the whole country (e.g., Estonia, Slovenia; Table 12.5) or from a particular region (e.g., Armenia). In decentralized systems, such as Australia and the USA, the authors have selected several

Table 12.5 Samples and their characteristics

Country	Delivery method	Sampling method	Size	Response rate
Armenia	Paper	Population of all police stations in one region	969	N/A
Australia	Online	Population of police officers from two police agencies	856	N/A
Croatia	Paper	Representative sample	966	88%
Estonia	Online	Population of police officers	147	N/A
Russia	Paper	Convenience sample of police officers	106	N/A
Slovenia	Paper	Population of police officers from all local and regional police agencies	583	N/A
South Africa	Paper	Convenience sample from all regions	871	88%
South Korea	Paper	Convenience sample	379	74%
Thailand	Paper	Representative sample	280	94%
The USA	Online	Population of police officers from 11 police agencies	664	37%

police agencies and tried to survey all police officers employed in these agencies. Several countries included convenience samples (e.g., South Africa, South Korea).

In terms of their demographic characteristics, respondents from different countries exhibited both similarities and differences (Table 12.6). As expected, the overwhelming majority of respondents—between 70 and 90%—were male (Table 12.6). At the same time, the overwhelming majority across all countries were experienced police officers with more than 5 years of experience (Table 12.6). On the other hand, the percentage of nonsupervisors among the respondents from each country varied from as low as 27% in Slovenia to as high as 90% in Korea. There was substantial variation in the assignments as well; although in none of the countries the majority of the respondents were assigned to patrol, the percentage was the highest in Korea and the lowest in Russia (Table 12.6). Similarly, some countries had virtually no community policing officers among the respondents, while in others that percentage was as high as 47% (Table 12.6).

Table 12.6 Respondent characteristics

Country	% Non supervisors	% Below 5 years of service	% in Patrol	% in COP	% Male
Armenia	81.2	35.5	13.1	47.2	90.8
Australia	59.0	14.3	28.2	6.0	71.5
Croatia	81.0	12.3	36.9	10.6	88.2
Estonia	63.3	11.9	27.5	32.1	72.5
Russia	46.2	11.3	0.9	3.8	80.2
Slovenia	26.5	7.6	18.1	22.1	88.5
South Africa	62.5	18.0	27.9	12.9	70.8
South Korea	90.0	14.4	46.0	N/A	92.0
Thailand	52.9	10.7	40.4	9.3	91.2
The USA	72.6	14.6	55.2	3.7	N/A

Results

Seriousness

The respondents were asked to evaluate how serious they perceive the behaviors described in the scenarios, as well as how serious they think that their fellow police officers would evaluate such behavior. The respondents could have selected an answer from a five-item Likert scale, ranging from "not at all serious" to "very serious."

The results, shown in Table 12.7, contain mean values and ranks for each country. With the exception of Russia, the respondents in 9 out of 10 countries evaluated most of the behaviors described in the scenarios as being on the serious side of the scale; mean values across the 11 scenarios range from about 3, the midpoint of the scale, to about 5, the serious end of the scale (Table 12.7). The perceptions of scenarios seem to be more tightly clustered together in some countries than in others. For example, in some countries (e.g., South Africa, Estonia) the difference across scenarios between the smallest mean and the largest mean is barely 1, while in other countries (e.g., Russia, Slovenia, Australia, the USA) the difference between the smallest mean and the largest mean is close to 2 or even 3 (e.g., Thailand; Table 12.7).

The exploration of country rankings of seriousness reveals common themes across countries. In particular, the respondents in virtually every country other than Russia (Table 12.7) evaluated the theft of knife from a crime scene (scenario 3: theft of knife from crime scene) as the most serious out of all 11 scenarios (Table 12.7). This uniformity should not be surprising—opportunistic theft is among the most serious forms of corruption in Barker and Roebuck's typology of corruption (1974). Furthermore, in their analysis of the application of the first questionnaire in 14 countries, Klockars et al. (2004, p. 14) document that an earlier version of this scenario, describing a theft of watch from the crime scene, that the respondents

Table 12.7 Police officers' perceptions of seriousness (Means/Ranks)

Scenario number and description	Armenia	Australia	Croatia	Estonia	Russia	Slovenia	South Africa	South Korea	Thailand	The USA
Scenario 1: free meals, gifts from merchants	4.02 (2)	3.47 (2)	3.48 (2)	3.77 (1)	1.82 (7)	3.64 (2)	3.88 (1)	3.78 (5)	1.42 (1)	3.16 (1)
Scenario 2: failure to arrest friend with felony warrant	4.43 (8)	4.56 (6)	4.71 (10)	4.40 (7)	1.54 (2)	4.7 (10)	4.61 (10)	4.25 (7)	3.58 (8)	4.35 (5)
Scenario 3: theft of knife from crime scene	4.83 (11)	4.94 (11)	4.74 (11)	4.89 (11)	2.02 (8)	4.87 (11)	4.77 (11)	4.77 (11)	4.47 (11)	4.97 (11)
Scenario 4: unjustifiable use of deadly force	4.19 (4.5)	4.88 (10)	4.47 (8)	4.56 (8.5)	4.46 (9)	4.55 (7)	4.56 (9)	3.34 (1)	3.38 (7)	4.84 (9)
Scenario 5: supervisor offers holi-day for errands	4.52 (9)	3.94 (3)	4.33 (6)	4.31 (5)	1.55 (3)	4.45 (6)	4.33 (6)	4.44 (9)	3.23 (6)	4.24 (4)
Scenario 6: officer strikes prisoner	4.19 (4.5)	4.29 (4)	3.59 (3)	4.27 (4)	N/A	4.13 (4)	4.29 (4)	3.42 (2)	3.20 (5)	4.40 (6)
Scenario 7: verbal abuse of motorist	4.40 (7)	3.02 (1)	3.86 (4)	3.98 (2)	4.98 (10)	3.66 (3)	3.90 (2)	3.59 (3)	2.37 (3)	3.41 (2)
Scenario 8: cover-up police DUI and accident	3.42 (1)	4.39 (5)	3.06 (1)	4.02 (3)	1.27 (1)	2.87 (1)	3.98 (3)	3.64 (4)	2.09 (2)	3.70 (3)
Scenario 9: auto body shop 5 % kickback	4.34 (6)	4.82 (8)	4.46 (7)	4.56 (8.5)	1.77 (5.5)	4.63 (8)	4.30 (5)	4.68 (10)	2.57 (4)	4.64 (8)
Scenario 10: false report of drug possession	4.67 (10)	4.85 (9)	4.54 (9)	4.63 (10)	1.76 (4)	4.67 (9)	4.50 (8)	4.40 (8)	3.77 (10)	4.91 (10)
Scenario 11: Sgt. fails to halt beat-ing of child abuser	4.07 (3)	4.56 (7)	4.01 (5)	4.39 (6)	1.77 (5.5)	4.34 (5)	4.47 (7)	4.05 (6)	3.64 (9)	4.56 (7)

from almost every country evaluated it as the most serious or second most serious scenario.

Two other scenarios are perceived as most serious. In particular, unjustifiable use of deadly force (scenario 4) and official report falsification (scenario 10) were also evaluated as the most serious by the respondents from the majority of the countries. A striking finding is that, in a number of countries (e.g., Croatia, Slovenia, Thailand), falsifying the official record (scenario 10) is viewed as more serious than abusing deadly force (scenario 4), the application of the gravest type of force.

This issue is particularly pronounced for South Korea, in which abusing deadly force is evaluated as the least serious scenario of all (Table 12.7). As Kang and Kutnjak Ivković (2015) emphasize, the use of deadly force is evaluated as less serious than the acceptance of gratuities (scenario 1) and verbal abuse of a citizen (scenario 7). In fact, three out of four use of force scenarios are evaluated as the least serious ones in the questionnaire. As Kang and Kutnjak Ivković (2015) argue, this circumstance probably stems from the relatively tolerant attitudes toward the use of force in South Korea, a likely consequence of the efforts undertaken by the Grand Reform to curtail corruption, with its simultaneous neglect to address the problems associated with the use of excessive force.

Respondents from various countries share assessments of the least serious scenarios in the questionnaire. In particular, respondents in 8 out of 10 countries evaluated the cover-up of police DUI and accident (scenario 8) and the acceptance of gratuities (scenario 1) among the three least serious scenarios, followed by verbal abuse of motorist (scenario 7; 7 out of 10 countries). These findings are by no means surprising. Giving verbal commands is on the bottom of the use of force scale and, thus, abusing these verbal commands should be viewed as the least serious form of use of excessive force. Similarly, the acceptance of gratuities or the abuse of authority (Roebuck and Barker 1974) is the least serious of all types of corruption, least likely to lead to reporting and to result in a discipline.

Spearman's correlation of country rankings shows that the ranking of the seriousness of these scenarios is very similar across most of the countries (Table 12.8). In particular, with two exceptions (Russia and South Korea), the rankings in all countries are closely associated with the rankings in other countries (i.e., these countries have large and statistically significant correlation coefficients with at least 6 out of 9 other countries).

Especially strong are the connections among four East European countries—Armenia, Croatia, Estonia, and Slovenia. Similarities in their political, legal, economic, and social environments have historic roots. Until about two decades ago, they were part of the former Soviet Union (Armenia and Estonia) and the former Yugoslavia (Croatia and Slovenia), both former communist countries. Indeed, the results indicate that, despite the passage of two decades and diverse histories since their independence, their rankings are the most closely related among all (Spearman's correlation coefficient = 0.982, $p < 0.001$; Table 12.8).

Strikingly, the ranking from the Russian sample is quite different from the rankings in other four East European countries. In fact, it is quite different from the ranking in *any* other country in the sample—there are no strong and statistically

Table 12.8 Country Spearman's rank correlations of own seriousness evaluations

	Armenia	Australia	Croatia	Estonia	Russia	Slovenia	South Africa	South Korea	Thailand	The USA
Armenia	1.00									
Australia	0.346	1.00								
Croatia	0.806**	0.727*	1.00							
Estonia	0.642*	0.929***	0.888***	1.00						
Russia	0.079	0.109	0.067	0.046	1.00					
Slovenia	0.797**	0.736*	0.982***	0.907***	0.024	1.00				
South Africa	0.615*	0.809**	0.909***	0.875***	−0.055	0.891***	1.00			
South Korea	0.624*	0.355	0.555	0.542	−0.261	0.627*	0.409	1.00		
Thailand	0.665*	0.736*	0.827**	0.834**	0.018	0.818**	0.909***	0.436	1.00	
The USA	0.515	0.936***	0.755*	0.952***	0.109	0.782**	0.791**	0.382	0.818**	1.00
# of countries with Sig. correlations	6/9	6/9	7/9	7/9	0/9	8/9	7/9	2/9	7/9	6/9

* $p < 0.05$; ** $p < 0.01$; *** $p < 0.001$

significant coefficients at all (Table 12.8). This absence of similarity in ranking is driven by the fact that our Russian respondents evaluated the acceptance of gratuities (scenario 1) and verbal abuse (scenario 7) as much more serious than the respondents in any other country and, at the same time, evaluated the failure to exercise the arrest warrant (scenario 2) and falsifying the official report (scenario 10) as much less serious than the respondents from any other country (Table 12.7). In fact, many of the mean evaluations across scenarios for the Russian sample are very similar; 8 out of 10 scenarios have closely clustered means ranging, on a 5-point scale, from about 1.20 to 2.00. On the other hand, only two scenarios stand out as very serious (with the means between about 4.5 and 5). One of these two scenarios is verbal abuse (scenario 7), which the Russian respondents evaluated as *the* most serious scenario and the overwhelming majority of the respondents from other countries found to be in the group of least serious scenarios. One of the explanations why verbal abuse was perceived by the officers as more serious than other scenarios could be tied to the overall self-image perceptions of the Russian police officers. According to one of the authors of the Russian chapter, police officers' demeanor toward the public is part of their professional image that is tied, very closely, to their ability to exercise the profession in an effective way. In other words, responding to a member of the public in a way described in the verbal abuse scenario would show a weakness on the part of the officer, a situation in which the citizen was successful in provoking the officer to use an obscene language and, by doing so, detracting from the officer's authority.

Another group of countries with special connection in rankings is the group of countries in which the dominant religion is either Protestant or Anglican (Australia, Estonia, the USA). Correlation coefficients for these three countries are all above 0.900, suggesting a very strong connection among the countries. While South Africa has been an English colony for a long period of time, the influence of the Anglican religion is not as strong; consequently, the correlations between South Africa and the three Protestant/Anglican countries (Australia, Estonia, and the USA) are not as strong.

South Korea stands out from the group as well. It is the only true Asian democracy in the sample. However, the underlying reasons for the relatively unique ranking (it is statistically significantly correlated with the rankings in two out of nine countries; Table 12.8) may be related to the Grand Reform. In particular, while the Reform has been targeting corruption in its public announcements and the applications of internal discipline, the use of excessive force has been neglected. Indeed, Korea's ranking reflects this fact; all three scenarios evaluated as the least serious describe the use of excessive force (scenario 4: unjustifiable use of deadly force; scenario 6: officer strikes prisoner; scenario 7: verbal abuse of motorist). On the other hand, scenarios describing typical corrupt behaviors, including kickbacks, thefts, and internal corruption (scenario 3: theft of knife from crime scene; scenario 9: auto body shop 5 % kickback; scenario 5: supervisor offers holiday for errands), are all viewed by the respondents as very serious. In fact, as Kang and Kutnjak Ivković (2015) note, accepting free meals (scenario 1) is viewed as more serious than abusing deadly force (scenario 4).

In almost all countries, there were statistically significant differences between the respondents' own evaluations of seriousness and the estimated evaluations of se-

Table 12.9 Police officers' perceptions of seriousness: own versus others (statistically significant differences and substantive differences)

Scenario number and description	Armenia	Australia	Croatia	Estonia	Russia	Slovenia	South Africa	South Korea	Thailand	The USA
Scenario 1: free meals, gifts from merchants	***	***	***	***	***	***	***			***
Scenario 2: failure to arrest friend with felony warrant	***	***	***	***	***	***	***	**		***
Scenario 3: theft of knife from crime scene	***	***	***	***	***	***	***	**	***	***
Scenario 4: unjustifiable use of deadly force	***	***	***	***	***	***	***			***
Scenario 5: supervisor offers holiday for errands	***	***	***	***	***	***	***	**		***
Scenario 6: officer strikes prisoner	***	***	***	***	N/A	***	***	**		***
Scenario 7: verbal abuse of motorist	***	***	***		***	***	***	**		***
Scenario 8: cover-up police DUI and accident	***	***	***	***	***	**	***	**		***
Scenario 9: auto body shop 5% kickback	***	***	***	***	***	**	***	**	***	***
Scenario 10: false report of drug possession	***	***	***	***	***	**	***	**		***
Scenario 11: Sgt. fails to halt beating of child abuser	***	***	***	***	***	**	***	**		***
Meaningful differences	NO (0/11)	NO (0/11)	YES (5/11) positive	NO (0/11)	YES (2/10) positive	YES (3/11) positive	YES (3/11) positive	NO (0/11)	NO (0/11)	YES (4/11) Positive

** $p < 0.01$; *** $p < 0.001$

riousness by fellow police officers (Table 12.9). Using the rule of thumb established in our prior work (Klockar et al. 2006, p. 26), we consider only the differences of 0.50 or larger to be meaningful.

We found meaningful differences in about one half of the countries (Table 12.9). Even in the countries in which we did find meaningful differences between the respondents' own evaluations of seriousness and the estimates of others' evaluations of seriousness, they appeared in a small number of scenarios (typically between two and four out of 11 scenarios, depending on the country; Table 12.9), but always pointing in the same direction (i.e., the respondents' own evaluations of seriousness were higher than the respondents' assessment of others' evaluations of seriousness). The scenario with the largest number of countries registering meaningful differences describes the acceptance of gratuities; in Croatia, Slovenia, South Africa, and the USA, the respondents thought that their fellow officers would downplay the seriousness of this behavior. In all other scenarios with meaningful differences (shaded gray in the table), only one or two countries featured meaningful differences (Table 12.9).

Violation of Official Rules

The respondents were asked whether the behaviors described in the questionnaire could be classified as rule-violating behavior. As discussed in the methodology section, the respondents in some countries (e.g., Croatia, Slovenia, South Korea, and the USA) could have selected an answer from the three possible choices: "yes," "no," and "not sure," and the respondents from some other countries (e.g., Armenia, Australia, Estonia, Russia, and South Africa) would select an answer from the 5-item Likert scale. To get the responses to be roughly comparable, answers 4 and 5 from the 5-item Likert scale were grouped together, representing the respondents who thought that the behavior would be a violation of official policy. To circumvent this methodological challenge, we avoid comparing the percentages across the countries directly and instead rely on rankings based on relative within-country assessments of how a particular scenario is viewed by the respondents from that country, a methodology more readily amenable to cross-country comparisons.

The respondents were least likely to recognize the behavior described in four scenarios (scenario 1: free meals, gifts from merchants; scenario 5: supervisor offers holiday for errands; scenario 7: verbal abuse of motorist; scenario 8: cover-up of police DUI and accident; Table 12.10) as rule-violating. One of the scenarios least likely to be viewed as a violation of official rules describes the acceptance of gratuities (scenario 1: free meals, gifts from merchants). At the same time, acceptance of gratuities is viewed as the least serious form of police corruption, likely tolerated by fellow police officers, and unlikely to result in any serious discipline if the police agency learned about it (Roebuck and Barker, 1974). The issue is further complicated with the fact that in many countries there may be a conflict between official rules and unofficial rules. Therefore, it is not surprising that it is one of the scenarios least likely to be evaluated as rule-violating behavior.

The scenario describing verbal abuse (scenario 7) is in the same group. Among the four scenarios featuring the use of excessive force in the questionnaire, this scenario is by far the least serious one. It describes the abuse on the lowest end of the use of force continuum and, not surprisingly, the respondents were least likely to recognize it as rule violating. Scenario 8 (cover-up of police DUI and accident) usually draws attention from the police officers because they view it as one of the least serious forms of police misconduct, least likely to be recognized as rule violating. Finally, scenario 5 (supervisor offers holiday for errands) focuses on internal corruption, a form of corruption not viewed as very serious either.

Four scenarios (scenario 3: theft of knife from crime scene; scenario 9: auto body shop 5% kickback; scenario 10: false report on drug possession; scenario 11: Sgt. fails to halt beating of child abuser; Table 12.10) were most likely to be recognized as rule violating by the respondents. Scenario 3, describing a theft of an item from the crime scene, was most likely to be evaluated as a rule-violating behavior in the whole questionnaire. In fact, in nine out of ten countries the respondents were so sure that the behavior was rule-violating that it was ranked 11th. Falsifying an official report (scenario 10)—an example of serious police misconduct—was also more likely to be evaluated as rule violating than other scenarios. With so much emphasis on police corruption, the respondents were also agreeing that the acceptance of a kickback (scenario 9) violates official rules and that the supervisor's failure of stopping the child abuser (scenario 11) is another such scenario.

Appropriate and Expected Discipline

The respondents were also asked to express their views about the appropriate and expected discipline for the behaviors described in the questionnaire. As discussed earlier (Table 12.4), answers provided in each country were individualized in accordance with the relevant legal and administrative rules. Because the scales used in the ten countries were not identical, we grouped the answers for each country into "no discipline," "some discipline other than dismissal," and "dismissal."

Table 12.11 contains the percentage of respondents in each country who said that either "no discipline," "some discipline other than dismissal," or "dismissal" was the appropriate discipline for the behavior described in each scenario. In seven out of ten countries, there was no scenario in which the majority of the respondents thought that the police officer who engaged in the misconduct described in the scenario should not be disciplined (Table 12.11). In six out of ten countries, there were a few scenarios in which a substantial minority (20% or more) of the respondents assessed that no discipline should be appropriate. Accepting free meals and gifts from merchants (scenario 1), striking a prisoner (scenario 6), and covering up a police DUI and accident (scenario 8) are examples of scenarios in which there was a substantial minority of the respondents in 4 or 5 countries who argued that no discipline was appropriate.

Table 12.10 Police officers' assessments of rule violations (percent yes)

Scenario number and description	Armenia %	Australia %	Croatia %	Estonia %	Russia %	Slovenia %	South Africa %	South Korea %	Thailand %	The USA %
Scenario 1: free meals, gifts from merchants	80.3 (2)	89.1 (3)	54.8 (1)	86.2 (2)	71.7 (4.5)	81.5 (2)	76.3 (3)	64.7 (5)	3.3 (1)	75.9 (1)
Scenario 2: failure to arrest friend with felony warrant	88.1 (8)	95.3 (5)	90.7 (10)	92.7 (8)	70.8 (2)	96.5 (8)	87.3 (9.5)	78.7 (7)	68.3 (10)	86.8 (5)
Scenario 3: theft of knife from crime scene	95.5 (11)	99.7 (11)	92.7 (11)	98.2 (11)	71.7 (4.5)	98.9 (11)	95.4 (11)	94.7 (11)	92.2 (11)	99.4 (11)
Scenario 4: unjustifiable use of deadly force	81.5 (3)	92.7 (4)	78.4 (7)	88.1 (3.5)	23.6 (1)	87.9 (4)	86.2 (7)	39.5 (1)	51.2 (6)	88.2 (6)
Scenario 5: supervisor offers holiday for errands	89.0 (9)	84.3 (2)	58.5 (2)	84.4 (1)	73.6 (8)	81.9 (3)	80.9 (5)	80.3 (8)	44.6 (5)	81.4 (3)
Scenario 6: officer strikes prisoner	84.7 (5)	96.8 (6)	59.7 (4)	87.2 (5)	N/A	95.1 (6)	82.9 (6)	48.1 (2)	51.3 (7)	97.0 (9)
Scenario 7: verbal abuse of motorist	87.3 (7)	80.7 (1)	65.6 (5)	88.1 (3.5)	71.7 (4.5)	89.8 (5)	69.0 (1)	50.1 (3)	17.3 (3)	86.7 (4)
Scenario 8: cover-up police DUI and accident	69.8 (1)	98.0 (7)	59.2 (3)	91.7 (7)	71.7 (4.5)	72.0 (1)	73.2 (2)	53.7 (4)	14.8 (2)	78.4 (2)
Scenario 9: auto body shop 5% kickback	85.0 (6)	99.2 (9.5)	79.8 (8)	89.0 (6)	91.1 (9)	95.4 (7)	77.6 (4)	87.0 (10)	25.5 (4)	94.3 (7)
Scenario 10: false report of drug possession	91.4 (10)	99.2 (9.5)	84.9 (9)	96.3 (10)	72.6 (7)	97.6 (10)	86.8 (8)	82.2 (9)	67.5 (9)	98.2 (10)
Scenario 11: Sgt. fails to halt beating of child abuser	83.5 (4)	98.9 (8)	75.0 (6)	95.4 (9)	98.1 (10)	96.7 (9)	87.3 (9.5)	67.3 (6)	62.3 (8)	94.5 (8)

Table 12.11 Police officers' views of appropriate discipline

Scenario number and description	Armenia %	Australia %	Croatia %	Estonia %	Russia %	Slovenia %	South Africa %	South Korea %	Thailand %	The USA %
(% None)										
Scenario 1: free meals, gifts from merchants	27.7 (10)	7.5 (11)	20.1 (9)	11.0 (11)	99.1 (5)	26.2 (10)	9.6 (8)	35.0 (8)	81.9 (11)	18.6 (11)
Scenario 2: failure to arrest friend with felony warrant	10.3 (3)	0.9 (4)	1.0 (2)	1.8 (3)	47.2 (3)	2.4 (2)	2.8 (2)	11.6 (4)	5.2 (2)	4.9 (6)
Scenario 3: theft of knife from crime scene	2.1 (1)	0.0 (1.5)	0.9 (1)	0.5 (1)	0.0 (1.5)	0.9 (1)	0.8 (1)	1.2 (1)	1.5 (1)	0.5 (1)
Scenario 4: unjustifiable use of deadly force	13.0 (4)	2.1 (6)	9.6 (5)	3.7 (4)	100.0 (8.5)	6.6 (5)	3.1 (3)	39.0 (9)	7.7 (3.5)	5.3 (7)
Scenario 5: supervisor offers holiday for errands	14.9 (5)	3.3 (8)	19.9 (8)	10.1 (9.5)	100.0 (8.5)	18.0 (8)	4.4 (5)	19.8 (6)	19.2 (7)	6.6 (8)
Scenario 6: officer strikes prisoner	22.5 (8)	3.6 (9)	25.3 (10)	5.5 (7)	N/A	13.6 (7)	4.8 (7)	40.6 (10)	12.9 (6)	3.0 (3)
Scenario 7: verbal abuse of motorist	21.8 (7)	6.5 (10)	17.9 (7)	8.3 (8)	0.0 (1.5)	25.1 (9)	14.5 (11)	50.0 (11)	37.3 (9)	8.3 (9)
Scenario 8: cover-up police DUI and accident	40.9 (11)	1.3 (5)	27.7 (11)	10.1 (9.5)	99.1 (5)	42.6 (11)	13.0 (10)	29.3 (7)	43.5 (10)	16.4 (10)
Scenario 9: auto body shop 5 % kickback	18.4 (6)	0.0 (1.5)	7.0 (4)	4.6 (5.5)	100.0 (8.5)	4.5 (4)	11.5 (9)	4.3 (2)	36.9 (8)	3.1 (4)
Scenario 10: false report of drug possession	7.3 (2)	0.3 (3)	4.9 (3)	1.3 (2)	100.0 (8.5)	3.8 (3)	4.5 (6)	8.0 (3)	8.9 (5)	0.7 (2)
Scenario 11: Sgt. fails to halt beating of child abuser	25.2 (9)	3.1 (7)	12.8 (6)	4.6 (5.5)	99.1 (5)	10.5 (6)	4.0 (4)	19.4 (5)	7.7 (3.5)	4.0 (5)

Table 12.11 (continued)

Scenario number and description	Armenia %	Australia %	Croatia %	Estonia %	Russia %	Slovenia %	South Africa %	South Korea %	Thailand %	The USA %
% Some Discipline, Other than Dismissal										
Scenario 1: free meals, gifts from merchants	61.3 (4)	89.9 (9)	73.3 (8)	71.6 (8.5)	0.9 (6)	66.1 (8)	74.3 (6)	59.7 (4)	17.0 (1)	80.0 (7)
Scenario 2: failure to arrest friend with felony warrant	69.9 (8)	76.1 (7)	61.8 (3)	57.8 (6)	52.8 (8)	46.1 (3)	76.4 (8)	72.5 (8)	72.0 (7)	85.4 (9)
Scenario 3: theft of knife from crime scene	45.5 (1)	21.4 (1)	47.0 (2)	16.9 (1)	100.0 (9)	13.1 (1)	49.5 (1)	70.1 (6)	42.4 (2)	25.7 (2)
Scenario 4: unjustifiable use of deadly force	54.6 (2)	26.3 (2)	38.1 (1)	36.7 (2)	0.0 (2.5)	31.2 (2)	55.1 (2)	57.9 (3)	79.3 (10)	17.2 (1)
Scenario 5: supervisor offers holiday for errands	78.6 (11)	93.8 (11)	75.3 (9)	72.5 (10)	0.0 (2.5)	70.5 (9)	84.7 (11)	72.8 (9)	73.1 (8.5)	90.4 (10)
Scenario 6: officer strikes prisoner	69.4 (9)	71.6 (6)	70.0 (7)	71.6 (8.5)	N/A	72.6 (10.5)	80.1 (10)	56.6 (2)	81.2 (11)	82.4 (8)
Scenario 7: verbal abuse of motorist	74.3 (10)	93.0 (10)	81.6 (11)	86.2 (11)	100.0 (9)	72.6 (10.5)	79.3 (9)	49.1 (1)	62.0 (6)	90.9 (11)
Scenario 8: cover up police DUI and accident	57.1 (3)	77.9 (8)	69.1 (6)	64.2 (7)	0.9 (6)	51.1 (6)	74.4 (7)	64.8 (5)	54.2 (3)	75.2 (6)
Scenario 9: auto body shop five percent kickback	64.2 (6)	39.8 (4)	62.5 (4)	47.7 (3)	0.0 (2.5)	46.5 (4)	64.3 (4)	70.3 (7)	60.1 (4)	61.8 (4)
Scenario 10: false report of drug possession	63.7 (5)	35.6 (3)	64.6 (5)	51.0 (4)	0.0 (2.5)	47.8 (5)	62.2 (3)	78.2 (11)	60.9 (5)	35.4 (3)
Scenario 11: Sgt. fails to halt beating of child abuser	66.5 (7)	67.3 (5)	76.6 (10)	54.1 (5)	0.9 (6)	58.7 (7)	69.9 (5)	73.5 (10)	73.1 (8.5)	71.7 (5)

Table 12.11 (continued)

Scenario number and description	Armenia %	Australia %	Croatia %	Estonia %	Russia %	Slovenia %	South Africa %	South Korea %	Thailand %	The USA %
% Dismissal										
Scenario 1: free meals, gifts from merchants	11.1 (6)	2.7 (2)	6.6 (5)	17.4 (2.5)	0.0 (5.5)	7.7 (3)	16.1 (5)	5.3 (4)	1.1 (2)	1.4 (2)
Scenario 2: failure to arrest friend with felony warrant	19.9 (8)	23.1 (5)	37.2 (9)	40.4 (6)	0.0 (5.5)	51.5 (9)	20.8 (6)	15.9 (9)	22.9 (9)	9.7 (5)
Scenario 3: theft of knife from crime scene	52.4 (11)	78.4 (11)	52.2 (10.5)	82.6 (11)	0.0 (5.5)	86.0 (11)	49.7 (11)	28.7 (11)	56.1 (11)	73.8 (10)
Scenario 4: unjustifiable use of deadly force	32.4 (10)	71.5 (10)	52.2 (10.5)	59.6 (10)	0.0 (5.5)	62.2 (10)	41.8 (10)	3.1 (3)	12.9 (7)	77.5 (11)
Scenario 5: supervisor offers holiday for errands	6.6 (3)	2.9 (3)	4.8 (4)	17.4 (2.5)	0.0 (5.5)	11.5 (4)	10.9 (2)	7.4 (7)	7.7 (6)	3.0 (3)
Scenario 6: officer strikes prisoner	8.1 (4)	24.9 (6)	4.7 (3)	22.9 (5)	N/A	13.8 (5)	15.1 (4)	2.8 (2)	5.9 (5)	14.6 (6)
Scenario 7: verbal abuse of motorist	3.9 (2)	0.5 (1)	0.6 (1)	5.5 (1)	0.0 (5.5)	2.4 (1)	6.2 (1)	0.9 (1)	0.7 (1)	0.8 (1)
Scenario 8: cover up police DUI and accident	2.1 (1)	20.8 (4)	3.1 (2)	25.7 (4)	0.0 (5.5)	6.3 (2)	12.6 (3)	5.9 (5)	2.2 (3)	8.4 (4)
Scenario 9: auto body shop five percent kickback	17.3 (7)	60.2 (8)	30.5 (8)	47.7 (8.5)	0.0 (5.5)	49.0 (8)	24.2 (7)	25.4 (10)	3.0 (4)	35.1 (8)
Scenario 10: false report of drug possession	29.0 (9)	64.1 (9)	30.4 (7)	47.7 (8.5)	0.0 (5.5)	48.4 (7)	33.3 (9)	13.8 (8)	30.3 (10)	63.9 (9)
Scenario 11: Sgt. fails to halt beating of child abuser	8.4 (5)	29.6 (7)	10.6 (6)	41.3 (7)	0.0 (5.5)	30.8 (6)	26.1 (8)	7.1 (6)	19.2 (8)	24.3 (7)

Relaxed attitudes toward the use of excessive force were noticeable in the Korean results; the majority of the respondents advocated that no discipline should be appropriate for a police officer who verbally abused a citizen (scenario 7). Furthermore, a substantial minority of the respondents advocated that no discipline be used in two other use of excessive force scenarios (about 40%; Table 12.11).

The results from Russia stand out from the group. In 7 out of 11 scenarios, literally all respondents (99 or 100%; Table 12.11) thought that the police officer should not be disciplined. These behaviors involved relatively benign scenarios in which the police officer accepted free meals and gratuities (scenario 1) or a supervisor engaged in internal corruption (scenario 5). However, they also involved some very serious scenarios, such as the police officer falsifying an official form (scenario 10), a supervisor who did not stop the beating (scenario 11), and even an officer who unjustifiably used deadly force (scenario 4). These attitudes are indicative of a police culture in which even serious misconduct is well protected.

We also studied the other end of the scale, the percentage of the respondents who viewed "dismissal" as the appropriate discipline (Table 12.11). While the respondents from Russia thought that a police officer who engaged in any of these behaviors should not be dismissed, the respondents in the ten countries occasionally (in 1–4 scenarios out of 11 for each country; Table 12.11) thought that "dismissal" was the appropriate response; in most instances, some discipline was thought to be appropriate, but not dismissal. The majority of the respondents in seven countries (Armenia, Australia, Croatia, Estonia, Slovenia, Thailand, and the USA) and a strong minority in two more countries (South Africa, South Korea) thought that the police officer who stole a knife from the crime scene (scenario 3) should be dismissed. Unjustifiably using deadly force (scenario 4) should also be a cause of dismissal according to the majority of the respondents in five countries (Australia, Croatia, Estonia, Slovenia, the USA) and a strong minority in two more (Armenia, South Africa). Finally, the majority of the respondents from the USA and Australian samples, and a strong minority in six more countries (Armenia, Croatia, Estonia, Slovenia, South Africa, and Thailand) assessed that the police officer who falsified the official report (scenario 10) should be dismissed as well (Table 12.11).

A strong minority of the respondents from various countries advocated for "dismissal" in several scenarios. In particular, the acceptance of a kickback (scenario 9) was the scenario that resulted in a strong minority of the respondents who supported "dismissal" in the largest number of countries (6 out of 11 countries) and the majority of the respondents in Australia. Falsifying the official report also generated a strong minority in six additional countries (Table 12.11). Similarly, the failure to execute a search warrant (scenario 2) should result in "dismissal," according to the majority of respondents in Slovenia and a strong minority in five countries.

We studied not only the respondents' own views about discipline but also what they assumed that their agencies would do (i.e., expected discipline Table 12.12). Table 12.12 contains the percentage of respondents in each country who said that "no discipline," "some discipline other than dismissal," or "dismissal" was the expected discipline for the behavior described in each scenario. In eight out of ten countries, there was no scenario in which the majority of the respondents thought

Table 12.12 Police officers' views of expected discipline

Scenario number and description	Armenia %	Australia %	Croatia %	Estonia %	Russia %	Slovenia %	South Africa %	South Korea %	Thailand %	The USA %
(% None)										
Scenario 1: free meals, gifts from merchants	21.2 (10)	5.8 (10)	24.3 (10)	15.6 (11)	1.9 (3.5)	32.4 (10)	12.4 (8)	30.5 (9)	80.8 (11)	19.9 (11)
Scenario 2: failure to arrest friend with felony warrant	7.5 (2)	1.6 (7)	4.2 (2)	1.0 (2)	47.2 (5)	7.9 (5)	3.9 (3)	12.4 (4)	5.2 (2)	6.0 (8)
Scenario 3: theft of knife from crime scene	2.3 (1)	0.2 (2)	3.1 (1)	0.1 (1)	0.9 (2)	1.4 (1)	1.1 (1)	2.2 (1)	1.8 (1)	0.8 (1)
Scenario 4: unjustifiable use of deadly force	9.9 (4)	1.8 (8)	7.2 (4)	2.8 (5)	96.2 (7)	3.5 (2)	2.6 (2)	23.0 (7)	7.0 (3)	4.3 (6)
Scenario 5: supervisor offers holiday for Errands	16.7 (8)	10.1 (11)	34.7 (11)	14.7 (10)	100.0 (9)	44.2 (11)	7.3 (7)	29.6 (8)	21.4 (7)	13.4 (10)
Scenario 6: officer strikes prisoner	15.3 (7)	1.3 (5.5)	18.7 (8)	2.8 (5)	N/A	11.8 (7)	6.7 (6)	34.0 (10)	13.3 (6)	2.4 (4)
Scenario 7: verbal abuse of motorist	15.0 (5)	3.5 (9)	17.0 (7)	6.4 (8.5)	0.0 (1)	28.3 (8)	14.2 (11)	41.9 (11)	38.4 (9)	4.5 (7)
Scenario 8: cover-up police DUI and accident	31.0 (11)	0.9 (4)	19.5 (9)	6.4 (8.5)	100.0 (9)	30.1 (9)	13.0 (9)	22.9 (6)	44.6 (10)	9.1 (9)
Scenario 9: auto body shop 5% kickback	15.1 (6)	0.1 (1)	9.3 (5)	3.7 (7)	75.5 (6)	7.8 (4)	14.1 (10)	5.1 (2)	38.0 (8)	2.3 (3)
Scenario 10: false report of drug possession	7.7 (3)	0.5 (3)	5.5 (3)	1.8 (3)	100.0 (9)	6.1 (3)	5.6 (5)	8.5 (3)	9.2 (5)	1.1 (2)
Scenario 11: Sgt. fails to halt beating of child abuser	17.0 (9)	1.3 (5.5)	13.9 (6)	2.8 (5)	1.9 (3.5)	9.4 (6)	4.0 (4)	19.7 (5)	8.5 (4)	3.0 (5)

Table 12.12 (continued)

Scenario number and description	Armenia %	Australia %	Croatia %	Estonia %	Russia %	Slovenia %	South Africa %	South Korea %	Thailand %	The USA %
% Some discipline, other than dismissal										
Scenario 1: free meals, gifts from merchants	65.0 (5)	89.6 (10)	65.6 (7)	52.3 (6)	98.1 (8.5)	56.9 (7)	74.2 (7)	62.3 (3)	17.7 (1)	78.4 (6)
Scenario 2: failure to arrest friend with Felony Warrant	70.4 (8)	78.2 (8)	62.2 (5)	61.4 (9)	52.8 (6)	55.6 (6)	74.6 (8)	68.8 (8)	70.5 (7)	84.0 (10)
Scenario 3: theft of knife from crime scene	42.8 (1)	30.5 (2)	48.6 (2)	16.4 (1)	97.2 (7)	26.3 (2)	49.5 (1)	66.2 (7)	42.1 (2)	31.5 (2)
Scenario 4: unjustifiable use of deadly force	48.9 (2)	23.0 (1)	27.8 (1)	26.6 (2)	1.9 (5)	23.5 (1)	54.6 (2)	70.7 (9)	78.2 (10)	17.0 (1)
Scenario 5: supervisor offers holiday for errands	76.6 (10)	87.8 (9)	60.8 (3)	71.5 (10)	0.0 (2.5)	50.0 (5)	79.7 (11)	64.7 (4)	70.8 (8)	83.6 (9)
Scenario 6: officer strikes prisoner	72.2 (9)	67.7 (6)	81.3 (10)	56.8 (8)	N/A	66.1 (10)	78.6 (9)	61.9 (2)	80.8 (11)	79.8 (8)
Scenario 7: verbal abuse of motorist	80.0 (11)	96.1 (11)	81.9 (11)	85.3 (11)	100.0 (10)	69.6 (11)	79.3 (10)	55.9 (1)	60.9 (6)	94.1 (11)
Scenario 8: cover up police DUI and Accident	65.2 (6)	69.6 (7)	75.2 (9)	53.2 (7)	0.0 (2.5)	57.0 (8)	72.5 (6)	65.8 (5)	53.5 (3)	79.2 (7)
Scenario 9: auto body shop five percent kickback	63.6 (4)	43.1 (4)	63.9 (6)	35.7 (3)	0.0 (2.5)	49.4 (3)	61.2 (3)	67.3 (6)	59.0 (5)	63.2 (4)
Scenario 10: false report of drug possession	58.4 (3)	37.9 (3)	61.6 (4)	43.2 (4)	0.0 (2.5)	49.6 (4)	62.3 (4)	74.5 (11)	58.7 (4)	37.7 (3)
Scenario 11: Sgt. fails to halt beating of child abuser	68.5 (7)	64.2 (5)	72.4 (8)	49.5 (5)	98.1 (8.5)	61.1 (9)	70.2 (5)	72.8 (10)	73.8 (9)	71.7 (5)

Table 12.12 (continued)

Scenario number and description	Armenia %	Australia %	Croatia %	Estonia %	Russia %	Slovenia %	South Africa %	South Korea %	Thailand %	The USA %
% Dismissal										
Scenario 1: free meals, gifts from merchants	13.8 (5)	4.6 (3)	10.1 (5)	32.1 (3)	0.0 (5)	10.7 (3)	13.4 (3)	7.2 (5)	1.5 (2)	1.8 (2)
Scenario 2: failure to arrest friend with Felony Warrant	22.1 (8)	20.1 (4)	33.6 (9)	37.6 (4)	0.0 (5)	36.5 (7)	21.5 (6)	18.8 (9)	24.4 (9)	10.0 (4)
Scenario 3: theft of knife from crime scene	54.9 (11)	69.2 (10)	48.3 (10)	83.5 (11)	0.0 (5)	72.3 (10)	49.4 (11)	31.6 (11)	56.1 (11)	67.7 (10)
Scenario 4: unjustifiable use of deadly force	41.3 (10)	75.3 (11)	65.0 (11)	70.6 (10)	0.0 (5)	73.0 (11)	42.8 (10)	6.3 (4)	14.8 (7)	78.7 (11)
Scenario 5: supervisor offers holiday for errands	6.7 (3)	2.2 (2)	4.6 (3)	13.8 (2)	0.0 (5)	5.8 (2)	13.0 (2)	5.7 (3)	7.7 (6)	3.0 (3)
Scenario 6: officer strikes prisoner	12.5 (4)	31.0 (6)	0.0 (1)	40.4 (5.5)	N/A	22.1 (5)	14.7 (5)	4.1 (2)	5.9 (5)	18.0 (6)
Scenario 7: verbal abuse of motorist	5.0 (2)	0.5 (1)	1.2 (2)	8.3 (1)	0.0 (5)	2.1 (1)	6.5 (1)	2.2 (1)	0.7 (1)	1.4 (1)
Scenario 8: cover up police DUI and accident	3.8 (1)	29.5 (5)	5.3 (4)	40.4 (5.5)	0.0 (5)	12.9 (4)	14.5 (4)	11.3 (7)	1.8 (3)	11.7 (5)
Scenario 9: auto body shop five percent kickback	21.3 (7)	56.7 (8)	26.8 (7)	60.6 (9)	24.5 (10)	42.8 (8)	24.7 (7)	27.6 (10)	3.0 (4)	34.5 (8)
Scenario 10: false report of drug possession	33.9 (9)	61.7 (9)	32.9 (8)	55.0 (8)	0.0 (5)	44.3 (9)	32.1 (9)	17.0 (8)	32.1 (10)	61.2 (9)
Scenario 11: Sgt. fails to halt beating of child abuser	14.3 (6)	34.5 (7)	13.7 (6)	47.7 (7)	0.0 (5)	29.5 (6)	25.8 (8)	7.5 (6)	17.7 (8)	25.3 (7)

that the police officer who engaged in the misconduct described in the scenario would not be disciplined (Table 12.12). In other words, the majority of police officers in eight countries expect at least some discipline for all the behaviors expected in the questionnaire. In addition, in seven out of ten countries, for a few scenarios a substantial minority of the respondents assessed that no discipline would be meted out. Accepting free meals and gratuities (scenario 1) and covering up a police DUI and accident (scenario 8) are examples of scenarios in which there was a substantial minority of the respondents in four or five countries who argued that no discipline would result.

South Korea has a large number of scenarios (7 out of 11) in which there was a substantial minority of the respondents who expected no discipline (Table 12.12). In addition to the two scenarios describing milder forms of police corruption (scenario 1: free meals, gifts from merchants; scenario 8: cover-up of police DUI and accident), all four scenarios describing the use of excessive force (scenario 4: unjustifiable use of deadly force; scenario 6: officer strikes prisoner; scenario 7: verbal abuse of motorist; scenario 11: Sgt. fails to halt beating of child abuser) had a large minority who thought that no discipline would result.

Russia again stands out based on what discipline the respondents expected. In five scenarios, the majority of the respondents—75 % or more—expected no discipline at all (Table 12.12). Although some of the scenarios were not evaluated as very serious across the countries (scenario 5: supervisor offers holiday for errands; scenario 8: cover-up of police DUI and accident), this group of scenarios included some very serious forms of misconduct, including the use of deadly force (scenario 4: unjustifiable use of deadly force), the acceptance of a kickback (scenario 9: auto body shop 5 % kickback), and falsification of the official form (scenario 10: false report on drug possession). These are the behaviors for which the majority or a strong minority of our respondents in other countries would expect dismissal.

We also explored the other end of the scale, the percentage of the respondents who expected that their agencies would dismiss police officers (Table 12.12). Overall, the respondents in these 10 countries only occasionally (0–4 scenarios out of 11, depending on the country; Table 12.12) thought that their agencies would dismiss a police officer if he engaged in the behavior described in the questionnaire; most of the times, they thought that their agencies would discipline, but not dismiss. Australia, Estonia, and the USA have the largest number of scenarios in which they expected dismissal (4 Australia, 4 Estonia, 3 the USA).

However, when the scenarios in which there was a substantial minority (20 % or more) are added, then four scenarios really stand out (scenario 3: theft of knife from crime scene; scenario 4: unjustifiable use of deadly force; scenario 9: auto body shop 5 % kickback; scenario 10: false report on drug possession). At the same time, these are the scenarios typically evaluated as the most serious. The majority of the respondents in two countries (Australia, Estonia) and a strong minority in seven more countries expected dismissal for a police officer who accepted a kickback arrangement (scenario 9; Table 12.12). Similarly, the majority of the respondents in six countries (Armenia, Australia, Estonia, Slovenia, Thailand, and the USA) and a strong minority in three more (Croatia, South Africa, and South Korea) expected dismissal for a police officer who stole the knife from the crime scene (scenario 3). Furthermore, the majority of the respondents in three countries (Australia, Estonia, the USA) and a strong minority in five more (Armenia, Croatia, Slovenia, South Africa, and Thailand) expected dismissal for a police officer who falsified the official report (scenario 10). In addition, the majority of the respondents in five countries (Australia, Croatia, Estonia, Slovenia, and the USA) and a strong minority in two more (Armenia, South Africa) expected dismissal for a police officer who unjustifiably used deadly force (scenario 4).

The respondents from Russia again showed a different pattern. While in other countries there was either the majority and/or strong minority of the respondents who expected dismissal for the behavior described in at least several scenarios, not a single Russian respondent expected dismissal in 9 out of 10 scenarios. In the remaining scenario (scenario 9: auto body shop 5 % kickback), about a quarter of the respondents expected dismissal.

Willingness to Report Misconduct

The last two questions after each scenario asked the respondents to express how willing they would be to report misconduct and to estimate how willing other officers in their agencies would be to do so. The answers ranged on a five-point Likert scale from "definitely not" to "definitely yes."

The results, shown in Table 12.13, contain mean values and ranks for each country. With the exception of Russia, Thailand, and South Korea, the respondents in seven out of ten countries had means clustered on the reporting side of the scale (mean values between about 3, which is the midpoint of the scale, and 5, the reporting end of the scale). The range of the means is the largest in Thailand (between 1.26 and 4.27; Table 12.13). Based on the range of mean values for each country, we can classify countries into four categories. First, the codes in Australia, Estonia, Slovenia, South Africa, and the USA are all on the reporting side of our scale (from about 2.5–3 to 5; Table 12.13). Second, Armenia, Croatia, and Thailand also have most of the means on the reporting side of the scale, but are somewhat lower and closer to the midpoint of the scale (means are somewhere between 2.5 and 4.2 or 1.26–4.3 for Thailand). This would imply that the codes in Armenia, Croatia, and Thailand seem to be somewhat stronger than the codes in Australia, Estonia, Slovenia, South Africa, and the USA (with the means between 2.5–3 and 5; Table 12.13). Third, the means for South Korea are closer to the midpoint of the scale than any of the two ends (means are from 2.0 to 3.6). This would imply that the code in South Korea is stronger than the codes in Australia, Estonia, Slovenia, South Africa, and the USA, and probably somewhat stronger than the codes in Armenia, Croatia, and Thailand as well. Fourth, the code of silence is by far the strongest in Russia; the mean values for all scenarios are clustered between the nonreporting side and the midpoint of the scale (mean values are from 1.0 to below 3.0; Table 12.13).

Table 12.13 Police officers' own willingness to report (Means/Ranks)

Scenario number and description	Armenia	Australia	Croatia	Estonia	Russia	Slovenia	South Africa	South Korea	Thailand	The USA
Scenario 1: free meals, gifts from merchants	2.97 (3)	3.35 (2)	2.84 (4)	3.14 (2)	1.37 (4)	2.76 (2)	3.61 (3)	2.36 (3)	1.26 (1)	2.39 (1)
Scenario 2: failure to arrest friend with felony warrant	3.36 (8)	4.37 (7)	4.05 (9)	3.86 (8)	1.80 (8)	4.14 (8.5)	4.20 (9)	2.98 (7)	3.44 (7.5)	3.61 (4)
Scenario 3: theft of knife from crime scene	3.83 (10)	4.83 (10)	4.11 (11)	4.41 (11)	1.78 (7)	4.60 (11)	4.36 (11)	3.57 (11)	4.27 (11)	4.65 (10)
Scenario 4: unjustifiable use of deadly force	3.93 (11)	4.89 (11)	4.09 (10)	4.39 (10)	2.87 (10)	4.42 (10)	4.32 (10)	3.20 (10)	3.84 (10)	4.79 (11)
Scenario 5: supervisor offers holiday for errands	3.27 (7)	3.76 (3)	3.04 (5)	3.68 (6)	1.56 (6)	3.47 (5)	3.84 (6)	2.84 (6)	2.84 (5)	3.67 (5)
Scenario 6: officer strikes prisoner	2.91 (2)	3.98 (4)	2.49 (2)	3.35 (3)	N/A	3.16 (4)	3.80 (5)	2.20 (2)	2.88 (6)	3.79 (6)
Scenario 7: verbal abuse of motorist	3.02 (5)	2.94 (1)	2.60 (3)	3.00 (1)	2.00 (9)	2.70 (3)	3.33 (1)	2.05 (1)	2.01 (3)	2.83 (2)
Scenario 8: cover-up police DUI and accident	2.70 (1)	4.10 (5)	2.43 (1)	3.36 (4)	1.00 (1)	2.27 (1)	3.47 (2)	2.41 (4)	1.92 (2)	3.07 (3)
Scenario 9: auto body shop 5% kickback	3.12 (6)	4.69 (8)	3.66 (7)	3.66 (5)	1.28 (3)	4.06 (7)	3.68 (4)	3.19 (9)	2.35 (4)	4.15 (8)
Scenario 10: false report of drug possession	3.71 (9)	4.71 (9)	3.78 (8)	4.20 (9)	1.01 (2)	4.14 (8.5)	4.07 (8)	3.18 (8)	3.75 (9)	4.59 (9)
Scenario 11: Sgt. fails to halt beating of child abuser	2.98 (4)	4.32 (6)	3.13 (6)	3.75 (7)	1.51 (5)	3.61 (6)	3.92 (7)	2.72 (5)	3.44 (7.5)	4.12 (7)

The exploration of the country rankings reveals common themes. To begin, the respondents from the majority of the countries were most likely to say that they would report a fellow police officer who engaged in a theft of a knife from a crime scene (scenario 3), unjustifiable use of deadly force (scenario 4), and falsified the official report (scenario 10). In fact, the use of deadly force (scenario 4) and the opportunistic theft (scenario 3) are viewed as *the* scenarios in which the respondents from most of the countries would be most likely to say that they would report (Table 12.13). Even in Russia and South Korea, two countries that often stand out in our cross-country comparisons, the use of deadly force—the abuse of the most serious type of force available—trumps the code of silence to the extent that it might lead to reporting.

On the other end, four scenarios (scenario 1: free meals, gifts from merchants; scenario 6: officer striker prisoner; scenario 7: verbal abuse of motorist; scenario 8: cover-up of police DUI and accident) were consistently viewed as those most likely to be protected by the code of silence (Table 12.13). Accepting gratuities and small gifts (scenario 1) has been perceived as the least serious form of police corruption. Therefore, it is by no means surprising that all ten countries have it on their list as one of the four scenarios least likely to be reported and the most likely to be protected by the code of silence. Similarly, verbal abuse of a citizen (scenario 7) is the least serious form of police use of excessive force and, thus, eight out of ten countries find it to be one of the four scenarios most likely to be covered by the code (Table 12.13). The cover-up of police DUI and accident (scenario 8)—a relatively moderate case of internal corruption—is also a highly protected behavior; nine out of ten countries view it as one of the four scenarios most likely to be covered by the code of silence.

Furthermore, there seems to be a very strong negative relation between how serious particular scenario has been evaluated and how likely the respondents felt that the behavior would be protected by the code of silence. In eight out of ten countries, the strong and statistically significant Spearman's correlation coefficient (above 0.7) suggests that, the more serious the respondents evaluated the scenario, the less likely they were to say that they would protect it in silence. In Russia and Korea, the correlation coefficient is large as well (0.590 and 0.545). It is pointing in the same direction and is statistically significant at the 0.10 level.

In addition, we used Spearman's correlation coefficient to test whether the country rankings are correlated (Table 12.14). Indeed, for nine out of ten countries, their own ranking of scenarios based on how likely they were protected by the code of silence was aligned very closely with the ranking provided by other countries. Specifically, for nine countries, their ranking was very strongly correlated with the ranking of other eight other countries (with the exception of Russia; Table 12.14), regardless of whether they are located on the same continent, belong to the same legal tradition, or have common history.

The Russian ranking is again quite different from the rankings from other countries; it is not statistically significantly correlated with any of the other nine countries (Table 12.14), including those with historical similarities political, legal, and economic dimensions. This is partly a consequence of the fact that the Russian

Table 12.14 Country Spearman's rank correlations of own willingness to report

	Armenia	Australia	Croatia	Estonia	Russia	Slovenia	South Africa	South Korea	Thailand	The USA
Armenia	1.00									
Australia	0.718*	1.00								
Croatia	0.918***	0.818**	1.00							
Estonia	0.818**	0.891***	0.882***	1.00						
Russia	0.527	0.115	0.406	0.261	1.00					
Slovenia	0.907***	0.866**	0.961***	0.907***	0.432	1.00				
South Africa	0.800**	0.800**	0.882***	0.945***	0.370	0.916***	1.00			
South Korea	0.818**	0.909***	0.891***	0.891***	0.164	0.879***	0.791**	1.00		
Thailand	0.776**	0.799**	0.808**	0.904***	0.354	0.911***	0.932***	0.712*	1.00	
The USA	0.700*	0.891***	0.727*	0.818**	0.176	0.843**	0.764**	0.818**	0.845**	1.00
# of Countries with Sig. correlations	8/9	8/9	8/9	8/9	0/9	8/9	8/9	8/9	8/9	8/9

* $p < 0.05$; ** $p < 0.01$; *** $p < 0.001$

ranking does not correspond well in regard to two specific scenarios. In particular, Russian respondents ranked the scenario describing verbal abuse (scenario 7) much higher than the respondents from other countries (Table 12.14). At the same time, they ranked both the scenario describing opportunistic theft (scenario 3) and the scenario describing official report falsification (scenario 10) much lower than the respondents from other countries did (Table 12.14).

A comparison of the respondents' own assessments of how likely they were to report misconduct and their estimates of how likely their fellow officers were to do so offers several conclusions. In almost all countries, there were statistically significant differences between the respondents' own willingness to report and the estimated willingness to report by their fellow police officers (Table 12.15). Based on the previously developed rule of thumb (Klockars et al. 2006), we consider only the differences of 0.50 or larger to be meaningful.

In about one half of the countries (5 out of 10; Table 12.15), there were no meaningful differences between the respondents' own willingness to report and their assessment of how willing others in their agency would be to report. This finding implies that police officers in these five countries (Armenia, Australia, Estonia, South Korea, and the USA) have an accurate perception of how the code of silence in their agencies might look like. There is one scenario in which Russian respondents thought that other officers would have a different take; in that scenario (scenario 8: cover-up of police DUI and accident), they assumed that other officers would be more likely to say that they would report than they themselves were ready to do. This scenario is evaluated as the least serious, both in relative terms (i.e., it was as evaluated as the least serious scenario in the questionnaire) and in absolute terms (i.e., the mean value of 1.27, practically as close to the nonserious side of the scale as possible). In this case, it was clear from the mean value that virtually no respondent would report (mean value of 1; Table 12.13) and they probably regarded themselves as more loyal to their colleagues than others in the agency, translating into their perception that others might be somewhat more likely to report.

A comparison of four countries—Croatia, Slovenia, South Africa, and Thailand—features meaningful differences between the respondents' own willingness to report and perceived willingness to report by other officers in the agency in at least two scenarios (Table 12.15). In all these instances, the respondents seemed more willing to report than they thought other police officers in their agency would be to do so. This discrepancy is particularly pronounced for the respondents from South Africa (there were 7 out of 11 scenarios with meaningful differences) and Thailand (there were 10 out of 11 scenarios with meaningful differences). For several scenarios in which there seems to be a meaningful discrepancy, the discrepancy existed for two, three, or sometimes even four countries (Table 12.15). Two of these scenarios (scenario 3: theft of knife from crime scene; scenario 10: false report of drug possession) are viewed as the most serious in the questionnaire.

Table 12.15 Police officers' willingness to report: own versus others (statistically significant differences and substantive differences)

Scenario number and description	Armenia	Australia	Croatia	Estonia	Russia	Slovenia	South Africa	South Korea	Thailand	USA
Scenario 1: free meals, gifts from merchants	***	***	***	***	***	***	***	*		***
Scenario 2: failure to arrest friend with felony warrant	***	***	***	***	***	***	***		***	***
Scenario 3: theft of knife from crime scene	***	***	***	***	***	***	***		***	***
Scenario 4: unjustifiable use of deadly force	***	***	***		***	***	***		***	***
Scenario 5: supervisor offers holiday for errands	***	***	***	***	***	***	***	**	***	***
Scenario 6: officer strikes prisoner	***	***	***	***	N/A	***	***		***	***
Scenario 7: verbal abuse–"Arrest an Asshole Day"	***	***	***	***	***	***	***		***	***
Scenario 8: cover-up police DUI and accident	***	***		***	***	***	***		***	***
Scenario 9: auto body shop 5 % kickback	***	***	***	***	***	***	***		***	***
Scenario 10: false report of drug possession	***	***	***	***	***	***	***	**	***	***
Scenario 11: Sgt. fails to halt beating of child abuser	***	***	***	***	***	***	***		***	***
Meaningful differences	NO (0/11)	NO (0/11)	YES (2/11) positive	NO (0/11)	YES (1/10) negative	YES (5/11) positive	YES (7/11) positive	NO (0/11)	YES (10/11) positive	NO (0/11)

* $p < 0.05$; ** $p < 0.01$; *** $p < 0.001$

Conclusion

The comparative exploration of police integrity is riddled with inherent challenges, from adjusting the wording of the scenarios, to offering different options as answers to the same questions. We took a cautious approach, while, at the same time, trying to capture the key similarities and differences in the contours of police integrity across ten countries. Our analyses revealed a number of key conclusions.

First, although absolute evaluations of seriousness and willingness to report vary across countries, relative rankings of seriousness and willingness to report (i.e., how scenarios are evaluated compared to other scenarios in the questionnaire) tended to be similar across most of the ten countries. In all of these comparisons, the results from Russia and, to a certain degree, from South Korea, stand out from the remaining countries.

Second, there seems to be an underlying hierarchy of misconduct seriousness. Stealing from a crime scene, unjustifiably using deadly force, and falsifying official reports are consistently evaluated as the most serious forms of misconduct. Similarly, illegitimate use of deadly force represents the abuse of the most severe level of force at the police disposal. In the use of force continuum, used in different versions across the U.S. police agencies, deadly force always comes on top of the continuum. Consequently, it is by no means surprising that it has been evaluated as one of the most serious forms of misconduct described in the questionnaire.

The respondents from the majority of the surveyed countries agree on what scenarios should be viewed as the least serious. Covering up a police DUI and accident, accepting gratuities and free meals, and verbally abusing a citizen are consistently evaluated as the least serious forms of police misconduct. Similarly, verbal abuse of citizens involves the least severe violation on the use of force continuum—issuing verbal commands. It is by no means surprising that police officers across the world evaluate this behavior as one of the least serious in the questionnaire. Finally, the cover-up of the police DUI and accident is an example of a milder form of internal corruption.

Third, behaviors evaluated as more serious were also more likely to be viewed as violations of official rules. There is more consistency for the more serious misconduct than for examples of misconduct on the other end of the scale. With one exception, stealing a knife from a crime scene—evaluated as the most serious scenario in the questionnaire—generated most uniformity because it was evaluated as rule violating by 90 % or more of the respondents across the countries. About 80 % or more of the respondents from different countries recognized falsifying an official report or unjustifiably using deadly force as rule violating. On the other hand, covering up a police DUI and accident, by far the least serious scenario in the questionnaire according to the respondents, has generated the greatest diversity of opinion; it has been evaluated as rule violating by between 45 and 98 % of the respondents. Similarly, accepting gratuities or verbally abusing citizens, some of the least serious examples of misconduct in the questionnaire, were viewed as rule violating by 60 to 90 % of the respondents.

Fourth, with one exception, it is comforting that the majority of the respondents from nine countries support and expect some discipline for all or most of the forms of misconduct featured in the questionnaire. Not only did the respondents deem some discipline appropriate and expected for the most serious scenarios (theft from a crime scene and the unjustifiable use of deadly force) but they also indicated that they would support and expect that some discipline would follow even for less serious misconduct (acceptance of free meals and gratuities, verbal abuse of a citizen, and cover-up of police DUI and accident).

Fifth, the results tell us that these police agencies create vastly different disciplinary environments. Based on the evaluations provided by our respondents, some countries create environments in which police officers neither support nor expect dismissal for any of the forms of misconduct described in the questionnaire; our respondents thought that a police officer who steals from a crime scene, who unjustifiably uses deadly force, or who falsifies the official report quite likely would not be dismissed. By contrast, the overwhelming majority of our respondents from Estonia, Australia, and the USA expected and supported dismissal for such behaviors.

Sixth, dismissal is neither expected nor supported discipline for the majority of the scenarios. Whereas dismissal would seem very appropriate for police officers who participate in kickbacks, use deadly force unjustifiably, steal from the crime scene, or falsify official reports, it would be surprising if police agencies fired police officers for verbally abusing citizens or accepting gratuities. Accordingly, our results indicate that the respondents thought that the severity of the discipline should be proportionate to the seriousness of the misconduct. The majority of the respondents expected that some discipline, but not dismissal, would follow for the scenarios evaluated as the least serious. On the other hand, the majority or a strong minority expected discipline for the most serious cases in almost all countries.

Seventh, police officers differentiate across scenarios and neither expect nor support the same type of discipline for every type of misconduct. Even in Estonia and Australia, whose respondents portrayed the harshest disciplinary environments, very few respondents expected that somebody would be dismissed for accepting free meals or gratuities or for verbally abusing a motorist. On the other hand, the majority of the respondents in these countries expected and supported dismissal for police officers who stole from the crime scene, used deadly force unjustifiably, or falsified an official report.

Eighth, it should come as no surprise that the code of silence is present in each and every country. However, in a manner fully consistent with the theory of police integrity upon which we rely in this work (Klockars and Kutnjak Ivković, 2004), what seems to be protected by the code varies greatly across the ten countries. Yet, there are reverberating common themes. A police officer who accepts free meals and verbally abuses citizens would likely be protected by fellow police officers in any surveyed country. On the other hand, respondents indicated that stealing at the crime scene or abusing deadly force probably would not go unreported in most surveyed countries.

Ninth, the responses from two countries stand out. Russian respondents stand out virtually for almost every measure. Although their evaluations of rule violations are not that different from the evaluations provided by respondents from other countries, with the exception of two scenarios, Russian respondents evaluated all other scenarios as much less serious than the respondents from any other country. The respondents were also very certain that no discipline would result in almost one half of the scenarios and the majority did not expect dismissal for any of the behaviors described in the scenarios. In fact, there was only one scenario—a kickback—in which about one quarter expected dismissal. Finally, the code of silence was extremely strong; based on the results, it seems that the code in Russia would protect all types of misconduct included in the study. However, given the widespread nature of corruption in Russia, where police officers have been exposed to various types of corrupt behaviors, it is not surprising that our respondents from Russia would exhibit such attitudes tolerant of various forms of police misconduct. In comparison to some truly egregious behaviors occurring both within and outside the police organization, the scenarios described in our questionnaire do not seem to reach levels of truly shocking examples of police misconduct.

South Korea also stands out from the group. Regardless of the measure—from estimates of seriousness, violation of the rules, or expected discipline—Korean responses tend to be similar to the responses from other countries for everything except the use of excessive force. All these measures indicate a more tolerant and relaxed stance toward the use of excessive force, from the verbal abuse of citizens to the use of deadly force. As Kang and Kutnjak Ivković (2015) noted, "the scenario describing the use of deadly force, the most serious form of force, has been recognized as a rule-violating behavior by only four out of ten respondents." The code of silence also seems to be very protective of the use of excessive force. Overall, the effects of the Grand Reform with the emphasis on corruption and little on use of excessive force are clearly noticeable.

Tenth, the contours of police integrity vary across the world. What is acceptable and tolerated in one country or one police agency may not be acceptable at all in another, and may be disciplined severely. Because police agencies are part of their societies at large, the larger environments setup and uphold the standards of acceptable and tolerated behavior. Legal, social, political, and historical conditions shape police agencies and the behavior of the police officers they employ.

References

Alain, M. (2004). An exploratory study of quebec's police officers' attitudes toward ethical dilemmas. In C.B. Klockars, S. Kutnjak Ivković, & M.R. Haberfeld (Eds.), *The contours of police integrity* (pp. 40–56). Thousand Oaks: Sage.

Andreescu, V., Keeling, D. G., Voinic, M. C., & Tonea, B. N. (2012). Future Romanian law enforcement: Gender differences in perceptions of police misconduct. *Journal of Social Research & Policy, 3*(1): 97–114. http://www.academia.edu/3114941/Future_Romanian_Law_Enforcement_Gender_Differences_in_Perceptions_of_Police_Misconduct.

Charles, S. (2009). Professional integrity, modern racism, self-esteem, and universality-diversity orientation of police officers in a large *urban police agency*. DigitalResearch@Fordham.

Chattha, Z. N., & Kutnjak Ivković, S. (2004). Police misconduct: The Pakistani paradigm. In C. B. Klockars, S. Kutnjak Ivković, & M. R. Haberfeld (Eds.), *The contours of police integrity* (pp. 175–194). Thousand Oaks: Sage.

Desta, Y. (2013). Applying a U.S. police integrity measurement tool to the Eritrean context: Perceptions of top-level Eritrean police officers regarding police misconduct. *Journal of Organizational Transformation & Social Change, 10*(3), 238–261.

Edelbacher, M., & Kutnjak Ivković, S. (2004). Ethics and the police: Studying police integrity in Austria. In C. B. Klockars, S. Kutnjak Ivković, & M. R. Haberfeld (Eds.), *The contours of police integrity* (pp. 19–39). Thousand Oaks: Sage.

Gottschalk, P. (2010). Police integrity surveys: A court-based survey approach. *International Journal of Management and Enterprise Development, 8*(3), 243–259.

Greene, J. R., Piquero, A. R., Hickman, M. J., & Lawton, B. A. (2004). *Police* Integrity and Accountability in Philadelphia: Predicting and Assessing Police Misconduct. National Institute of Justice. http://www.ncjrs.gov/pdffiles1/nij/grants/207823.pdf. Accessed 20 June 2014.

Haberfeld, M. R. (2004). The heritage of police misconduct: The case of the Polish police. In C. B. Klockars, S. Kutnjak Ivković, & M. R. Haberfeld (Eds.), *The contours of police integrity* (pp. 95–210). Thousand Oaks: Sage.

Haberfeld, M. R., Klockars, C. B., Kutnjak Ivković, S., & Pagon, M. (2000). Police officer perceptions of the disciplinary consequences of police corruption in Croatia, Poland, Slovenia, and the United States. *Police Practice and Research: An International Journal, 1*(1), 41–72.

Huberts, L., Lamboo, T., & Punch, M. (2003). Police integrity in the Netherlands and the United States: Awareness and alertness. *Police Practice and Research, 4*(3), 217–232.

Johnson, D. T. (2003). Above the law? Police integrity in Japan. *Social Science Japan Journal, 6*(1), 19–37.

Johnson, D. T. (2004). Police integrity in Japan. In C. B. Klockars, S. Kutnjak Ivković, & M. R. Haberfeld (Eds.), *The Contours of Police Integrity*. Thousand Oaks: Sage.

Kang, W., & Kutnjak Ivković S. (2015). Police integrity in South Korea. In S. Kutnjak Ivković & M. R. Haberfeld (Eds.), *Measuring police integrity across the world*. New York: Springer.

Khechumyan, A., & Kutnjak Ivković, S. (2015). Police integrity in Armenia. In S. Kutnjak Ivković & M. R. Haberfeld (Eds.), *Measuring police integrity across the world*. New York: Springer.

Klockars, C. B., & Kutnjak Ivković, S. (1999). The Measurement of police delinquency. In W. Laufer & F. Adler (Eds.), *The criminology of criminal law. advances in criminological theory*, (Vol. 8. pp. 87–106). New Brunswick: Transaction.

Klockars, C. B., & Kutnjak Ivković, S. (2004). Measuring police integrity. In M. J. Hickman, A. R. Piquero, & J. R. Greene (Eds.), *Police integrity and ethics*. Belmont: Wadsworth Publishing.

Klockars, C. B., Kutnjak Ivković, S., Harver, W. E., & Haberfeld, M. R. (2000). *The measurement of police integrity. research in brief. U.S. department of justice, office of justice programs, national institute of justice*. Washington: Government Printing Office.

Klockars, C. B., Kutnjak Ivković, S., & Haberfeld, M. R. (2004). Police integrity in the United States of America. In C. B. Klockars, S. Kutnjak Ivković, & M. R. Haberfeld (Eds.), *The contours of police integrity* (pp. 265–282). Thousand Oaks: Sage Publications.

Klockars, C. B., Kutnjak Ivković, S., & Haberfeld, M. R. (2006). *Enhancing police integrity*. Dordrecht: Springer.

Kremer, F. (2000). Comparing supervisor and line officer opinions about the code of silence: The case of Hungary. In M. Pagon (Ed.), *Policing in central and eastern europe: ethics, integrity, and human rights* (pp. 211–219). Ljubljana: College of Police and Security Studies.

Kremer, F. (2004). Police integrity in Hungary. In C. B. Klockars, S. Kutnjak Ivković, & M. R. Haberfeld (Eds.), *The contours of police integrity* (pp. 116–130). Thousand Oaks: Sage.

Kucukuysal, B. (2008). Determinants Of Turkish Police Officers' perception of integrity: Impact of organizational culture (Doctoral dissertation, University of Central Florida Orlando, Florida).

Kutnjak Ivković, S. (2004). Sharing the view: Line officer and supervisor evaluations of police corruption seriousness in Bosnia and Herzegovina. In G. Mesko, M. Pagon, & G. Dobovsek

(Eds.), *Dilemmas of contemporary criminal justice* (pp. 312–322). Ljubljana: Faculty of Criminal Justice, University of Maribor.

Kutnjak Ivković, S. (2005). Police (Mis)Behavior: A cross-cultural study of corruption seriousness. *Policing: An International Journal of Police Strategies and Management, 28*(3), 546–566.

Kutnjak Ivković, S. (2009). The Croatian police, police integrity, and transition toward democratic policing. *Policing: An International Journal of Police Strategies & Management, 32*(3), 459–488.

Kutnjak Ivković, S., & Kang, W. (2011). Police integrity in South Korea. *Policing: An International Journal of Police Strategies and Management, 35*(1), 76–103.

Kutnjak Ivković, S. (2012). Exploring the relation between police integrity and rank a Croatian example. *International Criminal Justice Review, 22*(4), 372–396.

Kutnjak Ivković, S., & Khechumyan, A. (2013). The state of police integrity in Armenia: Findings from the police integrity survey. *Policing: An International Journal of Police Strategies and Management, 36*(1), 70–90.

Kutnjak Ivković, S., & Klockars, C. B. (1998). The code of silence and the croatian police. In M. Pagon (Ed.), *Policing in central and eastern europe: organizational, managerial, and human resource aspects* (pp. 329–347). Ljubljana: College of Police and Security Studies.

Kutnjak Ivković, S., & Klockars, C. B. (2000). Comparing police supervisor and line officer opinions about the code of silence: The case of Croatia. In M. Pagon, (Ed.), *Policing in central and eastern europe: ethics, integrity, and human rights* (pp. 183–195). Ljubljana: College of Police and Security Studies.

Kutnjak Ivković, S., & Klockars, C. B. (2004). Police integrity in Croatia. In C. B. Klockars, S. Kutnjak Ivković, & M. R. Haberfeld (Eds.), *The contours of police integrity* (pp. 56–74). Thousand Oaks: Sage.

Kutnjak Ivković, S., & Shelley O'Connor, T. (2007). Police integrity and the Czech police officers. *International Journal of Comparative and Applied Criminal Justice, 31*(1), 21–49.

Kutnjak Ivković, S., & O'Connor Shelley, T. (2008). The police code of silence and different paths towards democratic *policing. Policing & Society, 18*(4), 445–473.

Kutnjak Ivković, S., & Sauerman, A. (2012). The code of silence: Revisiting South African police integrity. *South African Crime Quarterly, 40,* 15–24.

Kutnjak Ivković, S., & Shelley O'Connor, T. (2010). The code of silence and disciplinary fairness: A comparison of Czech police supervisor and line officer views. *Policing: An International Journal of Police Strategies and Management, 33*(3), 548–574.

Kutnjak Ivković, S., Klockars, C. B., Cajner-Mraovic, I., & Ivanusec, D. (2002). Controlling police corruption: The Croatian perspective. *Police Practice and Research: An International Journal, 3*(1), 55–72.

Kutnjak Ivković, S., Cajner-Mraovic, I., & Ivanusec, D. (2004). The measurement of seriousness of police corruption. In G. Mesko, M. Pagon, & G. Dobovsek (Eds.), *Dilemmas of contemporary criminal justice* (pp. 300–311). Ljubljana: Faculty of Criminal Justice, University of Maribor.

Kutnjak Ivković, S., Haberfeld, M., & Peacock, R. (2013). Rainless West: The integrity survey's role in agency accountability. *Police Quarterly, 16*(2), 148–176.

Lee, H., Lim, H., Moore, D. D., & Kim, J. (2013). How police organizational structure correlates with frontline officers' attitudes toward corruption: A multilevel model. *Police Practice and Research, 14*(5), 386–401.

McDevitt, J., Posick, C., Zschoche, R., Rosenbaum, D. P., Buslik, M., & Fridell, L. (2011). Police integrity, responsibility, and discipline. National Institute of Justice. http://www.nationalpoliceresearch.org/storage/updated-papers/Police%20Integrity%20Responsibility%20and%20Discipline.pdf. Accessed 20 June 2014.

Newham, G. (2004). Out of step: Integrity and the South Africa Police Service. In C. B. Klockars, S. Kutnjak Ivković, & M. R. Haberfeld (Eds.), *The contours of police integrity* (pp. 232–247). Thousand Oaks: Sage.

Pagon, M., & Lobnikar, B. (2000). Comparing supervisor and line officer opinions about the code of silence: The case of Slovenia. In M. Pagon (Ed.), *Policing in central and eastern europe: ethics, integrity, and human rights*. Ljubljana: College of Police and Security Studies (pp. 197–209).

Pagon, M., & Lobnikar, B. (2004). Police integrity in Slovenia. In C. B. Klockars, S. Kutnjak Ivković, & M. R. Haberfeld (Eds.), *The Contours of police integrity* (pp. 212–231). Thousand Oaks: Sage.

Pagon, M., Kutnjak Ivković, S., & Lobnikar, B. (2000). Police integrity and attitudes toward police corruption: A comparison between the police and the public. *Policing in Central and Eastern Europe: Ethics, integrity, and human rights*, 383–396.

Pagon, M., Lobnikar, B., & Anelj, D. (2004). Gender differences in leniency towards police misconduct. In G. Mesko, M. Pagon, & B. Dobovsek (Eds.), *Policing in central and eastern europe-dilemmas of contemporary criminal justice* (pp. 1–16). Ljubljana: Faculty of Criminal Justice, University of Maribor.

Porter, L. E., Prenzler, T., & Hine, K. (2015). Police Integrity in Australia. In S. Kutnjak Ivković & M. R. Haberfeld (Eds.), *Measuring police integrity across the world*. New York: Springer.

Pounti, A., Vuorinen, S., & Kutnjak Ivković S. (2004). Sustaining police integrity in Finland. In C. B. Klockars, S. Kutnjak Ivković, & M. R. Haberfeld (Eds.), *The contours of police integrity* (pp. 95–115). Thousand Oaks: Sage.

Punch, M., Huberts, L. W. J. C., & Lamboo, M. E. D. (2004). Integrity, perceptions, and investigations in the Netherlands. In C. B. Klockars, S. Kutnjak Ivković & M. R. Haberfeld (Eds.), *The contours of police integrity* (pp. 161–175). Thousand Oaks: Sage.

Roebuck, J. B., & Barker, T. (1974). A typology of police corruption. *Social Problems, 21*, 423–437.

Rothwell, G. R., & Baldwin, J. N. (2007). Whistle-blowing and the code of silence in police agencies policy and structural predictors. *Crime & Delinquency, 53*(4), 605–632.

Sauerman, A., & Kutnjak Ivković, S. (2008). Measuring the Integrity of the South African police service during transitional times. *Acta Criminologica, 2*, 21–39.

Torstensson Levander, M., & Ekenvall, B. (2004). Homogeneity in moral standards in Swedish police culture. In C.B. Klockars, S. Kutnjak Ivković, & M.R. Haberfeld (Eds.), *The contours of police integrity* (pp. 251–265). Thousand Oaks: Sage.

Vito, G.F., Wolfe, S., Higgins, G. E., & Walsh W.F. (2011). Police integrity: Rankings of scenarios on the Klockars scale by "Management Cops". *Criminal Justice Review, 36*: 152–164.

Westmarland, L. (2004). Policing integrity: Britain's thin blue line. In C. B. Klockars, S. Kutnjak Ivković, & M. R. Haberfeld (Eds.), *The contours of police integrity* (pp. 75–93). Thousand Oaks: Sage.

Westmarland, L. (2005). Police ethics and integrity: Breaking the blue code of silence. *Policing and Society, 15*(2), 145–165.

Yun, I. (2003). A study of police officers'perceptions of police deviance: From an occupational socialization perspective. ProQuest Dissertations and Theses, pp. 89–89. http://ezproxy.msu.edu/login?url= http://search.proquest.com/docview/305329643?accountid=12598. (305329643). Accessed 20 June 2014.

Yunus, O. M., Bustaman, H., & Khalid, K. (2013). Conducive business environment: A measurement of local authority integrity. *The Journal of Interdisciplinary Networks, 129*, 213–220.

About the Authors

Serguei Cheloukhine is an Associate Professor at the Department of Law, Police Science and Criminal Justice Administration, John Jay College of Criminal Justice. Dr. Serguei Cheloukhine's areas of expertise are Corruption, Corrupt Networks, Organized Crime, Anti-Money Laundering and Financing Terrorism, Criminal Justice and Policing. Cheloukhine worked as a police officer in Caucasus and Chechnya, and then professor and the Department of Social Sciences chairperson at the Rostov-on-Don Law School (former Higher Police Academy) for ten years. From 1997–2001, he was the first Russian police officer working at the Nathanson Center for the Study of Organized Crime and Corruption (Toronto, Canada) as a researcher.

Qasim Haq is a Research Associate at PROVE (Project for Return and Opportunity In Veterans Education) at the Silberman School of Social Work, Hunter College. PROVE engages recently separated veterans in transition to civilian life, with emphasis on higher education. Qasim is an adjunct lecturer in the Law and Police Science Department at John Jay College of Criminal Justice where he has taught a number of courses including Seminar in Terrorism, U.S. Law Enforcement, and Introduction to Criminal Justice and Corrections. Qasim's research interests include police integrity, police performance, and policing in minority communities. Qasim holds a Master of Arts in Criminal Justice from the John Jay College of Criminal Justice, and Bachelors' of Science in Psychology with Human Biology from the University of Plymouth, United Kingdom.

Kelly Hine is a Doctoral Candidate in the School of Criminology and Criminal Justice, Griffith University, Australia and a member of the ARC Centre of Excellence in Policing and Security (CEPS). She attained a double degree in Psychological Science and Criminology and Criminal Justice and was awarded First Class Honours in Criminology and Criminal Justice for her dissertation on the potentials of using situational crime prevention as an alternative approach to preventing police deviance. In addition to her research interests on police corruption and misconduct, her doctoral thesis investigates police use of force and the decision making processes of police. Specifically, it focuses on the individual and situational factors that impact on police officers' decisions to use force. Her thesis explores how these difficult

S. Kutnjak Ivković, M. R. Haberfeld (eds.), *Measuring Police Integrity Across the World,*
DOI 10.1007/978-1-4939-2279-6

decisions are made in difficult situations in order to provide officers with optimal information to best prepare them for situations that potentially require force.

Wook Kang is an Assistant Professor in the Department of Public Administration at the Korean National Police University. He received a Ph.D. in criminal justice from Michigan State University. Dr. Kang underwent Specialized Statistical Training for several years at the Center for Statistical Training & Consulting (CSTAT) at Michigan State University. He worked at the University of Central Oklahoma as an assistant professor. He delivered presentations on various topics at international conferences such as the American Society of Criminology (ASC) and Academy of Criminal Justice Sciences (ACJS). He is the author of two books: *Public Security* (2005*), Police Administration* (2013). He wrote chapters in several books such as *Global Community Policing: Problems and Challenges* (2012) and *Community Policing in Indigenous Communities* (2013). He also published several articles in peer-reviewed journals such as *Policing: An International Journal of Police Strategies & Management, Asian Journal of Criminology, Korean Journal of Defense Analysis,* and *Korean Public Administration Review*.

Aleksandr Khechumyan is a Doctoral Fellow at the MaxNetAging Research School (MNARS) and is affiliated with the Max Planck Institute for Foreign and International Criminal Law. He holds a diploma in law (equivalent to an LL.B) from the Police Academy of the Republic of Armenia (2000) and an LL.M degree in International Human Rights Law from the University of Essex, UK (2010). Aleksandr has an extensive practical experience of working both at governmental and non-governmental sectors. Prior to his doctoral research, he worked at the Police of the Republic of Armenia, first as a pre-trial investigator (2000–2005) and subsequently as a research and teaching fellow at the Police Academy (2005–2009). He also worked as a researcher at Penal Reform International, an NGO in London. Aleksandr's research interests focus on implementation of human rights standards in criminal justice and police corruption. He has published in journals such as *Policing: An International Journal of Police Strategies and Management*; *European Journal on Criminal Policy and Research; International Journal of Comparative* and *Applied Criminal Justice*

Branko Lobnikar is an Associate Professor of Police Management and Police Administration and Head of the Policing and Security Studies Chair at the Faculty of Criminal Justice and Security, University of Maribor, Slovenia. As former police officer and police supervisor, he serves as OSCE international expert in Bishkek, Kyrgyzstan, and in Baku, Azerbaijan, on community policing, was a member of management board of European Diploma in Policing, an international Leonardo da Vinci project of senior police managers training, a short time expert of Council of Europe in Tirana, Albania, and Ankara, Turkey in area of maintaining police corruption and short time expert of DCAF (Swiss) on motivation and maintaining discipline at the workplace for police managers of border police from area of West Balkans in Macedonia, and police corruption management in Belgrade, Serbia. He participated as trainer at seminar in Moldova in the field of anti-corruption and police reform. His areas of expertise comprise issues of contemporary policing, human resource management, and deviant behavior management within organizations. He has authored several papers on various aspects of policing and police deviance management and recently (2013) co-edited *Handbook on Policing in Central and Eastern Europe* for Springer. Currently, he is involved in the studies of police integrity and police legitimacy.

Gorazd Meško is a Professor of Criminology and Dean at the Faculty of Criminal Justice and Security, University of Maribor, Slovenia and a visiting scholar at the Institute of Criminology, University of Cambridge, UK. He has been a leading editor of *Understanding and Managing Threats to the Environment in South Eastern Europe* (Springer 2011), *Handbook on Policing in Central and Eastern Europe* (Springer 2013), and *Trust and Legitimacy in Criminal Justice—European Perspectives* (Springer 2014). Professor Meško's work appeared also in the *Journal of Criminal Justice, Policing—An International Journal of Police Strategies and Management, Psychology, Crime and Law, The Prison Journal, Crime, Law and Social Change, European Journal of Criminal Policy and Research, European Journal of Criminology, and British Journal of Criminology*. He also edited special issues of the *Journal of Criminal Justice and Security* on the development of criminology is Southeastern Europe (2008), Rehabilitation of prisoners (2010), Unconventional deviance (2010), Fear of crime (2012), Criminal justice in Central and Eastern Europe (2013), Prevention of juvenile delinquency (2013), and Legitimacy of policing in Central and Eastern Europe (2014) His research interests include comparative criminology, crime prevention, and policing.

Robert Peacock is a Doctoral Candidate at the School of Criminal Justice, Michigan State University, and currently manages the U.S. Department of Justice ICITAP Regional Program Office in Kyiv, Ukraine. He holds an MBA in Finance from Ohio University and a BA in Public Policy from the University of Michigan. His research focuses on law enforcement personnel performance, agency accountability, and the prerequisites of institutional legitimacy and public trust in police. Mr. Peacock previously coauthored *Rainless West: The Integrity Survey's Role in Agency Accountability* (Police Quarterly 2013).

Narin Phetthong is a Doctoral Student at the College of Criminal Justice, Sam Houston State University. He has a Bachelor of Arts degree in Public Administration and a Master of Science in Computer Security. His research interests are police crime control strategies. His rank is a Police Major of the Royal Thai Police and he has been serving in the RTP for over a decade.

Louise Porter is a Lecturer in the School of Criminology and Criminal Justice, Griffith University, Australia, and a member of the Australian Research Council Centre of Excellence in policing and Security (CEPS). Louise is a British Psychological Society Chartered Psychologist, holding previous appointments at the University of Liverpool, University of Birmingham and, more recently, the ARC Centre of Excellence in Policing and Security at Griffith University. Her research applies social psychology to forensic contexts, including co-offending as well as police corruption and misconduct. Her work on police misconduct has focused on types of misconduct behavior, its causes, and the systems in place to address such behavior. She teaches courses in professional ethics and corruption and forensic psychology and is coauthor of *Police Integrity Management in Australia* (CRC Press—Taylor and Francis 2012).

Tim Prenzler is a Chief Investigator in the Australian Research Council Centre of Excellence in Policing and Security (CEPS) and a Professor in the School of Criminology and Criminal Justice, Griffith University, Brisbane, Australia. In CEPS, he manages the Integrity Systems Project and works in the Frontline Policing Project. He teaches courses in situational crime prevention and security management, and criminal justice ethics and corruption prevention. He is the author of *Police Corruption: Preventing Misconduct and Maintaining Integrity* (CRC Press—Taylor and Francis 2009); coauthor, with Adam Graycar, of *Understanding and Preventing Corruption* (Palgrave Macmillan 2013); editor of *Policing and Security in Practice: Challenges and Achievements* (Palgrave Macmillan 2012); and editor of *Professional Practice in Crime Prevention and Security Management* (Australian Academic Press 2014).

Adri Sauerman is a Doctoral Candidate at the School of Criminal Justice, Michigan State University. A Fulbright alumni (Florida State University), he has a professional background as advocate (barrister) to the High Court of South Africa with a history of interactions with both the South African Department of Justice and the South African Police Service. His research work with Prof. Kutnjak Ivković on international criminology, criminal justice, and law have found inclusion in several leading academic journals, such as *Policing and Society*; *Policing: An International Journal of Police Strategies and Management*; *South African Crime Quarterly;* and *Acta Criminologica*. He is also a coauthor of *Police Management Beyond 2000* (Juta 2001).

Birgit Vallmüür is a State Budget Strategy Adviser, Estonian Ministry of Finance. Birgit holds a master's degree in public management (BA, internationally equivalent to MA, Tallinn University). Immediately following these studies she was employed as an adviser at KPMG Baltics Ltd and simultaneously enrolled into a Ph.D. program in Government and Politics at Tallinn University. She received an invitation for a one year full-time public management lecturer position at Tallinn University followed by a coveted full-time public management lecturer position for the next four years. During her Ph.D. studies, she developed an interest for researching informal responses to observed misconduct, integrity in organizations, and police misconduct. As she was leaving the lecturer position, Birgit created a course titled *Ethics in the Public Sector* for the Open University at Tallinn University. She also continued to expand her skill set and passion for teaching and research at a research-based boutique consulting firm, BV Consulting Ltd. She advanced her teaching skills by participating in the International Teachers Programme at the Kellogg School of Management at Northwestern University in 2011, and was recruited to the Ministry of Finance of the Republic of Estonia where she is currently employed as the State Budget Strategy Adviser, a post she has held since 2011.

Index

S. Kutnjak Ivković, M. R. Haberfeld (eds.), *Measuring Police Integrity Across the World*,
DOI 10.1007/978-1-4939-2279-6

MIX
Papier aus verantwortungsvollen Quellen
Paper from responsible sources
FSC® C105338

If you have any concerns about our products,
you can contact us on
ProductSafety@springernature.com

In case Publisher is established outside the EU,
the EU authorized representative is:
Springer Nature Customer Service Center GmbH
Europaplatz 3, 69115 Heidelberg, Germany

Printed by Libri Plureos GmbH
in Hamburg, Germany